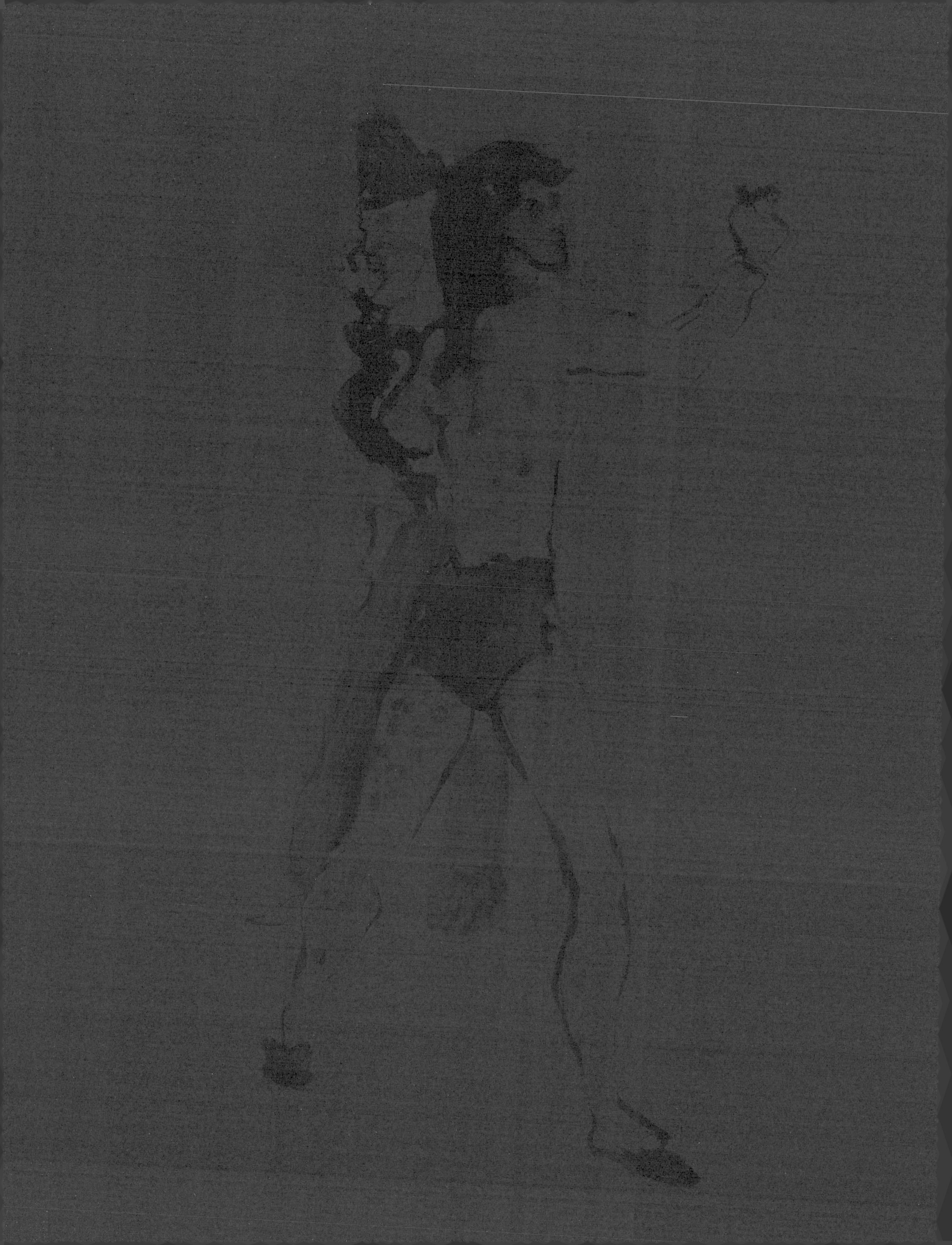

THEATRES OF MELANCHOLY

THEATRES OF MELANCHOLY

The Neo-Romantics in Paris and Beyond

PATRICK MAURIÈS

With over 250 illustrations

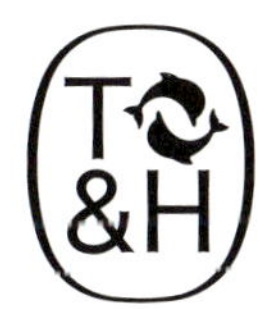

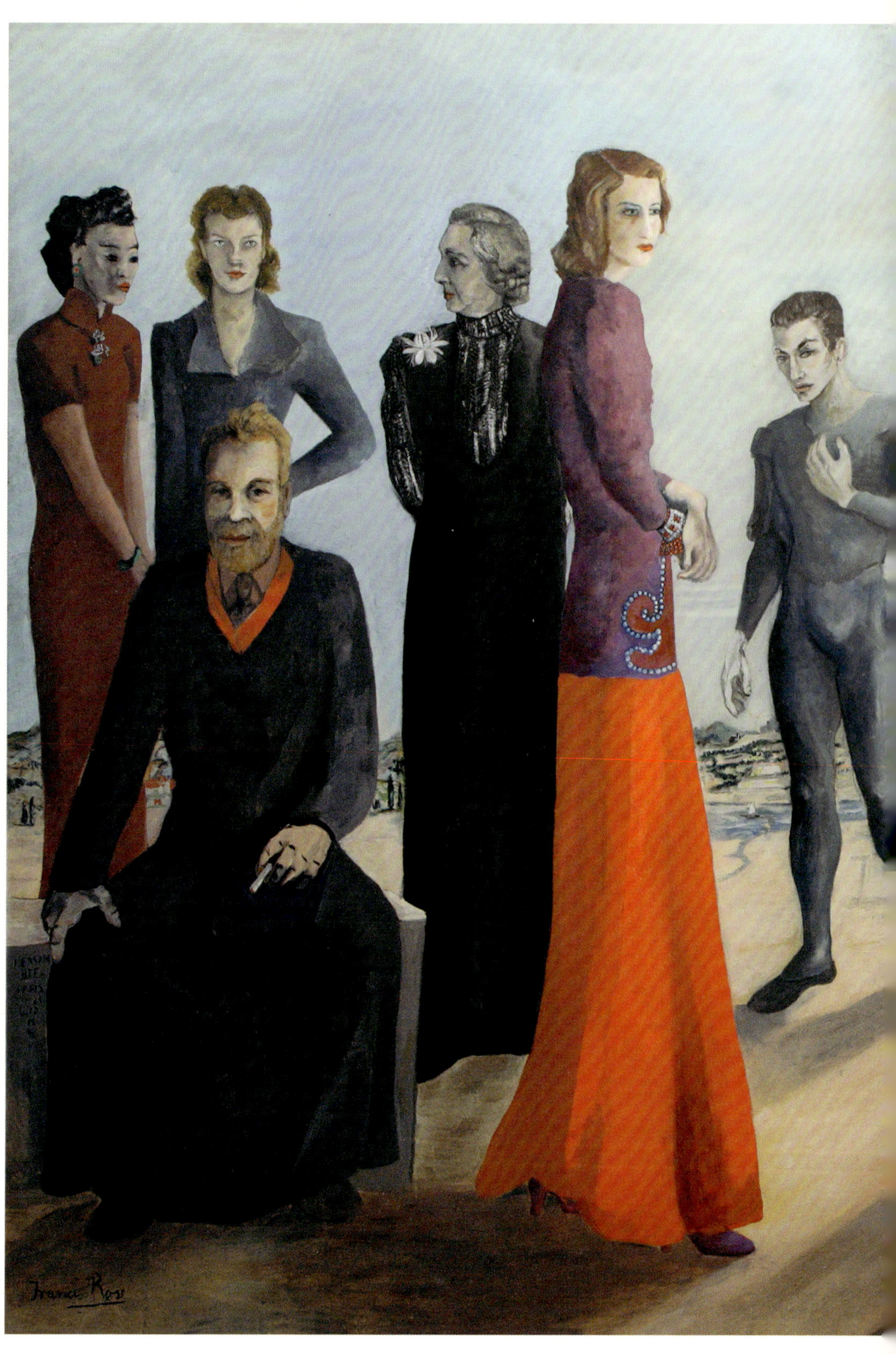

Sir Francis Rose, *L'Ensemble*, oil on canvas, 200.6 × 350.5 cm (79 × 138 in.), 1938, exhibited in 1939 at Le Petit Palais, Musée des Beaux-Arts, Paris: (from left) Madame Wellington Koo, Emmy Sommermann, Henry-Russell Hitchcock, Natalie Barney, Diana Varé, Serge Lifar, George Maratier, Francis Rose, Christian Bérard, Pavel Tchelitchew, Alice B. Toklas, Gertrude Stein, Jean Cocteau, Louis Bromfield, Tyrone Power, Virgil Thomson, Francis Picabia and Billy Mayor

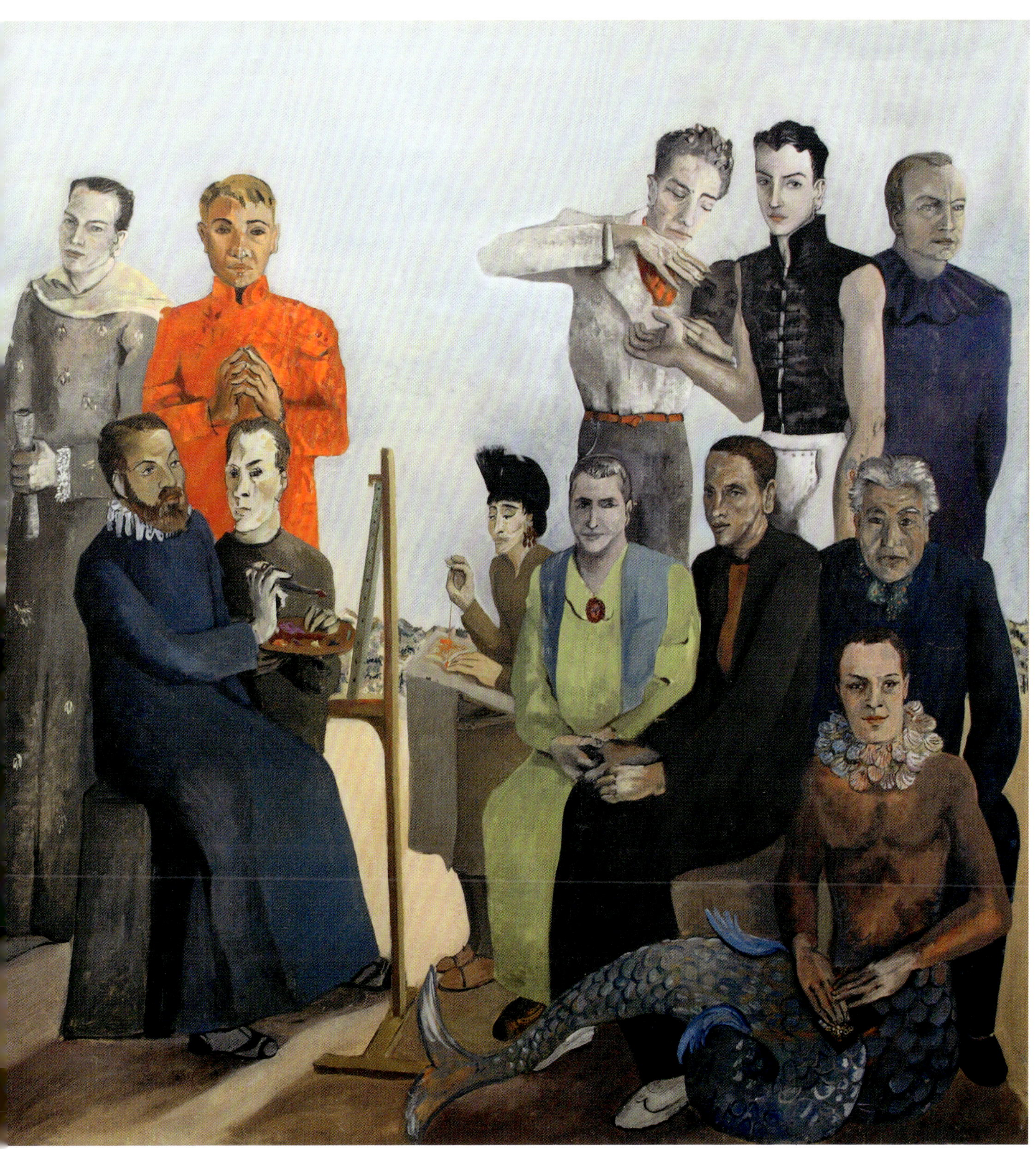

AUTHOR'S NOTE

This book examines a forgotten episode of modern art history. Although it was brief and marginal, it nevertheless inspired a significant body of writing, by both well-known authors (Gertrude Stein, Edith Sitwell, Julien Green) and lesser-known ones (James Thrall Soby, Virgil Thomson, Sir Francis Rose). Many of these texts – in the form of essays, diaries and memoirs – are no longer readily available, but as they provide eye-witness accounts of Neo-Romanticism and its main players, it seemed vital to draw on them as accurately as possible.

As a result, the following pages are, to echo the words of the great British historian Keith Thomas at the start of one of his books, 'thickly studded with direct quotations'. Thomas admits that: 'Some may find this practice ungainly. As the natural philosopher Robert Boyle remarked in 1665: "I know it would be more acceptable to most readers, if I were less punctual and scrupulous in my quotations; it being by many accounted a more genteel and masterly way of writing, to cite others but seldom, and then to name only the authors, or mention what they say in the words of him that cites, not theirs that are cited."'

Having said that – via a quotation of a quotation – the author freely acknowledges a certain predilection for what he considers not just a collection of telling references but rather a dialogue with distant voices that come together like lines of convergence; and he finds further justification for this predilection in the fact that it was shared by the Neo-Romantics themselves.

CONTENTS

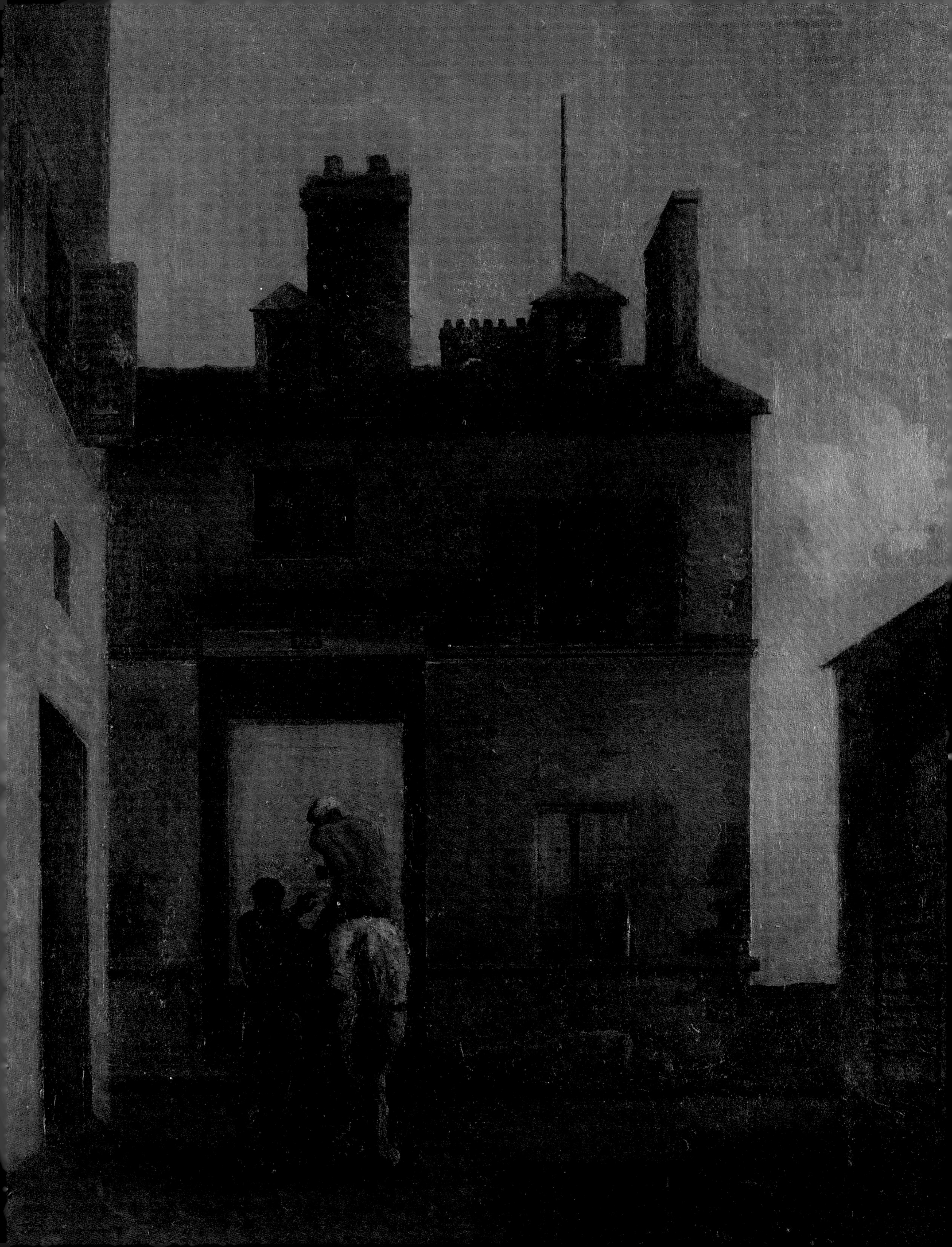

PROLOGUE

'Neo-Romantic, Neoclassical, Surrealist, all these names are both true and false. As art is made up of a thousand possibilities and contradictions, it is important to abstain from that all too general and easy tendency to immediately catalogue and lay down the law about those affirmations of our times that are viable and the directions that have to be followed!'

Eugene Berman, 'Declaration of Independence', 1964

In late February 1926, the Druet Gallery on rue Royale in Paris presented the work of a handful of young painters for a few days. Most of them were exhibiting for the first time, thanks to the efforts of one of their number, who had taken advantage of his connections with the gallery to obtain free use of its walls and picture rails.

The various participants had little in common, although most of them had passed through the Académie Ranson, where they had studied under Maurice Denis, Paul Sérusier, Édouard Vuillard and Félix Vallotton. The disparate group comprised two brothers (Eugene and Leonid Berman) and one of their friends (Pavel Tchelitchew), who had all fled the Russian Revolution; a member of a solidly bourgeois Parisian family (Christian Bérard); a young Dutch prodigy (Kristians Tonny); and a young woman who has left few traces (Thérèse Debains). An attentive viewer would have noticed some shared features, however: a taste for thick, grainy paint that sometimes mixed pigment with sand and coffee grounds; a predilection for soft, muted light; a renunciation of strong contrasts in favour of subtle tonal variations that pushed the surface of their pictures to the limits of monochromatism and of readability; and, finally, above all, a return to figures and landscapes at the very height of abstraction and Cubism.

The show was a commercial failure that served merely as an intermission in the gallery's regular programme. However, it had a considerable impact, as it launched the artists' careers and brought their work to the attention of their future dealers.

The unheralded event would also be recognized as a phenomenon of major importance by a no less disparate group of visitors, including a critic embarking on a long but chequered career, a future world-famous fashion designer, a figurehead of American letters, a ballet-mad aesthete from New York, and two elegant Bostonians. These various witnesses saw the signs of an unobtrusive but substantial artistic revolution that showed up the exhaustion of the trend that had dominated painting for the previous twenty years and had already solidified into a new academicism.

The enthusiasm of such major figures, and the subsequent publication in 1935 of an important book analyzing the themes and ideas behind this new tendency, was not enough, however, to ensure its longevity, as it was soon eclipsed by major players like the Surrealists. The shift of the art world's centre from Paris to New York after World War II and the subsequent emergence of Abstract Expressionism further helped to obscure it from view.

A simplistic view of art history, complete with adulation of heroes and euphoria over the latest big names, could never find room for the essential hybridity of artists who loved to play with forgotten references and outmoded visual devices such as trompe-l'œil, as well as being open to secondary forms of expression such as theatre, decoration and ballet (and, in some cases, to hobnobbing with socialites). These artists shied away from the gravitas inextricably bound up with the cult of the Great Painter, that exemplary figure of modernity. It is hardly surprising, therefore, that one of the high priests of that cult, Clement Greenberg, fulminated against an aesthetic that was totally foreign to him. The excommunication endured, unchallenged, throughout the latter half of the twentieth century. In fact, it is only in the last few decades that the embargo has begun to be lifted, coinciding with a deconstruction of the teleological view of twentieth-century art and the very notion of a canon.

Now, with almost a century of distance, the time seems to have come to rescue this distinctive episode from the footnotes of modern art history and to reassess the artists who were its prime movers. Such a re-examination also necessarily embraces the critics, patrons and collectors in Paris, London, New York and Rome who stuck their necks out for a bunch of fledgling painters. Finally, we also need to consider the long-term impact of an aesthetic stance that would come to be known, albeit tentatively, as 'Neo-Romanticism'.

PREVIOUS PAGE: Eugene Berman, *The Farm*, oil on canvas, 92 × 73 cm (36⅛ × 28¾ in.), 1930 (detail)
OPPOSITE: Kristians Tonny, drawing, ink on paper, 44 × 59 cm (17⅜ × 23⅛ in.), n.d. (detail)

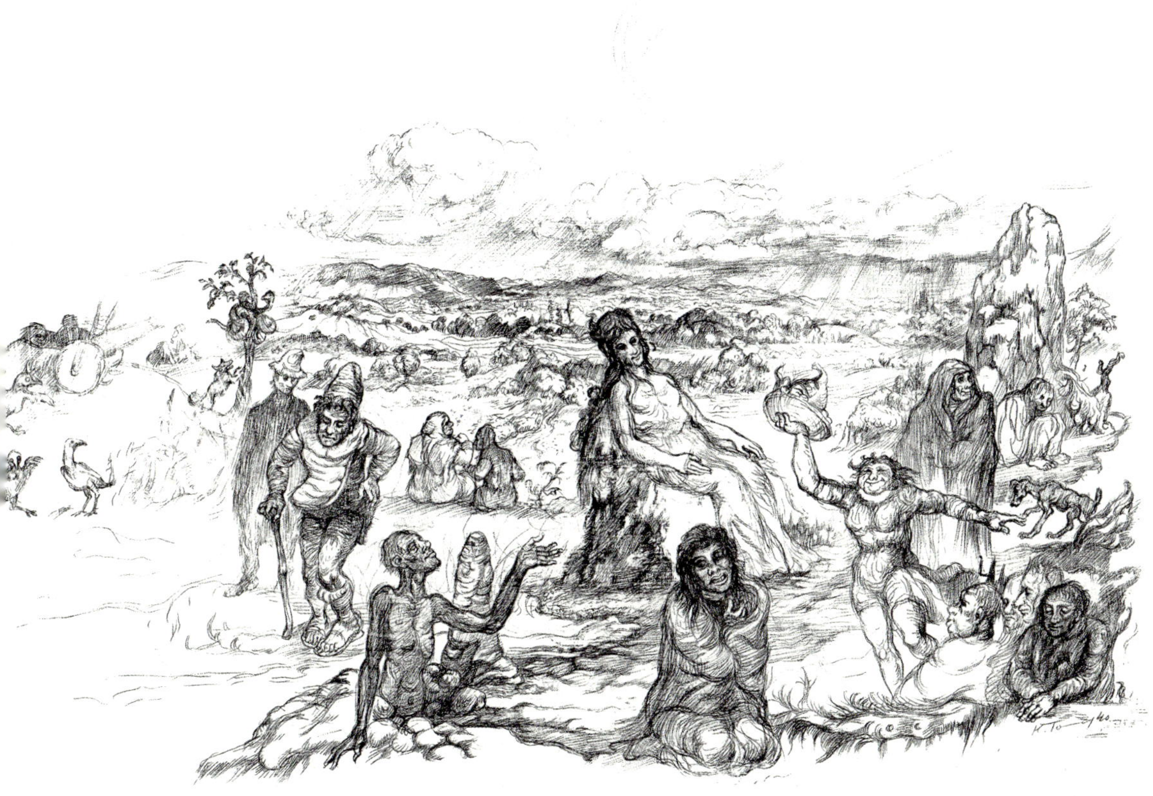

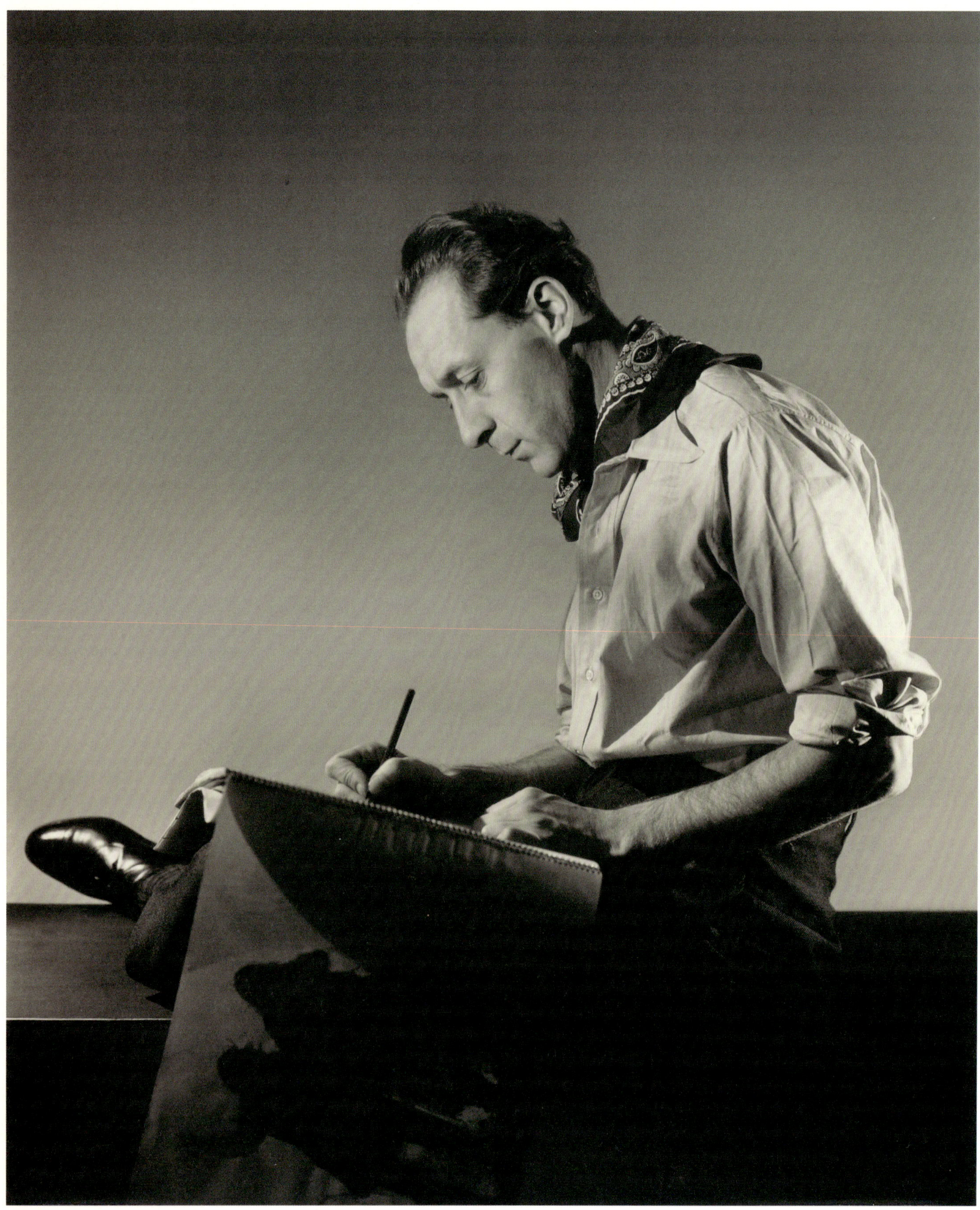

ABOVE: Pavel Tchelitchew,
December 1934, by George Platt Lynes
OPPOSITE: Portrait of Christian Bérard,
c. 1945, by G. R. Aldo

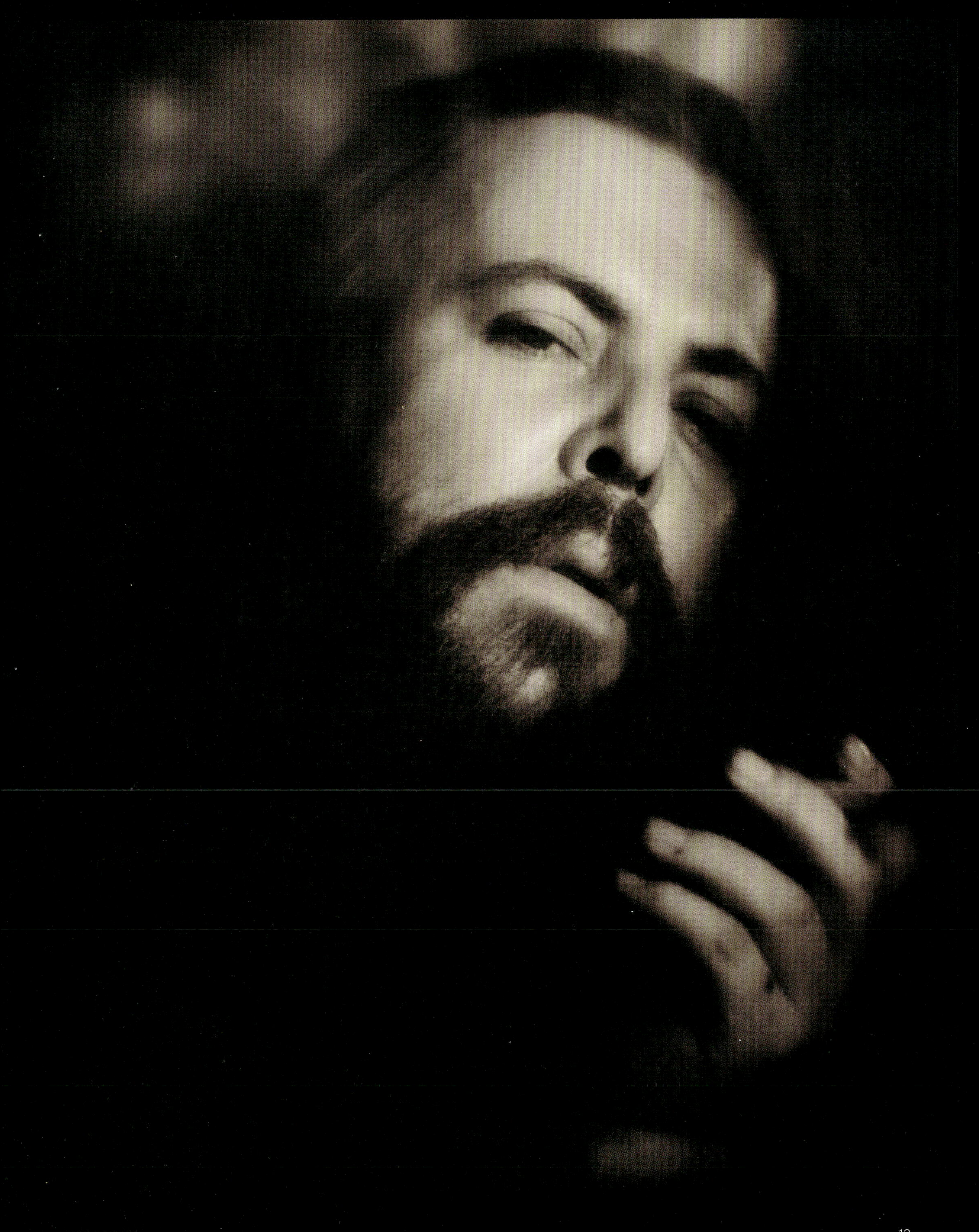

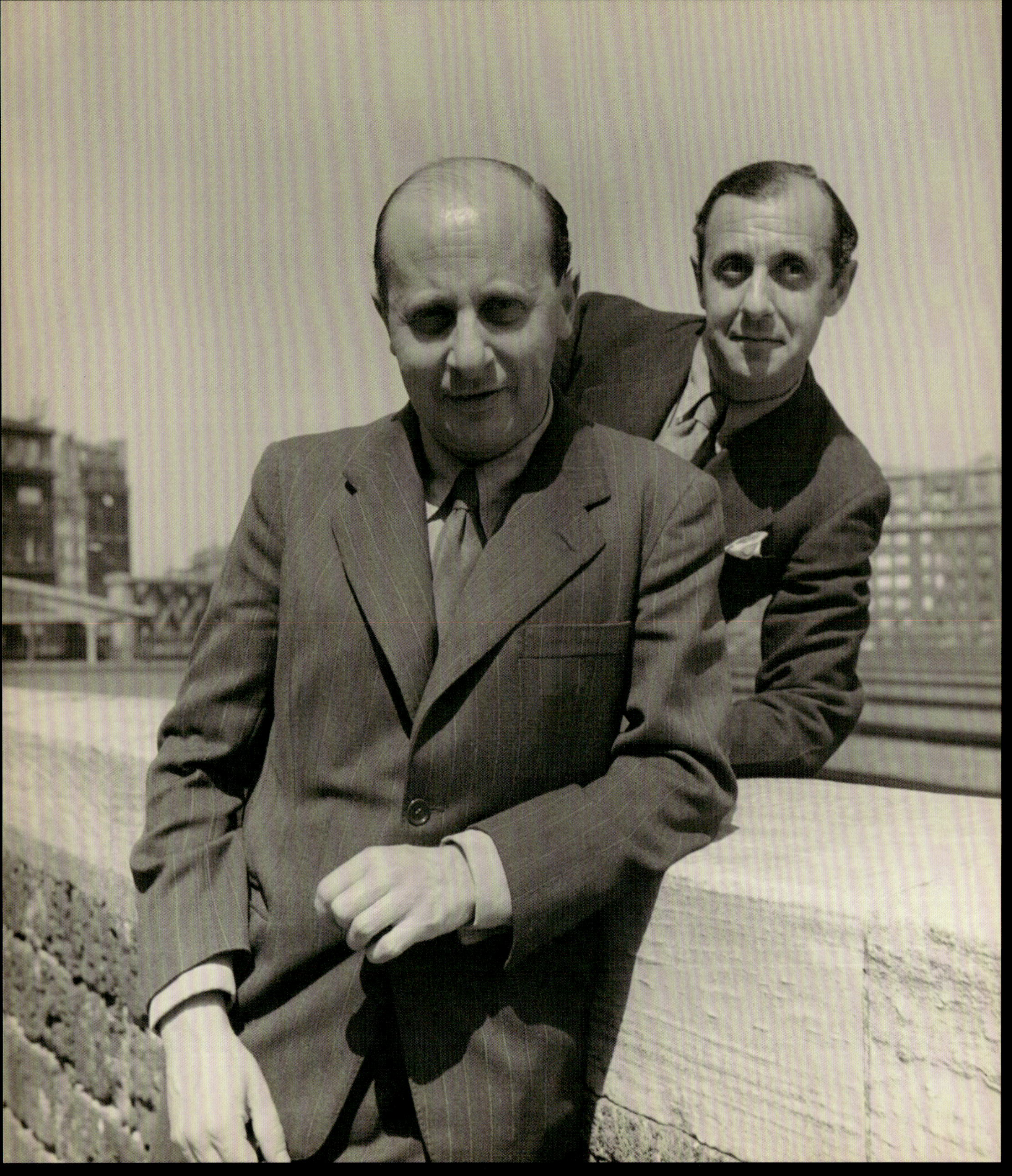

ABOVE: Eugene and Leonid Berman, *c.* 1937–39, by James Thrall Soby
OPPOSITE: Kristians Tonny, 1930, by Man Ray

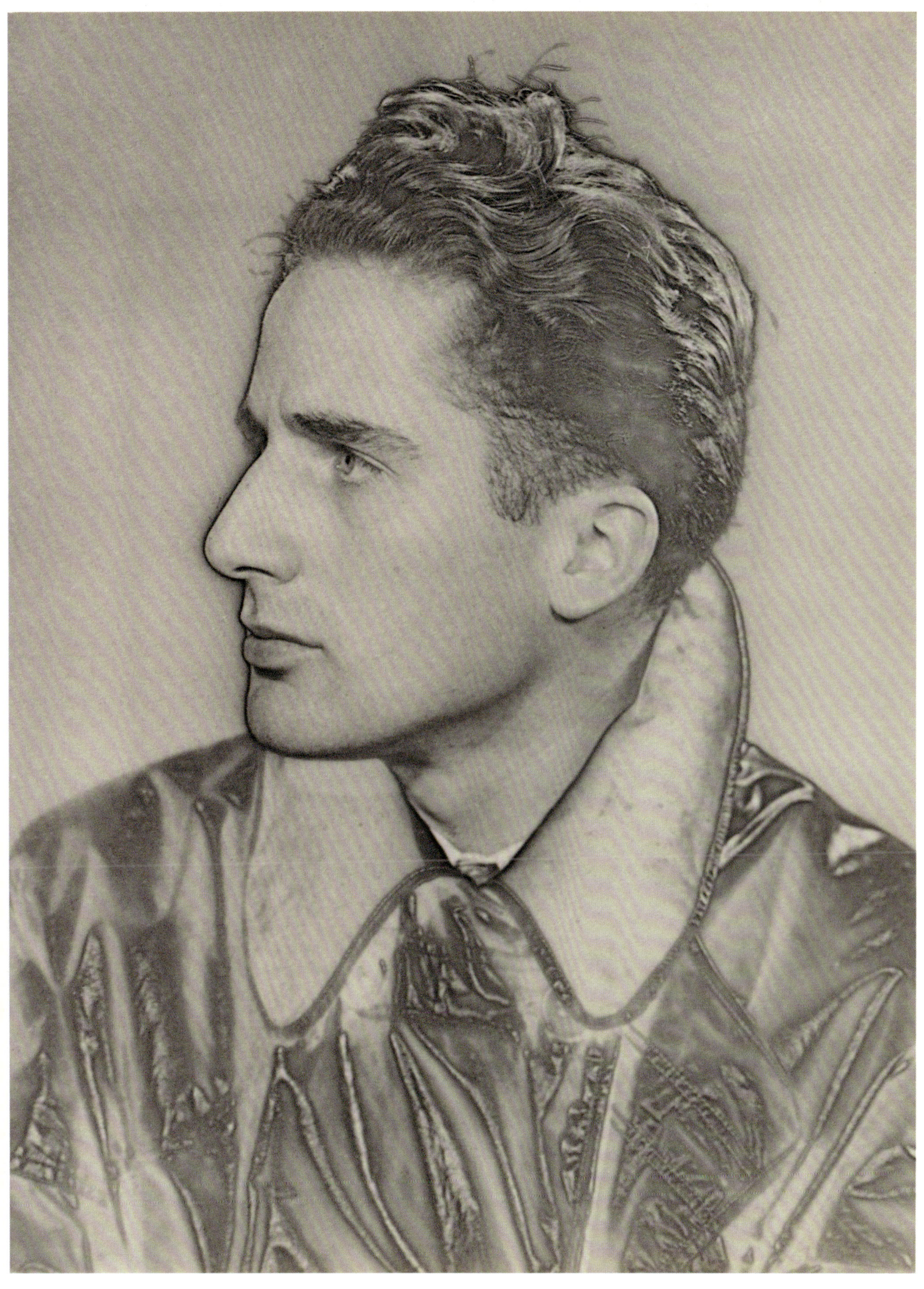

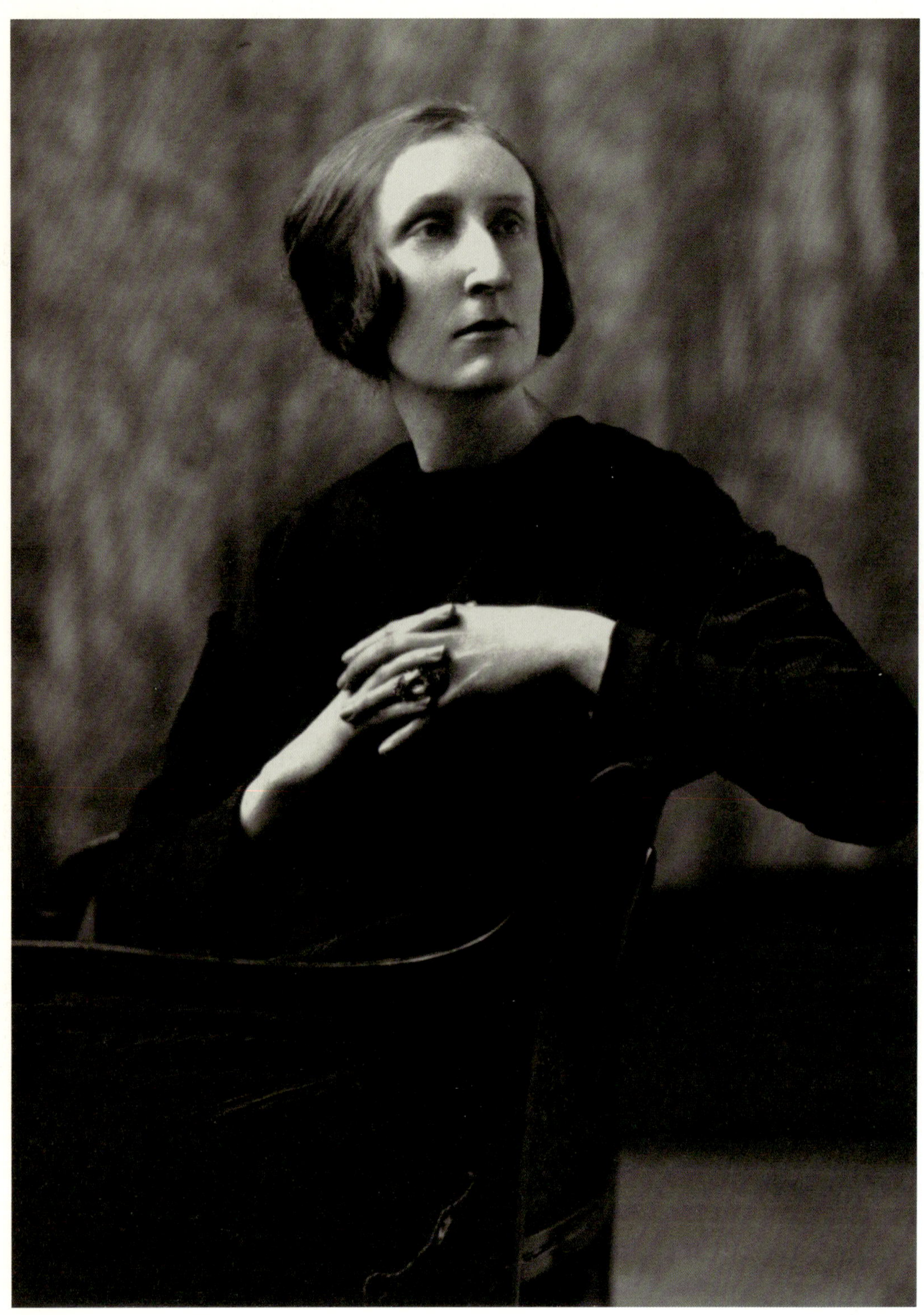

ABOVE: Edith Sitwell, 1925
OPPOSITE: Jean Cocteau, Paris, 1947

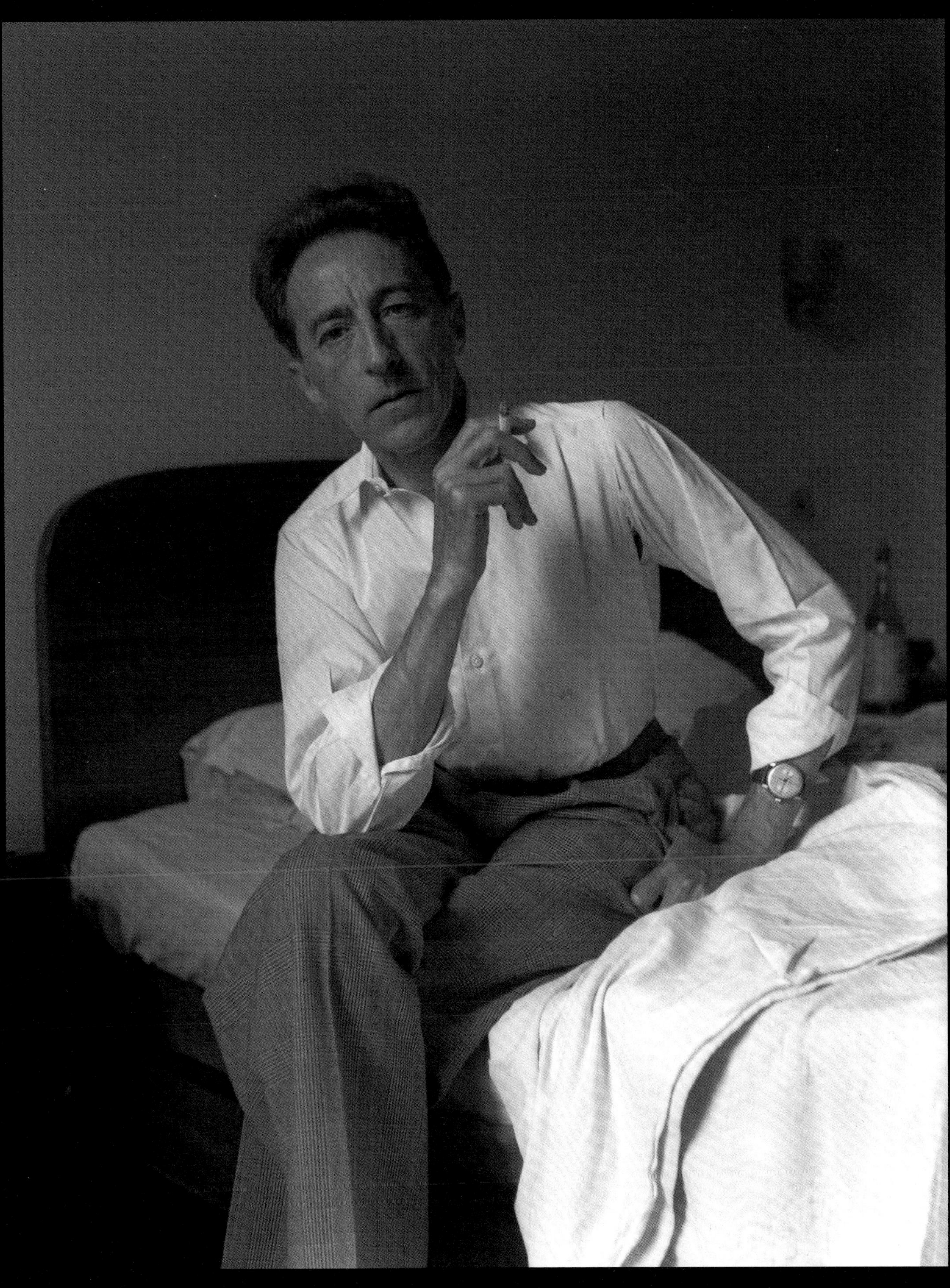

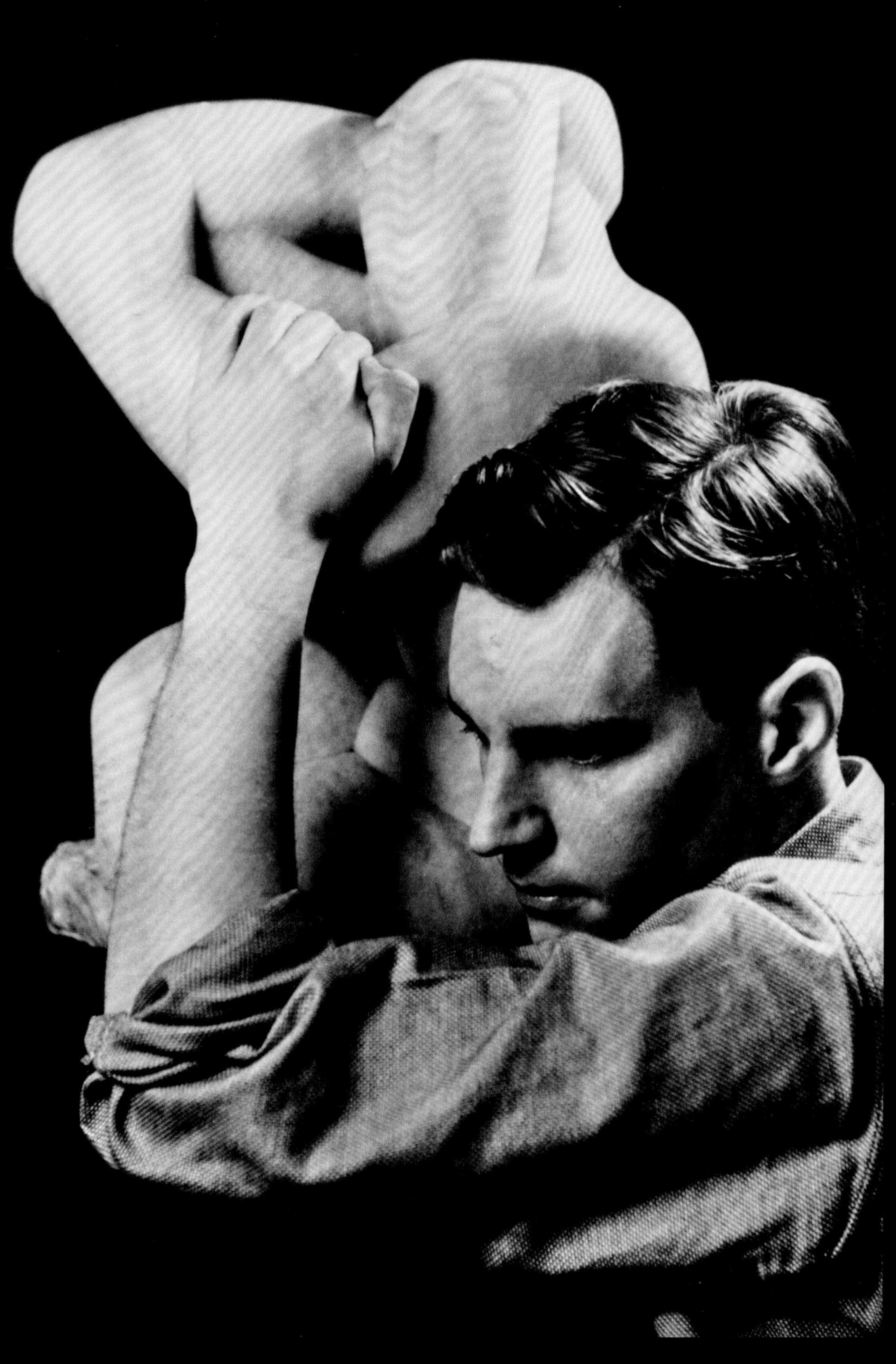

ABOVE: Chick Austin with a sculpture by Henri Gaudier-Brzeska, 1936, by George Platt Lynes

OPPOSITE: Lincoln Kirstein, 1940s–1950s, by George Platt Lynes

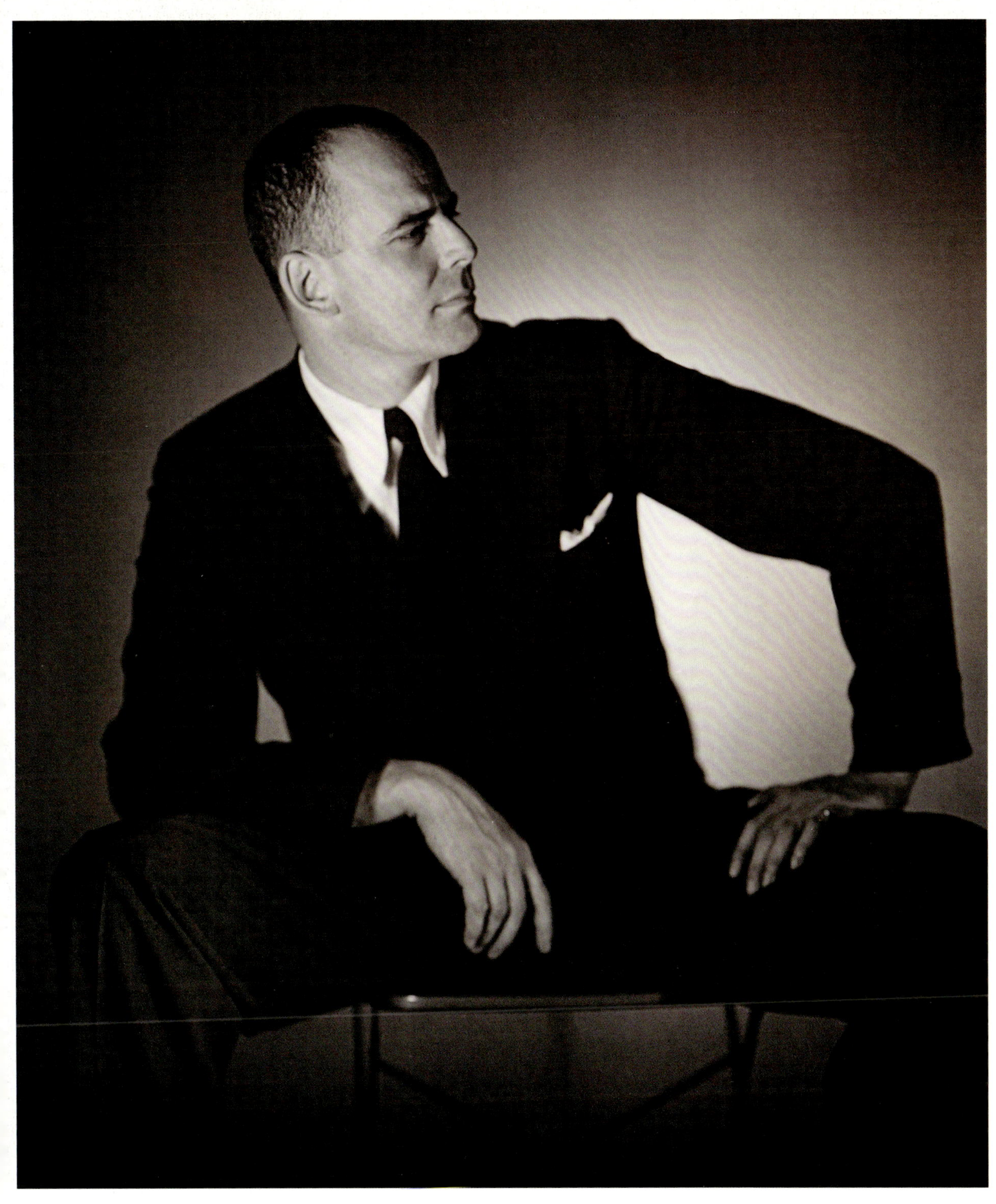

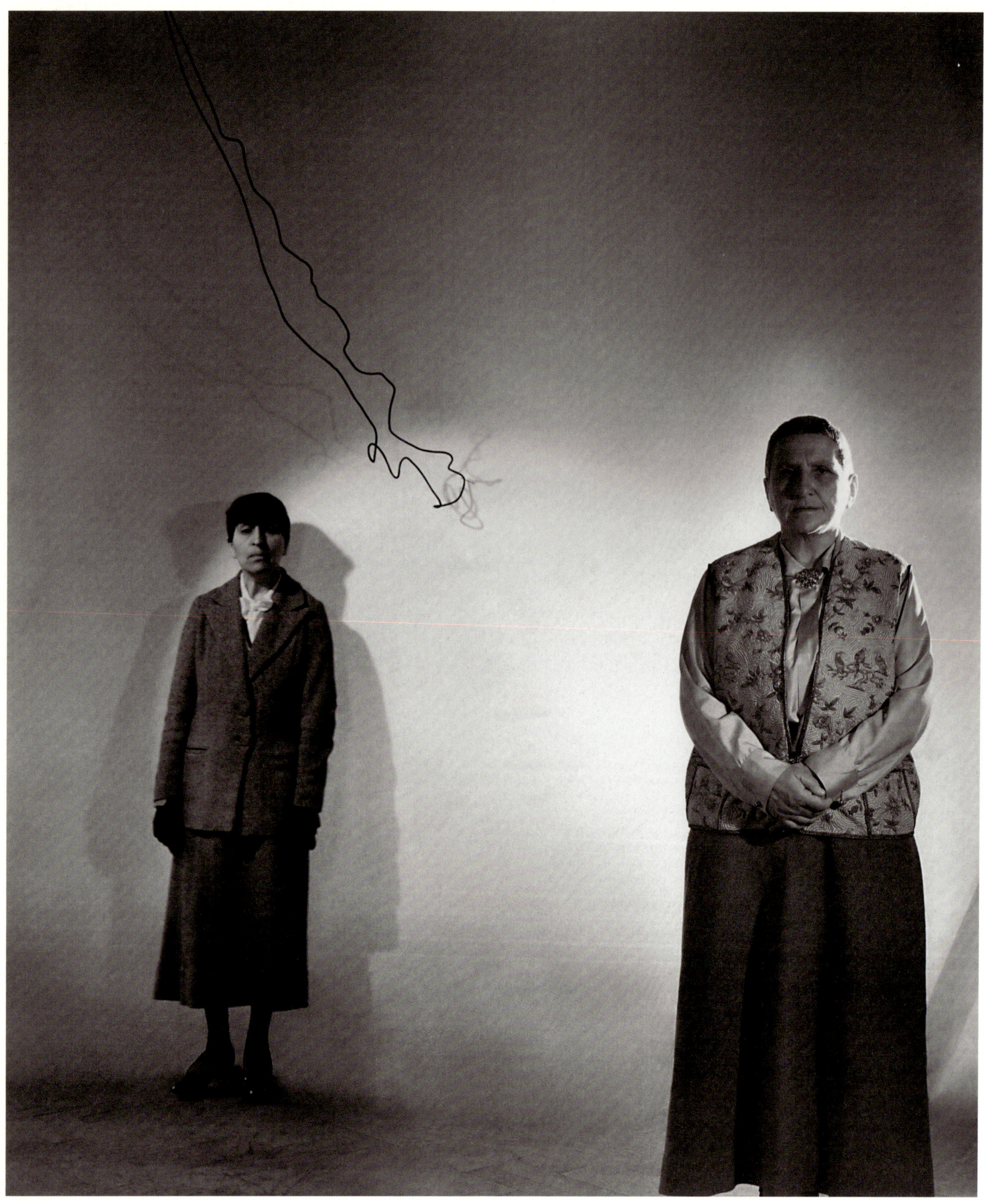

ABOVE: Gertrude Stein, in foreground, and Alice B. Toklas, in background, standing on either side of a wire sculpture, photograph by Cecil Beaton for *Vogue*, 1951

OPPOSITE: Portrait of Georges Hugnet, 1934, by Dora Maar

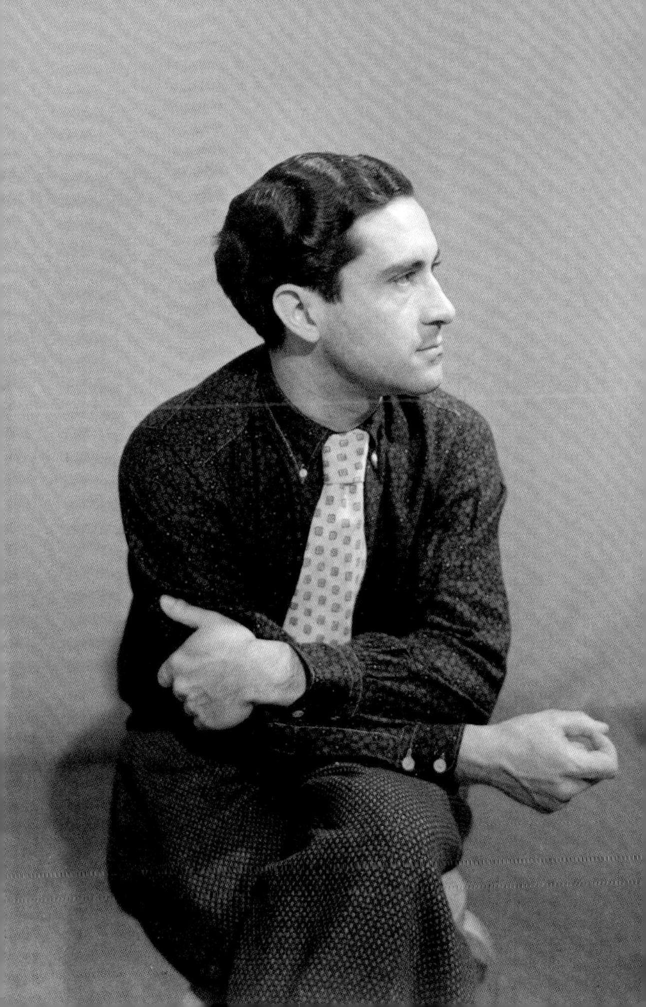

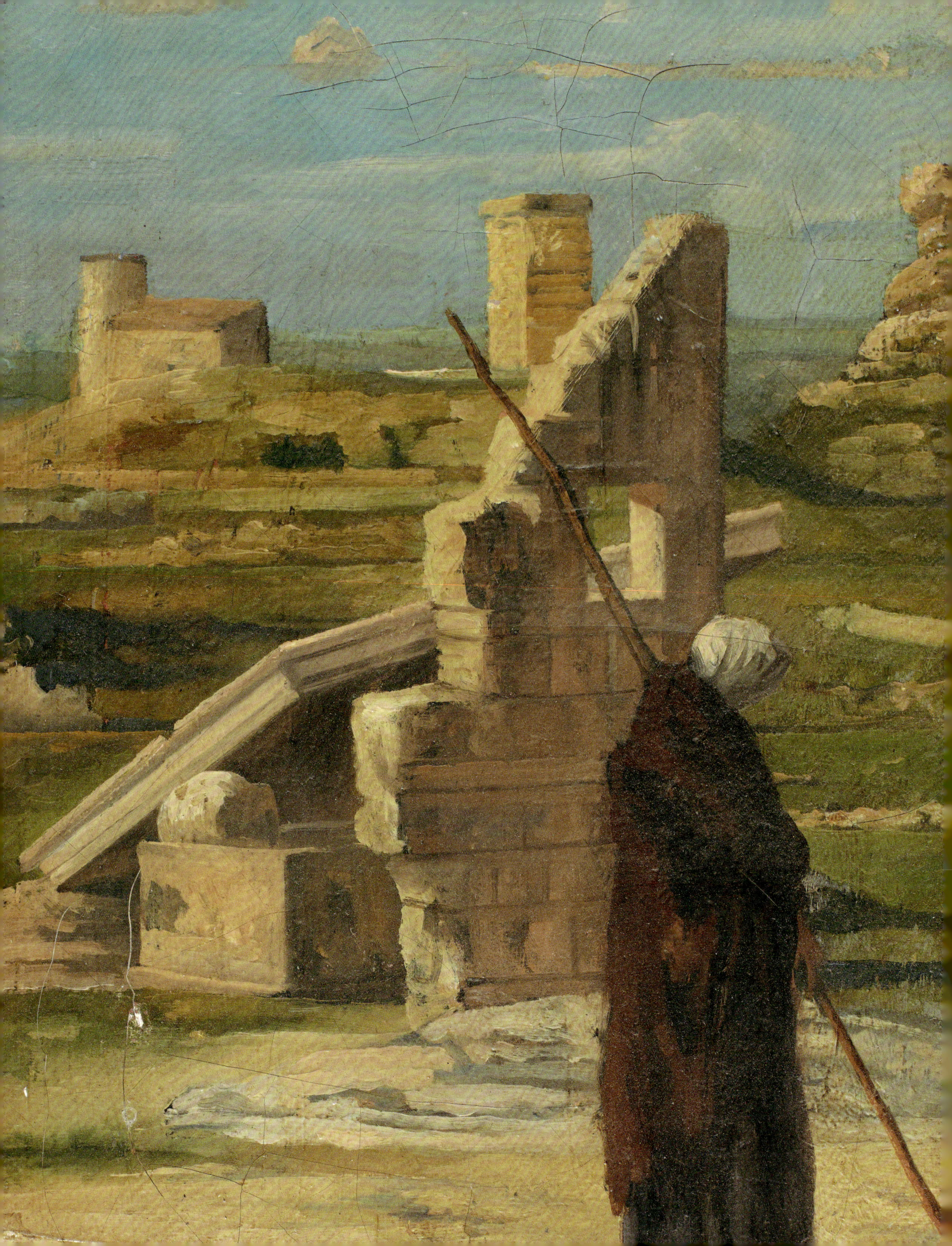

ACT I

1926

Exiles

While still a student at the Académie Ranson, Pierre Charbonnier (1897–1978) was able to invite some friends and classmates to participate in an impromptu exhibition at the Druet Gallery, thanks to the generosity of his father-in-law, Alfred Natanson (the gallery's artistic director and one of the co-founders, along with his brothers Alexandre and Thadée, of the *Revue Blanche*). Natanson agreed to make the gallery walls available for a few free days that fell between two scheduled exhibitions. The fact that Maurice Denis had once been one of the gallery's leading lights and now taught the budding artists at the Académie Ranson can only have helped their cause. Curiously, the instigator of the exhibition that would crystallize the 'Neo-Romantic' sensibility would remain outside the movement. Charbonnier is best known today for his work as art director on several of Robert Bresson's films, but his own work has been unjustly overlooked. He directed movies himself (including the remarkable animated film *La Fortune enchantée*, released in 1936), and he continued painting until the 1970s, building up a sophisticated body of work that was admired by the poets René Char and Francis Ponge.

Another of the participants in the Druet show, Leonid Berman (1896–1976) – one of the major figures of Neo-Romanticism, along with his brother, Eugene (1899–1972) – has left us a first-hand account of those exciting days in a brief memoir entitled *The Three Worlds of Leonid* (New York, 1962). He recalled that the months leading up to the exhibition were extremely hectic ('a season of *sturm und drang*') but helped seal the emotional and artistic bonds between the young artists.

In the summer of 1925, Leonid met up with Charbonnier and his wife Annette somewhere between Sainte-Maxime and the then-obscure village of Saint-Tropez, along with some other artists – Louis Marcoussis and his wife, Alice Halicka; the writer René Crevel and his lover, the American painter Eugene MacCown; the critic Raymond Mortimer, who was close to the Bloomsbury group; and another student from the Académie Ranson, with the air of a dilettante, the young Christian Bérard. ('Two seventeen-year-old Parisians also came,' recalled Leonid ironically, with reference to the Ranson, 'one to talk, the other to fetch him at noon: Christian Bérard, nicknamed Bébé, and one Christian Dior.') Bérard owed his nickname to his resemblance to the famous 'pink baby with round cheeks' in the Cadum soap adverts that 'then covered the walls of Paris'.

Leonid's memoir depicts a colony of artists gripped by tumultuous passions and amorous comings-and-goings to rival those that were similarly shaking up the Bloomsbury group on the other side of the English Channel in this same period. Charbonnier made a pass at his sister-in-law; MacCown soon abandoned Crevel for one of their friends; Leonid was mad about Thérèse Debains but was being pursued by Bérard, who was himself in the sights of Thérèse... 'This summer,' concluded Leonid philosophically, 'was a mixture of chastity and vice, of affairs and breakups... Crevel and Bébé were always crying. Bébé in fact pursued me so with his jealous scenes that finally I beat him up [...] on the beach.'

However inconsequential this convulsive interlude may appear, it would have a decisive and formative influence on the young painter and his friends: 'Finally and truly,' declared Leonid, 'I would stop being an amateur and become a professional. All this happened this summer.' He captured the youthful intensity of the bonds between the different members of the group, which would in turn shape the aesthetic vision and values often associated with the Neo-Romantics. Above all, he sketched in the backdrop against which the group's key figures would shine.

Like the Ballets Russes, Chanel N°5 and Nabokov's novels, the Neo-Romantic movement was, obliquely, an after-effect of the 1917

PREVIOUS PAGE: Eugene Berman, *Provence*, oil on canvas, 41 × 24 cm (16⅛ × 9⅜ in.), 1934 (detail)
ABOVE: Pierre Charbonnier, *Portrait of a Man*, oil on paper, 28 × 23 cm (11 × 9 in.), *c.* 1930

OPPOSITE, ABOVE: Christian Bérard, *Portrait of René Crevel*, ink on paper, n.d.
OPPOSITE, BELOW: Christian Bérard, *Portrait of the Poet René Crevel*, oil on cardboard, 99.7 × 65.4 cm (39¼ × 25¾ in.), 1925

Revolution. Just as Diaghilev had to flee from St Petersburg, Ernest Beaux (the creator of N°5) from Moscow, and Nabokov from his family estate, three of the protagonists of the 1926 exhibition – the Berman brothers and their friend Pavel Tchelitchew (as well as the painter Léon Zack [1892–1980], who was associated with the movement in its early days) – were obliged to go into exile in 1918 and ended up finding refuge in France.

Leonid was born on 6 June 1896 into a Jewish family from Peterhof, near St Petersburg. He was three years older than Eugene. ('It was always I who led, who took the initiative,' explained Leonid, 'and he who was the imitator.') After the death of their father and their mother's remarriage to a rich banker, the two brothers enjoyed a life of privilege, surrounded by a dozen servants, a governess and a French chef, before being abruptly dispossessed by the Revolution. The Berman brothers shared with Tchelitchew (and, incidentally, Nabokov) the subject matter of a life on the run, a naturally cosmopolitan aristocracy and a lost splendour, and the violence of this upheaval was one of the sources of the melancholy that suffuses their paintings. A fleeting but arresting reference in the *Journal* of Julien Green, one of the first collectors of the Neo-Romantics, reveals the trials that Eugene underwent: '[He] told us about his flight from Russia in 1919. He had been imprisoned for two months by the Cheka and was freed through a caprice of the administration. The account of his flight into Finland was thrilling. At that time, there was a whole secret organization that helped suspects escape.

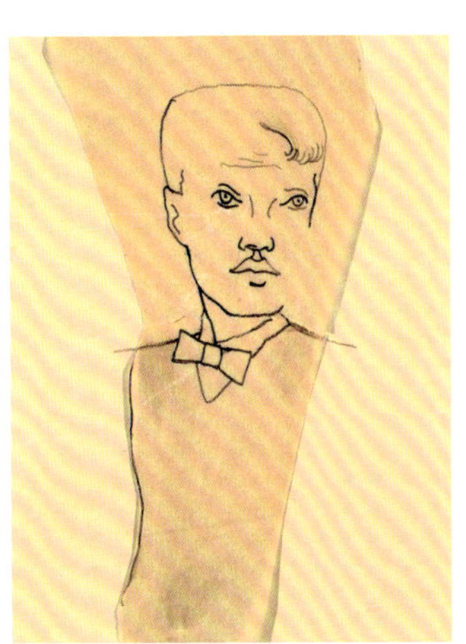

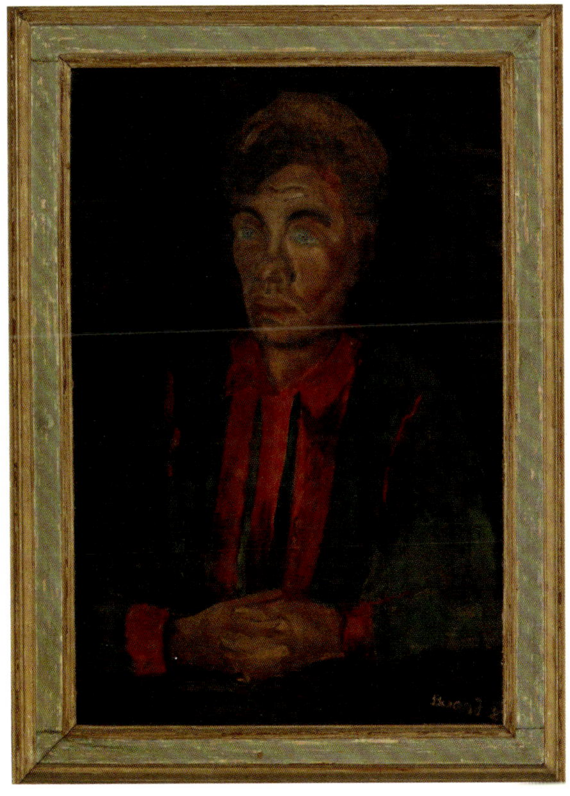

'They would hide in the bottom of a cart that would take them to such-and-such a place. There, a child would be waiting, and he would lead the way through the wood to a car that would take them somewhere else, and, stage by stage, after enormous detours and innumerable terrors, they would reach the border. He told me, with great simplicity, that prison had been good for him, that it had corrected his somewhat capricious nature, the fads of a spoilt child.'

The fascinating personality of a rebellious cousin called Anatole, an aesthete and avid collector, made such a lasting impression on the two brothers that, according to Leonid, he would have a decisive influence on their future artistic careers. ('Anatole, the visionary, liked to turn human beings into masterpieces. Eugene remained his spiritual creation for a long time [...] and my brother always retained his taste for luxury, for theater sets and ballets, a love of detail and a passion for collecting art.')

The Berman brothers arrived in Paris armed with a letter of recommendation from the painter Nicholas Roerich to his friend Maurice Denis. (Roerich had lived in Paris for a long time, where his achievements had included the costumes for Stravinsky's *Rite of Spring*.) Denis naturally steered them towards the Académie Ranson, where he was teaching. This was a less popular school than the Académie de la Grande Chaumière, but it was more prestigious, as Leonid explained, 'because of the great number of famous painters who taught there'. Maurice Denis was joined on the teaching staff by Sérusier, Bonnard, Vallotton, Roussel and Vuillard (albeit only 'on Saturday at noon').

The two brothers started off by following the somewhat rigid rules of the Nabis, dividing their palette into two colour sections (hot and cold), sketching the subject in dark colours with a stiff brush before adding light and shade to convey the illusion of volume, and renouncing the use of black 'because it didn't exist in nature'. Like most rules, these were made to be broken, and, after two years at the Académie, Eugene and Leonid had well and truly forgotten them.

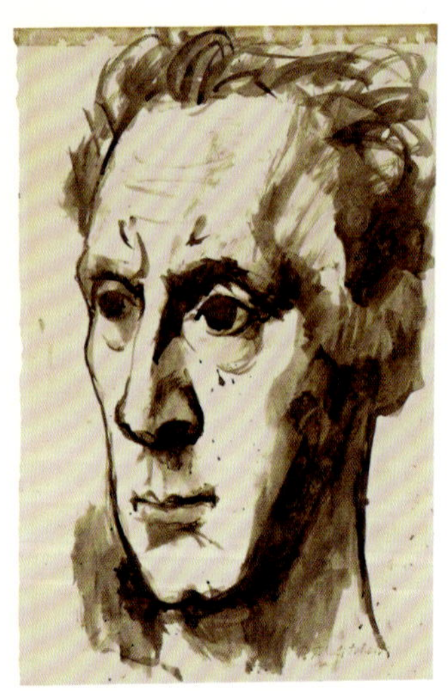

They immediately found a place in Parisian artistic circles, particularly a small group of painters and sculptors from Central Europe, bound together by the memory of exile: Jacques Lipchitz, Louis Marcoussis (both already quite well known), Alice Halicka and Marc Chagall, as well as critics such as André Salmon and Florent Fels. The Berman brothers were regular visitors to the galleries of Paul Rosenberg and Paul Guillaume (at 21 and 59, rue La Boétie, respectively). They were particularly struck by a retrospective of the Douanier Rousseau at Guillaume's gallery and then, in 1922, by Giorgio de Chirico's first solo show in Paris. (De Chirico's influence can clearly be seen in Eugene's early works.)

The two brothers were introduced by their cousin Anatole to Pavel Tchelitchew ('whom we called Pavlik'). The latter two had first met in Berlin, on a stopover on their journey into exile, and as Anatole was sharing a 'sumptuous' apartment with Eugene on rue des Lions Saint-Paul in the Marais (in a shaky ménage à trois with Anatole's wife, Claudia), a meeting of the future protagonists

ABOVE: Pavel Tchelitchew, *Self-Portrait*, ink and wash on paper, 30.5 × 18.4 cm (12 × 7¼ in.), *c.* 1933
OPPOSITE: Christian Bérard, *Boris Kochno*, oil on cardboard, 109.2 × 78.7 cm (43 × 31 in.), 1930

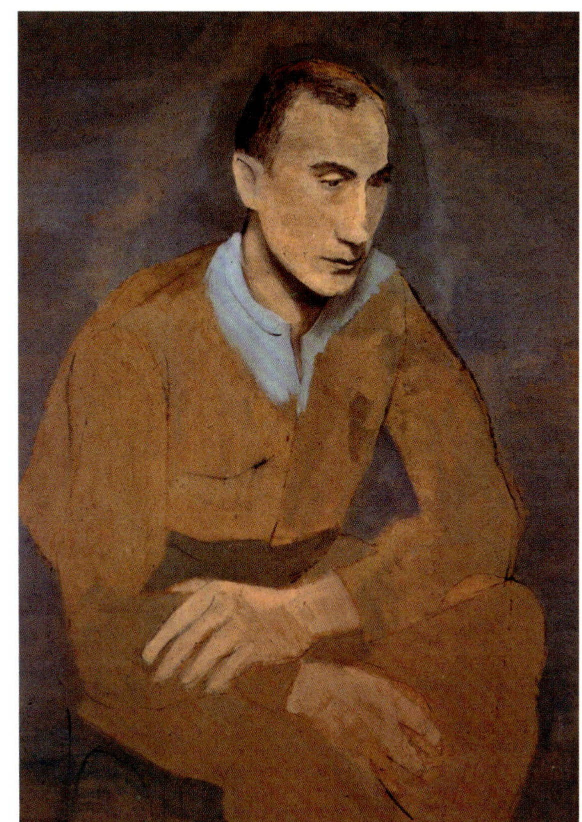

of Neo-Romanticism was inevitable. Only the final member of the founding quartet was missing: 'Bébé' Bérard, whom 'Pavlik' met at around the same time. The relationship between these two was immediately marked by an ambivalence that would never go away: 'The two geniuses got along badly, jealous or admiring, in accordance with the mood of the day.' (In corroboration of this summary, Julien Green noted in his *Journal* on 2 April 1931: 'Bérard came to see me in the afternoon. He spoke about Tchelitchew with great moderation and sometimes fairly. [...] When I told him that Tchelitchew praised his way of drawing ("I don't know how to draw. Bébé, he draws well"), he simply said: "That's his way of saying that great painters don't always draw well." They undoubtedly barely like each other, but Bérard's barbs are fired with greater finesse. Tchelitchew brandishes a club.' The source of this antipathy seemed to be fairly mundane – yet another reverberation of the group's amorous seesawing. Two years later, on 29 June 1933, Green recorded: 'The other day, Berman told me that Bérard and Tchelitchew had quarrelled in 1926 over Crevel. Bérard was besotted with him, but Crevel had thrown himself at Tchelitchew. Their falling-out dates back to that time.')

Bérard, however, felt at ease in this small group, as, according to Leonid, he had always been fascinated by Russians and their culture. (Bérard would later form a relationship with Boris Kochno, another Russian exile who was Diaghilev's secretary at the time of their meeting, and the couple would remain together until Bérard's untimely death in 1949.) All in all, Leonid's memoir shows that Dorothy Parker's famous description of the Bloomsbury group was equally applicable to the Neo-Romantics: 'They lived in squares, painted in circles and loved in triangles.'

The complications of this emotional geometry did nothing to prevent Bérard and the Berman brothers from setting off to Venice together in 1922, or from going on to spend 'three unforgettable months' in Rome, Florence and Tuscany. It is impossible to overestimate the importance of this trip in the young artists' development and in the formation of the sensibility that they would later espouse.

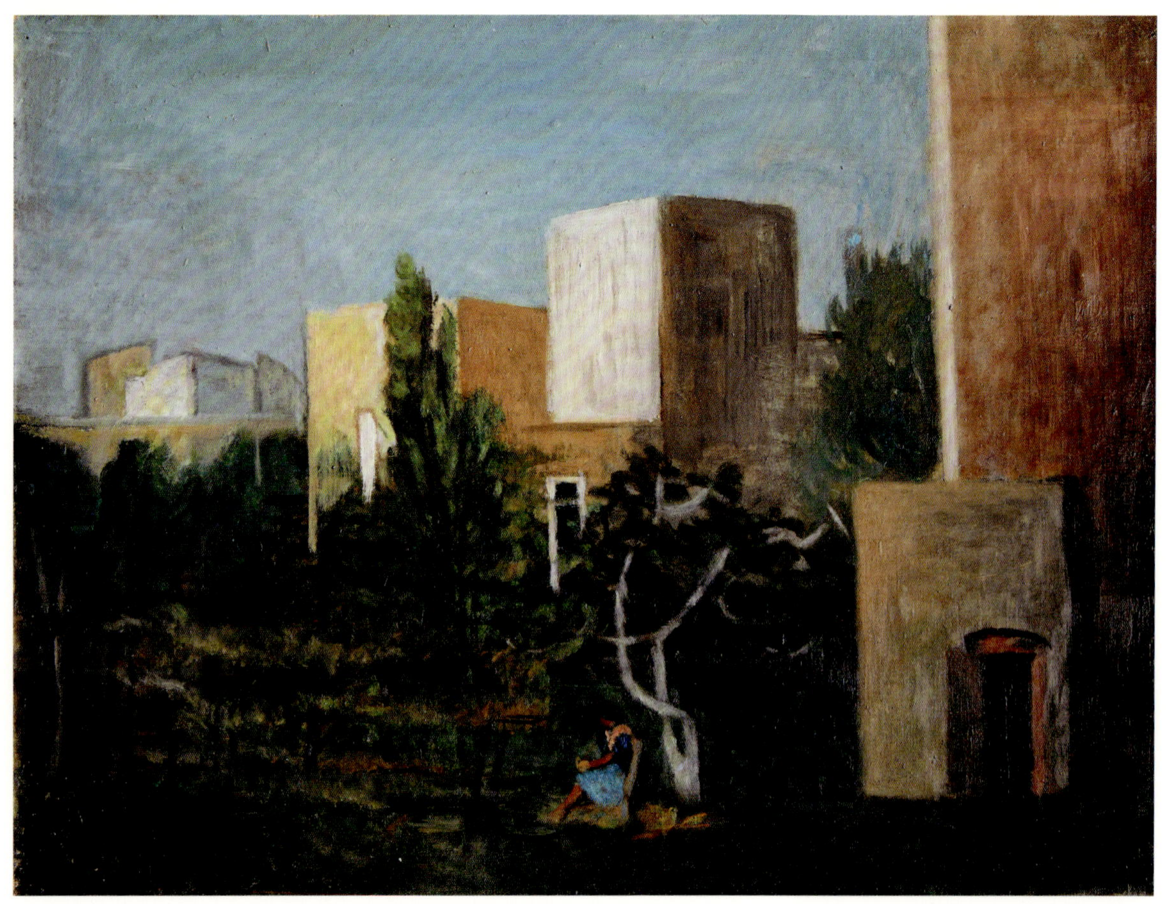

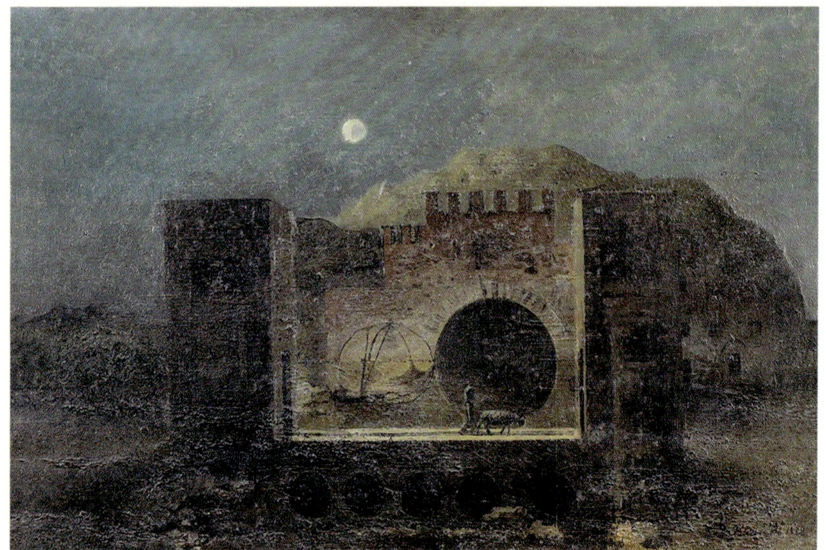

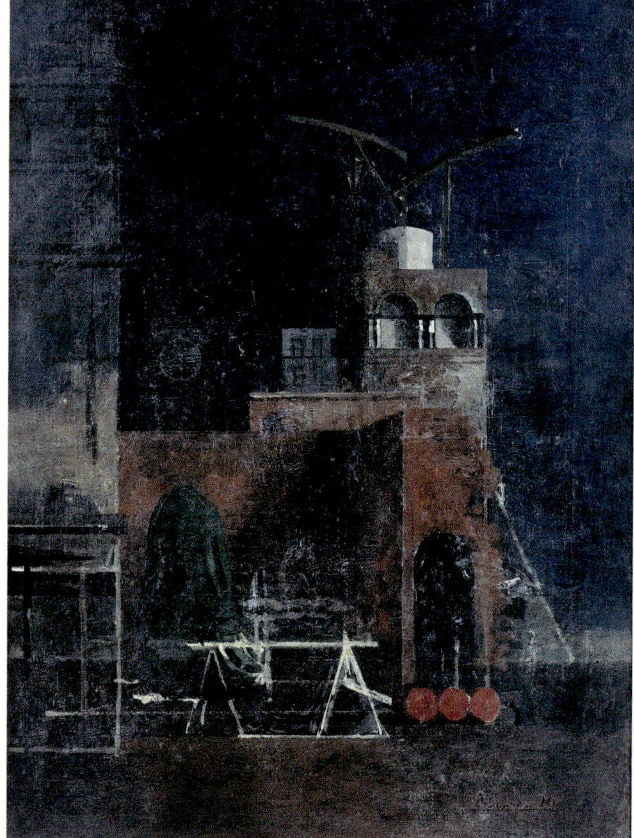

THIS PAGE, CLOCKWISE FROM TOP: Leonid Berman, *Landscape with Figure*, oil on canvas, 54 × 72 cm (21¼ × 28⅜ in.), *c.* 1930; Eugene Berman, *Nocturne*, oil on canvas, 99.5 × 72.5 cm (39 × 28½ in.), 1930; Eugene Berman, *Clair de Lune*, oil on canvas, 65 × 100 cm (25 × 39 in.), 1928
OPPOSITE: Piero della Francesca, *Legend of the True Cross: Verification of the True Cross*, fresco, 356 × 747 cm (140⅛ × 294 in.), *c.* 1452

Leonid's Travels

Italy was a recurring leitmotif in the lives and work of the four leading Neo-Romantics. Initially, it provided a revelation of a heritage that had hitherto been diluted and deformed by mechanical reproduction (which did not prevent the travellers from spending a small fortune on postcards and Alinari photographs), but it eventually led to a real dialogue with contemporary Italian painters, and the ways in which they were interpreting their own tradition. The first trip undertaken by Bérard and the Bermans coincided with the emergence in Rome and Turin of the Novecento, an artistic movement with some interests similar to their own. (The first Novecento exhibition outside Italy took place at the Carminati Gallery in Paris in May 1926 – only a couple of months after the show in the Druet Gallery.) We shall go on to explore in greater detail these complex and tortuous entanglements with the Italian culture of the 1920s, in which a 'return to order' manifested itself in a return to the figure and to formal purity, as well as a celebration of Latinity rooted in antiquity.

Some members of the Novecento (most notably Margherita Sarfatti, an art critic and devotee of Mussolini) formulated ideological positions in 1925 that would be taken up in France by the critic Waldemar-George (whose importance will emerge in due course). Whether or not Bérard and the Berman brothers subscribed to these views, they did share their Italian counterparts' fascination with the masters of the Quattrocento, whose works they were now discovering, and the 'taste of the primitives', to quote the title of the book published by Lionello Venturi in 1926 that gave full expression to this rediscovery. 'We were most impressed by the works of Carpaccio, Masaccio, Mantegna and especially Piero della Francesca. We went back to Paris exhausted, thinner and very

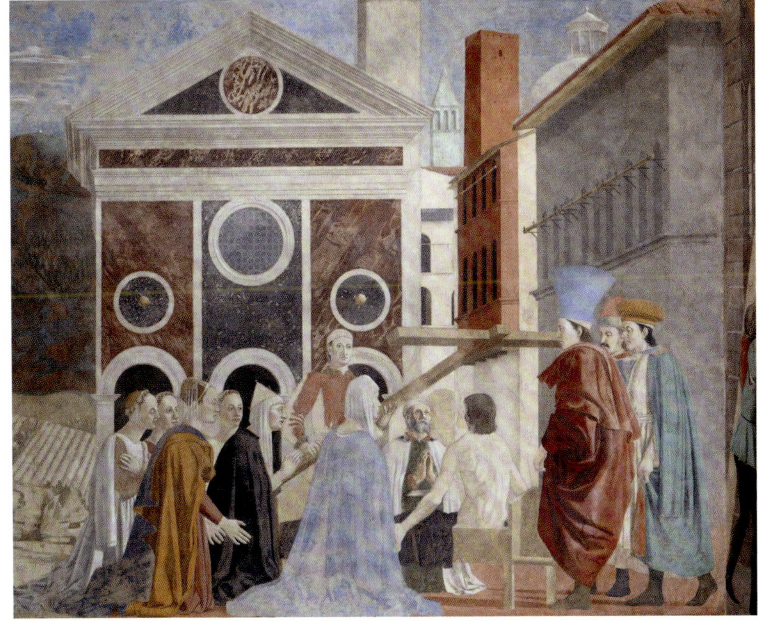

happy.' Following this impetus, the two brothers went further afield the following year, to Orvieto, the countryside around Rome, Tivoli and Naples.

This Italian inspiration is more noticeable in the early works of Bérard and Eugene than in those of Leonid, who would soon go on to explore other avenues. ('He [Eugene] preferred Italy, and I France,' observed Leonid, laconically.) Of the three, Eugene was undoubtedly the one who assimilated most enthusiastically the influence of Italian culture, light and landscape. He made several trips to Italy in the 1930s and went back often in the 1950s (by which time he had settled in the United States), before finally making his home there in 1956.

The years following the two brothers' first visit to Italy would bring them into the limelight under the banner of Neo-Romanticism, but it would also mark a parting of ways, in both personal and artistic terms. Leonid displayed a fierce desire for independence that was not shared by the more easy-going Eugene. Leonid also went through several rocky periods during these years, not least due to his unhappy relationship with Thérèse Debains. While Eugene quickly found his place on the Parisian scene, 'seeing the architect Emilio Terry, Marc Chadourne, a writer, Gertrude Stein and the Polignacs, and painting a big portrait of Marie-Laure, Vicomtesse de Noailles', Leonid preferred to explore the region that was yet to be christened the Côte d'Azur (he would later take some credit for the invention of this concept), staying in small hotels within his limited means around Marseille, Toulon, Sainte-Maxime and Saint-Tropez. There, he met up with both former classmates such as Pierre Charbonnier and established artists (Jules Pascin and Moïse Kisling, Louis Marcoussis and Alice Halicka), as well as composers and writers such as Henri Sauguet, René Crevel, Jean Cocteau, Glenway Wescott and Monroe Wheeler. He also began to establish the rudiments of a personal idiom and subject matter that would endure throughout his life. ('More and more, I was giving up portraits, nudes, and still-lifes for landscapes.')

The death of Leonid's father-in-law in the winter of 1928 triggered both a personal and family crisis. ('After his death came the deluge. [...] Slowly, the family began to disintegrate.') By his own admission, a journey to Boulogne-sur-Mer the following year marked a turning point, as it solidified his topographical repertoire and his colour scheme. As he recalled in 1962: 'It immensely furthered my paintings. What I began to paint then, I am still painting today. I had found my theme: sea, space and solitude. My Boulogne paintings were the first "Leonids".'

The Riviera gave way to the expansive beaches of northern France, the colours of sand and water, the muted light of the Somme Bay and the Opal Coast. Over the next ten years, Leonid would explore the coastlines of the North Sea, Brittany, Normandy and the Atlantic, as far down as Arcachon. In 1934, he benefitted from the hospitality of Christian Dior, with whom he had struck up a friendship after being introduced by 'Bébé', for he spent several weeks in the Villa Les Rhumbs in Granville. The following year, he travelled from Étretat to the Île d'Oléron, stopping in Port-en-Bessin and Genêts. In 1938, he stayed in Ambleteuse, not far from Boulogne-sur-Mer, and painted 'some of [his] best pictures'. Over the course of many years, he tirelessly captured the shores and light of these regions in a totally original way, far removed from the work of painters who had previously mined this subject matter (particularly the Impressionists). Enthralled by the distinctive topography of the coastlines, he homed in on the distorted perspectives of mussel fields, fish houses and salt marshes, punctuated by people gathering shellfish, with boats and nets, like signs suspended on the 'infinity of equinoctial sands'.

These explorations were brought to a halt in the autumn of 1939 by the vicissitudes of history. After the declaration of war, Leonid joined a regiment in Melun whose soldiers found themselves in Dordogne after the Nazi occupation of France in June 1940. He was subsequently demobilized and returned to Paris, but left again in 1942 for a village close to La Rochelle. He was then called up to work on the construction of the 'Atlantic Wall' but he was spared the persecution to which he was exposed by his Jewish origins. He went back to Paris after the Liberation, but in 1946 he settled in the United States (following in Eugene's footsteps, some ten years earlier), where, as we shall see, his work took new stylistic turns.

Even apart from the historical circumstances, the Neo-Romantic episode had long been over. With its prime movers now dispersed in Europe and the United States, all memory of it was obscured by the attention devoted to the more prominent currents that had emerged in modern art.

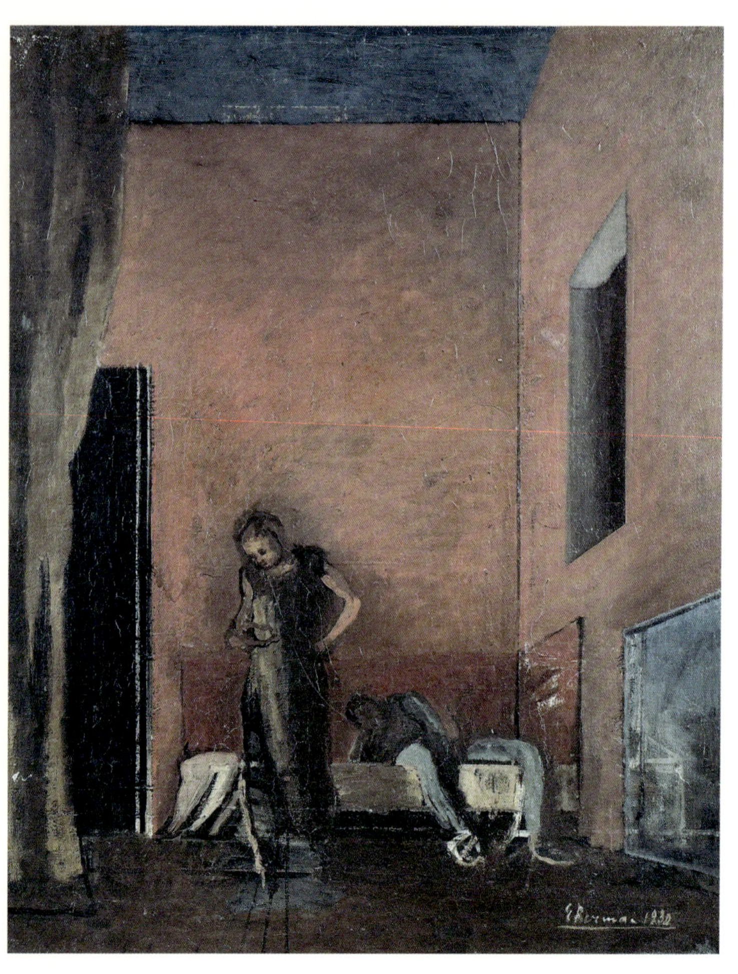

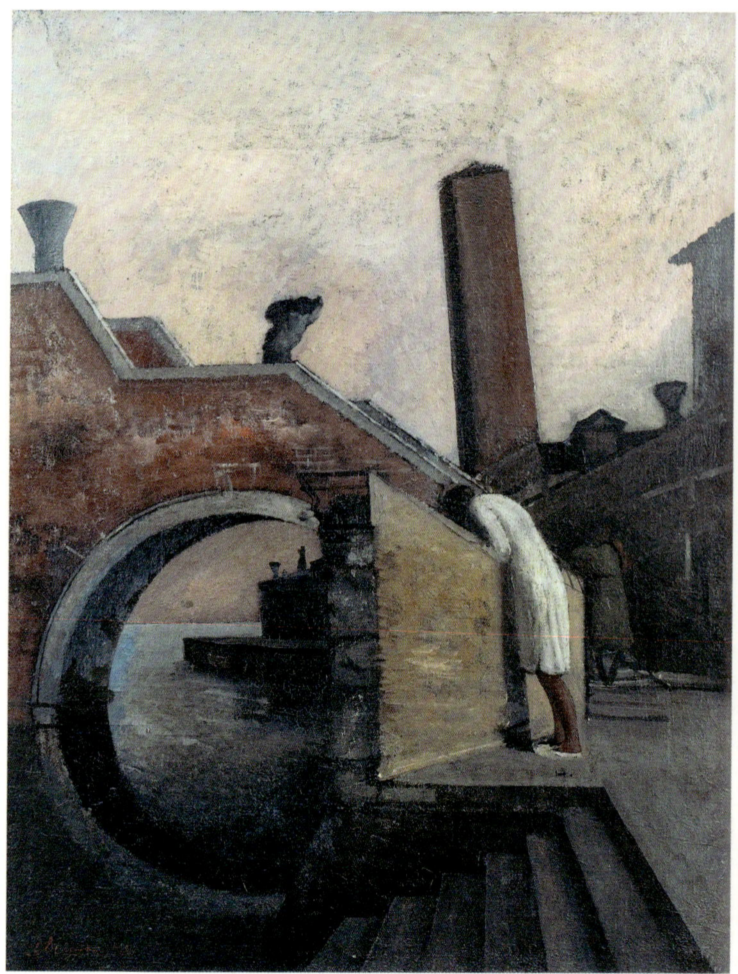

ABOVE, LEFT: Eugene Berman, *Red Interior*, oil on canvas, 81 × 64.5 cm (32 × 25⅜ in.), 1930
ABOVE, RIGHT: Eugene Berman, *Venice*, oil on canvas, 92 × 73 cm (36½ × 28¾ in.), 1931
OPPOSITE: Eugene Berman, *Verona*, oil on Masonite, 100.3 × 73 cm (39½ × 28¾ in.), 1931

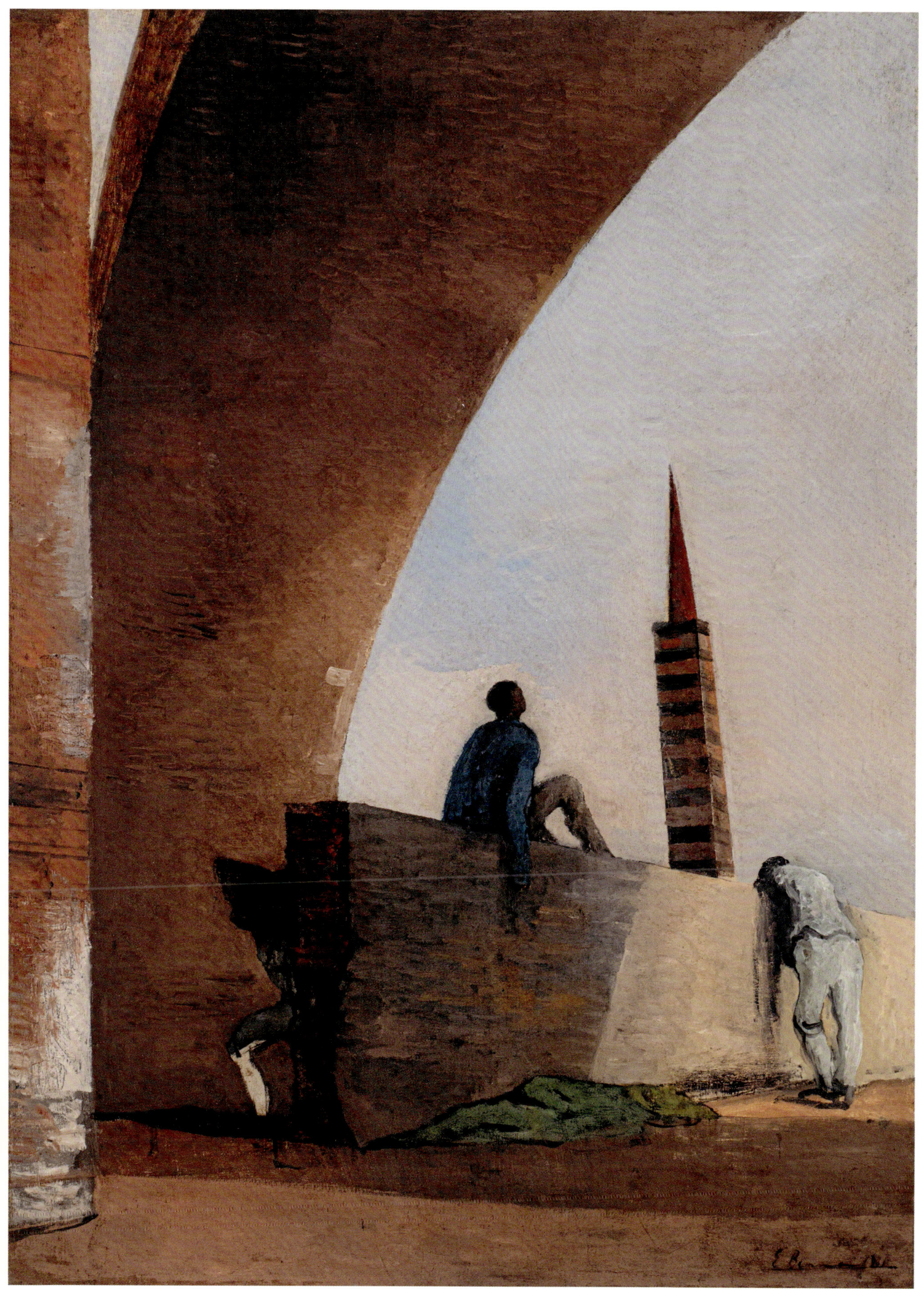

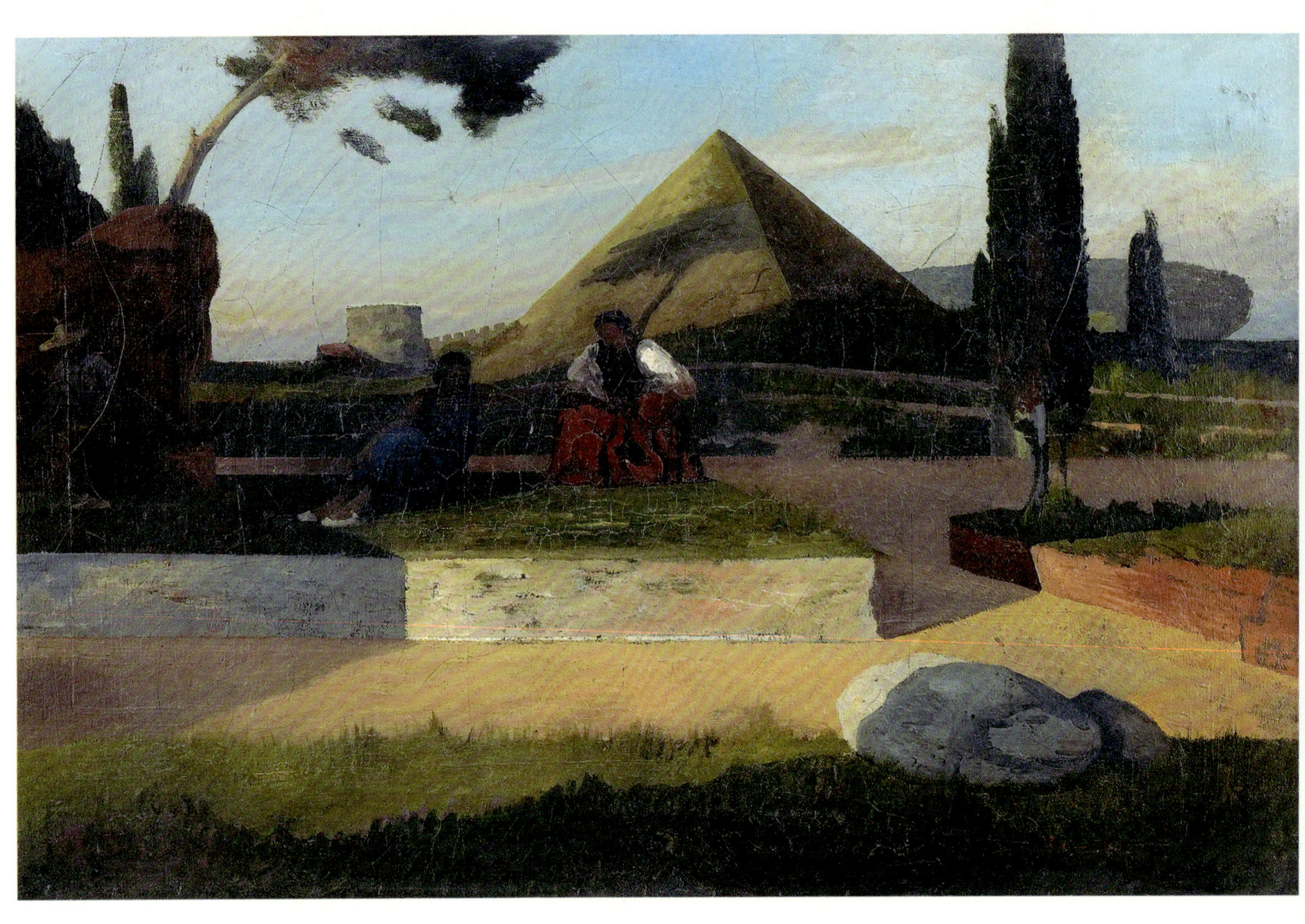

ABOVE: Eugene Berman, *Pyramid Landscape*, oil on canvas, 65.5 × 99 cm (25½ × 39½ in.), 1933
OPPOSITE, CLOCKWISE FROM TOP LEFT: Eugene Berman, *Mutilated Statue – Umbria Valley*, oil on canvas, 100 × 81 cm (39½ × 32¼ in.), 1932–33; Eugene Berman, *Apollo and Daphné – The Olive Trees*, oil on canvas, 92 × 73 cm (36 × 28½ in.), 1932–33; Eugene Berman, *The Meal in the Quarries*, oil on canvas, 61 × 49.5 cm (24 × 19½ in.), 1934; Eugene Berman, *Stones and Rocks*, oil on panel, 62 × 49 cm (24⅜ × 19⅜ in.), 1933

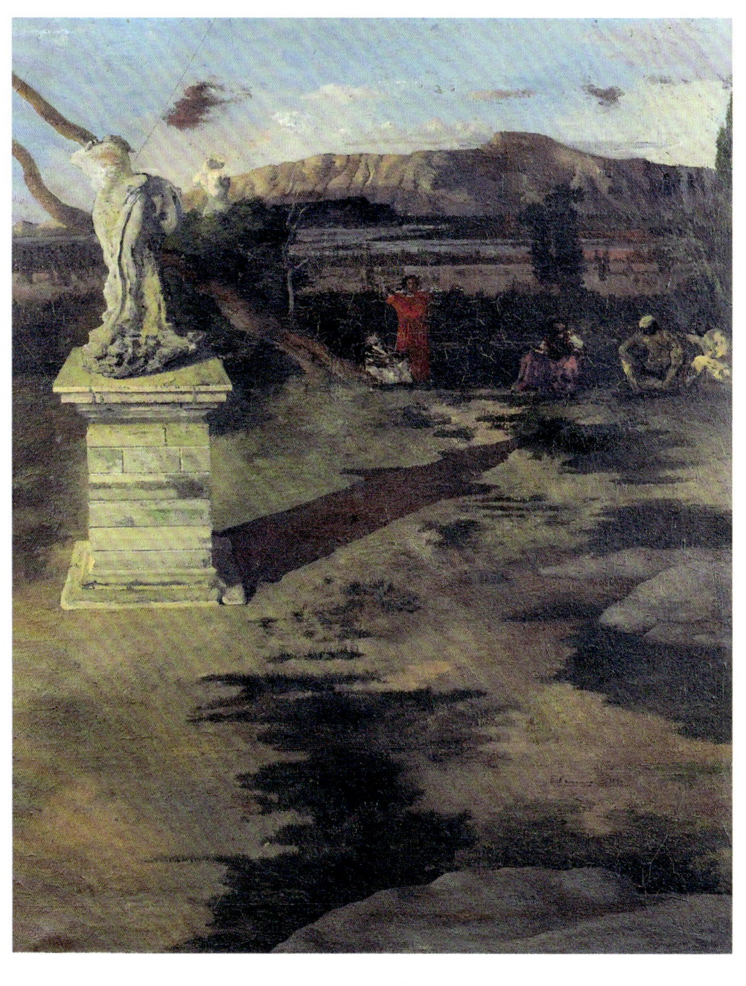

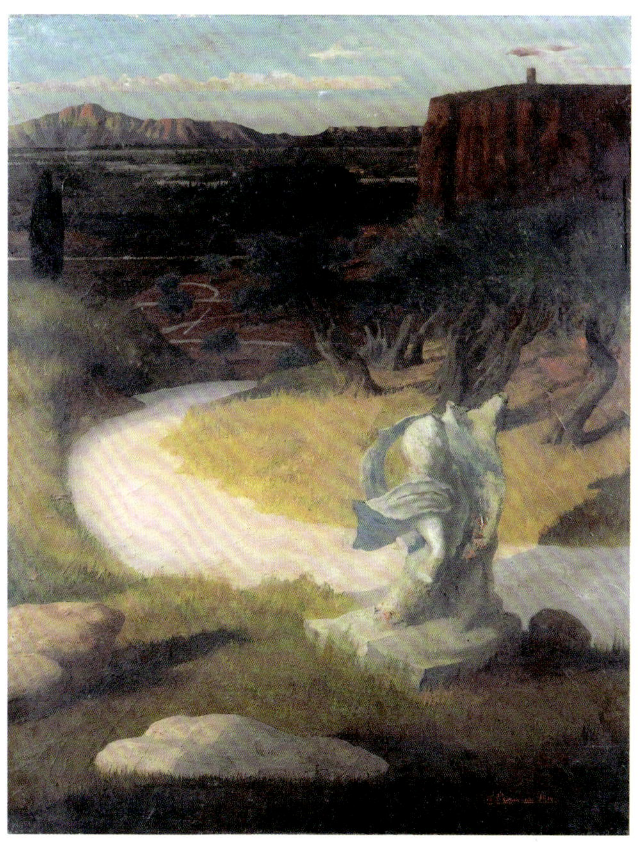

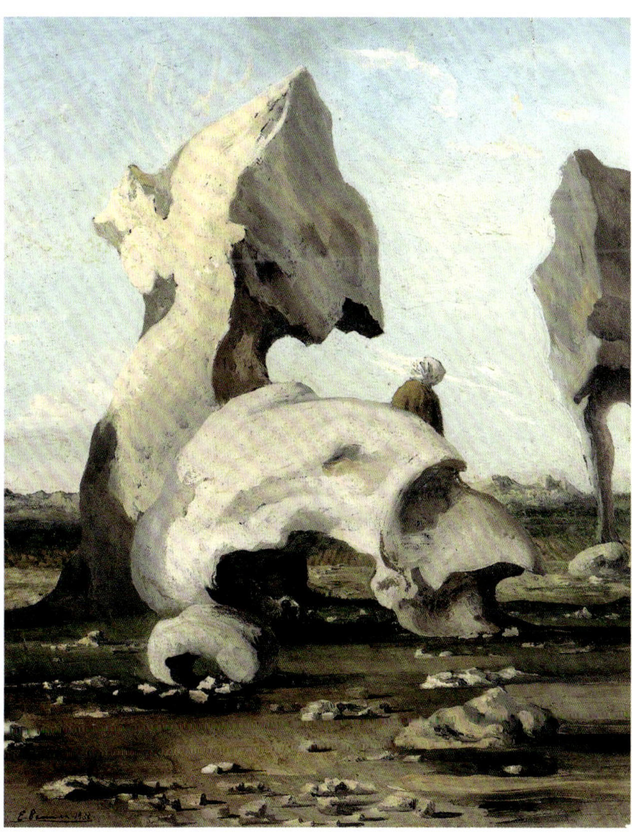

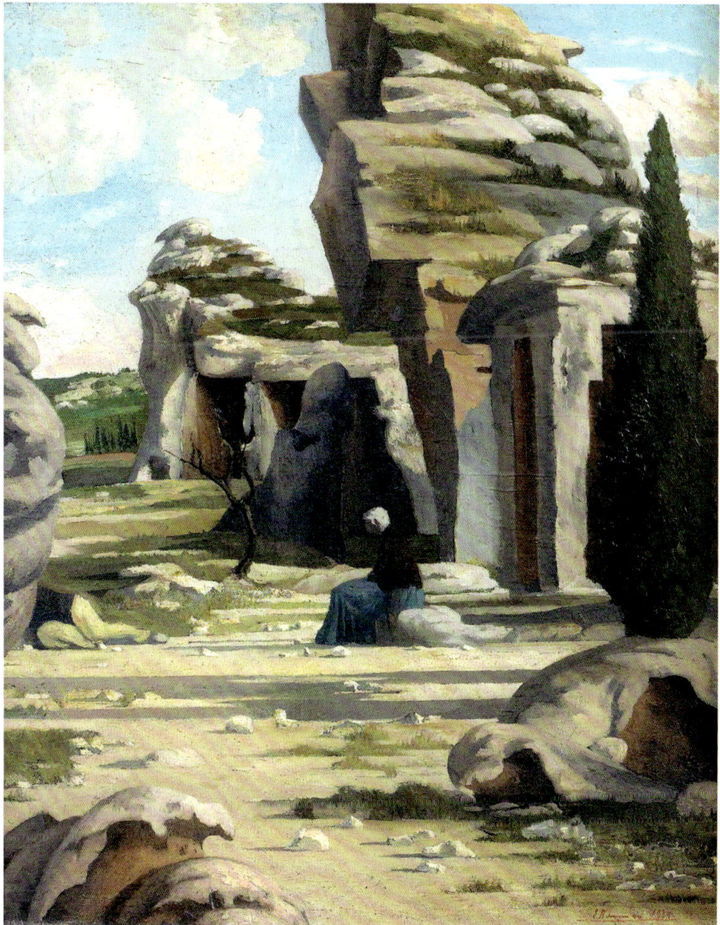

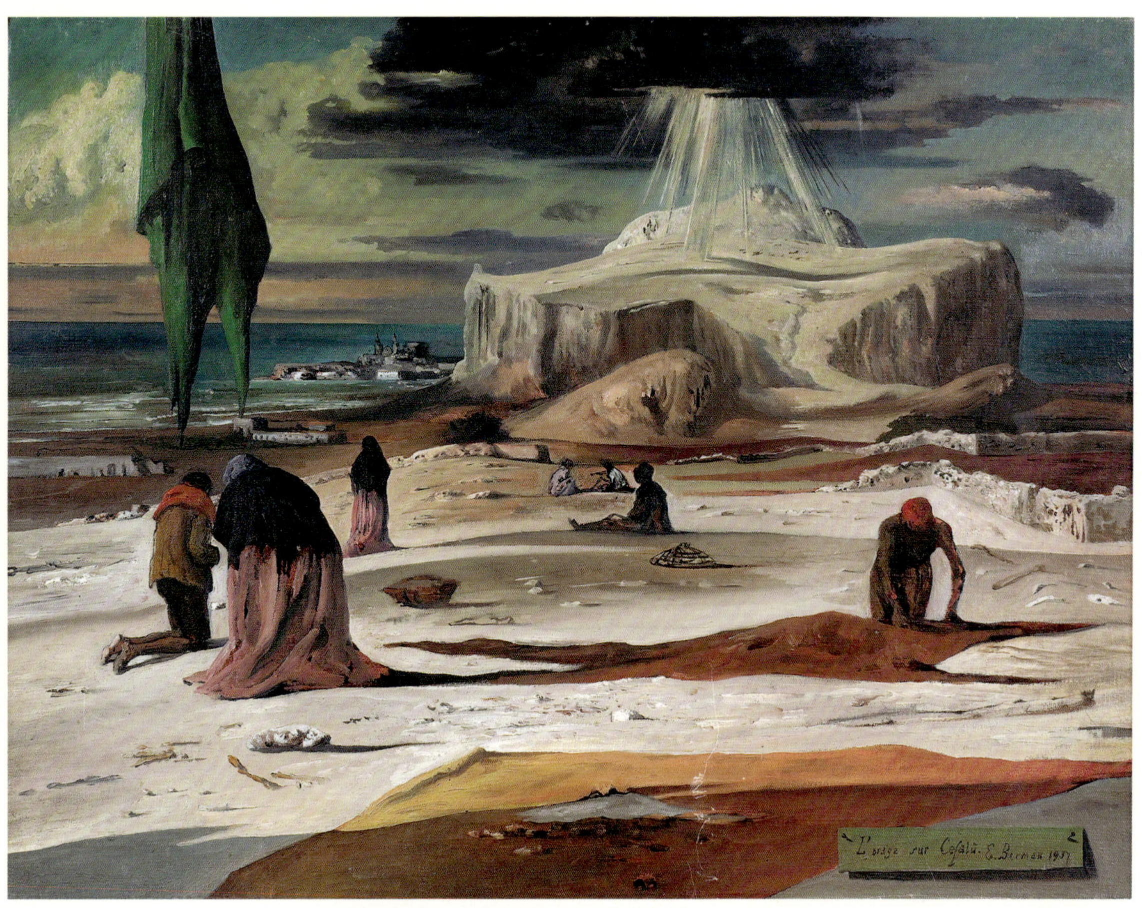

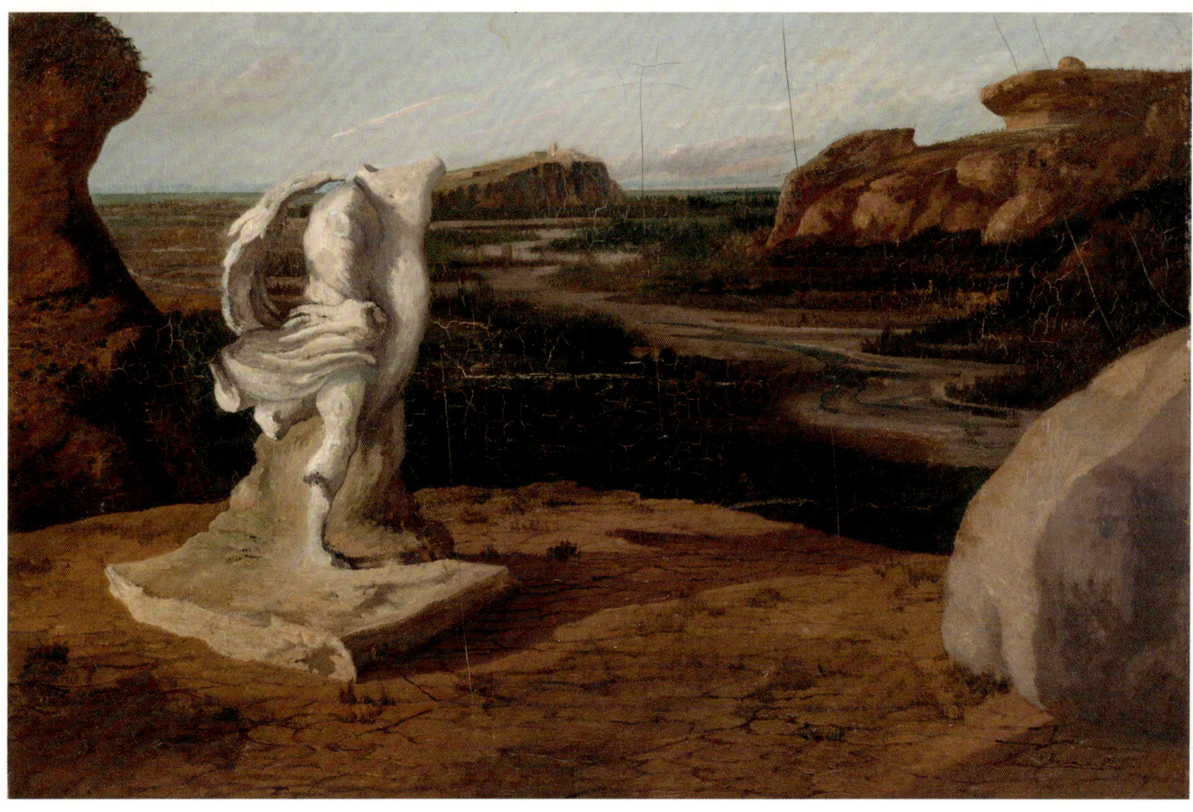

TOP: Eugene Berman, *Storm on Cefalú*, oil on canvas, 61.5 × 81 cm (24¼ × 31⅞ in.), 1937
ABOVE: Eugene Berman, *Apollo and Daphné (The Valley)*, oil on canvas, 64.2 × 100.1 cm (25¼ × 39⅜ in.), 1933

OPPOSITE: Eugene Berman, *Orvieto, July 1934*, oil on canvas, 50 × 62 cm (19⅝ × 24⅜ in.), 1934

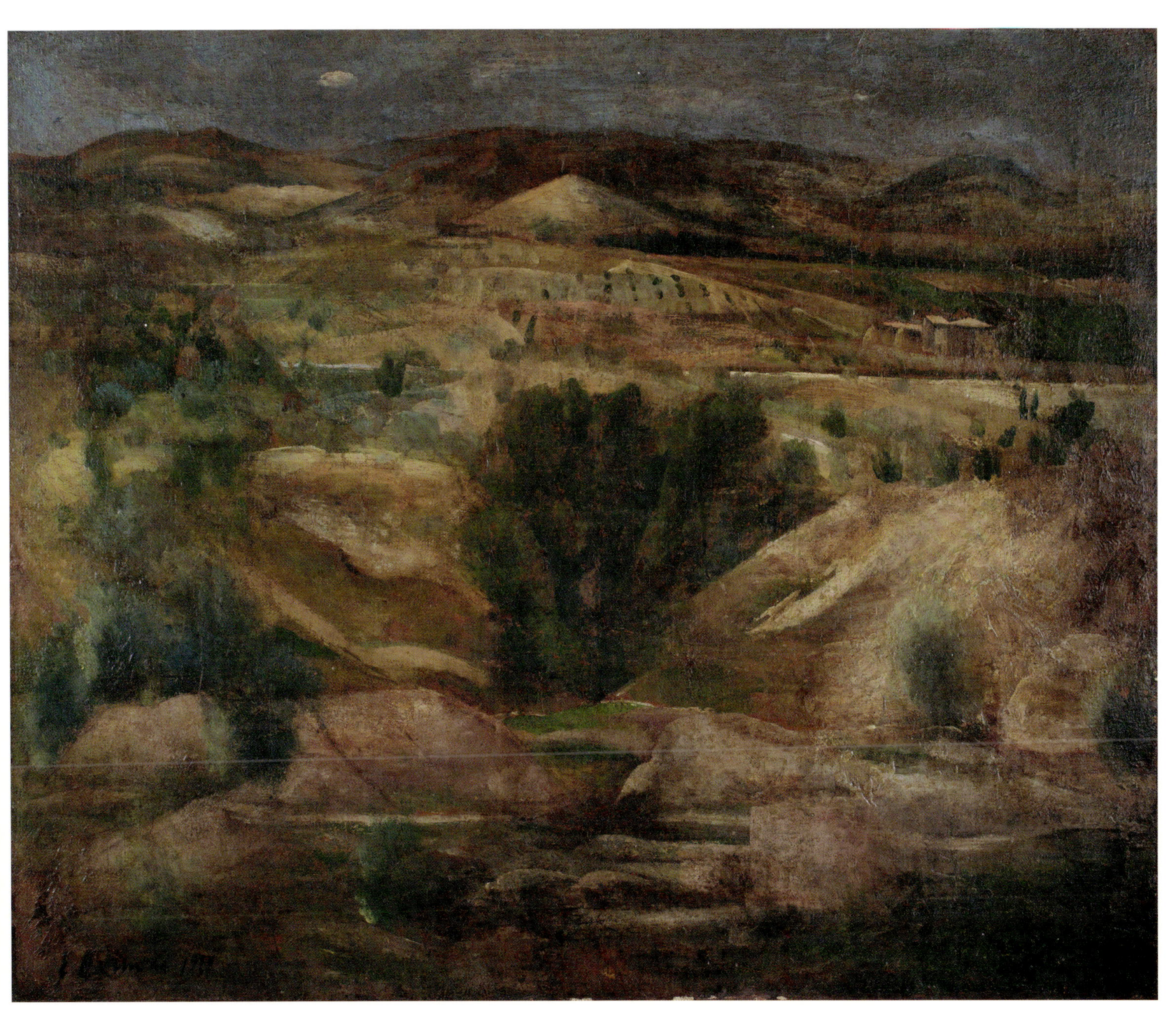

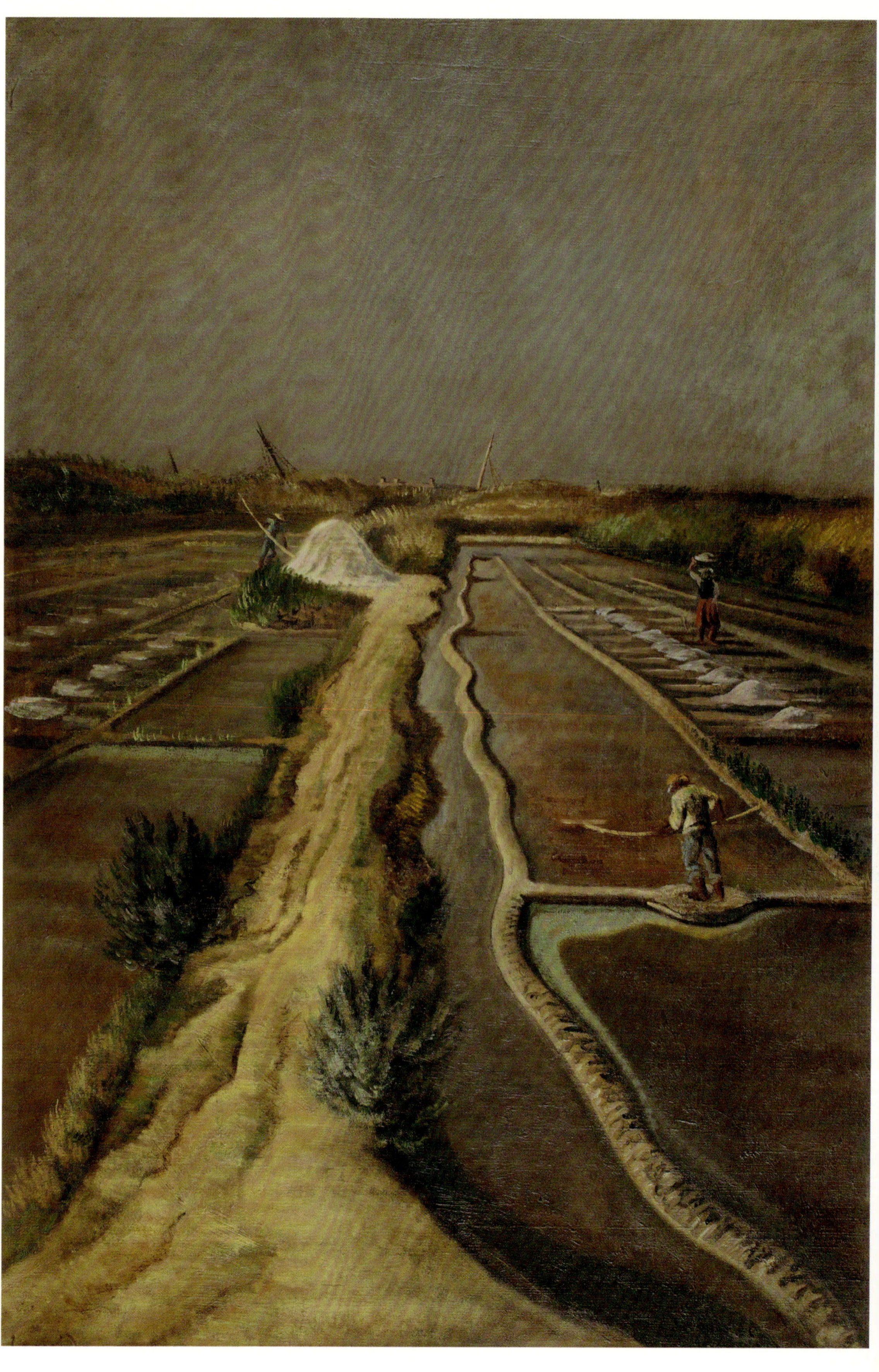

OPPOSITE, CLOCKWISE FROM TOP LEFT: Leonid Berman, *Small Fisherman*, oil on canvas, 23 × 17 cm (9 × 6⅝ in.), *c.* 1928; Leonid Berman, *Oyster Farm*, oil on canvas, 54 × 82 cm (21½ × 32¼ in.), 1935; Leonid Berman, *Shrimp Fisherwomen*, oil on canvas, 27 × 45 cm (10⅝ × 17⅝ in.), 1934; Leonid Berman, *Shrimp Fishermen*, oil on canvas, 27 × 46 cm (10⅝ × 18⅛ in.), 1939

ABOVE: Leonid Berman, *Salt Marshes*, oil on canvas, 81.3 × 54 cm (32 × 21¼ in.), 1931

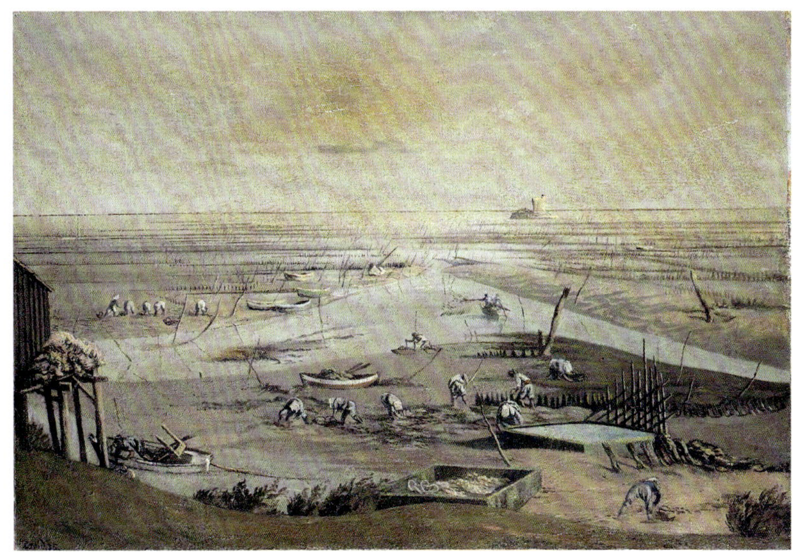

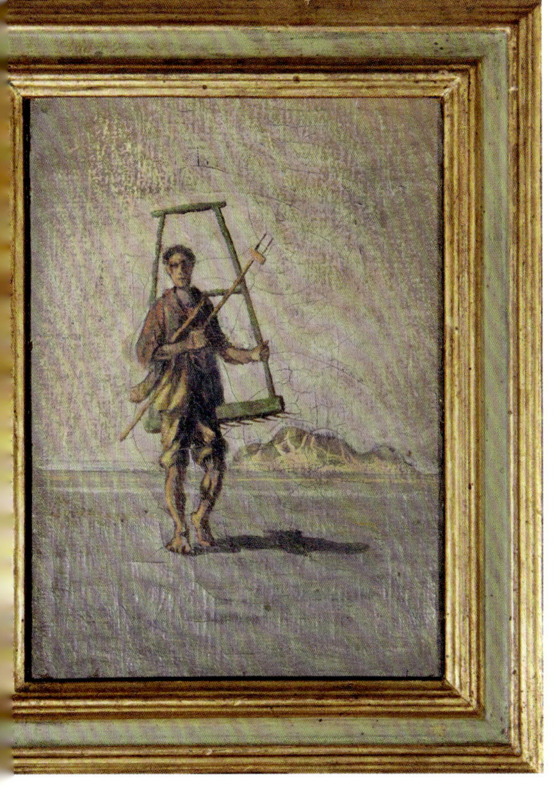

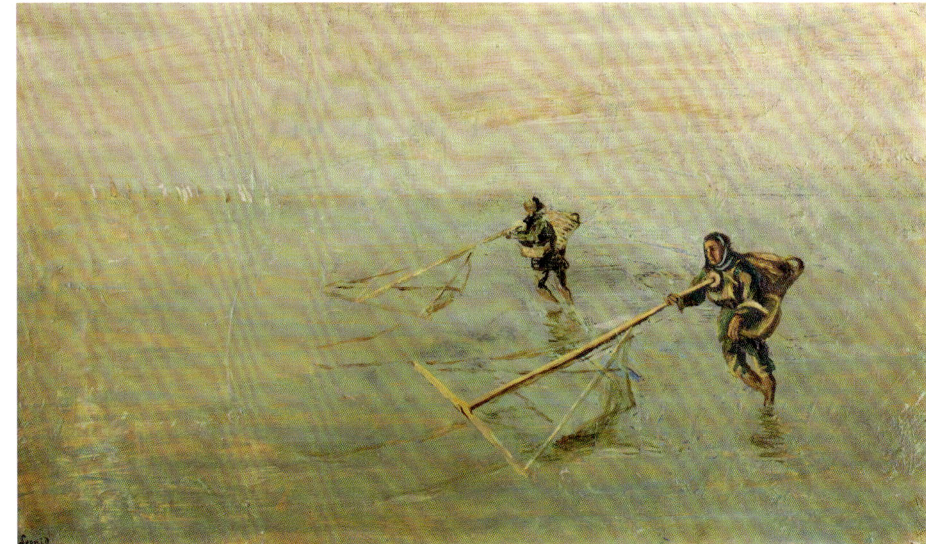

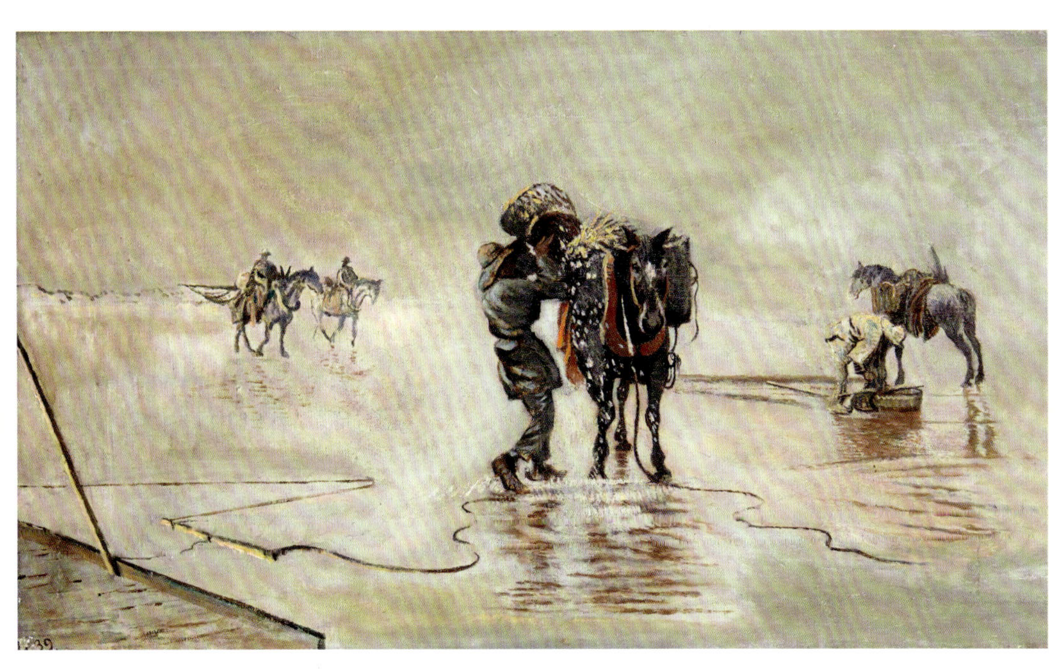

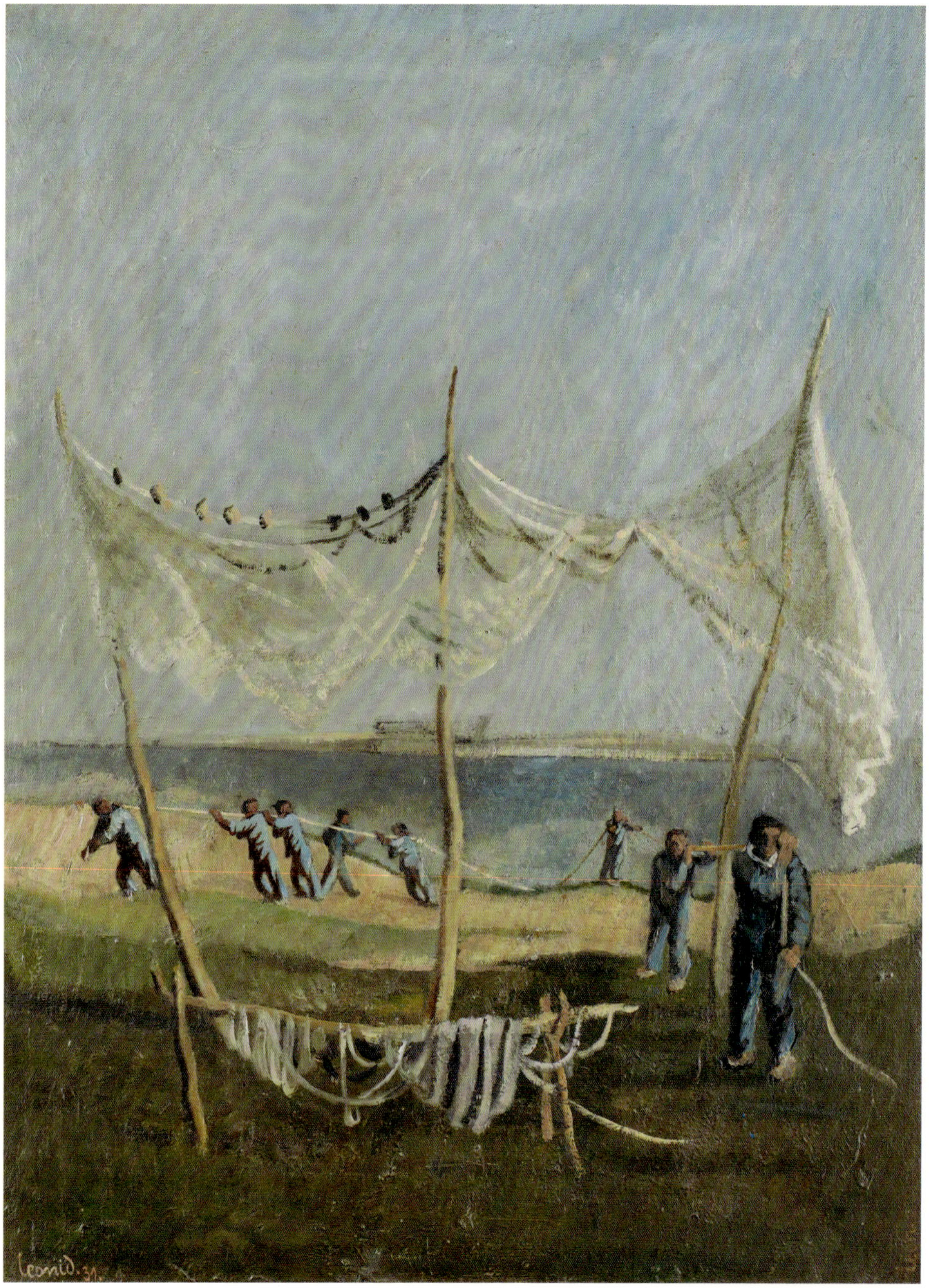

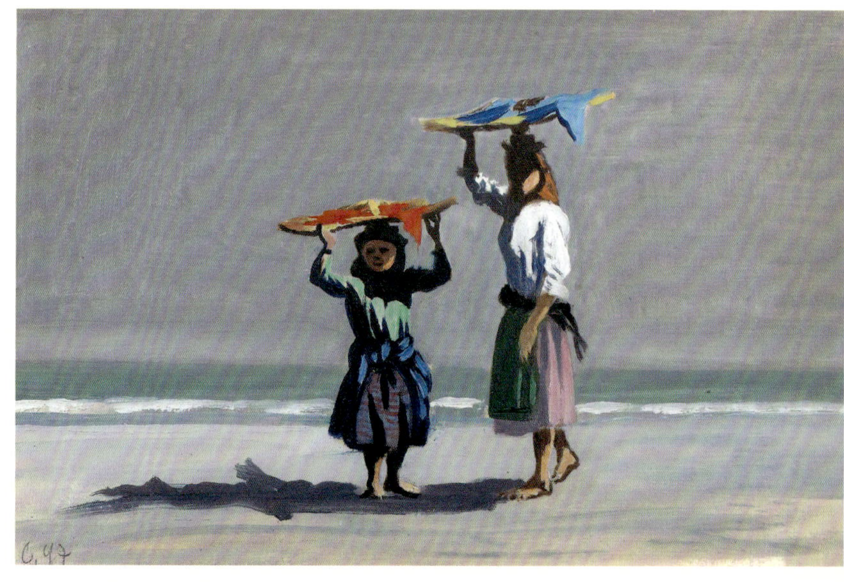

ABOVE: Leonid Berman, *The Nets*,
oil on canvas, 73 × 54 cm (29 × 21 in.), 1931
RIGHT: Leonid Berman, *Untitled*,
gouache on paper, 21 × 33 cm (8½ × 13 in.), 1947
OPPOSITE, FROM TOP TO BOTTOM: Leonid Berman,
Oyster Farm, oil on canvas, 51 × 81 cm (20 × 32 in.), 1935;
Leonid Berman, *Shrimp Fisherwomen in Brittany*, oil on
canvas, 54 × 81.4 cm (21¼ × 32 in.), 1946; Leonid Berman,
Le Chalutier, oil on canvas, 31 × 54.5 cm (12⅛ × 21⅜ in.), 1935

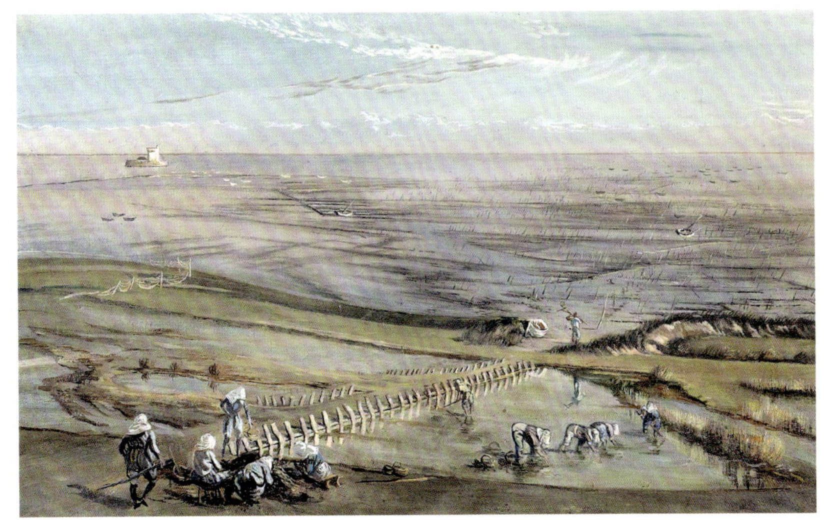

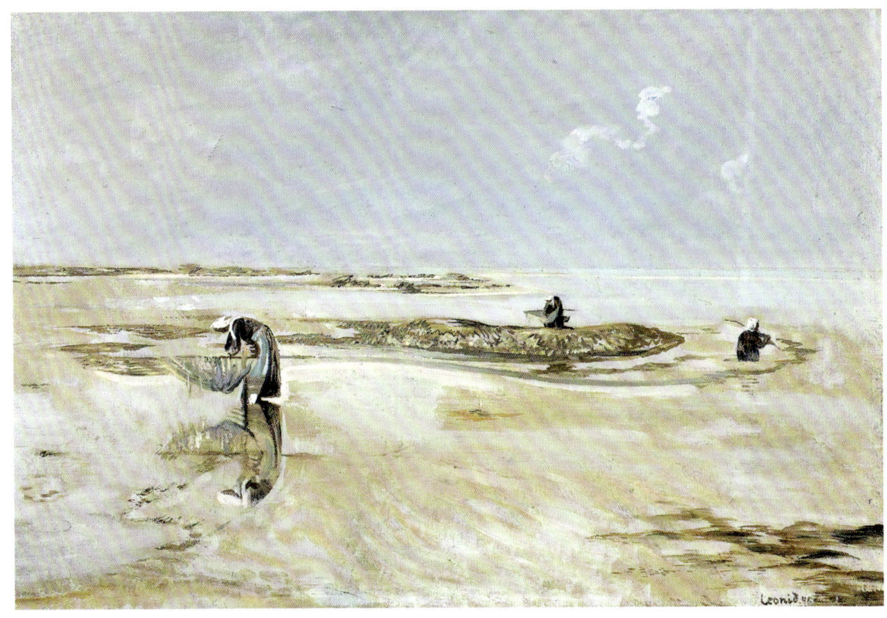

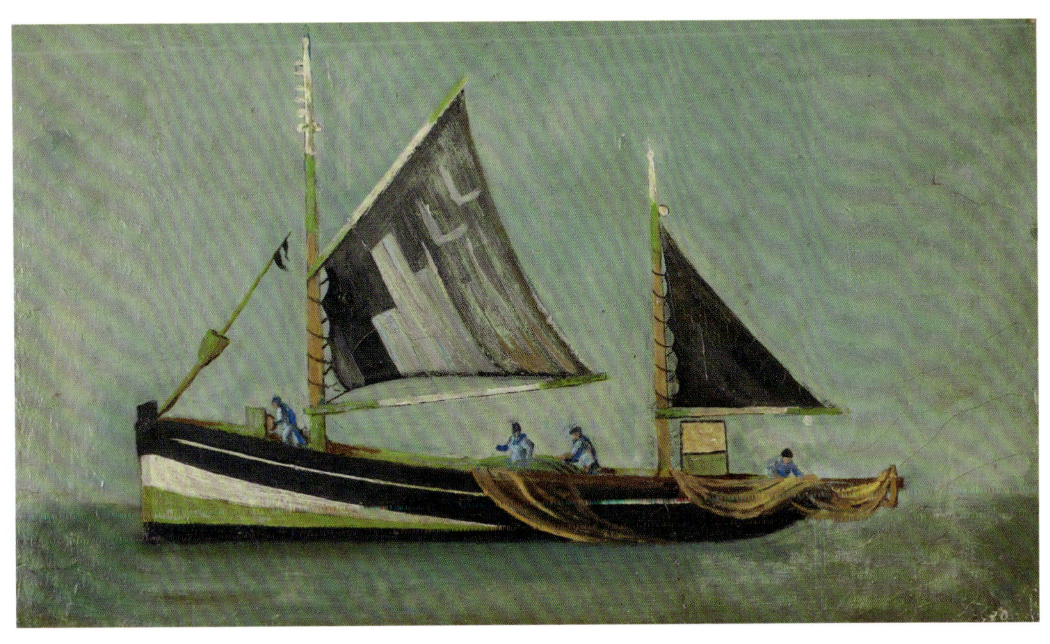

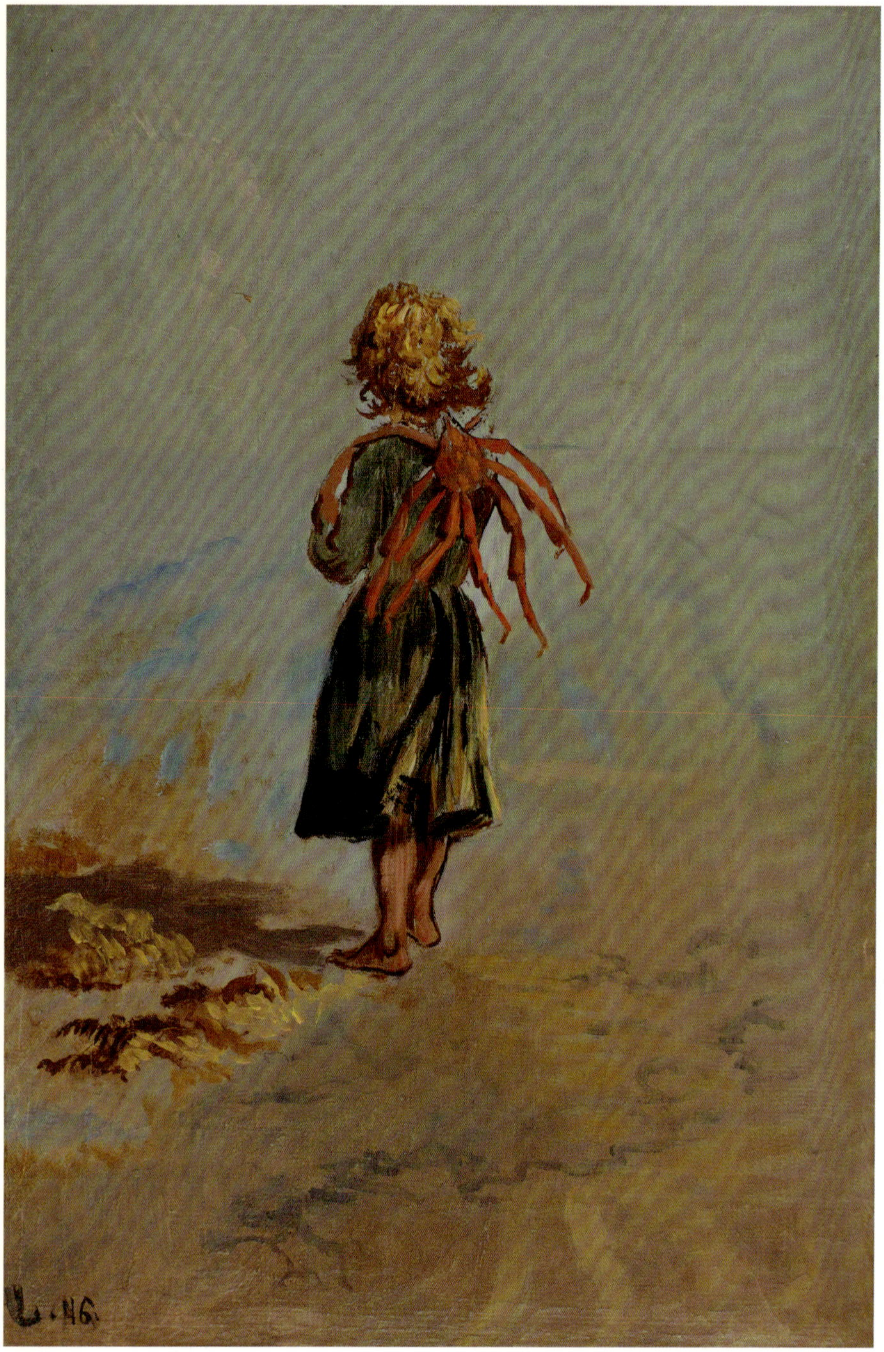

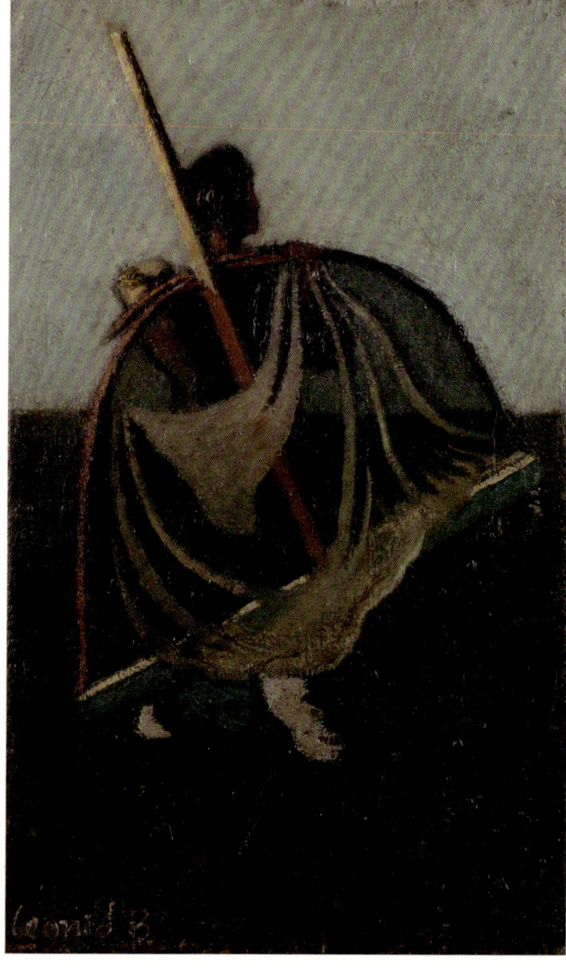

ABOVE, LEFT: Leonid Berman, *Little Girl with Spider Crab*, oil on canvas, 41 × 27 cm (16 × 10¾ in.), 1946
ABOVE, RIGHT: Leonid Berman, *Fisherman with Net*, oil on canvas, 35 × 22 cm (13¾ × 8⅝ in.), *c.* 1930
OPPOSITE: Leonid Berman, *Boat in Italy*, oil on canvas, 51 × 62 cm (20 × 24⅜ in.), 1947

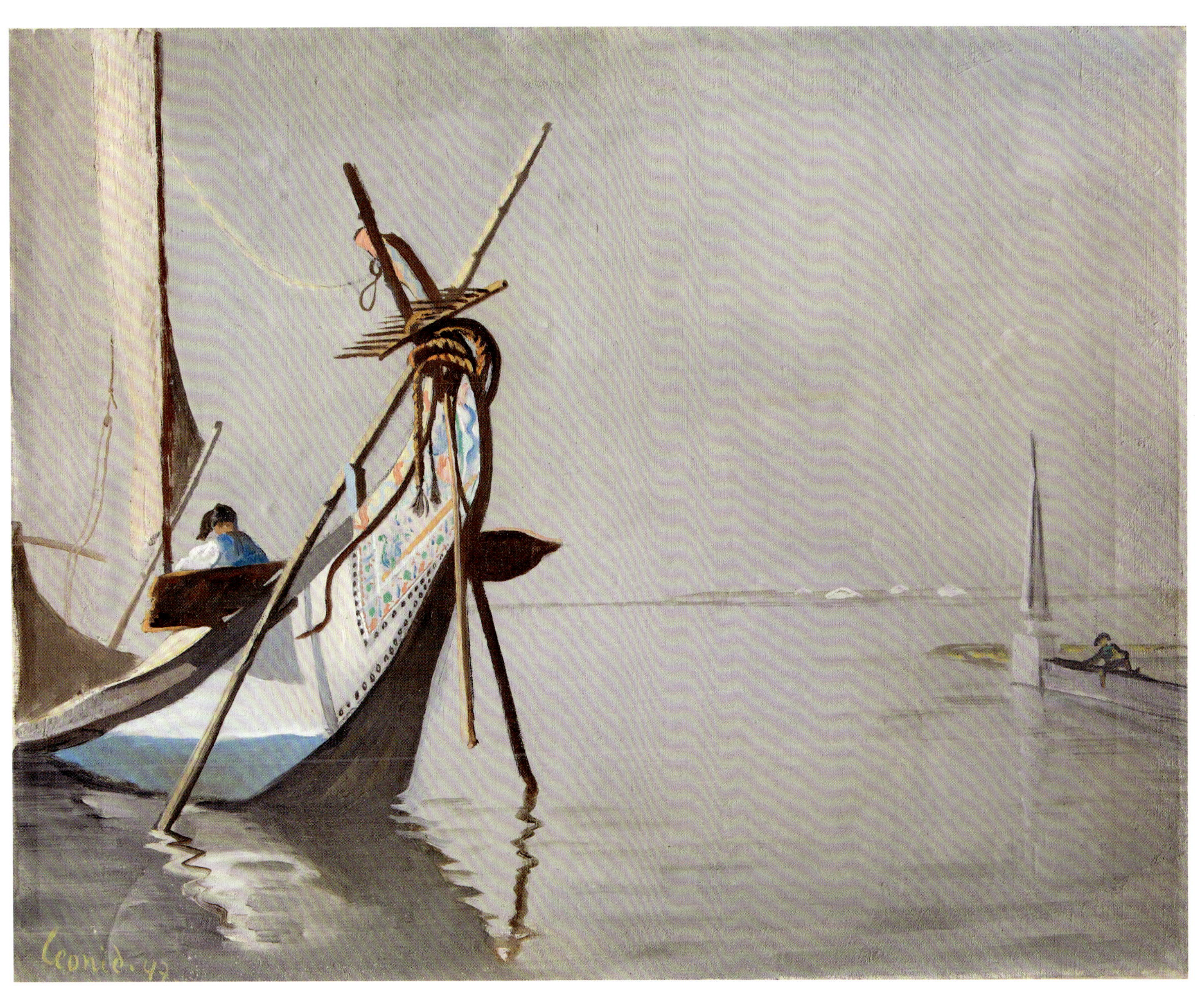
Leonid. 47

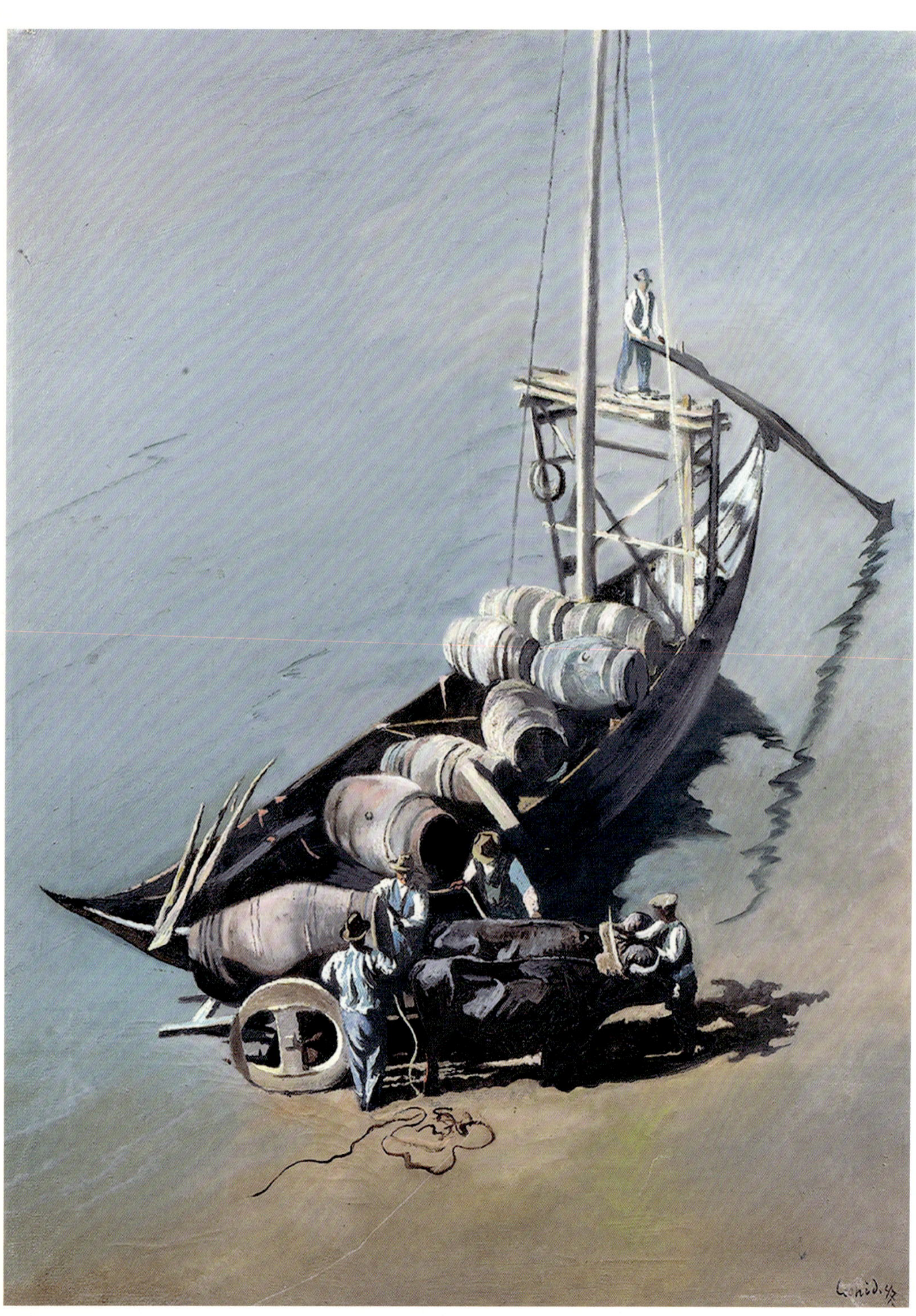

ABOVE: Leonid Berman, *Loading Wine in Porto*, oil on canvas, 80 × 60 cm (32 × 23½ in.), 1947
OPPOSITE: Leonid Berman, *Sachuest Point, Sakonnet River, Rhode Island*, oil on canvas, 91.4 × 127 cm (36 × 50 in.), 1951

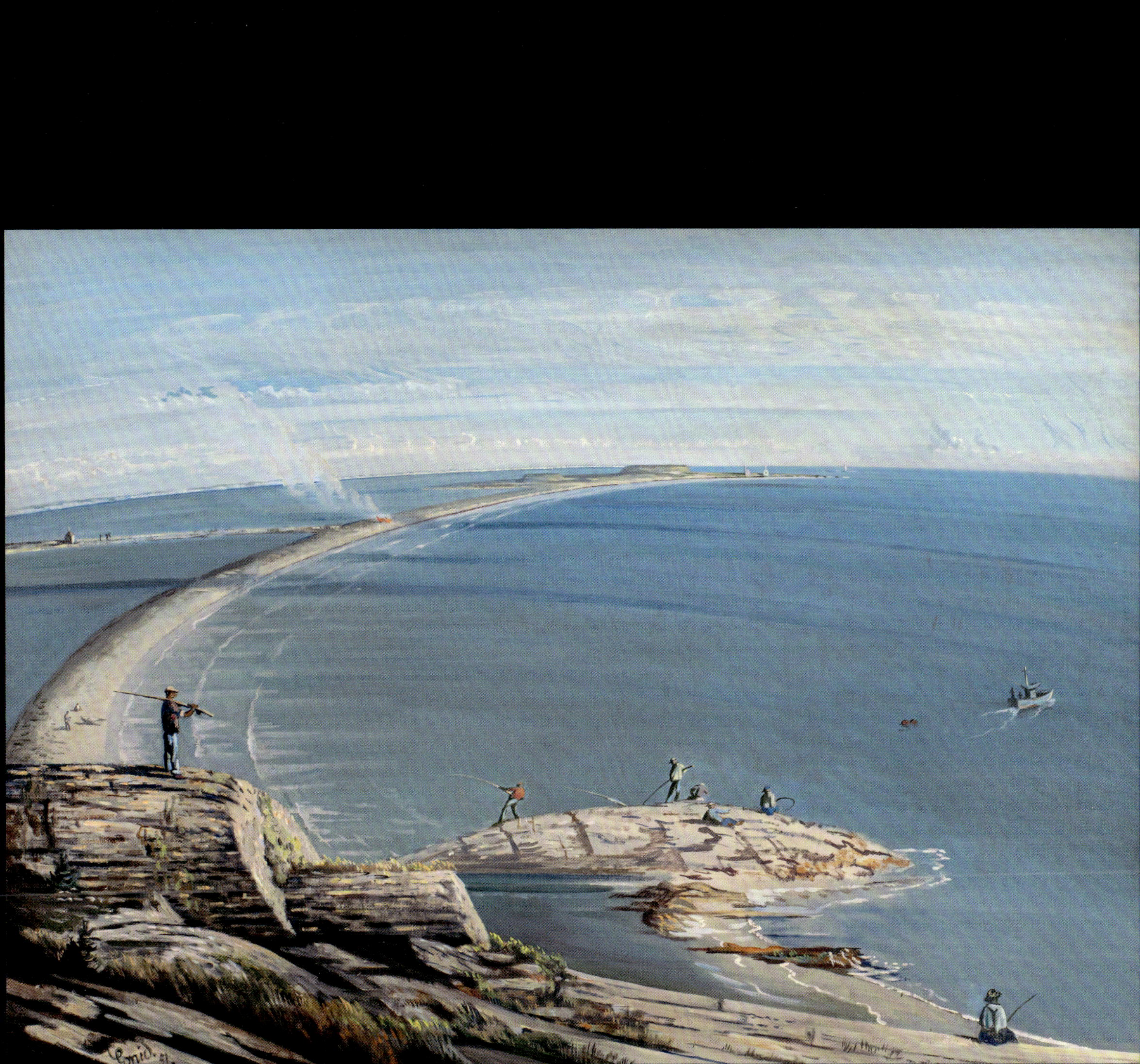

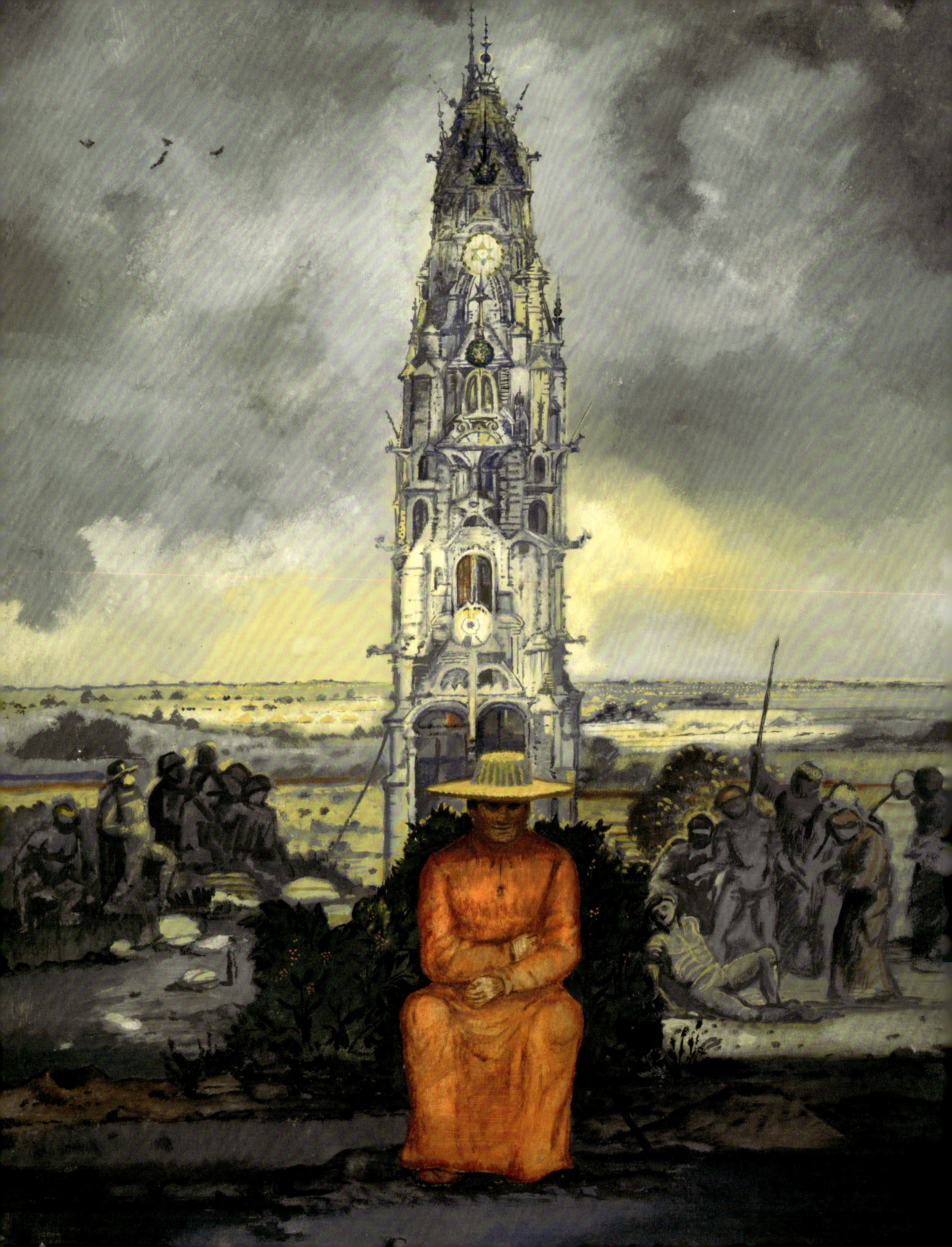

ACT II

AGAINST THE TIDE

Miss Stein's Prevarications

> 'We were all going to be great artists and we had all sat with Alice and we had all given our homage to Gertrude [...] "the greatest artist in the world".'
>
> Bravig Imbs, *Confessions of Another Young Man*, 1936, p. 171

A century on, the panorama has changed, clearing the way for a new assessment of the significance of the Neo-Romantic group, or rather the fleeting conjunction of sensibilities that arose in 1926. According to the prevailing history of modern art, there was a decisive rupture with figuration in the early years of the twentieth century. This upheaval was characterized by the abandonment of the illusionist construction of space, the skewed perspectives of Cubism, the use of collage and the emergence, around 1910, of abstraction. These developments were seen as stages that were destined to be continued – after the parenthesis of the war and the displacement of the artistic centre of gravity from Paris to New York – in Abstract Expressionism and successive waves of new American painting. (Julien Levy, one of the key dealers for the Neo-Romantics, who played a major role in their introduction to the United States in the 1930s, wrote in his memoirs that the eruption of Abstract Expressionism in the 1950s led to it becoming

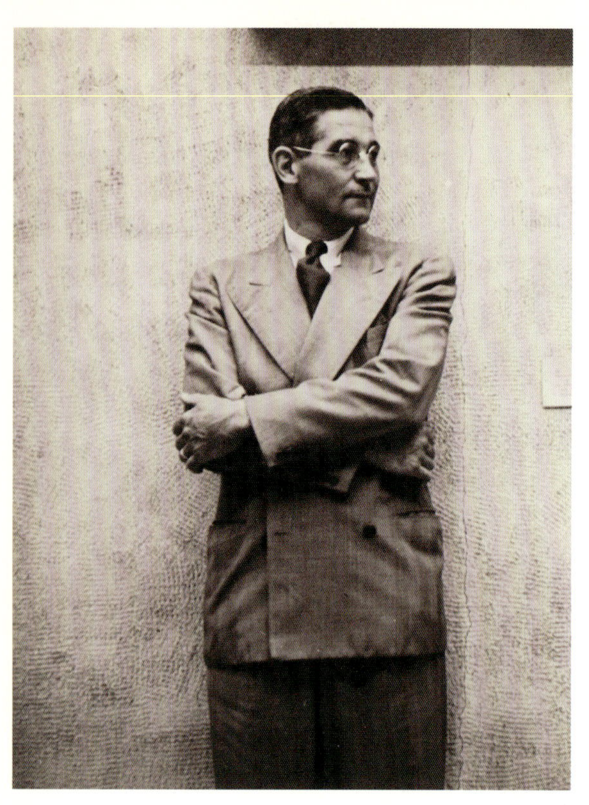

the 'new international school', carrying away 'like a tornado, everything else, good or bad', all but obliterating the artists that he himself had championed.)

There is no place in this accepted narrative, therefore, for a small handful of painters who, at the start of their careers, resolutely swam against the tide and swore no allegiance to any credo or charismatic figure (unlike most of the artistic movements of the time) but were brought together by serendipity and geographical proximity. Half a century later, the poet and critic James Schuyler, prompted to reflect on the Neo-Romantics by a retrospective of Leonid's work in New York, expressed surprise that '[the group] was bound by neither dogma nor true affinity of style' and had little in common outside of their collective shows. We shall see later how Eugene viewed this aspect in his musings on the nature and course of Neo-Romanticism in the final years of his career.

The Neo-Romantics were not even united by an urge for reaction or for a return to tradition, as a retrospective simplification would suggest. They were, in fact, highly tuned to the latest developments in modern art, but they were not afraid to test the limits of these developments. Twenty years after the invention of Cubism and the emergence of abstraction, the initial inventiveness and daring of these explorations had gradually been dissipated by dogmas and formulas. Modernist architecture, meanwhile, was adopting a similarly intellectual and formalist approach, stripped of any aesthetic dimension, and proclaiming a desire for a *tabula rasa*. It advocated unyielding purism, a radical back-to-basics that subordinated form to function, and saw ornamentation, in the famous declaration by Adolf Loos in 1908, as a 'crime'.

Neo-Romanticism was one of the first movements to resist or question this abstract modernity, which was presented as the natural endpoint, and indeed the culmination, of artistic exploration. (This conviction was not seriously challenged until the latter decades of the twentieth century.) The importance of these young artists' stance lay precisely in their clearing of the decks, as recognized in 1935 by James Thrall Soby in the only book thus far devoted to the group, tellingly entitled *After Picasso*. '[They] deliberately renounced the value of all abstract art, whether classic or romantic,' declared Soby

PREVIOUS PAGE: Kristians Tonny, *After van Eyck [Gertrude Stein]*, black ink over tempera on Masonite adhered to cardboard, 61 × 45.4 cm (24 × 17⅞ in.), *c.* 1930–36 (detail)
ABOVE: James Thrall Soby, 1954

in its opening pages. 'Their first works showed that they intended to abandon non-representational painting for a return to sentiment in subject-matter and in the handling of subject-matter. [...] Being young, they were able to accept Picasso's upheaval of tradition as an accomplished fact and to proceed with a counter-revolution.' What Soby saw as supplantation, as a passing of the dialectic baton, has more recently been interpreted in terms of an alternation between baroque and neoclassical poles in twentieth-century art. By this score, the Neo-Romantics would be the first representatives of a sensibility that would be dubbed 'post-modern' in the last quarter of the century.

Soby's proximity to the group's artists and the perspicacity of his analyses make *After Picasso* a foundational text, and its author – the first to discern these young painters' significance, coherence and worth – one of the true 'inventors' of Neo-Romanticism, along with Waldemar-George. James Thrall Soby (1906–1979) was a critic, curator, patron and collector who formed part of the European and transatlantic literary and artistic circles that were the Neo-Romantics' natural habitat. He can be seen as the embodiment of a milieu that included not only writers and artists but also collectors. The curiosity, cosmopolitanism, openness of spirit, and acceptance of both old and new that characterized this scene would be lost after the war, together with a particular kind of sociability.

The young artists were promoted by adherents to the more carefree branches of modernism: in the United States, Julien Levy (whose gallery championed both the Surrealists and the Neo-Romantics), Lincoln Kirstein (co-founder of the New York City Ballet) and Chick Austin (the adventurous director of the Wadsworth Atheneum, a focal point for the movement); in Britain, the Sitwells; and in France, the Noailles, the Beaumonts and, last but by no means least, that imposing oracle of the avant-garde, Gertrude Stein.

The Neo-Romantics play a supporting role – incidental but decisive – in Stein's most famous book, *The Autobiography of Alice B. Toklas*. This was published in 1933, only a few years after that seminal exhibition at the Druet Gallery (which is mentioned in passing in the book). The Neo-Romantics' paintings appear in the closing sections of this classic of *faux naïveté* as a pretext for a final discussion of the course of modern art in the early years of the twentieth century, from the time when Stein arrived in Paris, with the companion who would serve as her alias, to the six weeks that it took her, a quarter of a century later, to write a text that was primarily intended to bring in some money.

Invoking herself in the supposed words of her soulmate, Stein starts off with a fallacious declaration, albeit one delivered with all the authority for which she was renowned: 'In *How To Write* Gertrude Stein makes this sentence, "Painting now after its great period has come back to be a minor art." She was very interested to know who was to be the leader of this art.'

Having opened up this quest for a new leader, the explorations of Bérard and company found themselves on the receiving end of a wily repertoire of prevarications, omissions and paradoxes of varying degrees of sincerity. In keeping with the stylistic tone of the book, these interrogations also served, above all, as a means for demonstrating the difficulty, or indeed the impossibility, of pinning down the Neo-Romantic movement with any single idea or description. Stein used her novelistic skills to establish, in her own inimitable style, the themes that would underlie and structure her discussion of Neo-Romanticism. Moreover, whatever her criticism (in every sense of the term) of the group's leading lights, Stein was still willing to collaborate with them.

A chance meeting – with Jane Heap, a friend of Stein and Toklas, and the publisher of Ezra Pound, T. S. Eliot and William Carlos Williams in her avant-garde magazine *The Little Review* – allowed Stein to introduce her motif: 'Jane Heap had been telling us of a young russian in whose work she was interested. As we were crossing a bridge in Godiva [Stein's car] we saw Jane Heap and the young russian. We saw his pictures and Gertrude Stein too was interested. He of course came to see us.' The young Russian – none other than Tchelitchew, of course – would provide the connection with the rest of the group, which was shot through with the enmity, described above by Leonid, between its two aspirants to pre-eminence: 'The young russian was interesting. He was painting, so he said, colour that was no colour, he was painting blue pictures and he was painting three heads in one. Picasso had been drawing three heads in one. Soon the russian was painting three figures in one. Was he the only one? In a way he was although there was a group of them. This group, very shortly after Gertrude Stein knew the russian, had a show at one of the art galleries, Druet's I think. The group then consisted of the russian, a frenchman, a very young dutchman, and two russian brothers. All of them except the dutchman about twenty-six years old. [...] The russian Tchelitchev's work was the most vigorous of the group and the most mature and the most interesting. He had already then a passionate enmity against the frenchman whom they called Bébé Bérard and whose name was Christian Bérard and whom Tchelitchev said copied everything.'

Leaving aside any speculation about the artists' reaction to Stein's crafty indiscretions – they were surely accustomed to crossing the path of the redoubtable *grande dame* – the passing reference to Picasso is most worthy of our attention. His shadow hangs over the final part of the *Autobiography*, which is haunted by the radical innovation of his work and the possibility of a succession, coupled with the quest for a new figurehead (thus anticipating Soby's stance two years later).

One by one, three of the Neo-Romantic artists were summoned by this exacting arbiter of taste to submit their work for her appreciation. Tchelitchew was the first candidate, but he would end up being brutally rejected: 'Gertrude Stein was at first not interested in this group of painters as a group but only in the russian. This interest gradually increased and then she was bothered. Granted, she used to say, that the influences which make a new movement in art and literature have continued and are making a new movement in art and literature; in order to seize these influences and create as well as re-create them there needs a very dominating creative power. This the russian manifestly did not have. Still there was a distinctly new creative idea.'

Bérard, who had initially been brushed aside, then became a suitable pretender to the throne. He came back into Stein's orbit thanks to the American composer Virgil Thomson, who greatly admired his work and also formed part of Stein's inner circle (he would provide the music for her opera *Four Saints in Three Acts* in 1934). Although Stein was always on the lookout for a new standard-bearer, she could not make up her mind about Bérard. 'Virgil had in his room a great many pictures by Christian Bérard and Gertrude Stein used to look at them a great deal. She could not find out at all what she thought about them. [...] Virgil said he knew nothing about pictures but he thought these wonderful. Gertrude Stein told him about her perplexity about the new movement and that the creative power behind it was not the russian. Virgil said that there he quite agreed with her and he was convinced that it was Bébé Bérard, baptised Christian. She said that perhaps that was the answer but she was very doubtful. She used to say of Bérard's pictures, they are almost something and then they are just not.'

In order to sharpen her thinking, and justify this piece of something and nothing, the Stein of *Four Saints in Three Acts* came to the fore by bizarrely applying to aesthetics the religious register that would emerge in her libretto for Thomson. Bérard suddenly fell from grace: 'As she used to explain to Virgil, the Catholic Church makes a very sharp distinction between a hysteric and a saint. The same thing holds true in the art world. There is the sensitiveness of the hysteric which has all the appearance of creation, but actual creation has an individual force which is an entirely different thing. Gertrude Stein was inclined to believe that artistically Bérard was more hysteric than saint.'

Bérard having therefore been cast into the rubbish bin of history – the appropriate place for a hysteric, according to Jacques Lacan – Eugene Berman took centre stage via an exhibition in 1929 at the gallery of Jacques Bonjean, who, along with his associates, would later become one of the main pillars of support for the Neo-Romantics. '[W]e happened to go to a show of pictures at the Galerie Bonjean. There we met one of the russian brothers, Genia Berman, and Gertrude Stein was not uninterested in his pictures. She went with him to his studio and looked at everything he had ever painted. He seemed to have a purer intelligence than the other two painters who certainly had not created the modern movement, perhaps the idea had been originally his. She asked him, telling her story as she was fond of telling it at that time to any one who would listen, had he originated the idea. He said with an intelligent inner smile that he thought he had. She was not at all sure that he was not right.'

By now, the reader has become familiar with Stein's affected reservations and circumlocutions, and is thus not wholly unprepared for the following breathtaking flourish of contradictions: 'He came down to Bilignin to see us and she slowly concluded that though he was a very good painter he was too bad a painter to have been the creator of an idea.' Coincidentally, what might be described as a variation on this theme can be found in Julien Green's *Journal*: '"Berman is a bad painter who will one day paint quite good pictures. He may well finish up in the collection of a provincial museum in a hundred and fifty years' time. Bérard has the charm of his race and he may, after endlessly debating between beauty and fashion, opt for beauty, but he is in danger of falling into fashion, and staying there." Who says this? Miss Stein. She is half stretched out on a black horsehair sofa with her hand plunged into the white fur of her poodle. She has the strong, tranquil air of a menhir.'

OPPOSITE: Virgil Thomson and Gertrude Stein at 27 rue de Fleurus, Paris, *c.* 1932

It was Stein herself who brought this series of frustrating advances to a conclusion: 'So once more the search began.' The Neo-Romantics had merely marked a brief episode in her fruitless yearning for a changing of the guard.

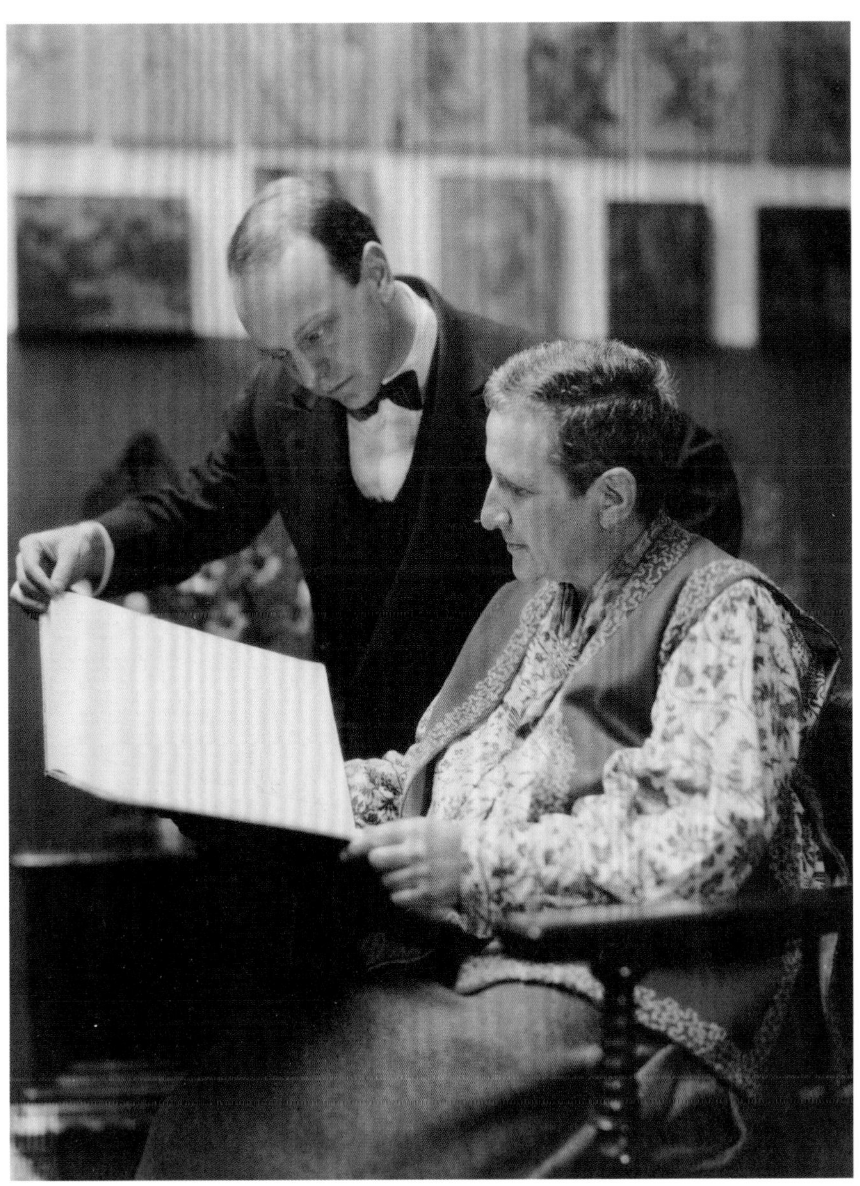

Ten Portraits

> 'Monsieur Bérard, another artist who became such a lion in Parisian society he grew a red beard to look the part. Famed for his smart fashion drawings, his peppery *bon mots*, his elusively sinister paintings. French, and a friend of Cocteau.'
>
> Bravig Imbs, *Confessions of Another Young Man*, 1936, p. 11

There was, however, more to the relationship between Gertrude Stein and the Neo-Romantics than this disheartening to-and-fro. More tangible evidence of her interest can be seen in the very pages of her *Autobiography*, and in her account therein of her own beginnings as a writer. By 1930 she had published only a handful of books in limited editions (including *The Making of Americans* in 1925) and she eagerly welcomed the publishing proposals of a young poet whom she met through Virgil Thomson.

Georges Hugnet (1906–1974), the son of a cabinet-maker from Faubourg Saint-Antoine, became interested very early on in the most radical movements of the day, Dada and Surrealism. A neighbour in his apartment building, Marcel Jouhandeau, had introduced him to Max Jacob, who, in turn, presented him to the *crème de la crème* of literary and artistic Paris, from Picasso to Duchamp, from Cocteau to Tristan Tzara. Hugnet stood on the threshold of a highly productive and varied career that is still undervalued, even today (he was a poet, memoirist, playwright, film director, graphic designer, publisher, book binder, painter and creator of collages). In 1929, he decided to establish a small publishing house, Les Éditions de la Montagne, which he launched by translating and introducing selected extracts from *The Making of Americans*, which Stein had

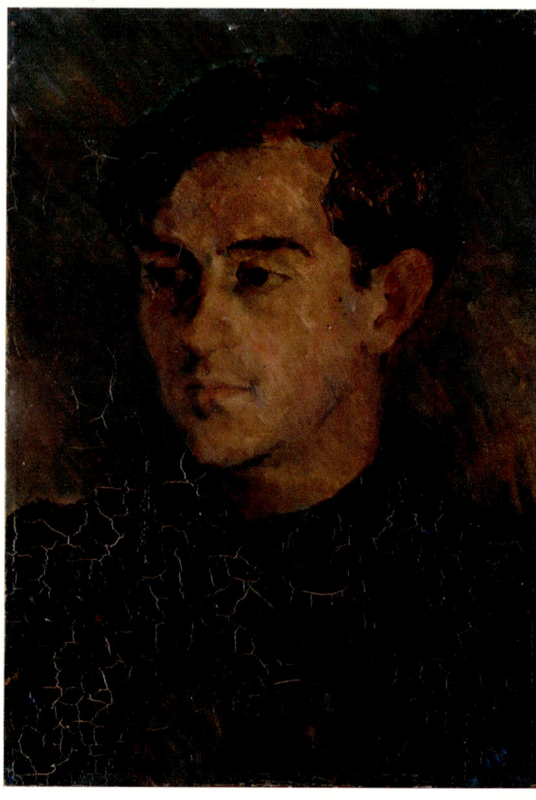

ABOVE: Maurice Grosser, *Portrait of Georges Hugnet*, oil on canvas, 46 × 27 cm (18⅛ × 10⅝ in.), 1931
OPPOSITE: Engravings and drawings from *Ten Portraits* and *Le Droit de Varech*: (clockwise from top left) Christian Bérard, Virgil Thomson, Eugene Berman, Kristians Tonny and Pavel Tchelitchew

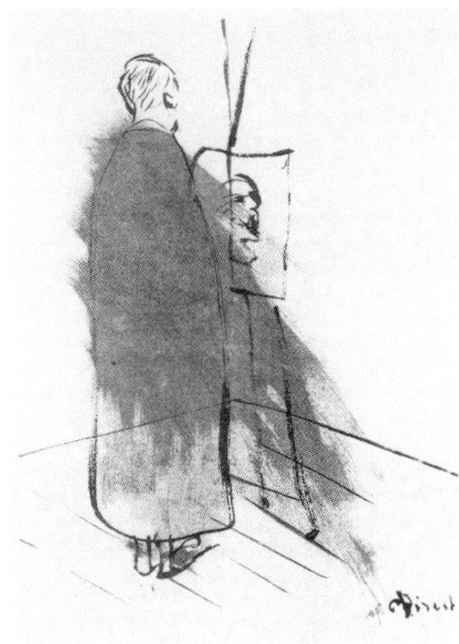
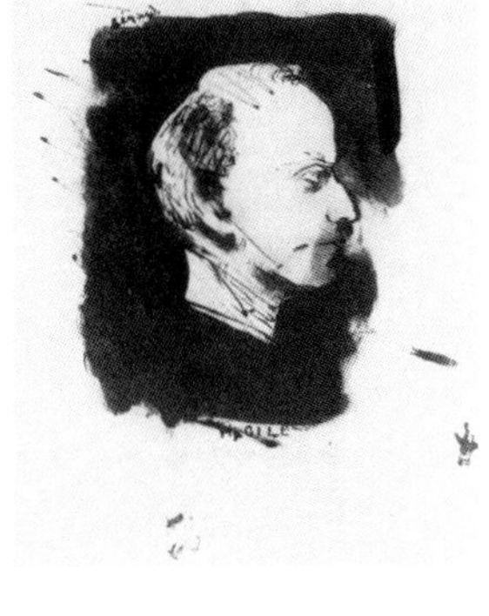
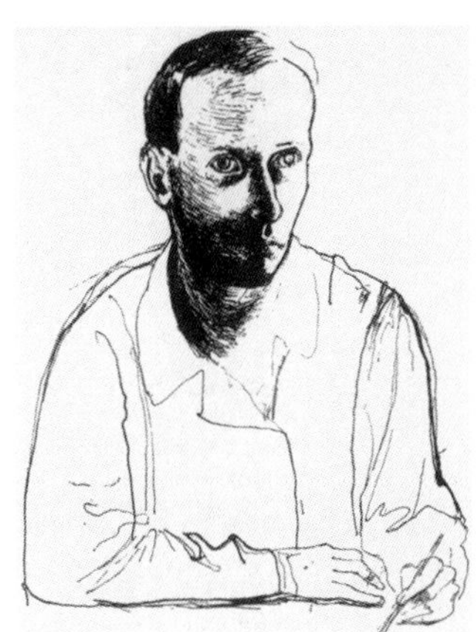
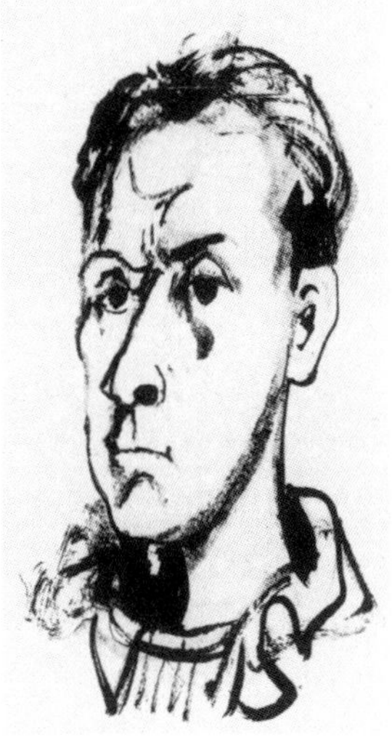
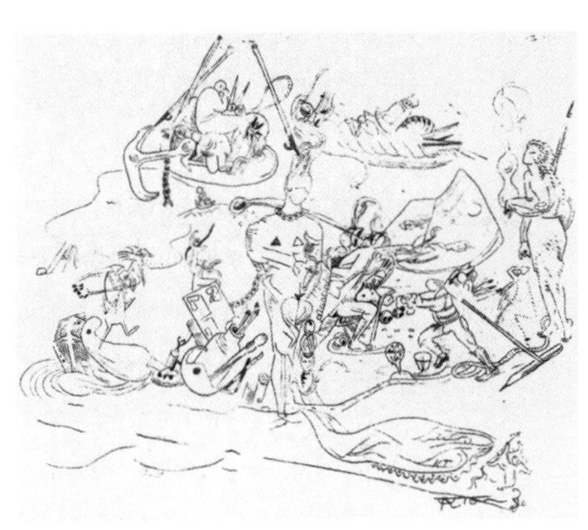
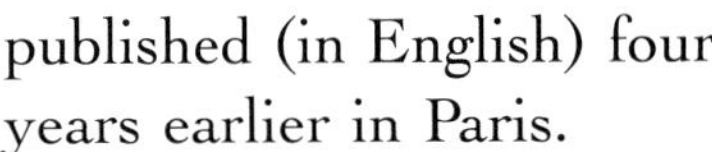

published (in English) four years earlier in Paris.

Hugnet continued along the same lines the following year by publishing a second book by Stein. Starkly entitled *Ten Portraits*, with a curious preface by the young Dadaist Pierre de Massot, it comprised the original English text, its translation by Hugnet and Thomson, and a series of drawings that linked the two versions. Stein chose to gather this collection of portraits of friends and acquaintances, written between 1913 and 1929, 'to clarify her mind, as she said', in the words of the *Autobiography*.

The subjects were, in the following order, Picasso, Apollinaire, Satie, Tchelitchew, Thomson, Bérard, the historian Bernard Faÿ, Hugnet himself, the young Dutch painter Kristians Tonny, and Eugene Berman. The Neo-Romantics are thus shown, somewhat audaciously, running with the baton passed on by the trailblazers that preceded them. And it is not by chance that Picasso starts off the proceedings. *Ten Portraits* legitimizes the young artists by connecting them with the tutelary figure of modern art (who was responsible for three of the book's drawings). It also indirectly sets them apart, and moreover affirms their own urge to set themselves apart. The portraits and self-portraits that accompany the text convey a desire to return not only to the figure, but also to 'the expression of sentiment' and distinctive individuality, as opposed to the cerebrality and coldness of abstraction, the dryness of the *cosa mentale*. Virgil Thomson referred to this desire on several occasions, particularly in his memoirs, and it would go on to constitute one of the main arguments in Waldemar-George's defence of the Neo-Romantics.

It is barely necessary, then, to underline the leading role played by Georges Hugnet in the presentation of the new movement's artists, far beyond his Dadaist leanings and the flurry of his various activities. Having gathered them together in *Ten Portraits*, in the following months he entrusted the illustration of the third book published by Les Éditions de la Montagne – *Prolégomènes à une éthique sans metaphysique* by Pierre de Massot – to Kristians Tonny, and then, in 1931, that of his own work, *Le Droit de Varech*, to Eugene Berman. Hugnet also sat for numerous drawings and paintings by Eugene, as well as for portraits by Pierre Charbonnier and Virgil Thomson's partner, Maurice Grosser. Even more decisively, a letter from Tonny to Gertrude Stein dated 1928 reveals that Hugnet saw the Neo-Romantics as a genuine new wave, and was eager to see it take form and become more substantial. ('I am once again full of ardeur and projects', wrote Tonny, 'and my anemic spirit from before the vacation has vanished with the wind. [...] Next year, if we have a larger sailboat as I hope, we will invite all the future celebrities: Bébé Bérard, Bravig, Virgile, Hunier ... etc. ... We'll found a school... It's Georges Hunier's dream, *une école* [*sic*].')

Hugnet was fascinated by the matriarch of modernism (although he would soon fall out with her), but he did not share her doubts about the role and importance of his group of friends. Virgil Thomson states in his memoirs that the publication of *Ten Portraits* played a key role in launching the Neo-Romantics and opening up new horizons in modern painting. (Thomson would go on to attribute their failure to follow through to their lack of 'a personnel sufficiently tough to face, as artists, a lifetime of persecution from the collectors of pre-World-War-I modern art – in other words, from the Picasso marketeers.')

As a mere five hundred copies of *Ten Portraits* were published (with only the first hundred containing the illustrations), it would have remained a private affair, just a footnote in literary history, if recent examinations of the book through the prism of gender studies had not thrown the spotlight back on its author and endowed it with new importance. It can be read today as a manifesto for a dissenting viewpoint, a work whose erasure can be explained by its 'eccentricity', which chafed against 'ostensibly hegemonic cultural contexts'. It is now possible to see this perceived weakness, or fundamental flaw, as its abiding strength. Georges Hugnet's venture, and the support provided to him by Virgil Thomson, has thus been belatedly and unexpectedly vindicated, but before we follow the various stages of this turnaround, and of changes in taste over time, let us return to the group's initial project and its members, who, apart from Leonid, have so far only been evoked in passing.

Gertrude Stein's sly prevarication with respect to the Neo-Romantics was counterbalanced by the proselytism imparted at the same time by Virgil Thomson, who, as we have seen, was a friend and admirer of most of these young artists. Thomson provides an invaluable counterpoint, enabling us to view the early days of the group from a completely different perspective. Thomson was an ideologue in his way and, far removed from Stein's vacillations, he resolutely established the criteria for a definition of the movement that would later be developed by Waldemar-George and then by James Thrall Soby: 'Tschelitcheff, Bérard, and Eugene Berman (or "Pavlik", "Bébé," and "Genia") were in full reaction against cubism and striving steadfastly to express, as Picasso had loved to do two decades earlier, tenderness, mystery, and compassion. Pavlik and Bébé painted only people; Genia preferred deserted architecture. Leonid's subject even then was ships, the sea, and fishermen. Tonny, much younger, was a virtuoso draftsman of Flemish fantasy.'

Taking advantage of the privileged position afforded by his proximity to the artists, Thomson categorized them in clear-cut stylistic terms, while also contrasting them with the versatile Picasso, whom he never seemed to like very much. He even went as far as daringly suggesting a role reversal: 'Their movement had influence not only among the twenty-to-thirty-year-olds but also among the older artists. Picasso himself, about 1930, essayed to take over the mystery, humanity, and ink blots of Bérard; but he could never quite get back for use again the compassion he had felt when young and poor.'

This view of the relationship between Picasso and Bérard may seem surprising now, given the superficiality associated with Bérard as a result of his later incursions into fashion and theatre, which still hinder a full appreciation of his work. Thomson's remarks do reveal, however, the esteem with which he was regarded at the start of his career, when he was Tchelitchew's rival for the leadership of the group.

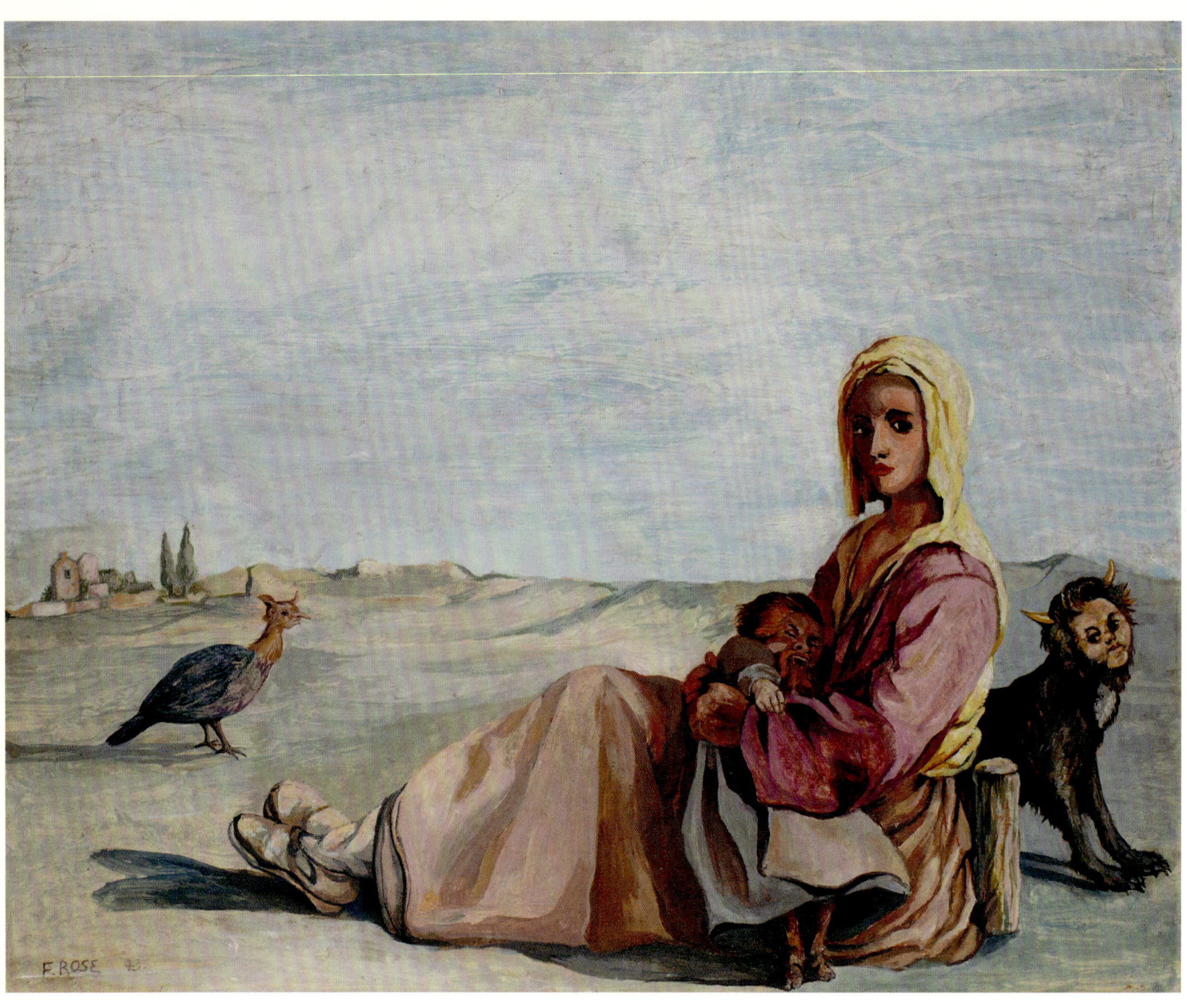

A few years later, James Thrall Soby, in his turn, described an indefinable aura around Bérard, set off by virtuosity, brilliance and a seemingly nonchalant mastery. Bérard was born in Paris in 1902, into an upper-middle-class family (his mother was the heiress of France's most famous funeral parlour, founded in 1820 by Henri de Borniol), and he was thus set apart from the exiles in the group by both his social status and his deep French cultural roots. Leonid was alluding to this anomaly when, as mentioned above, he reproached his brother for integrating too fast, too easily, into the Parisian bourgeois set that was Bérard's natural milieu. Similarly, Boris Kochno, who first heard about Bérard from Tchelitchew before actually meeting him, recorded that 'to Tchelitchew's impoverished bohemian circle, Bérard, the only son of a middle-class family, seemed little more than a spoiled young man who painted as a hobby'. This imputation of

ABOVE: Sir Francis Rose, *Character after Le Nain*, oil on panel, 56 × 70 cm (22 × 27½ in.), n.d.
OPPOSITE: Sir Francis Rose, *Still Life: A Plant*, watercolour on paper, 52 × 65 cm (20½ × 25½ in.), n.d.

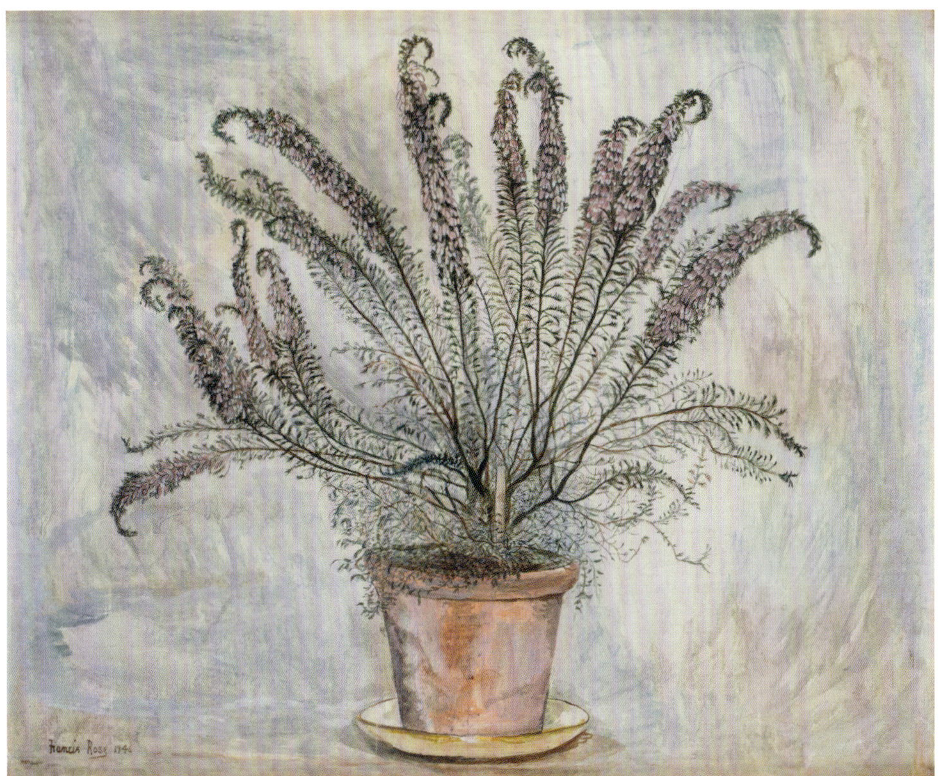

high-society dilettantism would pursue Bérard throughout his career and obscure his reputation as a painter, even after his death.

Soby also pointed out another distinguishing characteristic. He maintained that – unlike the Berman brothers and Tchelitchew, who were already extremely proficient technically – Bérard could barely paint at all in the early days. His palette was virtually monochrome: muffled and murky, with dark blues, deep blacks, sooty greys, ochres and dirty whites. Bérard's early works, from the years 1925–26, are also characterized by their thick surface, clumsy drawing and stiff lines – in stark contrast to his subsequent vibrant style and luminous colours.

According to one eye-witness of the times, Sir Francis Rose (1906–1979), an illustrator and painter to whom we shall return in due course, Bérard's early paintings looked as if they were covered with thick layers of wax. In his (admittedly somewhat unreliable) memoir, Rose explained that this effect could be traced back to a time spent with Jean Cocteau in Villefranche in 1925, and more particularly the decor that he found there. 'Jean's room had an influence on Bérard. There were also an early Greek silver coin and a Graeco-Egyptian money mask, which rested on cotton wool in a tiny packing case next to Cocteau's bed. These objects definitely inspired Bérard to create a type of face which distinguishes his work. The money mask was in

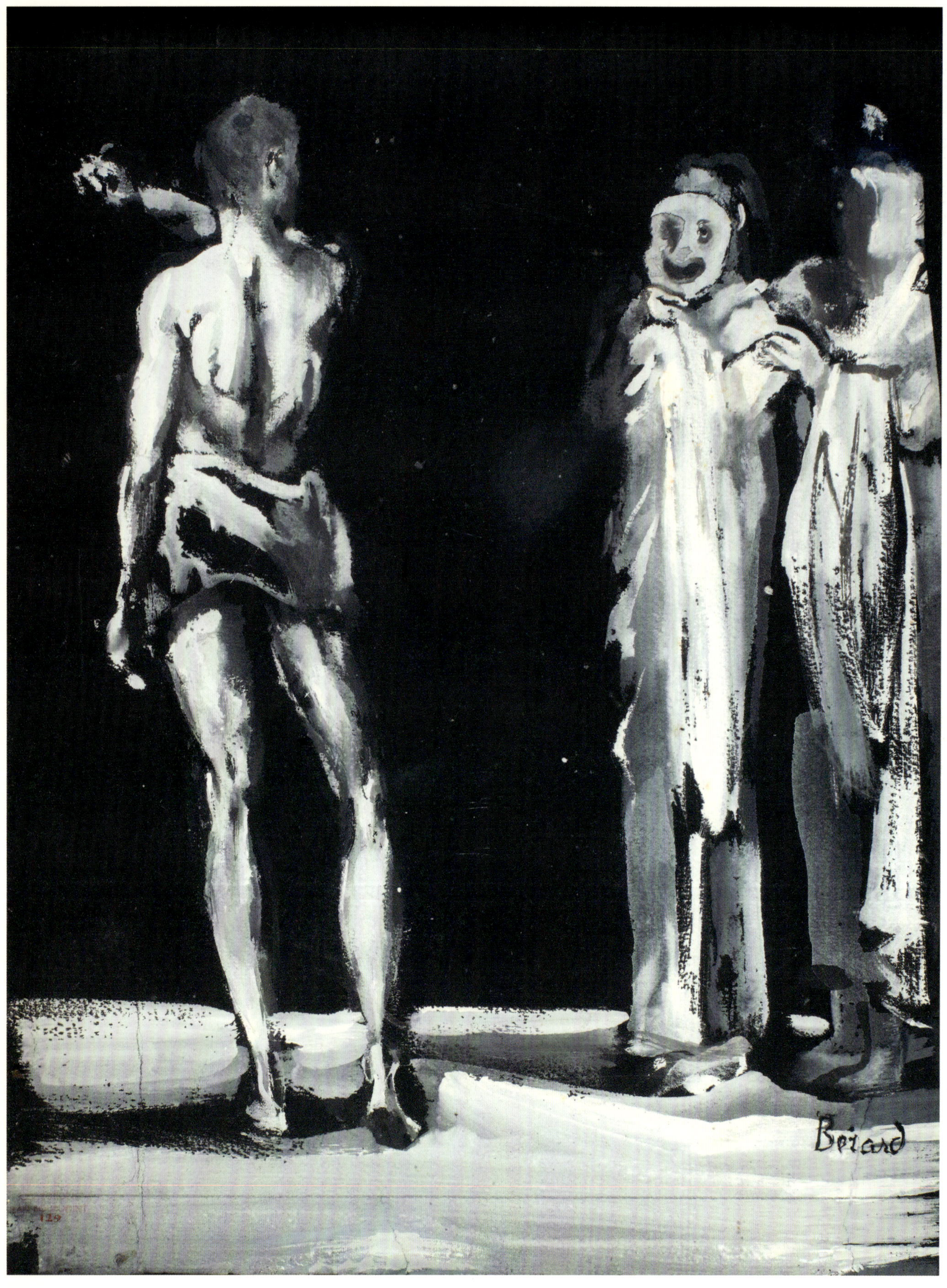

ABOVE: Christian Bérard, *Antique Scene*, gouache on paper, 37 × 25 cm (15½ × 9⅞ in.), *c.* 1930?

OPPOSITE: Christian Bérard, *Portrait of a Woman in the Style of Fayoum*, ink, watercolour and wash on mounted paper, 55 × 36 cm (21⅝ × 14⅛ in.), 1926

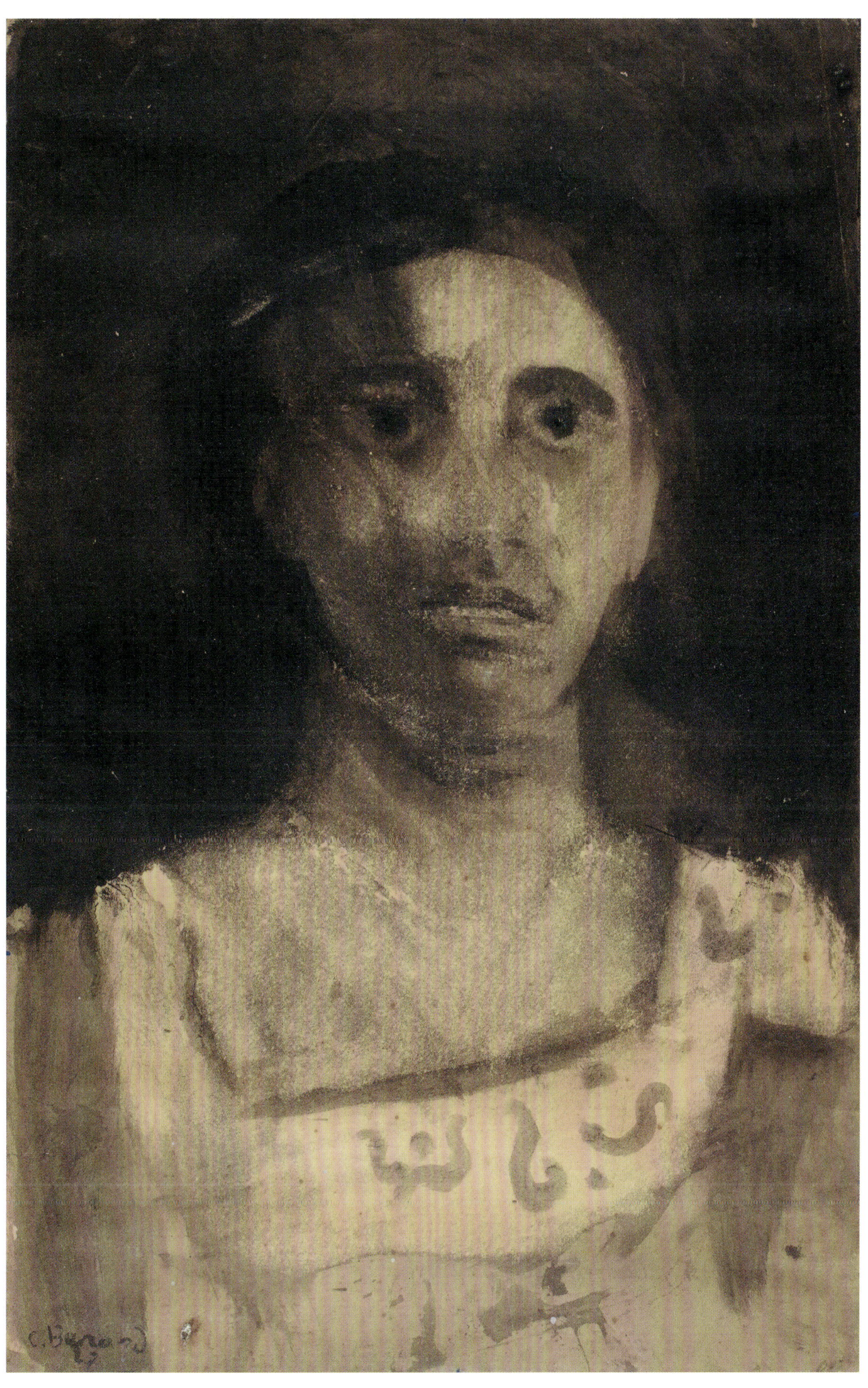

clay which had been decorated in polychrome; traces of coloured wax remained on the rounded grey surfaces and gave Bérard the idea of experimenting with candlegrease mixed with oil paint on canvases and boards. I followed his example, and we painted portraits and compositions with this medium.'

Whether this explanation is true or false, or at least oversimplified, it does not detract from the expressive power (albeit austere, even coarse) of this early style. Bérard's first efforts drew on various sources, such as Fayum mummy portraits, Ancient Roman frescoes and the Italian primitive painters, and, in all their clumsiness and imperfection, they summon up a ghostly, spellbinding presence and invoke mournful, crepuscular apparitions.

The contrast between these apprentice pieces and the portraits that Bérard produced barely three years later could hardly be more striking. Soby rightly stresses the importance of the double self-portrait entitled *On the Beach*, painted in 1934 (once owned by Soby and then bequeathed to the Museum of Modern Art in New York): a disturbing, surreal image of an androgynous, two-headed creature shrouded in a large tunic, set against a bluish-grey mountain that contrasts with the pale yellow sand on which it lies outstretched. A second 'Self-Portrait on the Beach', now in a Parisian collection, displays a similarly sophisticated use of colour, this time dominated by ochre and yellow against a dappled blue background, with touches of purple and white. Here, as in the myth of Plato's *Banquet*, the androgynous body is split, giving rise to two incarnations of the painter, who strangely seems to be taking leave of himself.

It is impossible to disagree with Soby's assertion that close study on the part of Bérard, particularly of portraits by Degas, played a key role in the emergence of this new style, as regards both the streamlining of forms and the delicacy of the colour scheme. Bérard also found inspiration in Picasso's rose period, and in André Derain and Modigliani. Another (seldom acknowledged) reference in Bérard's later work would be Félix Vallotton (who taught at the Académie Ranson), particularly in the use of blocks of pure, strongly acid colour and sharp chromatic contrasts.

Bérard's enthusiasm for Degas is evident in a dramatic anecdote recounted by Boris Kochno: 'On the eve of one of our moves, Bérard had just purchased a large canvas by Degas from a sale at the Hôtel Drouot, the great Parisian auction house. He paid three thousand francs – a trivial sum, but enormous to us at the time for this full-length picture of two standing men, one of whom had a green parrot perched on his hand. After admiring his acquisition for a long time, Bérard intended to wrap it up, but instead he laid it down in the middle of the room and covered it with old newspapers. Unexpectedly the door flew open, and our old friend Froska Munster swept in. Crossing the room, she stepped right on the picture hidden under the newspapers. [...] When we removed the newspapers we found a huge hole in the middle of the canvas. Naturally our friend was terribly upset when she realized what she had done, but Bérard, thinking only of consoling her, managed a pitiful smile and mumbled weakly: "It's nothing ... anything can be mended."'

This sum of influences cannot fully explain, however, these paintings' mesmerizing attraction, their 'magic' and 'poetic sentiment', in the words of Soby, who distinguished them from more calculated works by other members of the group: 'Curiously enough, in this art which seems accidental and barely dependent on composition, every accent must be in its right place or the emotional edifice falls down. Bérard's painting cannot be redeemed by occasional fine passages; it is so closely knit and so intense, that it exists as an impulsive, complete entity or it goes to pieces entirely.' Bérard was the type of artist (like, for example, his contemporary Filippo de Pisis [1896–1956]) whose *alla prima* technique owes its impact to a visual epiphany.

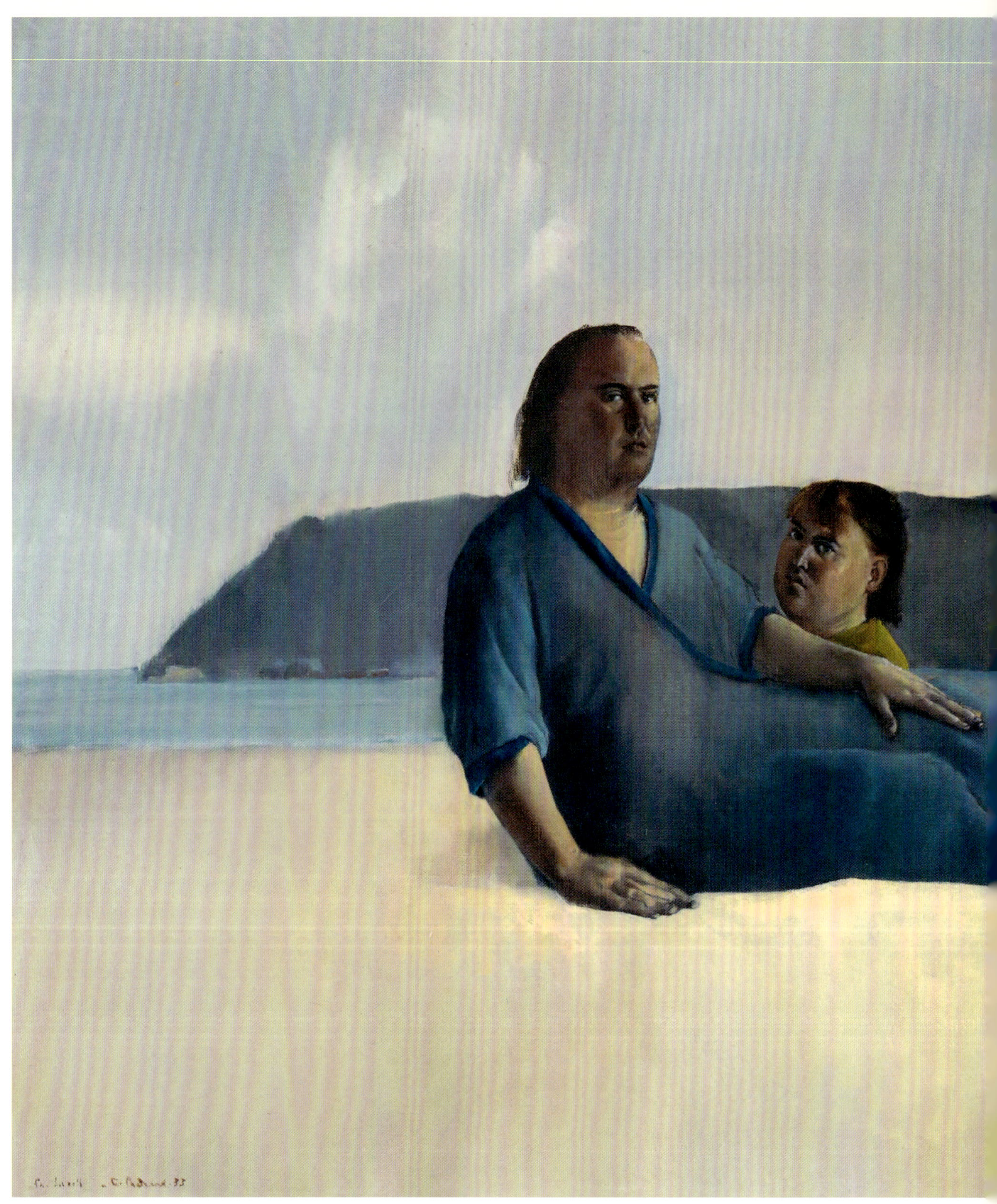

Christian Bérard, *On the Beach (Double Self-Portrait)*,
oil on canvas, 80.8 × 116.7 cm (31⅞ × 46 in.), 1933

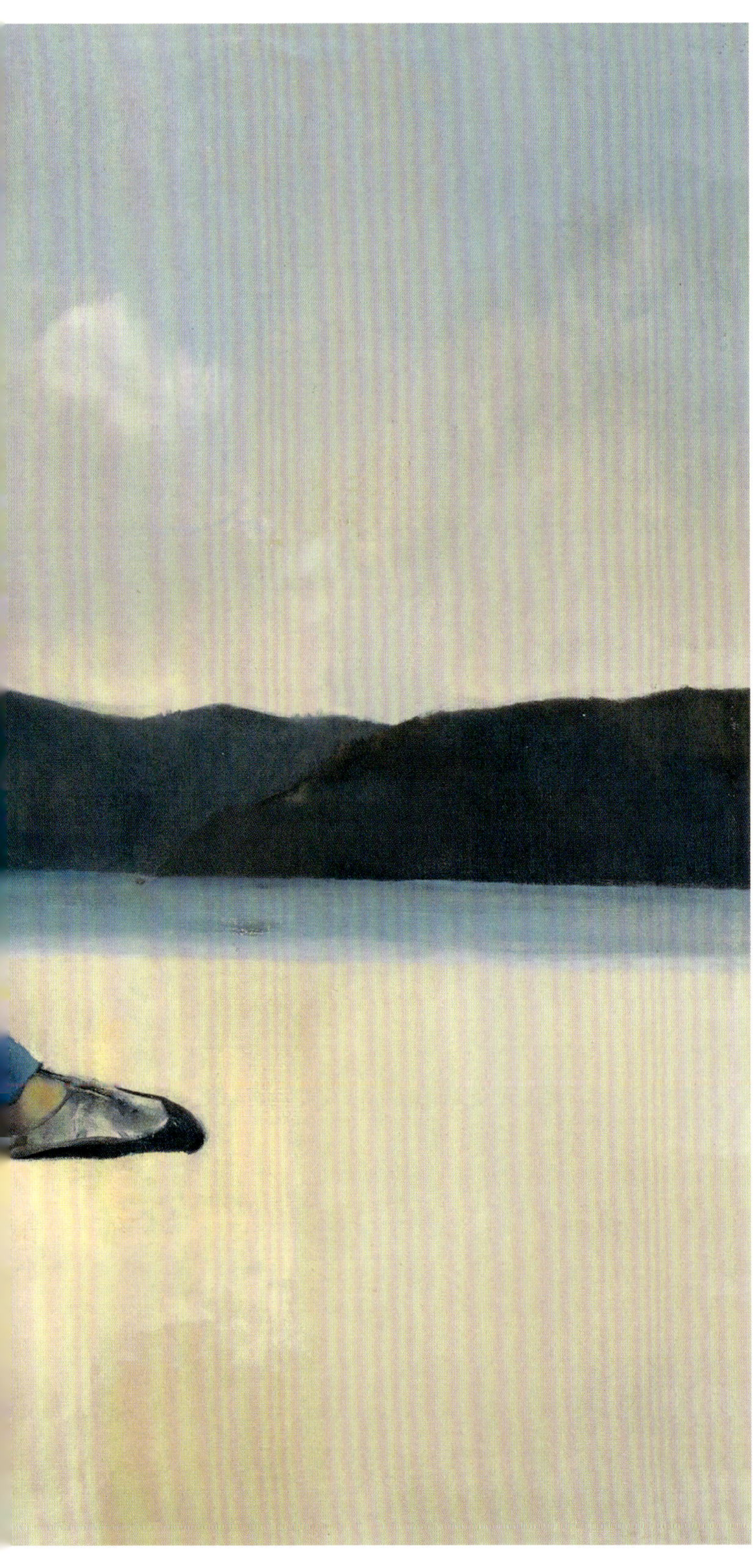

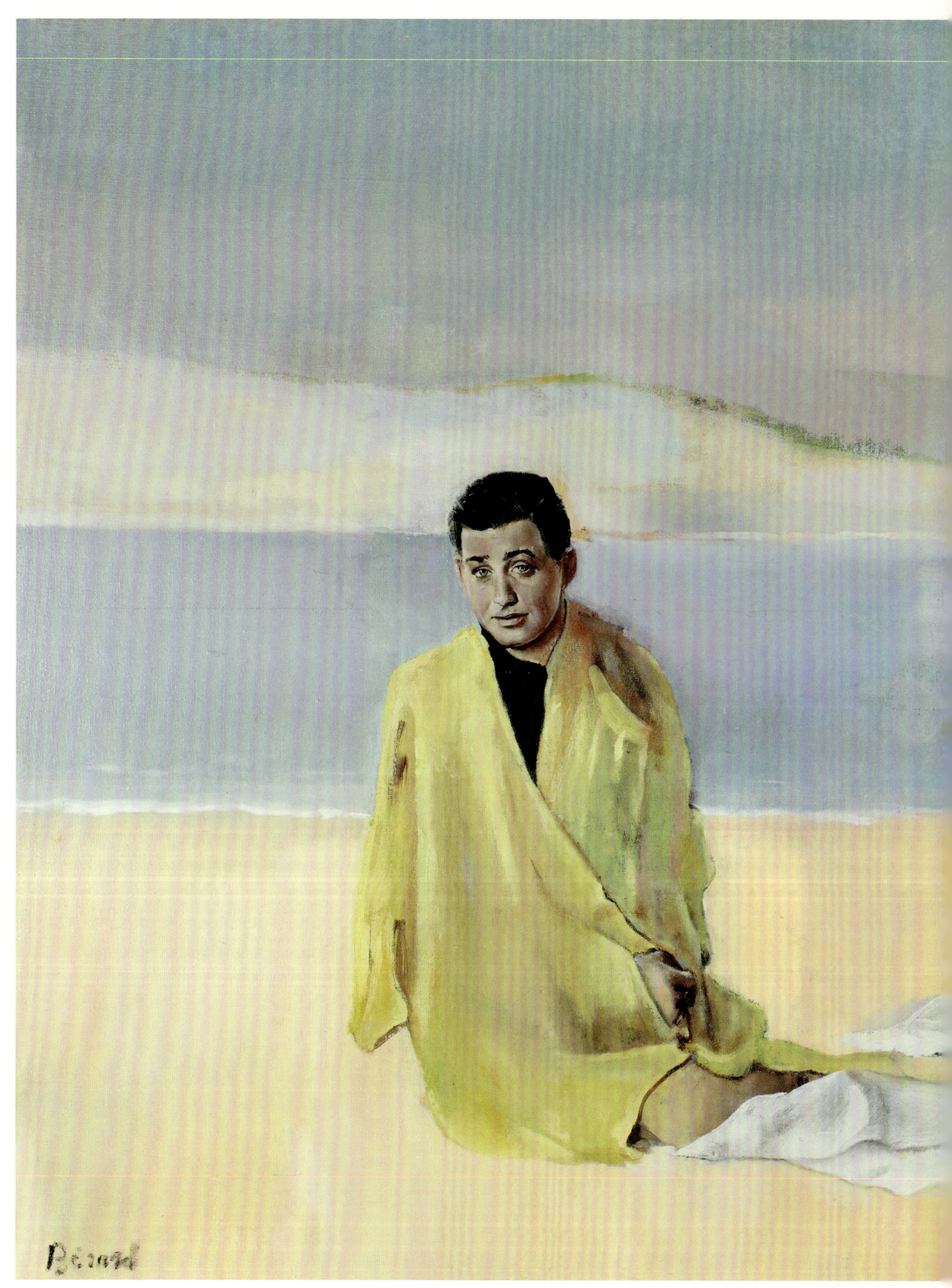

Christian Bérard, *Two Self-Portraits on the Beach*,
oil on canvas, 79 × 114 cm (31⅛ × 44⅞ in.), 1933

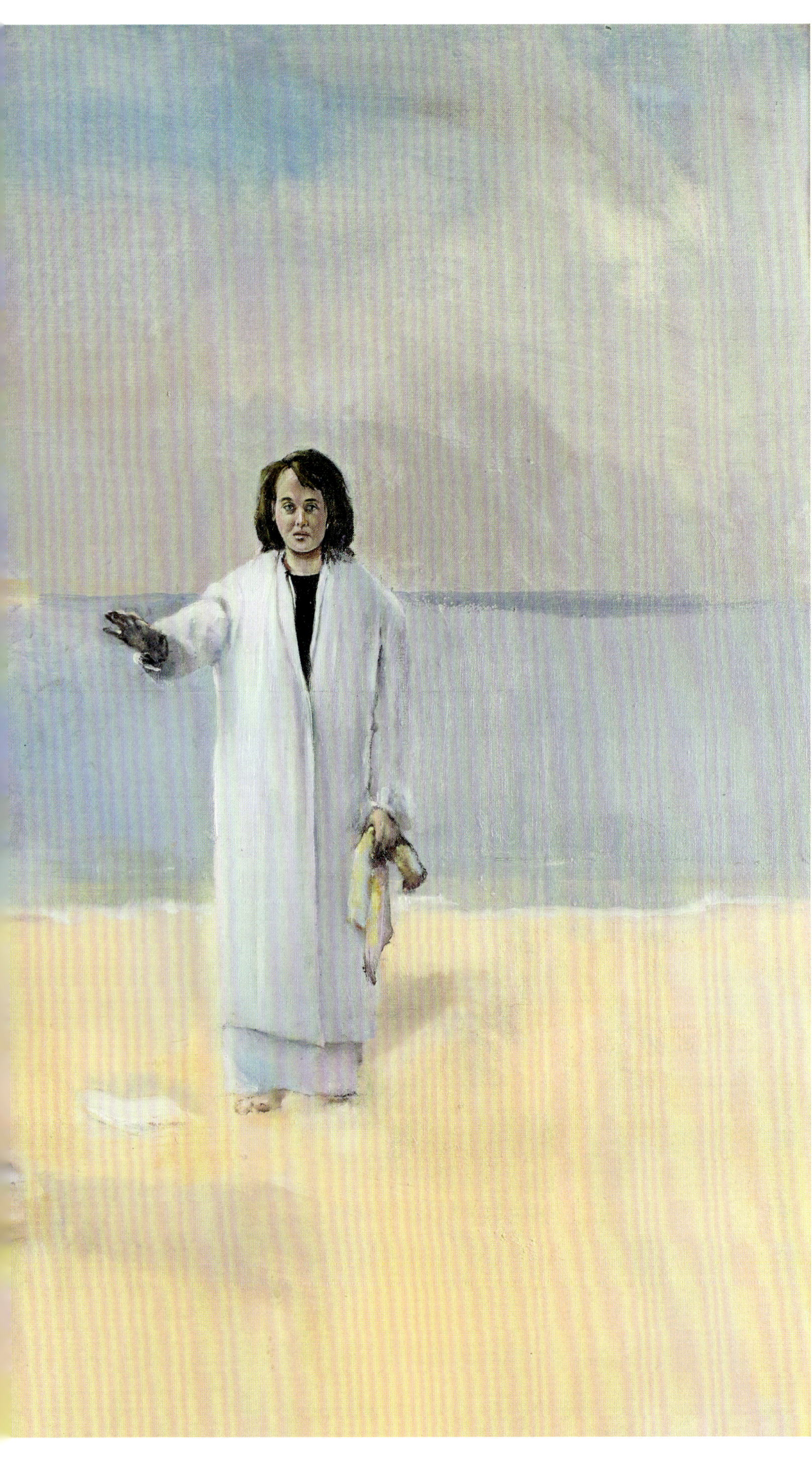

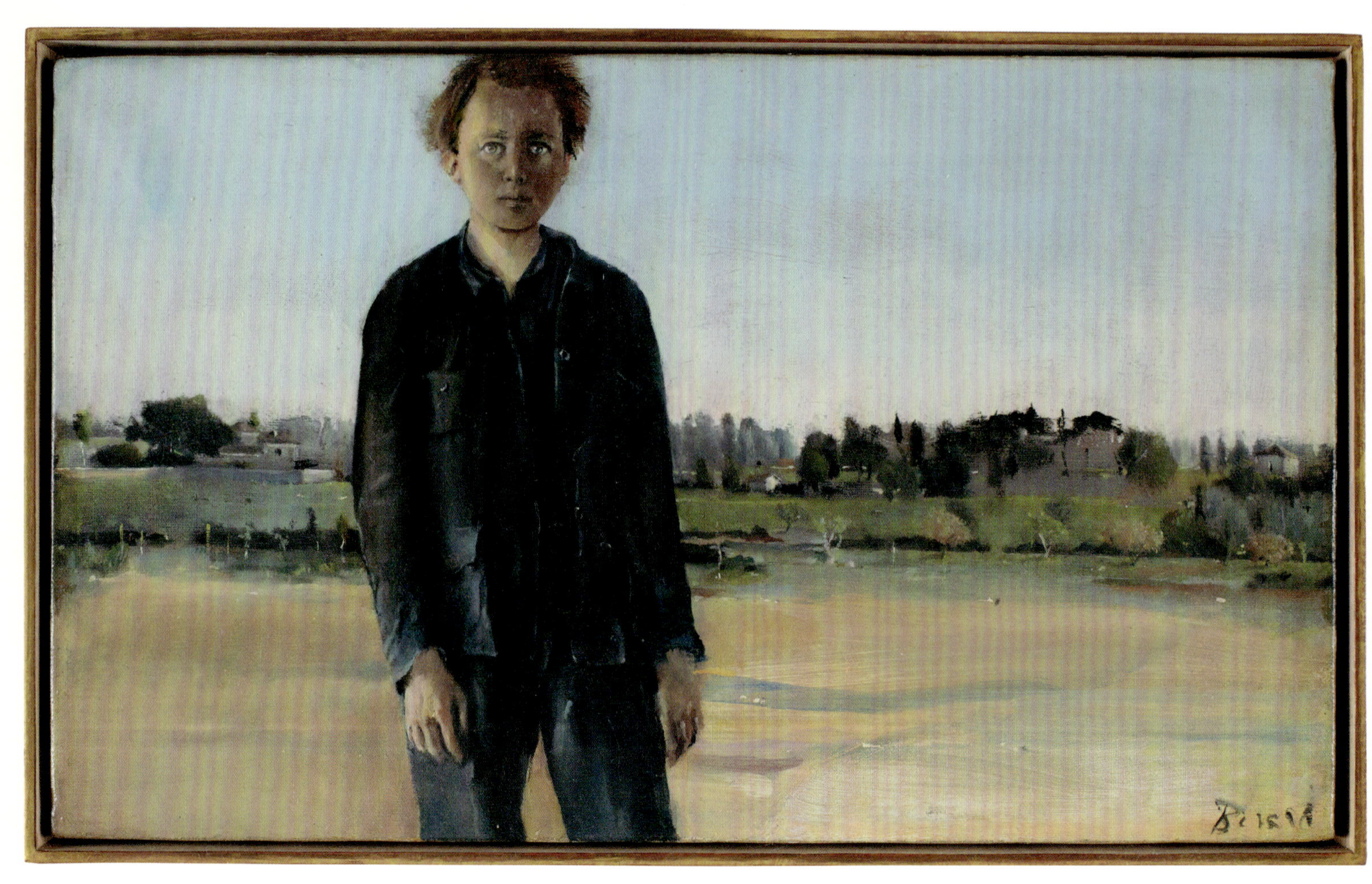

ABOVE: Christian Bérard, *Portrait of a Young Man with Landscape*, oil on canvas, 27 × 45 cm (10⅝ × 17⅝ in.), n.d.
OPPOSITE: Christian Bérard, *Self-Portrait*, oil on canvas, 41.5 × 27 cm (15¾ × 10¼ in.), *c.* 1934

‘The Bérard Era’

Bérard thus found and reinvented himself in the course of only a few months. With the encouragement of a small group of friends and young dealers convinced of his genius, he exhibited on a regular basis. These enthusiasts unexpectedly included the very same Christian Dior who would come every day to collect Bérard from the Académie Ranson, under the watchful eye of Leonid. In fact, Dior (who enjoyed the financial support of his parents, provided the family name never appeared ‘on the façade of a shop’) played an active role, as he recalled thirty years later, by which time he had become one of the world’s most celebrated fashion designers: ‘In partnership with a friend, Jacques Bonjean, I opened a little gallery at the end of a rather squalid dead-end street, the rue de la Boétie. Our ambition was to show the masters we admired the most – Picasso, Braque, Matisse, Dufy – and the younger painters we knew personally and already held in high esteem: Christian Bérard, Salvador Dalí, Max Jacob, and the Berman brothers.’

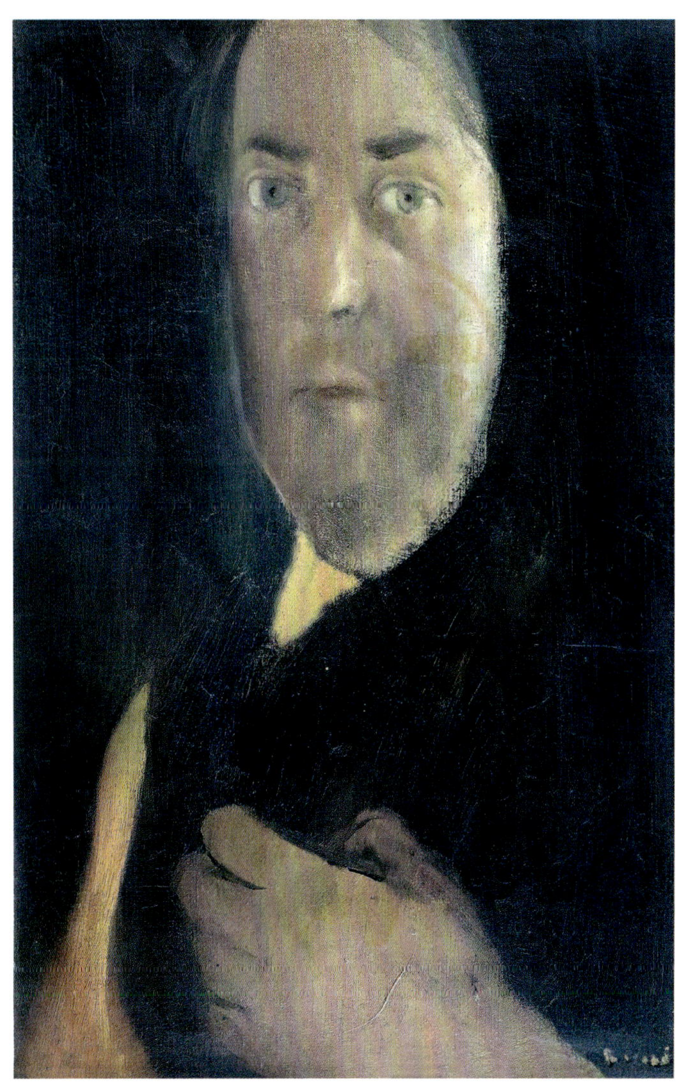

Dior saw Bérard along similar lines to Thomson and Soby, as ‘a fair young fellow, slender and smooth cheeked, whose enormous blue eyes had already told him that the human face and people’s lives were worthy of far greater attention than the simplified still lives of the Cubists or the geometrical figures of the “abstract” painters’. He also dwelt on another attribute, shared by the other members of the group: ‘His drawings taught one to transform daily life into a magic world of passion and nostalgia.’

Dior’s gallery presented an initial exhibition of Bérard’s drawings in May 1930, followed by another one the following year. This bold venture, driven by youthful fervour, was subject, however, to an unperceived threat from the start; as Dior himself drily observed: '1929. The Wall Street crash, forerunner of a world-wide depression, passed almost unnoticed in Paris.' Bonjean was soon forced to pull out, and Dior looked for help from a young poet in Max Jacob's circle, Pierre Colle, who 'soon left poetry to be a picture dealer'. Dior formed a new partnership, 'only to share in the even worse luck of Pierre Colle', although not before their gallery had organized a new Bérard show in May 1931, this time showcasing portraits.

Soby also mentioned another exhibition in May 1930, at the Vignon Gallery (run by Marie Cuttoli, a friend of Picasso, Matisse and Jean Lurçat, known for introducing tapestry into modern art), but he overlooked Bérard's very first exhibitions, in 1925 and 1927, at the Pierre Gallery, recently opened by Pierre Loeb. (The latter exhibition is mentioned by Boris Kochno, however.)

Bérard's work was also shown in New York by Julien Levy in 1934, and in Paris, in the same year, by Étienne Bignou, in his gallery on rue La Boétie. (Bignou represented Matisse, Derain and Picasso, among others, and advised the famous American collector Albert Barnes.) This brief survey indicates both Bérard's intense activity between 1925 and 1930 and the immediate acclaim that it aroused. His exhibitions were put on by some of the leading gallery owners of the day, some of whom would remain extraordinarily loyal: Lucie Weill (Marie Cuttoli's business partner in her final years) and Pierre Loeb's son, Albert, both exhibited Bérard's work in the 1970s in their respective galleries on rue Bonaparte and rue des Beaux-Arts.

The 1934 exhibition at Bignou's gallery brought this run to an abrupt halt, however, for, as Kochno recorded, it would be 'the last show of Bérard's work in Paris during his lifetime' (Bérard would die, prematurely, fifteen years later). His life and career had already taken a radically different turn in December 1929, when he took his first step into the world of theatre, after being asked by Jean Cocteau to design the scenery and costumes for his play *La Voix humaine*. He went on to become a major figure in stage design.

The relationship that Bérard forged with Boris Kochno can only have encouraged him in that direction. (The pair started living together in Le Marquis, a seedy hotel in Pigalle, in 1930, before moving to the First Hôtel, in the 15th arrondissement, for a ten-year spell.) Kochno had been Diaghilev's secretary and had witnessed the development of the Ballets Russes during a period of almost ten years.

OPPOSITE: Christian Bérard, *Anubis*, study for *The Infernal Machine*, ink on paper, 36.5 × 30.5 cm (14⅜ × 12 in.), *c.* 1934

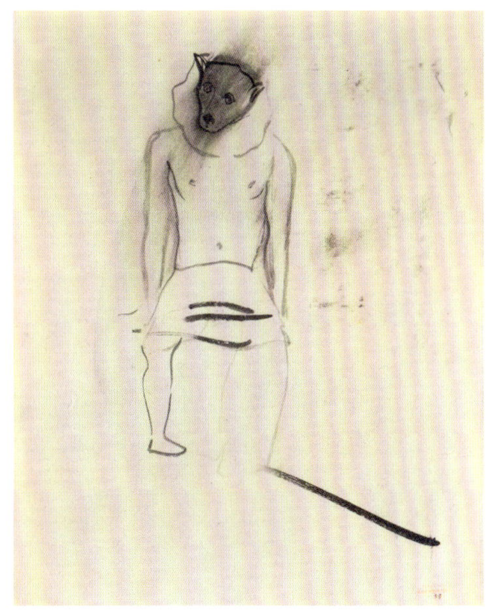

After Diaghilev's death in 1929, Kochno pursued a career as an impresario and stage designer in his own right. He liked to point out that he had anticipated Cocteau's commission to Bérard for *La Voix humaine* some time before, when he co-designed with Bérard the scenery and costumes for a ballet entitled *La Nuit*, with music by Henri Sauguet and choreography by Serge Lifar.

Bérard went on to have a dazzling, far-ranging career – in theatre, ballet, cinema, fashion and event design – that demonstrated an inexhaustible inventiveness that would make him famous; and, in the eyes of many critics, would divert him from his true calling as a painter. That seems to have been Soby's opinion in 1935: 'The extreme instability of his genius (and the word "genius" fits Bérard better than it does any young painter alive) made it inevitable that he would often waste himself on minor projects.' And Soby would be endorsed thirty years later by Virgil Thomson, writing in his memoir: 'Bébé did what he could; he was not self-deceived. But he did not, he could not persist as in France Degas had persisted, and Renoir and Monet and Bonnard. So he made stage designs. These were beautiful and appropriate. But all who were touched by his painting, especially his painting of people, came to regret, as he did too, that he had not been able to live up to his genius – for his talent, intelligence, and depth of directly expressed feeling did amount, I think, to that.'

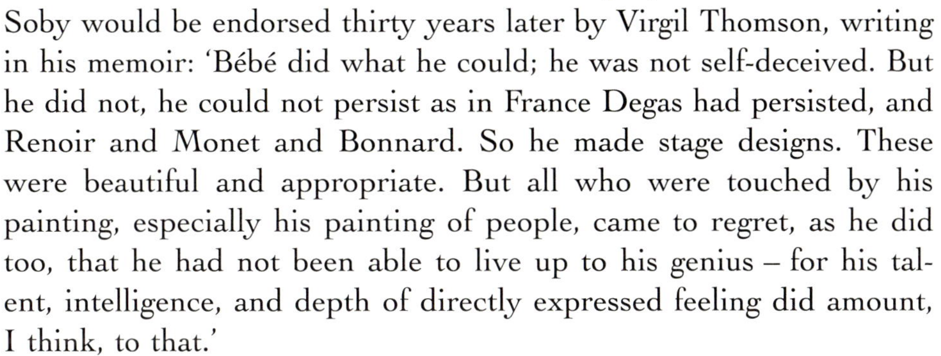

The choices that Bérard made could be debated endlessly, and they have been frozen in time by his premature death – a death which could be seen to have its own poetic justice, as he collapsed in an aisle of the Théâtre Marigny, while making adjustments to his set for Louis Jouvet's production of *Les Fourberies de Scapin*, and died on 12 February 1949. According to several contemporary witnesses, he was at this point planning to return to painting. Most evaluations of Bérard's work and career tend to be tinged with judgments that are more moral than artistic; according to Thomson, for instance, he was 'self-indulgent in every way [...] and quite without self-discipline. [...] He was also to smoke opium and drink a great deal.' Bérard was allotted the role of a high-society tramp, a frivolous genius who squandered his gifts. In this respect, there is a curious overlap with another 'irregular', Gabriel de Saint-Aubin (Bérard even owned a copy of the latter's biography, written by Émile Dacier). Both were reproached for betraying their

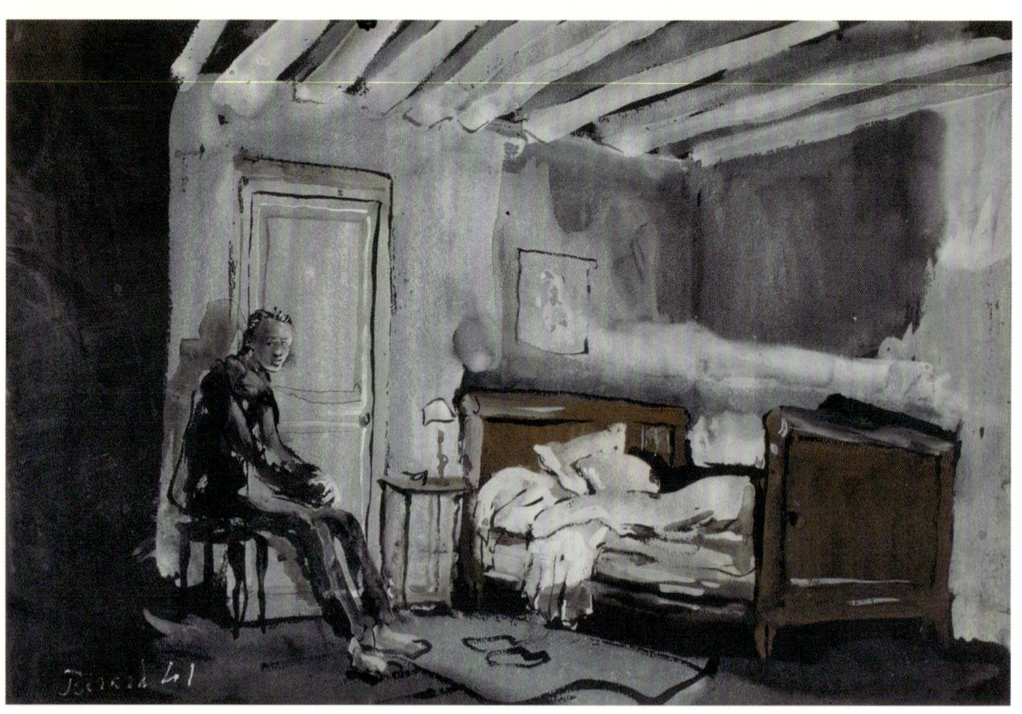

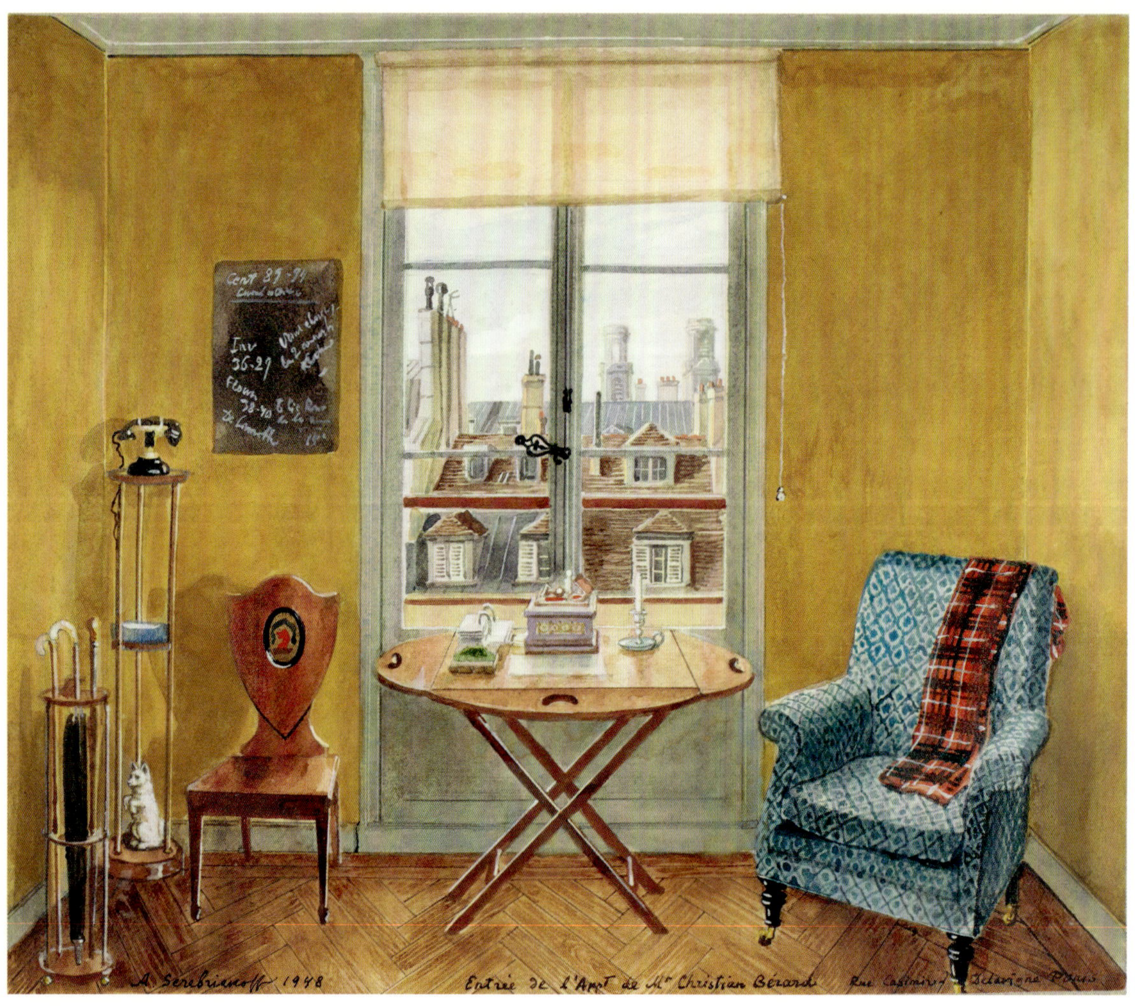

TOP: Christian Bérard, *The Poet's Room*,
gouache on paper, 32 × 47 cm (12½ × 18½ in.), 1941
ABOVE: Alexandre Serebriakoff, *The Antichamber of Christian Bérard and Boris Kochno, rue Casimir Delavigne*,
watercolour on paper, 33 × 39 cm (13 × 15⅜ in.), 1948

talent in an almost priapic eagerness to produce work quickly, while they also shared a lack of concern about posterity, a disregard for their own personal appearance, and a tendency to leave work unfinished, whether on their own account or due to outside forces.

Nevertheless, Bérard's works for the theatre, cinema and ballet were memorable, ranging from Cocteau's *Infernal Machine* (1934) to Louis Jouvet's production of *The School for Wives* (1936), from Henri Sauguet's *Fairground People* (1945) to *The Madwoman of Chaillot* by Jean Giraudoux (1945) and *Don Juan*, again for Jouvet (1947). He also worked on two splendid films directed by Cocteau: *Beauty and the Beast* and *The Eagle with Two Heads* (1946 and 1948).

Bérard also left an indelible mark on the history of fashion by illustrating the latest creations from Parisian designers in the leading magazines of the time, such as *Vogue*, *Harper's Bazaar* and *Album du Figaro*. According to the memoirs of Edna Woolman Chase, the formidable editor-in-chief of *Vogue* from 1914 to 1952, Bérard was first approached by Solange d'Ayen, a contributor to Paris *Vogue*, with the backing of Michel de Brunhoff, its managing editor, and, despite her initial reticence, Chase herself: 'Solange knew him as one of the spectacular figures of Paris and [...] De Brunhoff persuaded him to do fashion work for *Vogue*. A fat, grossly untidy man, a victim of drugs and liquor, it is probably true to say he died of his own excesses, yet he had enormous vitality, astringent wit, and great decorative talent. [...] His vogue was enormous, and it was politic to publish him.'

Bettina Ballard, another fashion editor for Paris *Vogue*, also remembered Bérard, and like Green and Thomson, she evoked his charisma: 'Bébé usually appeared about six in the evening set to work through the night. His black beard was full of spaghetti and little active pets who lodged there and he never dreamed of wiping his brushes any place but in it. He had a slashing wit and the wickedest tongue in Paris, but he could still draw more graphically than he could talk. He was ambidextrous, drew equally well with both hands, and he'd pick up pencils or brushes and before he'd finished describing a party it was before your eyes on paper, the drawing room where it was held, the women in their elegant dresses – the evening had come alive.'

'To facilitate Bérard's task,' explained Chase, 'Michel and Bettina offered themselves as models. [...] Bettina would hold up the dresses against her slim figure and Bérard would draw furiously, like most

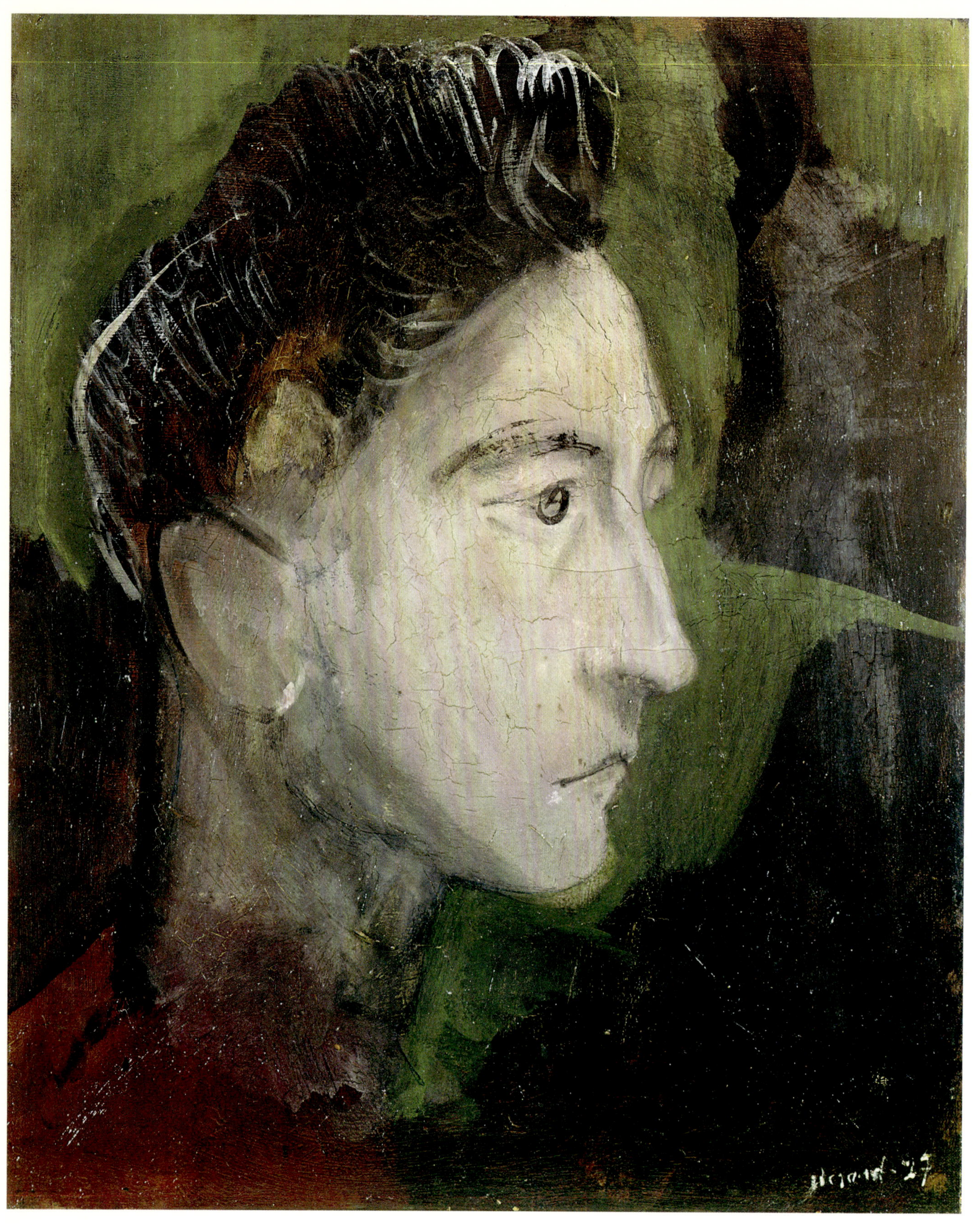

ABOVE: Christian Bérard, *Portrait of Jean Cocteau*, oil on canvas, 1927

OPPOSITE, CLOCKWISE FROM TOP LEFT: Christian Bérard, studies for *Margot* by Édouard Bourdet, ink, gouache and watercolour (double-sided), 31 × 19 cm (12⅛ × 7⅜ in.), 1935, with reverse showing costume studies; Christian Bérard, *Dancers* (with dedication, 'à Bolette, avec toute l'amitié de Bébé, [signed] Bérard'), oil on paper, 37 × 27 cm (14½ × 10⅝ in.), n.d.; Christian Bérard, *Sphinx*, gouache on paper, 23 × 31 cm (9 × 12⅛ in.), *c.* 1934

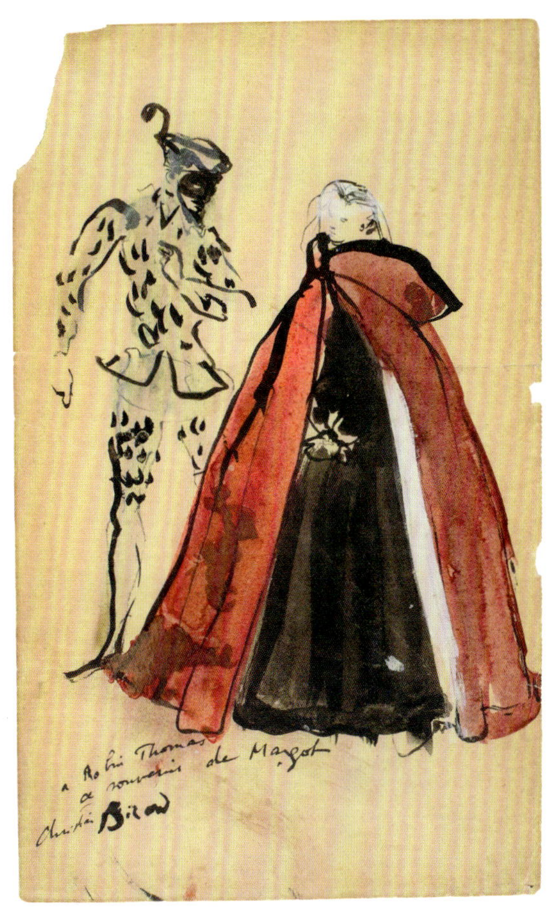
a Robin Thomas
en souvenir de Margot
Christian Bérard

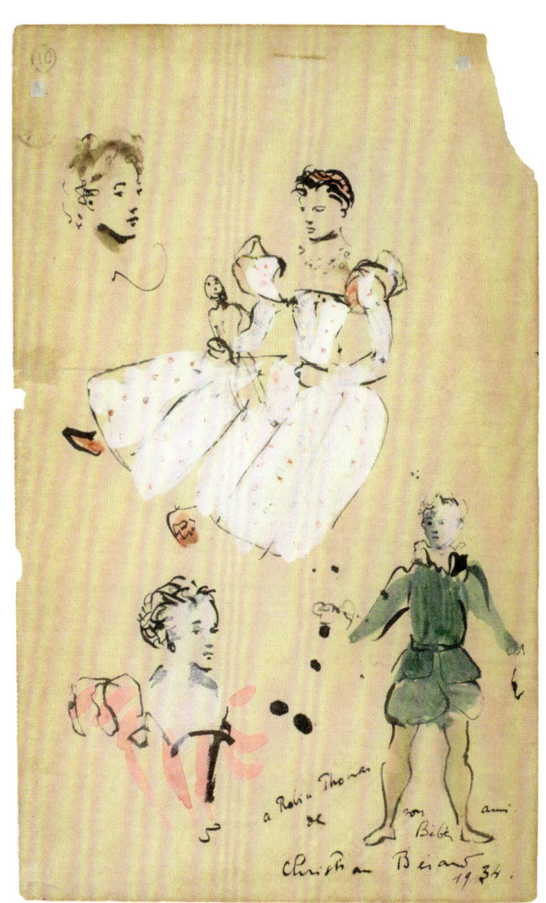
a Robin Thomas
de son ami Bébé
Christian Bérard 1934.

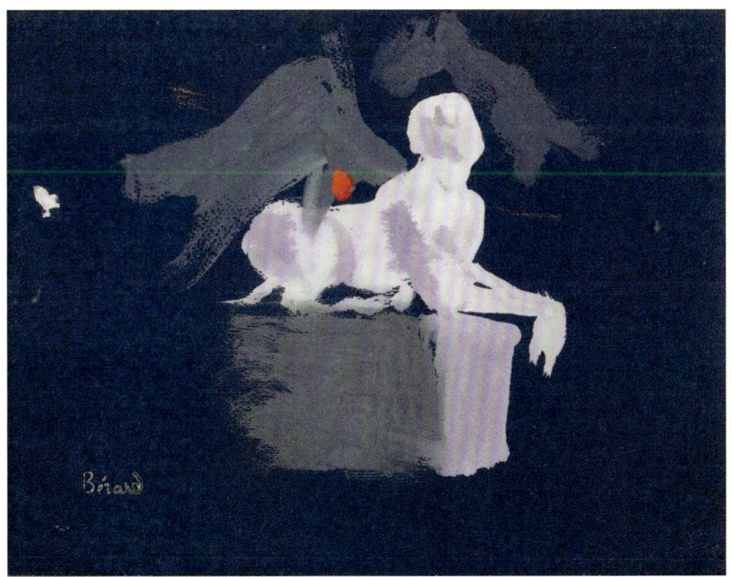
Bérard

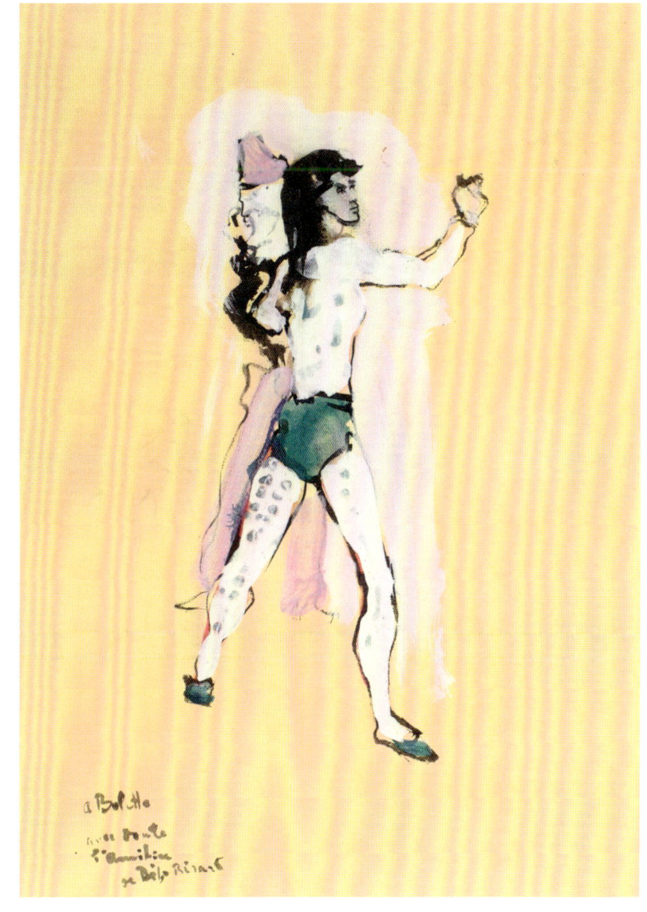

drug addicts, sweating profusely. Drops of sweat fell on the paper and he instantaneously converted them into windows or butterflies, charming imaginative bits of decoration, which gave individuality to his pictures and were vastly admired.' Chase concluded her account with a discreet euphemism: 'Despite the fact that his interests lay elsewhere, women fawned upon him, for he was an excellent dancer, his taste was exquisite, and there was a time when his approval or disapprobation could make or break the season for a couturier.'

The other *grande dame* of American fashion publishing, Carmel Snow, who had left *Vogue* – and the shadow of its all-powerful editor – to run its main competitor, *Harper's Bazaar*, was anxious to keep up with the latest trends and similarly sought out Bérard, under the auspices of another leading light of the jet set: 'I was very much on the *qui vive* to develop artists for the *Bazaar* – that's why I had sought out the avant-garde Jean Cocteau – and when Daisy Fellowes introduced me to a pink-faced, bearded cherub known as "Bébé" Bérard, I asked him to do some sketches of her. If they were "stylized" (Bébé drew only the outline of a face), they also had all the vitality and chic I was looking for.' In an effort to prise Bérard away from *Vogue*, to which he was formally contracted, Carmel Snow turned to her magazine's Paris correspondent, Marie-Louise Bousquet, a celebrated

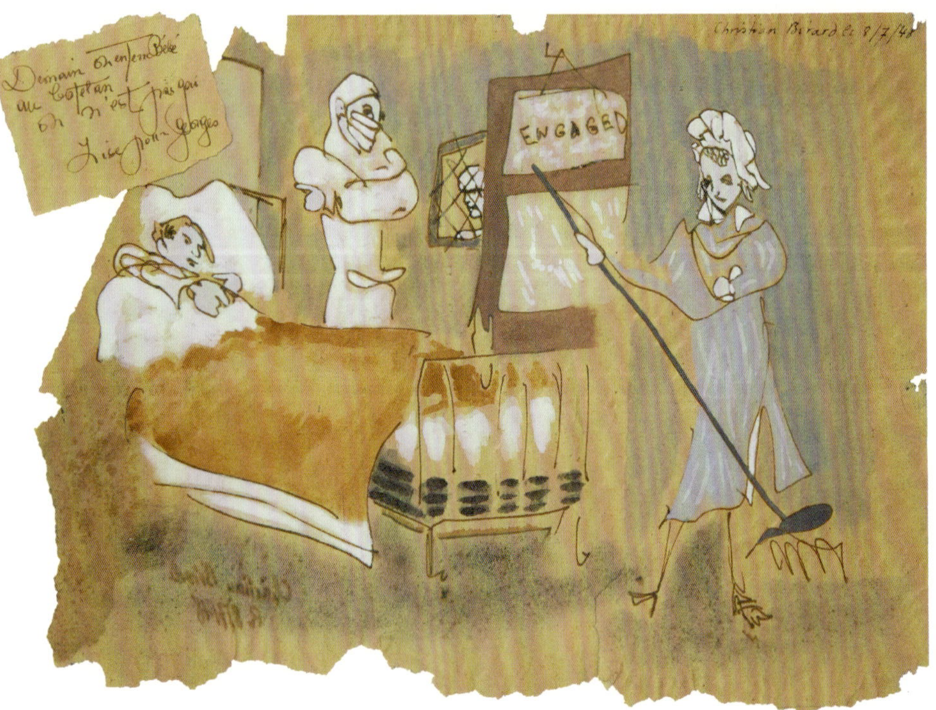

ABOVE: Christian Bérard, *'Tomorrow Bébé will be buried at the Catalan'*, gouache and pastel on section of tablecloth from Le Catalan restaurant, collage by Lise Deharme, 26 × 36 cm (10⅛ × 15⅛ in.), 1948

OPPOSITE, LEFT: Christian Bérard, perfume box for Cœur Joie by Nina Ricci, 11 × 10 cm (4⅜ × 3⅞ in.), 1946
OPPOSITE, RIGHT: Christian Bérard, original drawings, featuring female figures and costume studies, ink, pastel and gouache, various dimensions, n.d.

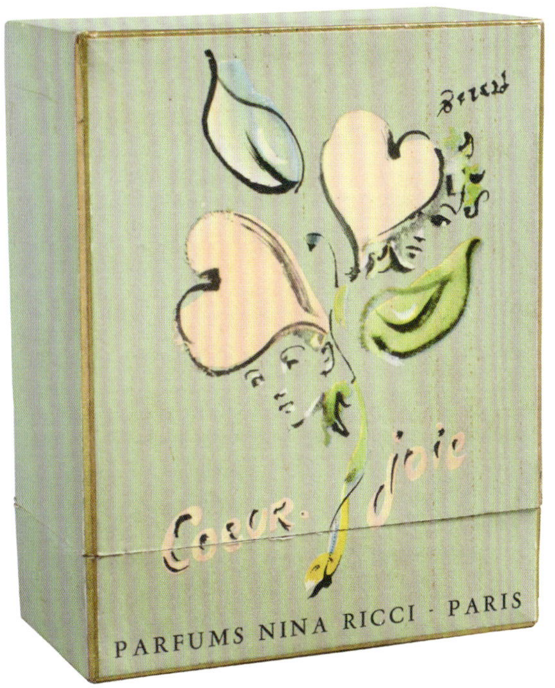

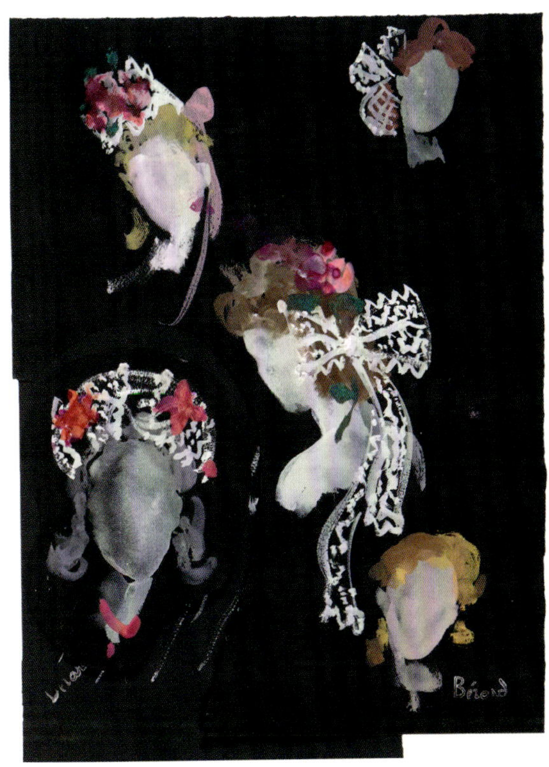

hostess and close friend of Bérard, whom he preserved in a touching portrait. The rivalry between the two editors over Bérard's services would sometimes involve a certain sleight of hand: 'Bébé's allegiance was always to his friends rather than to his business connections. He couldn't work for *Harper's Bazaar* when he had a contract with *Vogue*, but during the war, when I was desperate for Paris news, he sent over some radio sketches of the remarkable new designer, Castillo, which appeared in the *Bazaar* signed "Sam." To me they were unmistakably Bérard, though Edna Chase apparently didn't catch on.'

Soby's account of Bérard's fashion work is less gossipy and focuses on the artist's desire to adopt new means of expression and broaden his range 'to do for his generation what Van Dongen failed to do for his: to document, like Proust, the *haut monde* of society and art'. In this respect, Bérard was entirely successful, as he is now considered the creator of an outstanding visual record of his time; the chronicler of a society, who would later define a moment in history (just as René Gruau would do for the subsequent generation).

The boldness and rapidity of Bérard's technique and the precision of his line manifested an eagerness to capture the 'fugitive aspects of life' – along the same lines, in different eras, as Saint-Aubin,

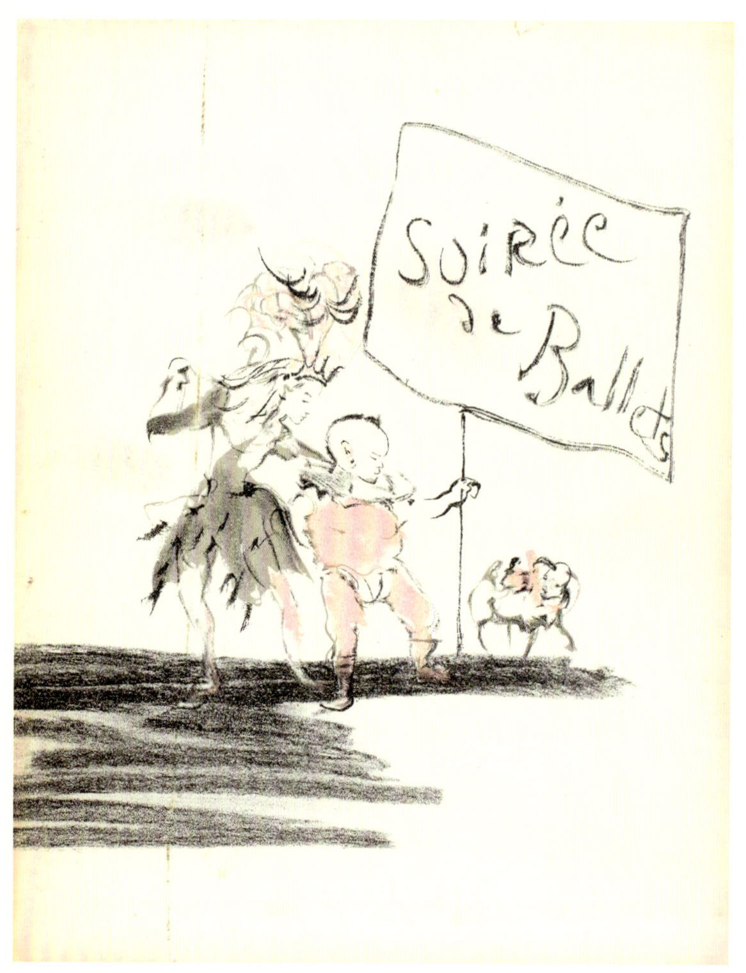

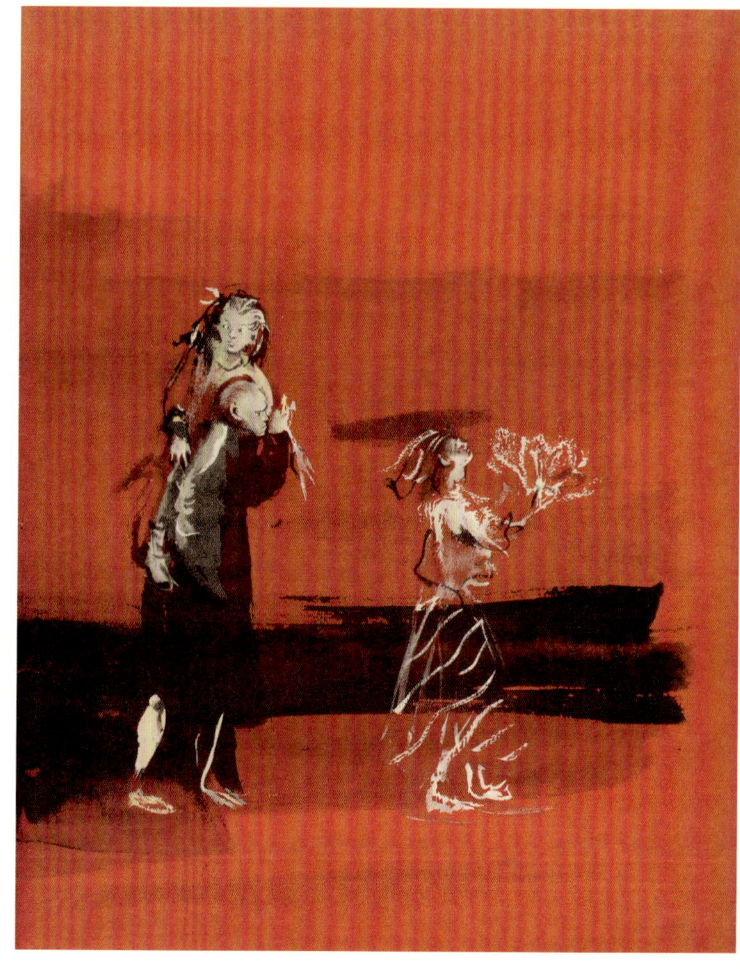

ABOVE, LEFT: Christian Bérard, *Soirée de Ballets*, lithography for programme cover, Éditions du Chêne, Paris, June 1945, 33 × 26 cm (13 × 10⅛ in.)
ABOVE, RIGHT: Christian Bérard, lithography for programme cover for the Ballets des Champs-Élysées, Spring 1946 season, 33 × 25 cm (13 × 9⅞ in.)

OPPOSITE, LEFT: Christian Bérard, lithography for programme cover of 'Dédié à l'Élégance', evening programme for 22 December 1945, Théâtre des Champs-Élysées, 33 × 26 cm (13 × 10⅛ in.)
OPPOSITE, RIGHT: Christian Bérard, lithography for programme cover for the Ballets des Champs-Élysées, April 1949, 32 × 25 cm (12½ × 9⅞ in.)

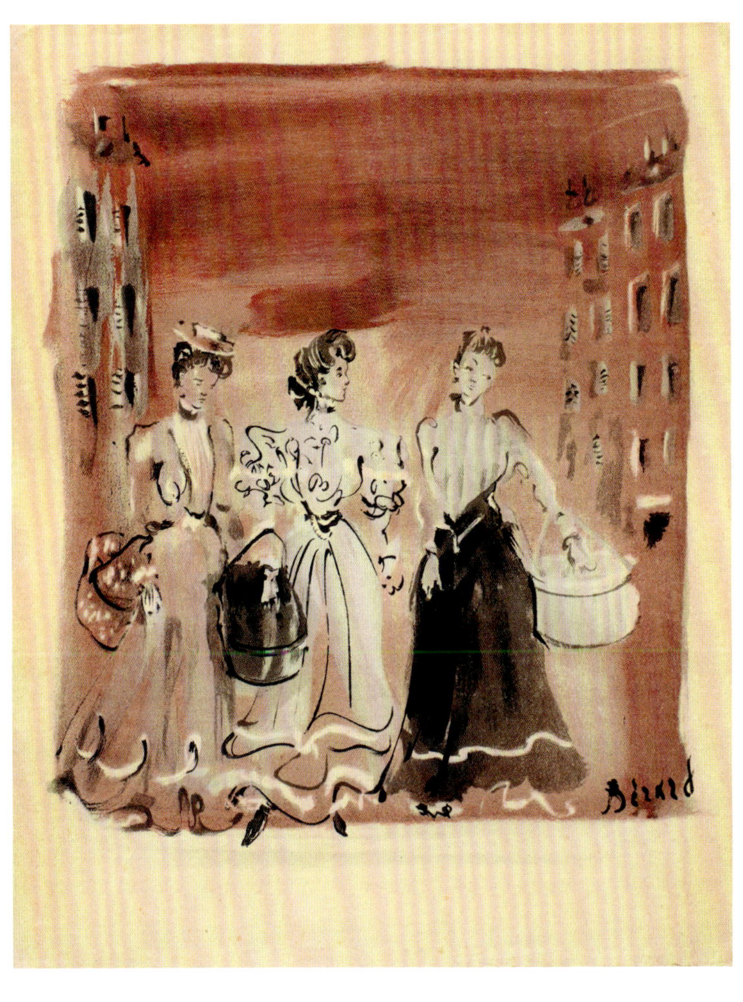
Bérard

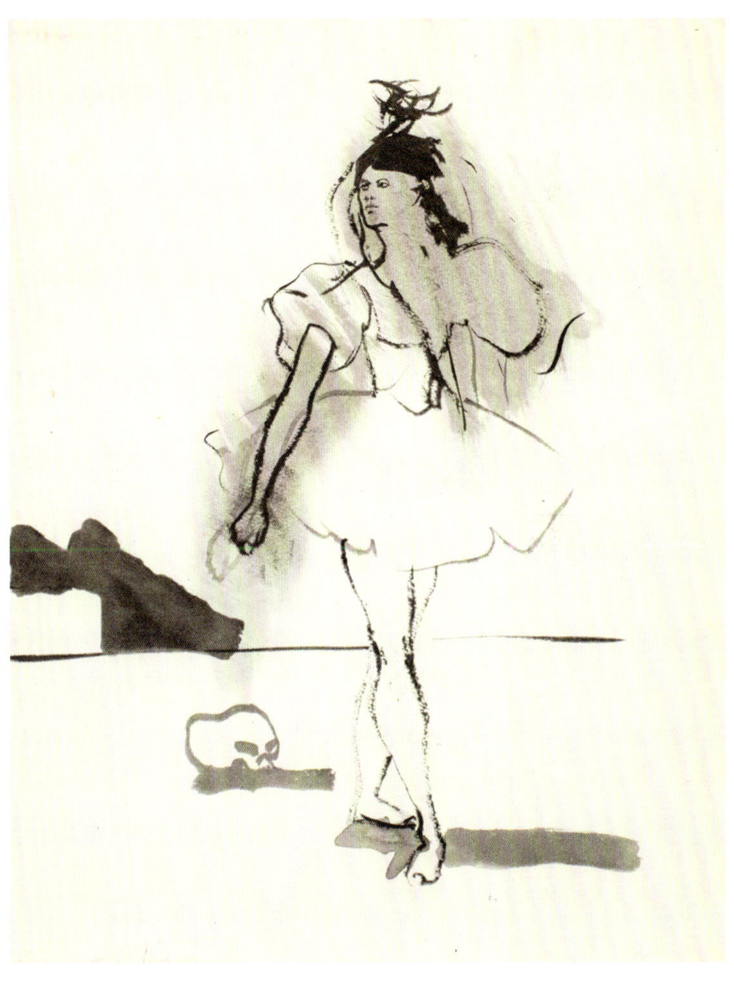

Constantin Guys (Baudelaire's 'painter of modern life') and the previously mentioned Filippo de Pisis, whom Bérard probably ran into in Parisian artistic and social circles.

The love of theatricality, dressing up and spontaneity was shared by the Neo-Romantics, to the extent that it informed their very ethos, but, as we shall see, it was also used to explain their perceived 'weaknesses'. Fashion and stage design have traditionally been looked down upon because they mix multiple media and are subject to the constraints and contingencies of collaborative work; they are further considered unworthy due to their ephemeral nature. The decorative arts were seen as superficial, standing in opposition to the true, 'superior' form of Art. Accordingly, this facet of Bérard's work was viewed as an expression of a dilettantism that was only reinforced by his dalliances with high society. This evaluation has made a lasting contribution to his reduced critical standing, although there has been some recognition of the extent, and tragic curtailment, of his artistic vision, and of the elements that bound him closely to the other members of the group in the rudiments of a Neo-Romantic 'identity'.

In recent years, the emergence, particularly in the United States, of cultural studies as a discipline, with a concomitant focus on queer history and feminist theory, has given rise to a totally different view of Bérard (and the Neo-Romantics in general). His supposed 'failure' can now be interpreted as a discreet, displaced form of resistance or protest against the traditional, normative account of modern art arranged around the white, male and heterosexual figure of the 'great painter'.

As Tirza True Latimer explained in her book on 'eccentric modernisms': 'To the extent that such failures as Bérard's point to alternative possibilities in ostensibly hegemonic cultural contexts, failure can be understood as a perverse form of success. Moreover, because failure exposes the criteria for success [...] that otherwise remain invisible, it has subversive potential.' Some theorists, she pointed out, go still further by elevating failure to 'a quintessentially queer form of cultural critique, arguing that "success in a heteronormative, capitalist society equates too easily with specific forms of reproductive maturity combined with wealth accumulation." [...] In contexts where success equates with permanence, failure is the place where transience, instability, incertitude, and mortality reside.' However extreme such approaches may seem, only time will tell whether they are valid, but they have already served to dismantle one

OPPOSITE, LEFT: Christian Bérard and Coco Chanel in the Italian pavilion at the 1937 Exposition, Paris, by Roger Schall

OPPOSITE, RIGHT: Christian Bérard, *Portrait of a Woman*, pastel on paper, 54.5 × 46 cm (21⅜ × 18⅛ in.), 1947

of the stereotypes to which Bérard's work is all too often reduced by dramatizing and enriching our view of his career and turning his seeming failure into an existential and affirmational choice.

The significance and reality of Bérard's failure has resonated still further, however, for it undoubtedly stood apart from any of the setbacks of the other Neo-Romantics – on account of his 'flaw' (i.e., his diversification, or even profligacy) – to such an extent that it captured the imagination of the age. Four years after his death, Jean Hugo (who was Bérard's friend and witnessed the effects of his influence first-hand) declared in a letter to Jean Cocteau: 'Broadly speaking, the half-century that interests you can be divided into two periods: 1925–1935, the rise and fall of the Chanel era, which in 1918 had succeeded the Poiret era; 1935–1950, the Bérard era, which is still going on.'

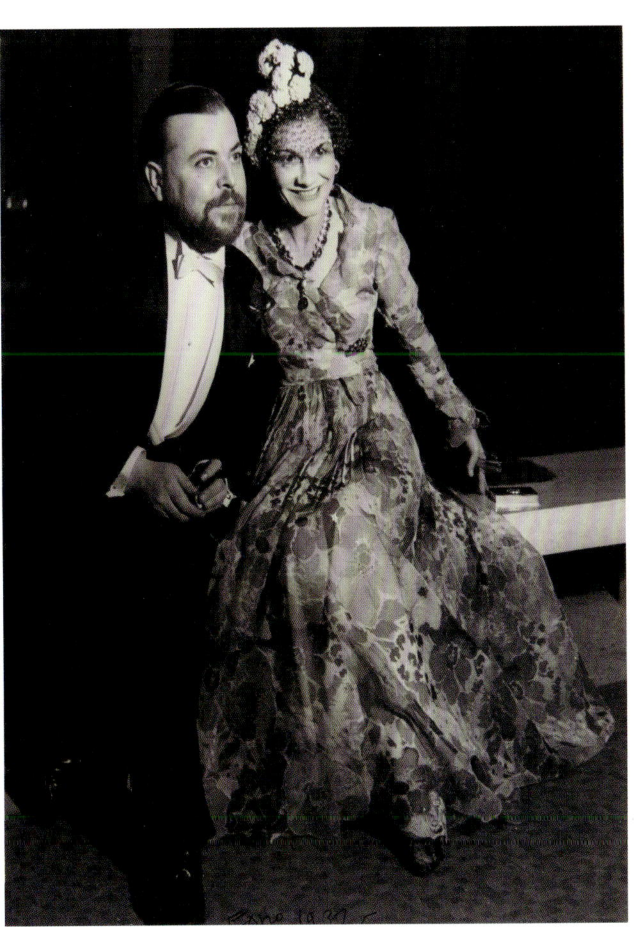

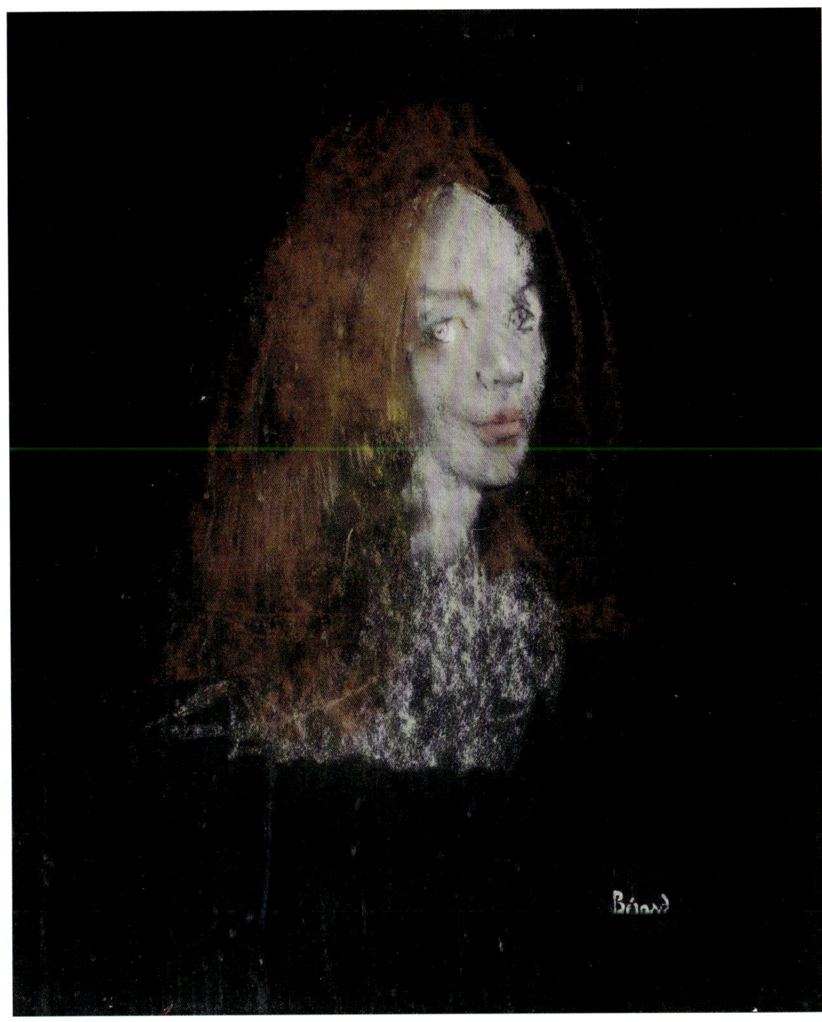

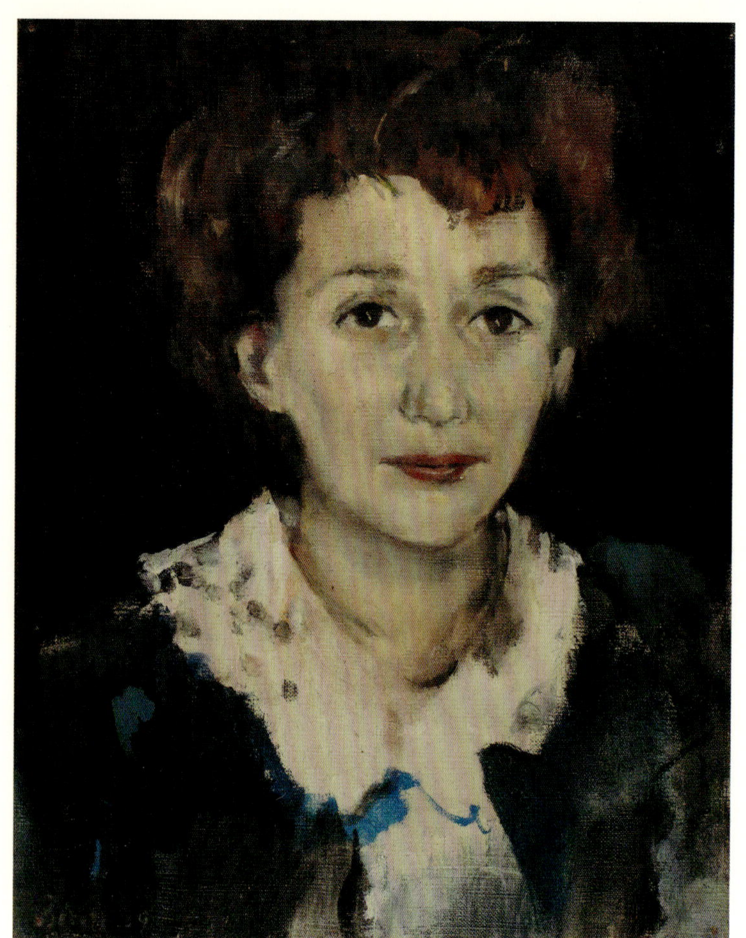

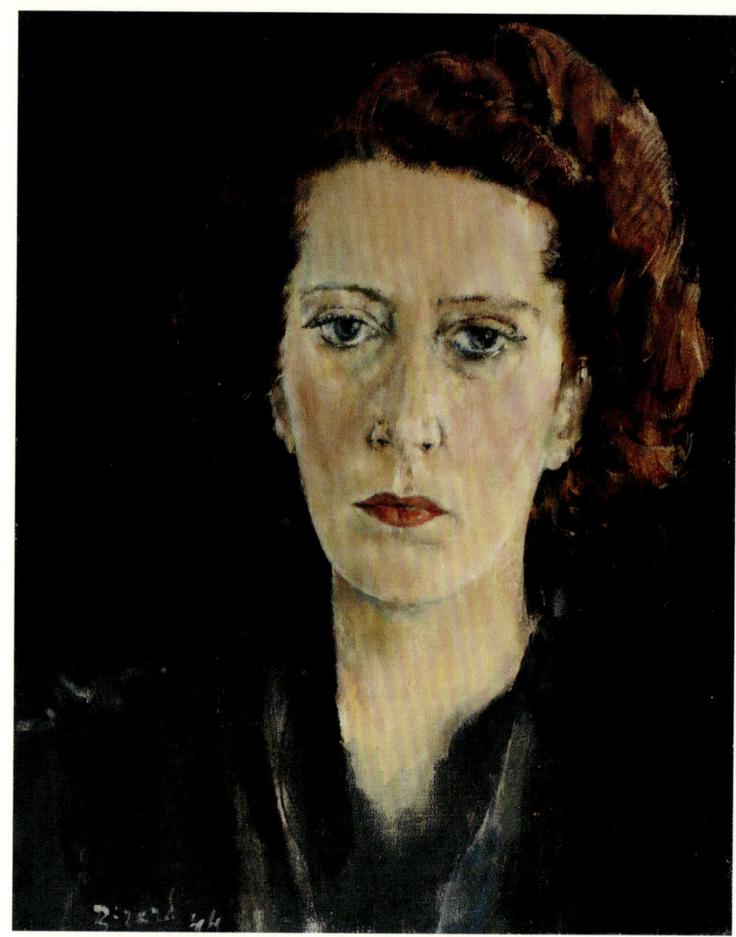

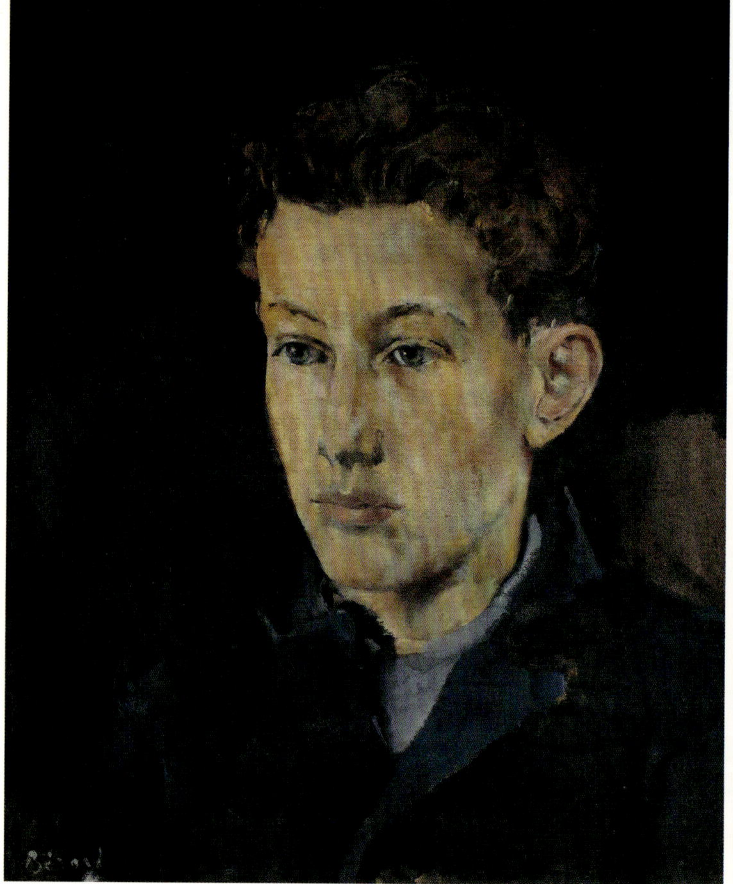

CLOCKWISE, FROM ABOVE LEFT: Christian Bérard, *Portrait of a Woman*, oil on canvas, 28 × 22 cm (11 × 8⅝ in.), 1939; Christian Bérard, *Portrait of a Woman*, oil on canvas, 41 × 33 cm (16⅛ × 13 in.), 1944; Christian Bérard, *Portrait of a Young Man*, oil on canvas, 47 × 39 cm (18½ × 15⅜ in.), 1945
OPPOSITE: Christian Bérard, *Portrait of a Woman*, oil on canvas, 60 × 50 cm (23⅝ × 19⅝ in.), 1948

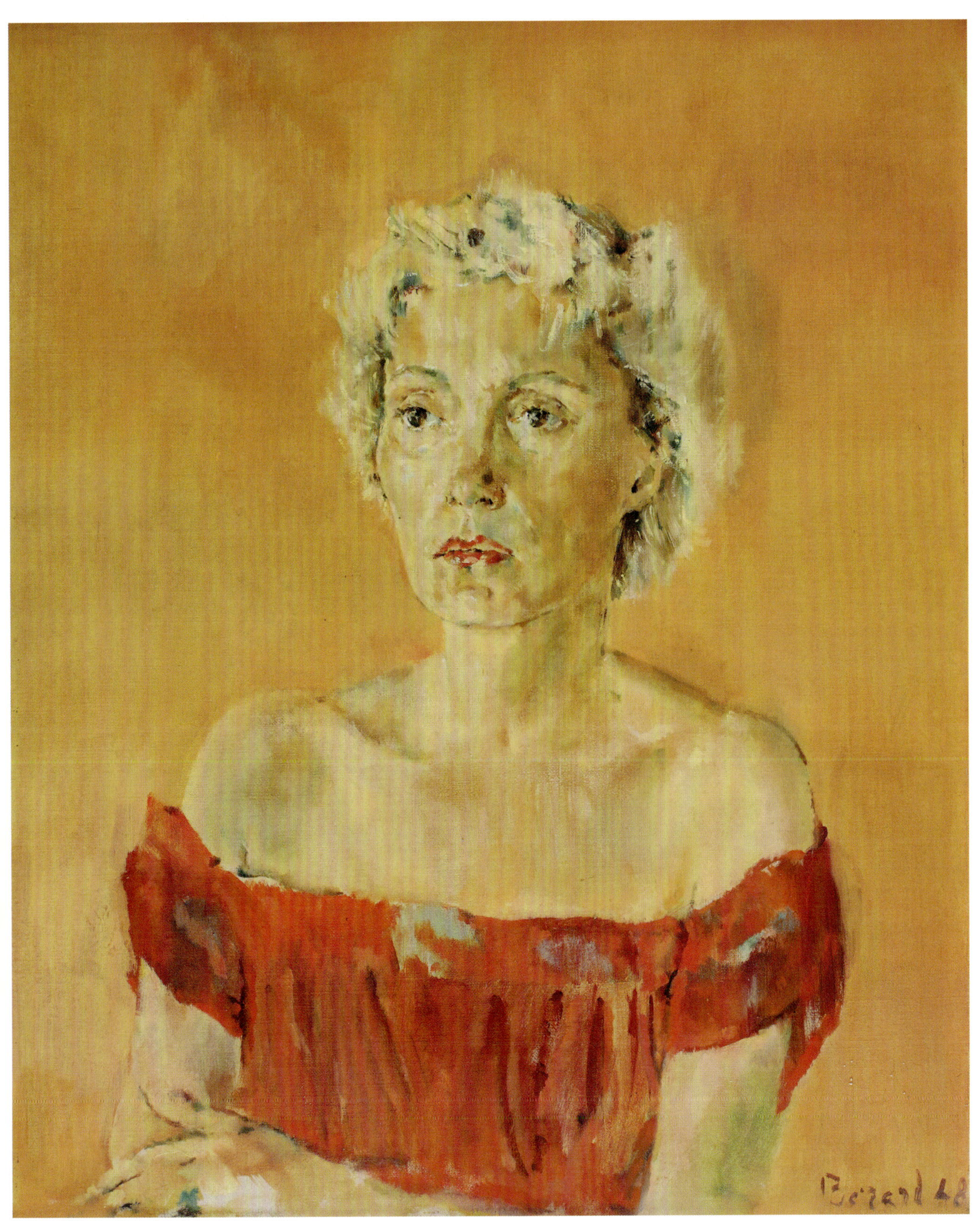
Bérard 48

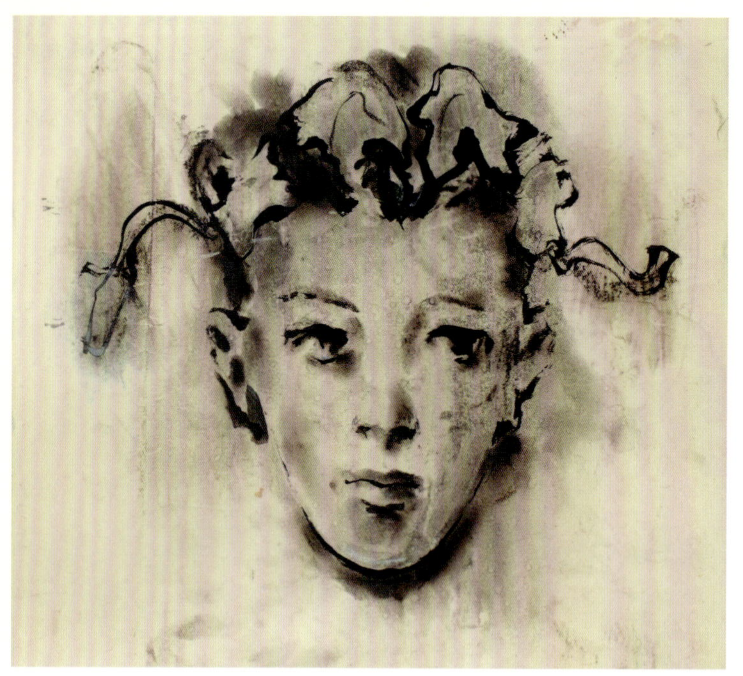

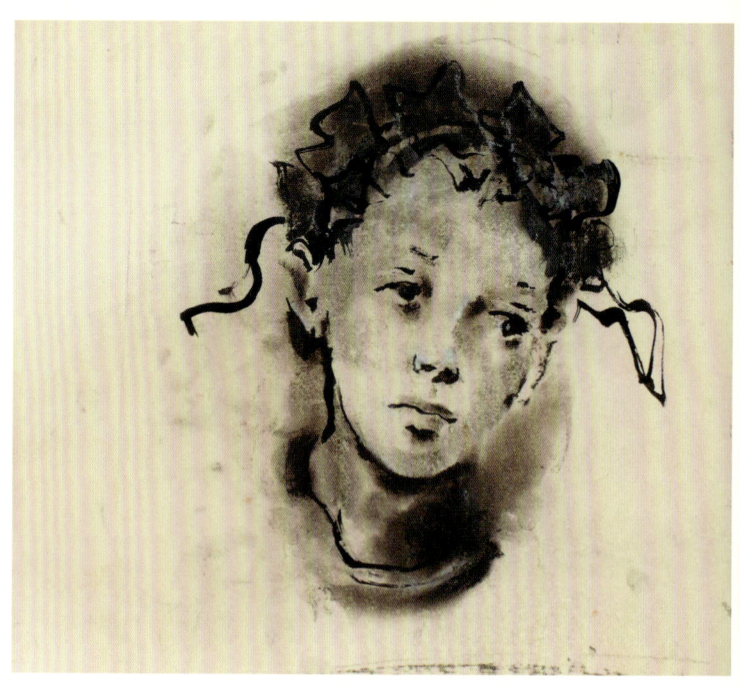

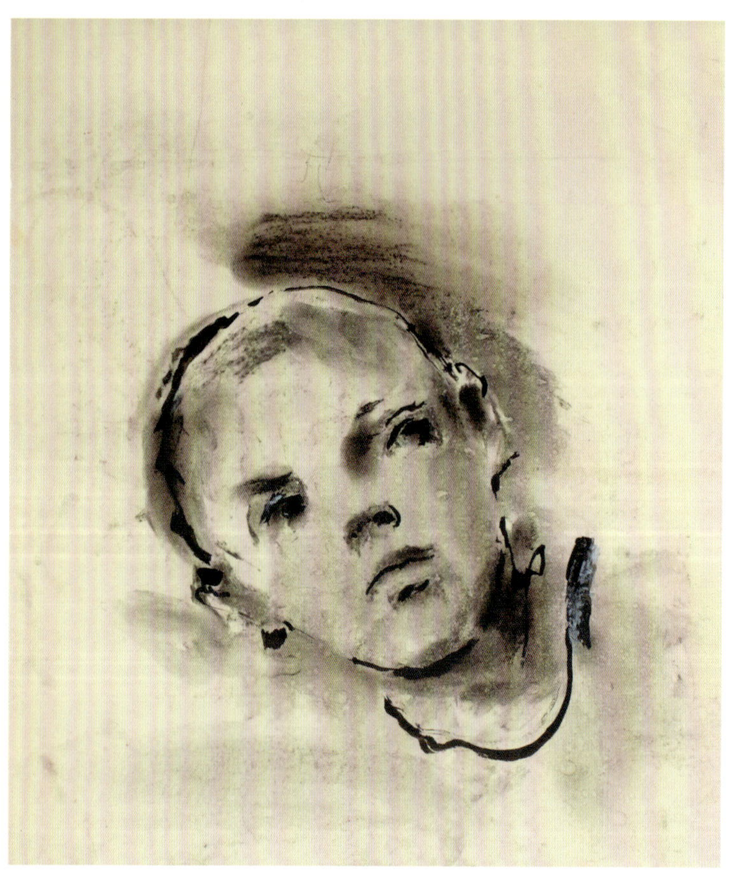

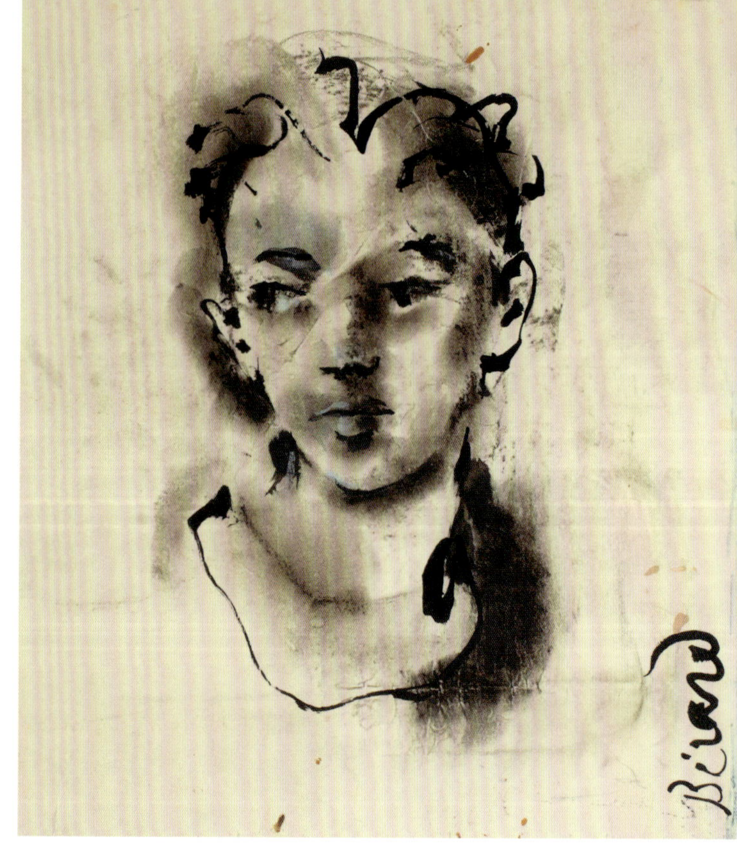

ABOVE: Christian Bérard, *Head of a Child*, four drawings, design for screen, ink on paper, 37 × 33 cm (14½ × 13 in.), n.d.
OPPOSITE, ABOVE: Christian Bérard, *Female Profile*, gouache on paper, 29 × 22 cm (11⅜ × 8⅝ in.), *c.* 1940
OPPOSITE, BELOW: Christian Bérard, *Imaginary Profile*, gouache on paper, 29 × 22 cm (11⅜ × 8⅝ in.), *c.* 1940

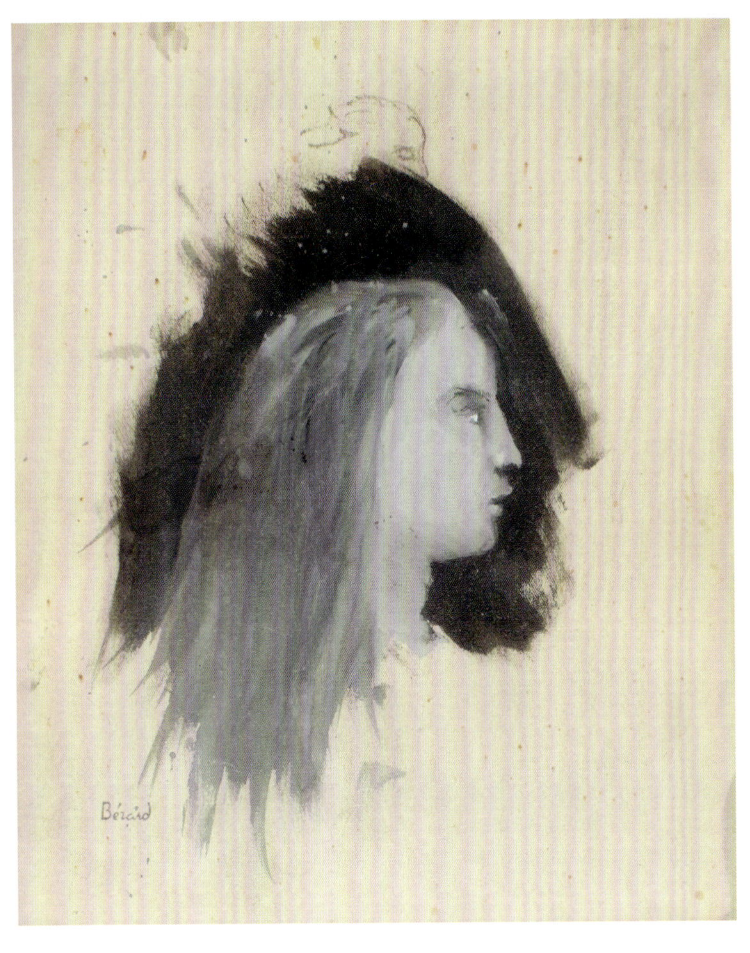
Bérard

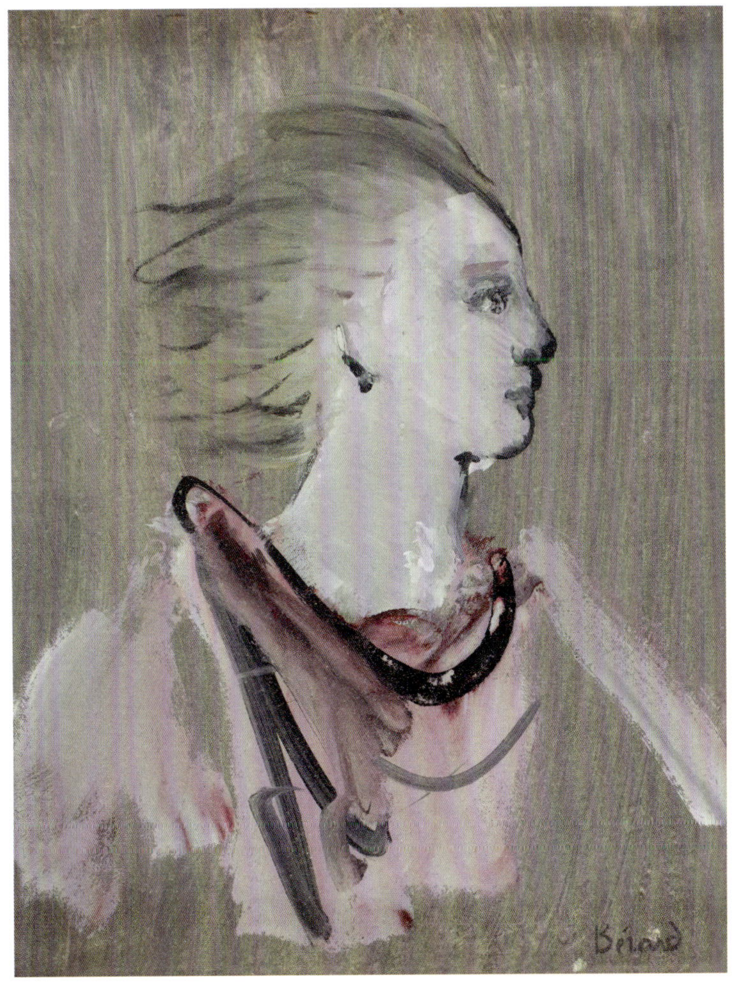
Bérard

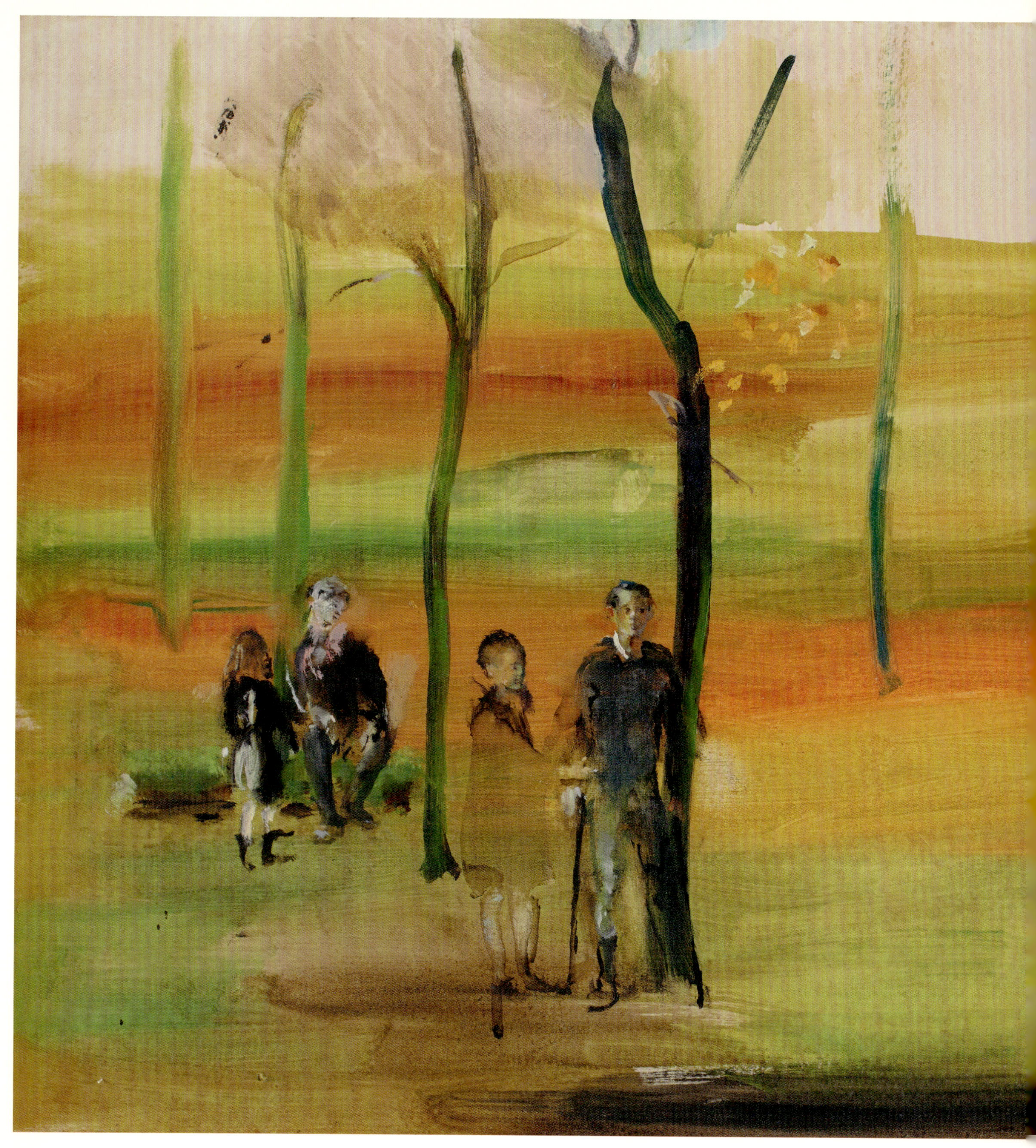

ABOVE: Christian Bérard, *Children in a Field with Trees*, oil on panel, 38 × 46 cm (14⅞ × 18⅛ in.), n.d.
OPPOSITE: Christian Bérard, *Rooftops*, oil on panel, 51 × 64 cm (20 × 25⅛ in.), n.d.

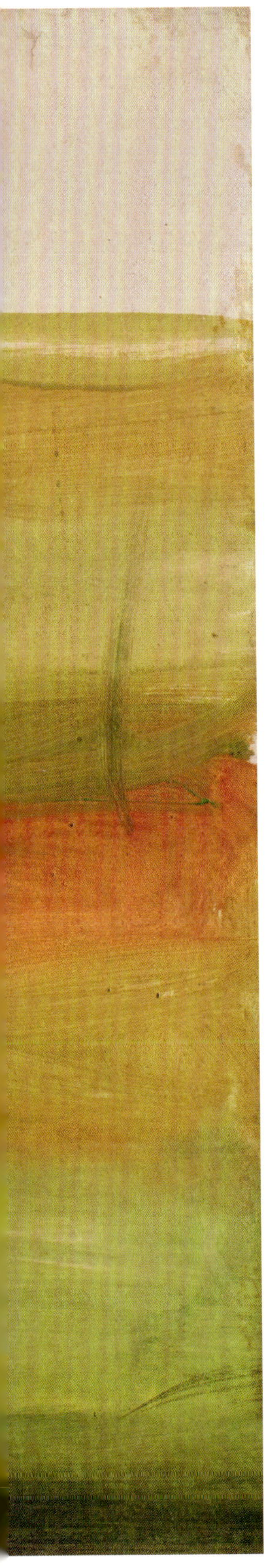

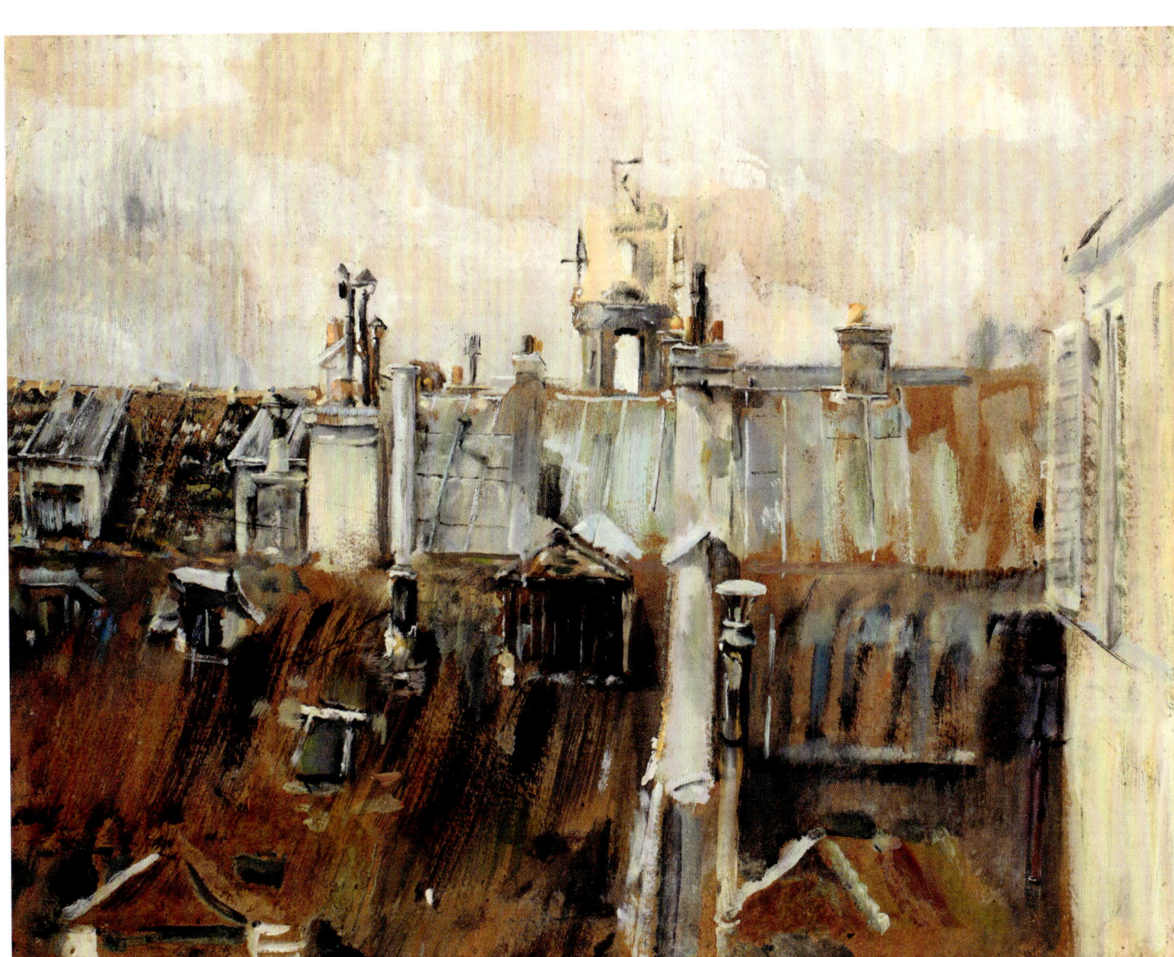

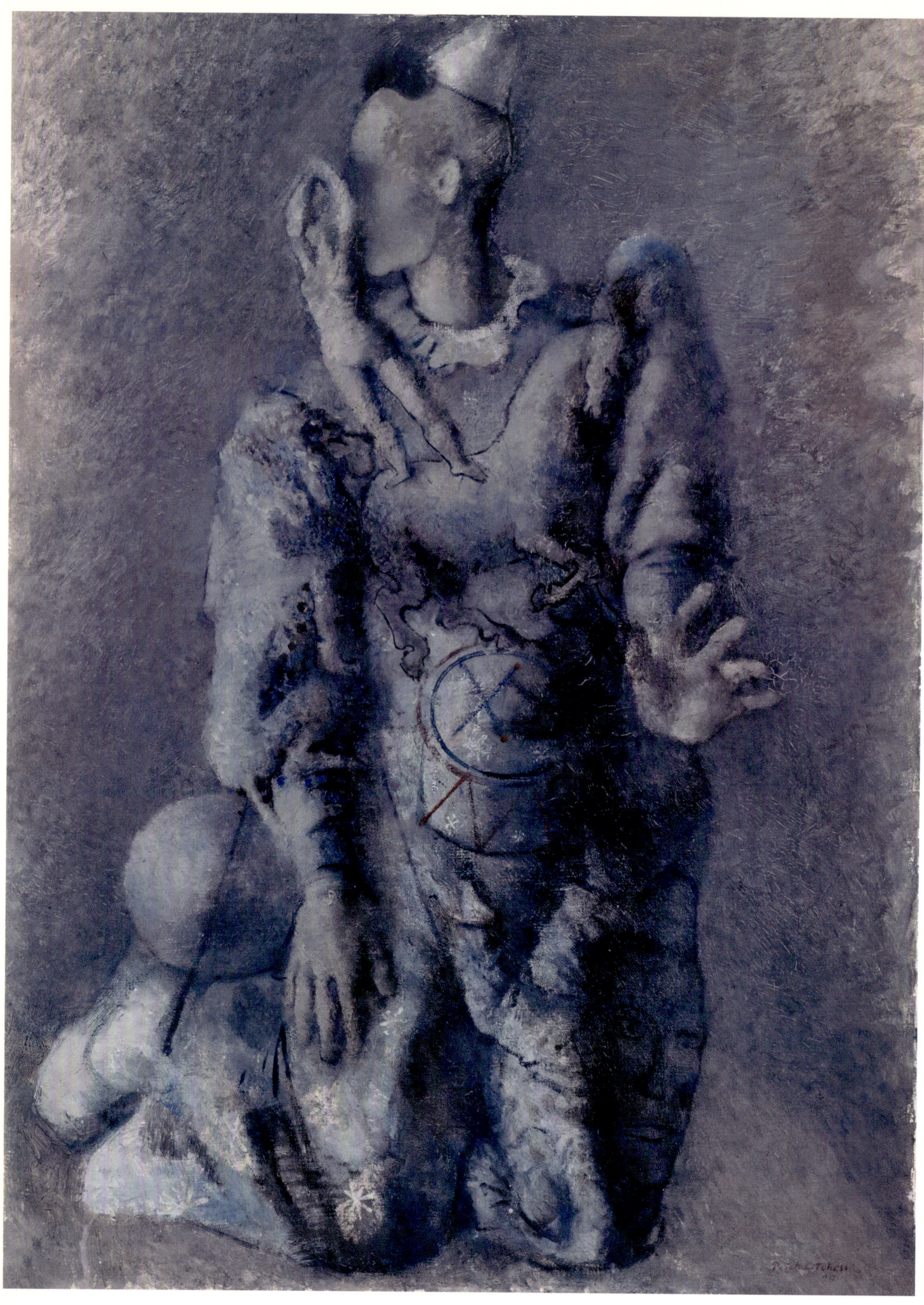

Pavel Tchelitchew, *Blue Clown*, oil on canvas,
81 × 59.7 cm (31⅞ × 23½ in.), 1929

Tchelitchew: Weightiness and Grace

> 'Mr. Pavel Tchelitchew, a sensitive, capricious painter of flowers, cabbages, eggs, clowns, lovely youths, lovely ladies. True Russian exuberance, true Russian blues. Candid, curious, intuitive.'
>
> Bravig Imbs, *Confessions of Another Young Man*, 1936, p. 11

Both Eugene Berman and Pavel Tchelitchew were born in Russia in the closing years of the nineteenth century, and they were as familiar with theatrical tradition as they were with the radical innovations of Diaghilev. Unlike Bérard, they were already immersed in theatre and ballet as teenagers. In fact, over the course of his wanderings, Tchelitchew worked as a stage designer before he ever became a painter; Berman, in contrast, developed this facet of his work after his arrival in the United States, and then in Italy.

Like the Berman brothers, Tchelitchew had been forced to flee Russia after the October Revolution. He left Moscow (where he had been born into an aristocratic family on 21 September 1898) for Kiev, which became the capital of a short-lived independent Ukrainian state. While there, he spent two years studying under the Constructivist Alexandra Exter, who had been Fernand Léger's student in Paris. He also took classes from two artists, one of whom, Isaac Rabinovitch, worked in the theatre. The influence of these two on Tchelitchew's early work is plain to see, and he would always retain a liking for geometric constructions and playing with volume. In 1919, when he was still only twenty-one, he designed his first set and costumes for *The Geisha*, an operetta by Ivan Caryll, for a theatre in Kiev, but the project never came to fruition because of the advance of the Bolsheviks and the resulting exodus.

After spells in, first, Odessa and, then, Istanbul, where he designed his first ballet scenery in 1921, Tchelitchew set off for the Berlin of the Golden Twenties, a boom period for cabaret and theatre. He worked in both these fields, most notably designing the set and costumes for Rimsky-Korsakov's *Golden Cockerel* in a style still marked by the spirit of Constructivism.

Tchelitchew's arrival in Paris in 1923 triggered a radical change in his approach, as Donald Windham, one of his close friends, explained: 'His interest turned to other problems of space, experiments in double

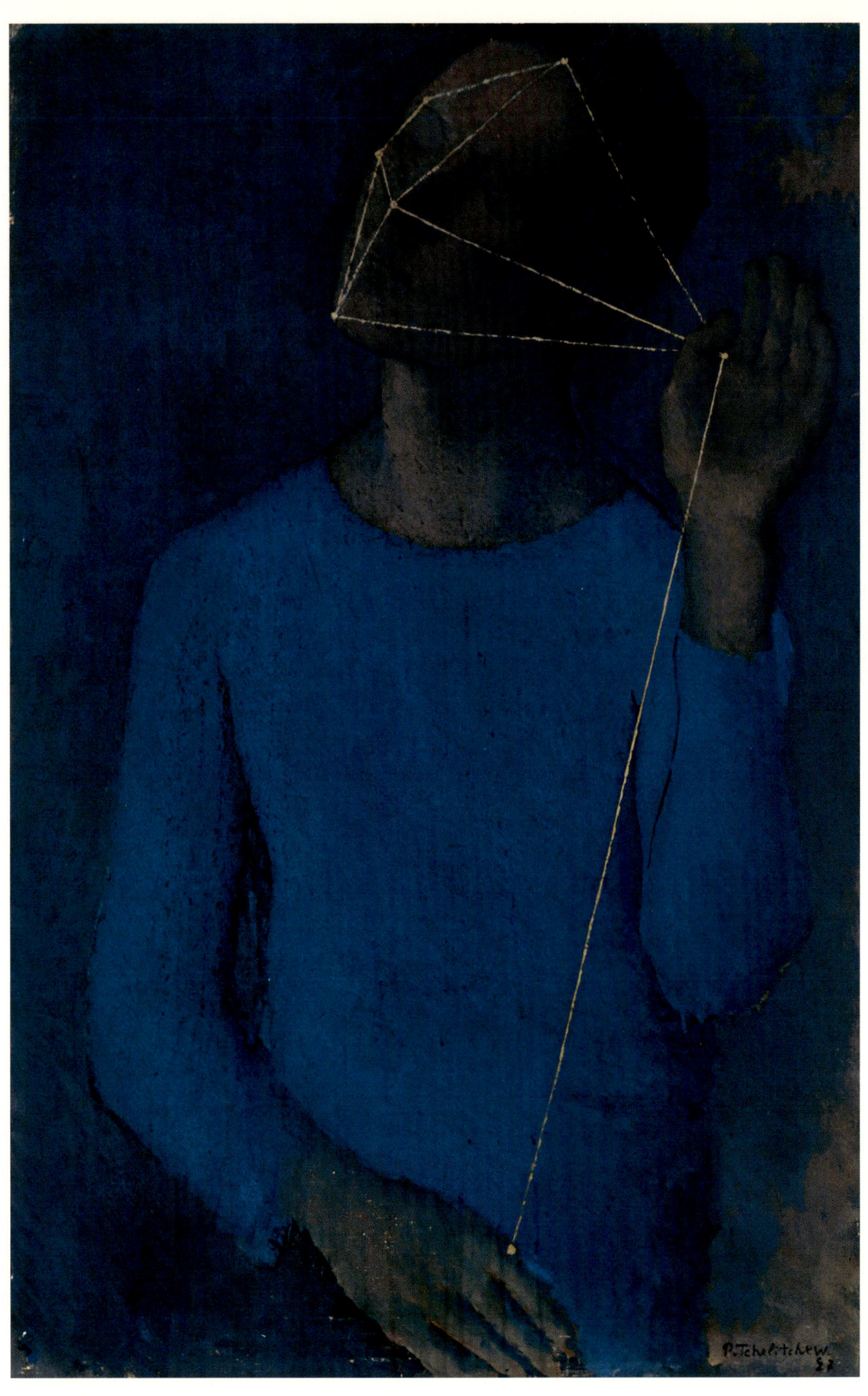

ABOVE: Pavel Tchelitchew, *Blue Boy with String*, oil on canvas, 97.2 × 64.1 cm (38¼ × 25¼ in.), 1927
OPPOSITE: Pavel Tchelitchew, *Personage*, oil and coffee grounds on canvas, 129.5 × 86.7 cm (51 × 34⅛ in.), 1927

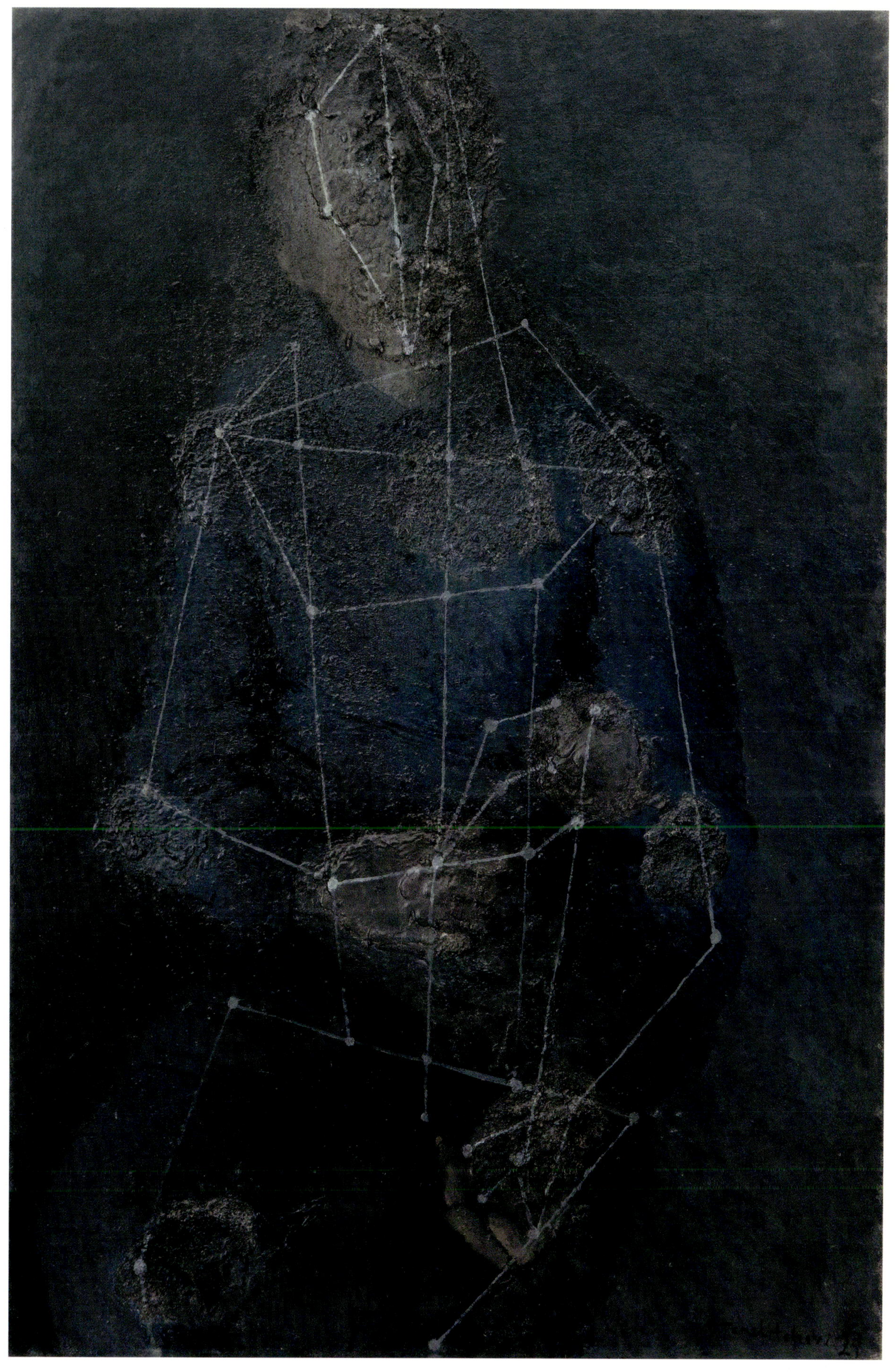

images and distortions formed by aerial perspective, and for five years he did no theatrical work. It seemed to him when he began to develop a new phase of painting that the work of stage designing was impossible. His new ideas had to find themselves on canvas.'

Tchelitchew abandoned the coloured spheres and kinetics of Constructivism to turn – like the Bermans and Bérard (to whom he was bound by 'a passionate enmity') – towards its exact opposite, characterized by melancholy and virtual monochromatism. The complexities of the biographical, aesthetic and psychological factors that led Tchelitchew to this transformation defy any glib summary, but we will remember that by the time Gertrude Stein came across the 'young russian' in the *Autobiography of Alice B. Toklas*, 'he was painting, so he said, colour that was no colour, he was painting blue pictures and he was painting three heads in one'. Similarly Soby, another eye-witness, portrayed a Tchelitchew who 'in most of his early pictures [...] restricted himself to artificially harmonized tones of a deep blue'.

Both Stein and Soby had a tendency to simplify their accounts, however. In fact, the first painting that Tchelitchew exhibited publicly in Paris, in the Salon d'Automne of 1925 – a *Basket of Strawberries* – revelled in a range of bright reds, pinks and oranges; and it was this painting (as much as the chance encounter on a bridge described in the *Autobiography*) that attracted Stein's attention, with its effects of reversed perspective and its delicate chromatic variations, and it was responsible for kickstarting Tchelitchew's career. (Several critics were equally impressed, including Florent Fels, as evident in the issue of *L'Art Vivant* published on 1 October 1925.)

A few months later, however, Tchelitchew decided to radically reduce his colour scheme and, in his own words, he 'threw away' everything except 'black, white, ochre, natural and burnt umber'. He combined a range of greys and browns with beige for a series of still lifes of eggs (whose symbolic charge was heightened by their presentation in threes, a magical number *par excellence*), while also indulging in the spatial deformations that so fascinated him. He thus confined himself to a colour spectrum resembling the one that would be used the following year by the

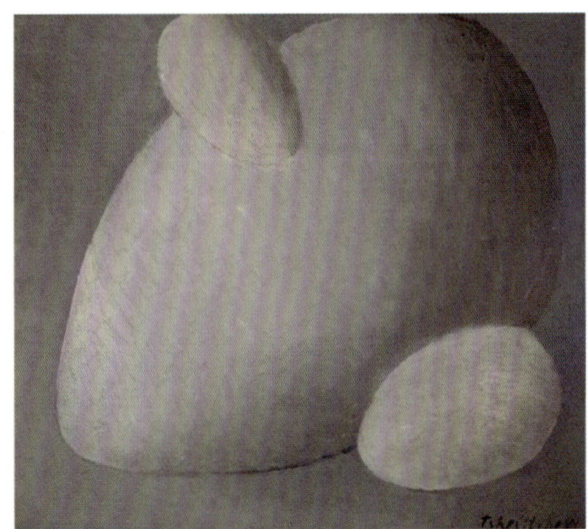

ABOVE: Pavel Tchelitchew, *Three Eggs*, oil on canvas mounted on board, 38.1 × 43.2 cm (15 × 17 in.), *c.* 1925
OPPOSITE: Pavel Tchelitchew, *Portraits of Joella Levy*, brown ink and wash on paper, 61 × 45.7 cm (24 × 18 in.), n.d.

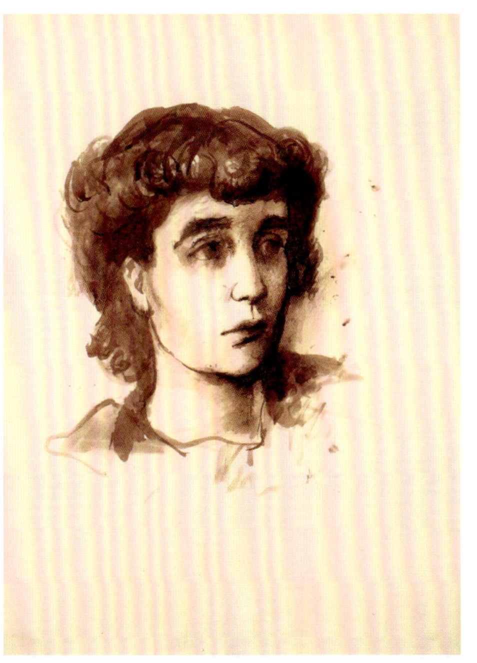
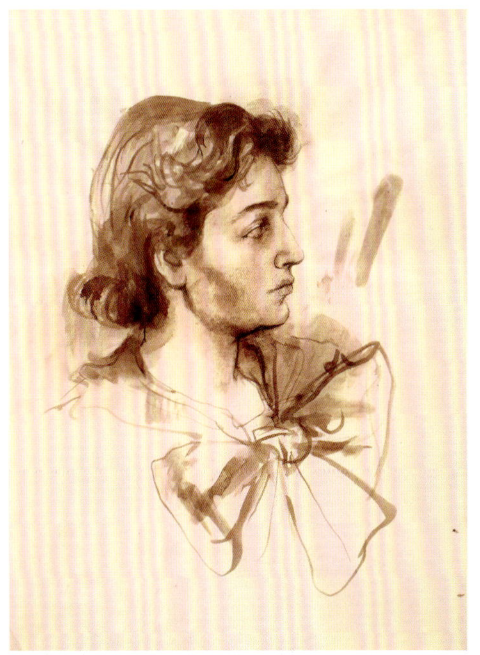
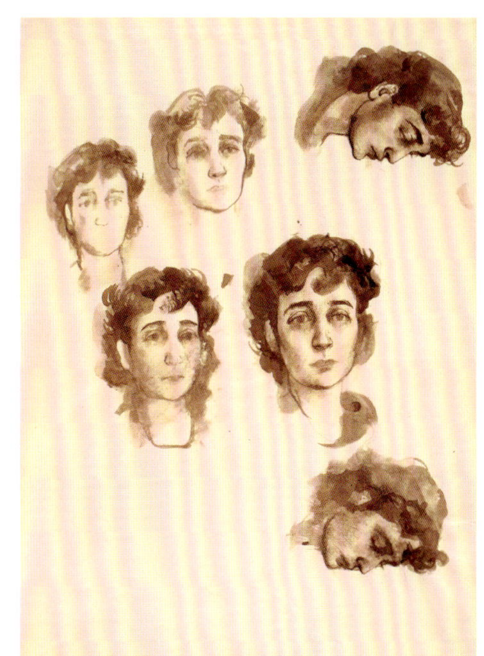

other participants in the exhibition at the Druet Gallery, making it a distinguishing feature of the Neo-Romantic sensibility.

During his progressive emancipation from abstraction and Constructivism, Tchelitchew also began to take an interest in a pictorial genre that would go on to form a major part of his oeuvre (both paintings and drawings). It was a genre in which he would excel: the representation of the human face, which, through the mimesis and psychological effects inherent in portraiture, provided another means of escaping from abstraction and embracing new values ('Gradually', observed Soby, 'the human face began to fascinate him above all other subjects.'). In 1925, he started working on a series of portraits of friends and relatives with his new range of colours, creating simplified, hieratic forms with a thick, grainy paste, sometimes mixed with sand or coffee grounds. ('[H]e piled up so heavy a texture', noted Soby, 'that, in his words, "The surface of my painting looked like maps of earth in low relief."') Some of these ghostly figures were uncannily similar to the sombre, hallucinatory apparitions that Bérard was producing at the time, using equally remarkable raw materials.

Tchelitchew subsequently went still further in his experimentation by trying to go beyond a static, stylized, frontal approach to his subjects. As Soby remarked, he took on 'one of the most persistent themes in 20th century painting: the simultaneous presentation of several different aspects of the human head and figure'. Tchelitchew embarked on a highly original attempt to inscribe the temporal dimension in space without resorting to the extreme deconstruction,

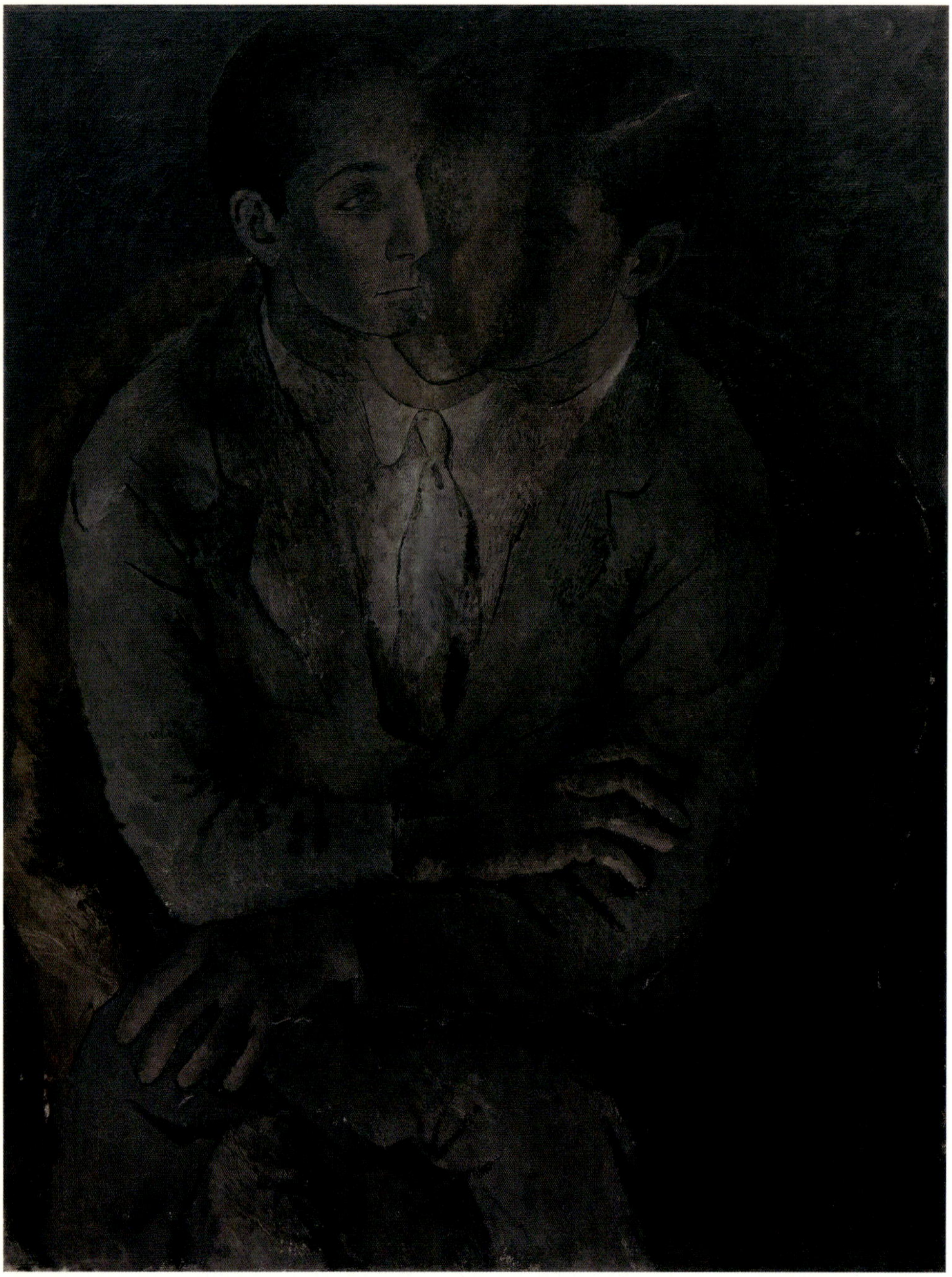

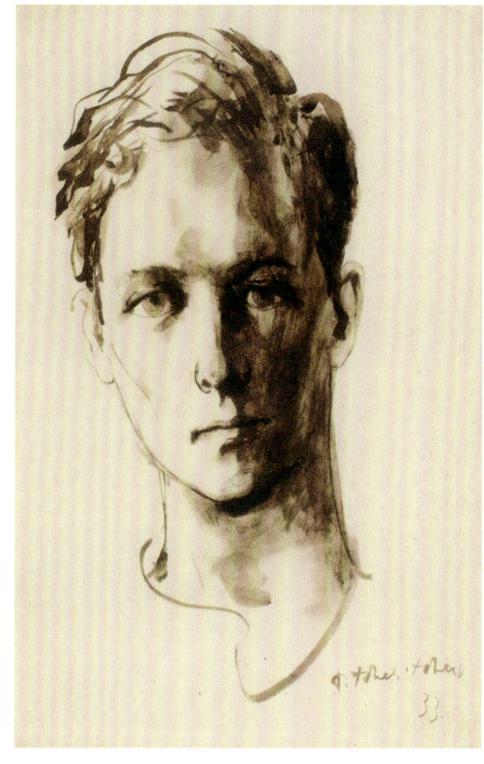

ABOVE, LEFT: Pavel Tchelitchew, *Untitled (Seated Man, Multiple Images)*, oil and coffee grounds on canvas, 116.8 × 89.5 cm (46 × 35¼ in.), 1927
ABOVE, RIGHT: Pavel Tchelitchew, *Portrait of Patrice de la Tour du Pin*, design for lithograph (wash on paper), 30 × 20 cm (11⅞ × 7⅞ in.), 1933

OPPOSITE, CLOCKWISE FROM TOP: Pavel Tchelitchew, *Untitled (Portrait of a Man)*, oil on canvas, 61 × 46 cm (24 × 18 in.), *c.* 1929; Pavel Tchelitchew, *Still Life with Hand*, oil on canvas, 100 × 80 cm (39⅜ × 31½ in.), n.d.; Pavel Tchelitchew, *Untitled*, oil on re-lined canvas, 45.7 × 38.1 cm (18 × 15 in.), n.d.

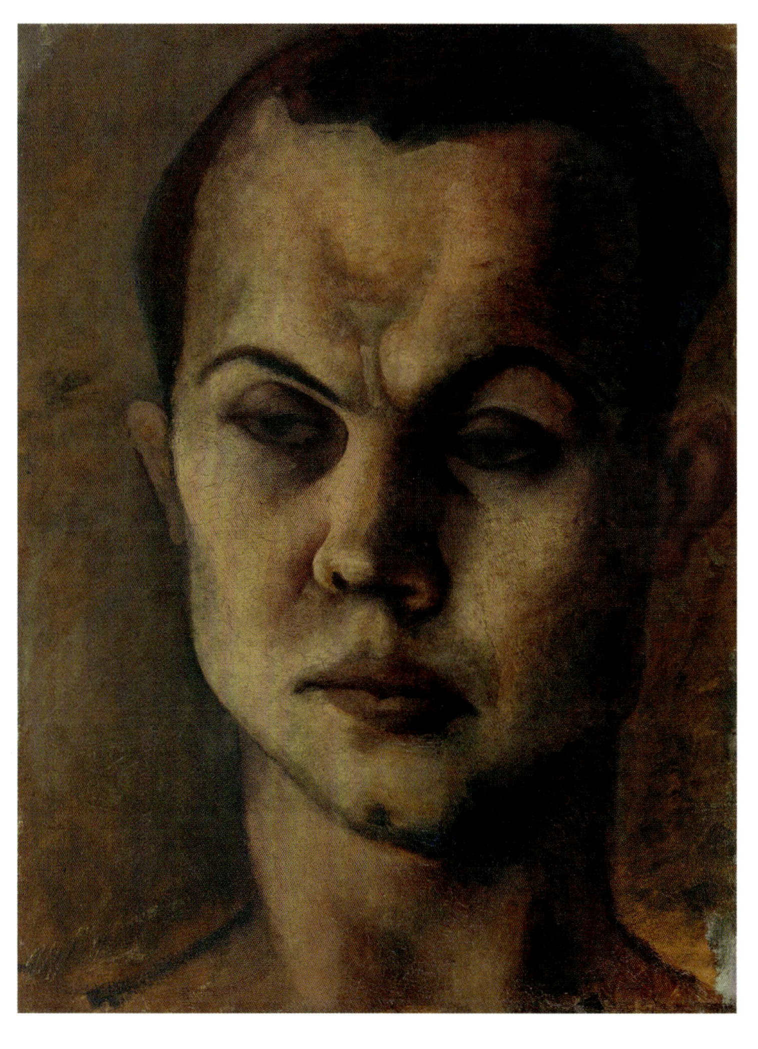

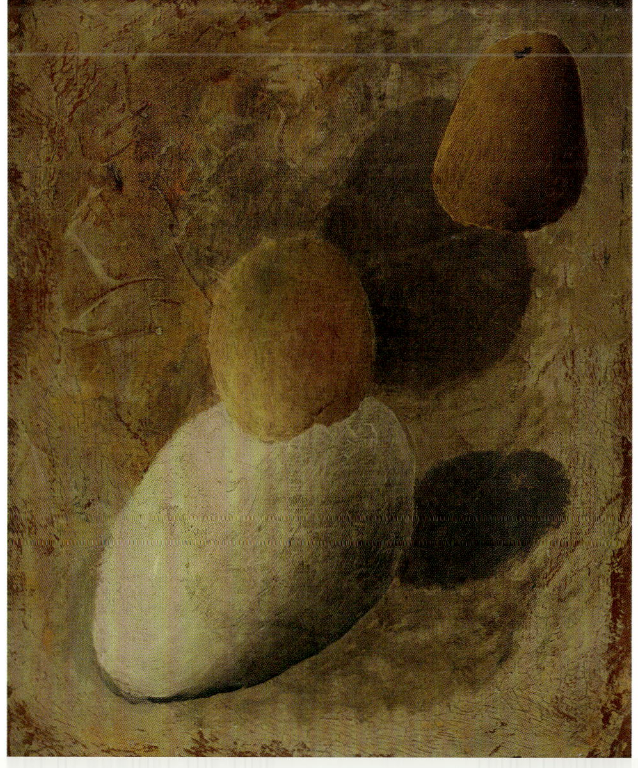

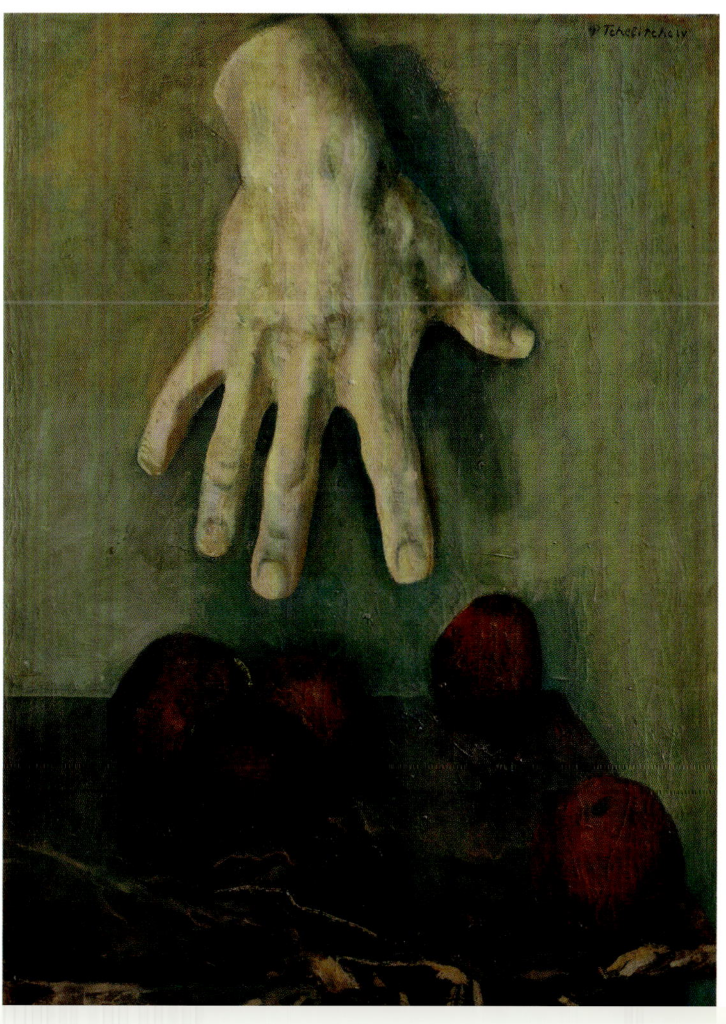

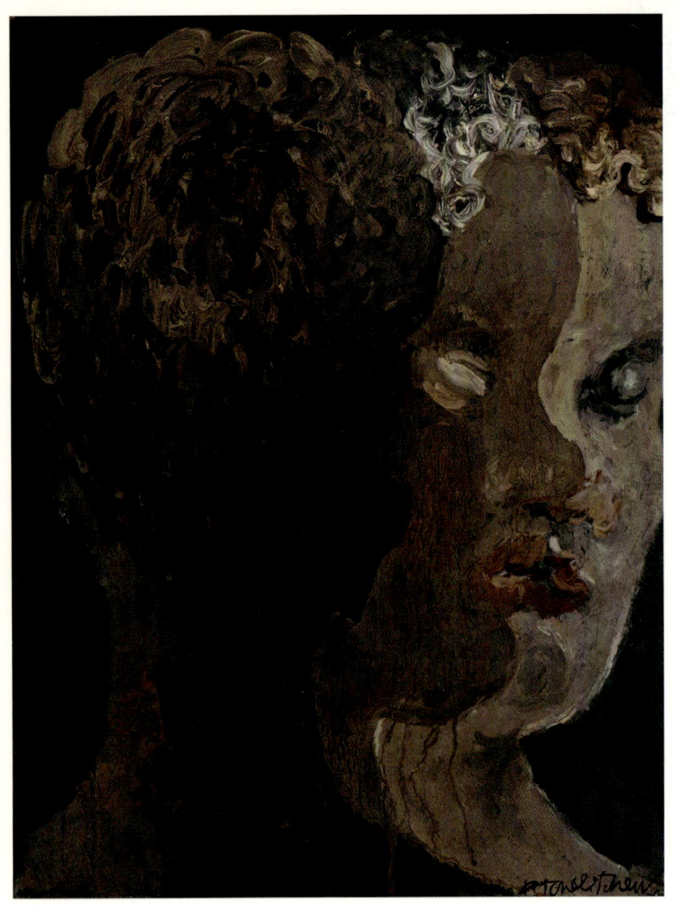

geometrization and fragmentation of Cubism – hence the 'three heads in one' mentioned in *The Autobiography of Alice B. Toklas*. One particularly striking example of this exploration is the portrait of René Crevel, which was painted in 1926 and bought by Stein. Tchelitchew's combination of dynamic representation and a faithful likeness foreshadows the experiments of David Hockney half a century later, with his successive photographic and pictorial images that evoked Cubism in their attempt to reproduce the movement involved in the act of seeing. (It is hard to imagine that Hockney was unaware of Tchelitchew, whose work has largely ended up in English-speaking countries, due to the subsequent developments in his life.)

Tchelitchew subjected the oval form of the face – reminiscent of the eggs in his still lifes – to a variety of deformations and stretches that are graphic translations of the sequential dimension of time in the immobility of space. He applied the same principles to the representation of the human body by elaborating a system of figuration which he described as 'laconic' to capture several 'states', or moments, of the same subject in a single image. The results were strange composite creatures whose egg-shaped heads recalled not only his own still lifes but also the dummies of de Chirico, while their bodies were regaled with multiple arms and legs, along the lines of certain Asian divinities or the chronophotographs of Étienne-Jules Marey and Eadweard Muybridge. This technique provides another demonstration of Tchelitchew's assimilation of the Constructivist obsession with kinetics long after he had distanced himself from the movement.

A stay in the South of France in the summer of 1926 sparked a new change in direction that Tchelitchew himself saw as a means of brightening his colour scheme: 'The predominant color of blue in this region surprised me greatly, and gradually indigo, Prussian blue, cerulean and cobalt came to my palette [...] against this blue, orange and yellow values appeared as ochre, sienna natural, golden ochre and burnt sienna.' A trip to Algiers the following year confirmed his new

ABOVE: Pavel Tchelitchew, *Three Heads (Portrait of René Crevel)*, oil on canvas, 47.6 × 36.8 cm (18¾ × 14½ in.), 1926
OPPOSITE: Pavel Tchelitchew, *Leopard Boy*, oil on canvas, 55 × 46.3 cm (21⅝ × 18¼ in.), 1935

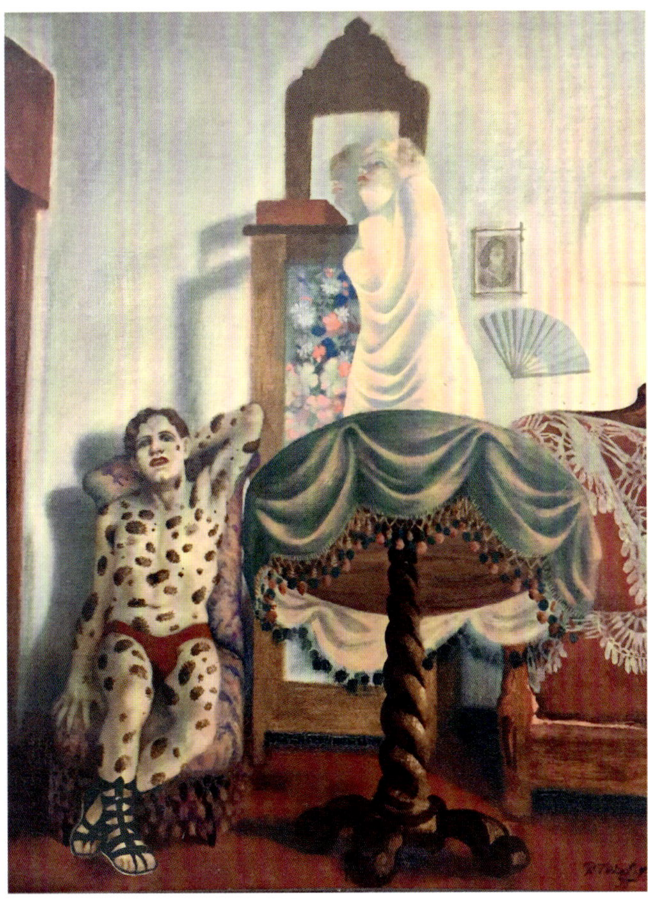

course, resulting in the first 'blue paintings' mentioned in both Stein's *Autobiography* and *After Picasso*. The works from the latter's rose period, which Tchelitchew had seen in the galleries on rue de Fleurus, surely enhanced the revelation of the colours that he encountered in the South: 'At Alfred Flechtheim's gallery in Berlin and in Parisian galleries and collections Tchelitchew had already seen innumerable Picassos, but they had been mostly of the Cubist and later periods. At Miss Stein's he saw the Rose period pictures of 1905–06 which were to have so vital an influence on his own paintings of 1929–32.'

Around this time a particular subject matter became the main focus of Tchelitchew's attention (and Bérard's, although both artists were once again following a trail marked out by Picasso in the early years of the century). Tchelitchew started a series of paintings of clowns and acrobats, and the world of the

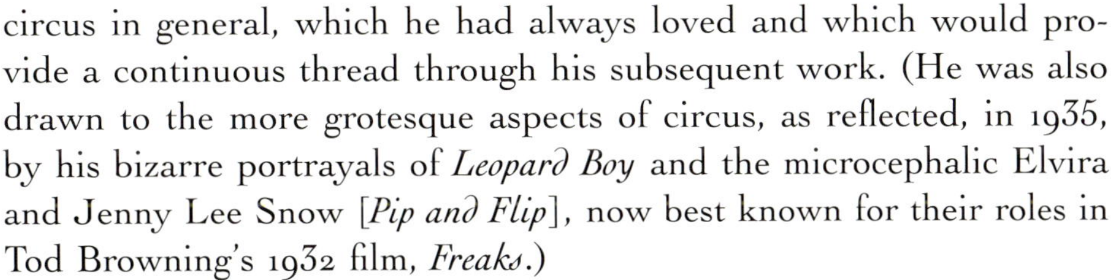

circus in general, which he had always loved and which would provide a continuous thread through his subsequent work. (He was also drawn to the more grotesque aspects of circus, as reflected, in 1935, by his bizarre portrayals of *Leopard Boy* and the microcephalic Elvira and Jenny Lee Snow [*Pip and Flip*], now best known for their roles in Tod Browning's 1932 film, *Freaks*.)

More generally, the image of the tumbling acrobat allowed both Tchelitchew and Bérard to explore two opposing aspects of human experience, namely grace and weightiness: on the one hand, the body's capacity to transcend itself, to defy the laws of gravity, and, on the other, the ineluctable fall back to reality, the melancholy heaviness of mortality. However, while Bérard tends towards the grace of nostalgic lightness, expressed through rapid, lively brushstrokes, Tchelitchew stands firmly on the side of corporeal weightiness. This is reflected not only in the pasty textures of his paintings but also in his depiction of bulky, distorted bodies, seemingly compelled to fall over and over, as if attracted by the earth. This vision is evident, for example, in Tchelitchew's drawings of sleeping or recumbent clowns, and in a splendid series of tellingly

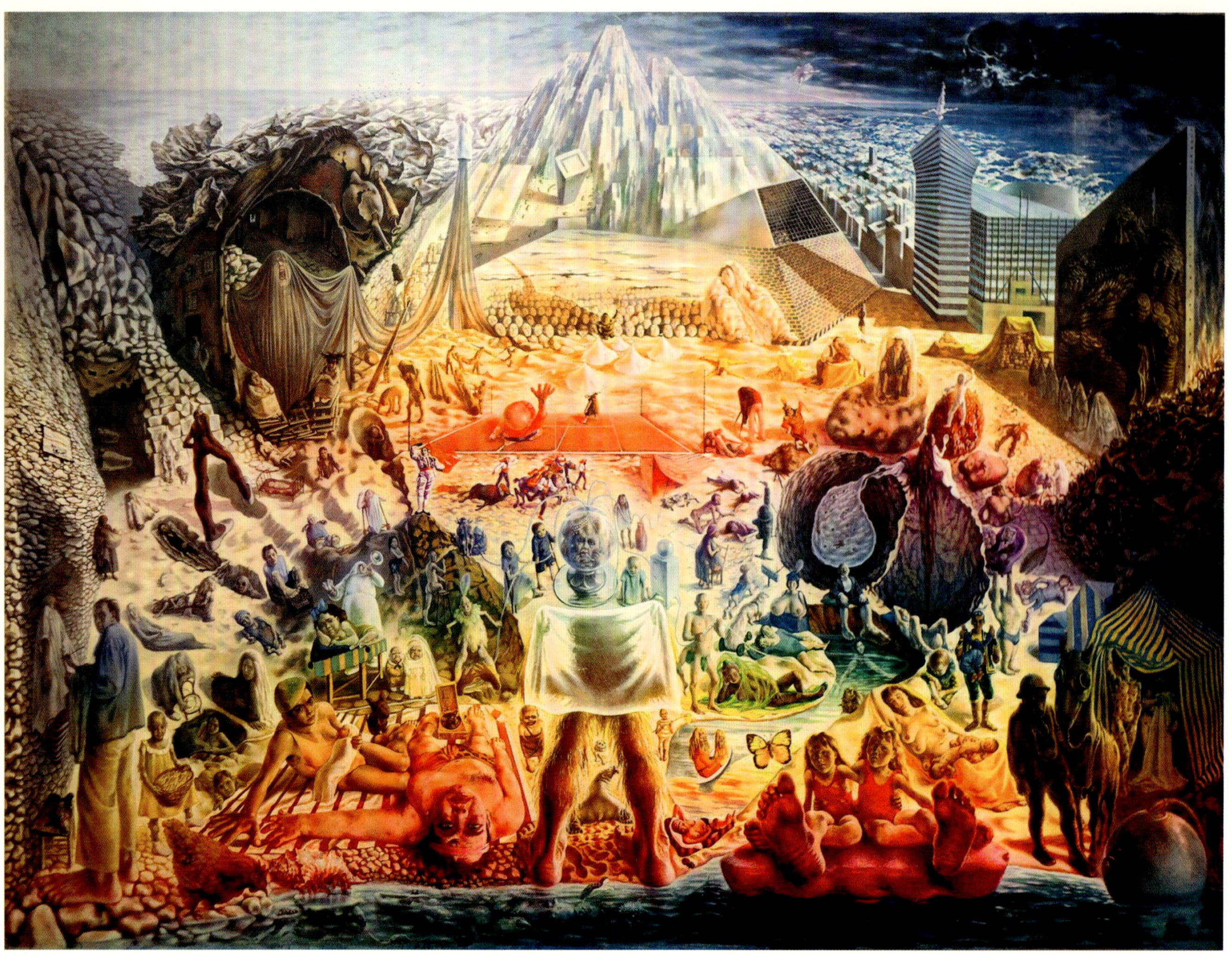

titled paintings dating from 1930: *Fallen Rider*, *Burial of the Acrobat* and the emblematic *The One Who Fell*.

Tchelitchew was a virtuoso draughtsman who loved line drawing, but he also enjoyed bringing out volume and relief, as well as structuring a composition. 'In contrast to the purely linear style of Picasso's well-known neo-classic drawings,' noted Soby, 'Tchelitchew's drawings make their statement through their dramatic qualities of light and shade.' His skills were so highly developed that, added Soby, '[h]is superiority at drawing has led him to make his sketches finished works of art rather than notes for later paintings'. This bold graphic force gave him, even more remarkably, a means of distancing and reducing the pathos inherent in the subject matter through sheer formal mastery. ('Less sensual and more of a theorist than Bérard, his nostalgia was to a certain extent forced through a process of formalization. It could not be expressed with instinctive ease; it had to be more ambitious, colder, and without the quick emotional release of less intellectual painters.')

Pavel Tchelitchew, *Phenomena*, oil on canvas, 200 × 270.5 cm (78¾ × 106½ in.), 1936–38

The young Russian was thus establishing one of his stylistic constants: while the Berman brothers played with perspective (topological in the case of Leonid, and architectural in that of Eugene), Tchelitchew used the human body as the raw material for 'grotesque tricks of perspective', subjecting it to a barrage of optical exaggerations and distortions. Furthermore, he set it in a dizzying abstract space, punctuated by multiple vanishing points that co-exist on the surface of his paintings, recalling primitive artists who merged the concepts of space and time. Some ten years later, this *modus operandi* would be spectacularly applied to a series of works that will be discussed below, as well as to one of his most famous paintings, *Phenomena* (1936–38), now in the Tretyakov Gallery in Moscow. This work is a kind of biographical diorama that assembles, under various guises, most of the protagonists of Tchelitchew's life since 1926, including Bérard, Eugene Berman and Gertrude Stein.

The same fascination with the geometry of the body inspired Tchelitchew's return to the theatre, after five years exclusively devoted to painting. In 1928, he was invited by Diaghilev to design the scenery and costumes for *Ode*, with a libretto by Boris Kochno, a score by Nicolas Nabokov and choreography by Léonide Massine. While retaining the essential elements of a ballet – to avoid alarming Diaghilev – Tchelitchew came up with a *Gesamtkunstwerk* that combined music, declamation, pantomime and dance, with acrobats and dancers moving in a floating, luminous and abstract space (created with the help of Pierre Charbonnier), which recalled his paintings. ('Mannequins, indistinguishable from the dancers and hung in space to create a false perspective, aided the light in creating an illusion of endless space in which the action was seen ideally, from all sides at once, as the acrobats in the ring are seen by the circle of spectators.')

The success of this unusual piece, and the association with Diaghilev, marked a decisive step in the recognition of Tchelitchew's work. Soby reported that he attracted 'a rapidly growing circle of critics and collectors'. This appreciation was consolidated by a debut solo show in London in July 1928, which received a tribute that was as extravagant as the figure who paid it.

Edith Sitwell (1887–1964), the dramatically attired poet and woman of letters, first met Tchelitchew in 1927 at Gertrude Stein's home, and she took over the role of principal cheerleader for his work (as well as succumbing to an unrequited love for the man himself). Never given to half-measures, Sitwell proclaimed, in *The Graphic* of

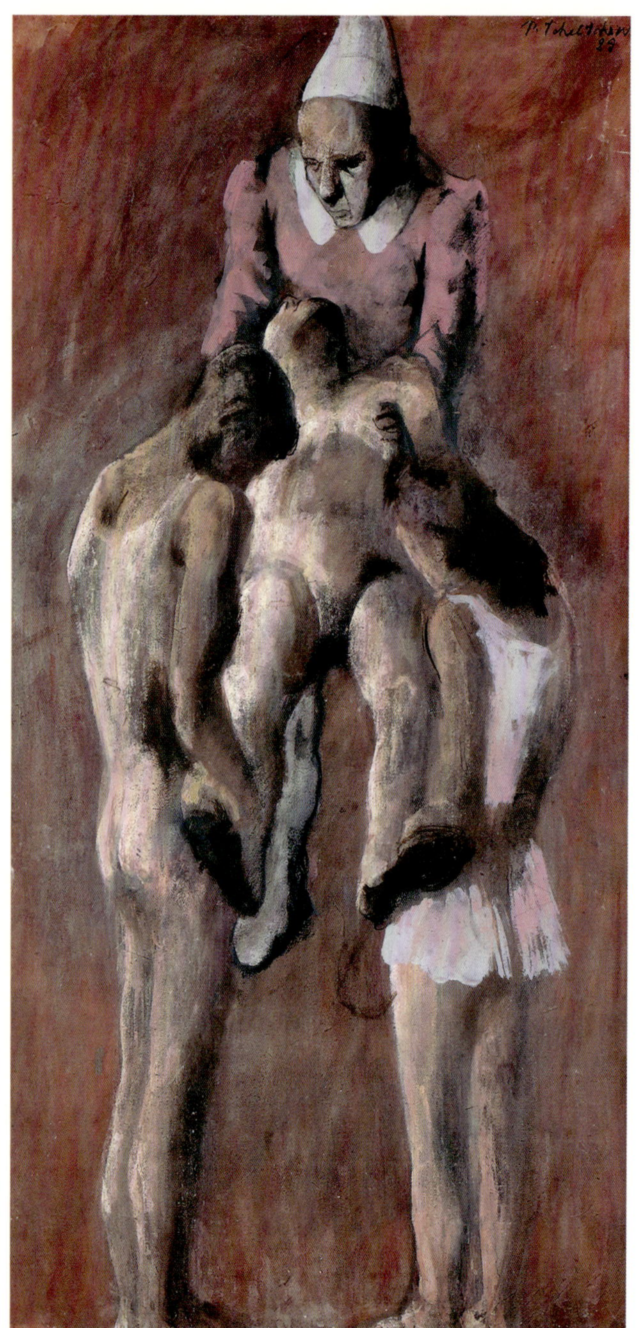

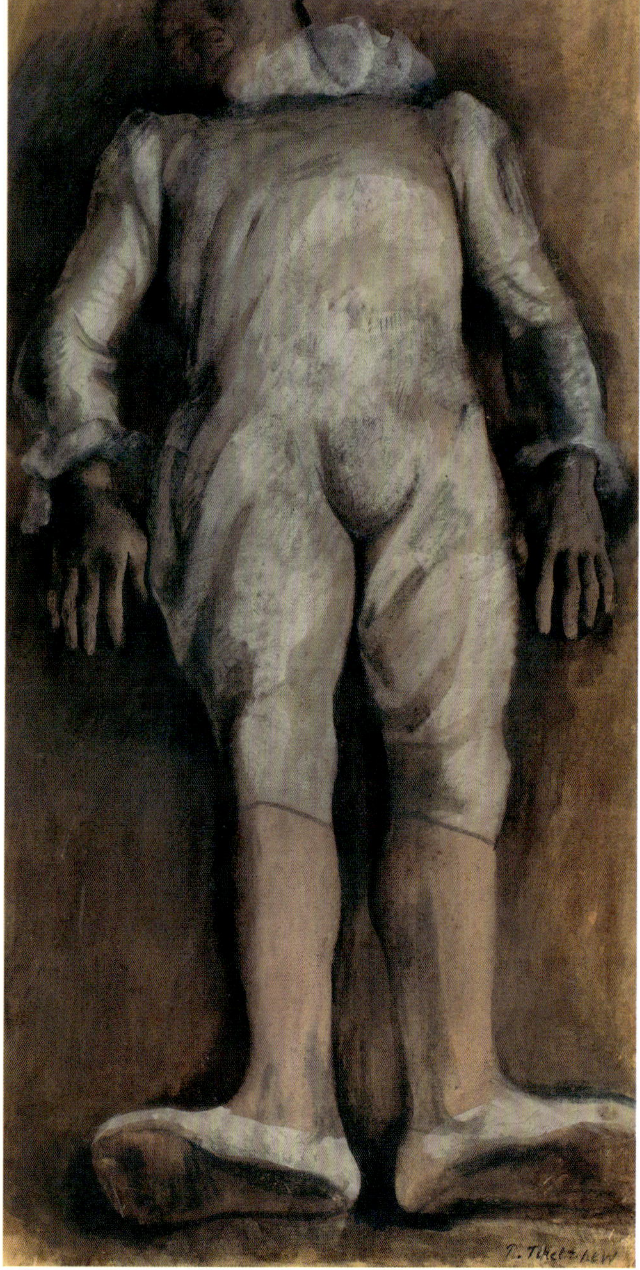

ABOVE: Pavel Tchelitchew, *Fallen Acrobat*, gouache on paper, 78.8 × 38.8 cm (30½ × 15¼ in.), 1929
RIGHT: Pavel Tchelitchew, *Untitled* (final study for *The One Who Fell*), gouache on illustration board, 79.7 × 40.6 cm (31⅜ × 16 in.), *c.* 1930
OPPOSITE, ABOVE: Pavel Tchelitchew, study for *The Fallen Rider*, gouache on canvas, 51.4 × 71.1 cm (20¼ × 28 in.), 1929
OPPOSITE, BELOW: Pavel Tchelitchew, *Fallen Rider*, oil on canvas, 54 × 73 cm (21¼ × 28¾ in.), 1930

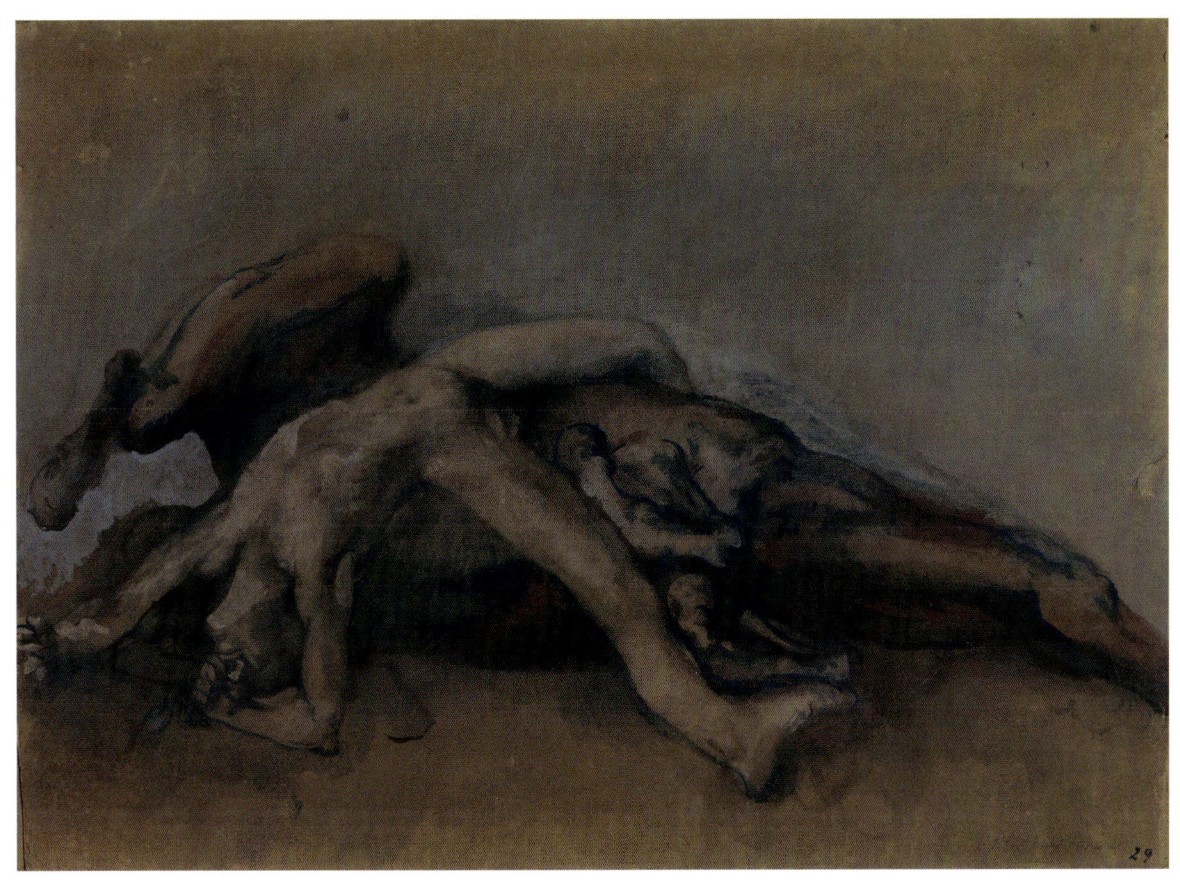
29

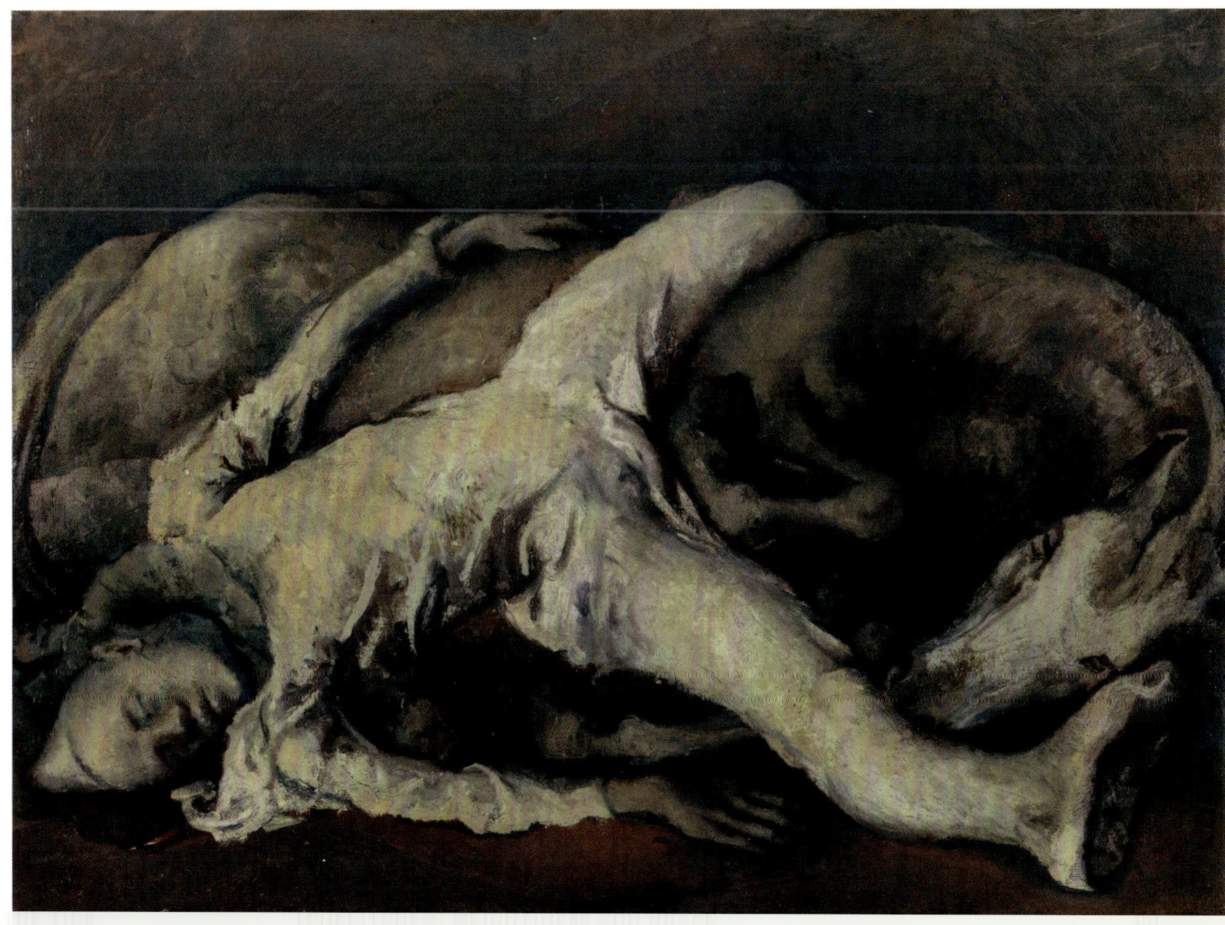

28 July 1928: 'London has been introduced to a really great new painter, Paul [*sic*] Tchelitchew. And when I say he is a really great painter, I mean what I say. He is not one of these new sensation-mongers that crop up every year, but a painter of the greatest powers, utterly individual, and his work has both majesty and beauty.'

Sitwell was a pioneer in the art of social networking, and she played a crucial role in the promotion and divulgation of the art of Tchelitchew (and of the Neo-Romantics in general), in England and beyond. Along with her equally versatile literary brothers Osbert and Sacheverell, she was one of the leading figures in a baroque revival which is currently being reassessed in a positive light – and which displays affinities with the Neo-Romantic sensibility. Tchelitchew was fascinated by this strange creature with 'a Plantagenet appearance' – elongated face, high forehead, prominent nose – and produced no fewer than six portraits of Sitvouka (as he nicknamed her) between 1927 and 1939.

These paintings serve to illustrate the evolution of his work over this period. He moved from the initial portrait from 1927 (now at the National Portrait Gallery in London) in shades of burnt earth, mixed with sand, set off by dashes of white, to an imposing full-length portrayal ten years later, where the palette is much paler, with her disproportionate hands reflecting the pallor of her face and the sculptural mass of her heavy tunic standing out against a bluish background and narrow-angle perspective. In his urge to accentuate the stylization that was an integral part of his subject, Tchelitchew even designed her clothes – much to her delight: 'I am awfully excited about my new clothes. Tchelitchew designed them all, and they look sometimes like a Della Francesca, sometimes like a Giotto!' Sitwell's arresting physiognomy, often described as Gothic, offered Tchelitchew resources for several different approaches, and his portraits of her (including an unusual effigy made with wax and wire) occupy a key position in his corpus.

OPPOSITE, LEFT: Pavel Tchelitchew, *Edith Sitwell*, gouache with sand, 62.5 × 47.9 cm (24⅝ × 18⅞ in.), 1927
OPPOSITE, RIGHT: Pavel Tchelitchew, *Edith Sitwell*, oil on canvas, 163 × 96.5 cm (64⅛ × 38 in.), 1937

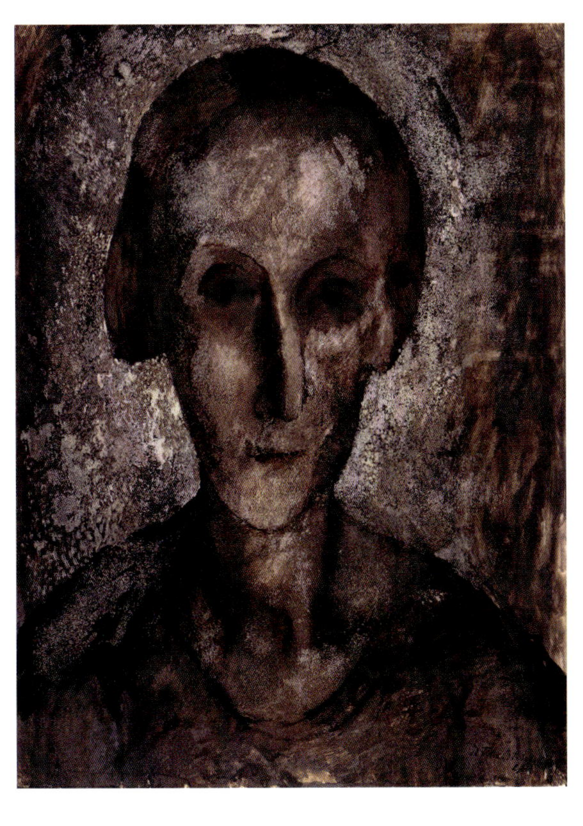

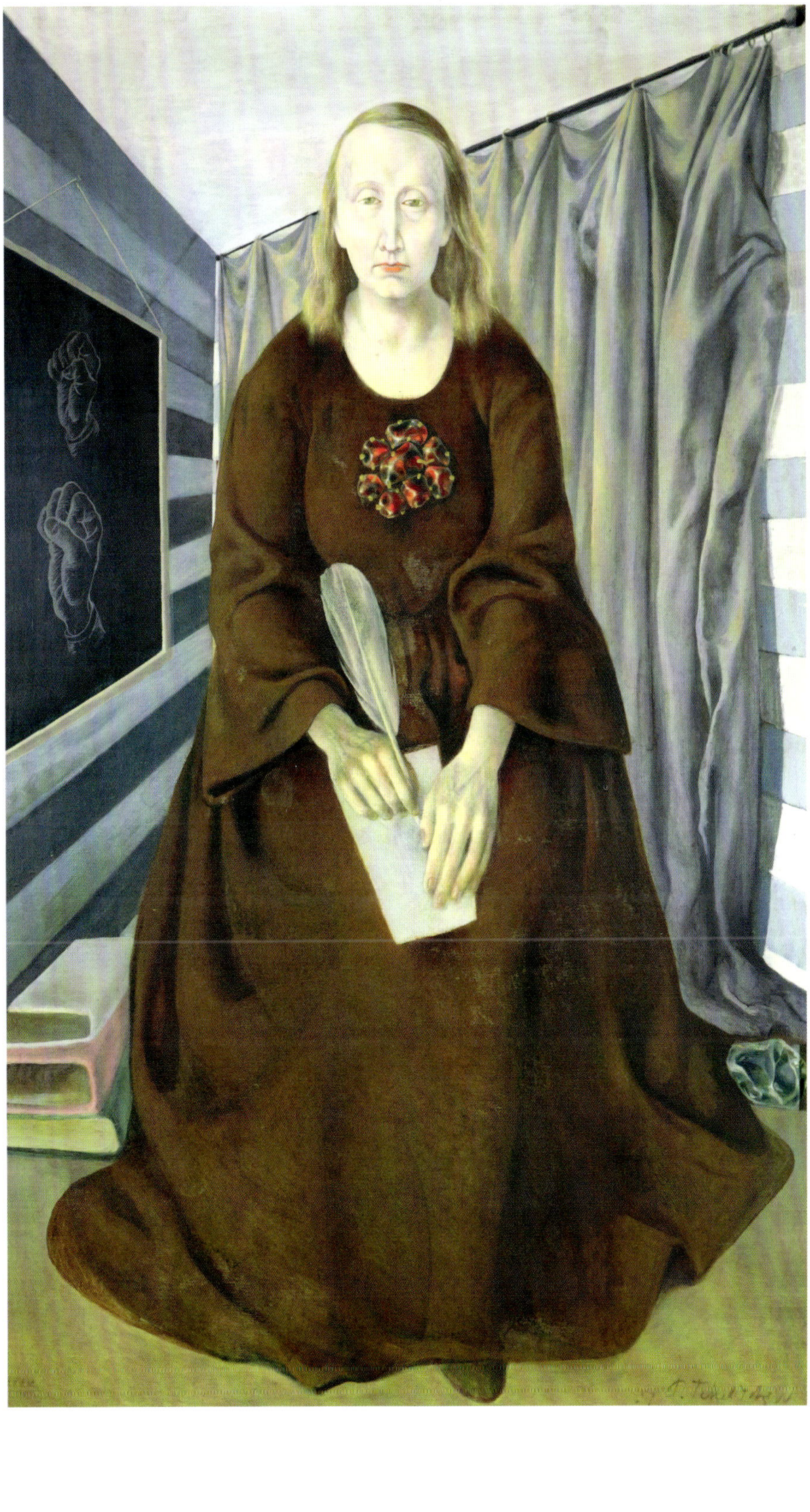

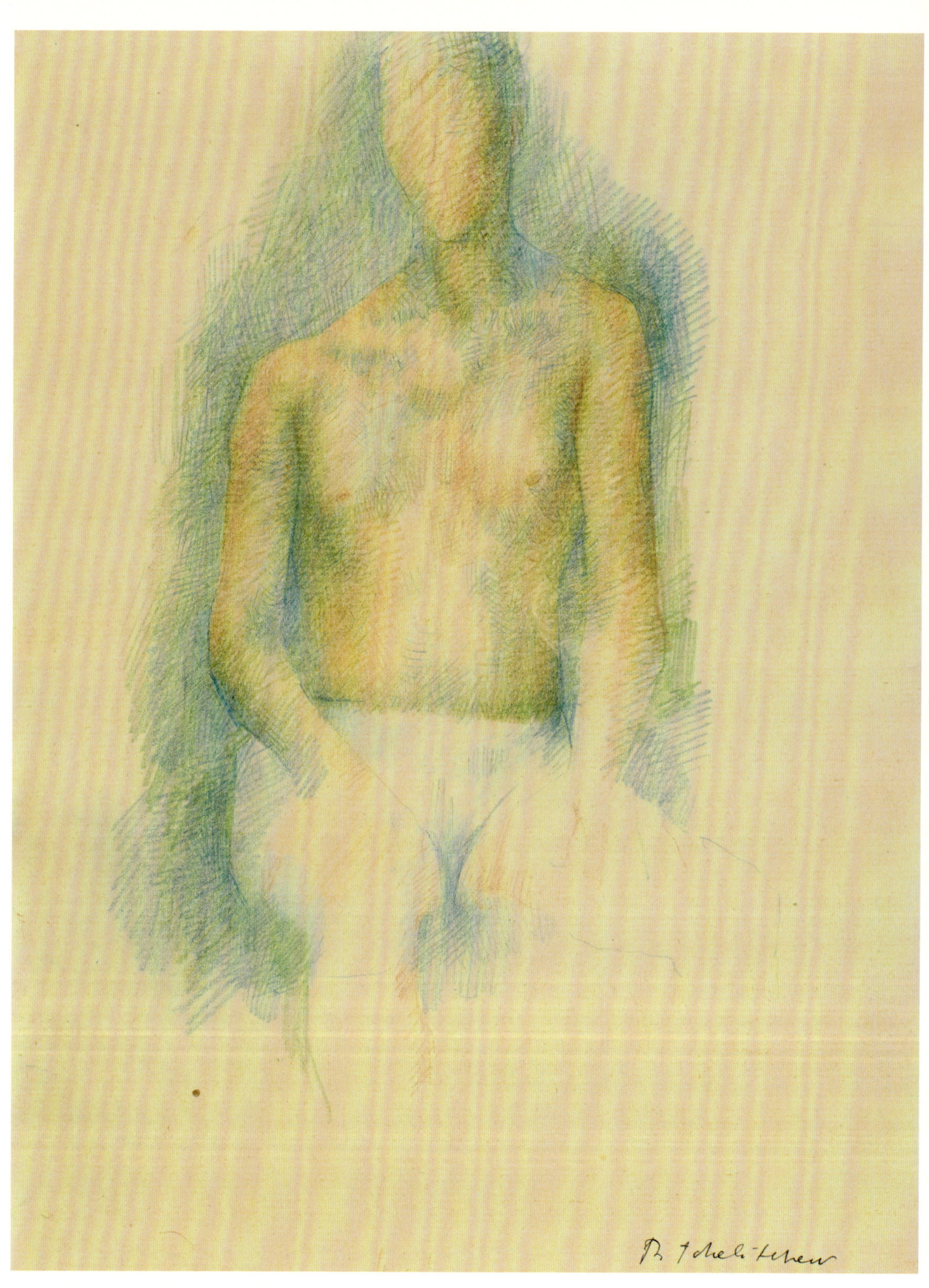

ABOVE: Pavel Tchelitchew, *Torso of a Man*, coloured crayons on paper, 26 × 22 cm ($10\frac{1}{8} \times 8\frac{5}{8}$ in.), n.d.
OPPOSITE: Pavel Tchelitchew, *The Clown* (aka *Green Clown*), oil on canvas, 189.2 × 87.6 cm ($74\frac{1}{2} \times 34\frac{1}{2}$ in.), 1929

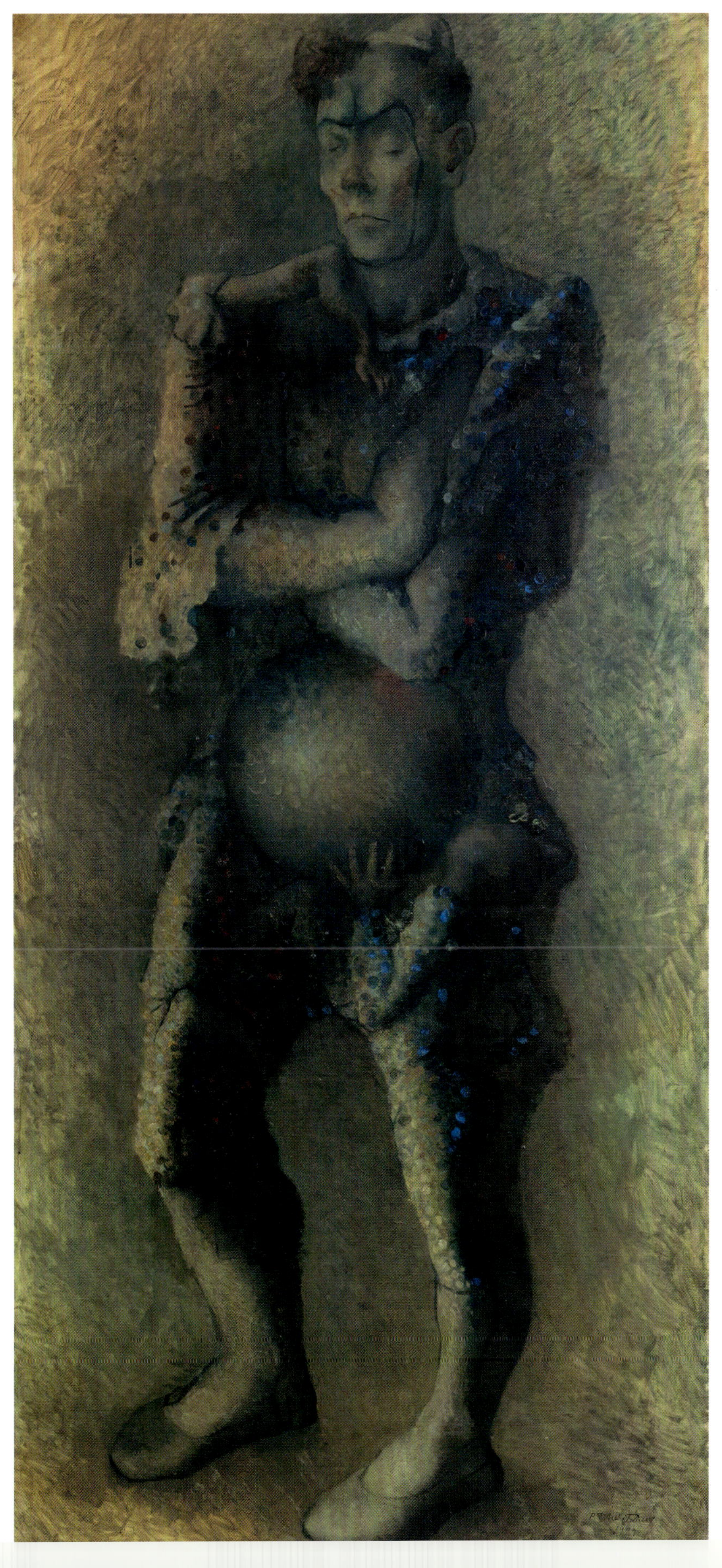

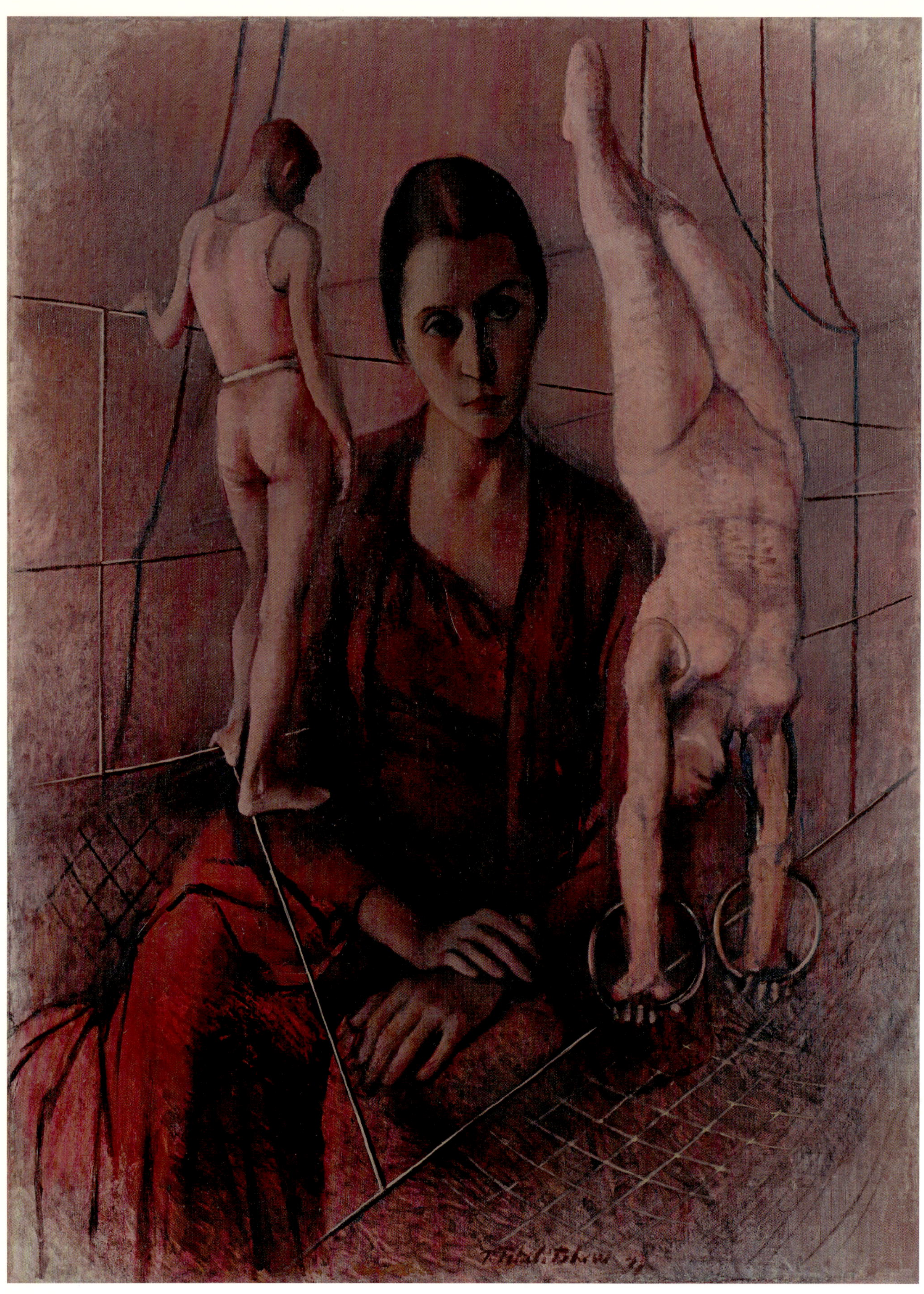

Pavel Tchelitchew, *Madame Bonjean*, oil on canvas,
100.3 × 64.8 cm (39½ × 25½ in.), 1930

Transparent Bodies

In the same period in which he was painting the portraits of Edith Sitwell and other friends and patrons, such as Elizabeth Kent (*Madame Sherman Kent*), Tchelitchew was continuing his investigation into the composition and decomposition of the body, now using a brighter palette featuring ochres, greys, sage greens and deep reds. Furthering the dynamics of his 'laconic' images, he started producing compositions that he now described as 'metamorphic', involving the overlapping of several images in a single picture, thereby giving rise to a double reading (just as Salvador Dalí would later do with his paranoiac-critical method). Tchelitchew's second solo show in Paris, at the Pierre Gallery in June 1929, featured these composite representations, many exploring the subject of clowns and acrobats. According to Soby, these new paintings had a lukewarm reception, particularly from Cocteau, and in the fallout Tchelitchew parted company with the gallery. He therefore moved closer to his British and American admirers, and these affiliations hastened his eventual departure to the United States five years later.

The metamorphic images marked a new stage in the process of destructuring the body. Tchelitchew's figures in this period were subjected to creepy deformations, often involving outsized hands that seemed about to detach themselves from the rest of the body, as if drawn by invisible forces. This dislocation was finally achieved in 1930, in a series of unsettling paintings (*Still-life Clown*, *The Lawyer*, *Spanish Dancer*) representing simulacra of bodies, with their limbs literally detached, in compositions that hover between still lifes (another of his favourite genres) and hallucinatory visions.

The world of the circus and its depictions – by Picasso, but also by Toulouse-Lautrec and Georges Rouault – continued to fuel Tchelitchew's imagination after the unsuccessful exhibition of 1929. In fact, it formed the nucleus of a subsequent show at the Vignon Gallery in Paris in June 1931, and Tchelitchew went on exploring this topic even as he transformed his colour schemes. 'The circus', wrote Soby, 'continued to supply Tchelitchew's subject matter in a majority of the pictures painted during the latter part of 1932. [...] The clowns of 1932 are usually rendered in high contrasts – green against yellow, blue against rose, with a liberal use of white. They wear bright

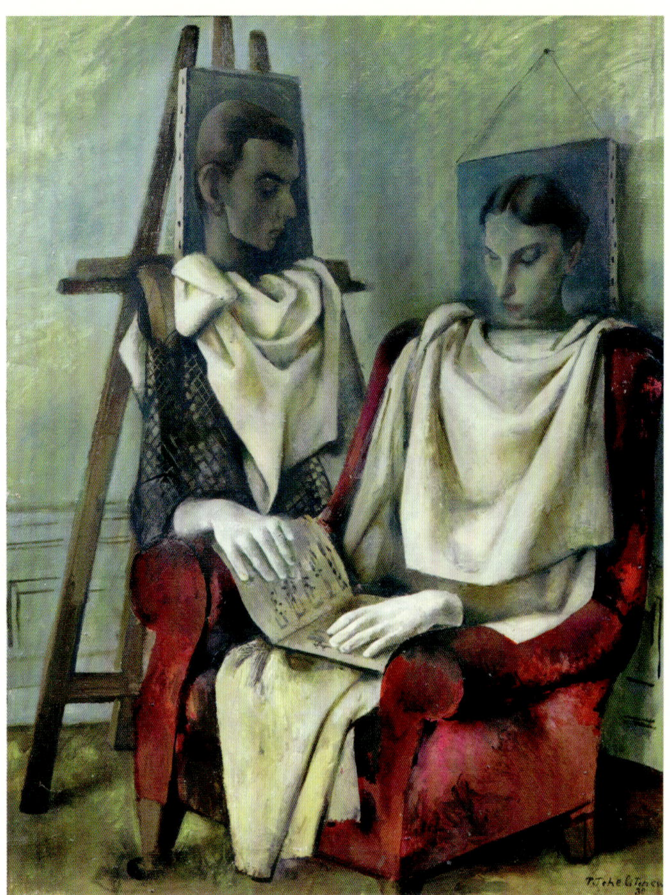

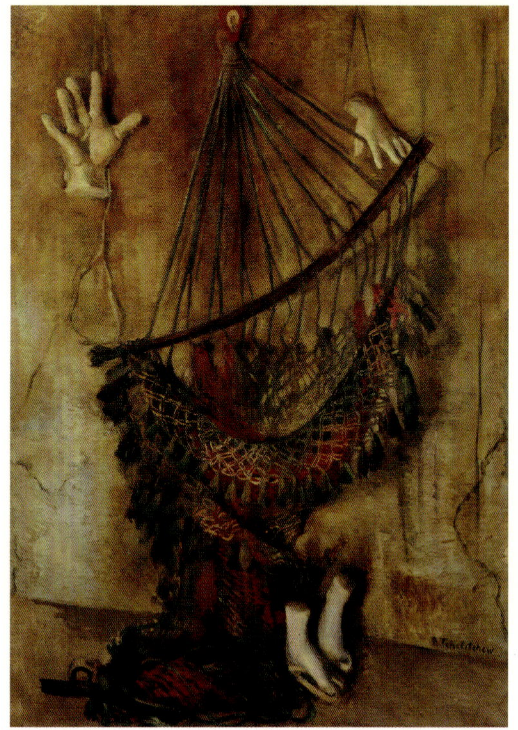

ruffles and spangled costumes, the latter painted in splashed dots of color which two years later led to the use of sequins affixed to the canvas.' By now, Tchelitchew had abandoned the sombre, monochrome palette of his early years. In fact, he went to the other extreme, using effects of transparency and diffuse light, while also incorporating bold dissonances that would find their full expression in the following decade in large-scale works such as *Cache-cache* and *Phenomena.*

In 1933, Tchelitchew found his (already large) circle of admirers on the other side of the Channel enriched by a new member who would go on to play a crucial role in his career. Edward James (1907–1984) belonged, like Edith Sitwell and her contemporary, Lord Berners, to the great tradition of British eccentricity. As the only son of an American industrialist who had settled in England, James inherited a vast fortune derived from copper mines and railroads in the United States. He was educated at Eton and Oxford, and, as he was acquainted with the upper reaches of the British aristocracy, he seemed predestined to become a fixture in high society. At a very early age, however, he decided to spurn that cosseted existence and live solely according to his aesthetic impulses (which would eventually lead him to spend the last part of his life building a utopian village in the

ABOVE, LEFT: Pavel Tchelitchew, *The Composer, Igor Markevich, and his Mother*, oil on canvas, 91.4 × 73 cm (36 × 28¾ in.), 1930
ABOVE, RIGHT: Pavel Tchelitchew, *Spanish Dancer*, oil on canvas, 100 × 73 cm (39½ × 28¾ in.), 1930

OPPOSITE, LEFT: Pavel Tchelitchew, *Penelope*, oil on canvas, 100.3 × 64.8 cm (39½ × 25½ in.), 1931
OPPOSITE, RIGHT: Pavel Tchelitchew, *Spahi*, oil on canvas, 100.3 × 81.3 cm (39½ × 32 in.), 1931

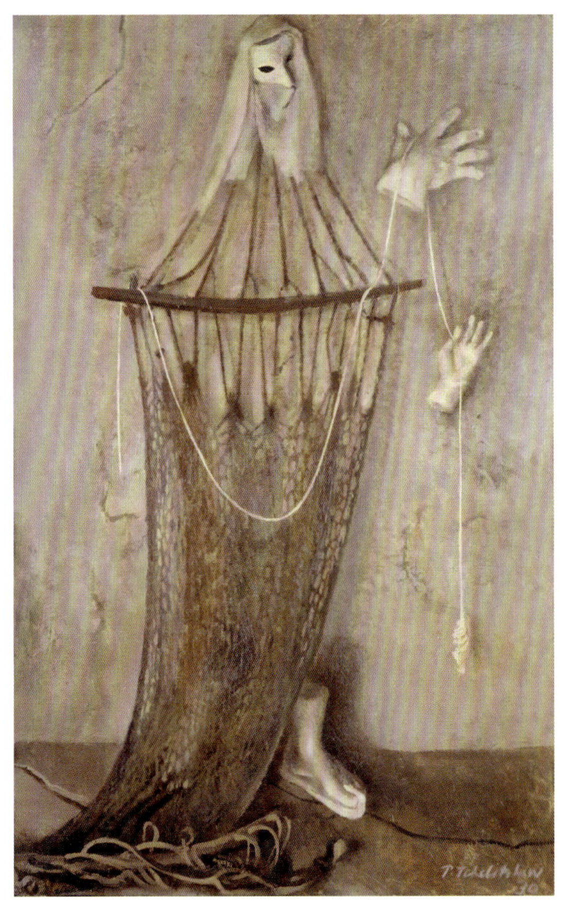

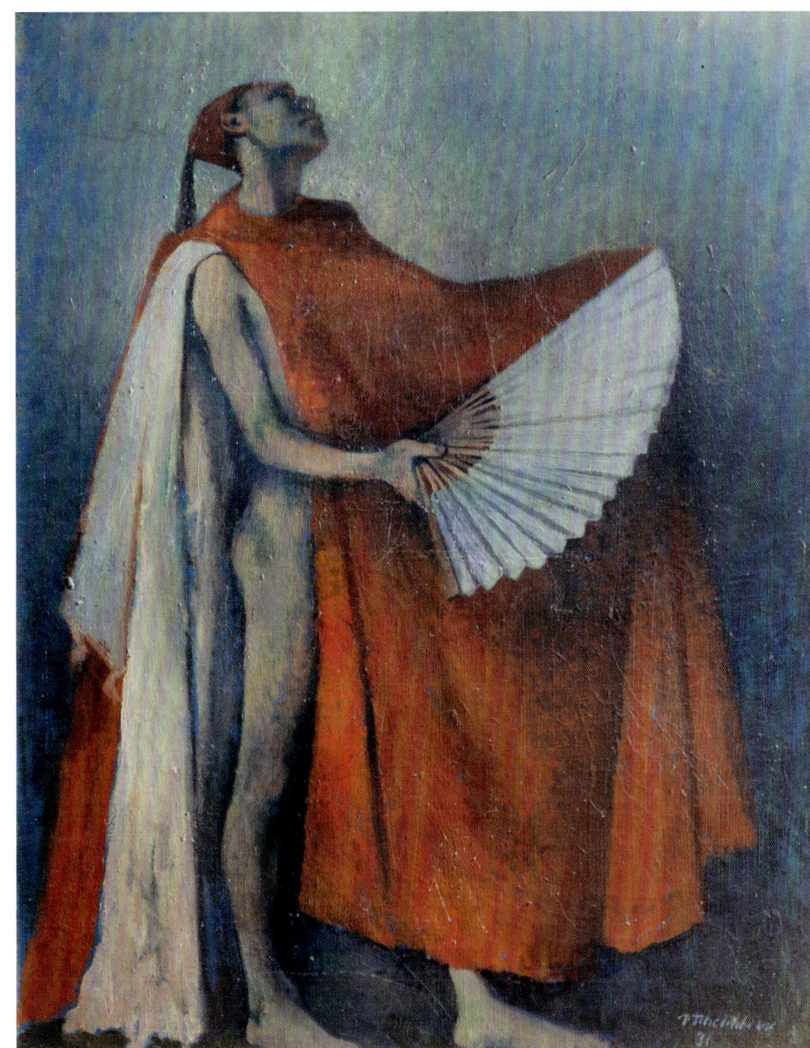

Mexican jungle). James was a friend and patron of Surrealists such as Dalí, Max Ernst, Magritte and Leonor Fini, and he took on the same roles with Tchelitchew, to the point of buying several paintings while they were still in progress. His collection would eventually include some of Tchelitchew's most important works (such as *The Concert*, 1933, *Excelsior*, 1934, and *Edith Sitwell*, 1937), as well as numerous drawings.

James had married a dancer, Tilly Losch, in 1931, and he also set about advancing her career. Accordingly, in order to give her starring roles, James provided financial backing for the company that George Balanchine and Boris Kochno were trying to create after the death of Diaghilev and the dissolution of the Ballets Russes. The resulting troupe, Ballets 1933, did not outlive that eponymous year, playing only to select audiences in a few theatres (such as the Champs-Élysées in Paris and the Savoy in London). Nevertheless, it gave rise to some memorable creations, including *L'Errante*, a ballet that marked Tchelitchew's return to the stage. Responsible for both

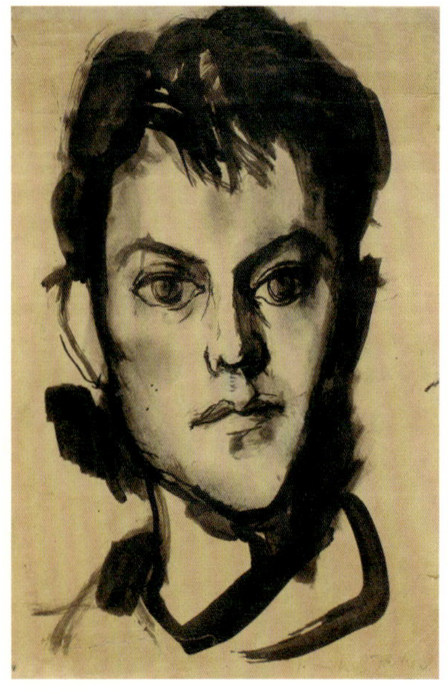

the libretto and the scenery, Tchelitchew continued on the path laid out by *Ode*: he left the space bare, demarcating it with a simple muslin curtain and transfiguring it with light. According to Donald Windham, 'Tchelitchew carried translucency further than in the previous ballet, creating on the stage by means of transparent fabrics and light a visual image as compact as the reflection in a drop of water.'

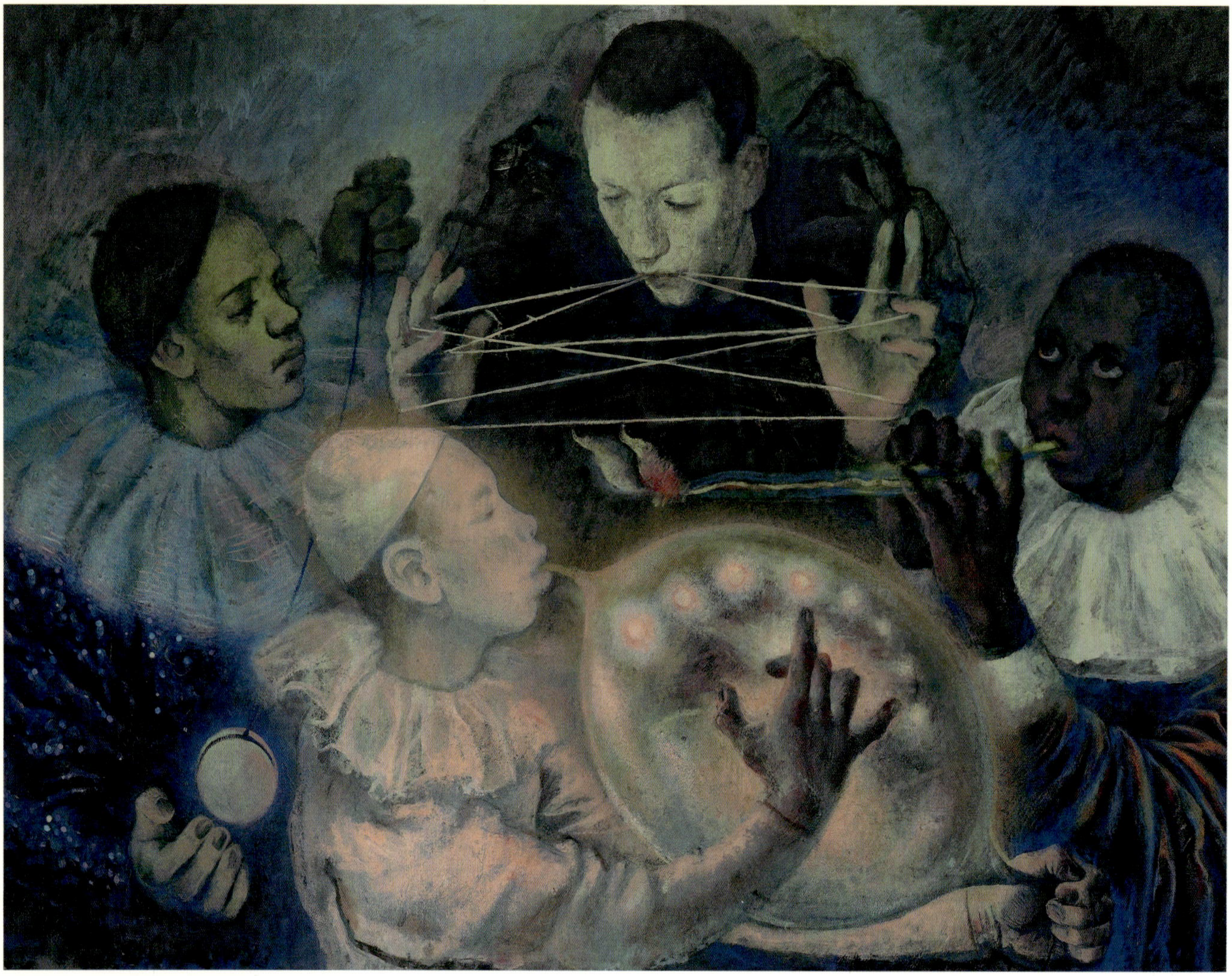

These effects of transparency and irradiating light signalled a new stylistic turn that is evident in paintings from this period: the portraits of the poet Charles Henri Ford (1934), whom Tchelitchew had just met and who would become his life-long partner, and Helena Rubinstein (1934), their surfaces studded with sequins, and the large-scale *Excelsior* (1934), which depicted different versions of Ford and continued Tchelitchew's experiments with the distortion of space. Here, as noted by Tchelitchew's

TOP: Pavel Tchelitchew, *The Concert*, oil on canvas, 89.5 × 116.3 cm (35⅛ × 45⅞ in.), 1933
ABOVE: Pavel Tchelitchew, *Portrait of Charles Henri Ford*, ink on paper, 29 × 20 cm (11⅜ × 7⅞ in.), *c.* 1945

OPPOSITE, ABOVE: Pavel Tchelitchew, study of 'Angels in White' for *L'Errante*, gouache and ink on paper, 43.2 × 22.2 cm (17 × 8¾ in.), 1935
OPPOSITE, BELOW: Pavel Tchelitchew, *Two Male Dancers*, study for *L'Errante*, gouache and ink on paper, 50.2 × 31.8 cm (179¾ × 12½ in.), 1935

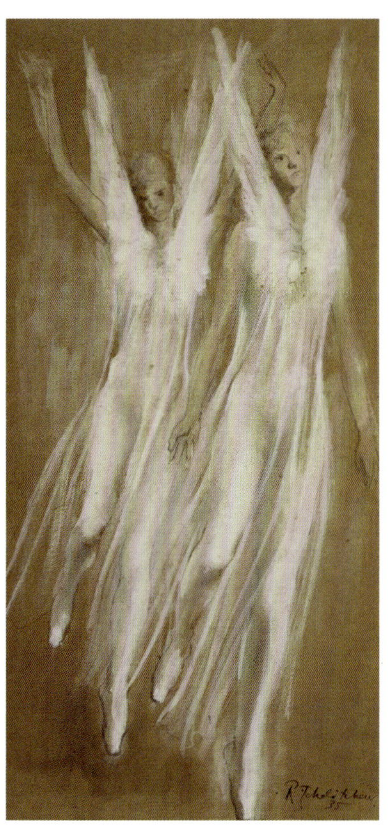

biographer Parker Tyler (who also appears in the picture), there were 'three distinct vanishing points in one pictorial space as each of the three heads is viewed head-on, from above and from below, self-designated as Body, Soul and Spirit'.

Excelsior was finished in the summer of 1934, after a stay at West Dean, Edward James's estate in Sussex, where its owner had retreated after a rapid and tumultuous divorce from Losch. Those few weeks spent in the English countryside stirred memories of Tchelitchew's carefree summers on his family's own estate in Russia. The tranquillity that he seemed to have found there, coupled with his relationship with his new lover, was reflected in the phosphorescent clarity of his new palette and his use of luminous glazes. Nowhere were these effects more evident than in the truly hypnotic portrait of Ford. Tchelitchew also found inspiration in the estate's tennis courts, which appeared in several drawings and paintings with unusual geometric and spatial configurations, complete with nets and rackets. The local trees, and those in the estate's own arboretum, also provided Tchelitchew with a new outlet for his obsession with transformation and metamorphosis, as evident in a series of variations on the theme of anthropomorphic plants. This subject would recur in his later work, taking on new elements after he settled in the United States (particularly after his sojourns in Vermont in 1940).

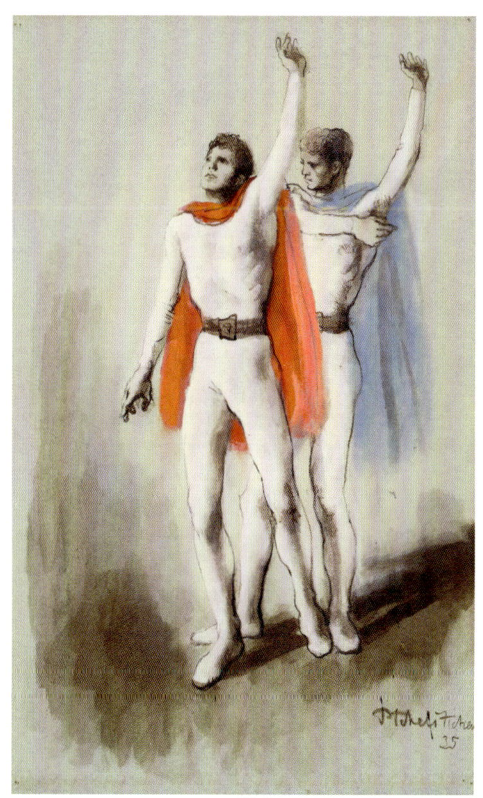

Meanwhile, Tchelitchew continued playing with the distortion of bodies and the exaggeration and deformation of space. A spell in Spain in the summer of 1934 made an 'enormous impression' on him, offering new colour schemes and opportunities to further his manipulations of perspective: 'The dry mother-of-pearl landscape of northern Spain, the characteristic proud faces of men and women, dressed in dark clothes, the bullfights, the towns, the Arabian vestiges, all combined to induce me to take a wholly new direction.' The *corrida*, in particular, provided a subject for several jerky paintings with intense colours in which he pushed still further the use of multiple,

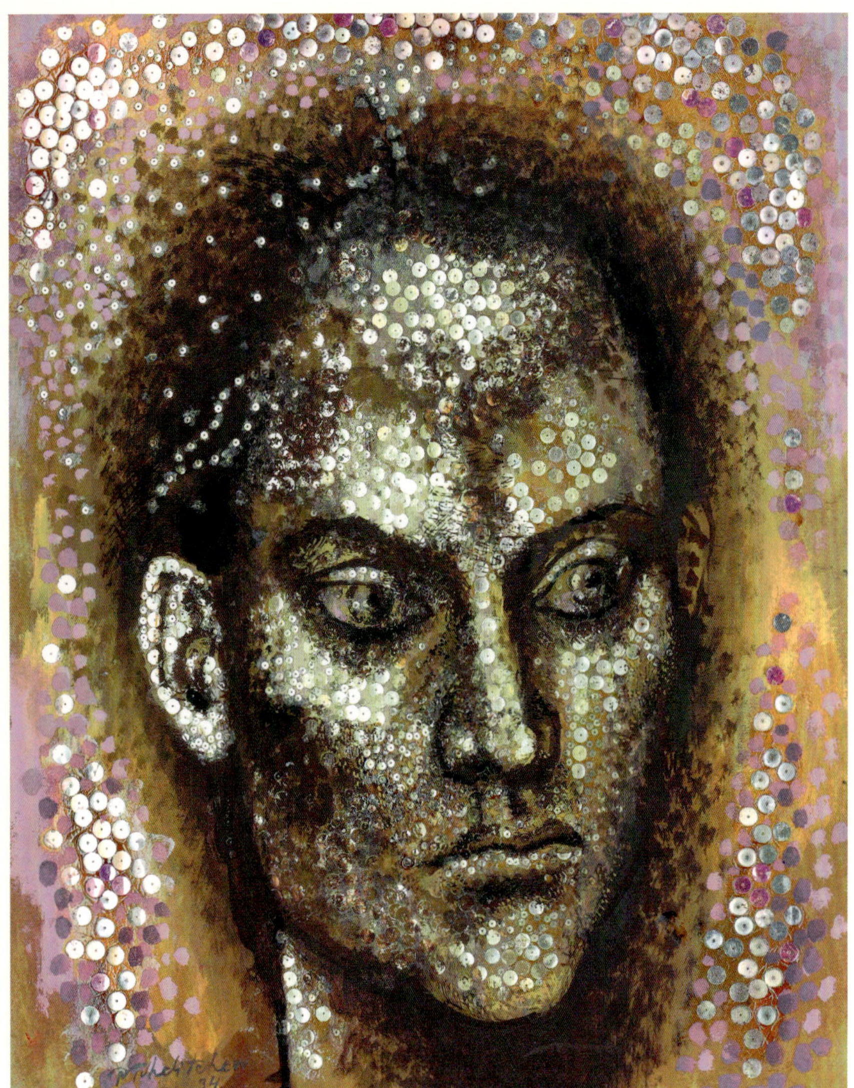

contradictory vanishing points within a single composition, as previously seen in *Excelsior*. Soby explained that '[t]here he first conceived the idea of presenting subject matter as seen simultaneously from three different angles of perspective – from below, straight-on and from above. The principle of simultaneity was not to be applied to a single object, as it had been in his multiple figures of 1926–27. Instead each object was to be rendered as a single image seen from a fixed viewpoint. But the viewpoint was to change from one object to the next, and within the same composition any object was to be represented as seen from any one of the three perspectives which suited his purpose.' The results were more radical than ever: space had become literally incoherent, or, to borrow a term from Leibniz, 'incompossible'. A flurry of abrupt ellipses, of perspectives all duly contracted or exaggerated, induces a vertiginous effect that Tchelitchew would take even further in the latter part of his career.

He embarked for the United States in October 1934, accompanied by Charles Henri Ford, and he was given his first solo exhibition in New York by Julien Levy in December of that year. Tchelitchew's move across the Atlantic would mark a 'before and after' in both his life and career: his Neo-Romantic period had ended and his 'American' period had begun. The latter would reach its apogee with *Phenomena* (1936–38) and *Cache-cache* (1940–42), a painting that, even when barely finished, was considered worthy of occupying the central position in a monographic exhibition organized by James Thrall Soby at New York's Museum of Modern Art (MoMA) in 1942.

ABOVE: Pavel Tchelitchew, *Portrait of Charles Henri Ford*, gouache, ink and sequins on board, 55.2 × 43.6 cm (21¾ × 17⅛ in.), 1934

OPPOSITE: Pavel Tchelitchew, programme cover for *Ode*, Serge Diaghilev's Ballets Russes, 13 June 1928

The hub of the art world was no longer London or Paris. It had shifted to the United States, and it was there that the second act of Neo-Romanticism would unfold. Eugene Berman first arrived in the country in 1935, followed by Kristians Tonny in 1937, and Leonid in 1946. The Neo-Romantics' patrons and admirers found themselves in a post-war era in which the artists whom they had so fervently promoted were relegated to the sidelines, while the intellectual and artistic circles of New York that had once given a second wind to the group's allusive, quirky and dramatic vision would now sweep it aside.

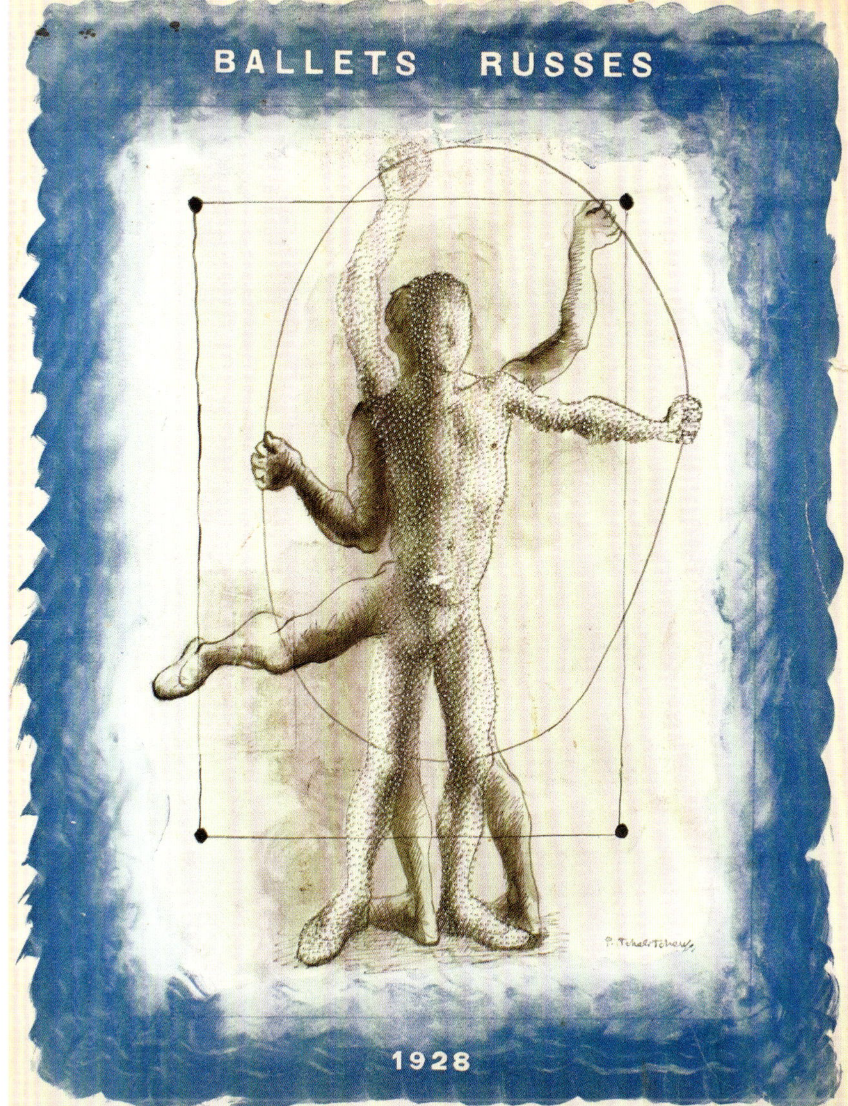

Nevertheless, Tchelitchew could count on some loyal and constant supporters, whose roles we will go on to examine in greater detail: Alfred Barr (1902–1981), the first director of MOMA; James Thrall Soby (1906–1979), whom we have already met as the Neo-Romantics' chronicler; Arthur Everett 'Chick' Austin (1900–1957), the director of the Wadsworth Atheneum in Hartford, Connecticut; Henry-Russell Hitchcock (1903–1987), the architectural historian; the art dealer Julien Levy (1906–1981); and the collector and ballet enthusiast Lincoln Kirstein (1907–1996). These admirers had followed the careers of Tchelitchew and his associates since 1926, and they remained unstintingly faithful to these artists (who, in many cases, were also their personal friends).

This constancy was particularly evident in Lincoln Kirstein, who had first met Tchelitchew when he was working on *L'Errante* in 1933 (when Kirstein had also taken the opportunity to persuade Balanchine to move to the United States, where they would eventually create the

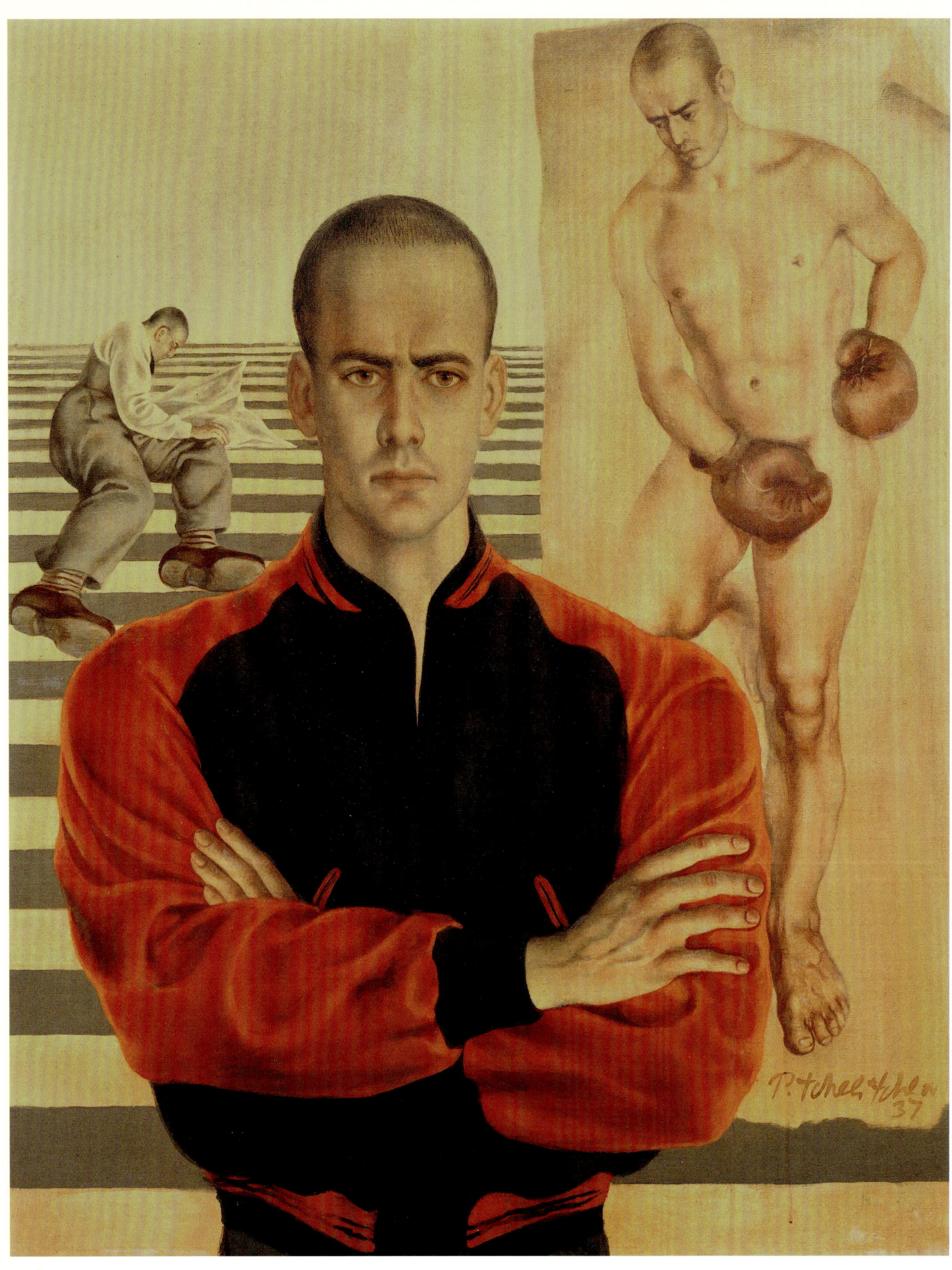

Pavel Tchelitchew, *Portrait of Lincoln Kirstein*,
oil on canvas, 1937

New York City Ballet together). On Tchelitchew's arrival in New York, Kirstein immediately commissioned a portrait (finished in 1937, and one of Tchelitchew's best). Much later, the unfailingly loyal Kirstein organized a major posthumous retrospective of Tchelitchew's work in 1964 (very much against the tide of then-current critical opinion), and in 1994 he published what would turn out to be his last book on the subject of his old friend.

A year after settling in the United States, Tchelitchew returned to Europe for a few months. Once there, he visited Italy for the first time, over ten years after Bérard and the Berman brothers' various trips to the country. This delay may seem astonishing, but it also reflects – as Soby, Tyler, Ford and others have observed – Tchelitchew's divergence from the other Neo-Romantic painters, especially Bérard and Eugene Berman. As Soby noted, somewhat peremptorily: 'Tchelitchew's romanticism by comparison with theirs is Northern both stylistically and in metaphysical approach.' His work displays no trace of the sensuality of the Cinquecento masters, the architectural extravagance of the Baroque or the pyrotechnics of a Tiepolo (at most, an argument could be made for the influence of Uccello's use of foreshortening and manipulation of perspective). None of the sources that so enriched Bérard in his early days, and that would sustain Eugene Berman right to the end, left any mark on Tchelitchew. His work, in contrast, was permeated with extreme tension, revolving around a core of dramatic and chromatic violence that seemed to come into its own in the United States.

'[I]n terms of fairly direct analogy,' Soby concluded, 'the name of Grünewald comes to mind rather than that of Raphael; that of Altdorfer or Bruegel rather than that of Piero della Francesca or Titian.' And Tchelitchew's output from the late 1930s onwards endorses these analogies. In his large portrait of Edith Sitwell from 1937, sometimes called *The Sibyl*, Tchelitchew exploited her striking appearance – high, exposed forehead, elongated nose, piercing gaze heightened by a lack of eyebrows, pale complexion, translucent skin – to accentuate a 'Nordic' quality in keeping with the formal severity of Flemish and Dutch primitive painters. In *Phenomena*, the space teeming with people, the flattened perspective and the hybrid creatures seem to have sprung from a vision of hell imagined by Bosch (also an important reference, in a completely different way, for another member of the group, Kristians Tonny). The jarring acid colours, shot through with bloody reds and pus-like yellows, with

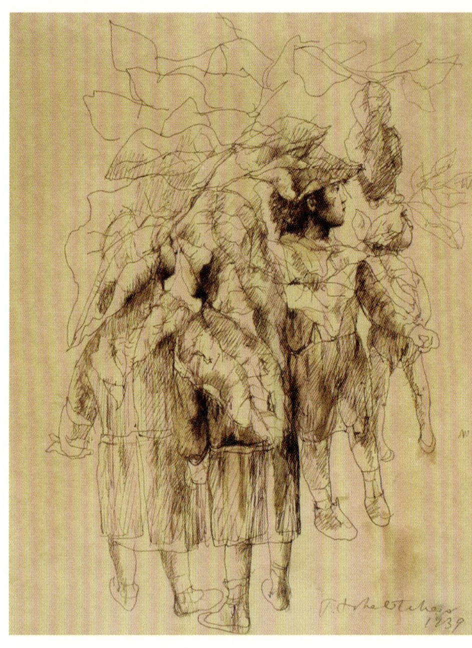

greens and purples that Huysmans would have described as 'chlorotic', anticipate the dazzling, morbid *Cache-cache*, imbued with echoes of the colours used by Grünewald.

Cache-cache can be interpreted in a number of ways. Its central anthropomorphic tree with hands and feet is surrounded by a mosaic of interlocking pieces (nine in all, according to Soby), displaying transparent images of children and foetal creatures. It recalls the plant hybrids Tchelitchew produced during his stay at West Dean, and he developed this theme further in a series of 'leaf-children' inspired by his stays in Vermont, in which tracings of serrated, curled leaves shelter, clothe or seemingly generate the bodies of children. Tchelitchew similarly explored anthropomorphism in landscapes (echoing paintings from the Renaissance and the Baroque), in which hills, mountains and other topological features double up as giant bodies and faces.

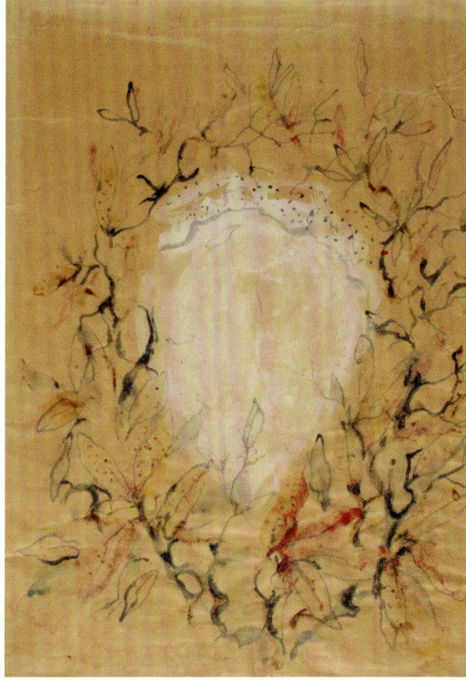

Some parts of *Cache-cache* also anticipate the 'interior landscapes' that would characterize Tchelitchew's final period: haunting cranial X-rays, heads literally in pieces, reduced to a network of blood vessels, nerves and synapses, as if traversed by an electrical current. In the mid-1940s, Tchelitchew would delve into this unsettling imagery obsessively, looking for inspiration in anatomical drawing from the sixteenth century and the work of Gautier d'Agoty – particularly his *Anatomy of the Head*, published in 1748, where some plates uncannily presage Tchelitchew's paintings from this period. Such influences were on display (even more literally than the 'interior landscapes') in the costumes that he drew up in 1941 for *The Cave of Sleep*, a ballet that was never in fact staged: here, the nervous, circulatory and muscular systems were painted onto the dancers' bodies, as if they had been skinned, directly evoking the work of Vesalius and his students.

TOP: Pavel Tchelitchew, *Leaf-Children*, ink and wash on paper, 27 × 20 cm (10⅝ × 7⅞ in.), n.d.
ABOVE: Pavel Tchelitchew, *Wreath of Foliage*, ink and gouache on wrapping paper, 35 × 24 cm (13⅞ × 9⅜ in.), n.d.
OPPOSITE, CLOCKWISE FROM TOP: Pavel Tchelitchew, *Cache-cache* (Hide-and-Seek), oil on canvas, 199.3 × 215.3 cm (78½ × 84¾ in.), 1940–42; Pavel Tchelitchew, *Head of Spring*, oil on canvas, 52.1 × 62.2 cm (20½ × 24½ in.), 1940; Pavel Tchelitchew, *Figure with Hand and Bull*, cover for exhibition catalogue (provenance Allen Porter), 23.5 × 29 cm (9¼ × 11⅜ in.), n.d.

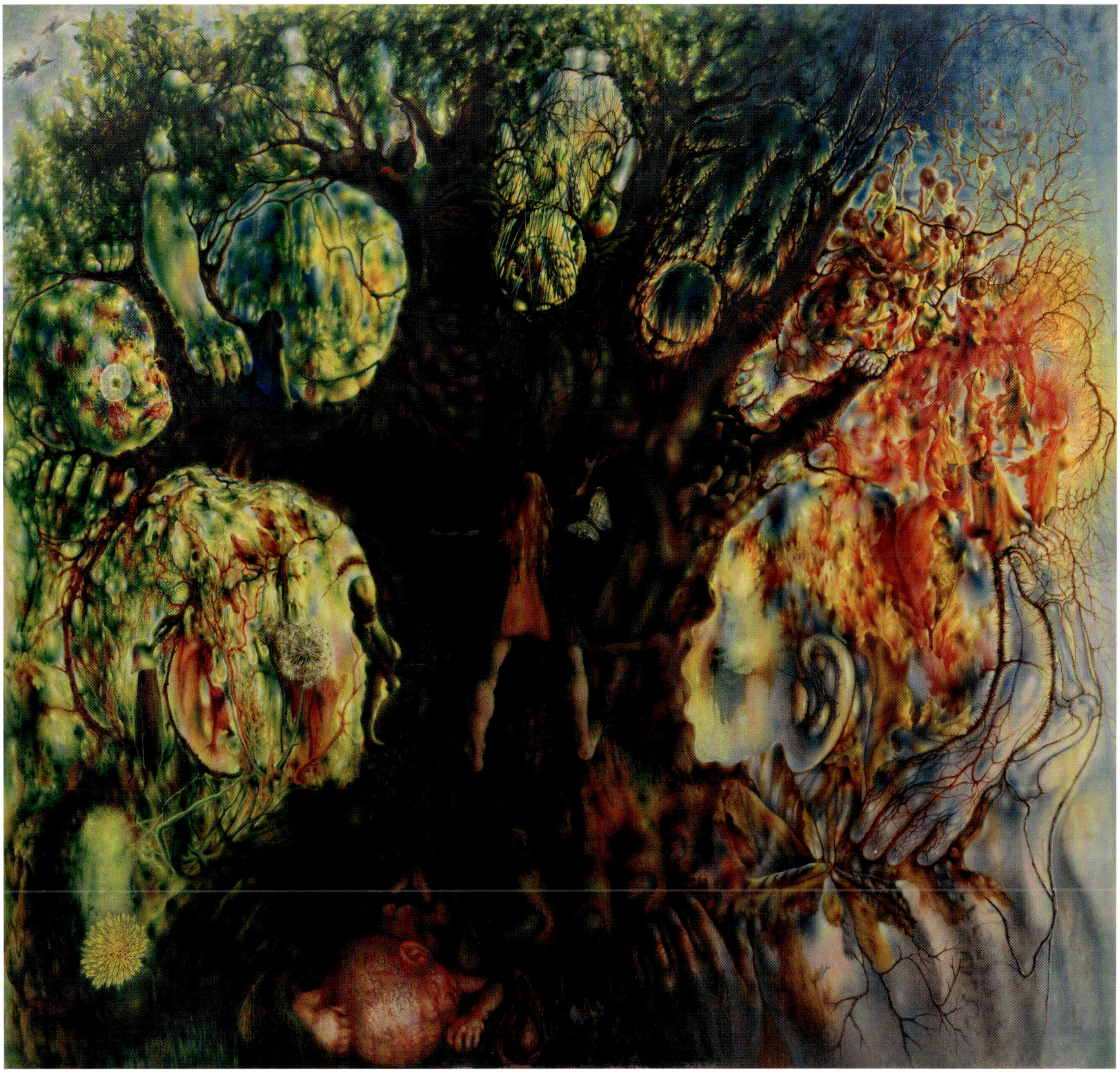

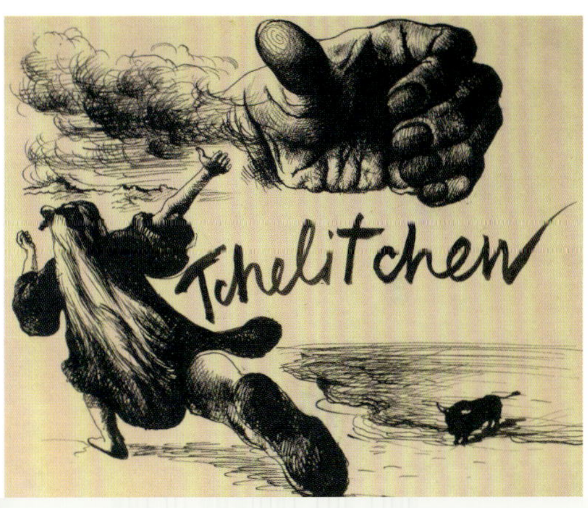
Tchelitchew

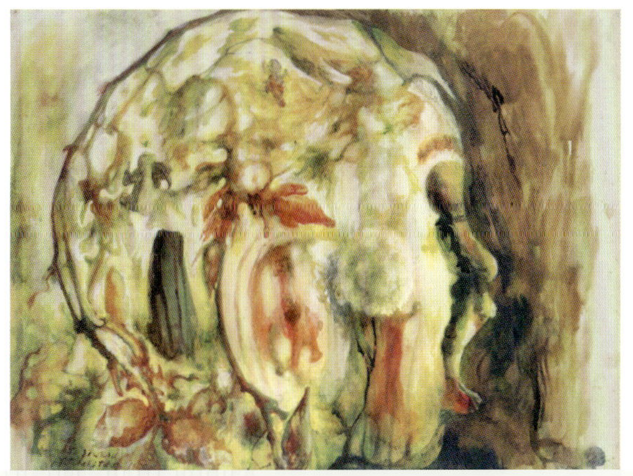

These transparent faces and bodies, in which inside and outside are as one, and these impalpable branching circulatory and nervous systems that make up the intimate parts of the human machine, provided Tchelitchew with new ways of representing, with an almost mystical intensity, the invisible dynamics, incessant flux, chemical transformations and processes of infinite metamorphosis that form the very wellspring of life. The 'interior landscapes' – translucent, electrified, bathed in pale coloured glazes – stand as the diametrical opposite of his initial works from 1926, with their thick paste, shadowy bodies and indistinct faces. Tchelitchew's work would end up being totally disembodied, for in his final years (spent, despite his Nordic propensities, in Italy, where he died in 1957) his figures would be reduced to strange geometric diagrams, to records of the traces or trajectories of atoms, to indefinable phosphorescence or to unseeing heads consisting of spirals of light, set in configurations that recall the abstract hoops of Constructivism. By returning to the human figure of his early days and the search for vibrant, densely carnal emotion, Tchelitchew ended up embarking on a metaphysical meditation on the mysteries of life.

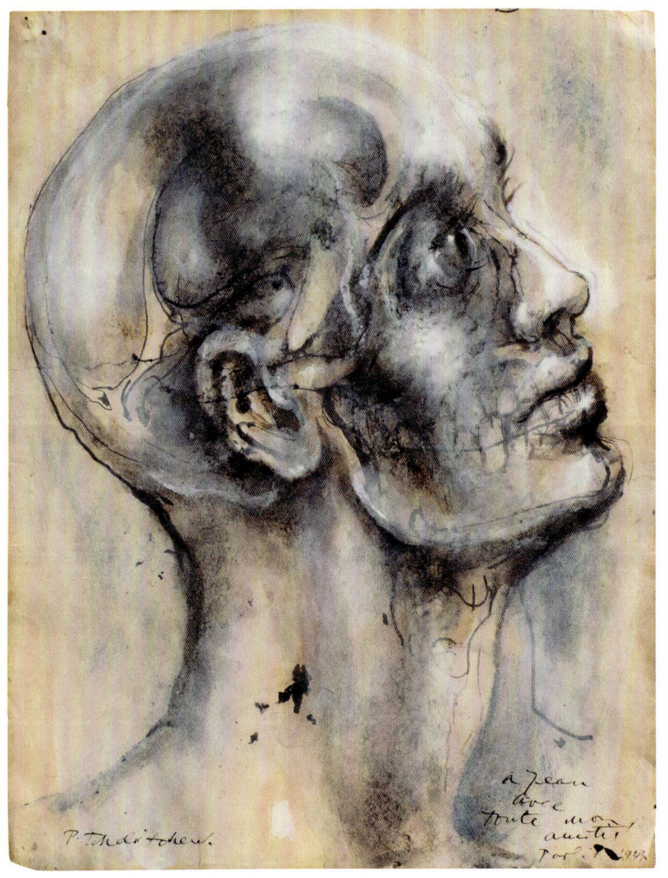

ABOVE: Pavel Tchelitchew, *Interior Landscape*, gouache and ink on paper, 27.3 × 21.6 cm (10¾ × 8½ in.), 1949
OPPPOSITE, CLOCKWISE FROM TOP LEFT: Pavel Tchelitchew, *Interior Landscape*, ink and watercolour on paper, 34.9 × 27.3 cm (13¾ × 10¾ in.), 1946; Pavel Tchelitchew, *Interior Landscape*, oil on canvas, 80.6 × 65.4 cm (31¾ × 25¾ in.), *c.* 1947; Jacques Fabien Gautier d'Agoty, 'Anatomy of the Head', plate from *Myologie*, 1746

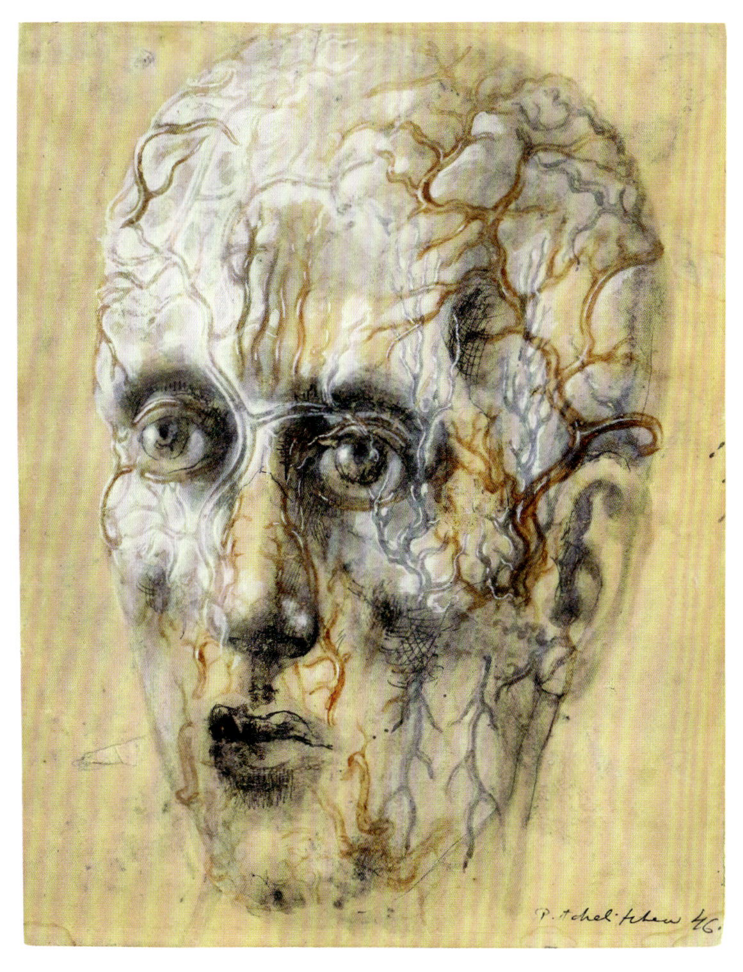
P. Tchelitchew 46.

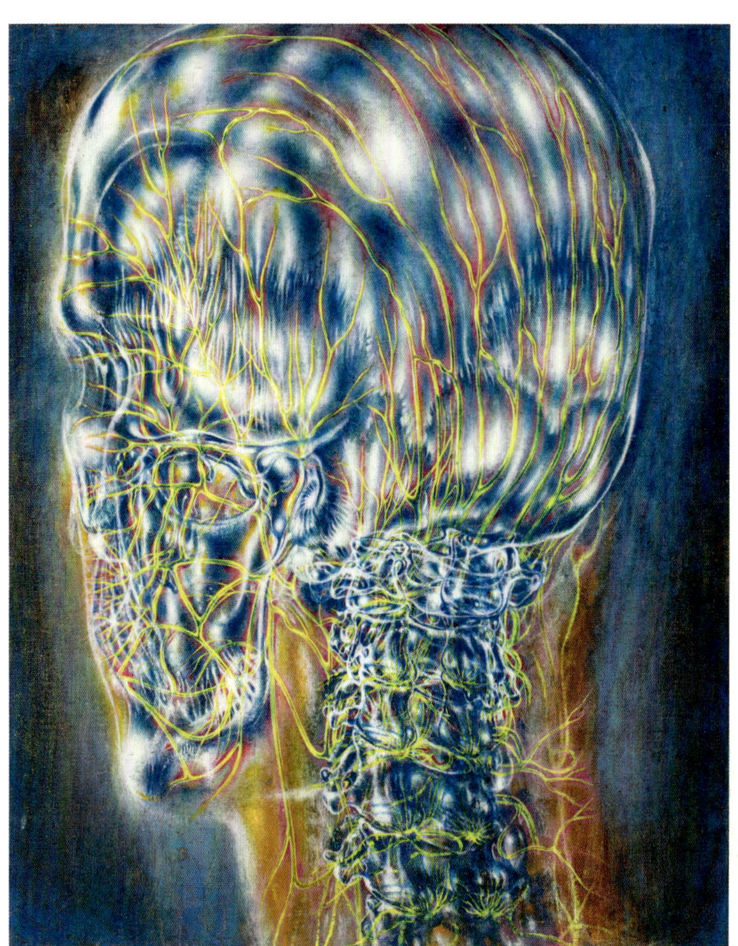

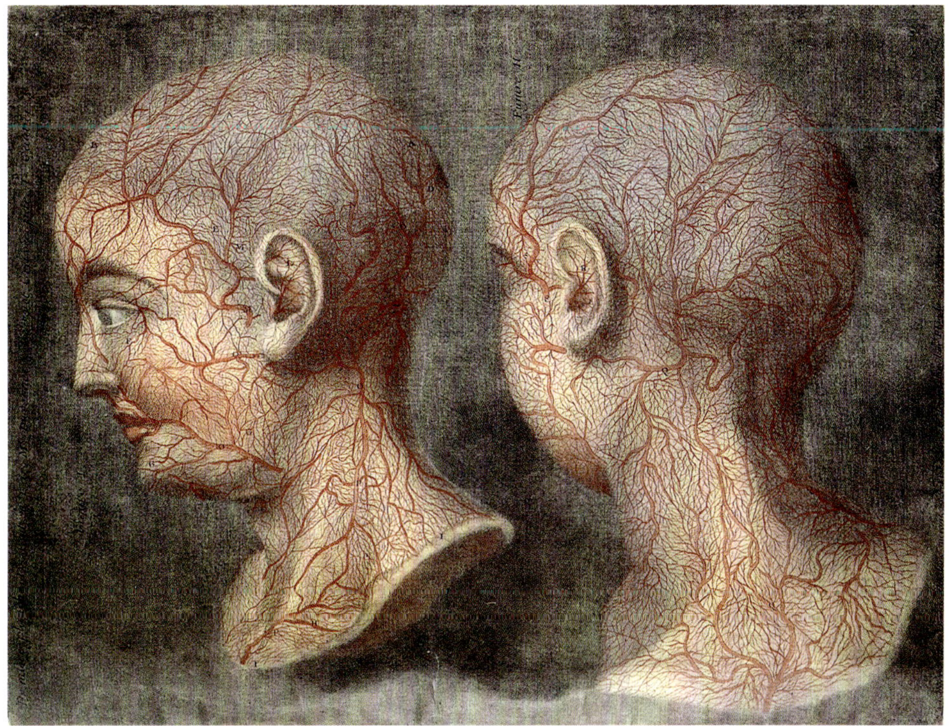

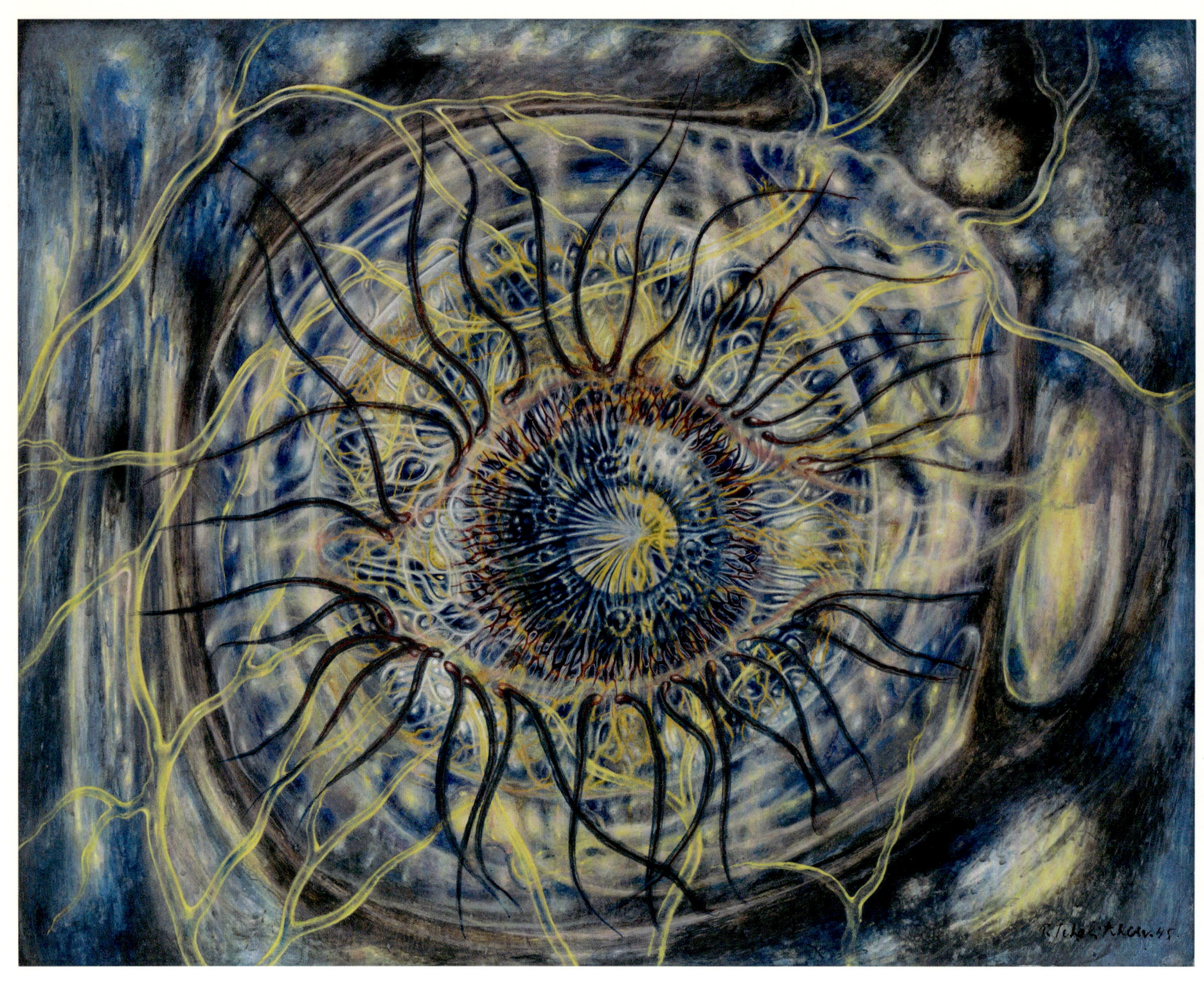

ABOVE: Pavel Tchelitchew, *The Sun*, tempera on Masonite, 55.9 × 71.1 cm (22 × 28 in.), 1945
OPPOSITE, CLOCKWISE FROM TOP LEFT: Pavel Tchelitchew, *Apoteosi*, oil on canvas, 67.3 × 51.8 cm (26½ × 20⅜ in.), 1954; Pavel Tchelitchew, *Castagna*, oil on canvas, 54.6 × 45.7 cm (21½ × 18 in.), 1954; Pavel Tchelitchew, *Wire Head From Side*, coloured chalk on dark green paper, 50.2 × 34.9 cm (19¾ × 13¾ in.), 1951; Pavel Tchelitchew, *Head*, pastel on paper, 50.8 × 34.9 cm (20 × 13¾ in.), 1950

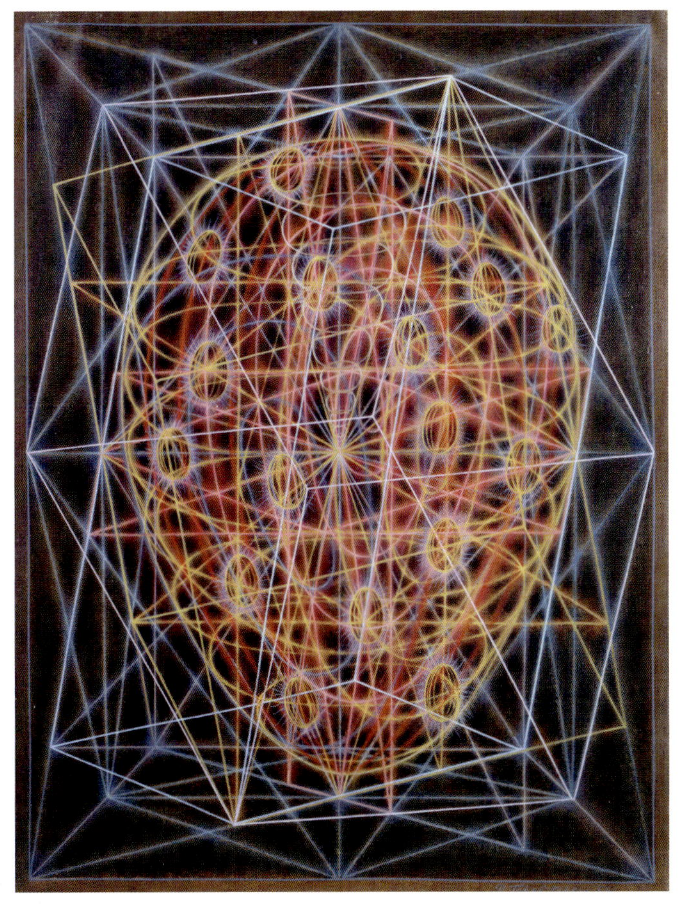

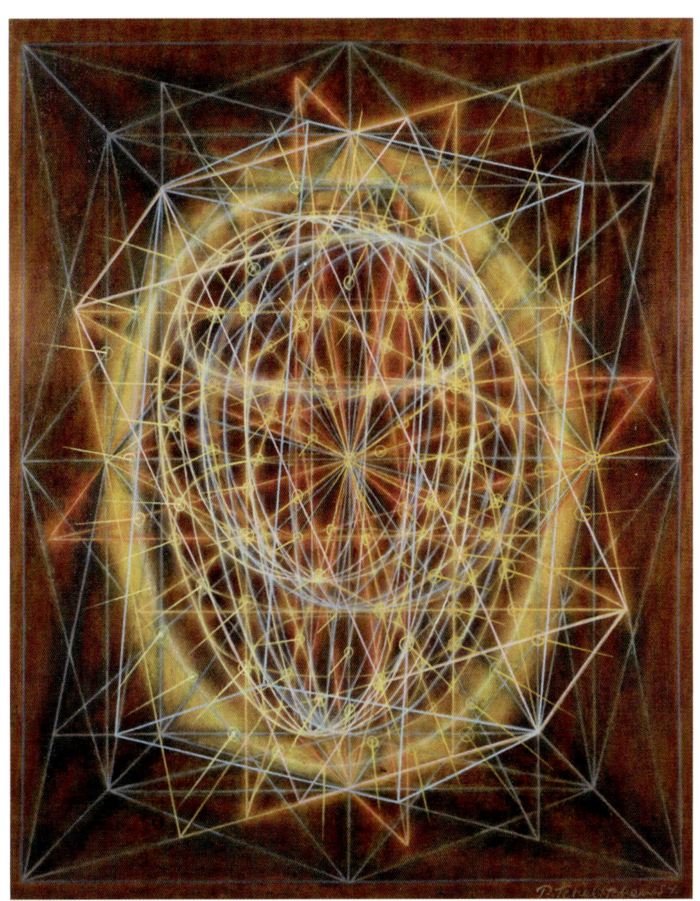

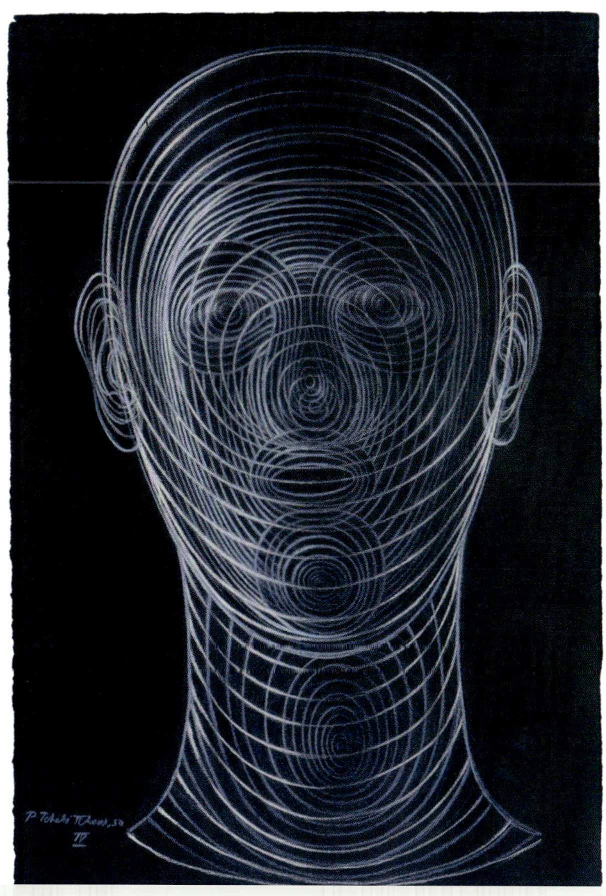

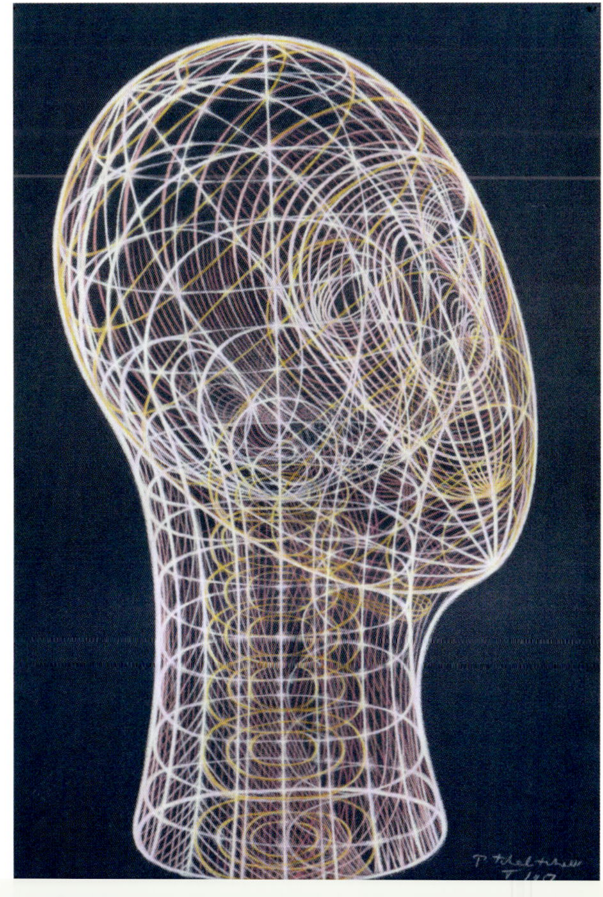

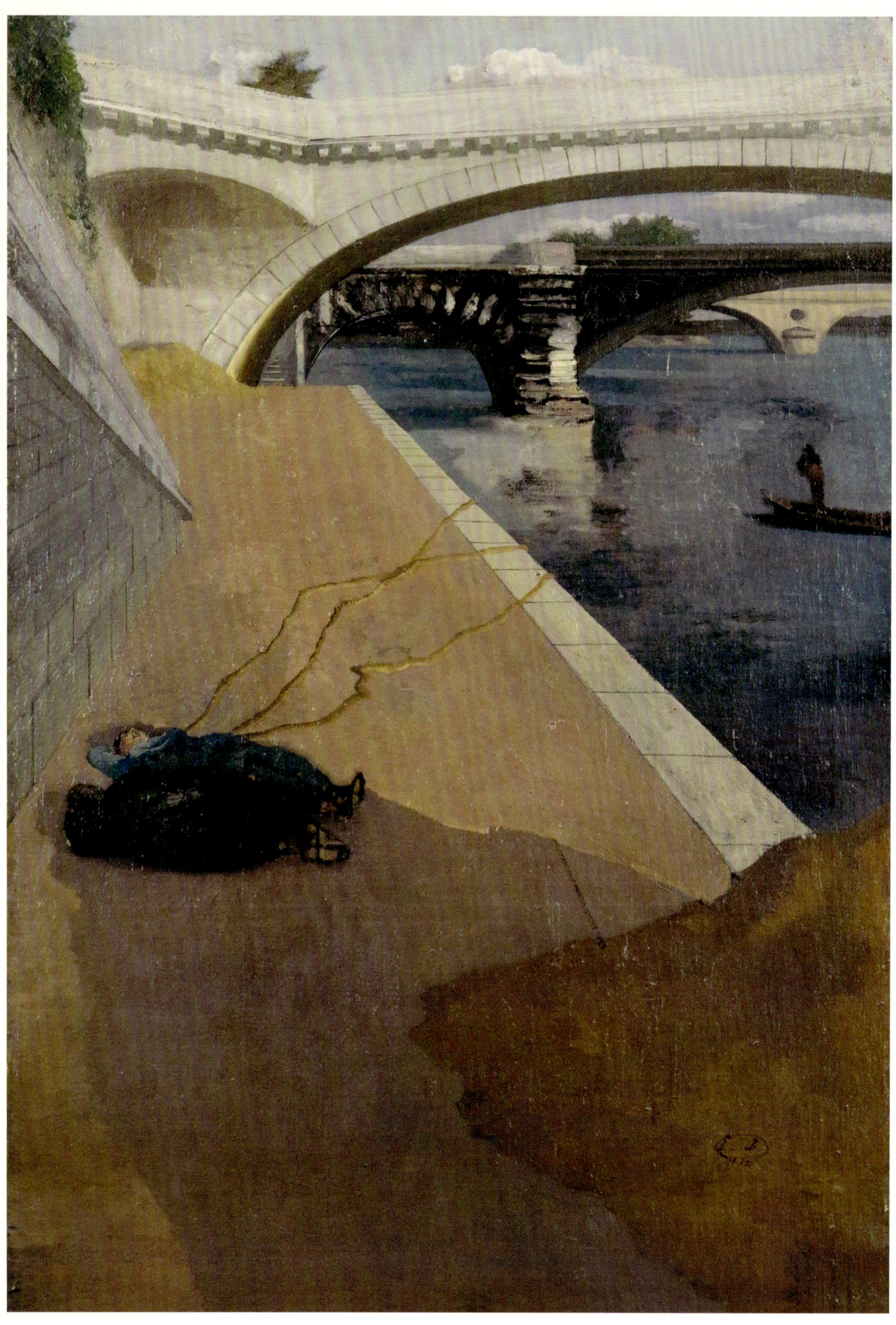

Eugene Berman, *Bridge of Paris*, oil on canvas,
91.9 × 64.8 cm (36³⁄₁₆ × 25½ in.), 1932

Eugene Berman: Dreaming of Architecture

Eugene Berman shared Tchelitchew's fascination for processes of transformation and transmutation, for ceaseless shifts in appearances and forms. Tchelitchew's focus was, however, more organic, almost alchemical, while Berman was more concerned with change derived from make-up, disguise and illusion; his metamorphoses were resolutely artificial.

Eugene was born three years after Leonid, in Peterhof, near St Petersburg, on 4 November 1899, and up until 1908 his childhood was divided between St Petersburg and Tsarskoye Selo. Like his brother, he showed a precocious talent for painting and drawing. After five years spent in Germany, Switzerland and Italy, Eugene returned to Russia in 1914 to study under the painter Pavel Semenovitch Naumov (1884–1942) and the young architect (and illustrator) Sergei Gruzenberg (1888–1934), who was a member of the Mir Iskusstva ('world of art') movement, along with Léon Bakst, Alexandre Benois, Ivan Bilibin and Dimitri Bouchène. (The group also founded a magazine called *Mir Iskusstva*, which was edited by Diaghilev.) This group's rejection of positivism, its emphasis on aesthetic emotion, and its taste for masques, theatre and historical references made it a forerunner of Neo-Romanticism.

Gruzenberg influenced Berman in several ways, but most particularly he initiated his young student in the monumental heritage of the urban architecture dreamed up by Italian masters such as Giacomo Quarenghi and Bartolomeo Rastrelli. Moreover, he taught Berman to look afresh at the architectural masterpieces dotted along the Neva River and to glean from them the lessons of Palladio, Neoclassicism and the Italian Baroque. Without doubt, these insights were the wellspring of the 'Italian dream' that ran through Berman's entire body of work. ('It is art that tends towards architecture', remarked Waldemar-George in 1930, while, some ten years later, the catalogue for a retrospective exhibition in Boston noted, rather stiffly, that 'Berman's interest in architecture [...] has remained undiminished since these first contacts and has motivated much of his painting'.)

The earlier chapters with reference to Leonid have already revealed the circumstances of the two brothers' exile in 1918 and their travels in Northern Europe, their arrival in Paris, their admission to the

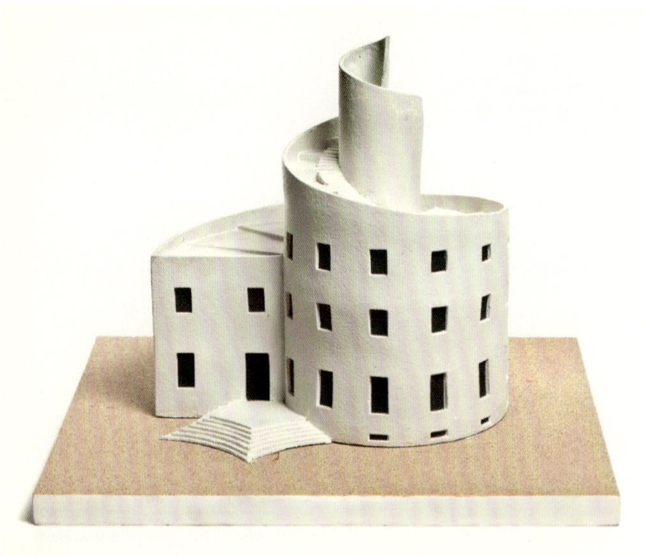

Académie Ranson in 1919, and the formation of a group of friends that would give rise to an exhibition in 1926. Prior to this, in 1920, Eugene's architectural inclinations were further intensified when he met the architect and decorator Emilio Terry (1890–1969). Eugene was drawn to Terry by a shared eclectic and historicist vision that blended allusions to eighteenth-century *vedutisti* and the ideas of Andrea Palladio and Claude-Nicolas Ledoux with a new repertoire of motifs, thus creating the basis for a style that Terry would describe, tongue in cheek, as 'Louis XVII'. (In 1931 Terry would pose for a superb portrait by Bérard but he was given short shrift by Leonid, who dismissed him as a socialite.)

Around the same time, Berman also struck up a friendship with another like-minded architect intent on adding an original twist to the legacy of Sebastiano Serlio and Palladio. Jean-Charles Moreux, born in 1889, had started off by following the principles of modernist rationalism, in an attempt to break free from the dogmatism of the École des Beaux-Arts. He came to realize, however, that 'the avant-garde movement [was ending up] in an impasse no less sterile than the academic style that had prevailed until then'. After 'a new intellectual volte-face, a definitive one this time', Moreux decided to go back to the principles of classical architecture, while giving them a new spin and using them as the source for an original lexicon. He became one of the major figures of the Neo-Baroque movement of the 1930s and '40s, alongside that other dreamer of architectural forms, Emilio Terry. The careers of these two mavericks, which ran parallel with those of the Neo-Romantics, provide a new example of the questioning and subsequent rejection – by artists working all over Europe in the 1920s, in various disciplines – of the diktats of a modernism that had ossified into a new conformism, leading to a return to imagination, ornament, playfulness and the accumulated stockpile of forms.

Berman almost certainly met Moreux through Bolette Natanson (1889–1936), the daughter of Alexandre, the oldest of the siblings with a connection to the Druet Gallery (location of the Neo-Romantics' inaugural show). Bolette is now a little-known figure in the history of decorative art but she was Moreux's muse, soulmate and associate, as well as a creator in her own right of remarkable picture frames and

Emilio Terry, *Snail House*, model in white-painted cork, wooden base and cork covered in sandpaper, 37 × 47 × 45 cm (14½ × 18½ × 17¾ in.), 1933

objects. She exhibited regularly in the gallery that she herself opened in 1930 on the rue du Faubourg Saint-Honoré. She played a key role in Moreux's 'volte-face', although the real catalyst seems to have been a trip to Italy in 1926, the year that the couple met – and also the year of the exhibition that launched the Neo-Romantics.

Berman had already discovered Italy four years earlier, and he would return there almost every year until his departure for the United States in 1938. The epiphany that both he and Moreux experienced on coming into direct contact with masterpieces of the Italian Renaissance and Baroque illustrates still further their shared tastes and character. In 1930, Waldemar-George stated, in one of the first texts devoted to Berman, appropriately entitled 'Calls of Italy': 'Eugene Berman's work signifies above all an aggressive return of the Italian spirit.' (We shall unpick this remark below, but it must be stressed that it does not necessarily reflect Berman's own point of view.)

The catalogue of the Berman retrospective organized by James Thrall Soby in Boston in 1941 was divided, apparently at the instigation of the artist himself, into phases revolving around these various stays in Italy. These pilgrimages were fired by passion but they also involved painstaking research, with each trip revealing a new region and landscape, as well as – literally – new colours. In 1928, 'repeated trips to Italy heightened his interest in Raphael and the renaissance masters; [he was] fascinated, in turn, by Italian landscape and remote coastal villages. [...] This phase was reminiscent of the architectural studies of Bramante and Luciano Laurana, the paintings of Fra Carnevale, the chiaroscuro painters of the 17th century.' In 1930, '[i]n Italy, he collected a library of architectural books and also made and studied scale models with reference to perspective and illusion'; in 1931 and 1932, 'he drew the streets and squares of Venice [...] and scenes along the Brenta. Expanded and clarified his palette, achieving in the Venetian landscapes a decorative richness recalling Veronese, Tiepolo and Guardi'; in 1935, 'Summer in Sicily and in the country surrounding the Bay of Naples. Much influenced at this moment by paintings of Mantegna, Hubert Robert, Canaletto and Panini.'

Waldemar-George, in his turn, pointed out that Italy had been, from the start, not so much an object of direct observation for Berman but more an indistinguishable mixture of dream and reality, of annotation and quotation, of restitution and flights of imagination. He showed how Berman proceeded on the basis of rhetorical devices (in the strict sense of the term), using synecdoche and enlargement of details of works presented in postcards or Alinari reproductions (of Raphael's frescoes in the Vatican, for example) to alter the 'proportional scale of the figure with respect to the canvas', or taking existing buildings to imagine an abstract architecture, 'pared down and free, comprising projects established by various builders, from Brunelleschi to Bramante, to Vignola', which offered him a host of ways 'to exteriorize a poetic state by means of associations'.

This methodical exploration was only interrupted by the war, and Berman's departure for the United States. It would be resumed in 1952, via long stays, until Berman finally settled in Rome six years later, finding refuge amid his collections in the attic of the Doria Pamphilj palazzo, which he gradually transformed into what his housemaid would describe as the 'Museo di papà Eugenio'. It was there that he died, in 1972.

Italy had also supplied the young Eugene with another formative influence. By his own admission, he was indelibly marked by the work of de Chirico and other 'metaphysical' artists. Berman's construction of space is clearly indebted to de Chirico, whom Julien Levy depicted, in his 1947 book on Berman, as a source of revelation: 'I do know that on a subsequent visit to Italy [after that of 1922] he met Giorgio de Chirico – another elder painter whose reputation in Paris was by no means so established as that of Picasso. This meeting provided the key which unlocked the doors of Berman's potential.'

De Chirico's first solo show in Paris took place in March 1922 at Paul Guillaume's gallery. This was followed by another, in the same location, four years later, and a third in July 1934, just before Guillaume's death. By then, de Chirico had returned to the tenets of Classicism, thereby earning the opprobrium of his former admirers among the Surrealists.

The mention of de Chirico's impact on Berman's development provides us with a cue for tackling the vexed question of the links between the Neo-Romantics and the Surrealists. Neo-Romanticism is often blithely,

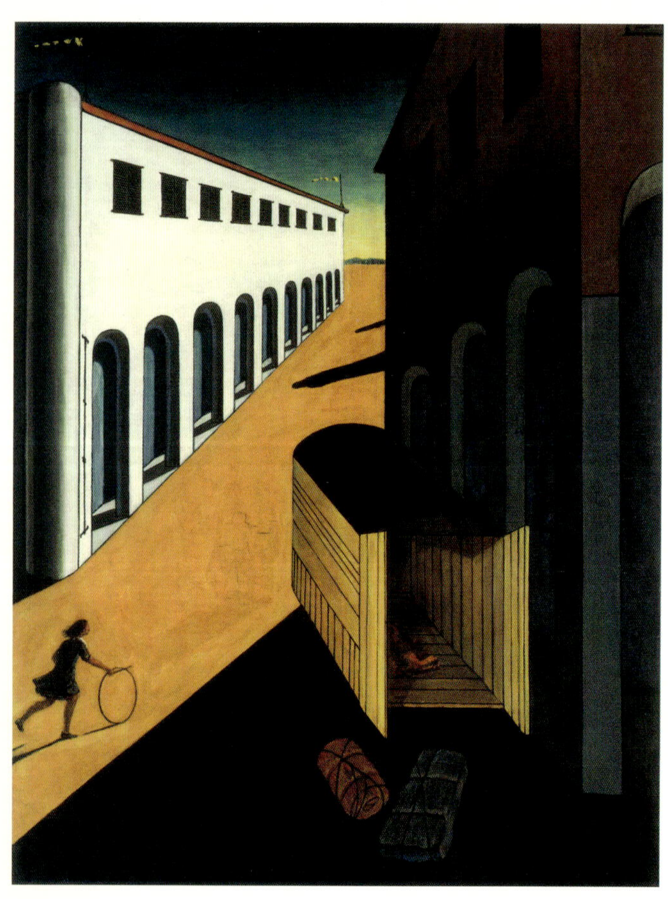

Giorgio de Chirico, *Italian Square, Girl with a Hoop*, oil on canvas, 75.2 × 58.1 cm (29⅝ × 22⅞ in.), 1948

and falsely, dismissed as a branch of Surrealism, or even a pale copy. (Bear in mind that André Breton's *Manifesto of Surrealism* came out in 1924, just two years before the exhibition at the Druet Gallery.)

In actual fact, the two groups had virtually nothing in common. The Neo-Romantics had no figurehead or spokesman, no doctrine or school of thought, no political position, and no sense of the sexual normativity that drove Breton's ideas, often violently. In Catrina Neiman's introduction to an anthology of texts drawn from the magazine *View* – the echo chamber of Neo-Romanticism in the USA, founded in 1940 by Charles Henri Ford – she commented that 'Breton's discomfort with homosexuality contributed not a little to his aloofness towards *View*. He was known to have been intolerant of Tchelitchew and other neo-romantics for this reason.' Without going into this particular aspect, Eugene Berman himself looked back in later years on the differences between the two groups in a lucid 'Declaration of Independence' that opened a catalogue published by Knoedler in 1964: 'Really, we have always refused to be classed as an organized group. Each of us has followed his own path, without worrying about the consolidation of a collective movement, as was the case with our Surrealist friends. We undoubtedly also lacked an ideological promoter capable of organizing us, spreading our ideas and aspirations, and conferring on them a vital cohesion. But we were not bothered about issuing manifestoes and endowing ourselves with formal labels and classifications.'

Berman had already made a similar pronouncement in his 'Notes for a Self-Portrait', published five years earlier in the catalogue for his first major Italian exhibition: 'We did not have the feeling of constituting a group or party, maybe because there were no more than three or four of us, and we were all too individualistic, too jealous of our freedom, too opposed to discipline and rules to form a stable and structured group. Above all, we were painters and we had no writer, poet or ideologue, no organizing personality who would have been able to maintain connections, to present, explain and spread our aspirations, to encourage the atmosphere of topicality and interest needed to popularize a new movement or an emerging trend. Little by little, the connections started to loosen; distance, travelling, the continents that separated us did the rest, not to mention the fact that our individual works were following ever more divergent paths.'

Going back to the early work of de Chirico, we can see that this common reference remained the essential point of contact between the

Surrealists and the Neo-Romantics – leaving aside the latter group's personal friendships with some of the Surrealists (often in defiance of decrees issued by Breton), including Max Ernst, Salvador Dalí, René Crevel and, later on (through Julien Levy), Joseph Cornell.

Levy was also – along with Waldemar-George, James Thrall Soby and Lincoln Kirstein – the closest anybody would get to Berman's 'ideological promoter' that the Neo-Romantics had hitherto lacked. Levy played a part in launching all the members of the group in the United States. In Eugene Berman's case, Levy put on his first New York show in 1930, at a time when such support was extremely welcome. (Julien Green, who had little time for Eugene and preferred Bérard and Tchelitchew, records in his *Journal* on 23 March 1931 a 'visit to Berman with Anne, who wants to buy a painting because it is said that this painter was in need'.)

It was in this period that Berman started to paint 'the bridges of Paris, first as unreal night scenes, later representing them more concretely in daylight'. Perhaps as a reflection of Berman's own precarious circumstances, these bridges are not uninhabited spaces but rather places of social desperation, haunted by groups of outcasts (with 'sleepers lying on improvised beds', in the words of Waldemar-George). Julien Levy captured the spirit of these times: 'The *clochards* finding shelter under the arches of the bridges of Paris, the *défaites champêtres* in the park of St. Cloud, beggars on the steps of Italian churches, [...] beachcombers living by the rocks and driftwood in Sicily, lost children of the roads, [...] all certainly prophetic of displaced persons and the fragmented structure of tomorrow!'

These marginal figures would reappear in Berman's work a couple of years later, but by then they would be stranded in huge dramatic landscapes with vast arid expanses and rocky craters hollowed out of dizzying gorges. Soby saw the influence of Dalí in these landscapes, but the primary source of inspiration was a trip to Les Baux-de-Provence in 1933. Berman's earlier paintings were characterized by stark, enclosed spaces (albeit with knowing allusions to Renaissance and Baroque architecture), but the natural scenery, eroded by time, that emerged in these later works seems just as artificial, just as much a product of composition and rarefied atmosphere. Les Baux (literally, the rocky outcrops) are, by their very nature, strikingly theatrical – thirty years later, Cocteau would go on to exploit this quality in the *Testament of Orpheus* – and they provided Berman with visual elements for the next phase of his work.

OPPOSITE, ABOVE: Eugene Berman, *L'Île aux Épaves*, oil on canvas, 59.5 × 92 cm (23 × 36¼ in.), 1929
OPPOSITE, BELOW: Eugene Berman, *The Red Houses*, oil on canvas, 81 × 100 cm (32 × 39 in.), 1929

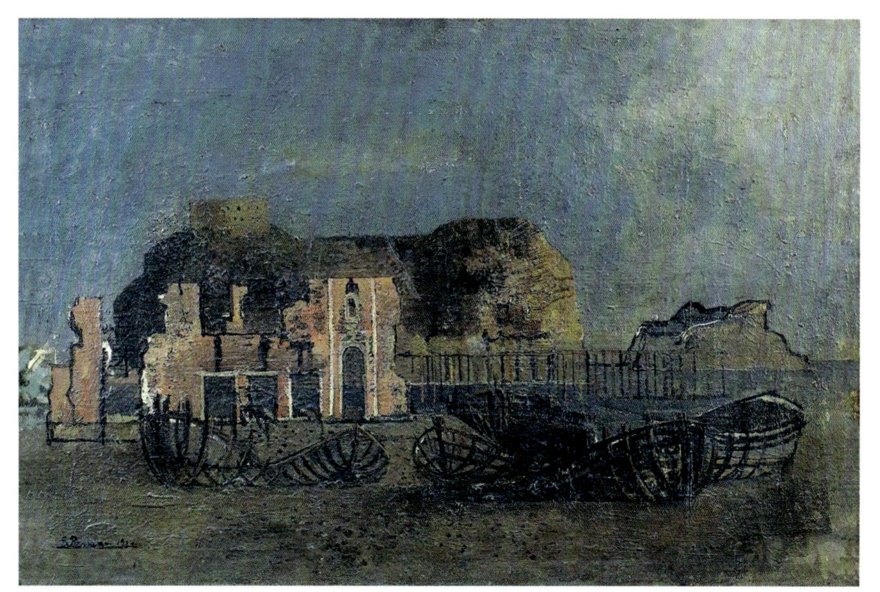

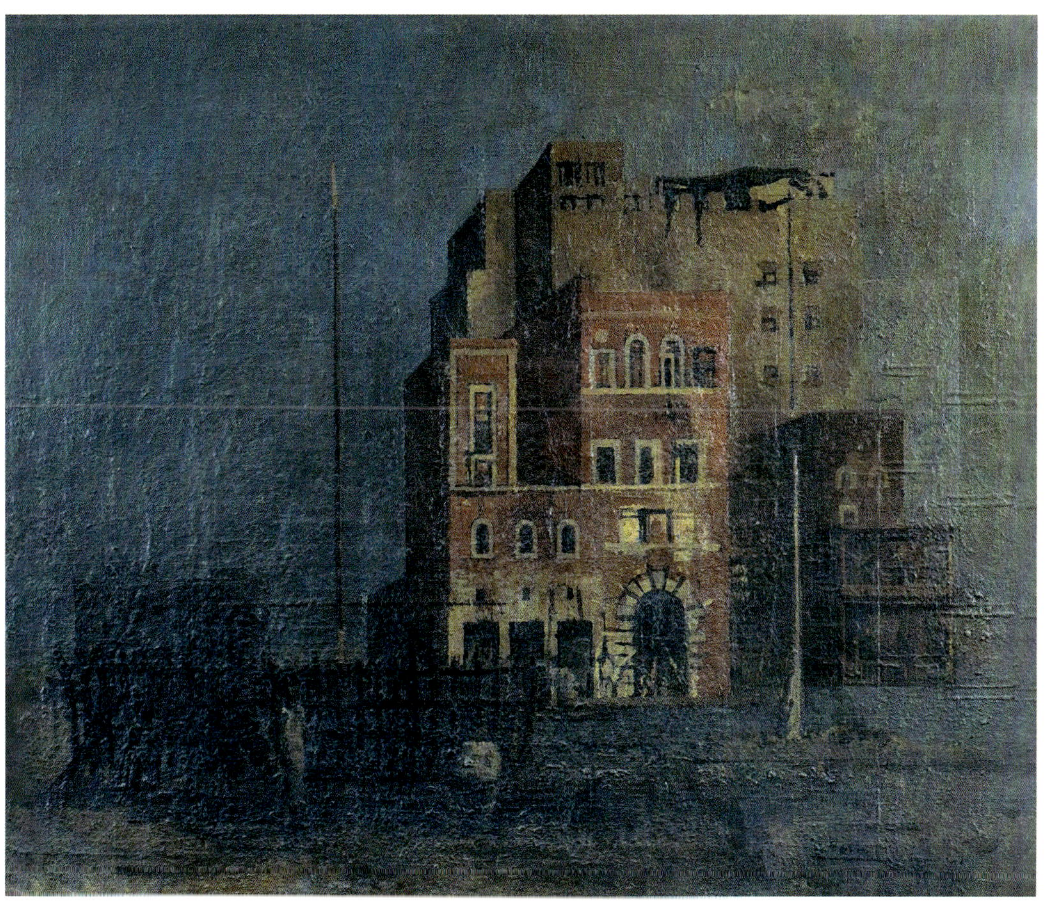

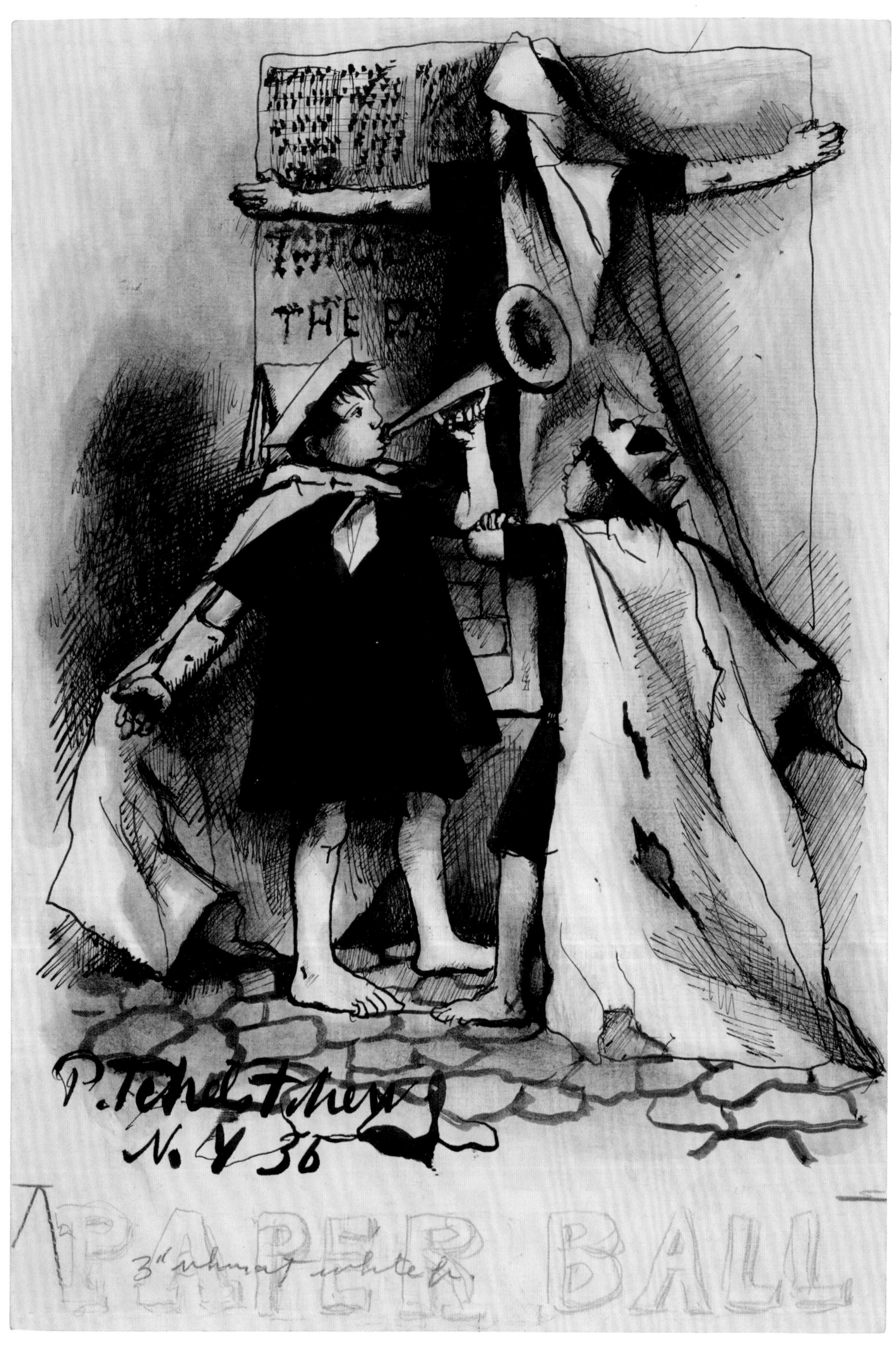

Pavel Tchelitchew, design for Paper Ball invitation, Hartford Festival, pen and ink and graphite on paper, 26.7 × 18.4 cm (10½ × 7¼ in.), 1936

A Paper Ball

Eugene Berman did not make it to New York for his 1930 exhibition and would have to wait until 1935 for his first visit to the city – a visit that would trigger a remarkable new development in his career. As Julien Levy recalled, 'In America the whole scale of his work underwent a dramatic change.' There was no stylistic rupture, as in the case of Tchelitchew, but rather new accomplishments, unexpected deviations, and the realization of a dream that had previously been held in check.

Eugene, even more than his brother, had been enthralled by the ballet productions that he had seen as a child. Alison Delarue learned from her conversations with Berman that '[a]t the age of five or six, [he] was taken for his first visit to the famous Marinsky Theatre. Significantly enough it was a matinee of Petipa's ballet *The Hunchbacked Horse*, a Russian fairy tale. The illusion was complete. [...] The occasion was unforgettable and Berman caught a glimpse of his Muse in this world of make-believe.' Moreover, his enchantment was only heightened by the sight of Nijinsky (who lived in the same building as his family) bounding up the stairs, four steps at a time, convincing Berman that 'the dancer was a supernatural creature or a bird'. Berman's teenage years coincided with Diaghilev's reinvention of ballet through his flamboyant productions for the Imperial Ballet in St Petersburg, which the young enthusiast lapped up. Bakst and Benois were responsible for the designs, but when Berman had the chance to see Diaghilev's Ballets Russes ten years later, in Paris, he found that he preferred the new sets and costumes by Derain (for *The Magic Toyshop*) and Picasso (for *The Three-Cornered Hat*).

The successes of Tchelitchew with *Ode* (1928) and *L'Errante* (1933), and of Bérard with *Cotillon* (1932) and *The Fantastic Symphony* (1936), only intensified what Levy described as Berman's 'longtime preoccupation with theatre' and his desire to become involved with it. Levy went on to explain that, 'impatient to work for the theatre, and envying the earlier debuts of his colleagues Tchelitchew and Bérard, he had begun to make numerous rough sketches for the use of architecture in relation to illusion on the stage – the two being forever linked together in his imagination since the revelation of the

Teatro Olimpico' (this refers to Palladio's masterpiece in Vicenza). These sketches remained on the drawing board for the moment, but they were only waiting for an excuse to come to life.

And this excuse arose on Berman's arrival in the United States: 'No sooner had I landed in New York than I was whisked away on my first week-end to see the Hartford museum and to meet the almost legendary man behind it: Chick Austin.' Austin, a fascinating multi-faceted figure – aesthete, magician, actor, collector – was also the first curator, and indeed the 'inventor', of the Wadsworth Atheneum as it is known today. He considerably expanded its collection, and under his auspices it became a veritable temple of Neo-Romanticism. Austin was appointed director of the institution in 1927, and he immediately launched a bold, wide-ranging programme that would include exhibitions of modern German and Mexican painting, contemporary photography, the Italian Baroque, eighteenth-century French art, and the watercolours of Edward Hopper.

Austin was at the forefront of a re-evaluation of nineteenth-century American trompe-l'œil painting (by the likes of William Harnett and Raphaelle Peale), as well as the work of Louis-Léopold Boilly, whose painstaking illusory effects were hyper-realistic and anticipated the unsettling paintings of both Pierre Roy (1880–1950), who was close to the Neo-Romantics, and Berman himself. Austin organized a de Chirico exhibition in 1930, and the following year he presented 'five young painters' – who included Tchelitchew, Bérard, and Leonid and Eugene Berman. Austin loved music (as well as parties), and he pioneered the organization of live events in the museum. In February 1934, Gertrude Stein and Virgil Thomson's opera *Four Saints in Three Acts* was staged there, in a production that broke new ground on account of its all-Black cast and unusual set (designed by Florine Stettheimer). By 1936, Austin had got the Hartford Festival off the ground, with a mixture of music, theatre and visual art. The first year's programme included the American première of Erik Satie's *Socrate* (with sets by Alexander Calder), a ballet by Balanchine based on a serenade by Mozart, and a masked ball that would be organized by Tchelitchew.

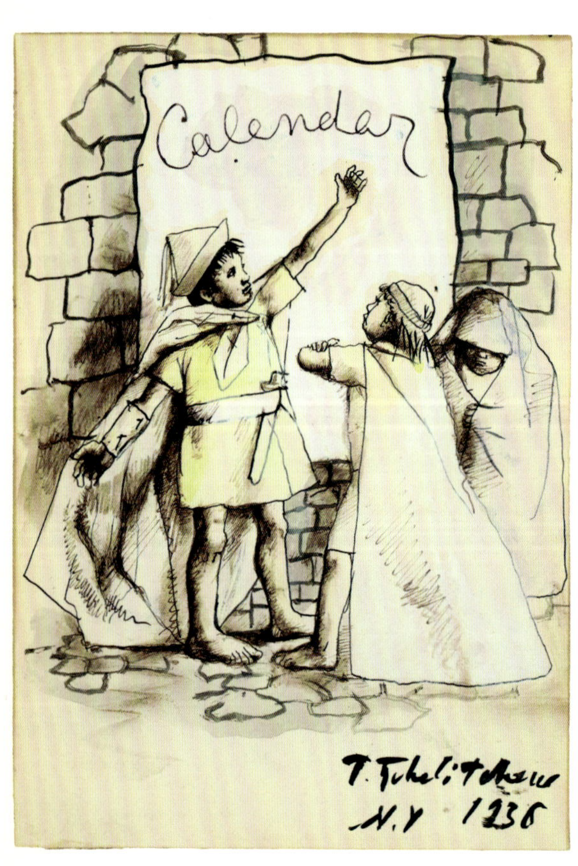

ABOVE: Pavel Tchelitchew, sketch for the Paper Ball, black ink and watercolour on paperboard, 25.4 × 17.8 cm (10 × 7 in.), 1936

OPPOSITE: Chick Austin, 'The Great Osram as "The Sea-God of Magic"', anonymous silver print, December 1944

Berman was taken under Chick Austin's wing as soon as he arrived in Hartford: he was entrusted with the design for a concert to be conducted by Virgil Thomson for the festival, before teaming up with Tchelitchew for the staging of a ball in the museum's atrium. Years later, Berman looked back with emotion on those first opportunities in the world of theatre, which turned out to be the first steps in an illustrious career: 'On that first visit to Chick's in 1935, immediate plans were laid out for the first Hartford Festival. For some five or six years I had been vainly waiting in Paris for an opportunity to complement my painting with stage work, an obsession I carried over from my boyhood years in St. Petersburg and my visits to the Imperial Ballet and to the Ballets Russes de Diaghilev in Paris, but here I was finally offered an almost immediate chance to try my hand on a special musical setting for a concert of XVIII century music.'

The decor for the ball, which might seem merely incidental, was in fact vividly recalled in Berman's memoirs. He found himself obliged to improvise 'a last minute decoration for the lobby of the auditorium in which all the spectacles and concerts took place, a decoration with contrasting vivid draperies and fake marbleized busts on pedestals for which I used whatever plaster heads of American statesmen I could lay my hands on in the cellars of the museum. By smashing a few noses and other features which betrayed too clearly the American origin of the model, by freely dousing them with running colors to achieve astonishing effects of real marble and painting in some cracks and characteristic features, I was able to transform them into roman emperors, matrons or baroque heroes.'

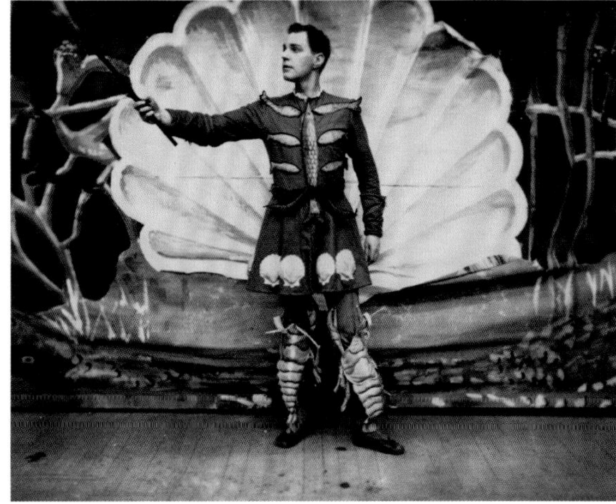

These busts were set off by a huge array of cut paper that covered 'the whole marble hall of the museum and all the costume of the guests' – hence the event's title of the Paper Ball. Berman remembered that this improvised decor, 'typical of the way things were done by Chick himself or by his friends and collaborators for such special occasions [...] was tremendously effective'. He went on: 'Shall I add that shortly upon my return to Paris I started getting offers to design stage productions and thus embarked on a parallel career in the theatre which was to last from 1936 to 1957?' (This text was

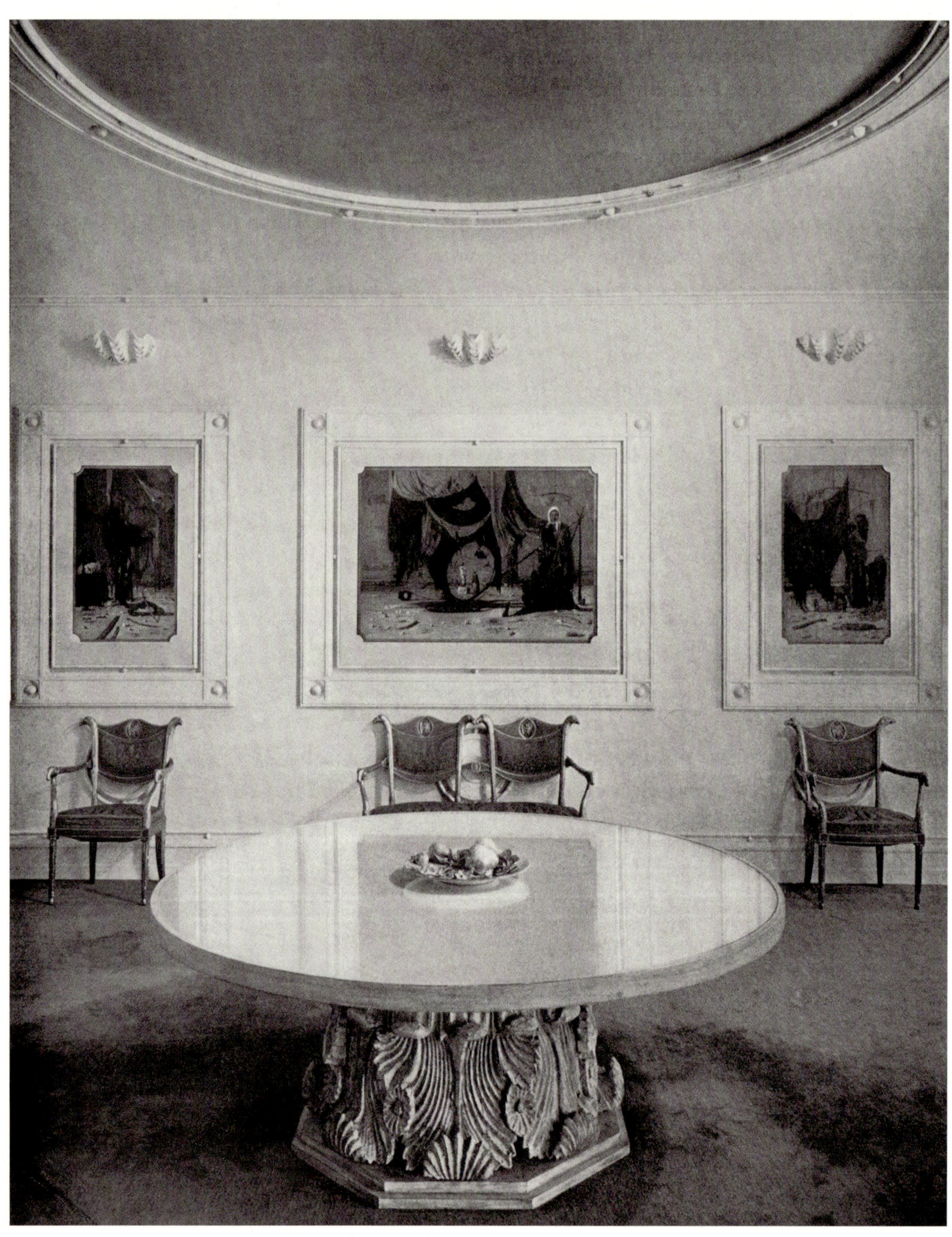

ABOVE: Eugene Berman, decorative wall panels in the dining room of James Thrall Soby, 1936

OPPOSITE: Eugene Berman, *Scène de la vie des Bohémiens*, oil on panel, 124.5 × 151.8 cm (49 × 59¾ in.), 1936

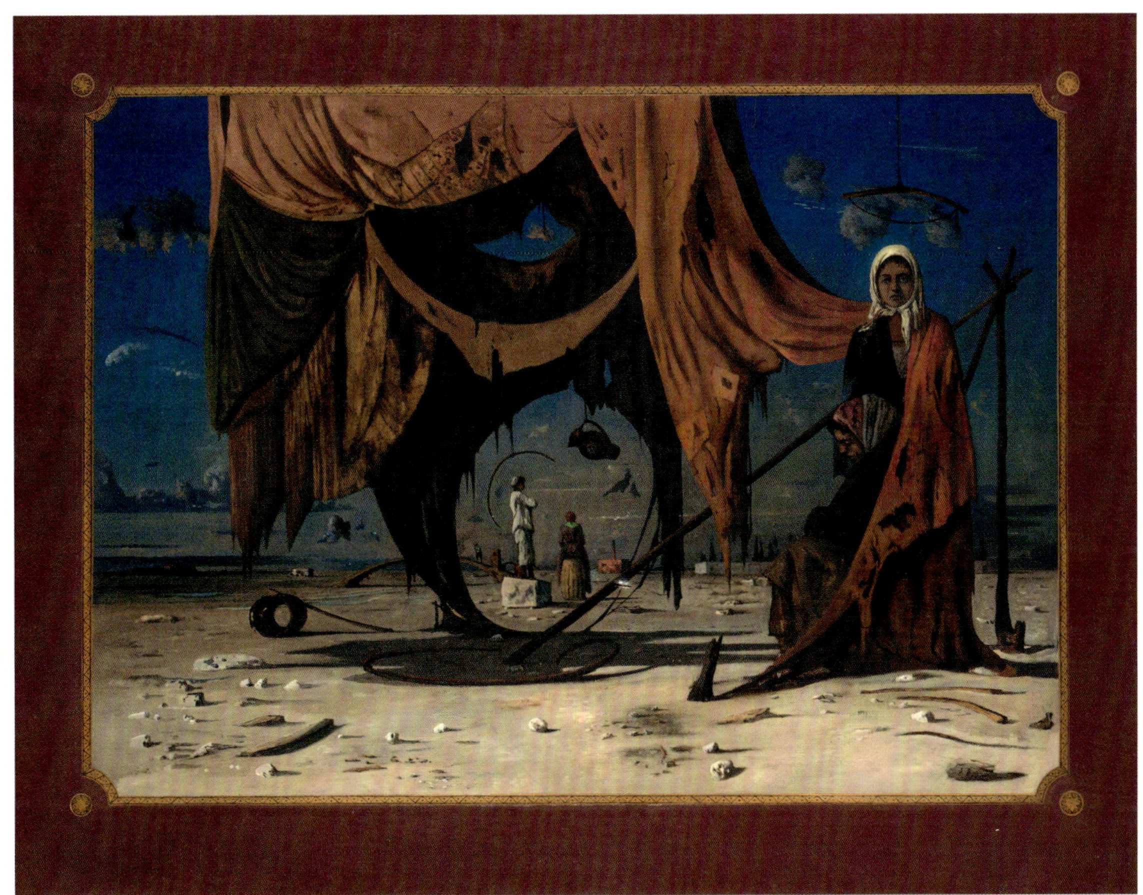

written in 1958; in fact, Eugene would continue to produce theatre work until his death fourteen years later.)

The ingenuity applied to the decor for the ball may seem merely the by-product of a hastily organized social event, but it nevertheless serves to illustrate a distinctive feature of the Neo-Romantic approach, also evident in the work of Bérard and Tchelitchew: a veritable passion for improvisation and for patching things together. This enthusiasm was coupled with a love of festivity and ephemeral creations, often involving 'poor' (but elegant) materials. The importance of these aspects of the Neo-Romantics' work has largely been overlooked, but they should be considered a bedrock to their whole aesthetic approach.

Berman's first visit to the United States not only enabled him to build up a new circle of buyers and admirers, which he would retain once he was back in Europe, it also provided him with the opportunity to expand his range and apply his vision to different kinds of media and occasions. In 1937, he produced 'a series of magnificent mural decorations' for Julien Levy's apartment in New York, before designing the decor and furniture, as well as a series of panels, for

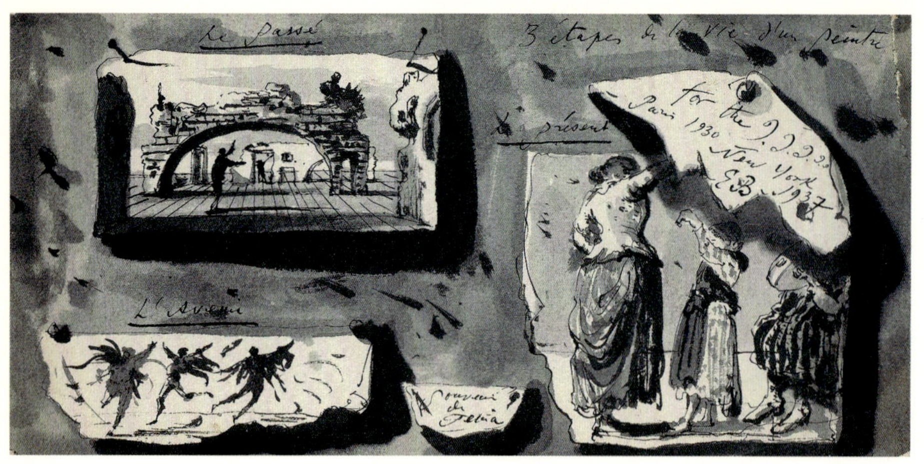

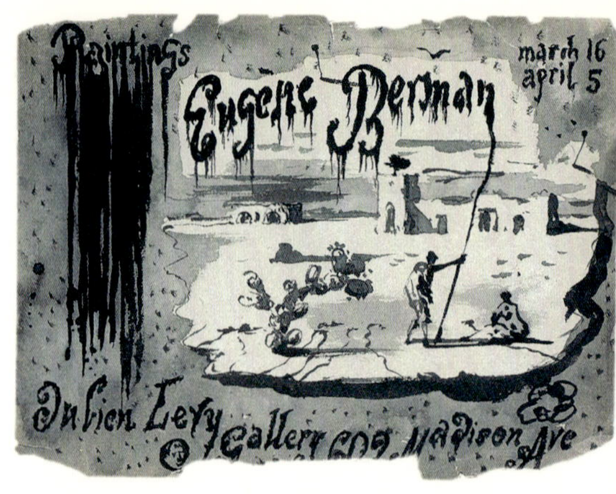

James Thrall Soby's residence in Farmington, Connecticut. The following year, he transformed the reception rooms of the collector Wright Ludington in Santa Barbara, and in 1941 he created striking decorative paintings for the architect John Yeon in Portland.

These various commissions allowed Berman to take the visual rhetoric of trompe-l'œil to new heights of virtuosity. Trompe-l'œil would become a central feature of his work, and Alison Delarue put it in a historical context: '"Of course," as Julien Levy has explained, "all perspective is *trompe l'oeil*, but in a special sense *trompe l'oeil* is more a Baroque innovation, used to break the plane not only backward but forward towards the spectator with startling effect."' Until then, Berman had drawn on his extensive knowledge of architecture and the memories of his Italian trips to play with the effects of monumental perspective and the illusionist construction of space. Now he sought to break the confines of a mere painting, as his works were now forming part of a larger decorative ensemble. So he developed another register of illusion, along the lines of the Baroque, blurring ever more playfully the boundaries between fiction and reality, between the plane of a picture and the viewpoint of its observer. He created the illusion that pieces of torn canvas or paper were pinned to or hanging from the surface of a picture, or inside an empty frame. These flimsy contrivances would split the pictorial space into two or more parts, giving rise to stories within stories, paintings within paintings, in the manner of the Italian virtuosos of the Seicento and the Settecento, as well as the less well-known nineteenth-century American painters currently being rediscovered by Austin, Levy, Soby and others.

Berman was thereby exposing himself to misconceived and reductive accusations of pastiche, or even plagiarism (and they duly arrived, from the likes of Clement Greenberg). Berman had foreseen these criticisms, however, and responded to them through the

ABOVE, LEFT: Eugene Berman, *Three Stages in the Life of a Painter*, ink and wash on paper, 21.5 × 45 cm (8⅜ × 17⅝ in.), 1937

ABOVE, RIGHT: Eugene Berman, design for the cover of the exhibition catalogue for *Paintings by Eugène Berman* at Julien Levy Gallery, 16 March–5 April 1937, ink and wash on paper, 22 × 30 cm (8⅝ × 11⅞ in.)

intermediary of Alison Delarue: 'Berman used these decorative elements because he felt a spontaneous relation to them, just as a dancer to-day may feel like a native in the tradition of Ballet. The original effect of Berman's style is definitely "Berman"; in using forms already established, he did not in the least restrict the manifestation of his own personality.' Berman's manipulation of the lexicon of classical forms and his joy in creating variations on these themes by rearranging them was one of the driving forces of his art, and it is far removed from any tired repetition of hackneyed expressive resources. It did, however, place him in direct opposition to the notion of originality as a rupture with the past or a radical transgression: for Berman, originality lay in the order of variations, of shifts and displacements, of a presence that could be described as ghostly.

The *cartellini* (derived from Bellini and Antonello da Messina) and the barely attached pieces of torn paper that distinguished Berman's scenery on this first American trip were repeated, as a further modulation of a single principle, in his first commission for theatre work in Paris, which awaited his return: the sets and costumes for Brecht's *Threepenny Opera*, staged in 1937 at the Theâtre de l'Étoile. Fired by enthusiasm for an opportunity he had so long anticipated, '[h]e made innumerable sketches and eight or nine impressive décors'. He took advantage of the fact that '[t]he action called for the introduction of explanatory placards' and integrated these into the set as quirky *cartellini* or pinned pieces of paper. They served as captions commenting on the action and thus translated Brecht's principle of *Verfremdungseffekt* or alienation, detachment from the action. One of Berman's favourite motifs, derived from Classical painting, was thus reworked and proved perfectly suited to its new use.

For Berman, just as for Bérard – whom Berman considered 'the most completely theatrical, resourceful and imaginative scenic designer of his generation' – the whole world was a stage. More than that, it was a Baroque stage that revelled in ambiguities and mirages, the dizzying divide between true and false, between the original and the copy, between allusion and quotation – and a painter was the architect of this stage. 'Theatre, it seems to Berman,' wrote Alison Delarue, still acting as his mouthpiece, 'is at once very real, very abstract and very fantastic; it requires all the arts to project its illusion [...] construction, painting, sculpture and light, and this he believes to be the goal of a designer-painter-architect.' As Delarue noted: 'He approaches theatrical work with all his painter's imaginations and invention but combines with these his architectural ability to build as well as ornament the stage for the performance.'

From 1937 onwards, Berman kept up a steady rhythm of designs for dance and theatre, in both Europe and the United States. Commissions came from private companies, such as the Ballets Russes de Monte-Carlo (Lifar's *Icare*, 1938; Frederick Ashton's *Devil's Holiday*, 1939; *Danses Concertantes* by Stravinsky and Balanchine, 1944; and, in the same year, Balanchine's *Malade Imaginaire*) and the Ballet Theatre (*Romeo and Juliet*, 1943; *Pas de Deux*, 1945; various productions of *Giselle* between 1940 and 1946). Berman's services were also solicited by major public institutions, such as the Sadler's Wells Ballet in London (*Ballet Imperial*, 1950) and the Metropolitan Opera in New York (*Rigoletto*, 1951; *The Force of Destiny*, 1952; *The Barber of Seville*, 1954; and Verdi's *Otello*, 1963).

In 1952, Berman designed the sets and costumes for a production of Pergolesi's *La Serva Padrona* for the Ringling Museum in Sarasota, now run by Chick Austin after his departure from the Wadsworth Atheneum. The piece was performed in the small Asolo Theater, which the museum had bought and shipped over from Venice. Berman was

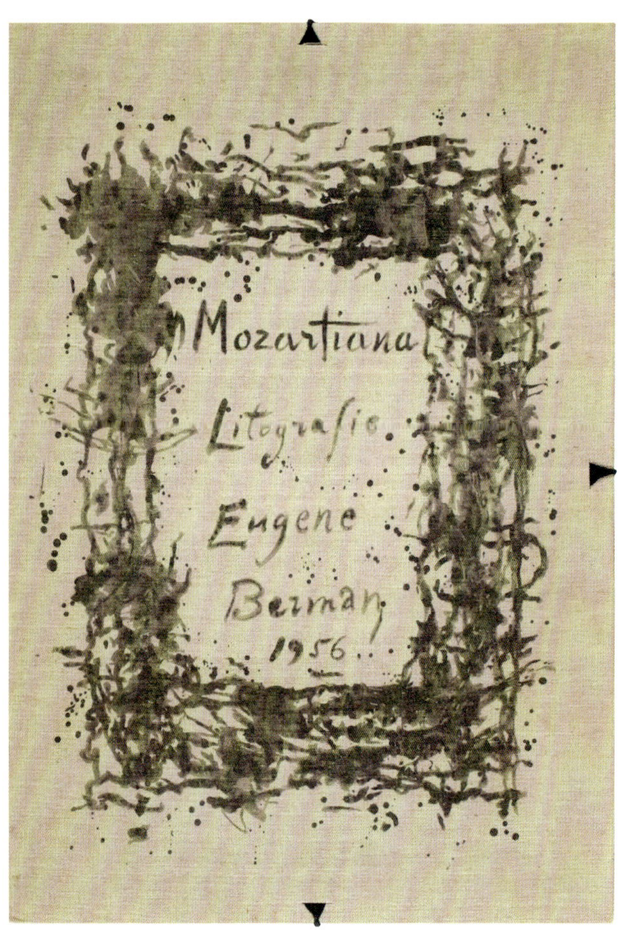

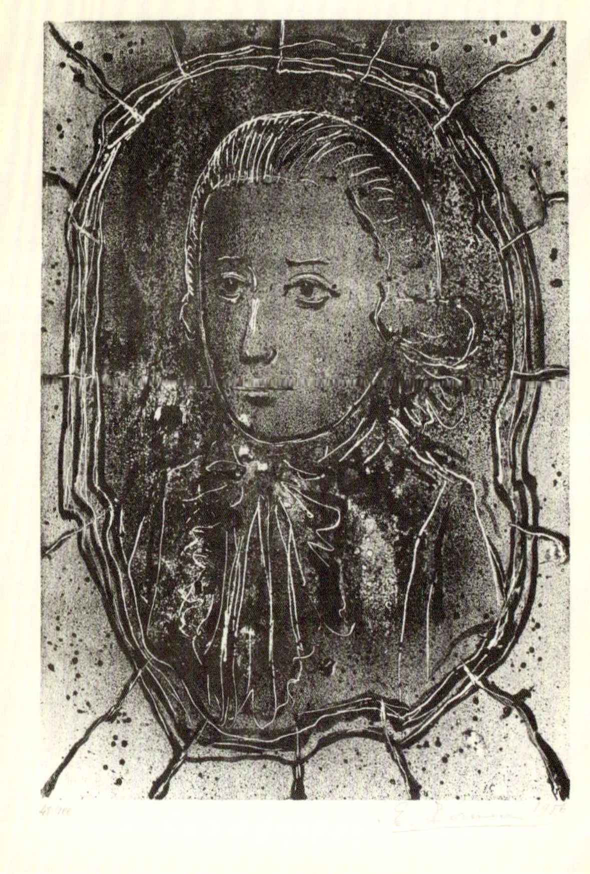

ABOVE AND OPPOSITE: Eugene Berman, *Mozartiana*, from portfolio of eight lithographs, 57 × 40 cm (22⅜ × 15¾ in.), Edizioni Beatrice d'Este, Milan, 1956

also a devoted Mozartian: in 1956, he produced a series of lithographs under the title of *Mozartiana*, and that same year he designed *Così Fan Tutte* for La Scala in Milan, before embarking, in 1957, on what was undoubtedly his most important work for the stage: a memorable *Don Giovanni* for the Metropolitan Opera in New York that remained in the repertoire until 1984. Berman's friendship with Stravinsky led to

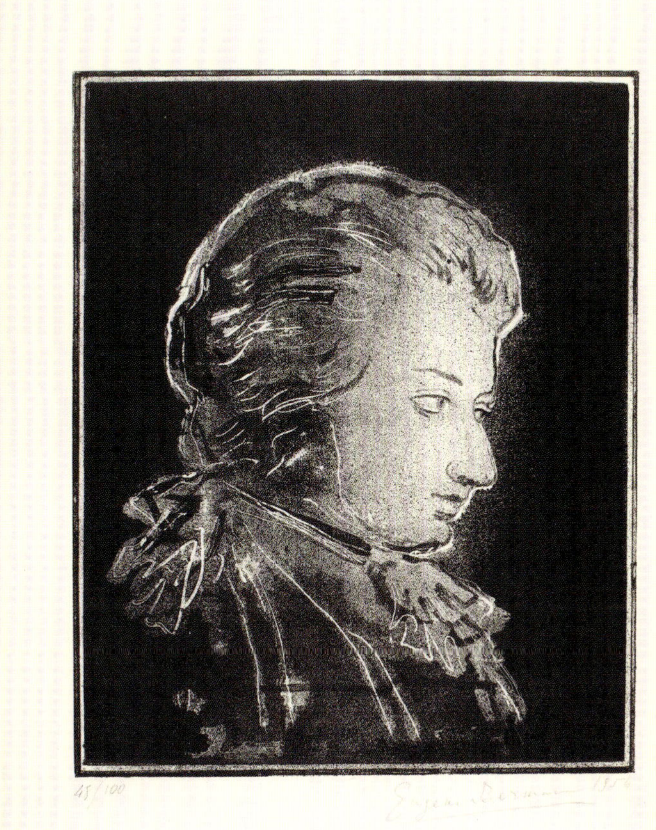

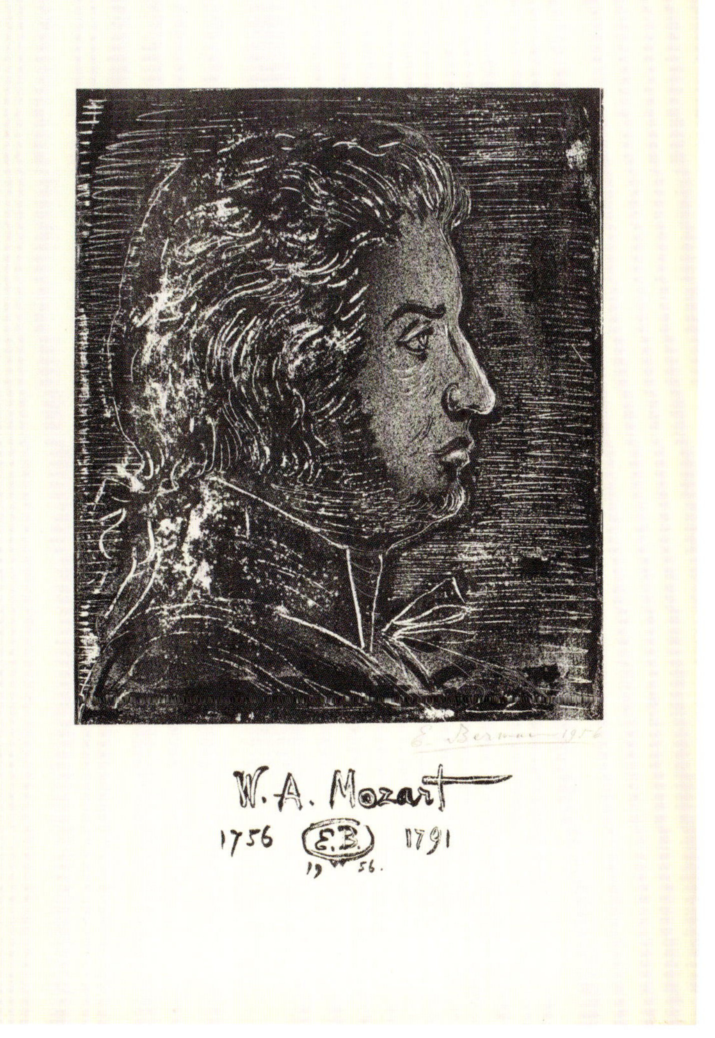

a commission to design the sets for the 'burlesque tale' *Renard* at the Accademia Filarmonica Romana in 1966, and he was also responsible for the sets and costumes for Stravinsky's *Pulcinella* (originally designed by Picasso for Diaghilev in 1920), with choreography by Balanchine, in 1972, the last year of his – and Stravinsky's – life.

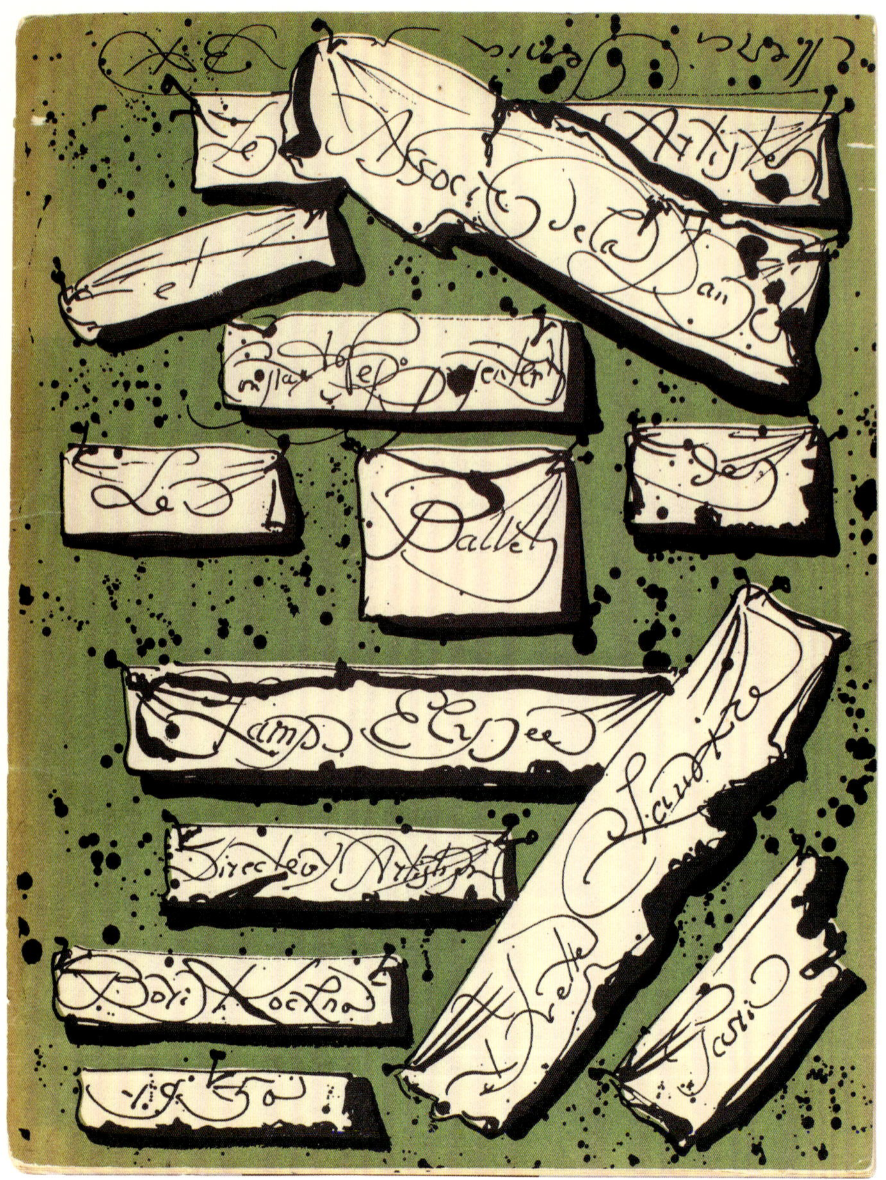

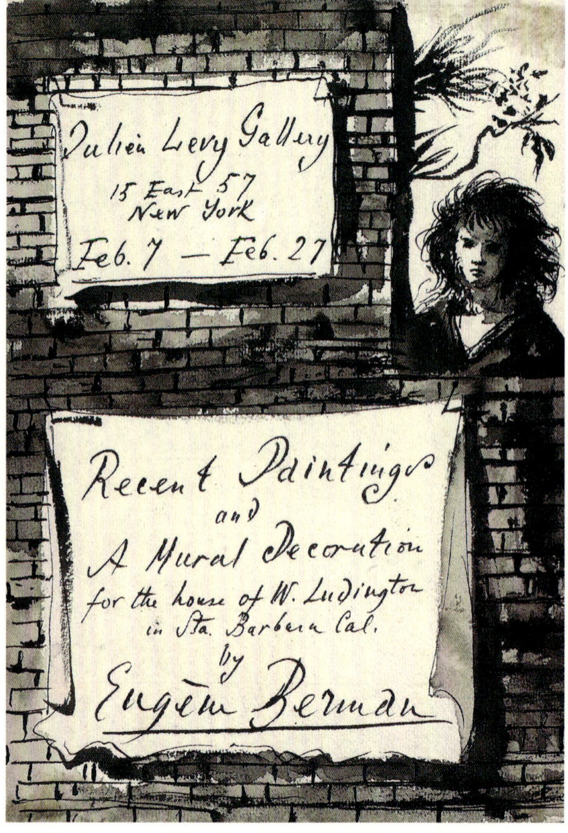

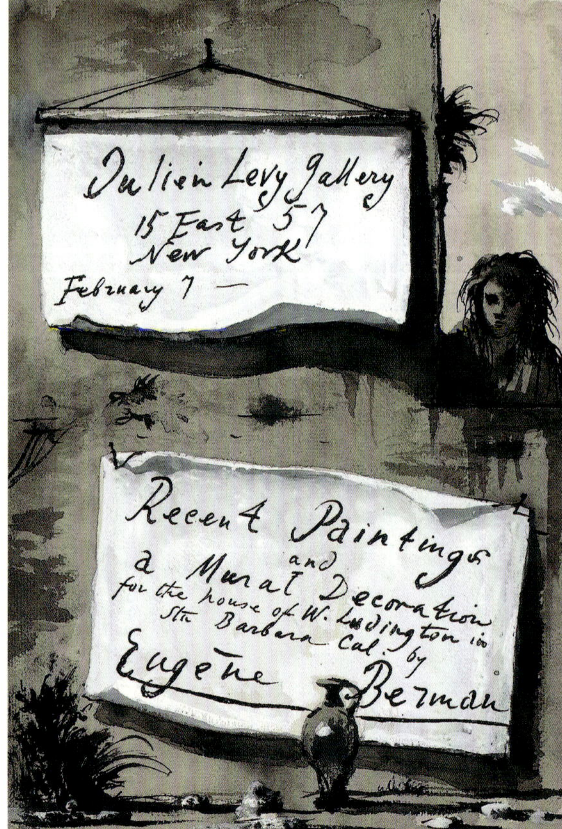

ABOVE: Eugene Berman, programme for the Ballets des Champs-Élysées (calligraphy by Boris Kochno), Paris, June 1950, 31 × 24 cm (12⅛ × 9⅜ in.)
RIGHT: Eugene Berman, designs for the cover of the exhibition catalogue for *Eugène Berman, Recent Paintings and Mural Decoration for the House of Wright Ludington in Santa Barbara, California*, 7–27 February 1939; (above) final design, ink and wash on paper, 29 × 19.2 cm (10⅞ × 7½ in.); (below) ink, wash and gouache on paper, 29 × 19.2 cm (10⅞ × 7½ in.)
OPPOSITE: Eugene Berman, *Trompe-l'œil*, oil on paper, 35 × 30 cm (13⅞ × 11⅞ in.), 1939

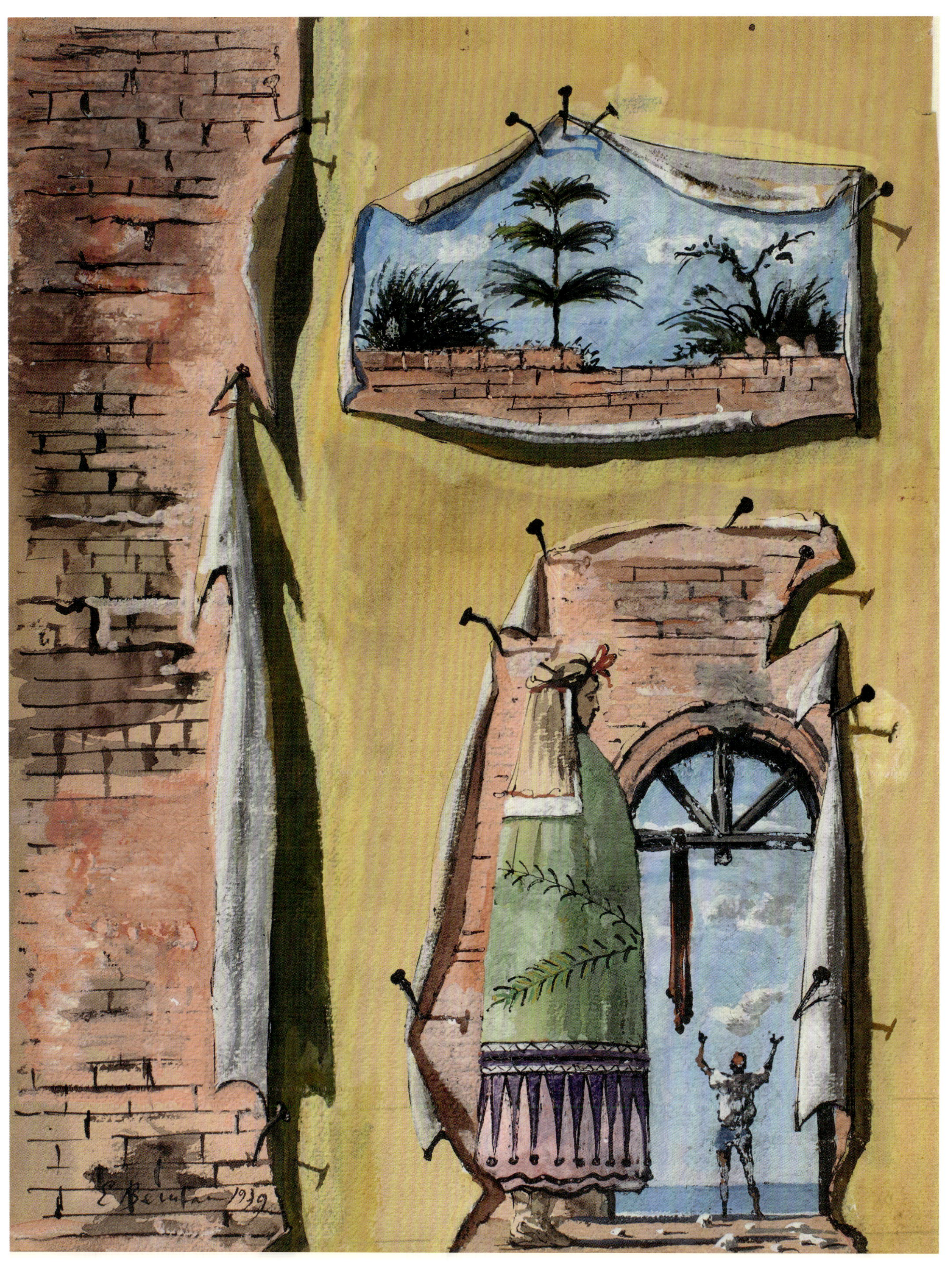

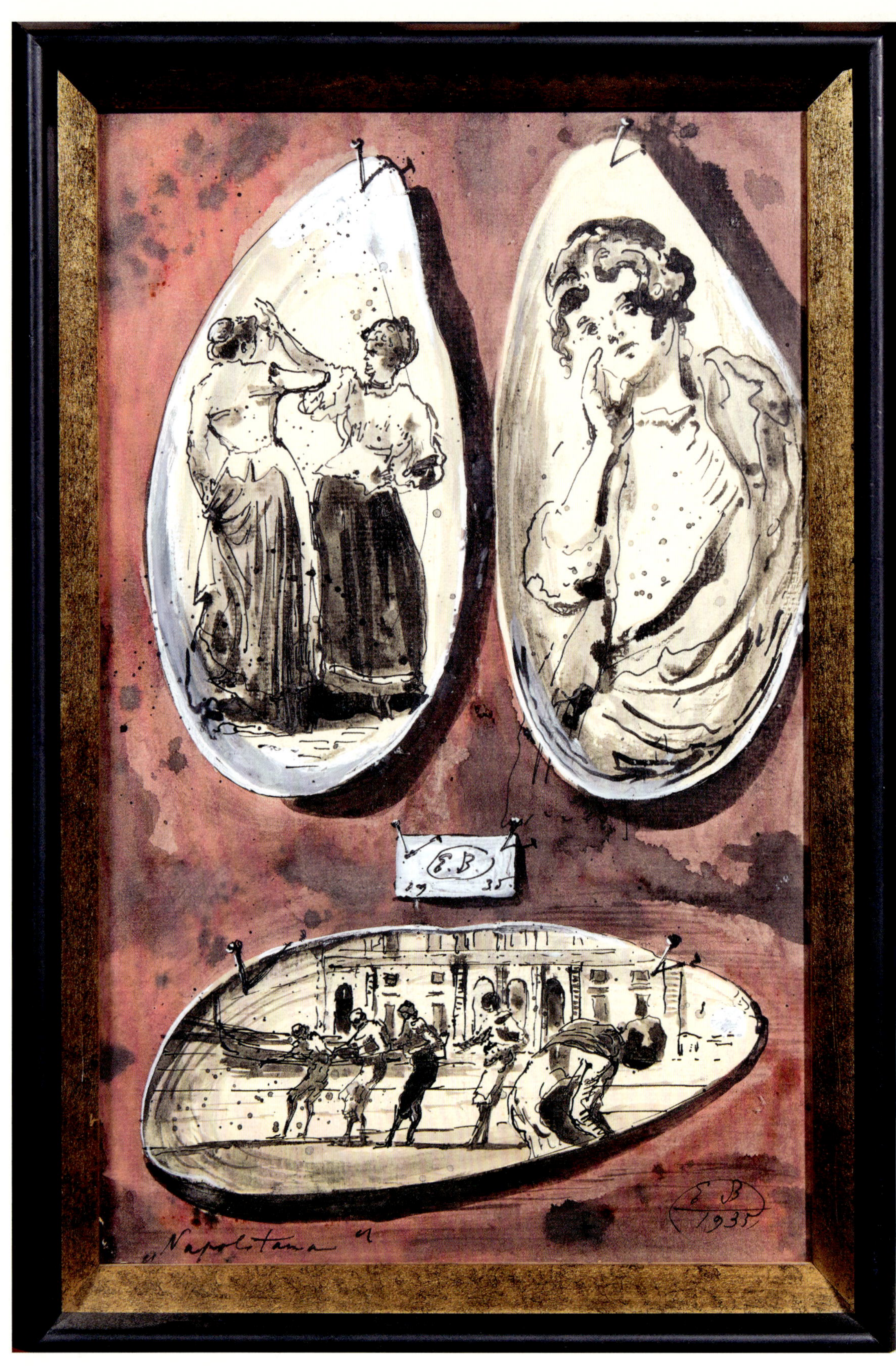

ABOVE: Eugene Berman, *Napolitaines*, ink and watercolour on paper, 45 × 26 cm (17⅝ × 10⅛ in.), 1935
OPPOSITE, CLOCKWISE FROM TOP LEFT: Eugene Berman, *Untitled*, ink on seashell, 13 × 11.5 cm (5⅛ × 4½ in.), 1944; Eugene Berman, *Untitled*, ink on seashell, 12 × 12 cm (4¾ × 4¾ in.), 1944; Eugene Berman, *Untitled*, painted stone, 21 × 15.2 × 15.2 cm (8¼ × 6 × 6 in.), 1945

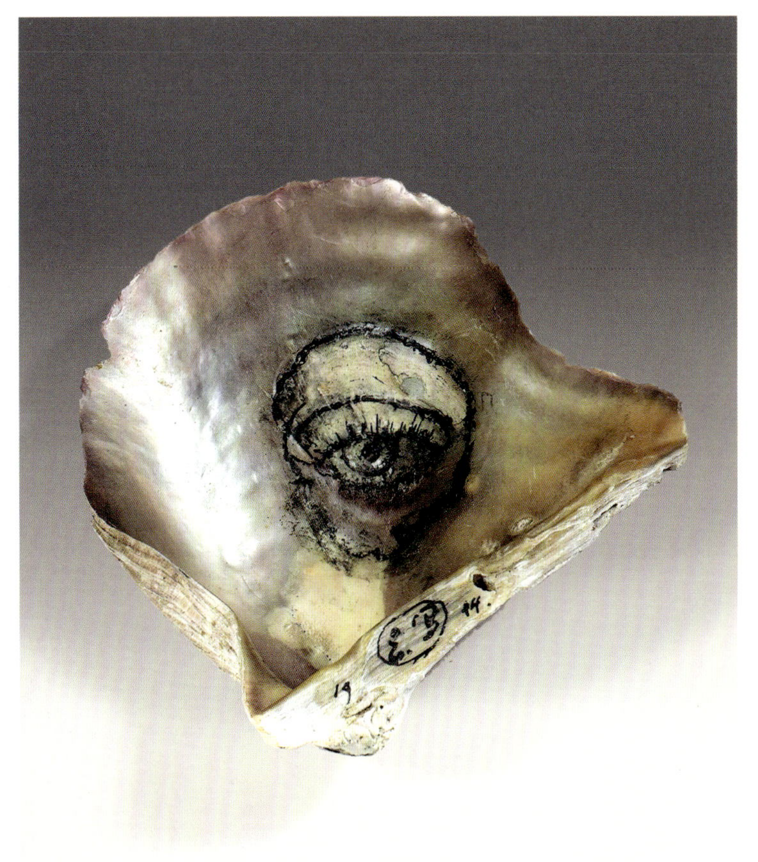

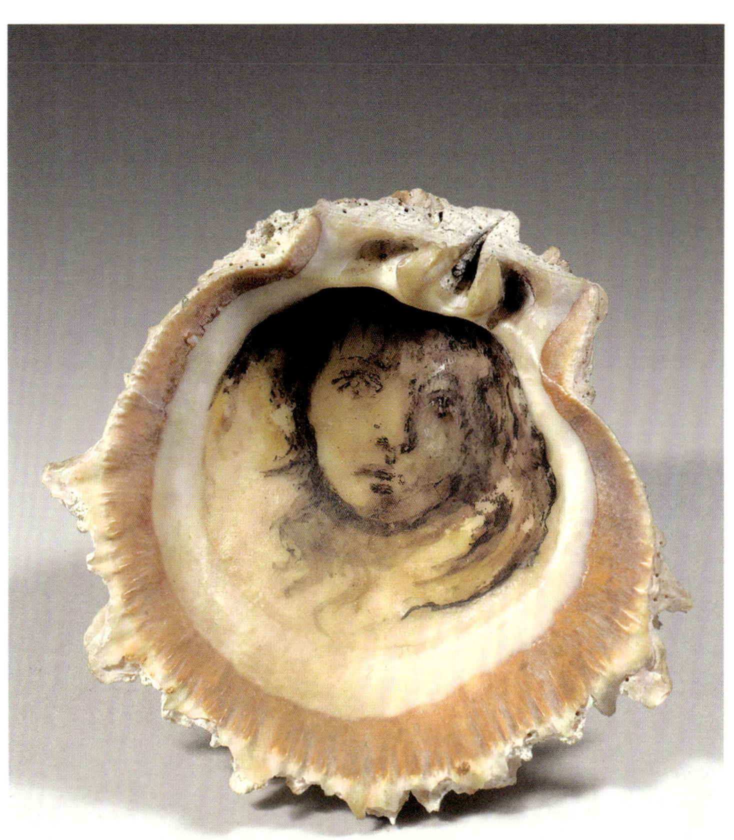

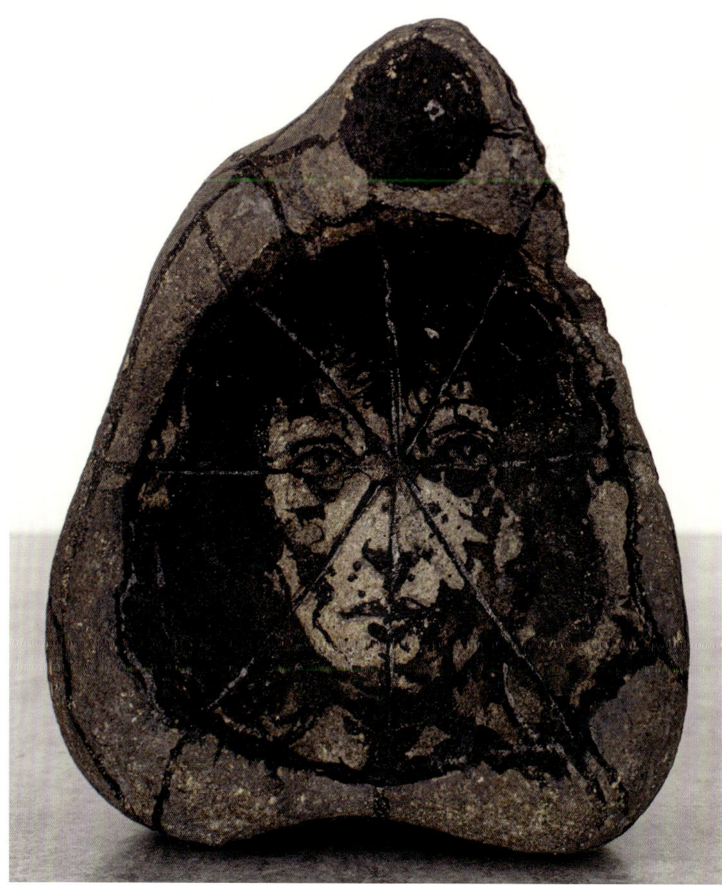

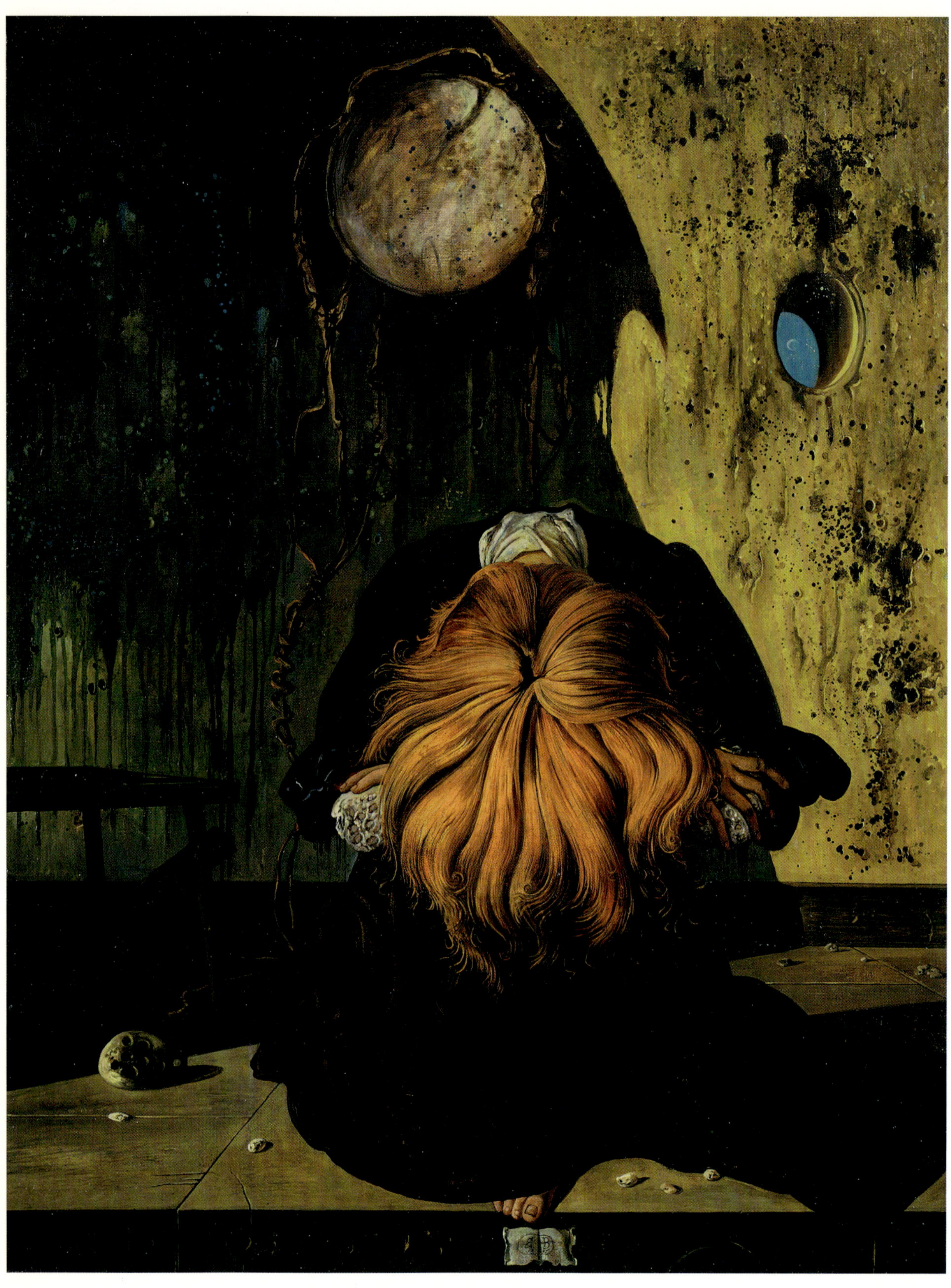

Eugene Berman, *Sunset Medusa*, oil on canvas, 146.4 × 114.3 cm (57⅝ × 45 in.), 1945

Eugene Berman's contact with the United States led to a decisive shift in his work that can be attributed to the visual impact of the landscape that he encountered. The commission for decorative work from Wright Ludington obliged Berman to cross the United States from east to west in 1938, taking him through the vast expanses of Arizona and New Mexico on the way to Santa Barbara in California. This confrontation with arid, unlimited, open spaces, pregnant with dreamlike power, sparked a 'brusque change-over from the Old to the New World' (Julien Levy). His work took on a far more intense register, both formally and chromatically, and its architecture took on a distinctly Latin American air: 'His busy imagination overran those barren "wide open spaces" with projects for architecture of a grandeur seldom seen before – Bermanesque arches and monuments, avenues and vistas, that would conquer the interminable horizon and tame the inhumanity of space.'

This new-found grandeur was complemented by a radical transformation in Berman's palette. His colours became the exact opposite of those of his earlier works: more dense and heavily saturated, with dramatic contrasts, sometimes pushing the limits of dissonance, as if subject to the searing light of these new lands. Soby summed up the effect somewhat drily: 'Strong impact of the brilliant color of the West, notably the Arizona desert, upon his painting.' (This remarkable epiphany was similar to the one experienced by Tchelitchew in another completely different landscape.)

Berman was thus laying the foundations for a 'flamboyant' period that would continue into the mid-1950s. Faced with this desolate barrenness, so different from the soothing plains of Italy, he introduced imposing figures, seemingly trapped by the endless vastness all around them. Two works from 1938, variations on a nocturnal theme – *Offering to the Night* and *Sentinels of the Night* – featured isolated subjects with their backs turned away from the viewer, set against an arid backdrop and a pale twilight sky. By 1941, and the enigmatic *Lorelei in Oregon*, such figures suddenly took on a dominant role, shrouded in opulent clothes and a dense mass of hair, lost in the contemplation of a horizon or an object that they themselves blocked from view. These were transitional bodies, on the border between two spaces, hiding as

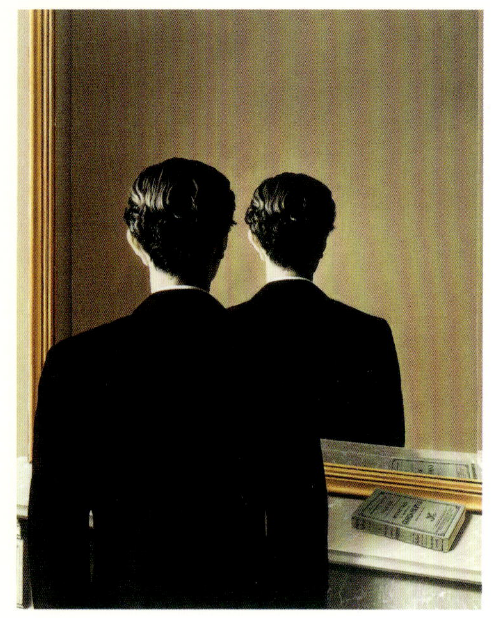

much as they revealed. They were the very incarnations of enigma. Berman was making his own version of one of the leitmotifs of Mannerist painting, and Parmigianino's in particular: the 'intermediary figure'. This is a subject in the foreground, often half-length, seen from the back, who serves as a nexus between the field of vision of the picture and that of the viewer, on whom it casts a kind of opaque reflection. (This format was used to spectacular effect by Magritte in his 1937 portrait of Edward James, appropriately entitled *Not to Be Reproduced*.)

Berman actively sought to avoid any communication, any dialogue, any exchange of looks with his subjects. His heroines – as in *Nike* (1943), *Medusa's Corner* (1943), *Sunset Medusa* (1945) – may sometimes face the viewer, but even then they are broken, folded in on themselves, masked by a mass of hair, isolated in their suffering, indifferent to their surroundings. Levy perceptively evoked an analogy with the poignant *Derelitta*, attributed to Botticelli, an androgynous figure (identified in 1940 by Edgar Wind as Mardocheus, from the Book of Esther), weeping into their hands, face hidden by hair, amid tattered clothes in front of a closed door. Caravaggio's *Penitent Magdalene* (1597, Galleria Doria Pamphilj) also comes to mind, but the most obvious source is surely *Malinconia* by Domenico Fetti (1589–1623), a reworking of Dürer's *Melencolia I* that is a veritable Berman *avant la lettre*. It was widely seen after its completion in 1618, and Berman would have been able to see both the version in the Louvre and that in the Accademia in Venice. Here, the protagonist sits immobile, in a dress with sculptural folds, the very image of an endless and purposeless wait, of withdrawal in the face of disaster, of the apprehension of a catastrophe as threatening as it is invisible. 'Just how much of despair and how much of hope there is in this figure is hard to ascertain. She seems somehow unresolved, waiting. Very soon she fills the whole picture frame, playing the heroine of a modern mythology in high tragic vein. *Proserpina* when she is in the dark and waiting for the light, *Muse of the Western World* when she is most glamorous, *Andromeda* abandoned and enchained, *Cassandra* as she faces the burning of her world.'

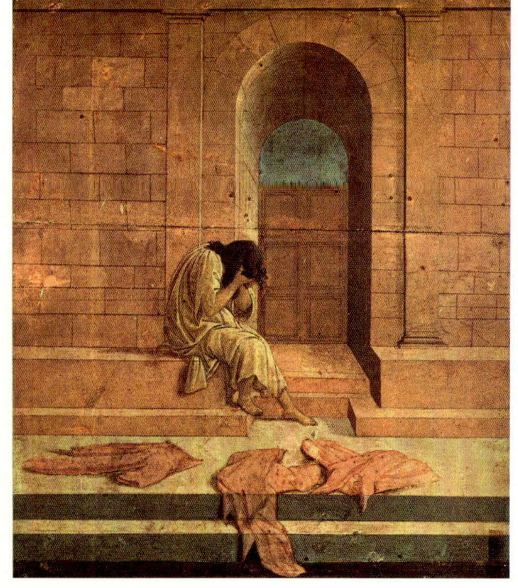

TOP: René Magritte, *La Reproduction interdite* (*Not to Be Reproduced*; portrait of Edward James), oil on canvas, 81.3 × 65 cm (32 × 26 in.), 1937
ABOVE: Sandro Botticelli, *La Derelitta* (*The Abandoned One*), tempera on panel, 47 × 43 cm (18½ × 16⅞ in.), *c.* 1495

OPPOSITE, ABOVE: Caravaggio, *La Maddalena* (*Penitent Magdalene*), oil on canvas, 122.5 × 98.5 cm (48⅛ × 38¾ in.), 1597
OPPOSITE, BELOW: Domenico Fetti, *La Malinconia* (*Melancholy*), oil on canvas, 171 × 128 cm (67⅜ × 50⅜ in.), 17th century

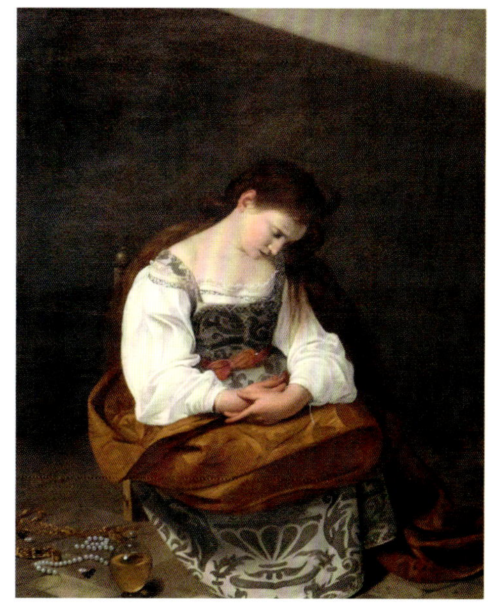

The emergence of these various female characters in Berman's work can be linked with the appearance in his life of the actress Ona Munson (1903–1955), whom he painted in 1942 (*Night Music, Imaginary Portrait of Ona Munson*). He went on to design the decor for her Hollywood home (photographed by *Vogue* in 1945), before marrying her 'in Igor Stravinsky's living room in Hollywood' in 1950. Munson is primarily known today for her role in *Gone with the Wind* and for her freewheeling and tumultuous love life. She met a tragic end: she committed suicide in New York at the age of fifty-one. And it befell Berman to discover her body on the afternoon of 11 February 1955, along with a chillingly laconic note: 'This is the only way I know to be free again... Please don't follow me.' In a sad overlap between art and life, the woman whom Berman had ceaselessly examined, and whose appearance he had modified to sublimate her into an icon of despair, finally chose to disappear by becoming the culmination of the melancholy that he had used to portray her.

Julien Levy considered *Proserpine II*, a painting from 1945/46, to be the most accomplished of Berman's series featuring muses of desolation. It is striking for its unusual treatment of the pictorial surface, with respect to both its materials and its representational devices. (The same is true of the *Imaginary Portrait of Isabelle d'Este in her Studio* from the same years and, above all, the splendid *Miserere* of 1945, in which the female figure is in three-quarter profile but nevertheless avoids the viewer's gaze; she stands out against a blind oculus that forms an unearthly halo edged with a profusion of stalactites.)

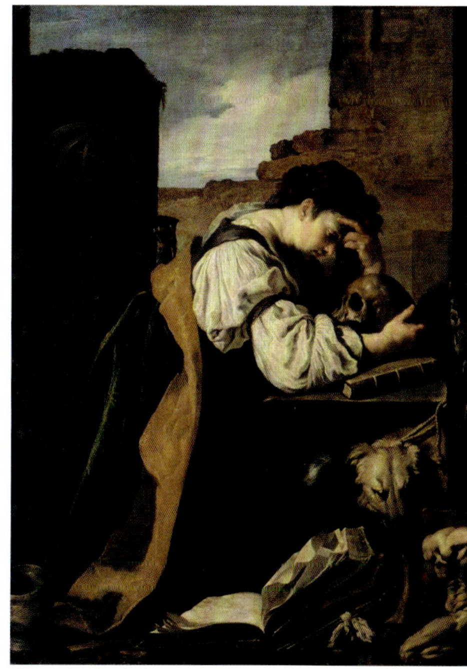

The surface of these pictures seems to be literally riddled with perforations (for Levy, it evoked 'the shrapnel-punctured architecture of the canvases during the years of World War II'). This is another trompe-l'œil effect – comparable to the broken-glass effect relished by Boilly, and sometimes used by Berman – but Berman unfurls it in an unusual way. It is the space of the picture itself, impalpable and abstract, that seems to be under attack. In a perverse game within a game, Berman pushes the limits of the credibility essential to trompe-l'œil by applying it to an object that is totally implausible: an invisible film stretched

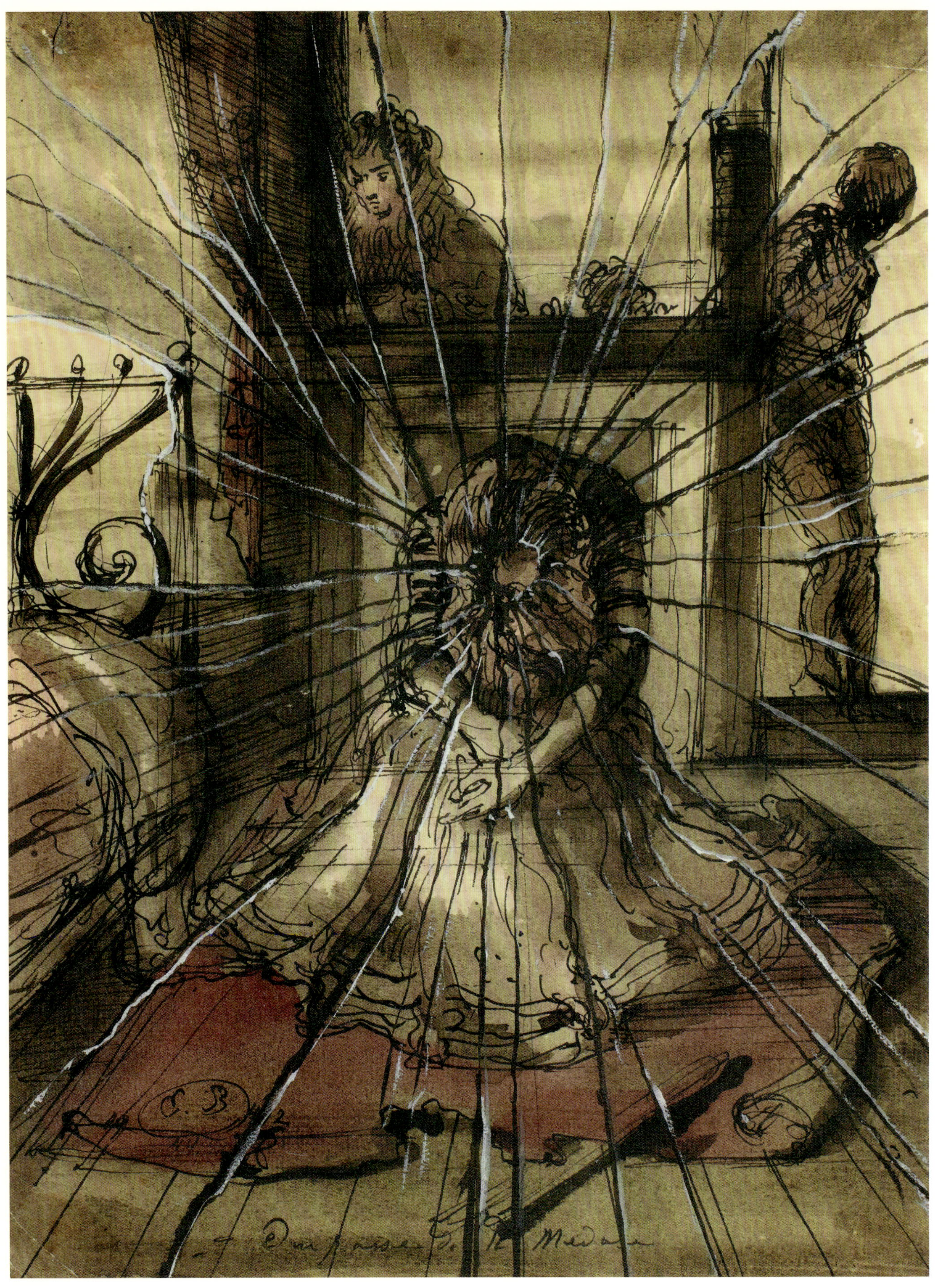

ABOVE: Eugene Berman, study for *Impasse of the Medusa*, ink, watercolour and wash on paper, 57 × 46 cm (22⅜ × 18⅛ in.), *c.* 1940

OPPOSITE: Eugene Berman, *Medusa*, oil on canvas, 30 × 40 cm (11⅞ × 15¾ in.), 1968

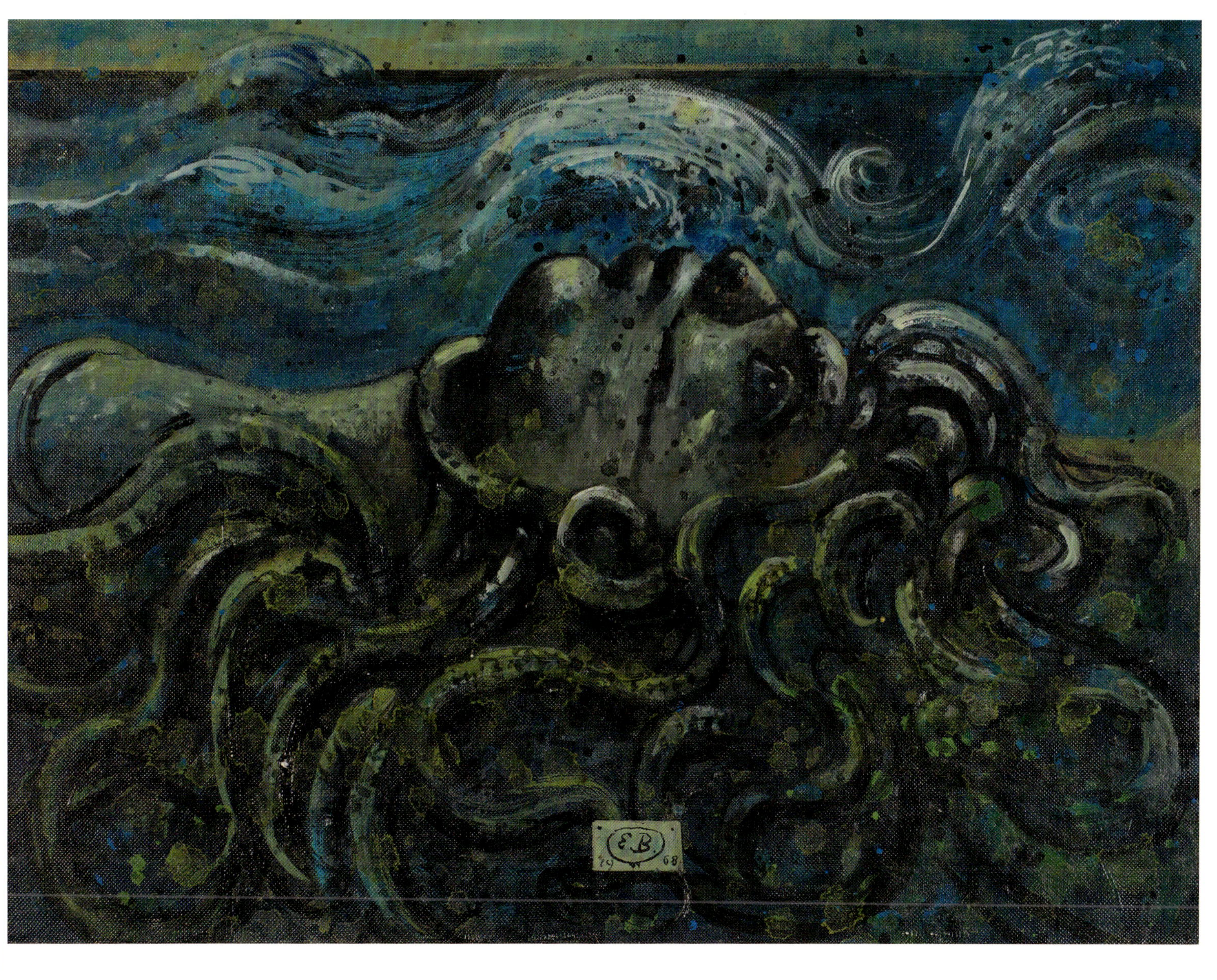

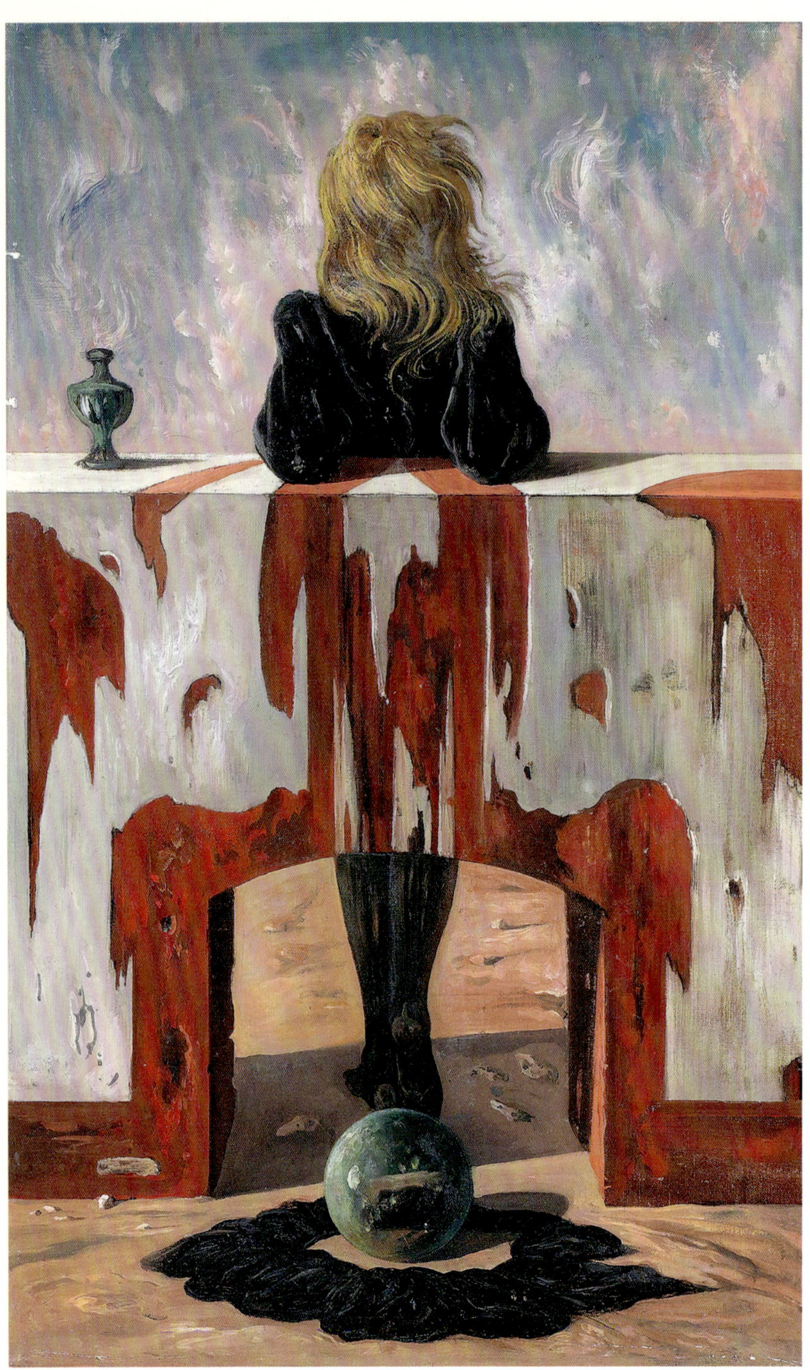

ABOVE: Eugene Berman, *La Petite Fortune*,
oil on canvas, 61 × 38 cm (24 × 15 in.), 1942
OPPOSITE: Eugene Berman, *Medusa's Corner*,
oil on canvas, 147.3 × 116.8 cm (58 × 46 in.), 1943

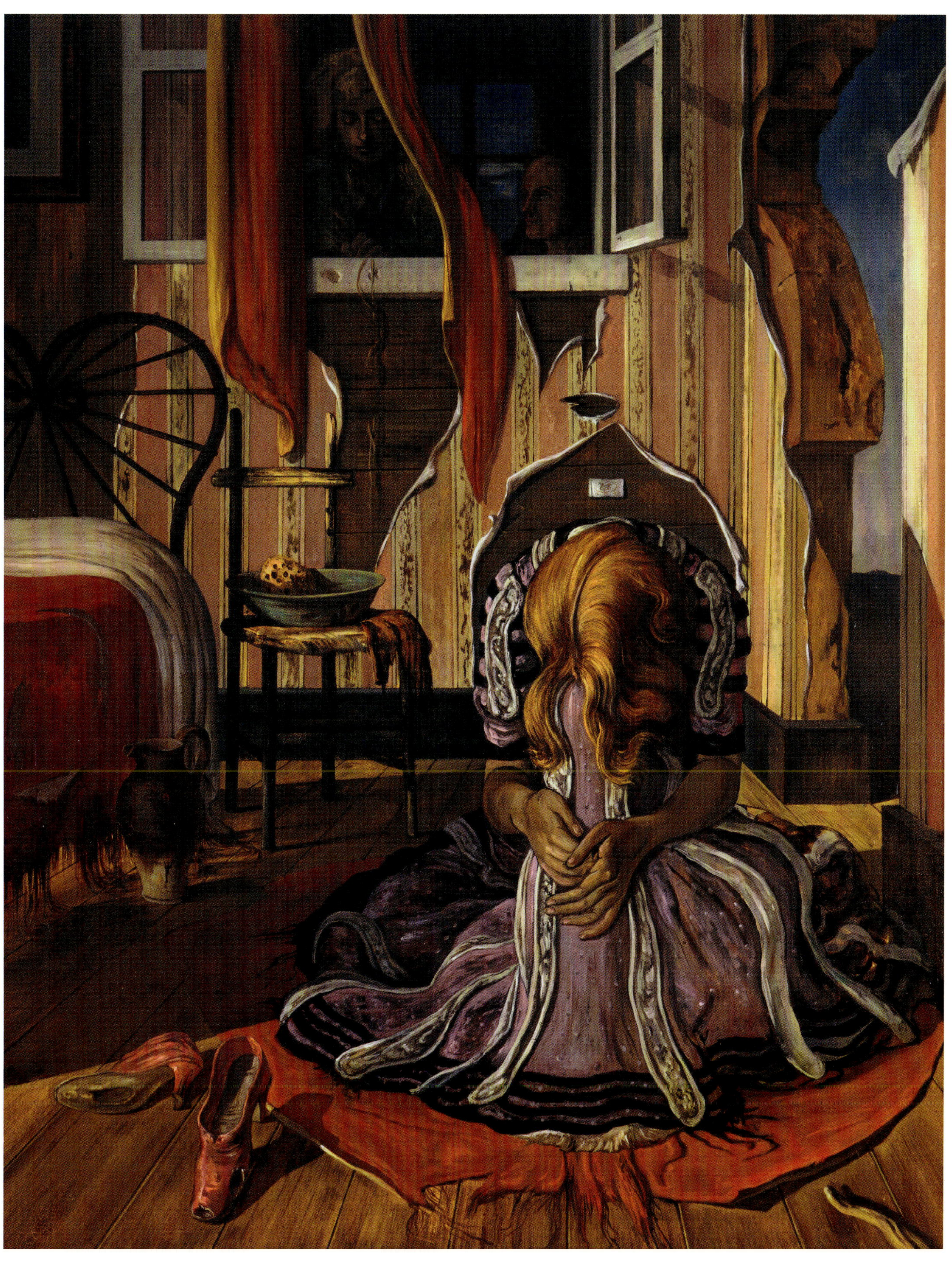

between the viewer and the image. That most perfect of illusionist techniques is here being used to uncover the fictitious transparency of space, in a serious game that is both cerebral and visual.

The end result is a mineralized necrosis, a depiction of a petrified world. These are truly Medusa pictures, capable of unflinchingly rooting the viewer to the spot. Levy saw Berman returning to his early days in these works and, once again, we find a device that is seemingly dictated by circumstances endowed with a new aesthetic purpose. One of the aspects 'common to all the neo-romantic painters', wrote Levy, 'was a persistent interest in fundamental mechanics of the painter's craft. They each had tried out various new media, such as pigments mixed with sand, Duco, wax, or even coffee grounds mixed with roofer's paint. Berman's particular contribution to these experiments was mothered by necessity: he could not afford many fine new canvases and the quantity of pigment needed to build the desired impasto of heavy under-painting, so he bought valueless old paintings at the Flea Market, repaired the canvases and primed them. [...] The texture of the earlier paint roughened the surface with lumps, lines, and ambiguous configurations which furnished provocative counterpoint to the shapes and perspectives of Berman's own composition.' This counterpoint between the two-dimensional surface of a canvas and the illusion of a third dimension never ceased to fascinate Berman, and it underlies the pictures 'invaded by deliberate spots, tears, and painted holes' that he would produce twenty years later.

Along the same lines, in 1945 Berman started creating a series of *Divertissements*, three-dimensional picture boxes in which found objects blend into the painted surface, in a new twist on the trompe-l'œil. The addition of organic matter – usually seashells – blurred still further the borders of illusion, as the 'natural' objects echoed the illusory mineral characteristics of the painted elements. (Back in 1939, Berman had already dreamed up a trompe-l'œil in three dimensions, but in the more traditional form of a cabinet simulating an architectural ruin: it had been commissioned by Leo Castelli for his first foray into the art market, an exhibition of Surrealist furniture and other objects that opened the René Drouin Gallery, on the Place Vendôme, in which Castelli was a partner.)

The 1940s were boom years for Berman in the United States. His admirers and buyers on the East Coast were joined by counterparts on the other side of the country; he was equally celebrated by aesthetes from Boston and New York as he was by Hollywood circles

OPPOSITE, LEFT: Eugene Berman, cover design for *Town and Country*, watercolour and ink on paper, 35 × 28 cm (13⅞ × 11 in.), 1939
OPPOSITE, RIGHT: Eugene Berman, *Town and Country*, 1939

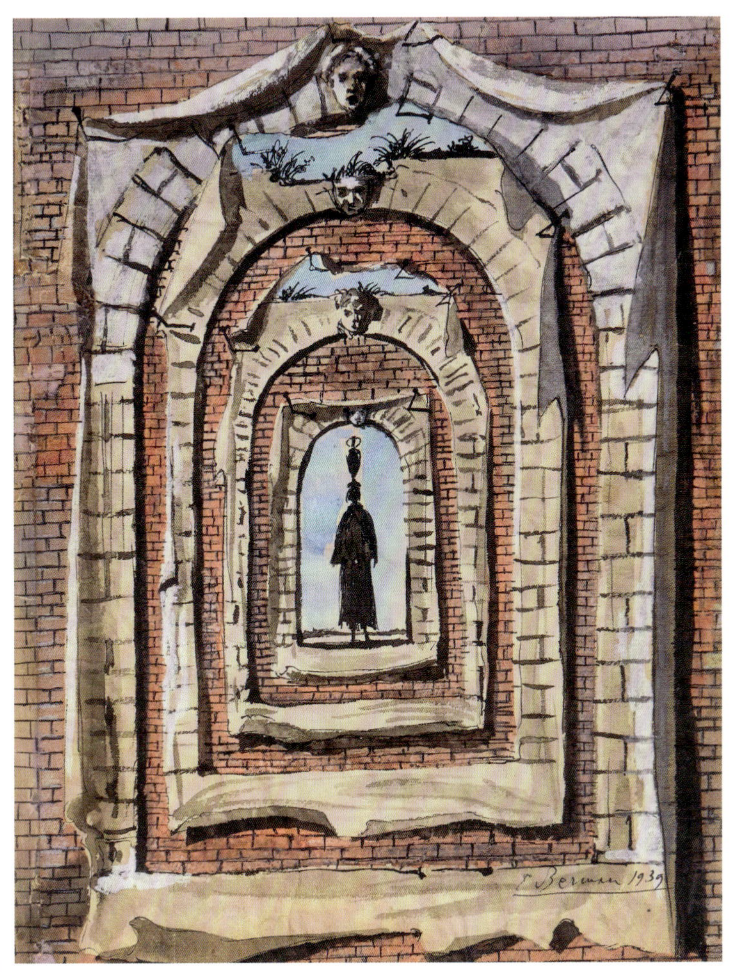

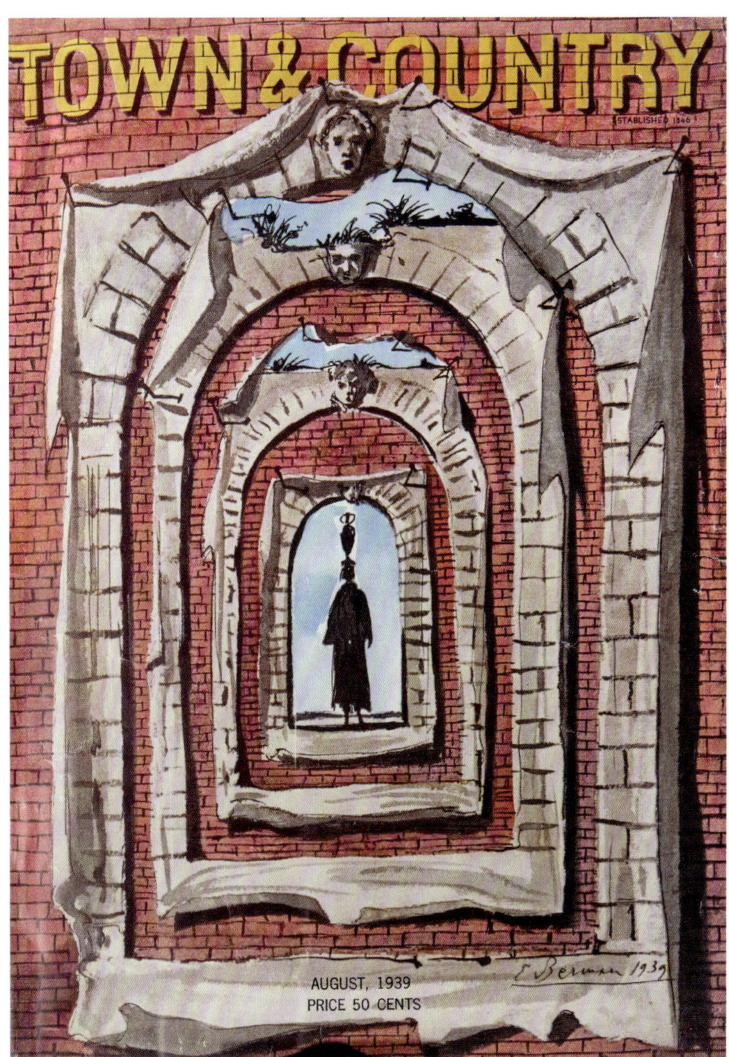

(through Ona Munson) and European émigrés in California (through Stravinsky). His commissions included work for theatre and opera, decor for private houses, and numerous covers for the major fashion and home decoration magazines, such as *Vogue* and *Town and Country*. Although Berman's magazine work never attained the astonishing richness and virtuosity of Bérard's ventures in this field, it was nonetheless often remarkable. And it further illustrates a shared tenet of the Neo-Romantics: their rejection of the opposition between 'high' art and applied (or commercial) art. This stance damaged their reputation in the post-war years, until the balance shifted again in the late 1960s, largely thanks to the pioneering work of Andy Warhol, which not only played with the tension between high and low art but also used it as subject matter.

This growing recognition undoubtedly prompted Berman's decision to apply for American citizenship in 1944. This step also

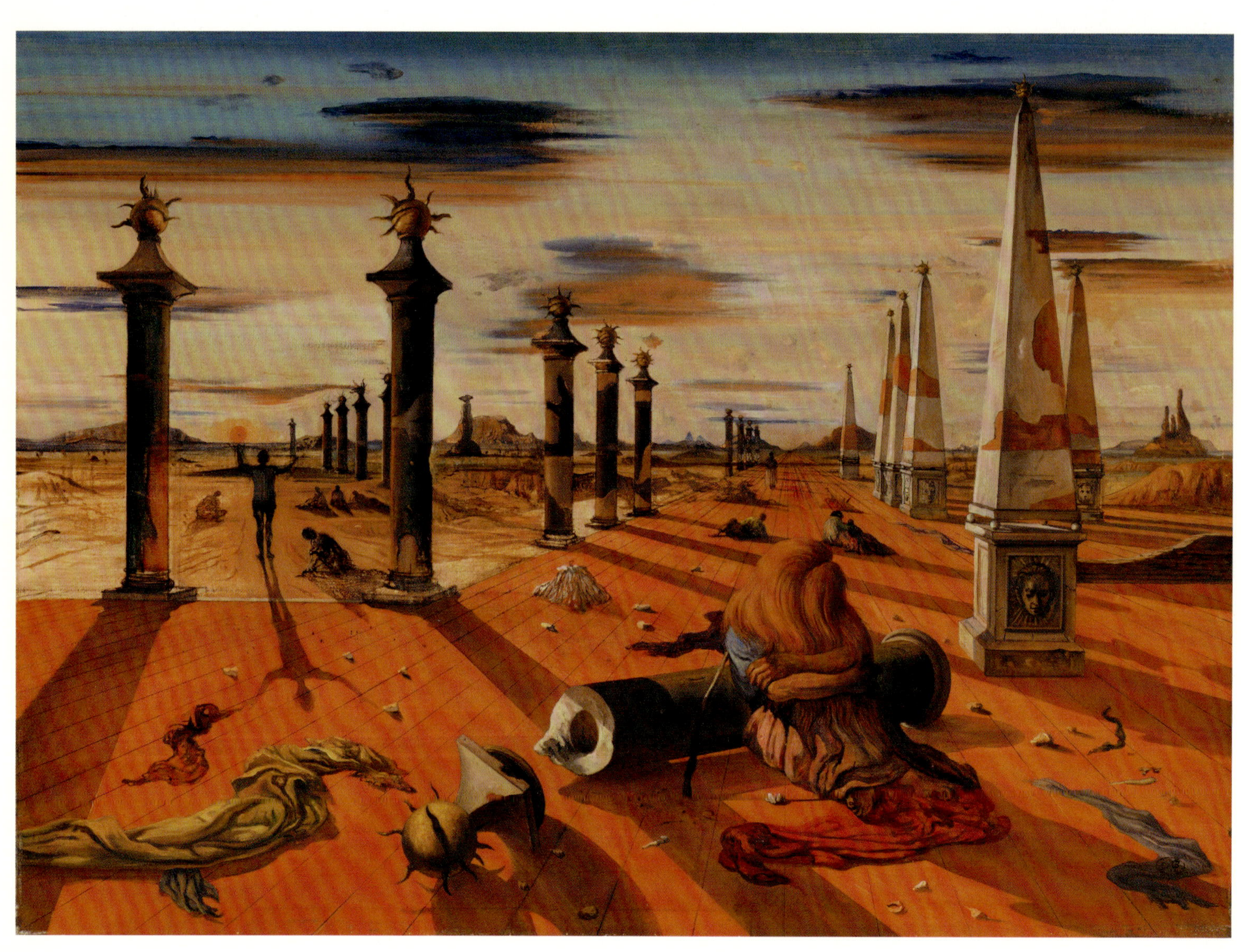

ABOVE: Eugene Berman, *View in Perspective of a Perfect Sunset*, oil on canvas, 91.6 × 127 cm (36 1/16 × 50 in.), 1941
OPPOSITE: Eugene Berman, *Noblissima Visione*, oil on canvasboard, 50.8 × 40.6 cm (20 × 16 in.), 1941

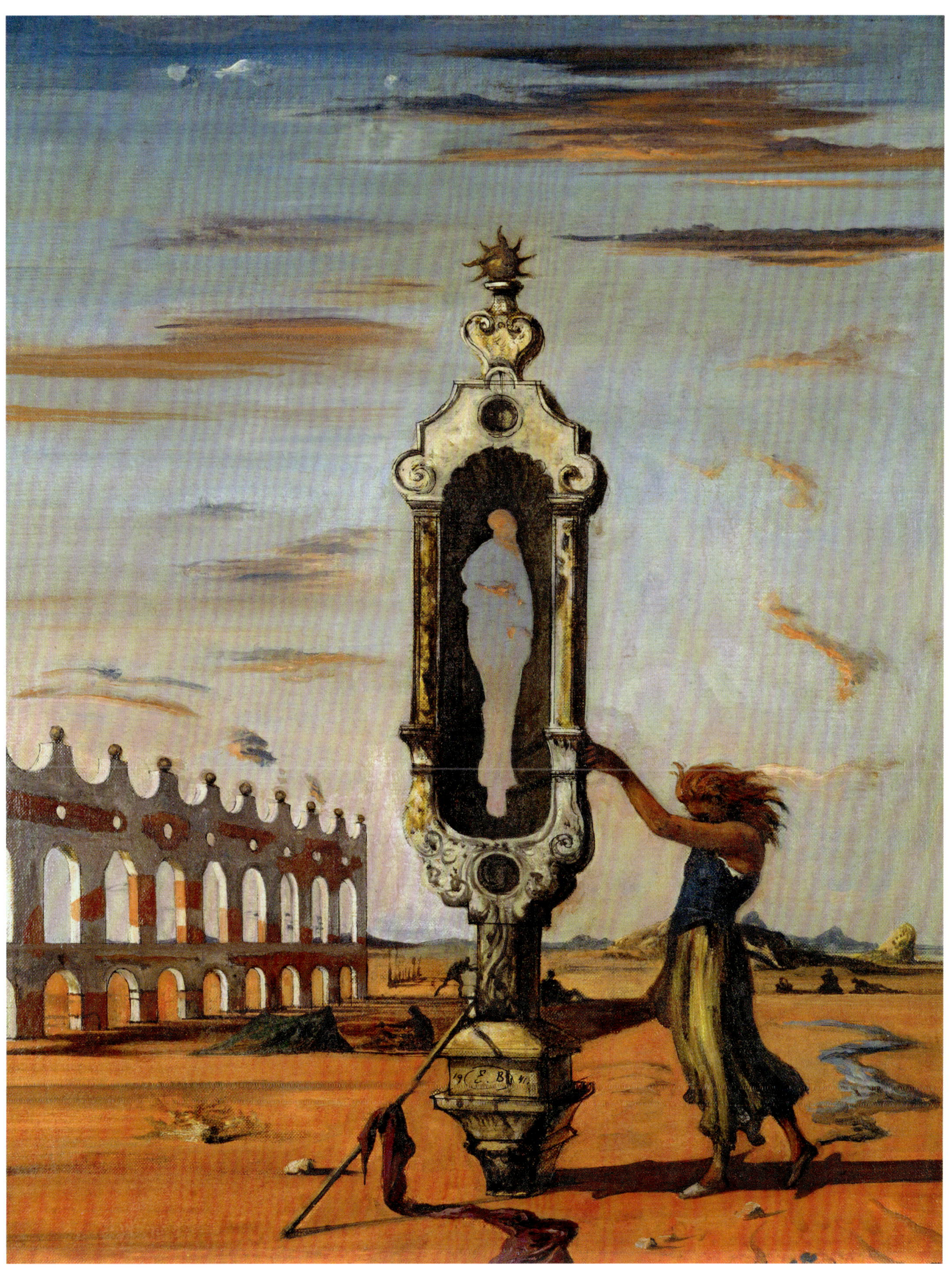

represented an acknowledgment of his debt to the country that had enabled him to take refuge from the Nazi persecution of Jews. Berman grasped the opportunities on offer with unremitting energy: in the first half of the 1940s alone, he exhibited, successively, in Boston, Chicago, St Louis, San Francisco, Cincinnati, New York, Los Angeles and Santa Barbara. The year 1947 was even more triumphant: his theatre work was the subject of a major exhibition at the Museum of Modern Art in New York; he received two grants from the Guggenheim Foundation for research trips to Mexico (which would give rise to a series of pictures that ushered in a new phase in his work); he was given a first solo show by Julien Levy; and he started an association with the Knoedler Gallery in New York that would last until the mid-1960s. All the while, he also continued with his work for theatre and opera.

After Ona Munson's death in 1955, however, Berman decided to leave the United States, and he only returned on a few brief occasions (most notably to renew his citizenship papers in 1963). He eventually settled in Rome in 1958, while maintaining a steady rhythm of exhibitions and stage work. Berman now complemented his network of American art dealers with prestigious European galleries, such as the Obelisco and the Medusa in Rome, as well as starting a collaboration with Alexandre Iolas, who would exhibit Berman's work throughout the rest of his life in Milan, Rome, Madrid and Geneva. By now, Berman had also acquired sufficient means to indulge his passion for collecting. More and more rooms in his home were taken over by Roman, Etruscan, Egyptian, Coptic, African and Pre-Columbian pieces that he had bought on his travels and visits to antique shops.

Berman's selection of objects – masks, ex-votos, funerary urns, fragments of antique sculptures – and their striking arrangement, reminiscent of old cabinets of curiosities, clearly establish his collecting activity as an extension of his work, or as a pursuit of the same goals by different means. Berman underlined the importance that he accorded to his collection, and his view of it as a single, far-ranging composition, by donating it to the Italian state. It is now preserved in Civita Castellana, near Rome.

The underlying unity of Berman's various activities was similarly demonstrated by visits that he made firstly to Egypt, in 1964, then to Libya two years later, as these countries not only inspired new thematic series, they also provided him with countless objects for his collection. The Knoedler Gallery in New York put on an exhibition of work inspired by the first trip, appropriately entitled *Return from Egypt*, in March–April 1965. This event sparked a rare declaration of intent (equally applicable to the paintings derived from his subsequent stay in Tripolitania and Leptis Magna in 1966): 'Don't search in "my" Egypt [for] any realistic intent or representation, even if at first sight some of my subjects may appear to be so familiar as to approach a truthful representation of existing places or monuments, easily identified by the beholder. This is the catch: one must not always trust in appearances, but rather look beyond. The more certain paintings seem real (and this is what interests me particularly in the works of other artists), the more likely they are the complex and cunning blend of fantasy, memory, of pure invention and of dreams. [...] These new images of Egypt are therefore in essence of their creative impulse not different from my previous work and continue the series of my imaginary Mexican landscapes, of the rocks and deserts of Arizona, of the columns of the Greek temples of Paestum and of Sicily, of the Roman or Parthenopean amphitheaters and of the pure architectural inventions of my earlier works.'

The catalogue for Berman's very last exhibition, organized by Iolas in 1972, illustrated this principle, and it can be read as a personal anthology of his subjects and motifs. There was a return to his rough surfaces, further damaged by trompe-l'œil effects in a work such as *The Death of Caravaggio* (1970–71). In other cases (*La Vida es Sueño*, 1970; *Landscape with Etruscan Tombs*, 1970; and, above all, *The Tempest*, 1970–71), the viewer was separated from the image by a strange, dense curtain of plant stalks, denoted by scratches or thick networks on the picture's surface. Meanwhile, *African Medusa* (1968), *The Shadow of Medusa* (1969) and *Medusa at Twilight* (1969) presented the latest versions of a figure that had come to truly obsess Berman after the death of Ona Munson: a face that could be made of stone as much as of flesh, with an alluring and deadly gaze, reigning over a desolate world of desert shores, of ruins and fragments. This emblem of solitude and despair could serve as an emblem for Berman's entire body of work.

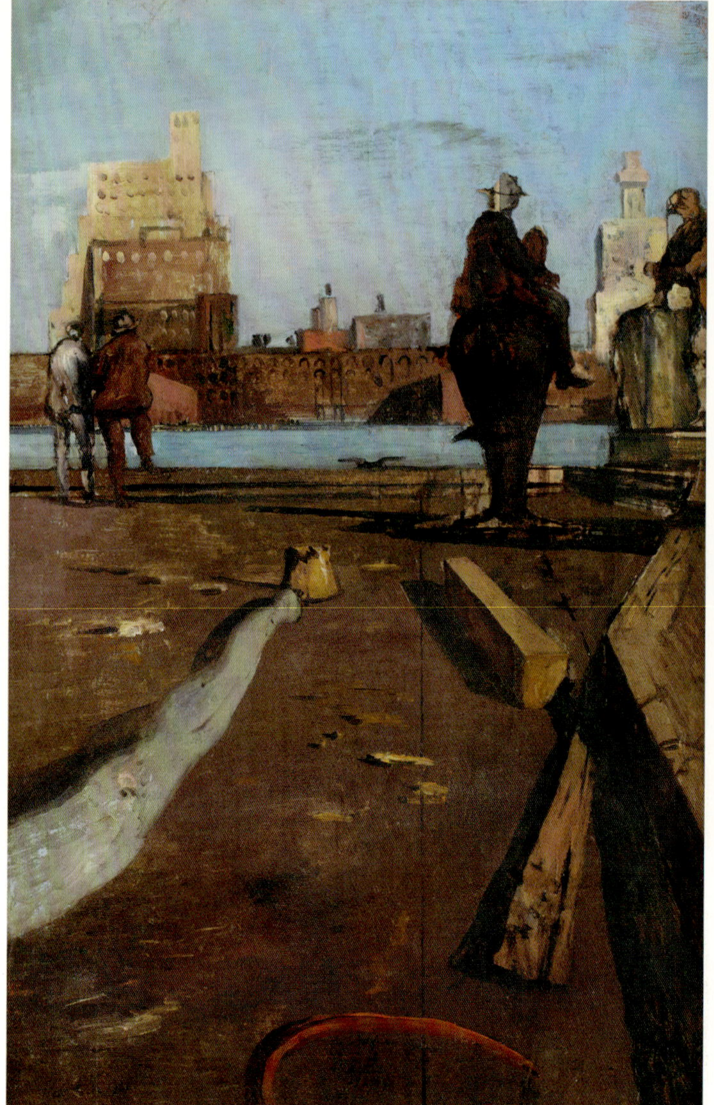

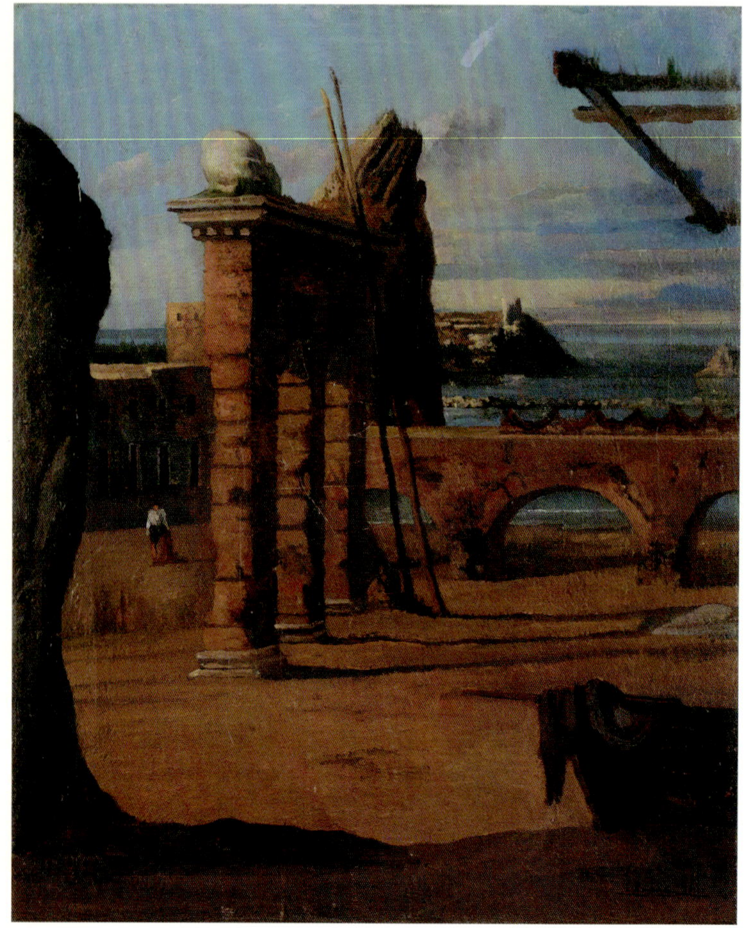

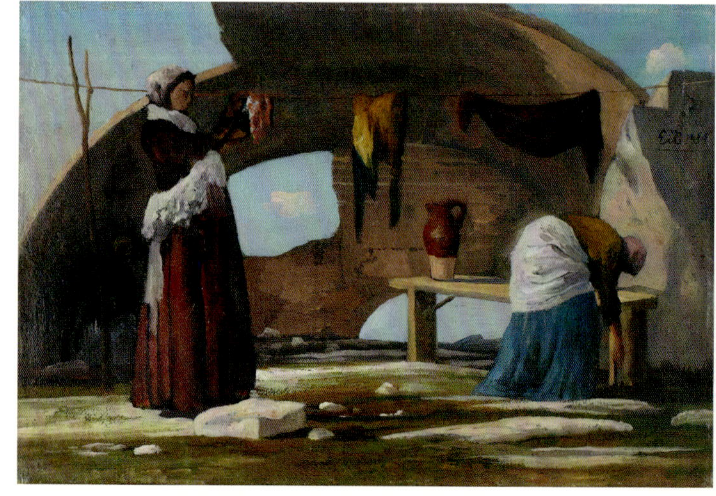

CLOCKWISE, FROM ABOVE: Eugene Berman, *Landscape*, oil on canvas, 65 × 53 cm (25½ × 20⅞ in.), n.d.; Eugene Berman, *Cityscape*, oil on canvas, 90 × 70 cm (35⅜ × 27½ in.), n.d.; Eugene Berman, *Scene in Ruins*, oil on canvas, 27 × 41 cm (10⅝ × 16⅛ in.), 1934

OPPOSITE, CLOCKWISE FROM ABOVE: Eugene Berman, *Landscape of Desolation*, oil on canvas, 71 × 101 cm (28 × 39¾ in.), 1936–37; Eugene Berman, *Collapsed Landscape at Dusk*, oil on canvas, 49 × 72 cm (19¼ × 28¼ in.), 1934; Eugene Berman, *Garden*, watercolour on paper, 23 × 17 cm (9 × 6⅝ in.), 1937

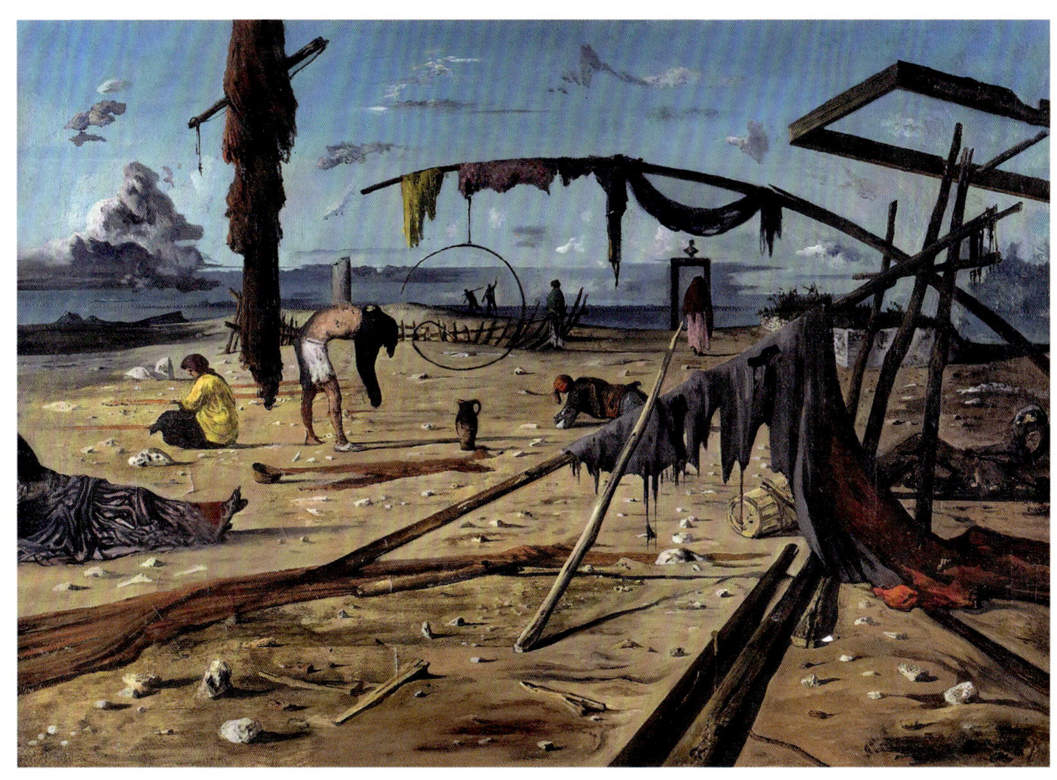

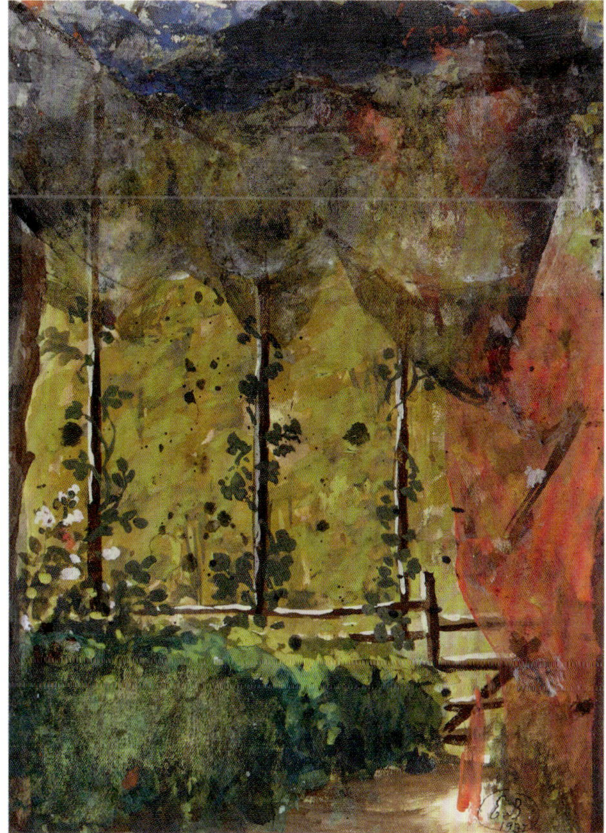

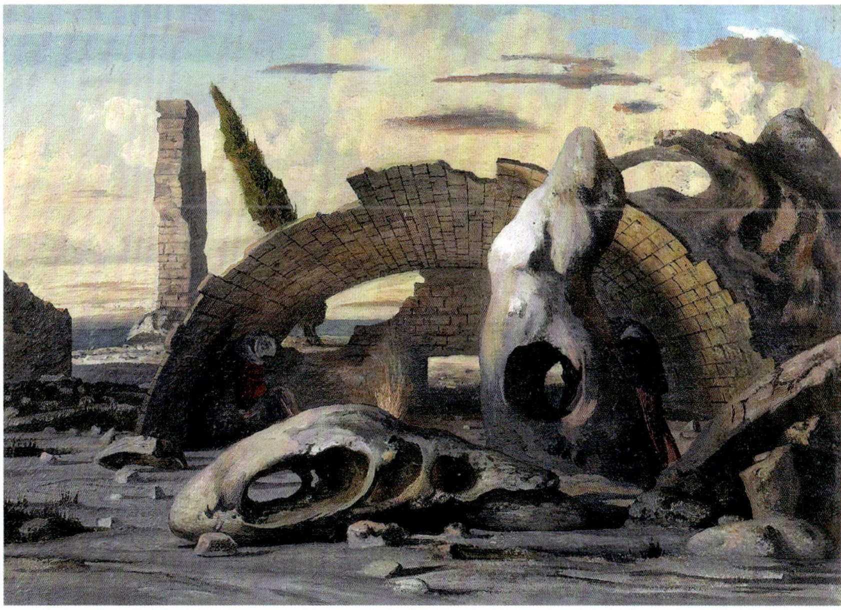

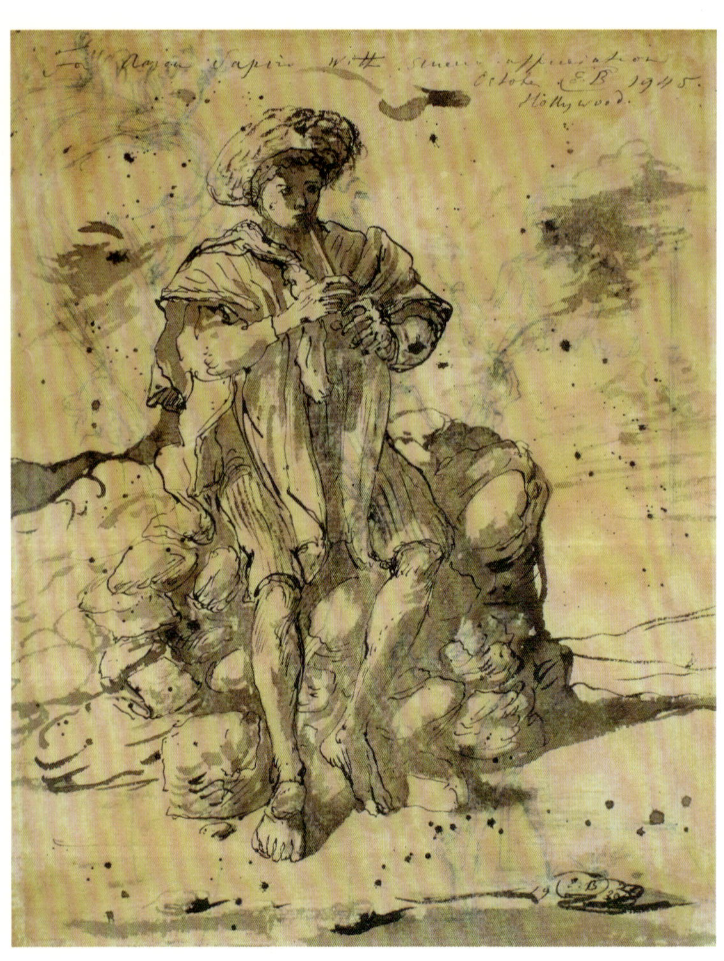

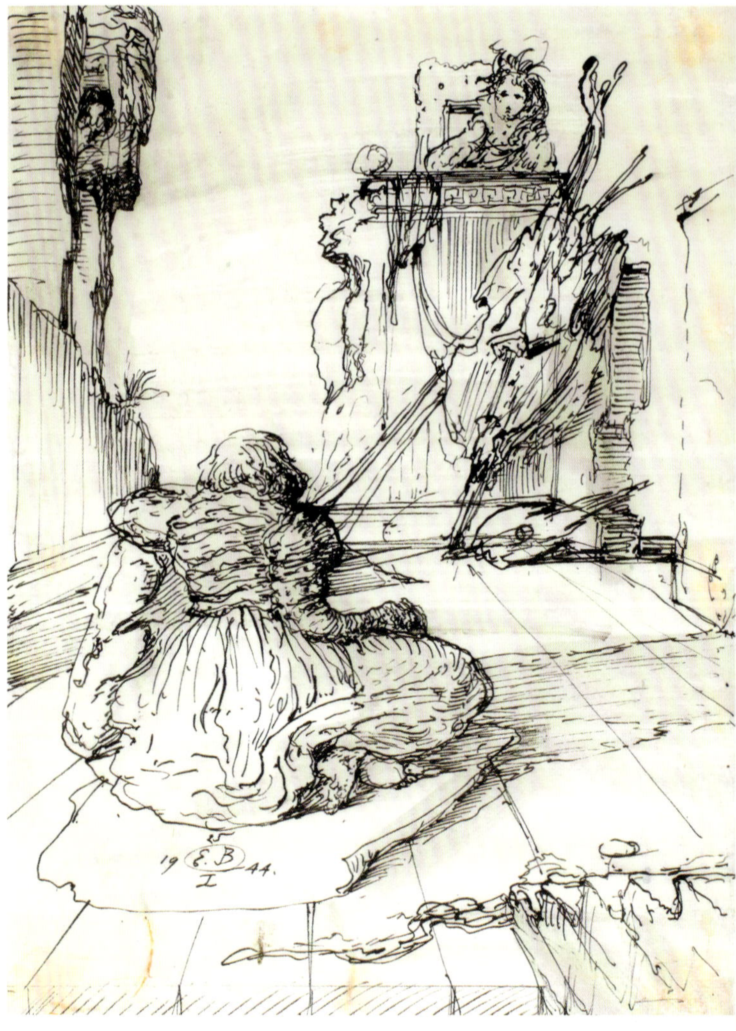

OPPOSITE, CLOCKWISE FROM TOP LEFT: Eugene Berman, *Indian Landscape*, ink and watercolour on paper, 21 × 28 cm (8¼ × 28 in.), 1941; Eugene Berman, *La Mozza*, ink and watercolour on paper, 18 × 23 cm (7 × 9 in.), 1940; Eugene Berman, *The Masque of the Red Death*, ink, gouache and watercolour on paper, illustrations for the story by Edgar Allan Poe, 31 × 22 cm (12⅛ × 8⅝ in.), 1945; Eugene Berman, *Green Hunting Man*, ink, oil and gouache on paper, 30 × 23 cm (11⅞ × 9 in.), 1941

ABOVE, LEFT: Eugene Berman, *Flute Player*, pen ink and wash on prepared paper, 27 × 22 cm (10⅝ × 8⅝ in.), 1930, with dedication in 1945
ABOVE, RIGHT: Eugene Berman, *Caprice*, pen and wash drawing on prepared paper, 36 × 27 cm (14⅛ × 10⅝ in.), 1944

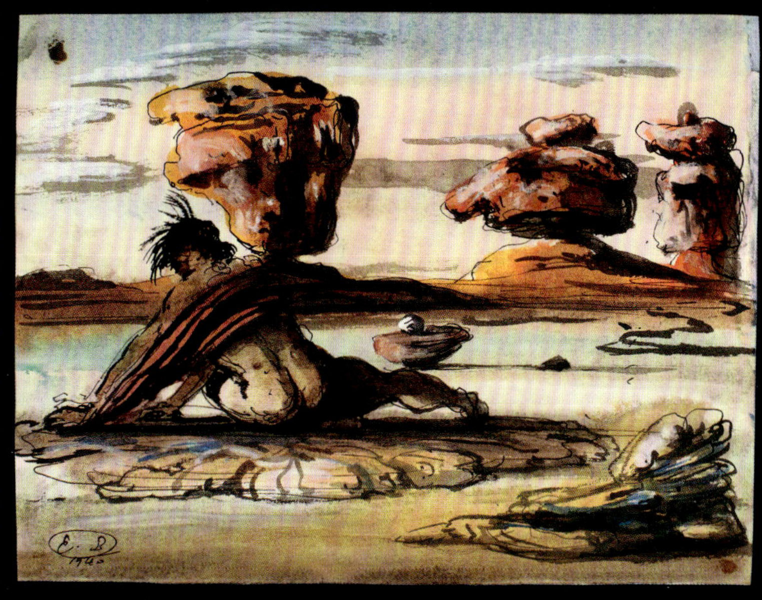

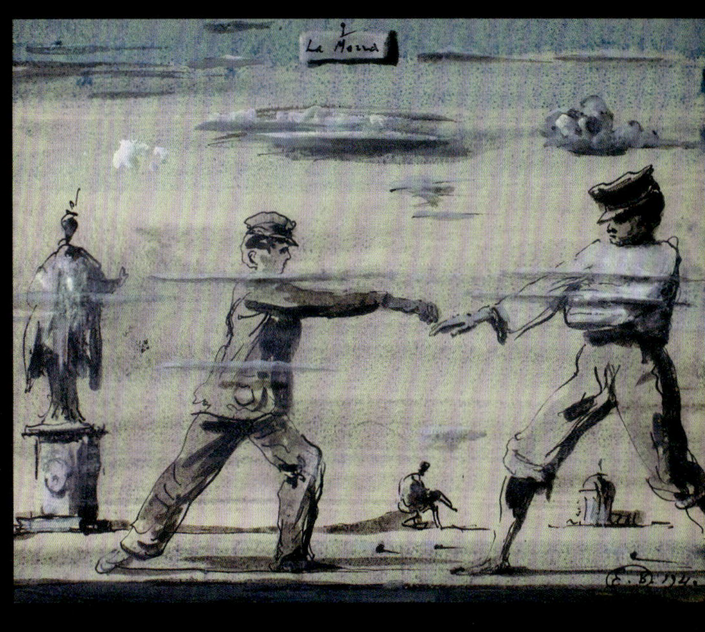
La Morra

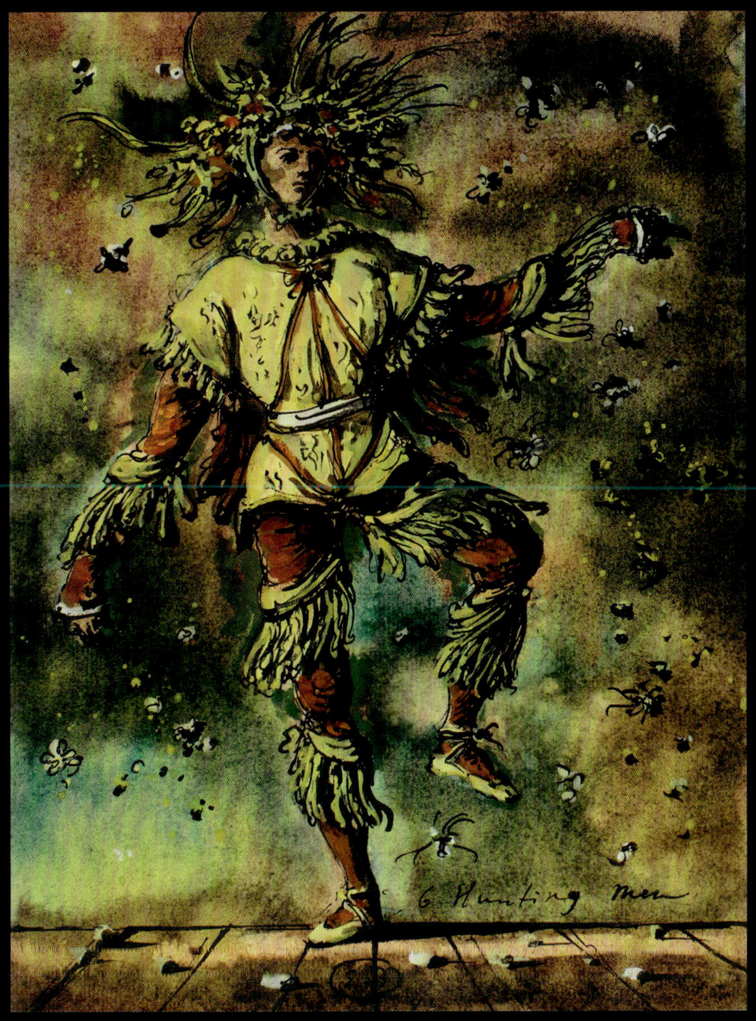
6 Hunting men

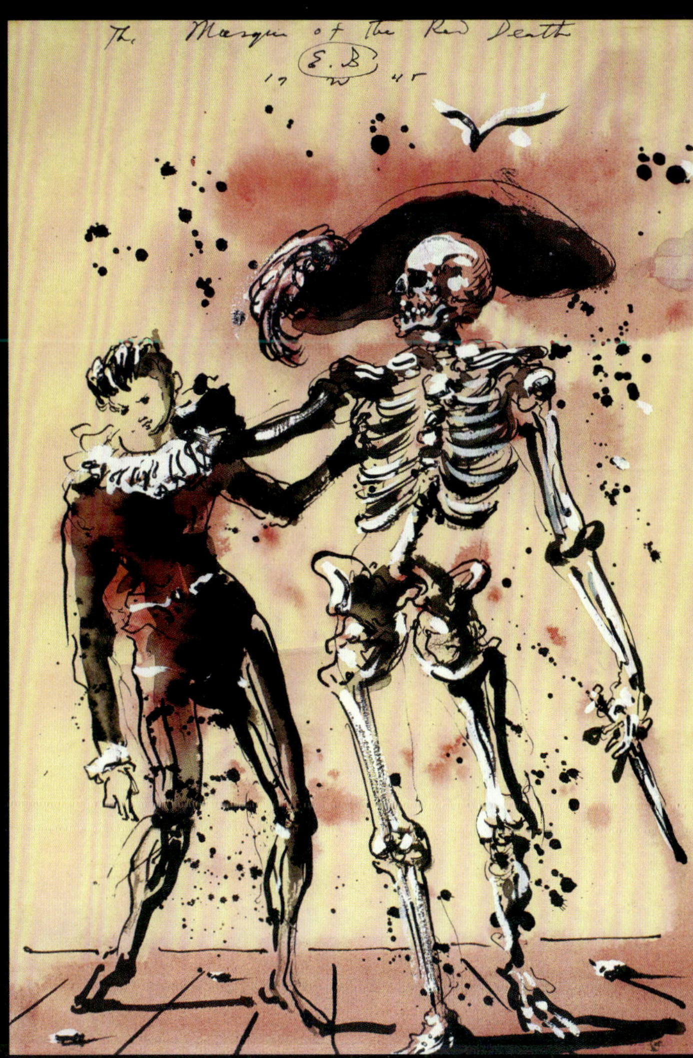
The Masque of the Red Death

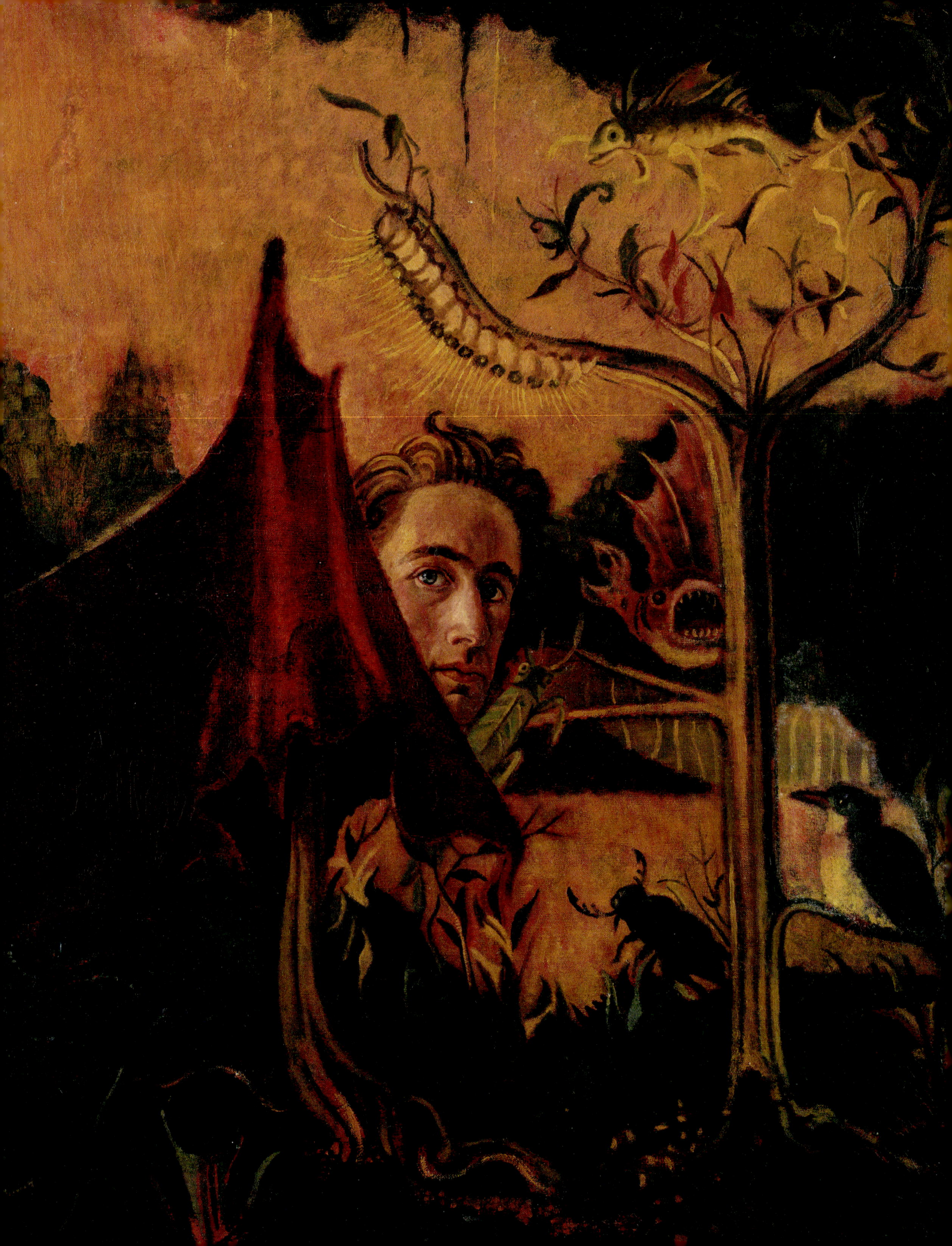

ACT III

FIGURES OF STYLE

Two Minor Arcana

The cards of Neo-Romanticism were not solely confined to the four major arcana so far discussed above. The movement's power of attraction in its early days was reflected by the number and variety of painters with which it was associated. These included Jean-Francis Laglenne (1899–1962), a friend of Bérard, Crevel and Charbonnier who was later drawn to the École de Paris, as well as Léon Zack (1892–1980) and Philippe Hosiasson (1898–1978). The latter two undoubtedly felt an affinity towards the group on account of their Russian origins and the shared formative experiences, exile and friendships that these entailed. (Both Zack and Hosiasson would move, like Tchelitchew, from figuration to a form of abstraction in their later periods.) However, if we return to the most direct and substantial account of the 1926 group (that of Leonid), then two other names stand out, no less worthy of attention for being minor arcana. (We shall leave aside the shadowy presence in the initial nucleus of a hairdresser from Ischia called De Angelis, who had been taken under Eugene's wing but has left no trace.)

Thérèse Debains (1897–1974) is a slightly less elusive figure, but nevertheless, despite a long and prolific career, her work is barely known, even though her paintings display refinement and skill. They

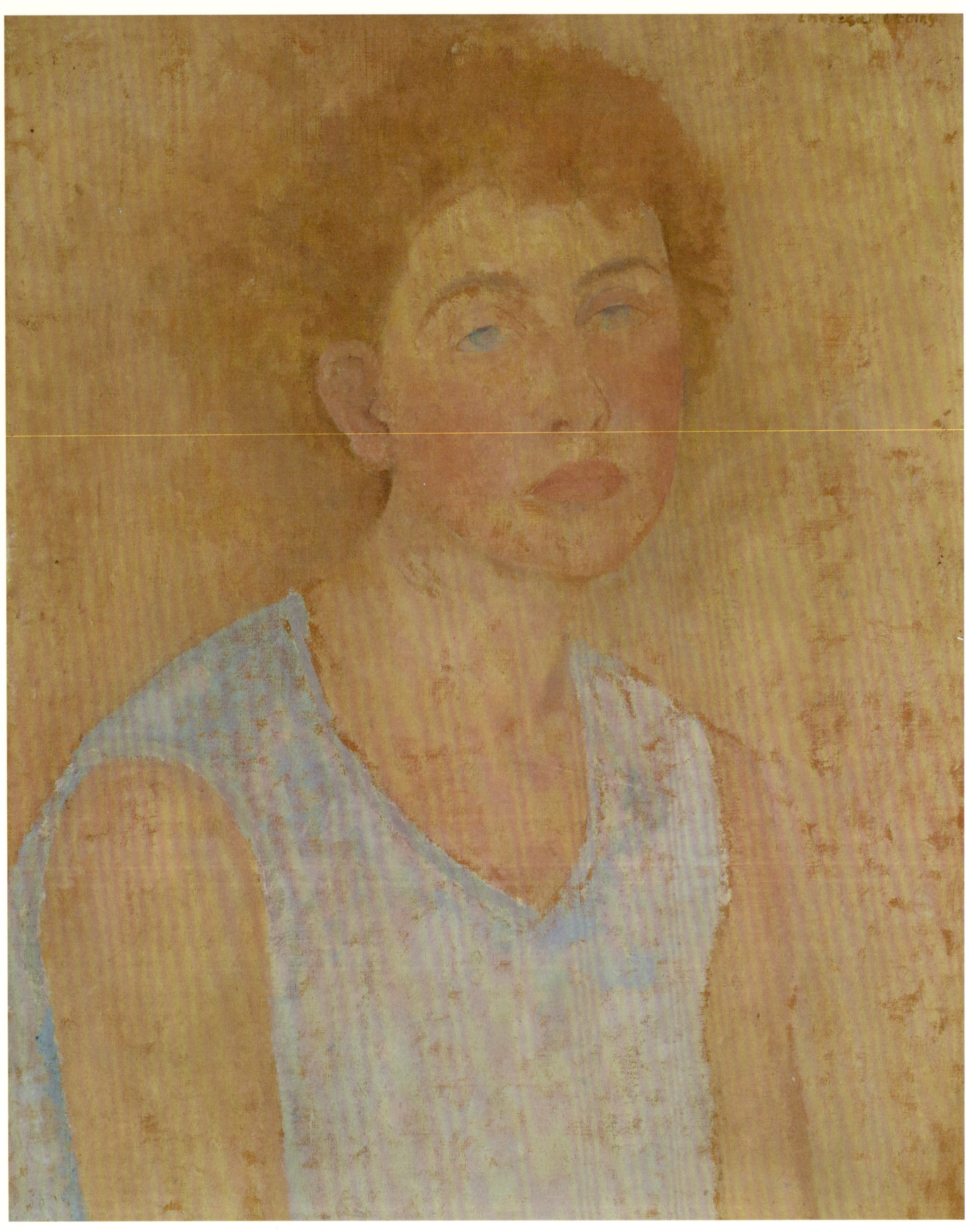

PREVIOUS PAGE: Kristians Tonny, *Self-Portrait*, oil on canvas, 95 × 75 cm (37⅜ × 29½ in.), n.d.

ABOVE: Thérèse Debains, *Portrait of a Young Woman* (Self-portrait?), oil on wood panel, 46 × 38 cm (18⅛ × 14⅞ in.), *c.* 1948?
OPPOSITE: Thérèse Debains, *Portrait of a Young Woman*, oil on canvas, 61 × 50 cm (24 × 19⅝ in.), 1924

come up for auction fairly regularly but her early decision to forge a solitary path, removed from the social circles of her companions, has led her tranquil lyricism to be undervalued. Once again, Leonid's memoir provides us with the only source of information about Debains (she was not considered worthy of more than a few lines in Édouard Joseph's *Dictionnaire biographique des artistes contemporains*, published between 1930 and 1936). She was a classmate of the Berman brothers at the Académie Ranson, where she showed a talent that elicited Leonid's admiration. ('Two girls, one fair, the other dark, Thérèse Debains and Isabelle Ischval, did wonderful drawings.') She was close in age to those 'two seventeen-year-old Parisians' Christian Bérard and Christian Dior, and in the eyes of the young Russian exile these bright young things embodied the spirit of a culture that fascinated him: 'I had been lucky to meet, in Thérèse and Bébé – right at the beginning of my stay in Paris – two cultivated people who were typically French, both physically and mentally. [...] Thérèse, who came in every day on the train from Versailles, where she lived with a widowed mother and two younger sisters, reminded me of the statue of justice in the Chartres cathedral. She was fair and wore her braided hair rolled up over her ears; she had blue eyes, thick arched eyebrows, and a very low voice. I liked listening to her discussions of painting with Bébé and to their commentary on the first volumes of Proust, which were then being published and which most people did not take seriously.'

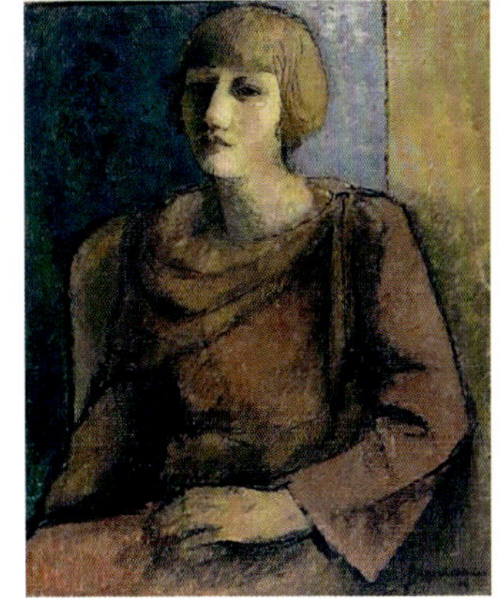

Leonid and Eugene quickly became part of the group, who were then discovering the artists whose influence would be crucial to the formation of the Neo-Romantic sensibility: 'Our little group from Rançon – Bébé, Thérèse, Genia, and I – when we went to the galleries went mostly to Paul Rosenberg on rue de la Boétie to see Picasso's latest cubist canvases, his ballet drawings, and his portraits, as admirable and realistic as those of Ingres; Rosenberg himself would show them to us in his office. At Paul Guillaume's, we looked at our first di [*sic*] Chiricos and Douanier Rousseaus. At Hessel's, our friend Jean Aron would show us paintings by Madame Hessel's old and faithful lover, Vuillard.'

Perhaps inevitably, these shared cultural and aesthetic enthusiasms soon became charged with erotic tensions, and Thérèse found herself at the centre of a romantic imbroglio that has already been alluded to. She became Leonid's lover, while 'what is certain is that, in his solitude, [Bébé] realized that he loved Thérèse, but told no one'.

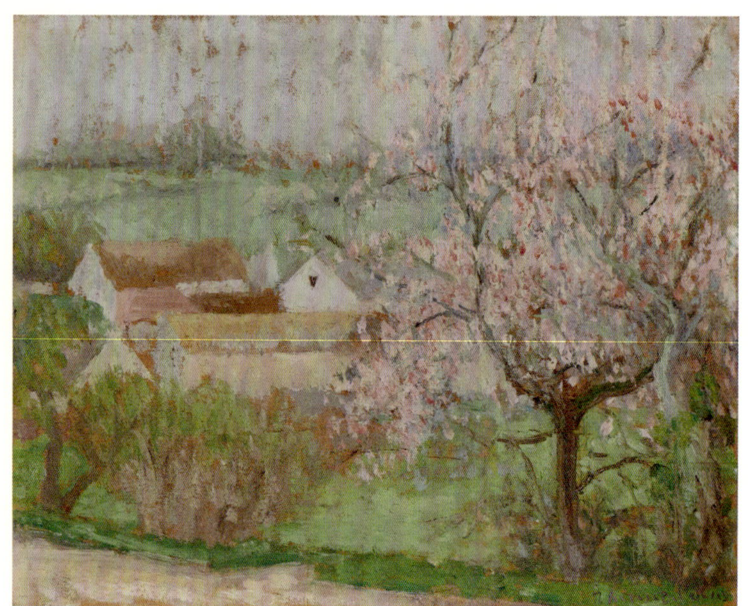

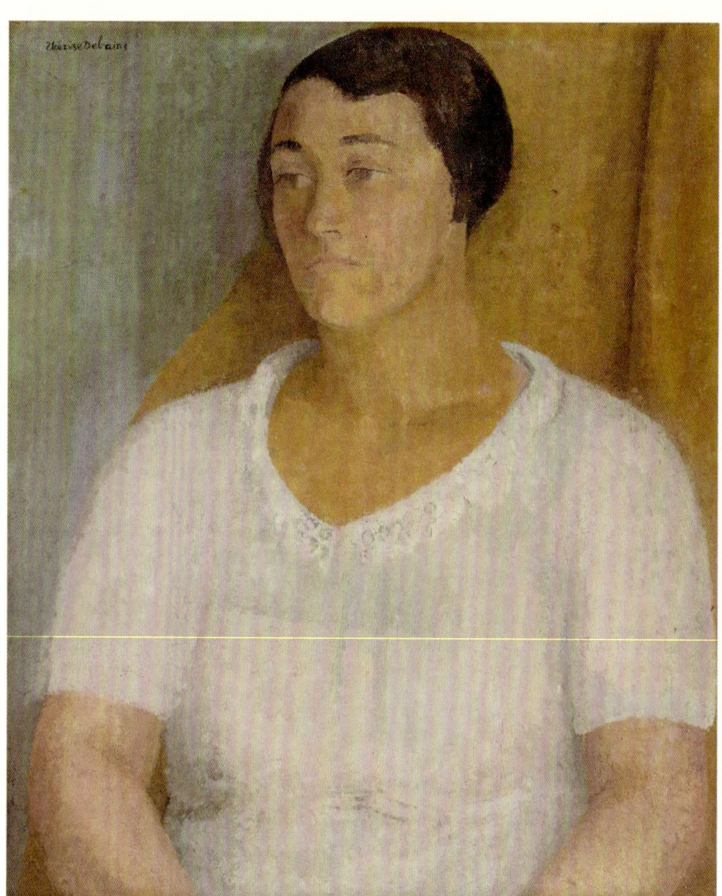

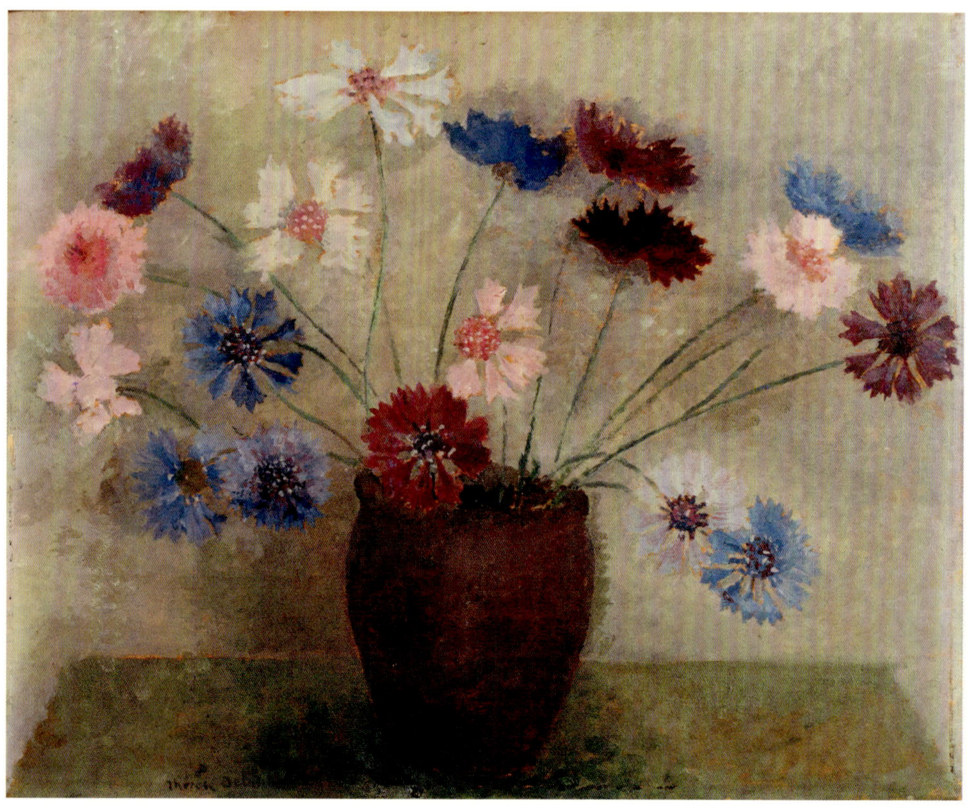

THIS PAGE, CLOCKWISE FROM TOP LEFT: Thérèse Debains, *Landscape and Tree in Bloom*, oil on panel, 22 × 25 cm (8⅝ × 9⅞ in.), n.d.; Thérèse Debains, *Portrait of a Woman*, oil on plywood, 54 × 45 cm (21¼ × 17⅝ in.), n.d.; Thérèse Debains, *Still Life*, oil on panel, 34 × 43 cm (13⅜ × 16⅞ in.), n.d.

OPPOSITE, CLOCKWISE FROM TOP LEFT: Thérèse Debains, *Portrait of a Man*, oil on canvas, 50 × 43 cm (19⅝ × 16⅞ in.), n.d.; Thérèse Debains, *Landscape*, oil on panel, 37 × 46 cm (14½ × 18⅛ in.), 1923; Thérèse Debains, *Le Belon (l'Aven)*, oil on canvas, 50 × 72 cm (19⅝ × 28⅜ in.), *c.* 1930?

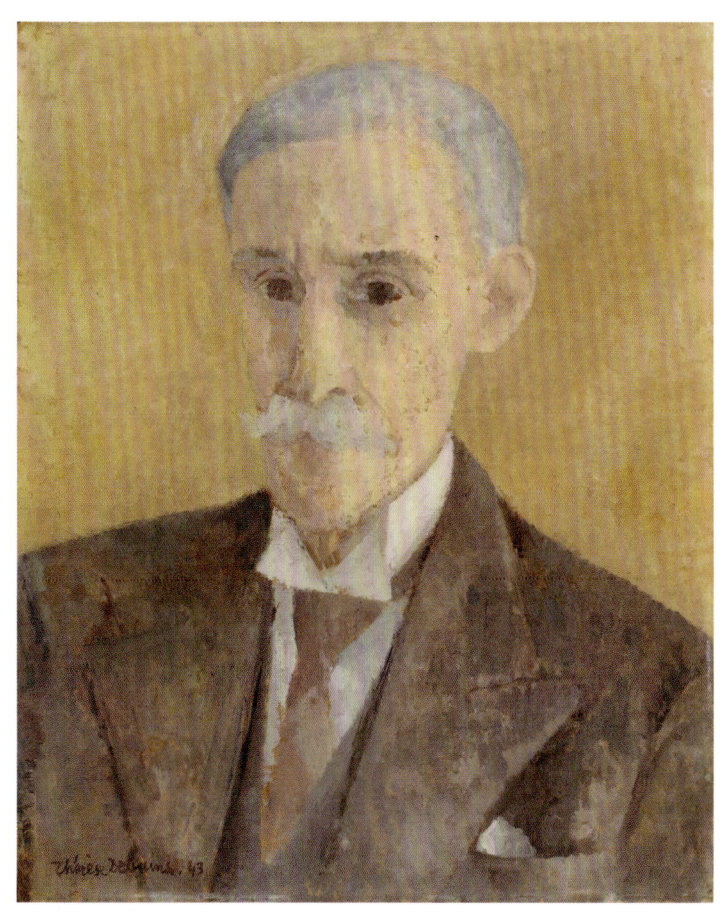

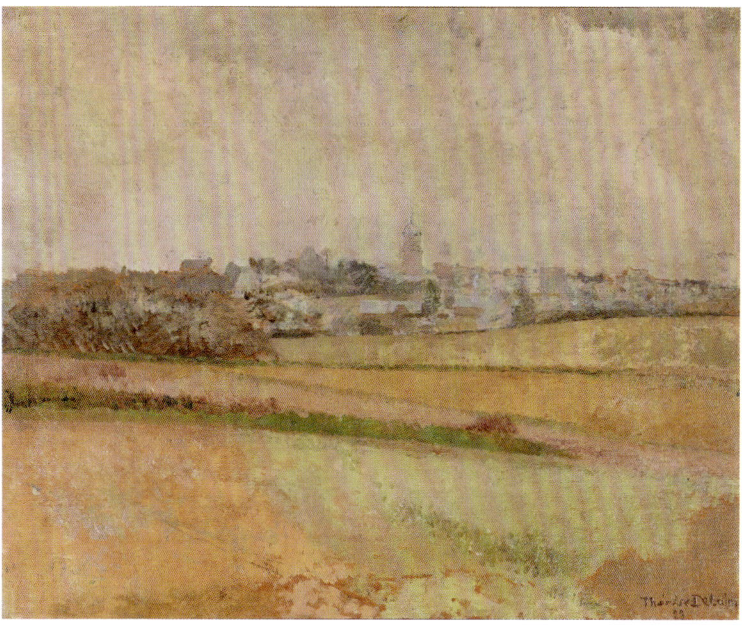

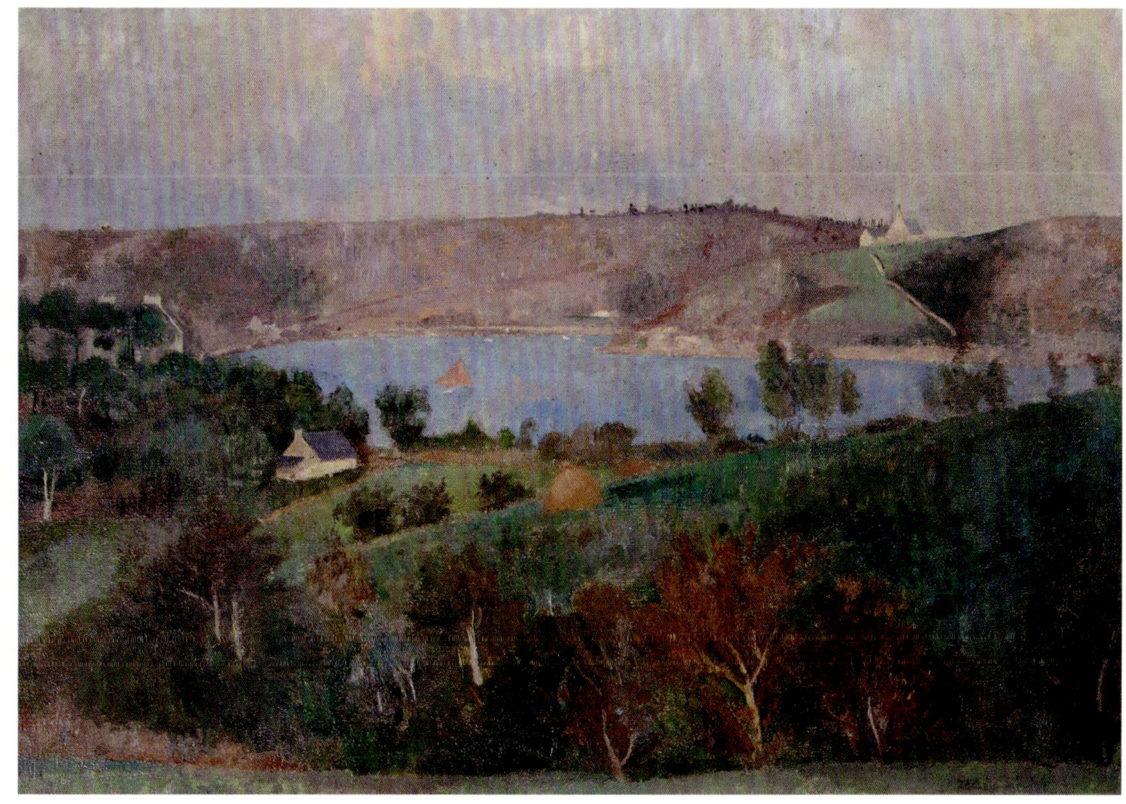

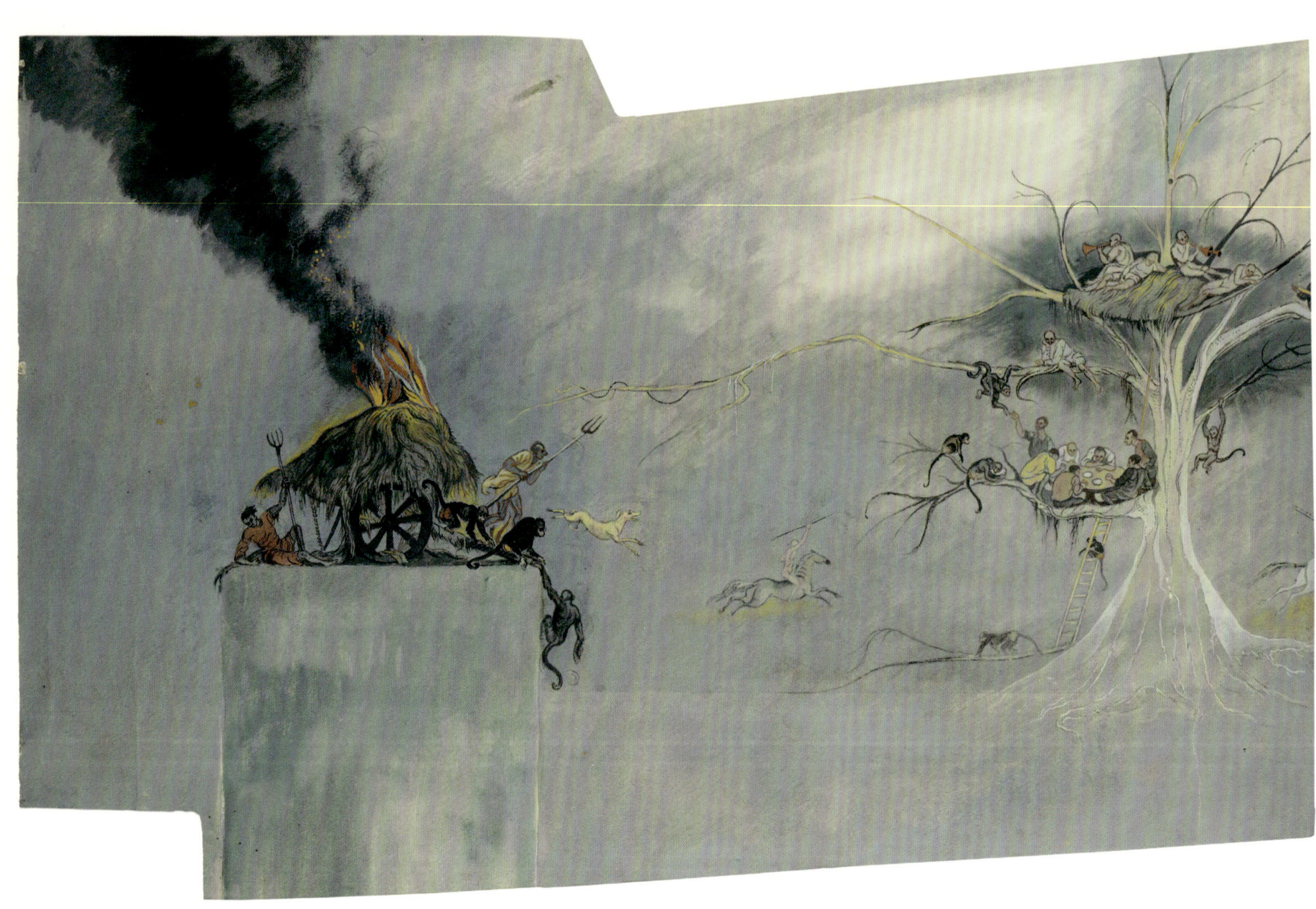

Kristians Tonny, sketch for a fresco at the Avery Theater, Wadsworth Atheneum, Hartford (right wall, with volcano), watercolour on wove paper, 55.3 × 81.3 cm (21⅞ × 32 in.), 1937

This silent passion ended up being briefly reciprocated, leading to an equation worthy of Racine that constitutes the kernel of our knowledge of this young woman. As Leonid recalled, with the benefit of hindsight: 'Actually, the needle had pointed the wrong way for all three of us: I loved Thérèse, Thérèse loved Bébé, and Bébé loved me. Thérèse abandoned me as Bébé did her and as I did Bébé as soon as I was myself again – which is to say, in love once more.' After this painful separation, which took place melodramatically during a thunderstorm in Brittany, Debains disappeared from Leonid's view and became just another artist erased from history.

Debains's work focused on the traditional genres of landscape, flower painting and portraiture. She seems to have resisted early on any temptation to indulge in the gloominess of her friends' early work and instead broke away to pursue a line of work influenced by her teachers Vuillard and Sérusier, the Post-Impressionists and, above all, Degas (whose importance to Bérard we have already seen). These affinities must only have been strengthened by the summer holidays that she used to spend with her mother and sisters in the village of Le Pouldu, near Quimperlé – the very same village where Sérusier had stayed in 1889, before forming the Pont-Aven school with Paul Gauguin and Charles Filiger. Debains seemed to have had a life-long attachment to this region (she died in Bégard, in the Côtes-d'Armor), and she undoubtedly introduced Leonid to it. *Le Bélon (l'Aven)*, her painting of an inlet to the south of Quimperlé, exemplifies both the type of landscape that attracted her and her style: simplified, streamlined forms; a harmonious composition; a thin layer of paint (unlike the thick paste of her friends); a play of transparencies and glazes; a palette of pale colours, with minute variations in their different shades; and a tranquil luminosity, also characteristic of her portraits, still lifes and flower paintings (which sometimes recall those of Odilon Redon).

Debains received some attention from Waldemar-George, even though she only fleetingly crossed the path of the Neo-Romantics, but, despite all her talent, she never gained the recognition that she deserved.

Meanwhile, we have already encountered the figure of Kristians Tonny (1907–1977) in the comings and goings of Gertrude Stein and, all in all, our picture of him is fuller than that of Debains. He came to Paris from the Netherlands in 1913 and soon attracted attention as a child prodigy. He first exhibited in a gallery in Paris in 1920, and his debut in Amsterdam came four years later. 'Before he was twenty,' remembered Soby, 'he had become widely known for the finished and refreshing quality of his drawings. [...] [T]hey were acquired by many of the discriminating supporters of modern art, among them the Americans, Gertrude Stein and Carl Van Vechten.' Like Tchelitchew and Eugene Berman, Tonny fleetingly became the object of Stein's enthusiasm, as Bravig Imbs observed: 'The newest excitement at Gertrude's was a young Dutchman named Kristians Tonny whose drawings gave evidence of tremendous talent. [...] I remember very well the first time I saw them, for it was such an electric shock. Gertrude simply withdrew some large sized drawings from a portfolio that leaned against the fireplace. "And what do you think about these?" she said quietly. [...] "These are Kristians Tonny's drawings," said Gertrude. "He's just a boy yet, but he's been painting and drawing since he was a kid. If he can only find a way to have as complete a communication with the exterior world as he has with his own inner world, he will be a very great artist indeed."' The young prodigy would soon meet his inevitable fate, however, and duly found himself excommunicated for reasons that had little to do with art.

Thanks to the help of Pascin, the 'Prince of Montparnasse' (1885–1930), Tonny seems to have built up a network of contacts from Eastern Europe to Munich, Berlin and Paris that rivalled those of Tchelitchew and the Bermans. Furthermore, he developed a distinctive graphic style that set him apart from his fellow Neo-Romantics. While it is perfectly possible to see links – despite the evident differences – between the work of Bérard and Debains (with the common influence of Degas) or between that of Debains and Leonid (in their approach to landscape), Tonny's was completely *sui generis*. (If any stylistic affiliation had to be established for Tonny, it would surely be with the Belgian painter and writer Jean de Bosschère [1878–1953], who shared his taste for linearity and vermiculated drawings teeming with life, almost overflowing from the paper; this affinity must have been sensed early on by the publisher and art dealer Robert Denoël, as he exhibited the two artists together in his gallery, Aux Trois Magots, in March 1928.)

Soby endorsed Bravig Imbs's opinion that Tonny's drawings drew heavily on the tradition of the Low Countries: 'In all essentials, they continued the Netherlandish tradition for extravagant fantasy laid down by Bosch and the elder Breughel. [...] The world described by Tonny's scenarios was a medieval world, bewitched by sinister emblems and symbols of the Black Sabbath and full of phalli and miniature eroticisms.' Tonny's art seems to be akin to automatic writing in its free associations, with one motif leading to another in a kind of perpetual motion that overturns the rules of classical composition.

This absence of polarity, of visible construction, in most of Tonny's works ('composed', according to Henry-Russell Hitchcock, 'solely by a sort of subconscious scenario and by no geometrical principles of design') can be partly explained by his technique, and a method that he had perfected alongside Pascin. This involved a transfer process that was described by Soby: 'A piece of paper is coated with oil pigment in one or more broad areas of color (often white, or gold and white, in Tonny's work). The coated paper is treated and dried until the pigment has reached the right consistency. It is then placed, coated side down, on another piece of paper which may be of any color, but with Tonny is often black. The artist now draws with a stylus on the back of the first piece of paper, and the pressure of the stylus transfers the image from the coated side of the first paper onto the second.' This method obliged Tonny to work 'in the blind', as his drawing was revealed only once the first sheet of paper had been removed. (This rejection of control in favour of surprise and accident explains why Tonny has often been ranked among the Surrealists, and in fact in 1925 he contributed to the movement's first major exhibition – the *Exposition Surréaliste* – at the Pierre Gallery.)

Tonny applied the same technique to paintings on canvas, often creating a disconcerting impression of an overexposed miniature that was oddly out of proportion. He even went as far as adapting this use of focal divergence to frescoes. The same tension is evident in a series of portraits of his friends – considered by Soby, in *After Picasso*, to be the most important paintings of Tonny's first period. In his memoir, Bravig Imbs, who was one of the subjects, evoked 'the time he painted everything in monumental terms and my portrait was at least twice life size'.

In contrast with the sinuous lines and painstaking detail of his drawings, Tonny's portraits subscribed to realist tradition at its purest, albeit embedded in a surrealistic setting, as in the case of his superb self-portrait. He moved into group portraiture in 1926 with the painting *Figures*, which, according to Soby, depicted the artist in the company of five of the participants in the Druet Gallery exhibition. He was eventually granted the honour of following in the footsteps of Picasso by being authorized, in 1930, to paint Gertrude

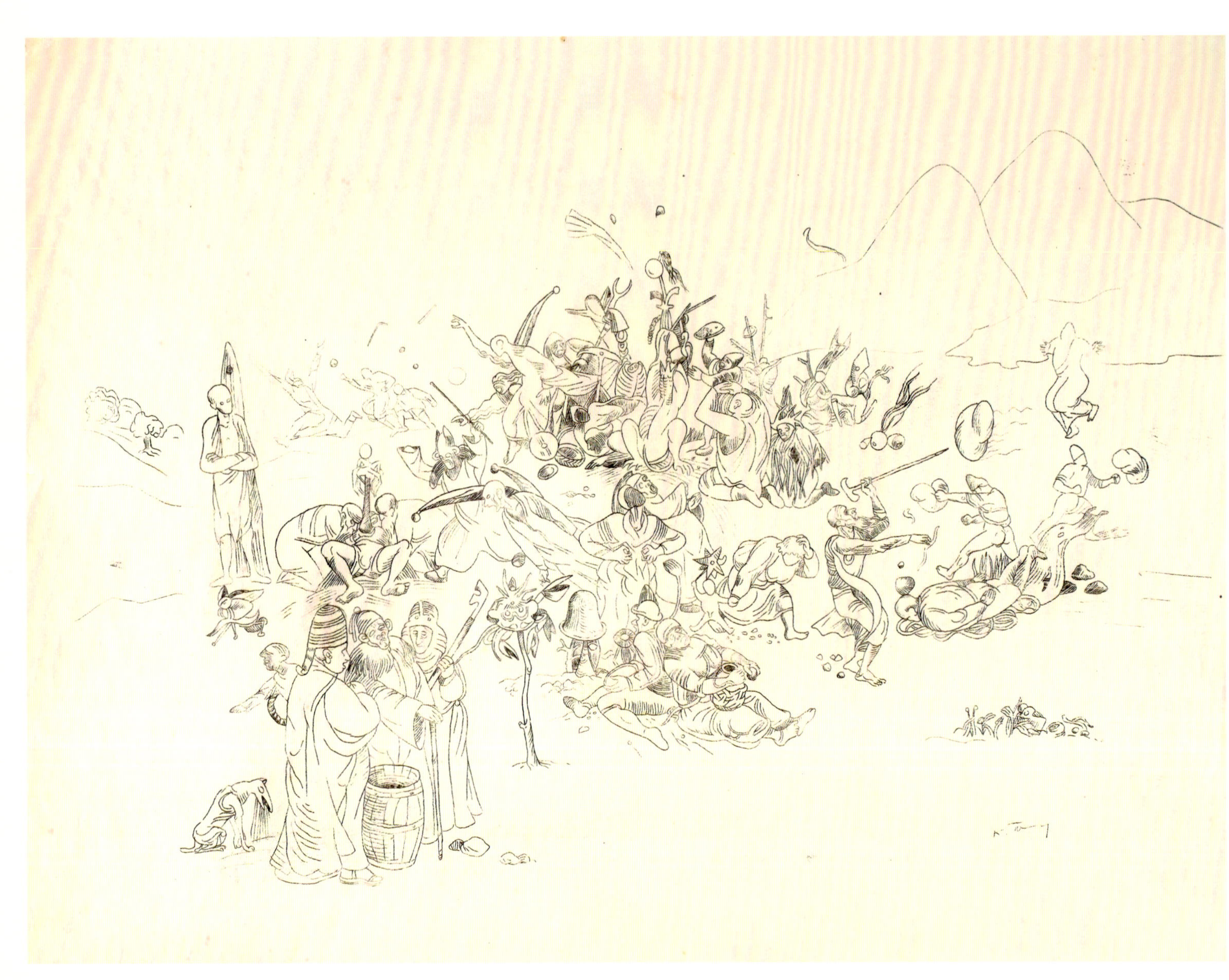

ABOVE: Kristians Tonny, drawing,
ink on paper, 44 × 59 cm (17⅜ × 23⅛ in.), n.d.
OPPOSITE: Kristians Tonny, drawing,
ink on paper, 30 × 50 cm (11⅞ × 19⅝ in.), n.d.

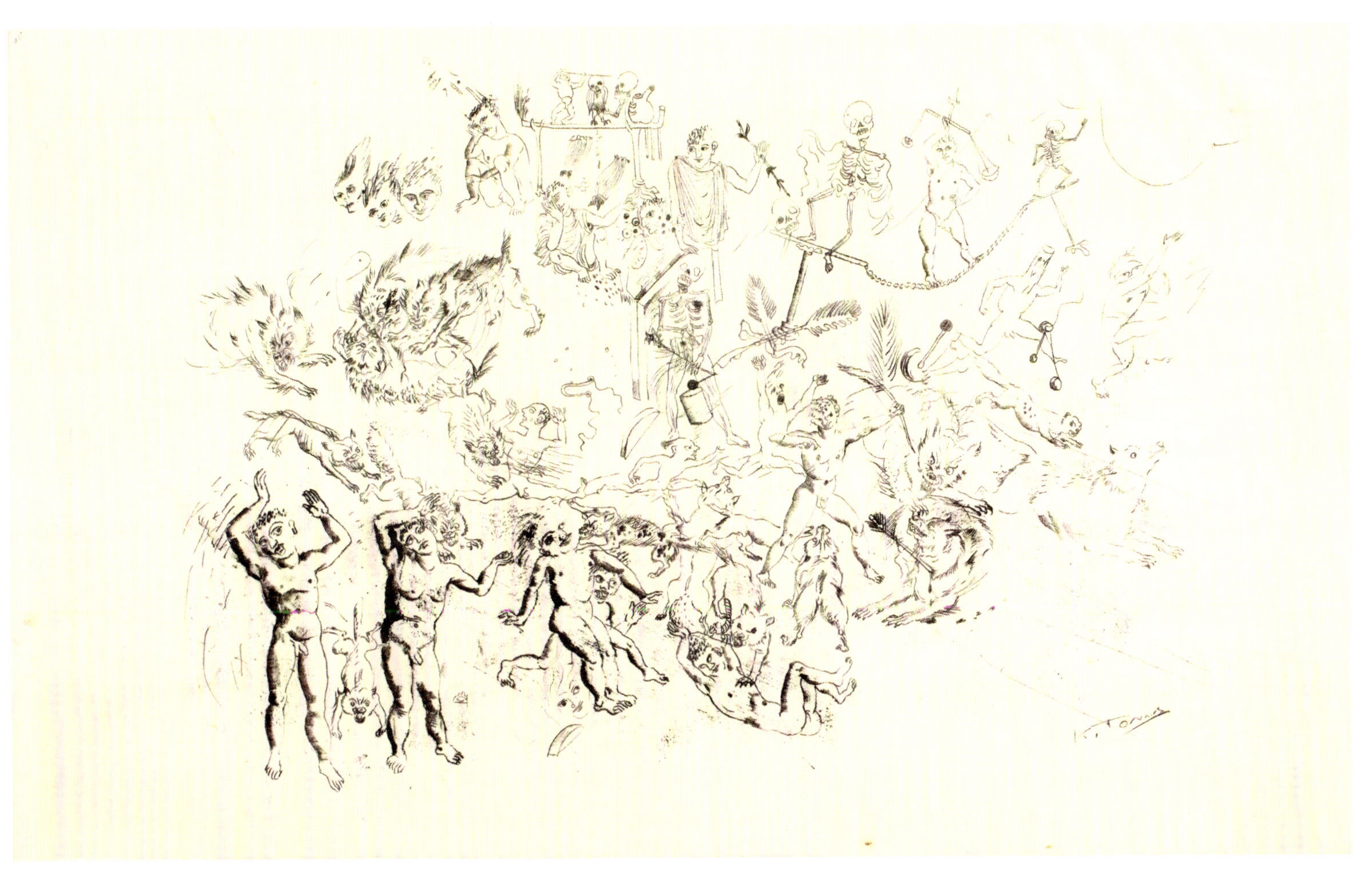

Stein, who had by then become, in the words of Bravig Imbs, 'an unofficial pontiff' of Parisian literary and artistic circles, who never hesitated to exercise her power of excommunication: 'His portraits of Gertrude Stein and other friends were Northern portraits, precise, rather than filled with sentiment as Bérard's were. Instead of portraying a mood and giving an illusion of emotional tension, Tonny's portraits communicated dispassionately the exact appearances of his subjects. The long observation, which made them possible, was essentially detached and unsentimental.' Tonny's laborious working methods soon exasperated Stein, giving rise to a few squabbles, although they invariably patched things up as both of them were eager to see the finished picture. Nevertheless, these quarrels turned out to presage one of the definitive ruptures that were Stein's forte, particularly when one of her protégés had the impertinence to fall in love. So, Tonny's name soon joined those of Georges Hugnet, Bravig Imbs, Pavel Tchelitchew and his then lover Allen Tanner on the blacklist of those ordered to never darken Stein's door on rue de Fleurus ever again. (Imbs mournfully recalled the chasm that appeared between Stein and the Neo-Romantics: 'It was amazing how rapidly the little court was dispersed. All the devoted admirers had become exiles, more or less chagrined. All the friends of the devoted admirers had left the salon as well, out of sympathy, and the rue de Fleurus must have seemed a desolate, deserted spot for a while. No more parties, no more teas, no more hours of gossip, no more recriminating against a common fate with publishers, no more dropping in after dinner, no more little cakes, no more exciting painter discoveries to discuss, no more manuscripts to criticize, no more voyages in the country – no more anything, but memories...')

Fleeing the ire of the grande dame of Modernism, Tonny followed his then-girlfriend, the actress and dancer Anita Thompson, to Tangiers, where he re-encountered another old acquaintance from Stein's house, Paul Bowles (then more of a composer than a writer), who was with his future wife, Jane Auer. He then returned to Europe for a few months before following the example of his artist friends and heading for the United States in 1937. Once there, Tonny soon received encouragement from the same circle of patrons and admirers that was supporting Berman and Tchelitchew. In the very year of his arrival, for example, Chick Austin commissioned him to paint a large fresco on the walls of the Avery Theater, an extension to the Wadsworth Atheneum that had been completed a few years earlier. Tonny then felt the pull of Mexico (long before Eugene Berman and Edward James), and continued from there to Guatemala, accompanied by Paul Bowles. According to Tonny's biographers, Frida de Jong and Laurens Vancrevel, this journey had a profound impact on his work.

On returning to Europe, just before the outbreak of World War II, Tonny found that the star of Neo-Romanticism had well and truly faded. He aligned himself once again with Surrealism by joining forces with Georges Hugnet to organize (under the supervision of André Breton) the first ever Surrealist exhibition in Amsterdam. (The movement had not taken root in the Netherlands as it had in Belgium, and the exhibition met with limited success.) Unable to leave Europe when war was declared, Tonny moved to the South of France, where he participated in several exhibitions, as well as having a solo show in Monte Carlo in 1942. He was back in Paris two years later, where he slipped back into the city's artistic circles and enjoyed an eventful love life. In 1949, Tonny decided to return to Amsterdam, which he had left over thirty years previously. Surrealism had still not gained a foothold in Dutch culture, however, and Tonny worked largely in isolation in his final period, although he remained productive until his death in 1977.

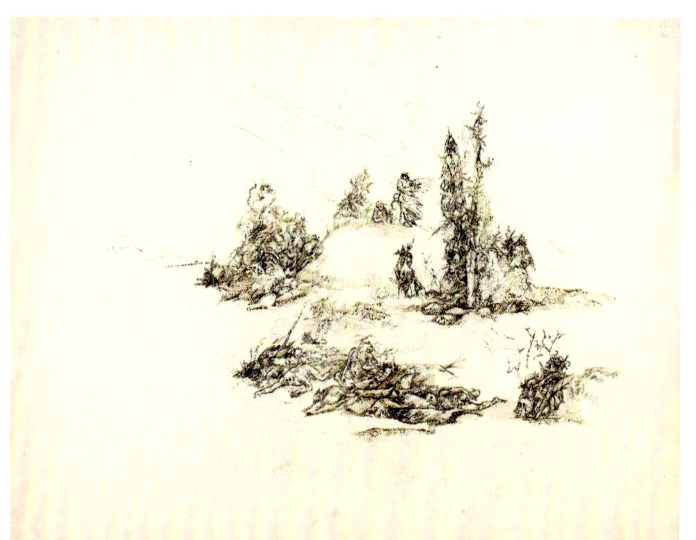

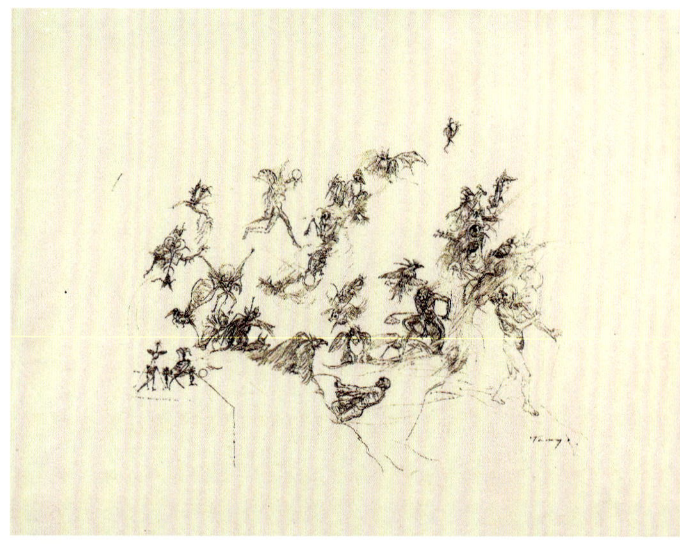

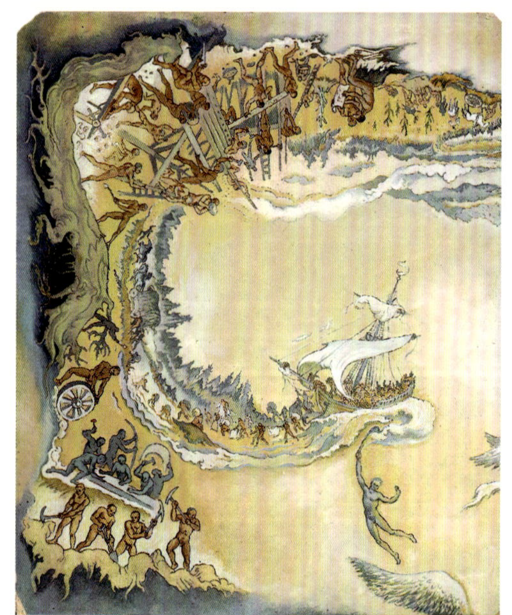

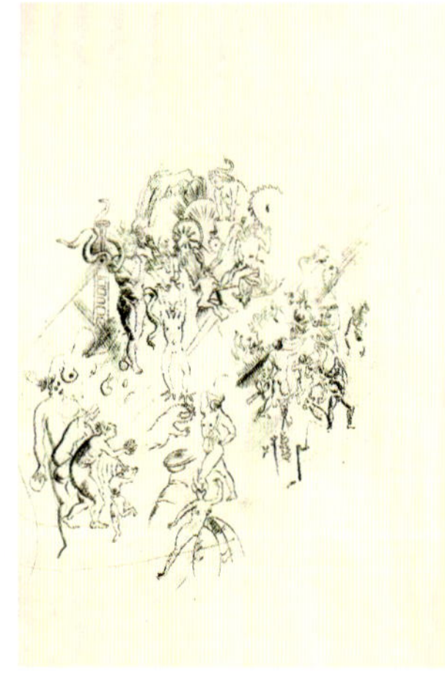

THIS PAGE, CLOCKWISE FROM TOP LEFT: Kristians Tonny, *Untitled*, ink on paper, 56.2 × 74 cm (22 × 29 in.), n.d.; Kristians Tonny, *Sans titre*, *Untitled*, ink on paper, 56.2 × 74 cm (22 × 29 in.), n.d.; Kristians Tonny, *Untitled*, ink on paper, 47.5 × 32.5 cm (19¼ × 13 in.), n.d.; Kristians Tonny, *Untitled*, oil on cardboard, 46 × 38 cm (18 × 15 in.), n.d.

OPPOSITE, CLOCKWISE FROM TOP LEFT: Kristians Tonny, *Untitled*, ink on paper, 49.6 × 64.8 cm (19½ × 25½ in.), n.d.; Kristians Tonny, *Untitled*, ink on paper, 49.6 × 64.8 cm (19½ × 25½ in.), n.d.; Kristians Tonny, *Untitled*, ink on paper, 42.5 × 53 cm (17 × 20½ in.), n.d.; Kristians Tonny, *Untitled*, ink on paper, 43 × 57 cm (17 × 22 in.), n.d.

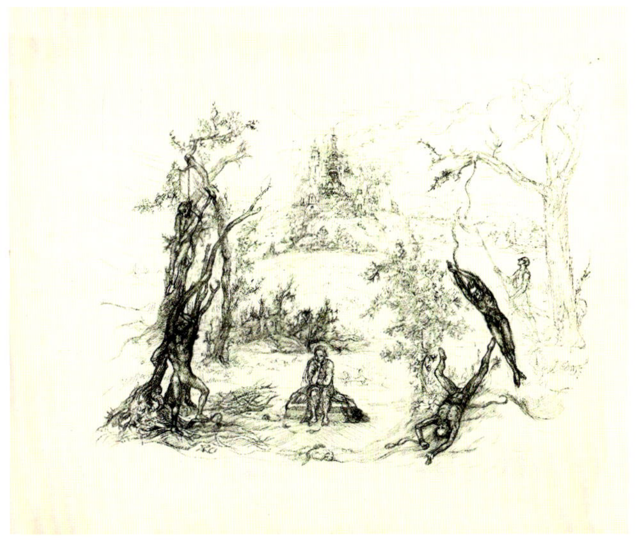

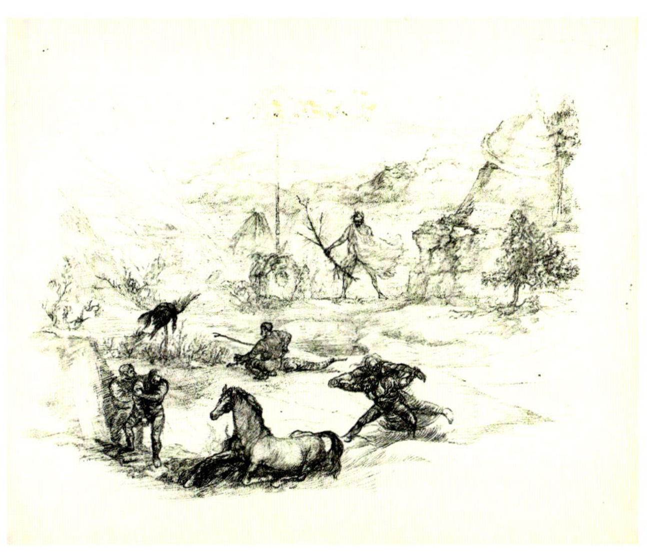

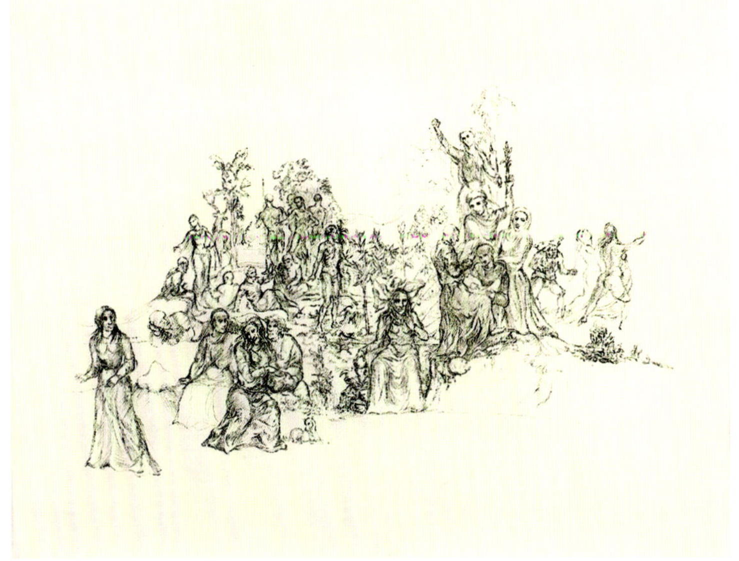

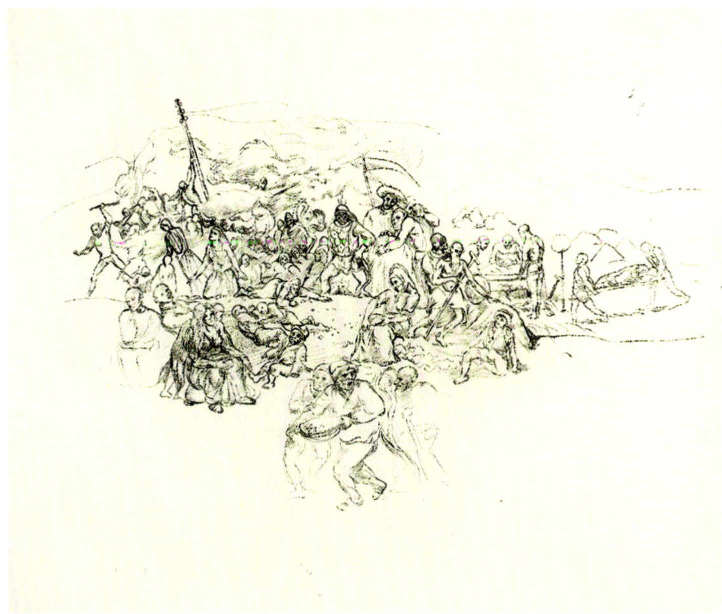

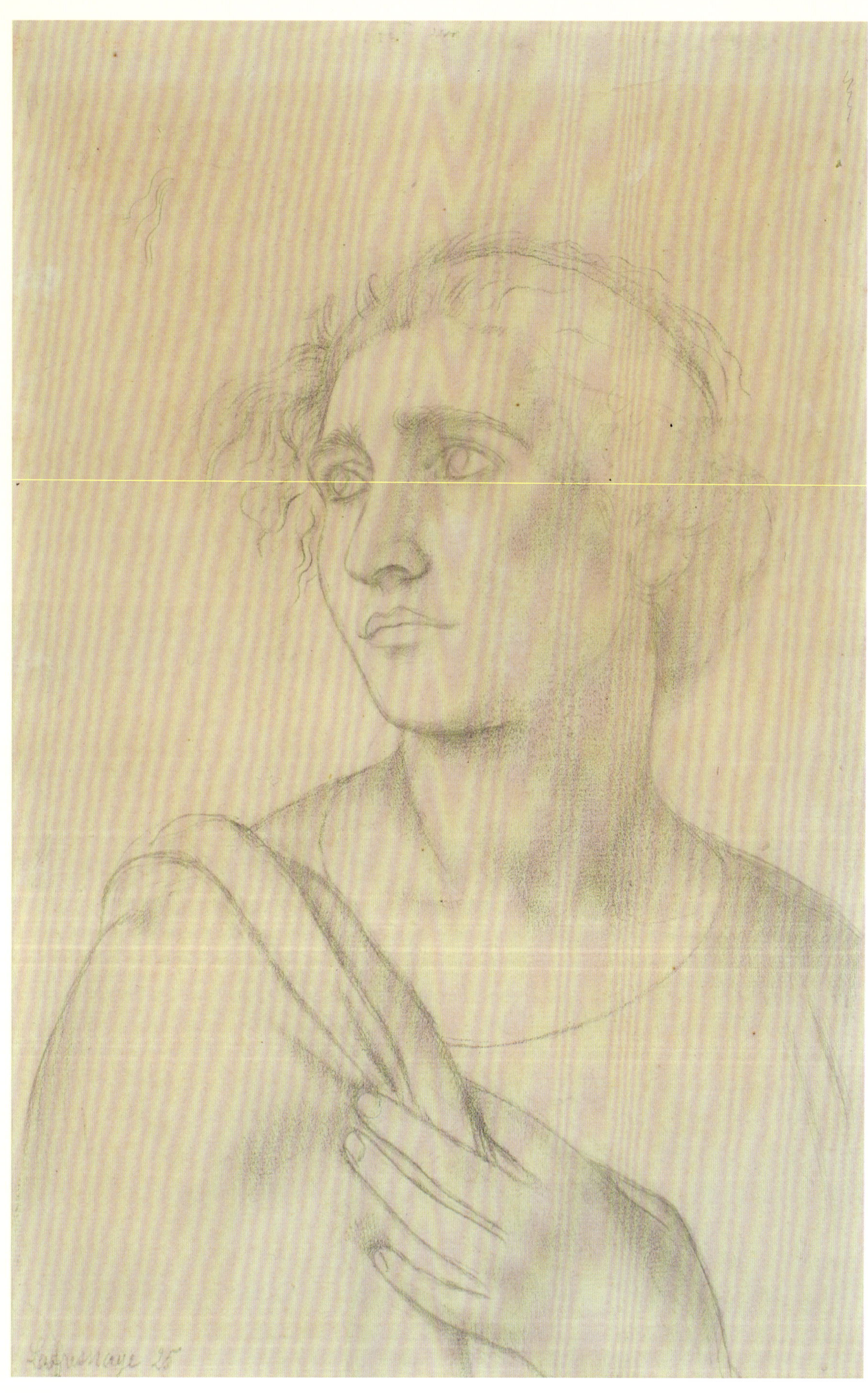

Roger de La Fresnaye, *Portrait of an Italian*,
graphite on paper, 39 × 30 cm (15⅜ × 11⅞ in.), 1925

The Strange Case of Waldemar-George

Thérèse Debains and Kristians Tonny were undoubtedly considered too distant from the sensibility that Waldemar-George was trying to define in *Formes*, the magazine he edited from 1929 to 1933, to warrant an essay on their work. Bérard, Tchelitchew and the Berman brothers were granted this honour, however, and Waldemar-George used *Formes* as a platform to formulate, before James Thrall Soby, both the idea of a movement called Neo-Romanticism (or Neo-Humanism) and the terms in which it should be discussed. He is largely forgotten today, but Waldemar-George (1893–1970) was one of the driving forces of art criticism in France from the 1930s to the 1970s, though his career was marked by various contradictions and ambiguities.

He was born Jerzy Waldemar-Jarocinski in Lodz, Poland, into a Jewish family of industrialists and bankers. He arrived in Paris in 1911, where he stayed with his uncle, Jean Finckelhaus, known as Jean Finot, a sociologist and journalist who had published an important book on racial prejudice in 1906. Finot would exert a significant influence on his nephew's thinking. (By a serendipitous twist of fate, in 1903 Finot had bought the magazine *La Revue Blanche* from the Natanson brothers, who would, of course, go on to play a crucial role in the exhibition at the Druet Gallery.) Following his uncle's example, Jerzy Waldemar-Jarocinski gallicized his name to Waldemar-George (thereby, like Kristians Tonny, inverting his original first name and surname). Finot provided the budding critic with a smooth introduction into the city's literary and artistic circles, and, in the very year of his arrival, Waldemar-George found himself working for *Paris-Journal*, where he made friends with writers as different as André Salmon and Louis Vauxcelles.

Waldemar-George enlisted in the Foreign Legion at the start of World War I, serving as an interpreter. After his demobilization in September 1919, he was appointed – at the instigation of Vauxcelles – director of the magazine *L'Amour de l'art*, whose first issue came out in 1920. This privileged position enabled him to firmly establish himself, in the words of his biographer, 'at the heart of the most effective of all set-ups, one that brought together artists and critics, galleries and magazines'. Eventually, however, Waldemar-George's uneasy relationship with the highly opinionated and dogmatic Vauxcelles led him to resign from his post in 1927. (Vauxcelles has gone down in history for the dubious honour of coining two neologisms – Cubism and Fauvism – which he had originally intended as insults.) In 1929, Waldemar-George founded *Formes*, which would become the vehicle for his critical vision and rebuttal of, as he saw it, 'the great imperatives of Modernist orthodoxy' via 'a heterodox conception of art'.

Unlike Vauxcelles, however, Waldemar-George was far from closed to new lines of expression and advances in modern art. He curated the first exhibitions of Emmanuel Mané-Katz in 1922, of Marc Chagall in 1924, and of James Ensor in 1926; he contributed to *L'Esprit Nouveau,* the magazine run by Amédée Ozenfant and Le Corbusier; he was friends with Robert and Sonia Delaunay; and he gave advice to Paul Guillaume and Alfred Barnes. Nevertheless, in 1925 he began to question the limits of a reified Modernism, criticizing the 'purely retinal vision' of Matisse and the primitivist fetishism or 'iconoclastic rage' that he perceived behind decompositions of the human figure. He saw a possible relief (in the Hegelian sense) from Cubist formalism in the paradoxical Neoclassicism of the recently deceased Roger de La Fresnaye. The evocation of this painter's tragic destiny and untimely death (aged only forty) allowed Waldemar-George to dialectically exalt the power of life, and its representation, in implicit opposition to the bloodless formulas of an abstraction that had become hegemonic. ('As [La Fresnaye's] strength abandoned him, he rediscovered the sentiment of Man, of the articulated body and the talking face. He rediscovered it in successive stages. His starting point was Antiquity and the drawings of the Masters. The sensitive understanding of Man not as a formal problem but as a thinking being would only appear in his work on the eve of his death.')

In Waldemar-George's view, Roger de La Fresnaye had become, along with de Chirico, the harbinger of a redefinition of an artistic practice that found its strength in a rediscovered tradition. The young Polish immigrant took the apparently paradoxical stance – although its logic is by no means unique to him – of invoking a timeless, mythical Frenchness (albeit tinged with Italianism) as the only possible recourse against the 'Esperanto' of a modern art based on formulas that had lost their meaning.

In a controversial book entitled *Profits et pertes de l'art contemporain* (Profits and Losses of Contemporary Art), published in 1933, Waldemar-George would develop this viewpoint into a theoretical system, which was summarized thus by Yves Chevrefils Desbiolles: 'Contemporary French art, as Waldemar-George envisaged it from then

OPPOSITE: Carlo Carrà, *Pine Tree by the Sea*, oil on canvas, 61 × 50 cm (24 × 19¾ in.), 1921

on, would be the fruit of a dynamism that took into account the long duration of civilization and a slow ripening process that integrates the contributions of successive generations. France is a "state of mind" that values order and good taste; like the Catholic Church, it knows how to maintain unity in diversity. This country bears within it the germs of the Neo-Humanism in painting that is "a discovery (or rediscovery) of the magic of the body and of human faces, of composition [...] and of the landscape that expresses the relationships between the inner life and the exterior world, between Man and his surroundings".'

André Derain and Aristide Maillol also earned Waldemar-George's praise in *Formes*; in fact, he saw them as the two leading figures in this resurgence, or re-imposition, of the genius of French art, standing in sharp contrast to the unclassifiable multiple identities and stylistic polymorphism of an artist like Picasso. And this quest for purity – which is, by definition, ideal – led Waldemar-George to look beyond even the great French tradition towards its very foundations: the culture of Ancient Rome (though not Greece), the 'core of the West', characterized by its celebration 'of inner life, of individual life', as evidenced, in particular, by the importance bestowed on the bust, on faces and gazes, from the era of the Etruscans to the Low Empire. As he proclaimed in the October 1930 issue of *Formes*, given over entirely to Italy, 'I declare that the Return to Rome is, in the present state of the visual arts, the only active and revolutionary posture that one can adopt.'

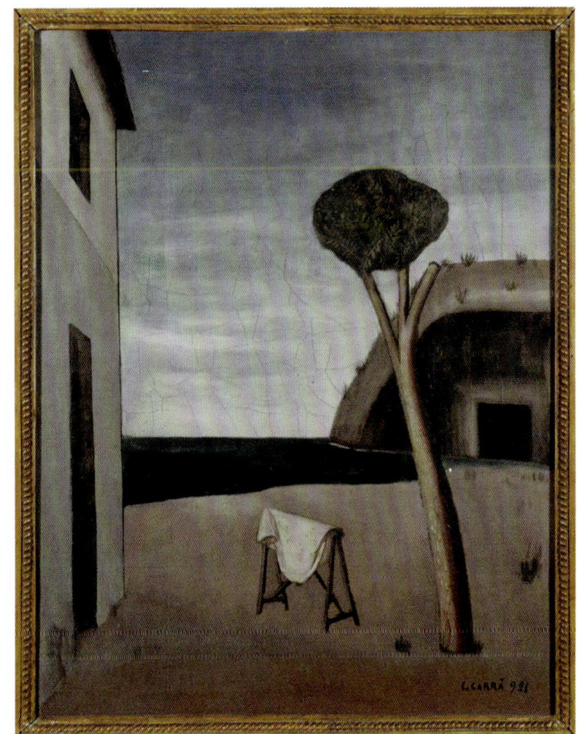

This search for a foundational origin or purity is as illusory as it is intellectually aberrant and symbolically loaded. Waldemar-George would soon answer a very particular call from Italy (to paraphrase the title of an exhibition that he curated). He followed a road parallel to that of the Novecento movement and its ideologue, Margherita Sarfatti (1880–1961). She was Jewish like him, and succumbed even more quickly than him to the seductive power of Fascism, playing an essential role in its upsurge in the Milan of the 1920s and eventually becoming its cultural spokesperson (and Mussolini's mistress until the early 1930s). In 1922, she assembled a group of painters under the banner of Novecento (1900s), featuring Mario Sironi, Achille Funi and Carlo Carrà (the latter's work would impress Bérard and the Berman brothers on their visit to Italy a few years later). These artists were united as much by the idea of a call to order (as reflected in Cocteau's manifesto of that name) as by a return to Rome. They advocated a reworked Neoclassicism, born of transgression rather than academism. The Novecento thus chimed with a trend that was manifesting itself in different ways throughout Europe in the late 1920s.

Like Waldemar-George, Margherita Sarfatti exalted Rome as the ultimate wellspring of culture and, more broadly, Latinity, and as a bulwark against abstraction, eclecticism, and the dehumanizing immoderation of the avant-garde and of Nordic cultures. 'Romanity or Italianity are synonyms of universality', declared Waldemar-George, unequivocally. He and Sarfatti joined forces with the painter Mario Tozzi (1895–1979) in 1928 to organize an exhibition at the Théâtre Louis Jouvet entitled *Italians in Paris*, which was intended to demonstrate the coherence of their ideas. Apart from Tozzi, the participants comprised Massimo Campigli, Filippo de Pisis, Alberto Savinio, Gino Severini and Alberto Giacometti.

Two years later, Waldemar-George used a report on the 17th Venice Biennale in *Formes* to highlight the affinity between the Neo-Romantics and contemporary Italian artists, thanks to a perceived common Italianness. In passing, he slipped in a tribute to their ideologue, whom he frequently invited to write for *Formes*: 'With the exception of Margherita Sarfatti, Marinetti and Prampolini, the sole defenders of modern painting in Italy, no critic has granted the painters of the *Calls of Italy* show, whether their names be Campigli or Savinio, Tozzi or Ozenfant, Bérard or Tchelitchev, Berman or even Roger de La Fresnaye [...], the status of Italians by adoption.'

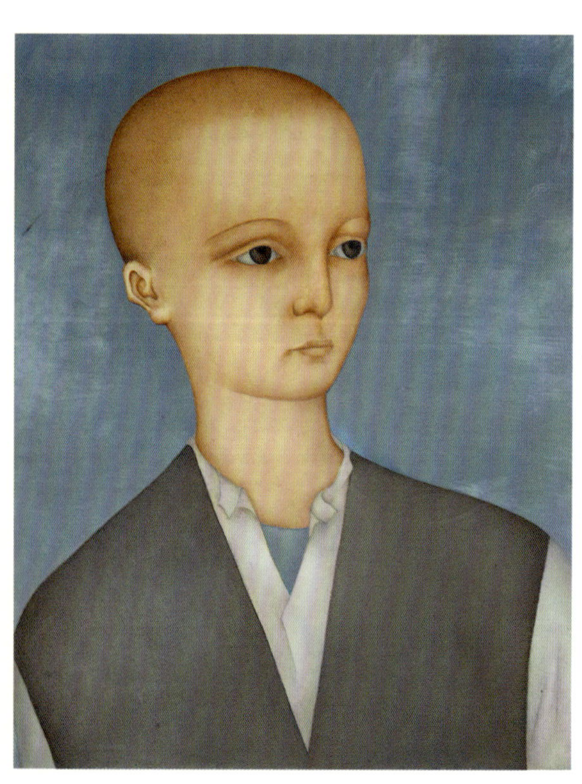

Waldemar-George took his enthusiasm for Italian culture a stage further in 1933 when he was invited to the country by the critic Pier Maria Bardi (who had replaced Margherita Sarfatti as the regime's cultural mouthpiece when she fell out of favour with Mussolini). Waldemar-George was received in the Palazzo Venezia by Il Duce himself, to whom he imparted 'some of [his] ideas about humanism in 20th-century art and the movement known as the "Return to Rome" that was manifesting itself in modern painting'.

Jean Martin-Roch, *Portrait of an Adolescent*, oil on canvas, 40 × 33 cm (15¾ × 13 in.), 1977

Waldemar-George's breathless account of this meeting obscures its negligible repercussions, as any hopes of winning over the dictator to his artistic cause would be shattered just as completely as those of Margherita Sarfatti. The parallels between the destiny of these two figures became even more pathetic when they both found themselves confronted with the consequences of their blind faith and the violence of their fellow travellers. After the enactment of race laws in Italy in 1938, Sarfatti took refuge in Uruguay. She did not return until 1947, when she withdrew to her home in the Como region. Although she made regular visits to Rome, she was shunned by cultural circles on account of her earlier political affiliations.

Meanwhile, the scales were finally falling from Waldemar-George's eyes. He had seen for himself the prevailing mood in Italy, but it was the German invasion of Austria in March 1938 that jolted him into seeing the catastrophe on the horizon. He got his mother out of Poland in July 1939, a month before it was occupied by the Nazis, and thus undoubtedly saved her life. He himself was subjected to virulent anti-Semitic attacks in the collaborationist press, and in 1941 he left Paris for the South of France under the auspices of Meraud Guinness-Guevara (1904–1993) and Jean Martin-Roch (1905–1991), two painters in tune with Neo-Romantic sensibilities who formed part of an artistic group that included the decorator André Arbus and fellow painters André Marchand and Pierre Tal-Coat. They were also active in the Resistance and Waldemar-George followed their lead; he had several close brushes with the occupying forces, sometimes in outlandish circumstances.

He eventually returned to Paris in August 1944 and immediately threw himself back into his work as a journalist. Furthermore, according to his biographer, he 'engaged in breathtaking activity; he was on all kinds of panels, and he formed part of juries and selection committees for exhibitions and salons'. And he had not forsaken his old battles or abandoned his aesthetic principles: 'his Fascism, or rather his "Mussolinism", had blown up in pieces but, as his fellow critic Léon Degand astutely observed, Waldemar-George's ideas "had, despite any changes in labels and expression, lost none of their vigour". Waldemar-George denounced not only abstraction but also any figuration that deformed the human body. He deplored the moral debilitation of France, as demonstrated by the interest shown by so many artists, critics and enthusiasts in barbaric arts.'

He was renamed by Jacques Prévert as Waldemar-George-Ohnet (playing on the name of a successful novelist 'well below the worst'), and it is tempting to cast him in the role of an unreconstructed reactionary, but such a judgment would belie his complexities and contradictions, as well as the perspicacity of some of his intuitions and the subtlety of his analyses, however biased they may have been.

In his persistent defence of a 'humanism' that went beyond 'a representation of the human figure respecting the main laws of perspective and anatomy', he exalted 'a feeling of the presence of Man in any work marked by his genius' (*Humanism and Universality*, 1950). This stance led Waldemar-George to see in the Cobra group and post-war Expressionism 'vehemence in the brushstrokes, unreal colour, hasty execution, independence of signs from subjects, drawing with a brush, curvilinear writing' and 'the last chance of the man who defends the instinct of liberty and the right to dream against cybernetics'.

The coherence of Waldemar-George's vision is also its limitation, because he often moulded works to fit into his theory. 'For George [*sic*],' concluded Christopher Green, 'where modernism had replaced God with formal experiments (abstraction) and "cabalistic" superstition (primitivism), humanism would restore that sense of each individual's human relationship with the world which had been threatened by the machine.' In his history of French art of the early twentieth century, Green not only disparaged this philosophy but also emphasized the opposition between 'what artists necessarily wanted their work to say' and 'what a strong critical voice wanted it to say'. Indeed, it is difficult to believe that the young painters of 1926 (hardly prone to staunchly defending any tenets other than their own right to freedom) subscribed to Waldemar-George's theoretical positions, or even concurred with everything that he saw in their work. At most, they would have recognized in him a fleeting connection and complicity, a shared spirit of the time, onto which Waldemar-George had pinned a label, however inadequate.

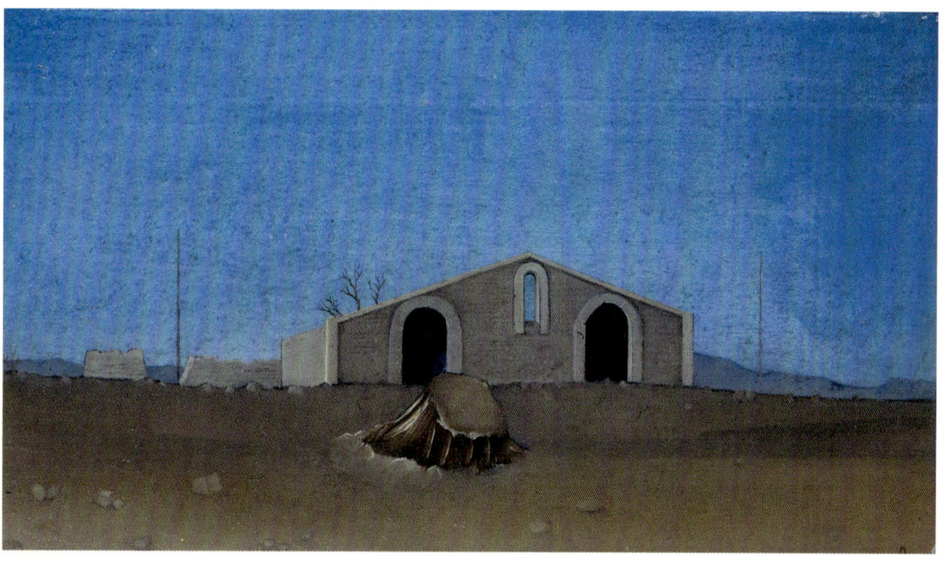

ABOVE: Jean Martin-Roch, *Ruins with Cut Trunk*, oil on mahogany panel, 16 × 27 cm (6⅜ × 10⅝ in.), 1940s

OPPOSITE, ABOVE: Jean Martin-Roch, *Landscape with Dead Tree*, oil on canvas, 30 × 60 cm (11⅞ × 23⅝ in.), *c*. 1960?
OPPOSITE, BELOW: Jean Martin-Roch, *Nocturnal Landscape*, oil on canvas, 20 × 41 cm (7⅞ × 16⅛ in.), 1945

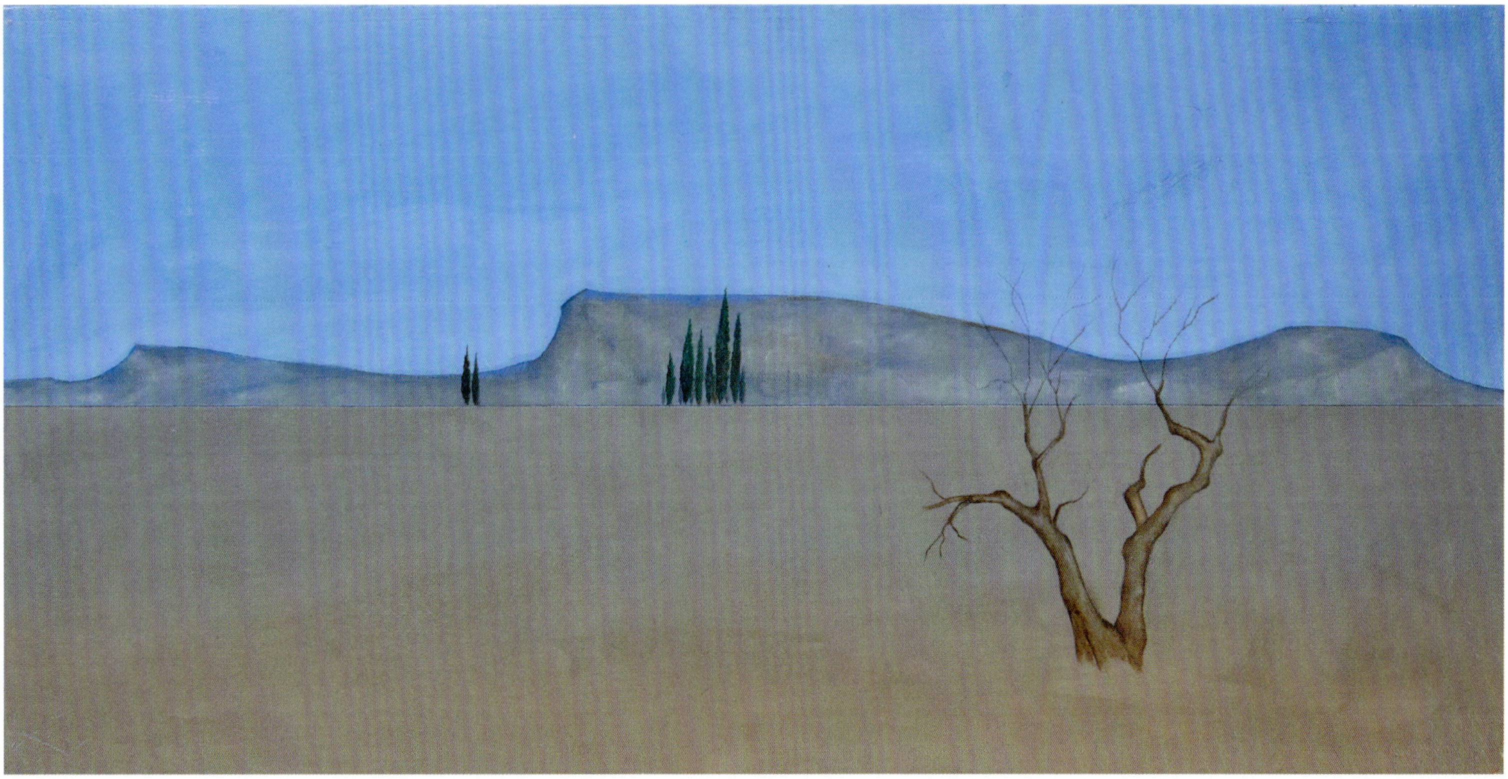

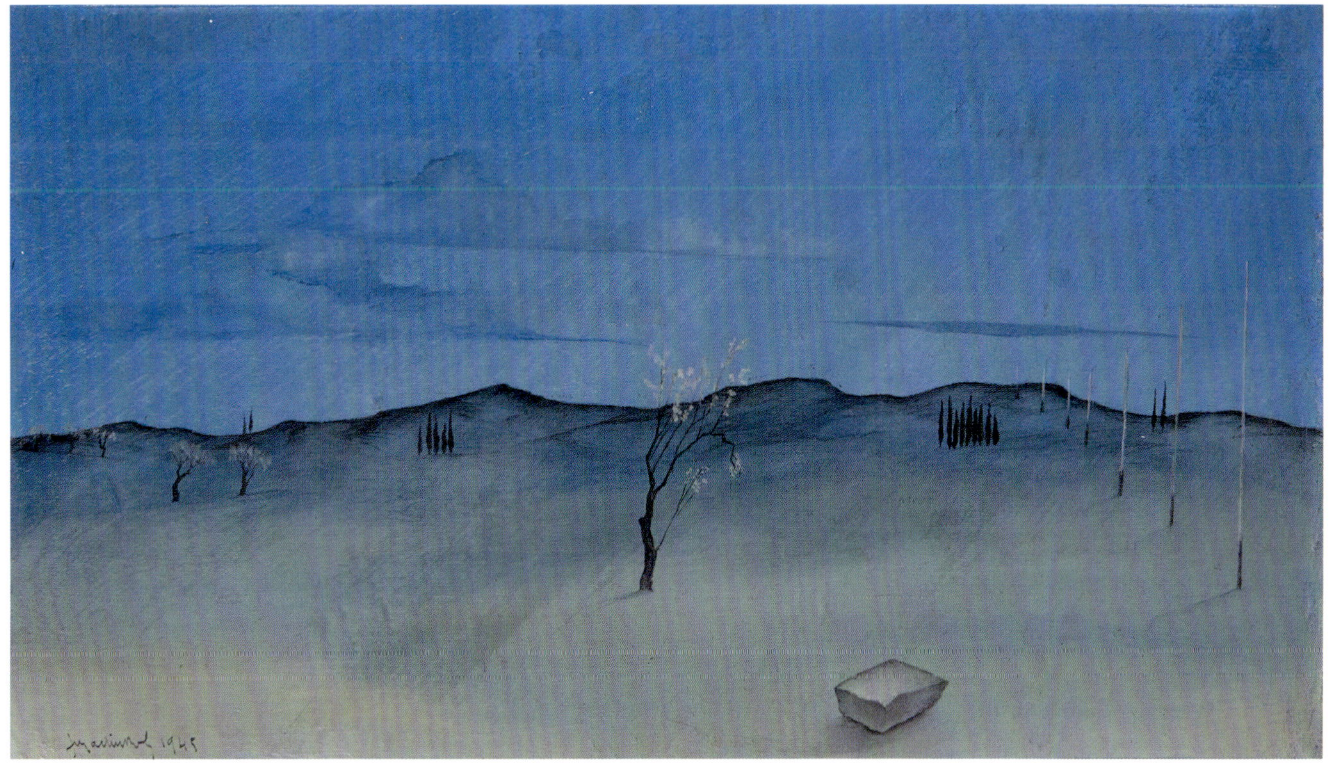

The Invention of Neo-Romanticism

Yves Chevrefils Desbiolles was thinking along the same lines when he described how Waldemar-George 'implicitly' grasped the work of the painters in the 1926 exhibition, through a kind of negative aesthetic: 'Waldemar-George extracted from his analysis of their works, all very different from each other, some generalities about a neo-humanism that is neither a repertoire, nor a vocabulary, nor a style, nor a fashion, nor even a movement seeking to revolutionize or merely renew the course of art. In short, he separated art from its formal history, through a series of subtractions, in order to submit it to a vaguely defined set of ethical rules that served to locate the presence of man in the work.'

The Neo-Romantic moment can, however, be better understood (this time more positively) by the opposition between the metaphors of the 'current' and the 'climate' explored by Jean Grenier in an essay in 1960. In these terms, it would be most appropriate to categorize the artists from the 1926 exhibition, who were too free and distinctive to form a *current*, as being part of a single *climate*: in other words, a set of informally shared values, references and aesthetic choices that served to bring them together. 'When we speak of "current", we think of the march of history, of the "sense" of history, of "progress", etc. – of all those attributes of the apparition of the modern god, whom we, with reason, gratify with a capital letter: History. [...] We fall therefore into that Hegelian conception which has come to us through Sartre, and which is responsible for all the nonsense spoken about what is "modern", what is "progressive" and "avant-garde" [...]. In contrast, the metaphor of "climate" signifies that a plant can only grow and develop if it is in harmony with a certain average temperature, a certain latitude and altitude. Its meaning is geographical rather than historical. It indicates that a painter cannot dispense with not only the society of the past (falsely referred to as Nature, since we see nature through the eyes of men who saw it before us) but also the society of the present and the society of the future, which is already prefigured in the society of today.'

Shared latitude, average temperature, skepticism about the 'avant-garde', a link with the past that does not rule out the present, opening towards the future: the metaphor of climate, and the factors that Grenier associates with it, correspond perfectly with the fluidity and 'indefinition' of Neo-Romanticism. And this corresponds with the way that Virgil Thomson described, as an insider, his experience of that time, as against the period that preceded it. 'The twenties', he wrote in his memoir, 'had been a peaceful and busy time, with lots of parties and dancing and casual sex-lives, and with minor new movements in music, art, and poetry every year. These were essentially a continuation under easy success conditions, of the modernist efforts that before the first World War had blossomed in far tougher weather.' The years after the Great War were marked not only by the famous incarnations of Modernism – Picasso, Joyce and Stravinsky – but also by what Thomson saw as an even greater cultural phenomenon: the Ballets Russes. In fact, he considered that a whole era came to an end with the death of Diaghilev in 1928: 'It was the choreographic stage that made the epoch shine. [...] Certain patrons were thereby led to furnish money for opera and ballet seasons in a climate of artistic (and sexual) cooperation that caused class barriers for a little time to disappear. After Diaghilev's death these barriers came right up again [...].'

At the same time, the artists who had created outrage at the start of the century saw their star quickly rise and even turn into marketable security: 'Characteristic of the whole new decade [...] was to be its preoccupation with the price of paintings. [...] In a decade of declining receipts from stocks and bonds, the buying of Modern Old Masters (Picasso, Braque, Matisse) and of the still inexpensive younger masters (Miró, Ernst, Arp, Dalí) was to be a source of rising wealth for the well advised, and a fascination to the public.'

In the face of this situation, and the concomitant reification of transgression, some young artists were drawn to affirm new values: 'Our new romanticism was no nostalgia for the warmths of World War I or for the gone-forever prewar youth of Stravinsky and Picasso, but an immersion complete in what any day might bring. *Mystère* was our word, tenderness our way, unreasoning compassion our aim. [...] Our novelty – and I am speaking of less than a dozen poets, painters, and musicians – consisted in the use of our personal sentiments as subject matter. Modern artists of the prewar time had mostly refrained from doing this.' Like Waldemar-George and (in a different way) James Thrall Soby, Thomson saw the return to emotion and subjective expression as the distinguishing feature of the Ranson alumni, but neither Soby nor Thomson associated themselves with any transcendental definition of 'Man' that could express a tradition or national genius, let alone any immutable essence. For them, it was more a question of a new *tone* within the tempo of artistic creation and the application of stylistic diversity.

'Neo-Romanticism', according to Thomson, in a key 1933 article in *Modern Music*, 'is the journalistic term for it. Spontaneity of sentiment is the thing sought. Internationalism is the temper. Elegance is the real preoccupation.' When Thomson honed his definition thirty years later, he drew on the authority of his partner, Maurice Grosser, a painter and critic who had known the original group: 'Neo-Romanticism in painting was defined twenty years later as "the personality of the painter reflected in the character of the thing seen." This from Maurice Grosser's book *The Painter's Eye*, where he also states that "by reintroducing humanity and personal feelings into an art that had become dehumanized, the Neo-Romantic painters made, I am convinced, the most important contribution to painting since the innovations of the great Moderns, and one which will have much influence in forming the painting of the second half of our century."'

Despite being situated at a different latitude from abstract art, and despite strategically shifting the centre of gravity of aesthetic interrogation, the Neo-Romantic climate stood apart from the current of Surrealism (even though they have often been lumped together, and some intermediary figures such as René Crevel, Georges Hugnet and Kristians Tonny had a foot in both camps). Surrealism has been defined as 'a particular blend of Marx-cum-Freud that constituted the philosophy of its poet-dictator André Breton'. The dogmatic pedantry of the 'Pope' of Surrealism was not the only point of contention, however, as even the two groups' subject matter was radically distinct: '[J]ust as the surrealists for their themes sought out the irrational, the subversive, and the cruel, the subjects of the neo-Romantics were predominantly humane and tender, the feelings you have when you let your mind alone. [...] Their chief defenders also were poets – Jean Cocteau, Max Jacob, and Gertrude Stein. And though their collectors in France were on the whole quite well-to-do (Paris millionaire bohemia), in America their work was bought only by intellectuals, chiefly the friends of Russell Hitchcock, who had been their earliest announcer. Edith Sitwell, who had formed with Tchelitcheff (over portrait sittings) a friendship of iron, managed to make a certain success for him in England.'

Nevertheless, Thomson could not deny that, despite their differences, Neo-Romanticism and Surrealism had in common a return to the figure, indicating the exhaustion of previous formal experiments. Even here, however, there was a clear divergence in the two groups' approach: 'It is worthy of note, moreover, that both of the chief contemporary movements, neo-Romanticism and surrealism, were concerned almost exclusively with figurative painting. Abstraction was still a note in sculpture (and in sculpturesque painting, such as that of Tanguy); but the newer painting of the time was generally concentrated on images. In this sense, it was all of it romantic, though surrealism spoke more directly to the mind, neo-Romanticism to the sensibilities.'

Although the two movements attracted some of the same patrons and champions (Marie-Laure and Charles de Noailles, Edward James, James Thrall Soby), their future destinies would diverge considerably. The Neo-Romantics enjoyed 'a certain prestige and some prosperity' in the years after they came onto the scene, but they would quickly find themselves victims of circumstance and see their market value plummeting (unlike that of the Surrealists): 'In 1935, [Tchelitchew] left both France and England for America; in 1938 Eugene Berman moved to New York; during 1939 and 40 Leonid Berman was in the French army, passing the Occupation underground; by 1937 or 38, Bérard, the leader of them all, had wholly given up painting in oil for fashion drawing and stage design. And so their side of the street lost its last contact with the European picture market.'

The effects of this dispersion, and of the war itself, were compounded by those of the displacement of the art scene from Paris to New York in the mid-twentieth century, as well as the emergence of new forms of that very abstraction that the Neo-Romantics had resisted. This abstraction would hold sway in the international art market for many years: 'It was only at the end of the decade, after the neo-Romantics (whom the French elegant world had begun to invest in, especially Bérard, who seemed possibly a new classical French painter) had either given up France or given up painting, that the French collectors, as the Americans had done already, settled for the abstract and the nonobjective.'

Thomson's account is personal (and sometimes extremely biased), but it has the virtue of taking into account the decisive economic factors – which he surely knew first-hand from Grosser's own travails – that would wipe Neo-Romanticism off the map: 'The grand return to painting nature and people that the neo-Romantics dreamed of bringing about had failed [...]. Hermetic art became therefore the only safe investment.'

Thomson's analysis of Neo-Romanticism is dispersed throughout his memoir (which he only published in 1966) and has attracted little attention, despite his position as an eye-witness. As we have seen, however, some thirty years earlier (when the Neo-Romantics were still in action), another account by a close observer, James Thrall Soby, did succeed in making waves. *After Picasso*, published in 1935, remains to this day the only work entirely devoted to the group, and it still stands as the seminal text on the subject. Soby's analyses are not encumbered by ideological premises, unlike those of Waldemar-George (who, in any case, never wrote a book on Neo-Romanticism but instead contented himself with a few magazine articles).

Like Thomson, Soby stressed the primacy of feelings, or what he termed 'unashamed poignancy', in the approach of these young painters whose art 'meant to touch the emotions rather than to appeal to the intellect'. Soby was therefore closer to Thomson than to Waldemar-George and, unlike the latter, he was never tempted by any return to an idealized 'humanity' that transcended history. Instead, he confined himself to a formal analysis of a series of dialectic reversals in artistic creation prior to the development of modern art, from the second half of the nineteenth century onwards. He thus saw Impressionism, and the movements that would follow it, as being in opposition to academic realism and workmanship; Impressionism was subsequently opposed by Expressionism (Fauvism), Expressionism by Cubism, and Cubism by Neo-Romanticism.

Accustomed as we now are to seeing the avant-gardes of the early twentieth century entirely as forces of transgression and innovation, as stages in a silent and progressive liberation, it is difficult to acknowledge, as Soby did in 1935, that the desire for 'personal expression' characteristic of certain sections of modern art had grown since 1908 into an article of faith 'as tiresome as the previous conceptions of Nature as Truth or Nature as Science'. It was these received ideas, which served as smokescreens for mediocrity, that led Braque and Picasso (otherwise an eminently romantic artist, in Soby's view) to go back to formal exploration and 'restore the rigid, architectural framework which had lain behind the painting of Poussin, Ingres and latterly, of Seurat and Cézanne'. This new direction would set the course for artistic creation for some fifteen years, brushing aside all forms of 'literary painting' (more aptly described as painting of the imaginary), such as the work of Klee and de Chirico – until, surprisingly, they inadvertently set in motion the backlash against Cubism:

'Few people thought that the literary painting of Chirico and Klee would so soon culminate in a revolt against Cubism [...]. Nevertheless, in 1924 the rapidly spreading fame of Surrealism announced the rebirth of literary, anecdotal painting, and Chirico and Klee had immediately to be reappraised as precursors of a new aesthetic.'

The emergence of the Neo-Romantics two years later undoubtedly marked the high point of this reaction, although, despite the best efforts of Waldemar-George, it was initially expressed in aesthetic rather than ideological terms. The openness to emotion, and even a degree of pathos, the representation of the human face and figure, and the taste for a poetic atmosphere all manifested a dialectical return to 'the very elements of sentiment which abstract art had been careful to suppress'. Even the minute chromatic variations of the early period of Bérard, the Bermans and Tchelitchew, which sometimes made their paintings virtually indecipherable, were a response to the violent contrasts and blocks of primary colours typical of abstraction: 'In reaction to what seemed to them the over-clear statement of abstractions, they attempted to cover their canvases with a mystifying veil.'

The Neo-Romantics also distanced themselves from another supposed hallmark of the avant-garde: an eagerness for transgression, scandal and provocation – 'shock value', sniffed Soby – that was being extravagantly displayed at that time by Dada and Surrealism but was totally alien to the Neo-Romantics. Their neutrality and lack of declarations, or even references to any kind of programme, were complemented by the accessibility of a new figuration that broke with 'the cult for the incomprehensible' that was part and parcel of modernity (Cubism being a prime example). This very accessibility, and the simplicity of these young painters' approach, would, however, undermine their credibility, as Soby observed: 'The painting of the Neo-Romantics [...] is, in fact, so easily enjoyed that people suspect it of being not altogether serious.' Even though such a line of reasoning may seem flimsy – inflated as it was by the creation of work for the fashion world and the stage, and by an implicit cultural hierarchization that would not be challenged until the latter part of the twentieth century – it would represent one of the key arguments in the case against the Neo-Romantics, especially from Greenberg, and it would be used to justify their poor critical standing.

Neo-Humanism is a Neo-Mannerism

Bearing these considerations in mind, it is the very title of Soby's book that provides the real clue as to his interpretation of Neo-Romanticism, which is undoubtedly the closest of all to the opinions of the artists involved: 'In calling this book "After Picasso",' he explained, somewhat provocatively, 'I have meant to imply two things: first, that in Paris certain painters younger than Picasso have already produced enough important work so that they, and not he, must stand for the latest developments in modern art; second, that much in the work of these younger painters was originally derived from Picasso.'

The question of age was paramount, in his view: 'Like Dalí, they belonged, in contrast to the early Surrealists, to a generation a quarter century younger than Picasso's. Their revolt against Cubism was more marked than that of the early Surrealists [...]. They had escaped the immense suction of his Cubist-architectural ideas by being too young to listen.'

The Neo-Romantics were not advocating, however, any return to an Edenic pre-Modernism. Nor did they reject Picasso's entire body of work, which had already acquired a stature sufficient to loom over all artistic creation. Instead, they pitted Picasso against himself, confronting him with the synthesis of emotion and form of his early periods, which he had now disavowed. Soby even evoked the Picasso who had once presided over an aesthetic of melancholy as a figure from a different life altogether: 'While Picasso's contempt for his own early periods had communicated itself to painters his age, the Neo-Romantics were able to discover his Blue and Rose periods as they would discover the work of a dead and neglected painter.'

If a work of art is, as George Kubler has claimed, a solution to a problem (in the same way as a tool or a scientific invention), then Picasso represented, as far as the Neo-Romantics were concerned, both the problem and the means to resolve it: '[T]he reaction against Picasso's kind of abstract art has paradoxically been given impetus by elements in Picasso's own work.' And, to continue in the terms proposed by Kubler in *The Shape of Time*, we can see Picasso as the 'first object' in a 'sequence' – that of Neo-Romanticism – that gathered together the solutions provided by the various painters involved, over the course of their development, in a series of variants and detours

OPPOSITE, ABOVE: Louis Le Nain, *Peasant Family in an Interior*, oil on canvas, 113 × 159 cm (44½ × 62½ in.), *c.* 1642
OPPOSITE, BELOW: Christian Bérard, *The Butcher's Children*, oil on cardboard, 54.6 × 46 cm (21 × 17½ in.), *c.* 1940

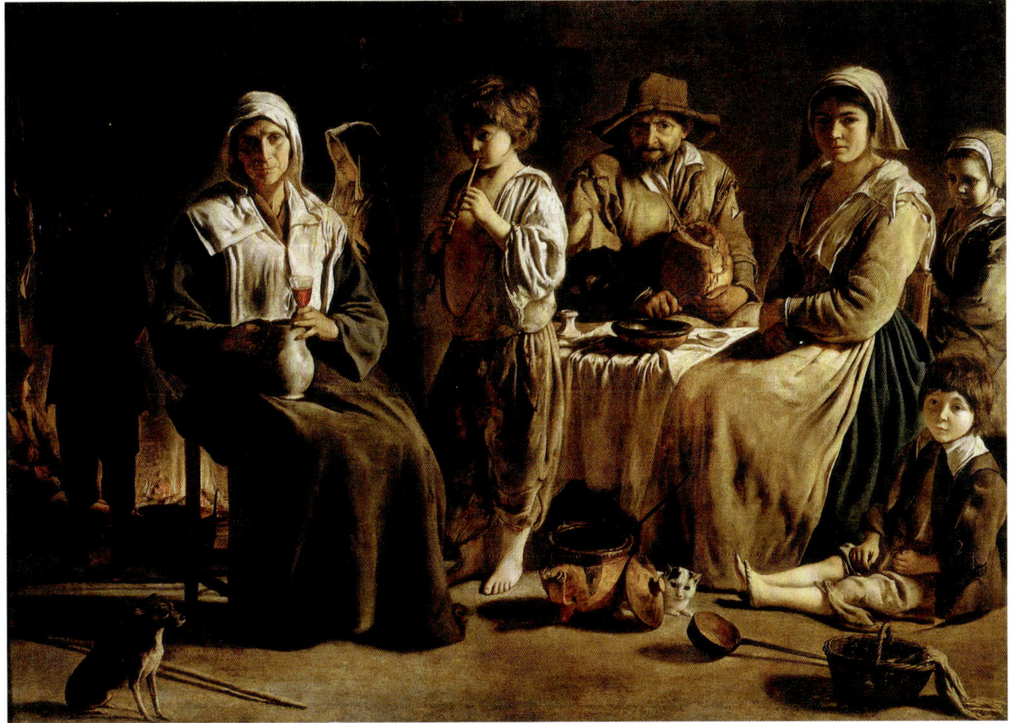

'also giving rise to change' through their stylistic differences.

From this viewpoint, it would be perfectly legitimate, and perhaps more accurate, to replace the notion of Neo-Romanticism with one of 'Neo-Mannerism', or at least to examine the aptness of this proposition by means of the group's paintings and historical circumstances, which they both reflect and stand apart from. There are clear links between, on the one hand, the work of Bérard, the Berman brothers and Tchelitchew, and, on the other hand, that of painters from the late sixteenth century. The Neo-Romantics had to face down radically innovative work from a previous generation that had marked a 'before and after' in the story of art, and the successors of Leonardo and Michelangelo must similarly have felt like interlopers. Both groups wore their knowledge

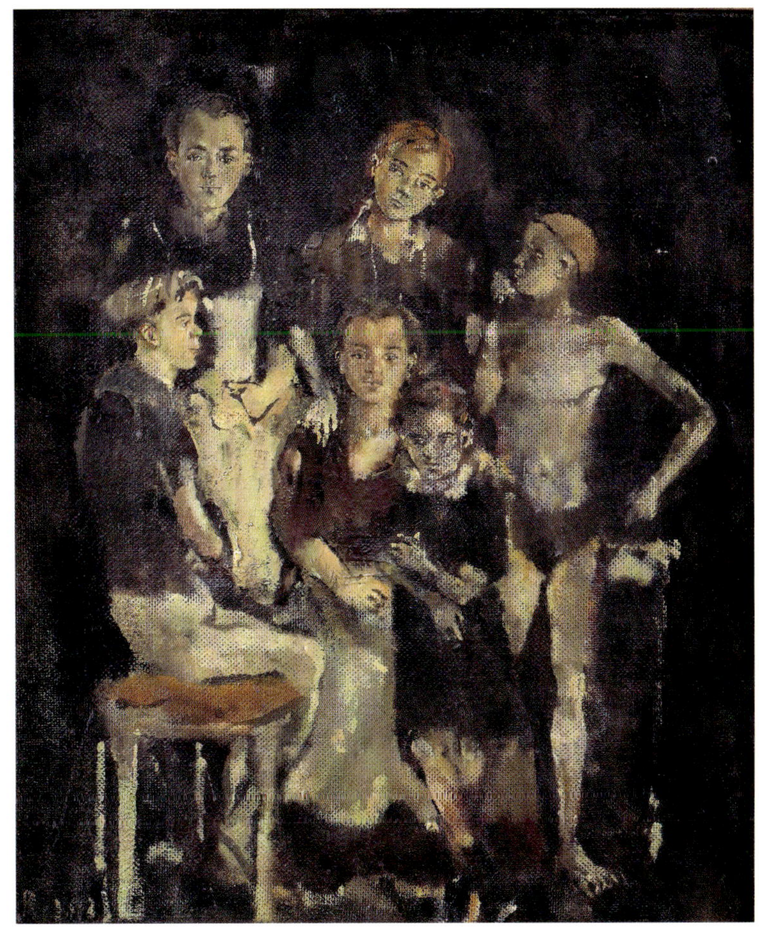

of art history lightly, applying technical virtuosity to memories of forms, deformations and visual quotations. Furthermore, they shared a melancholy palette, a ghostly atmosphere, with figures sleepwalking through a world that seemed to have been snuffed out.

This reading of Neo-Romanticism also makes it possible to reconfigure the crucial issue of the pathos and emotion in the painters from the 1926 exhibition. Their work cannot be reduced to an *illustration* of a universal aspect of human experience, as Waldemar-George would have us believe, because it ultimately springs from the *representation* of that experience. They were inspired in this respect by the formal interpretations of Picasso, but also by Derain, Degas and the French 'painters of reality' of the seventeenth century, such as Georges de La Tour and the Le Nain brothers, whose work had been re-evaluated in 1934 thanks to a revelatory exhibition at the Musée de l'Orangerie (their influence, particularly on Bérard, cannot be underestimated).

This coupling of Neo-Romanticism with Mannerism has barely been presented for inspection, however, largely because the epithet 'mannerist' has acquired irredeemably negative connotations. Nevertheless, there has been one notable exception to this reticence, in the form (unsurprisingly) of a historian with an enormous cultural range and an acutely observant eye: André Chastel. In his discussion of a 1946 exhibition by the artist who was undoubtedly most closely aligned with the Neo-Romantics (and who stayed in contact with Bérard, Eugene Berman and Tchelitchew until their deaths) – the indomitable and flamboyant Leonor Fini – Chastel raised the question of the 'resurrection of a mannerism'. He was speaking in general terms, but his remarks could easily be applied more specifically to the work of Fini's friends: 'Some spirits, in overstretched and troubled times, enjoy bringing to the fore the element of artifice and consensual lying that is indispensable to art. This is the origin of Mannerism. After the masters come the disciples, this cannot be denied; but the torment of the disciples, and more generally of artists who have been excessively cultivated, comes from that which they have been overly warned about: they know that there is a comedy, a game, in the principle of art, they know its resources, and, like the libertine who can never be satisfied by candid sensuality, they seek to play a subtler game in the very interior of the common game; they create an art full of reminiscences adroitly

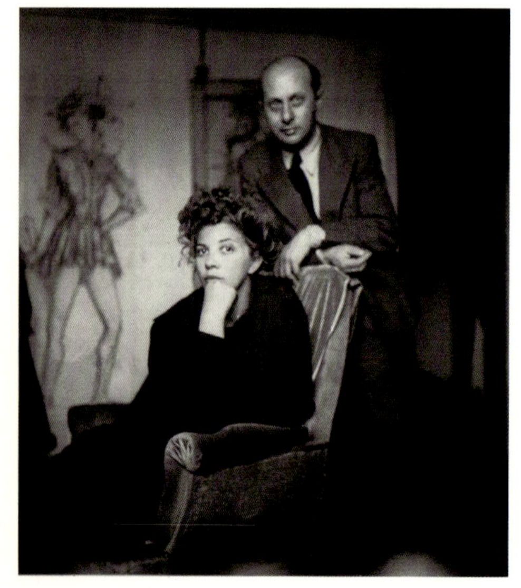

ABOVE: Eugene Berman and Leonor Fini, at the latter's apartment, Hôtel de Marles, Paris, *c.* 1938
OPPOSITE: Eugene Berman, with makeup by Leonor Fini, at the latter's apartment, Hôtel de Marles, Paris, *c.* 1938

used to unusual or surprising ends. A kind of technical perfection, an extreme subtlety of intentions, the quest for elegance in inordinately slender and elongated forms, a spicy mix of caprice and truth, and, to be frank, a sort of bad taste firing the sensibility of an aesthete: that is the basis of Mannerism, which was given varied, precious and extremely ingenious expressions around the middle of the 16th century by the art of Parmigianino, of Pontormo, of the Venetians and the Lombards.'

By insisting on the artificiality, sensuality and formal concerns of a 'manner' whose resurgence he found discernible in the mid-1940s, Chastel substantiates the redefinition proposed herein of a Neo-Romanticism that revolved around stylistic factors and not around a questionable 'Humanism', thereby releasing it from Waldemar-George's ideological cul-de-sac. This hypothesis can be further corroborated by drawing, paradoxically, on the indictment issued by Clement Greenberg against an exhibition of Eugene Berman's work at Julien Levy's gallery in 1943. This inculpatory and virulent text should be read, in a manner of speaking, the wrong way round, as Berman and his friends represented the exact opposite, the absolute counterpoint, of any definition of the legitimacy of art acknowledged by this champion of Abstract Expressionism and devotee of Hans Hoffman. (Like the Mannerists, the Neo-Romantics were frequently condemned by default for the principle underlying their aesthetic approach: an adverse reading was mistaken for an inverted one.)

'Eugene Berman, Neo-Romantic,' Greenberg began, 'is, I suppose, a painter. But we can save trouble by taking him as simple specialist in *frissons* for the cocktail hour. Given that he has discovered essentially nothing about his art that Raphael didn't know, he is very dextrous. That is, he can paint any way he wants to, provided the way has already been discovered by someone else. The prescription for Berman's thrill this year, and thrill it is, is to take a Florentine master, clean him thoroughly, rearrange the figures, reheat and remix the subject, and then freshen up everything with Böcklin syrup. [...] There is an effect, a wonderful-rich effect, but it belongs to journalism and mode. [...] Berman's pictures, crowded as they are into a relatively small space, are too overpowering, too decadent, too spurious, and, really, too well done to be dealt with in measured words. If this is art, the age is doomed.'

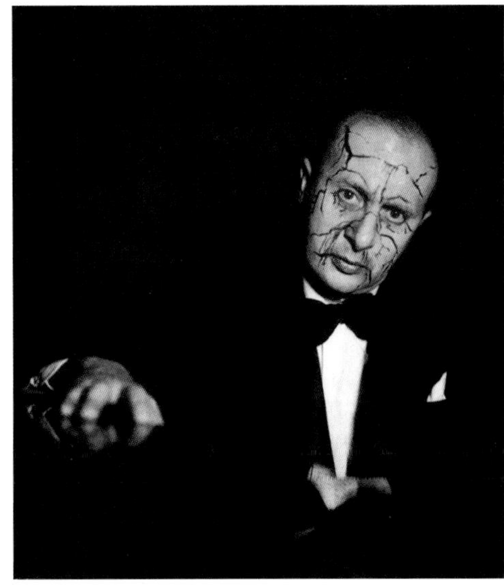

It is evident that the Neo-Romantic vision broke every tenet of Greenberg's supercilious dogmatism. In 1939, for example, he had famously made a distinction between 'high' and 'low' art, but the Neo-Romantics cast doubt on this dichotomy by denying any contradiction between 'pure' and applied art, or working in 'journalism and mode', or theatre and ballet, well before Pop Art mounted a radical challenge to such boundaries thirty years later.

So many of the terms applied to Eugene Berman also crop up in the criticism of historical Mannerism: derivative, minor, mimicry, tracings or copies merely striving for effect, lack of substance, hodgepodge of borrowings, calligraphy in a void... All these strictures were encapsulated in Greenberg's parting blow of 'spurious'. To him, Berman's painting was parasitical, adulterated and fallacious – especially in the light of his obvious enthusiasm for double images, trompe-l'œil, illusion and staging – and deserved to be dismissed outright as a counterfeit or a simulation of the 'truth' that exclusively manifested itself in abstraction, that summit of artistic expression and modernity.

There is no common ground between these two approaches. Towards the end of his career, however, Eugene Berman indirectly gave a positive twist to Greenberg's charge sheet in a few scattered, brief texts published in catalogues (they also stand in for the declarations that Bérard and Tchelitchew failed to make in their lifetimes). Berman interpreted all the supposed pastiche, distinguished only by dexterity (hollow virtuosity was another jibe directed at Mannerism) as a process of communing with the wellspring of memory, and he defined painting as a web of traces, reminiscences and lapses in which history and time are crucial protagonists.

In his presentation of his exhibition *Return from Egypt*, Berman contrasted the 'exact' view of a Canaletto (often reproduced by means of a *camera obscura*) to the composite reworking of a Carpaccio, whose lineage he claimed as his own: 'To a Canaletto we can oppose a Carpaccio and immediately see what creative difference there is between the painter of the real and the exquisite, fantastic visions of the painter of the more than real, of a real which never existed but which is actually more real than the documentary and real representations of the other. In fact, Carpaccio offers us a purely imaginary and impossible Venice and one could say verily that not content with the beauty of her most famous palaces, monuments and vistas, the Dalmatian painter wanted to prove that he could visualize, invent and build a city much more fantastic, splendid and visionary than the real city herself! And to me, he succeeded magnificently in this demonstration!' (Berman had already used the same example in a text which we shall return to later on: 'It is not a matter of visions of the real, of souvenirs of specific places or monuments or illusionist vistas, like the ones painted for 18th-century tourists by the Venetian vedutisti. [...] Think instead of the compositions of Poussin or Claude, of those heroic visions of Roman monuments, more invented than real, of those impossible seaports where the characters of Homer and Virgil disembarked, dressed in the "ancient" fashion of the time, of that elegiac painting of a Roman countryside that existed only in the mind of that artist from Lorraine. Think, above all, of the Venice of Carpaccio – of the landscapes and architectures that feature in the background of the pictures from the cycles of Saint Ursula, Saint George and Saint Jerome. A Venice that has never existed, has never been seen, emanating from a whimsical and ingenious imagination, and perhaps even more beautiful than the true Venice.')

According to Berman, the opposition between these two approaches hinges on the definition of truth in painting: 'the autobiography of Goethe was entitled "Dichtung und Wahrheit" [Poetry and Truth], a deft definition in one single brief phrase of the true significance of so much art. The truth then, is to be viewed not as a single realistic fact and a fleeting and fragmentary moment, but as a patient and ideal reconstruction and a summing up of our many visual and emotional experiences, buried in the moving sands of our memory and which aspire to give definite forms of expression to the many things we have dreamed, loved, sensed, discovered and invented.'

Although the art of Berman, and the Neo-Romantics in general, is often described as knowing or literary (with all the usual negative connotations implied by these terms), it is, above all else, an art of memory, a palimpsest of reminiscences and allusions, a game of borrowings and deformations. For all its pathos and emotional power, it is an art of *displacement* that draws on the past to nourish the present. Right from the start, it broke with what had already been enshrined as the tradition of the twentieth-century avant-gardes, but it did so not through opposition and rejection, but rather through continuity and contiguity. Rather than being anachronistic, it sought to be *uchronistic*. 'Berman thinks that art is "timeless"', wrote Julien Levy in 1946. 'To be classified as of the present day is alien to him – today being only the brief link between the great past and a limitless future.'

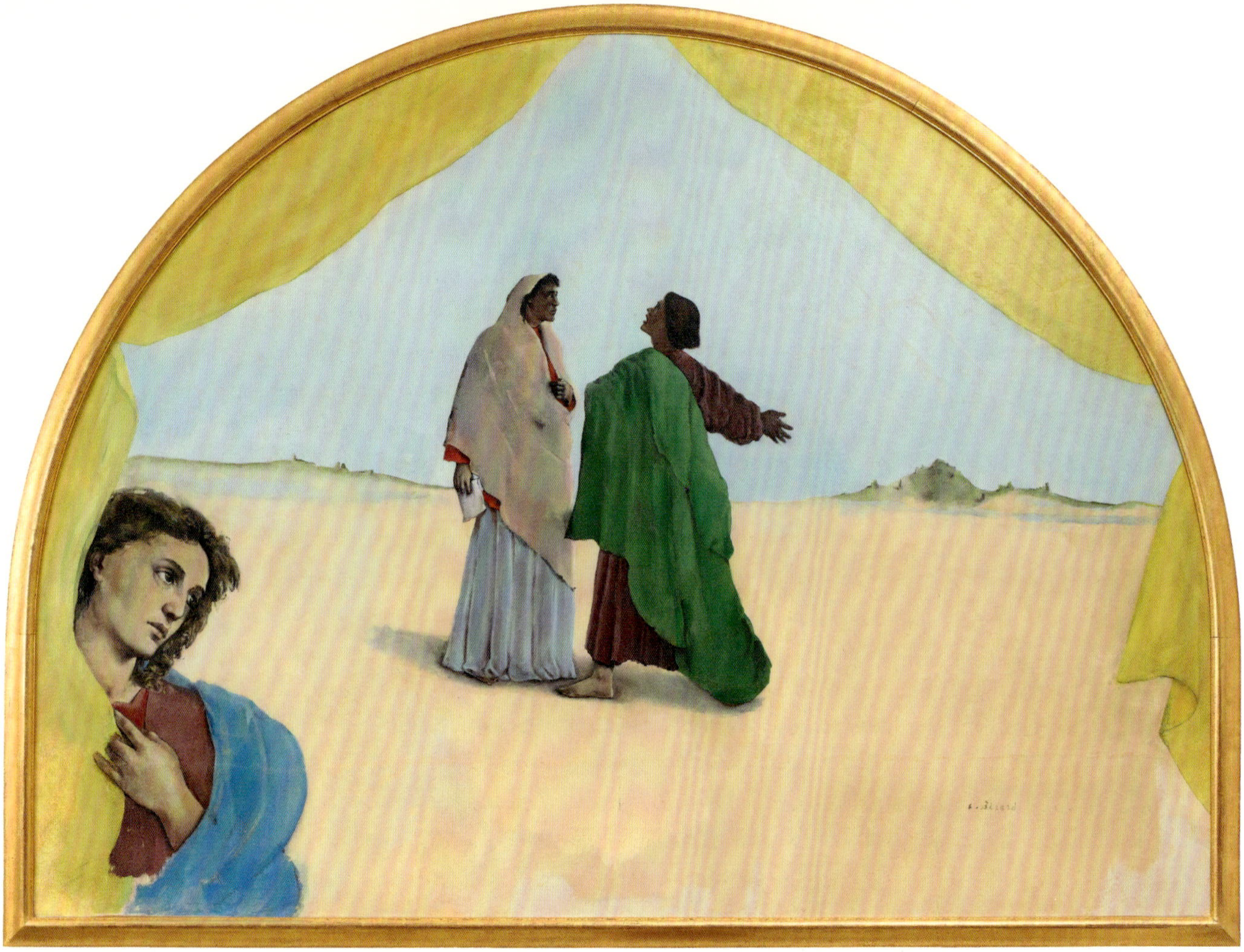

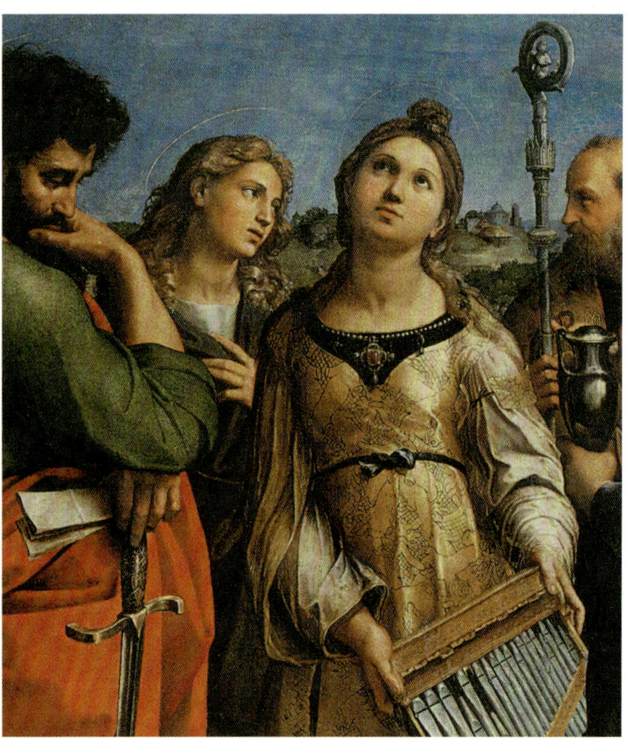

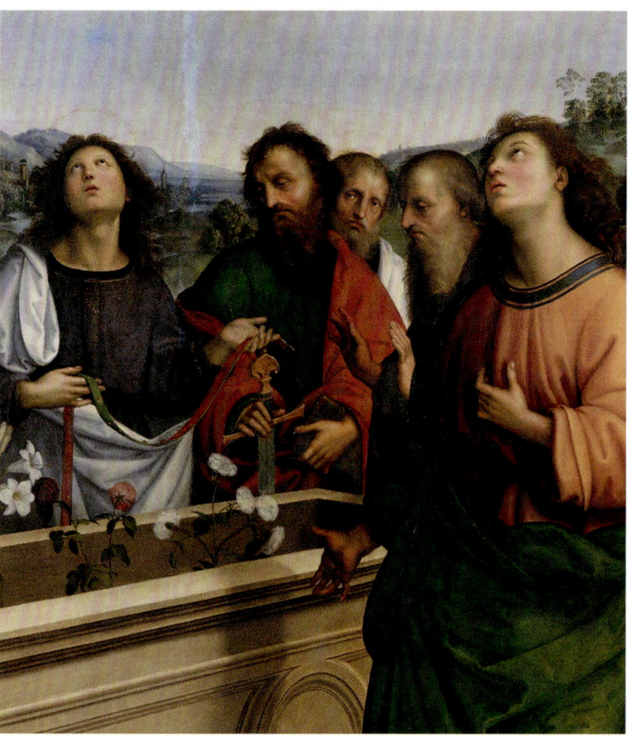

TOP: Christian Bérard, panel for Marie-Blanche de Polignac, oil on canvas, 140 × 190 cm (55⅛ × 74⅞ in.), n.d.

ABOVE, LEFT: Raphael, *Saint Cecilia*, oil on wood, transferred to canvas, 238.5 × 155 cm (93⅞ × 61 in.), 1516–17 (detail)

ABOVE, RIGHT: Raphael, *The Coronation of the Virgin* (Oddi altarpiece, Vatican), oil on wood, transferred to canvas, 267 × 163 cm (105 × 64 in.), *c.* 1503 (detail)

Landscapes of Fantasy

'We cannot escape history.' Berman borrowed this famous adage of Abraham Lincoln for a text, appropriately entitled 'Declaration of Independence', for a catalogue published by Knoedler in New York in 1964. (Several extracts from this text have already been quoted above.) This declaration was a reworking of 'Notes for a Self-Portrait', which he had written five years earlier for his first exhibitions in Rome, at the Obelisco and the Galleria San Marco ('my true beginnings as a painter in Italy'), and it serves to put his vision of art in context while, in passing, also providing an outline of the *modus operandi* of the Neo-Romantics.

While acknowledging the individuality of each of the Neo-Romantic artists, Berman affirmed their shared tastes and spirit, and delineated an approach that amounted to a profession of faith: 'We had common ideas and aspirations, we were interested in a poetic artistic expression, an imaginary vision of the visual world, a synthesis of realism and fantasy, of dream and reality.' Berman unhesitatingly traced this shared vision back to a source whose importance we have already seen: 'I spent my childhood between St. Petersburg and travelling, periods abroad, until, in 1920, I settled in Paris, where I lived for twenty years. During that time, I made frequent journeys to Italy and had some long stays there. Although Paris then seemed the ideal city for a young painter, the source of inspiration, the most fertile stimulants for my work come from those first stays in Italy, from the enchanted discovery of its landscapes, its architecture, its monuments, its ruins, its cities and its countryside.'

The attraction of contemporary Italy – 'the main influence on us was not Picasso (whom we greatly admired but also, in some respects, fought against) but rather the metaphysical painting of de Chirico' – was thus deepened by the allure of an origin story and a repository of memories and images whose contents could be rifled to form new compositions, in an endless game of destruction and reconstruction, 'a kind of *perpetuum mobile* that filled me with joy and exultation'. This dynamic and multi-faceted source of inspiration far outweighed the ideologically biased 'Romanity' of figures like Waldemar-George in his period of allegiance to the Duce. 'My true work', declared Berman, 'consists of accepting this universe that is visible, poetic and stimulating (at least in the elements that seem to be so to me) before submitting it to a poetic destruction. There now begins the process of a new creation, a patient and meditated reconstruction in which a new vision, thought up and invented by the painter, arises from the beloved and sacrificed universe.' And this methodology directly reflects the nature and status of the artist, defined by Berman with the term that was applied to the likes of Serlio, Palladio, Piranese and Carpaccio in their day: 'inventor'. This job description implies that originality is based on a store of memories and derivations: 'So, let us stop at this term of "inventor". The key word for my work, if anybody really wants to authorize me to declare a credo.'

All the Neo-Romantics, in fact, were 'inventors', particularly of an Italy which, for three of them, nestled St Petersburg in its shadow. As for Bérard, he made even fewer statements about art than the others, but some of his works speak for themselves: one panel that he painted for Marie-Blanche de Polignac, for example, featured key figures that were a direct quotation from Raphael's *Saint Cecilia* or from his *Coronation of the Virgin* in the Vatican. And Waldemar-George, in his 1934 article-manifesto in defence of Neo-Humanism, could not avoid underlining the importance of the formative Italian influence on the young painters, even while downplaying it in a desire to proclaim their originality: 'It is not Berman's stays and work in Rome that have made him contribute to a revival of classical landscape under a new guise. It is not by looking at the masters of the Quattrocento that Tchelitchew suddenly discovered the vocation of an anatomist painter. Direct influences play a secondary role in the aesthetic formation of artists, serving to confirm them in their own concerns and their own research.'

The Neo-Romantics were not alone in their fascination for Italy in the 1920s, and much could be said about the biographical, moral and aesthetic reasons that drove artists as different as Picasso (with his trip to Rome in 1917 and design for the stage curtain of *Parade*), Derain (who wrote to Daniel-Henry Kahnweiler in 1920, 'The journey to Rome has put me right off the Côte d'Azur, which I find very ugly'), Bérard and the Berman brothers towards an Italian motherland in search of a new formal register that could not be reduced to Neoclassicism, the tenets of the Novecento or a 'return to order', although these various currents did, as we have seen, overlap and intersect with each other.

To go back to Berman's 'Notes for a Self-Portrait', it is clear that the Italian flavour in his work was far more than a passing fancy.

OPPOSITE: Irene Brin, 1947, by Leslie Gill

Indeed, when he reworked the text in 1964, Berman bestowed a real ontological value on Italy, making it the justification for, and source of, a particular vision of existence: 'I feel Italian, in the sense that Stendhal felt Milanese (I would see myself more as Roman, Venetian or even Neapolitan). Just as at certain times Mozart, Goethe, Byron, Shelley and so many others felt Italian.' (In his *Orientamenti della scenografia*, published in 1960, the critic Carlo Rava also mentioned 'the constant backdrop of Italianness in his work, a feature that impregnates his entire corpus'.)

This substantial 'Italianness' did not have the same overtones in the late 1950s as it did in the early 1930s, when the country was heading for disaster. The Italy of that time presented a picture of poverty and ruins that seemed to bring to life Berman's perennial obsessions, to the extent that some critics, such as Marcel Brion, saw him as the prophet of 'post-catastrophe'. (Similarly, but in a completely different register, Tchelitchew was seen as a precursor of the extra-sensory experiments of the 1960s.) It was this Italy that Edmund Wilson described in the chronicle of his travels after the outbreak of the war, *Europe without Baedeker*: a land of destruction and deprivation but also a kind of joy, as the proximity of death heightened an unquenchable lust for life. In his attempt to capture the 'tragic paradox' of those years, Wilson evoked 'contrasts of brokenness and deadness with a warm and rich physical life'. This Italy also provided the stage for vibrant artistic and cultural activity. This was especially true of the Roman circles frequented by figures such as: the novelist Aldo Palazzeschi; the poet Sandro Penna; the eclectic and caustic Ennio Flaiano (all too often remembered nowadays only for his collaborations with Federico Fellini); the erudite and vaguely sinister Mario Praz; the punctilious de Chirico; the Neo-Baroque polymath Fabrizio Clerici; and the ironic and subtle Irene Brin, who combined fashion journalism under an array of pseudonyms with the management (alongside her husband, Gaspero del Corso) of a highly influential gallery, the Obelisco. It was there that Eugene Berman had his first major Italian exhibition, in May 1949, followed by two more in June 1959 and June 1961. (Tchelitchew also exhibited there in April 1950 and March 1955, as did Leonid in April 1954.)

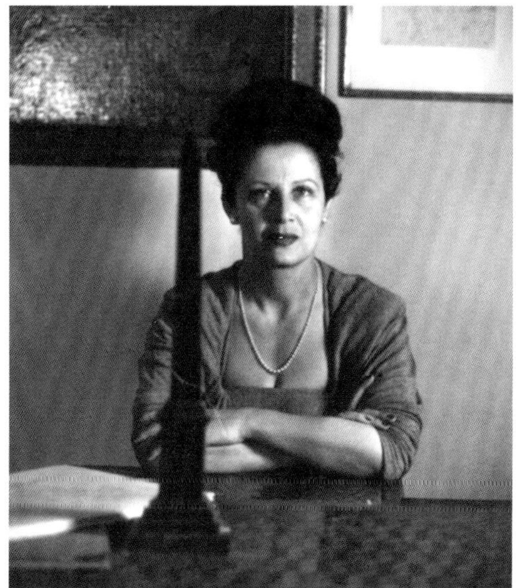

The Lightness of Life

Edmund Wilson was not the only American to leave an eye-witness account of these times. The journalist Peter Lindamood arrived in Italy as part of the US Army's Psychological Welfare Branch, which had as one of its missions the strengthening of cultural ties between the two countries. Lindamood was already an art enthusiast (he would go on to open an antiques shop in New York) and he immediately appreciated the vitality of Rome's cultural scene, and the crucial role of the Obelisco gallery. Not only did he present the city's leading lights to the American public in articles for magazines such as *Town and Country* ('Rome', March 1945) and *Harper's Bazaar* ('Italian Painting Today', February 1946), he also took an active part in the promotion and exhibition of their work in the United States. His connection with the editorial team of *View* (the magazine published by Charles Henri Ford, Tchelitchew's partner) allowed him to act as an intermediary between young Italian painters, the Obelisco and the New York art scene. His first port of call in the USA was the Hugo Gallery, founded in 1945 by Maria Ruspoli, the Duchess of Gramont, and run by Alexandre Iolas, formerly a dancer. (Iolas would become a top-rank art dealer in his own right, with a claim to fame as the organizer of Andy Warhol's first ever exhibition in 1952.) Iolas would remain loyal to Eugene Berman by exhibiting his work regularly in various locations in both Europe and the United States right up to the 1970s. He would thus become one of the last representatives of a network of gallery owners who would follow the precedents of Pierre Colle, Pierre Loeb, Christian Dior and Jacques Bonjean, Julien Levy, Marie Cuttoli and Lucie Weill by maintaining a low-key but constant support for the Neo-Romantics throughout the twentieth century.

The Obelisco would similarly go on to enjoy several decades as one of the nerve centres of a cosmopolitan milieu in which Eugene Berman felt very much at home. Its most prominent figures included Carmel Snow, the editor of *Harper's Bazaar* (who appointed Irene Brin as its Italian correspondent), Orson Welles, Gore Vidal, Tennessee Williams, Irving Penn, and the multilingual journalist and translator Henry Furst. Apart from these well-known names, another figure worthy of mention is Piero Fornasetti, originally from Milan. In 1951 Berman entrusted the young Fornasetti with the printing of his folio of magnificent lithographs collected under the title *Viaggio in Italia* (Journey in Italy). This series encapsulates Berman's vision of the country – both real and imaginary. Fornasetti was then just starting out as a printer, but he was a remarkable painter and draughtsman who would go on to be a major figure in post-war Italian design. He was highly versatile and created a wide-ranging body of work that embraced both graphic and decorative art that can legitimately be considered the continuation of Neo-Romanticism by other means.

It was another star of this artistic constellation, however, who would most fully capture the spirit of these post-war years in Italy. Alberto Savinio, de Chirico's brother, was both a writer and a painter, and he had been a fellow traveller with the Neo-Romantics since their early days in Paris. Savinio was able to transform the period into an instance of Nietzschean *Leichte Leben*, exemplifying that 'easy life' that enables human beings to endure, between mourning and lightness, the heaviness and horror of the real. ('*Nicht das Leben zu erleichtern sondern leicht zu nehmen* [Do not lighten life but take it with lightness]', wrote Nietzsche in one of his notebooks.)

This spirit runs through all of Savinio's work, and he made it manifest by dreaming up a 'conceptual character' whose multiple incarnations reappear throughout history. In an illuminating text written in 1944 as a preface to the works of Lucian of Samosata, Savinio made Lucian the prototype, or 'conceptual character', of the 'Great Dilettante', the precursor of a lineage that brought together Montaigne, Stendhal, Nietzsche (and Savinio himself) through a common vision of existence, morality and aesthetics. This 'dilettantism' is characterized by an untrammelled love of liberty, a critical spirit, a rejection of dogma and 'a single order, from a single principle', an innate cosmopolitanism, and a questioning of traditional definitions of genres and received hierarchies. Savinio thus handed to Berman – that 'Italian, in the sense that Stendhal felt Milanese' – the finest mask possible, and Berman seized it in his 1964 'Declaration of Independence', equally the work of a 'Great Dilettante': 'I believe more than ever in the necessity to probe every individual effort by tending to distance oneself from great collective movements that rapidly exhaust themselves. Taboos, arbitrary rules and shooting galleries, still so de rigueur in our days, are in reality merely the remains of a long totalitarian torment that has been exhausted and discredited. A spirit of submission to orders, decrees and pressures of all kinds continues nevertheless to govern our intellectual life in a disturbing fashion.'

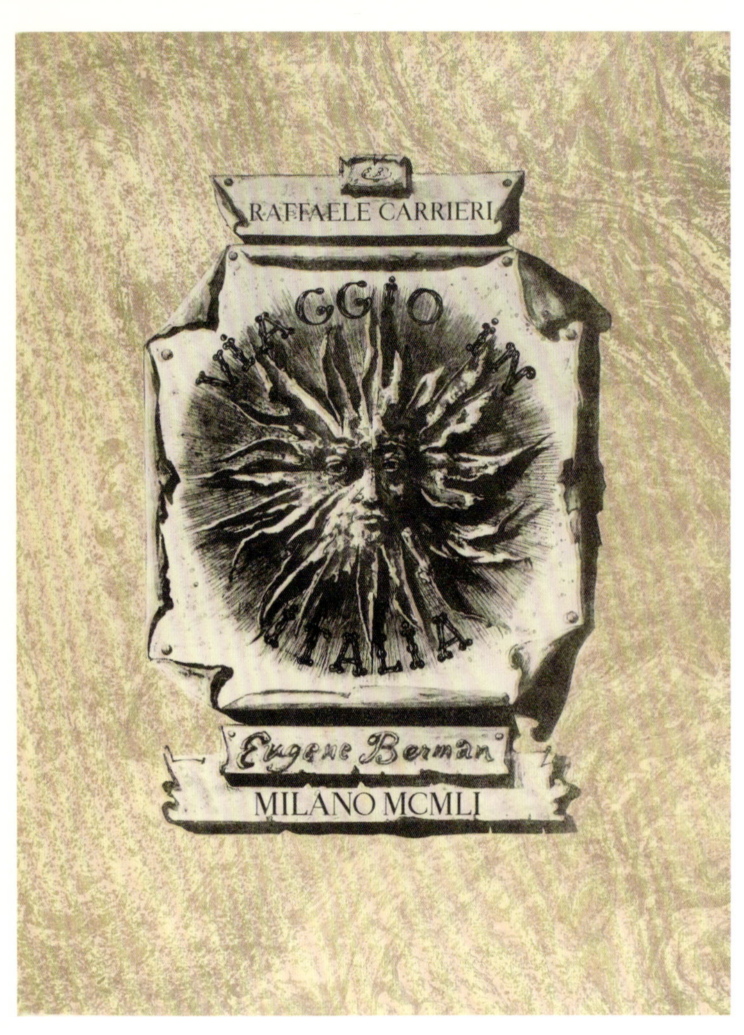

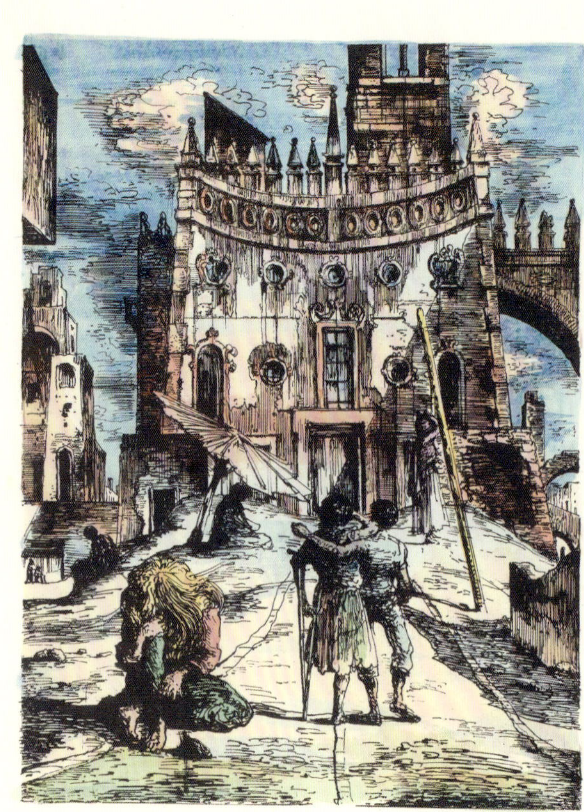

ABOVE AND OPPOSITE: Eugene Berman, lithographs from *Viaggio in Italia* by Raffaele Carrieri, album in folio printed by Piero Fornasetti, 1951

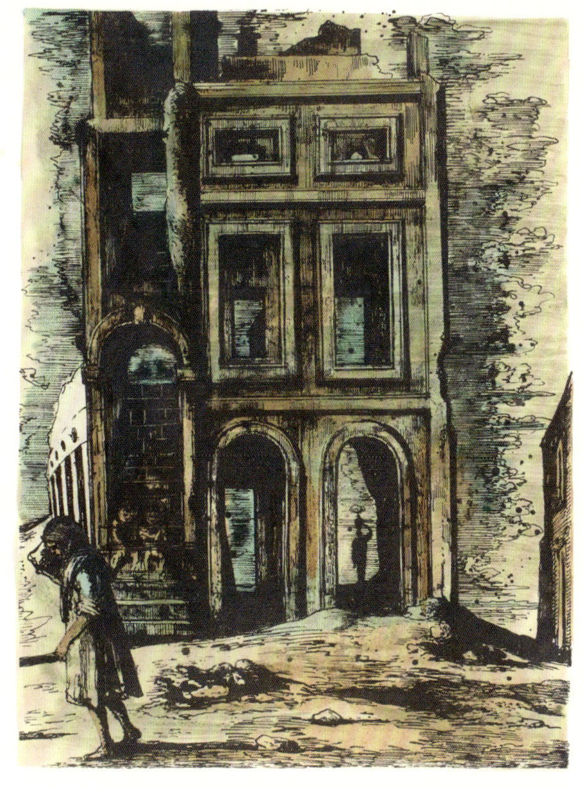

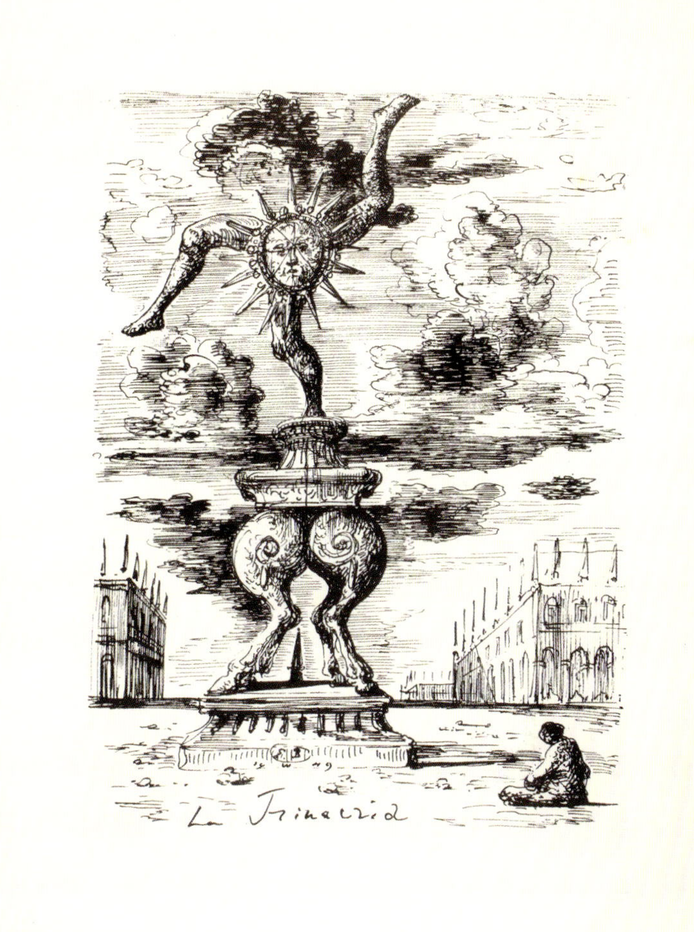

Unsurprisingly, these games of memory and 'invention', with their unabashed dilettantism, their quest for ontological lightness in the face of ruin and disaster, and their myriad facets of an Italianness as much dreamed as real, were also reflected in Bérard's body of work, which was steeped in melancholy. Bérard seemed unconcerned about posterity and projected a sense of nonchalance (as some critics were all too eager to point out), but this *sprezzatura* (to use the term coined by Castiglione in his *Book of the Courtesan*) was matched by a display of virtuosity and commitment to the bold, decisive gesture that exemplified Castiglione's concept of 'grace'.

This grace, rather than any slapdash offhandedness, was the driving force behind Bérard's accomplishments in fashion drawing, as a chronicler of the ephemeral who seized the moment with an élan that, in itself, seemingly conveyed or embodied the very nature of his subjects. Eugene Berman's contribution to this field would, in contrast, be much more marginal, but the fashion world knew that it was on to a good thing with Bérard. His drawings appeared in *Vogue*, *Harper's Bazaar* and the *Albums du Figaro*, and they turned him into a veritable interpreter of the age. (This aspect of Bérard's work was also reflected in a major exhibition that he curated, *The Theatre of Fashion*, inspired by the earliest mannequins from the eighteenth century; this show toured the world in 1944–45 in an effort to re-establish the primacy of Parisian couture.) This quality (in the philosophical sense) of Bérard's gestures was not confined to fashion, however, as it was equally characteristic of his approach to painting in general, including – perhaps most particularly – his remarkable portraits and his landscapes with metaphysical colour schemes.

If any single person can be considered emblematic of this combination of creative lightness and technical brilliance, it is surely the figure, or myth, of Mozart (another Italian by adoption, according to Berman). It is therefore unsurprising that both Bérard and Berman were so smitten by Mozart that each produced, albeit decades apart, a work entitled *Mozartiana*. Bérard, who had been given a biography of the composer by Marie-Laure de Noailles, not only designed the sets and costumes for Balanchine's ballet of this name in 1933, he also continued to create variations on the image of Mozart that, forebodingly, homed in on his truncated life and early death. Berman, in his turn, published *Mozartiana*, a collection of lithographic portraits celebrating the centenary of Mozart's death in 1956. This was the same year in which he designed *Così Fan Tutte* for the Piccola Scala in Milan, and

OPPOSITE: Christian Bérard, *Mozart*, gouache on black paper, 23 × 18 cm (9 × 7 in.), *c.* 1945

one year before he fulfilled a life-long dream by designing *Don Giovanni* for the Metropolitan Opera in New York. The Mozartian theme ran through the work of both painters and provided them with common ground. Mozart offered them not only an exalted model of the artist, and a possible object of identification, but also the imaginary representation of the marriage of melancholy and joy, of dynamism and nostalgia, that underlies human grace and that lay at the very heart of their own work.

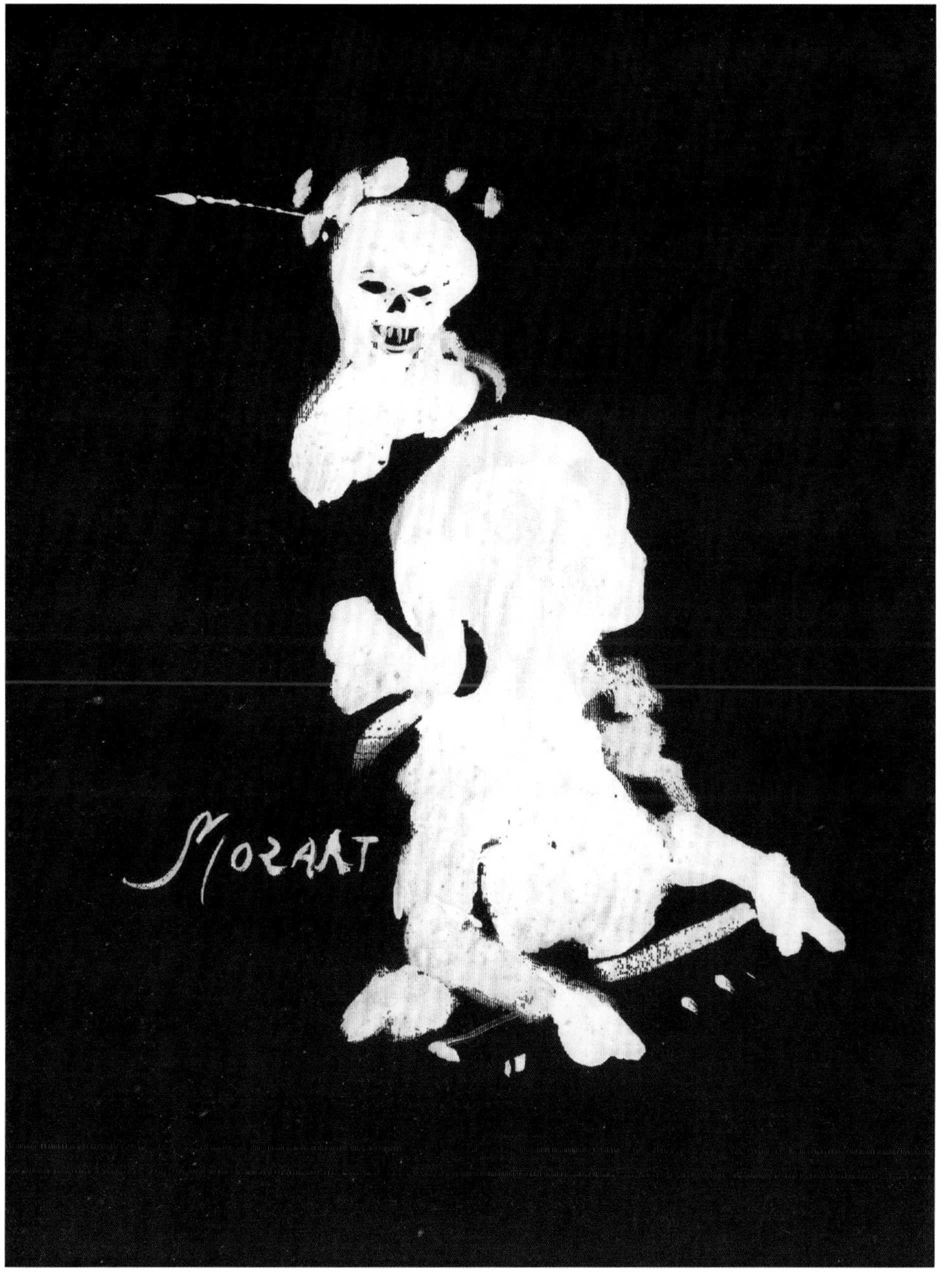

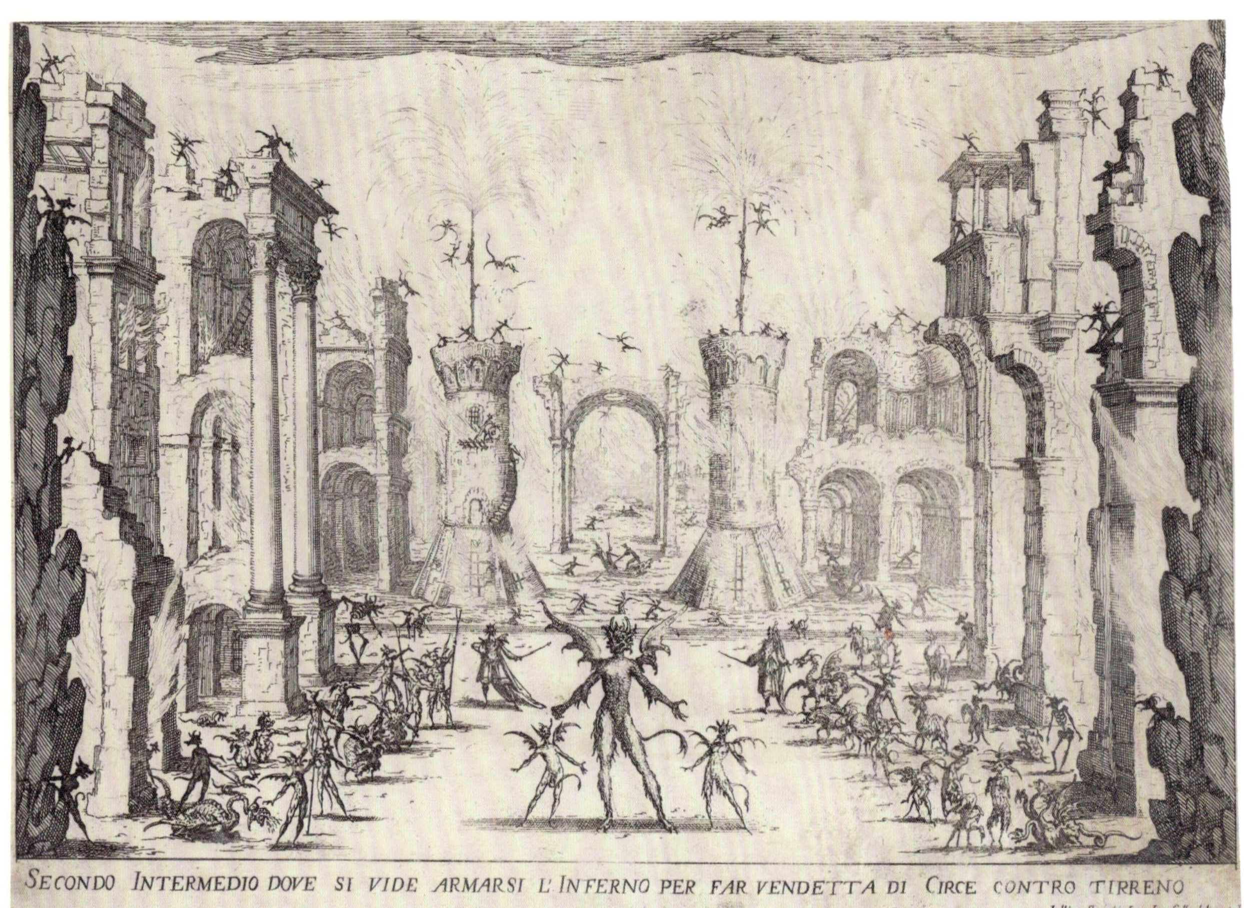

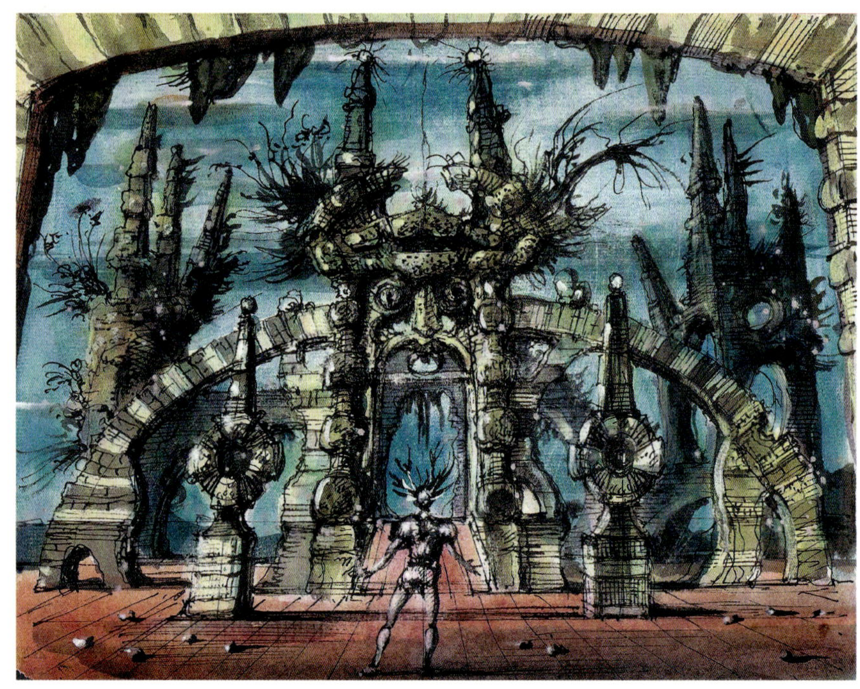

TOP: Jacques Callot, after Giulio Parigi, 2nd Interlude, from *The Interludes*, etching, 20.3 × 28.4 cm (8 × 11 in.), early 17th century
ABOVE: Eugene Berman, *Armida (Imaginary Ballet)*, ink and watercolour on paper, 24.5 × 30.5 cm (9½ × 12 in.), 1946

The Theory of the Saltimbanque

Italianness and its Mozartian ramifications were natural complements to another key Neo-Romantic subject: the world of the saltimbanques, including acrobats, clowns and characters from the *Commedia dell'arte*. Picasso's work from around 1905 is given particular prominence in this respect by Soby, but it in fact formed part of a line that various artists in distinct disciplines had already drawn on for their own purposes, particularly in the literature of the original Romantics (Théophile Gautier, Charles Nodier, Jules Janin, Baudelaire and others) between 1830 and 1870. In a brief but illuminating study of the subject, Jean Starobinski explained that 'the choice of the image of the clown is not just the selection of a pictorial or poetic motif but also a roundabout and parodic way of questioning art itself'. This results in 'deliberately distorting images that artists happily project of themselves and the condition of art', and this was nowhere more evident than in the early twentieth-century work of Picasso, who by then was already a master of self-representation.

Soby considered the theme of the saltimbanque (and of the circus in general, as a metaphor for the world) a crucial nexus between Picasso and the generation of 1926. Of the latter, Bérard, Eugene Berman and Tchelitchew displayed a shared passion for this subject matter, and each approached it from different angles at various points in their career. The image of the clown is inherently dualistic, even contradictory, as it is divided into two types, two physiognomies and two tensions in space. One is an ascending axis of agility, elegance and defiance of gravity, while the other is a descending axis of physical heaviness, earthly attraction and a clumsy, tangled body. As Starobinski elucidates: 'In the language of alchemical characterology, the agile clown corresponds to the mercurial type, while the awkward clown expresses the weightiness of the earth, as well as its coldness.' (There are echoes here of the duality of the Nietzschean *Leichte Leben*.)

The acrobats and clowns of Tchelitchew sometimes display an ascending dynamic, but they more usually belong to the second category. They are sometimes seen drowsily lying down, their bodies deformed, with narrow shoulders, wide hips, and outsize hands and feet, looking as if they have fallen heavily to the ground, trapped by

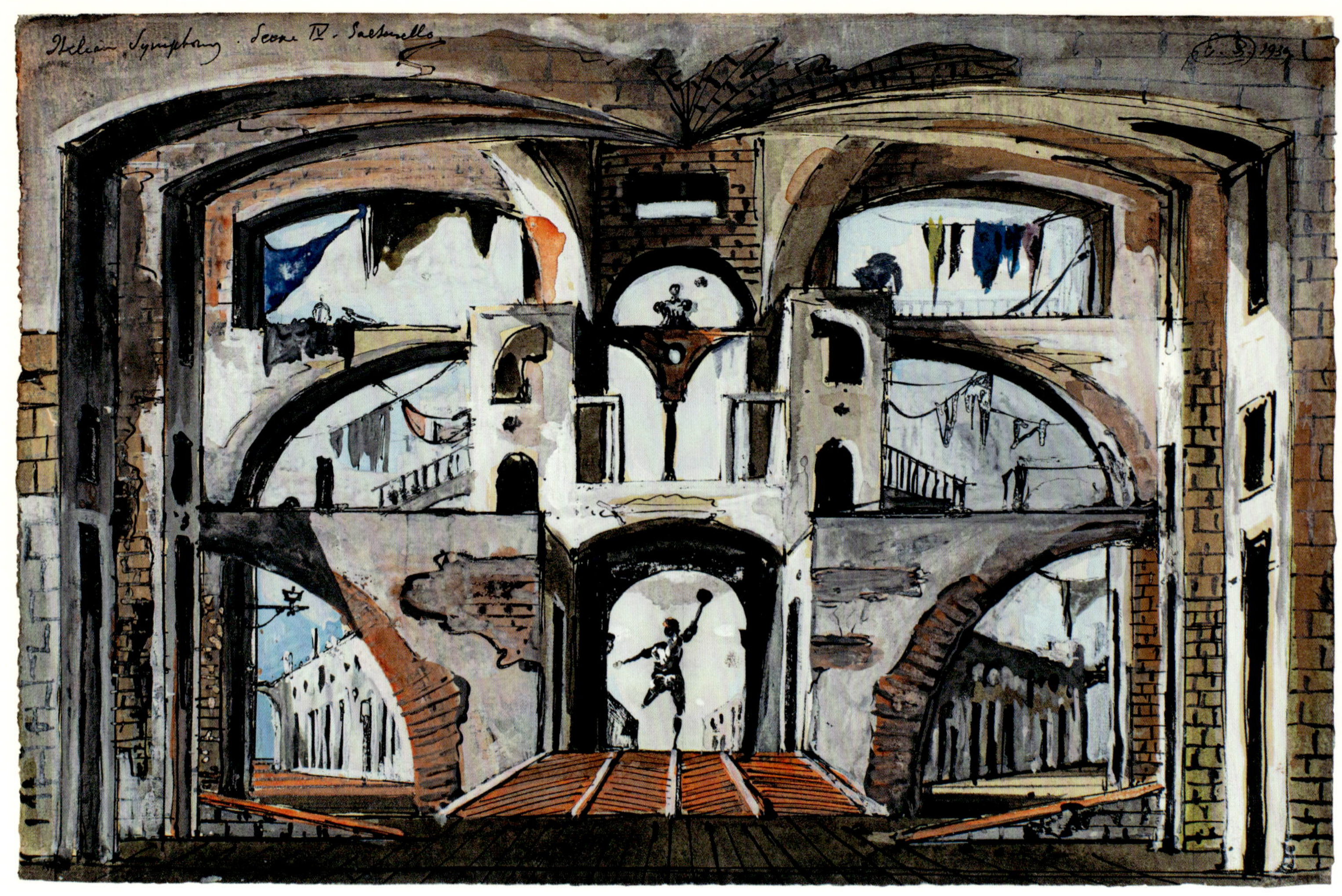

ABOVE: Eugene Berman, *Italian Symphony, Scene IV, Saltenello*, gouache and ink on paper, 24.4 × 38.1 cm (9⅝ × 15 in.), 1939
OPPOSITE: Jacques Callot, *Balli di Sfessania*, engraving, 7.3 × 9.6 cm (2⅞ × 3¾ in.), 1621–22

their fleshly envelope and incapable of resisting the force of gravity. Bérard, meanwhile, followed the example of Picasso in his reinterpretation of the traditional iconography of Fortune (as in the *Young Acrobat on a Ball* from 1905, now in the Pushkin Museum in Moscow). In a stunning series of wash drawings entitled *Aces of the Carpet*, Bérard contrasted the muscular corporeality of the fairground Hercules with the enormous suppleness of the acrobat and contortionist. More generally, however, he was drawn to the figure of a thin, androgynous, airy saltimbanque ('everything occurs as if the lightness *feminized* the acrobat', reflected Starobinski).

Bérard's outsider misfits – among whom he himself sometimes glides, barely disguised – wander in a desert-like void on the limits of abstraction, like the woebegone landscape that he dreamed up for Henri Sauguet's ballet *The Fairground People* in 1945. These mournful settings had been anticipated by a painter more drawn towards the clumsier type of clown – Georges Rouault – in a letter quoted by

Starobinski: 'That nomads' cart stopped on the road, the old emaciated horse grazing the sparse grass; the old clown sitting in the corner of his caravan putting on his shiny, glittery costume, that contrast of bright, gleaming things designed to amuse and this life of infinite sadness...' This bittersweet balance between pathos and display, between apparent nonchalance and underlying melancholy, was a key theme of the Neo-Romantics.

The two vertical axes of the rise and fall are complemented by a third, horizontal axis, characterized by the wanderings of the dispossessed, on the endless quest that gives sense to their lives as show folk, whose only destination is the next performance. This axis again had precedents, such as Gautier's *Captain Fracasse*, or, going further back, the prints of Stefano della Bella, or those of Jacques Callot for the *Balli di Sfessania*, where actors from the *Commedia dell'arte* are often set against a bare background or, at best, a distant horizon with the outlines of a few buildings.

The treatment of such subject matter provides a further rebuttal, if one is still needed, of simplistic readings of the Neo-Romantics, and a further demonstration that, for them, pathos is neither naive nor innocent. They went beyond a mere transposition of the reality of destruction and penury that history had thrust under their eyes to create, like E.T.A. Hoffmann (another miner of this seam), 'Fantasy Pieces in Callot's Manner'. They shared a vision of a destitute world that had basically ended, but one where the absence of materials and means paradoxically enhanced the importance of dressing up and festivity.

The entire history of Neo-Romanticism is shot through with what Lincoln Kirstein called, with respect to the Paper Ball organized by Chick Austin in the Wadsworth Atheneum in 1936, 'the pathos and the elegance of the *style pauvre*', both in their everyday lives and their aesthetic approach. Julien Levy recounts in his memoir, for example, how an impecunious Eugene Berman decided to live in an old mansion on rue des Lions Saint-Paul, in Le Marais, a neighbourhood that would wait many more years to be gentrified but perfectly satisfied the Bermans' taste for faded grandeur. The

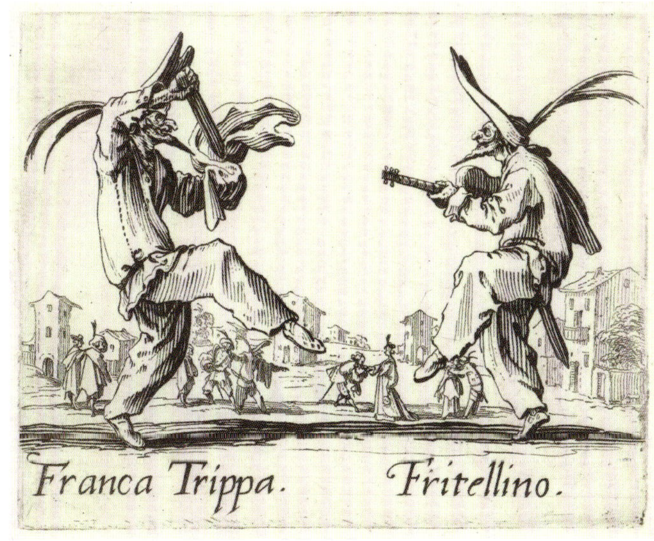

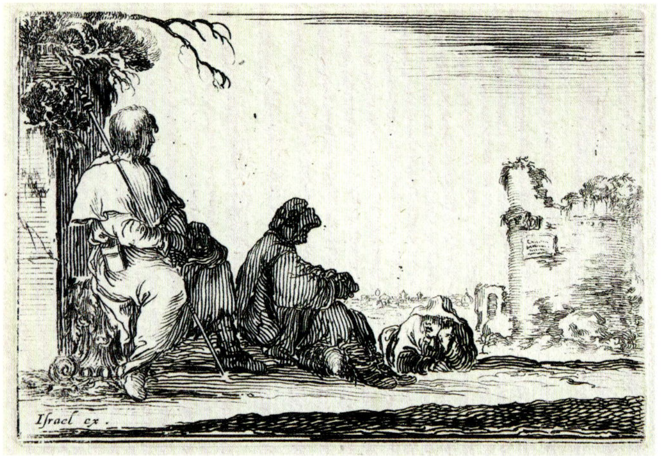

two brothers would also, like Bérard and Tchelitchew, paint on old canvases, bought in batches at flea markets, and the traces of these earlier pictures would sometimes remain visible. Kirstein also mentioned Tchelitchew's deployment of worn supports, such as paper too flimsy to last, for, as far as his work was concerned, he professed a 'rather recklessly aristocratic disdain'.

The Neo-Romantics were fired by a lack of materials, by a taste for improvisation as a means to transform the unbearable starkness of reality into a playful masquerade. (This stance was taken to even greater extremes by Leonor Fini, who lived in a state of perpetual fancy dress.) Starobinski identified this dialectic as the source of the mythology of the saltimbanque, endowing the latter, under the guise of insouciance, with all his gravitas: '[...] the leap of the acrobat, the skill of the contortionist serves to ward off death by imitating the irrepressible upsurge of life' in the middle of a stage that represents 'a world symbolically set between the sky and the earth, between life and death, but closer to death than to life, where everything is ordered around the secret of a passage'.

Thus, the wanderings of the saltimbanque, the poetry of the circus and the stylization of the *Commedia dell'arte* all lie at the heart of Neo-Romanticism. The barren, rocky landscapes, the abandoned, ruined cities, the improvised stages and desolate shores that reappear in so many of these painters' works are liminal spaces, great theatres of melancholy in which life is merely the shadow cast by death. As Starobinski concluded, 'Any real clown emerges from another space, another universe: his entrance must represent a liberation from the limits of the real, and he must appear to us, even in the greatest joviality, as a revenant.'

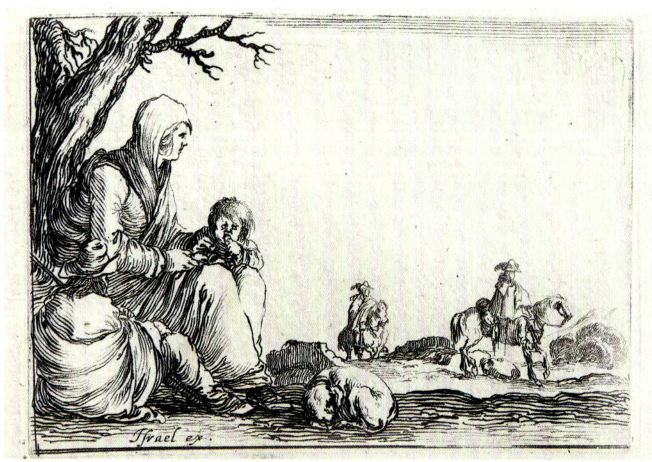

TOP AND ABOVE: Stefano della Bella, two plates from the suite *Caprice faict par Della Bella et mis en lumière par Israel*, etchings, 5.5 × 8.5 cm (2⅛ × 3⅜ in.), *c.* 1642

OPPOSITE, ABOVE: Stefano della Bella, plate from the suite *Diverse Figure e paesi*, etching, 9.5 × 15 cm (3¾ × 5⅞ in.), 1649
OPPOSITE, BELOW: Eugene Berman, *Fantaisie*, ink and watercolour on paper, 18 × 22 cm (7 × 8⅝ in.), 1944

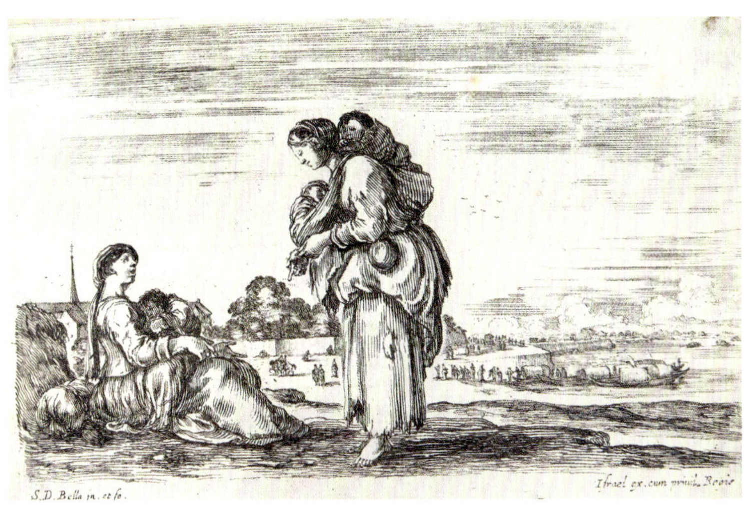
S.D. Bella in. et fe.
Israel ex. cum priuil. Regis

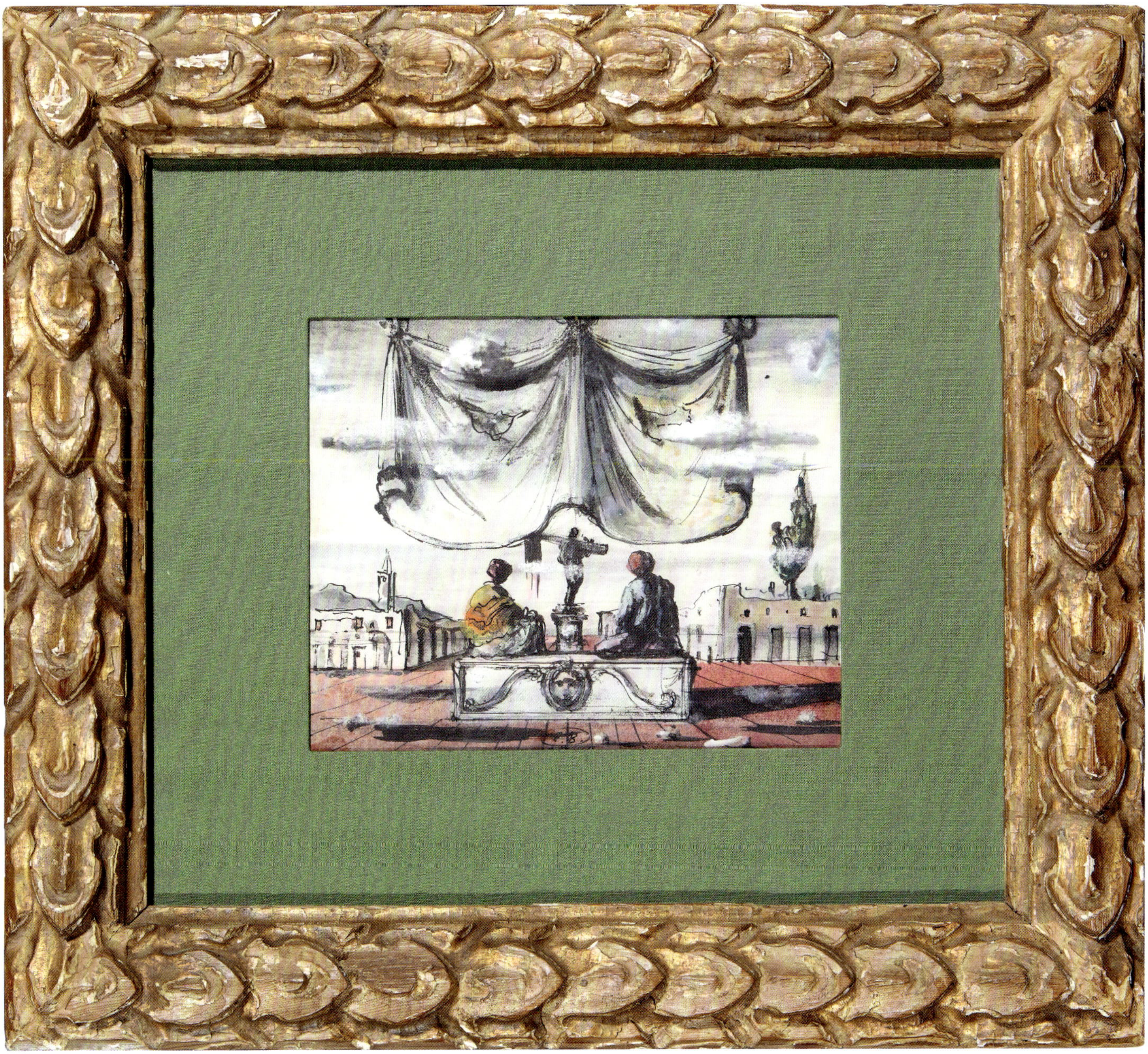

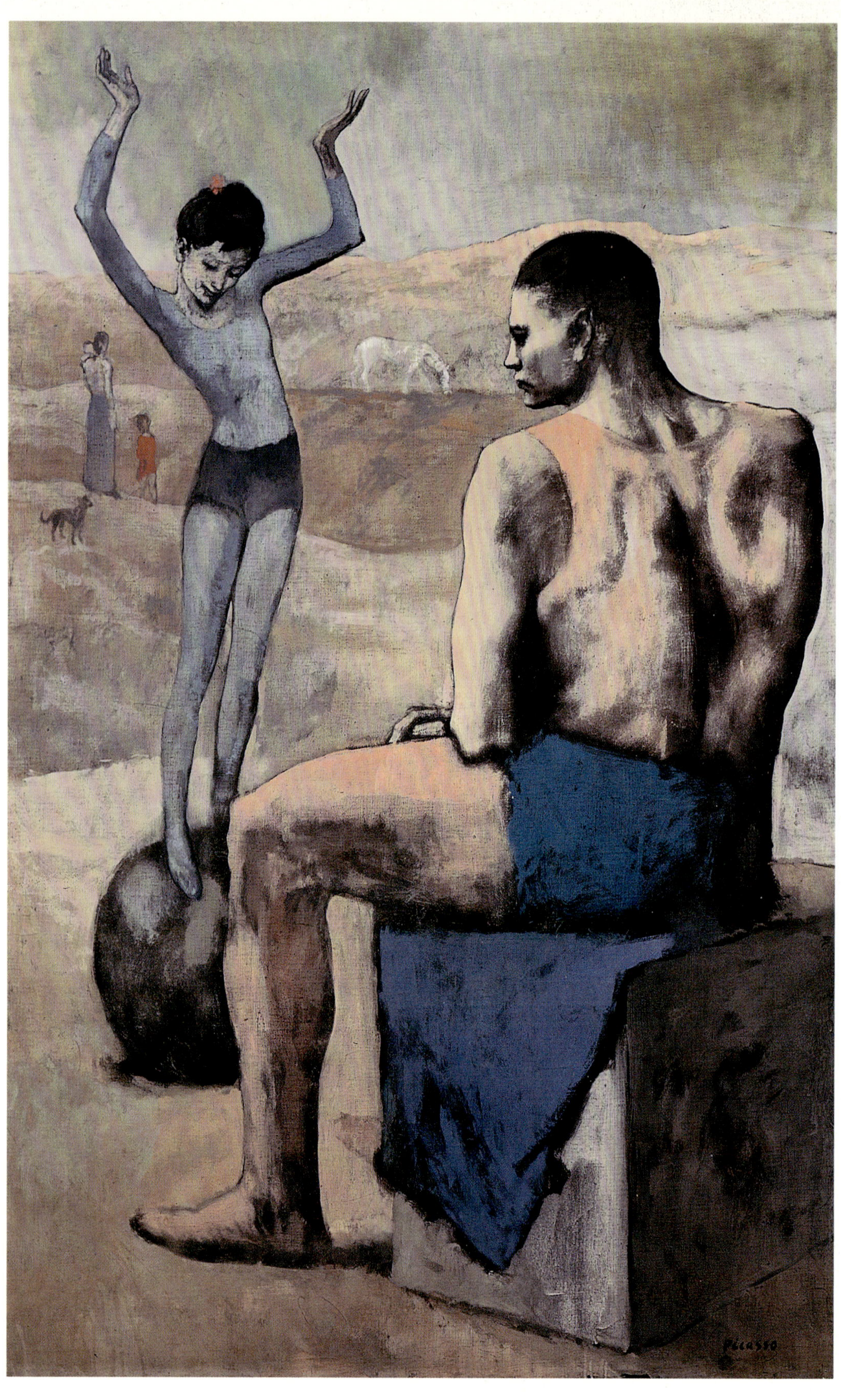

ABOVE: Pablo Picasso, *Young Acrobat on a Ball*, oil on canvas, 147 × 95 cm (57⅞ × 37⅜ in.), 1905

OPPOSITE, ABOVE: Christian Bérard, *Aces of the Carpet*, ink on paper, 37 × 22 cm (14½ × 8⅝ in.), page taken from a notebook containing variations on the theme, 1945
OPPOSITE, BELOW: Christian Bérard, costumes for the ballet *The Fairground People*, ink, ink wash and pastel, 33 × 30 cm (13 × 11⅞ in.), 1945

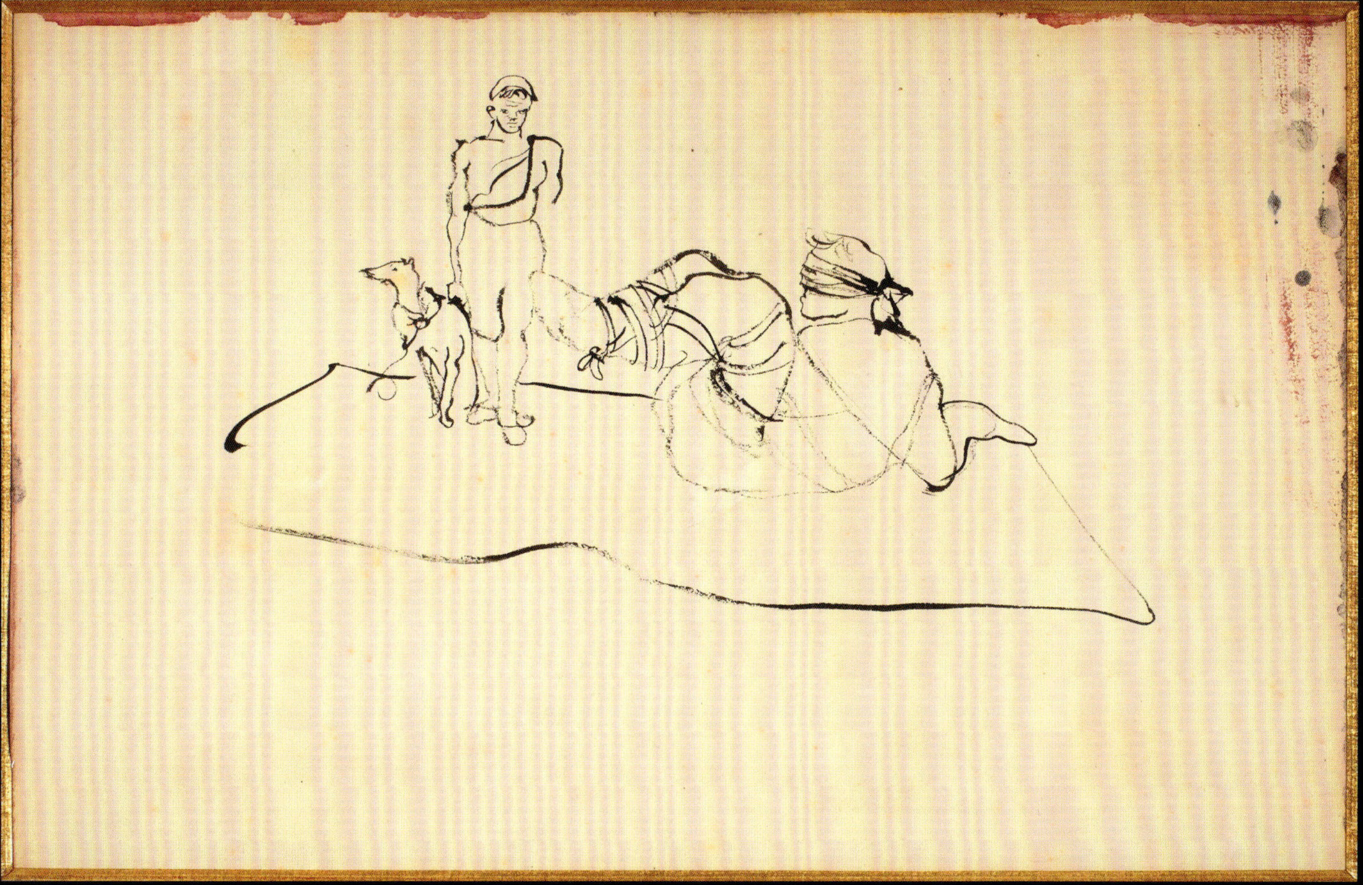

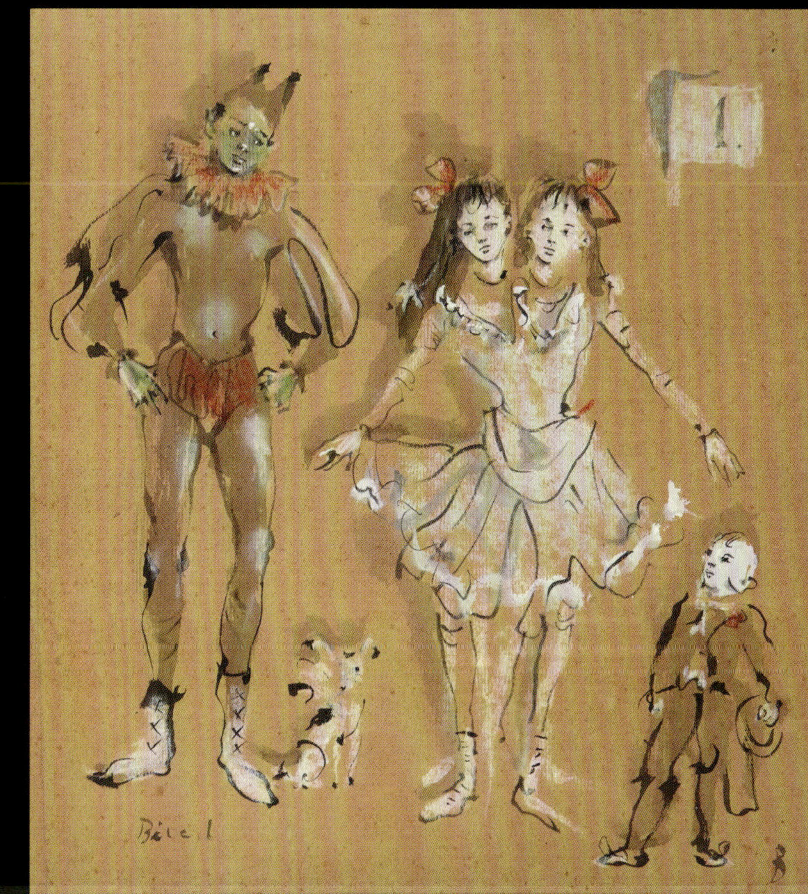
1

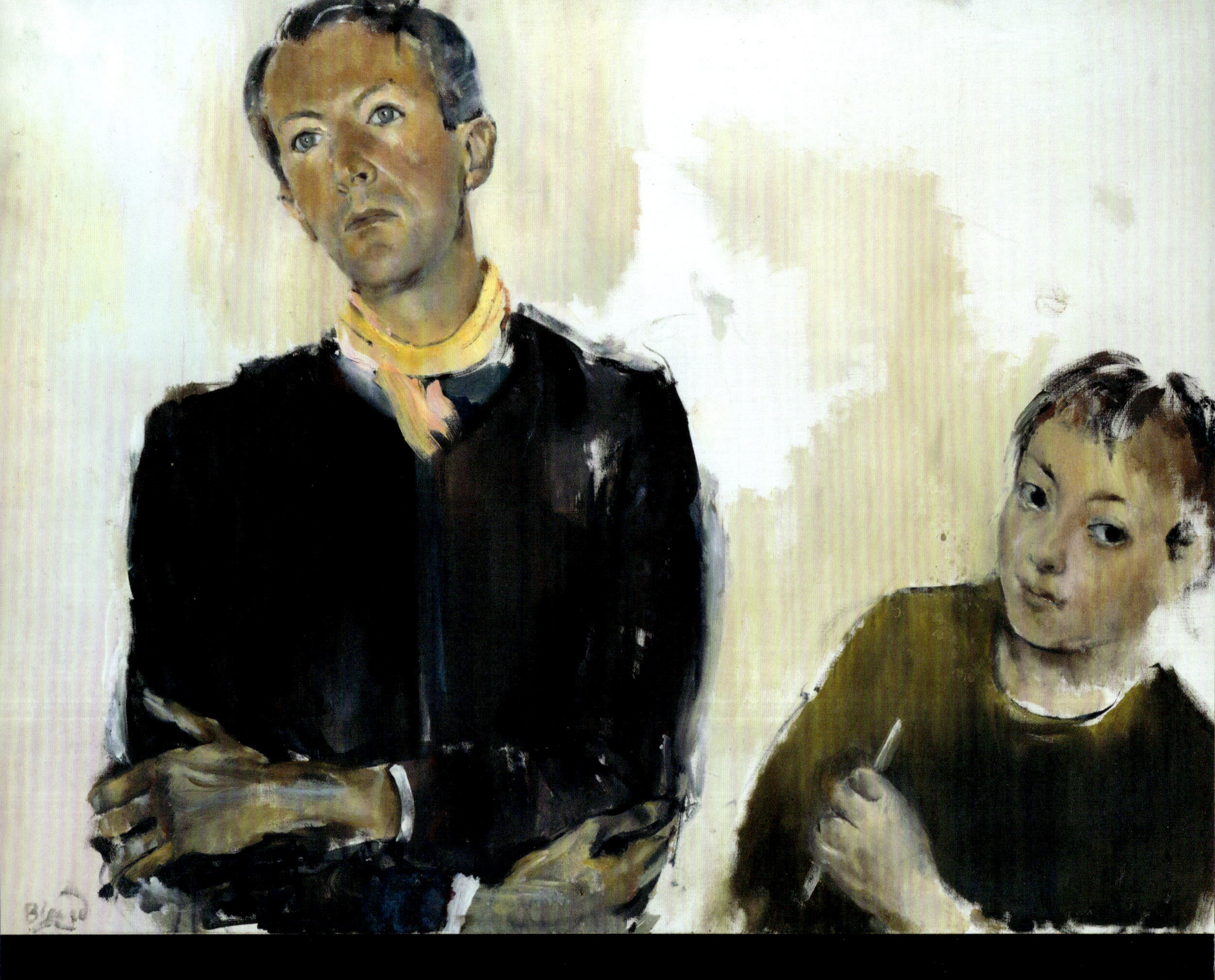

ACT IV

CONVERGENCE LINES

The English Scene

The duality described above, expressed through glittery but mournful imagery and a fascination with the *Commedia dell'arte* (and sophisticated theatricality in general), placed the Neo-Romantics in a field of artists, decorators, architects, writers and collectors who, from the 1930s to the late 1950s, unobtrusively stood against the received wisdom of modernity. Around the turn of the 1960s – when, significantly, pictorial values were being reassessed – two books by Martin Battersby, *The Decorative Twenties* (1969) and *The Decorative Thirties* (1971), tried to unravel the threads (albeit somewhat sketchily) of this body of work. Battersby (1914–1982) was primarily a painter (and a virtuoso of trompe-l'œil) rather than a historian, and he threw the spotlight on a broad community of like-minded spirits. Further publicity was forthcoming in the 1980s thanks to a 'Return of the Baroque' and the posthumous sales of several key collections (including those of Edward James in 1986, Stephen Tennant in 1987, Boris Kochno in 1991, Charles Henri and Ruth Ford in 2010, and Georges and Myrtille Hugnet in 2015). Meanwhile, academic research has continued apace, through works such as Jane Stevenson's *Baroque between the Wars* (Oxford University Press, 2018).

As we have seen, the Neo-Romantics enjoyed the patronage of the Noailles; Marie-Laure in particular sat for both Bérard and Eugene Berman, and she was happy to indulge their taste for dressing up. Nevertheless, it was probably the Sitwells in England who most fully appreciated the Neo-Romantic penchant for theatricality and the worlds of the saltimbanque and the *Commedia dell'arte*. Leaving aside Edith's support for Tchelitchew, her two brothers, the poets and writers Osbert and Sacheverell, both demonstrated similar enthusiasms. In 1922, Osbert commissioned from Gino Severini (who was just entering his Neoclassical period) a famous series of frescoes based on *Commedia dell'arte* characters for the family property in Montegufoni, Tuscany, while Sacheverell conducted in-depth examinations of the origins of the Baroque (in Germany, Spain, and elsewhere) and devoted numerous books and poems to the subject.

The Sitwells were hardly strangers to uninhibited theatricality in their everyday lives (indeed, they were often criticized for it). Edith, the eldest sibling, strove to exaggerate her unusual looks by wearing the long tunics that Tchelitchew had recommended to her and by decking herself out with outsize jewelry adorned with cabochon stones (on one occasion, during a fierce argument with Tchelitchew, she insisted above all that he did not touch the imposing amber necklace she was wearing that day). In the 1920s, Edith also willingly submitted to the settings proposed to her (when not proposing them herself) by an ambitious young photographer determined to propel her into the ranks of the idle aristocrats, lovable eccentrics and show-business figures known collectively as the 'bright young things'.

Cecil Beaton (1904–1980) thus played a major role in the construction of the Sitwells' image – literally, by photographing each of the siblings in highly artificial poses and lighting (including a famous picture of Edith lying in repose amid gloomy shadows typical of the Baroque). Beaton quickly made a name for himself through a calculated strategy of sophisticated lighting techniques, theatrical settings, striking poses and unusual angles. As his friend and model Sir Francis Rose observed, 'Cecil had already started to use glamour in his photography as a calculated asset. He is not a man who desires glamour, and he uses taste, fashion, and decor in a fascinating way, manipulating them as a stockbroker does stocks and shares.'

Riding on the wave of his success, Beaton worked for the leading fashion magazines of the time. He quickly struck up a friendship with Bérard (a leading light of the Parisian fashion scene), Eugene

Berman and Tchelitchew. The latter made an appearance in several photographs by Beaton and in his (somewhat catty) diaries, as well as in a 'panorama of elegance' entitled *The Glass of Fashion* (1954). Beaton deserves an important place in the story of Neo-Romanticism, not only because he clearly shared their aesthetic values but also because he had a foothold in several artistic and literary camps, enjoyed an international career, and helped push the group's leading players into the spotlight. Beaton's success and talent, along with his social skills, eclipsed the achievement of two other, equally versatile 'artist-photographers' whose vision was similar, each in their own way, to that of Neo-Romanticism: Peter Rose Pulham (1910–1956), who died relatively young and has been largely forgotten, and Angus McBean (1904–1990), who was long sidelined as a stage photographer before belatedly gaining recognition for the full range of his work in the early 1980s.

Beaton professed a sincere admiration for Bérard, and he kept Bébé's fine portrait of him until he died. He was also portrayed by Tchelitchew, in 1936, in a distinctive pen and wash drawing. At around the same time, Tchelitchew painted several portraits of the elusive but charismatic – and extremely rich – Peter Watson (1898–1957), for whom Beaton nurtured an unrequited love. (Bérard, never at a loss for a jibe about Tchelitchew, described one of these pictures, in which the subject was needless to say dressed up, as 'the English Joan of Arc done by the Russian Botticelli'). Watson would, in his turn, play a decisive role in the transplantation of Neo-Romanticism from France to England and its subsequent propagation.

Watson met Tchelitchew in 1932 through Beaton, and a few months later, still making light of the latter's feelings, Watson succumbed to the waspish charm of Charles Henri Ford on the terrace of the Deux Magots, in front of Tchelitchew, whose advances Watson had rebuffed a short while before. Ford claimed later that 'Pavlik' had deliberately used him as bait to take vengeance on Watson for the earlier rejection. Such calculating cynicism did nothing to diminish Watson's admiration for Tchelitchew's work, for he bought several paintings straight away and his enthusiasm never waned (the two men were eventually united by a genuine friendship).

Peter Watson's connection with the Neo-Romantic circle was not confined to this friendship with Tchelitchew. Watson professed to like '*beaucoup beaucoup*' Pierre Colle, the young dealer who started out with Christian Dior, after meeting him by chance on a cruise and then

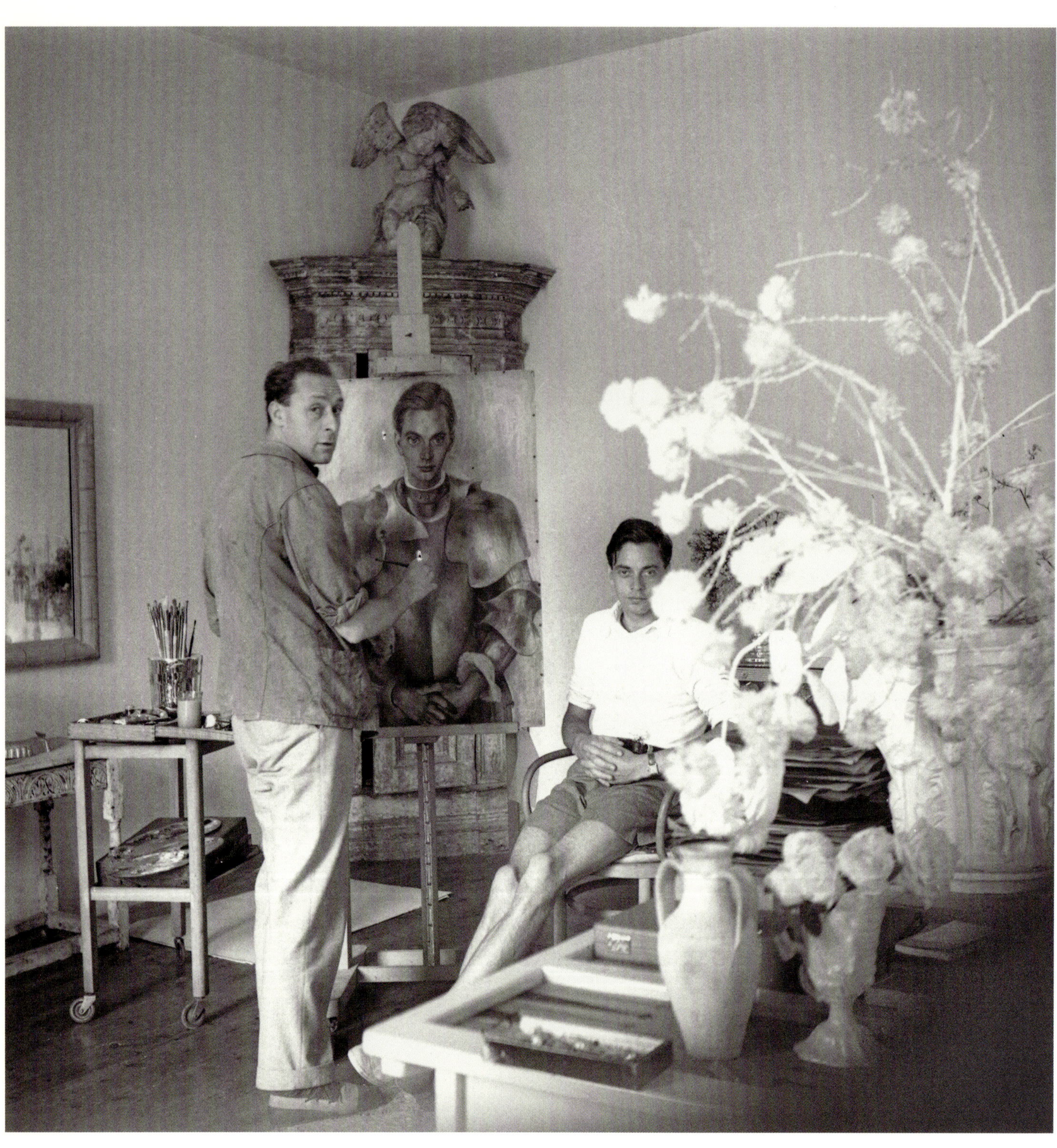

Pavel Tchelitchew and Peter Watson,
c. 1934, by Cecil Beaton

becoming his generous customer. Watson was also a friend of Christian Bérard and Boris Kochno. He amassed an impressive collection, in which Bérard and Tchelitchew rubbed shoulders with Dalí, Derain, Picasso and de Chirico, although this treasure trove would mostly be stolen from his apartment in Paris during the war. Watson also became a patron of *Horizon*, one of the most influential literary and artistic magazines of the time. *Horizon*, which lasted from 1939 to 1950, was edited by the sybaritic Cyril Connolly (1903–1974), who was also friendly with Beaton, Bérard and Kochno. The magazine publicized the new wave of British artists championed by Watson, who would, at a purely local level, bring to life a new vision of Neo-Romanticism.

Two young artists barely out of St John's Wood School of Art, Michael Ayrton (1921–1975) and John Minton (1917–1957), were bowled over by Soby's *After Picasso*, according to their biographer, Malcolm Yorke. Facing the same impasse of abstraction that a previous generation had confronted ten years earlier, they saw new horizons opening up for them after reading Soby's analyses. They were particularly attracted by the pictorial qualities and allusive theatricality of Eugene Berman's work and, accordingly, they sought him out when they went to Paris in 1938: 'For two young romantic English artists in search of a Parisian master who was neither a dogmatic abstractionist, nor a wilfully daft Surrealist, he seems to have been an ideal choice.'

Tchelitchew also exerted a notable influence, particularly on Ayrton, who would adapt his use of double and metamorphic images. The imminence of war prevented the two young artists from staying more than a few months in Paris, but this was sufficient to indelibly mark their work. By the time they returned to London, they had, wrote Yorke, 'packed in their mental luggage the tilted perspectives and dramatic lighting of de Chirico, the nostalgic and sweet harmonies of Picasso's Blue and Pink periods, and the stagey tableaux of the Parisian Neo-Romantics'.

Although less well-known than the painters with whom they are generally associated – Paul Nash, John Piper, John Craxton, Keith Vaughan, Robert Colquhoun and Prunella Clough – Ayrton and Minton belonged squarely in the English current of Neo-Romanticism. This was largely made up of artists from the generation that came immediately after that of Bérard and company. It fitted into a specifically British tradition, thus setting it apart from the Bloomsbury group, which emerged from a dialogue with the 'Continental' approach of Cézanne, Picasso, Matisse and Cubism under the auspices of the

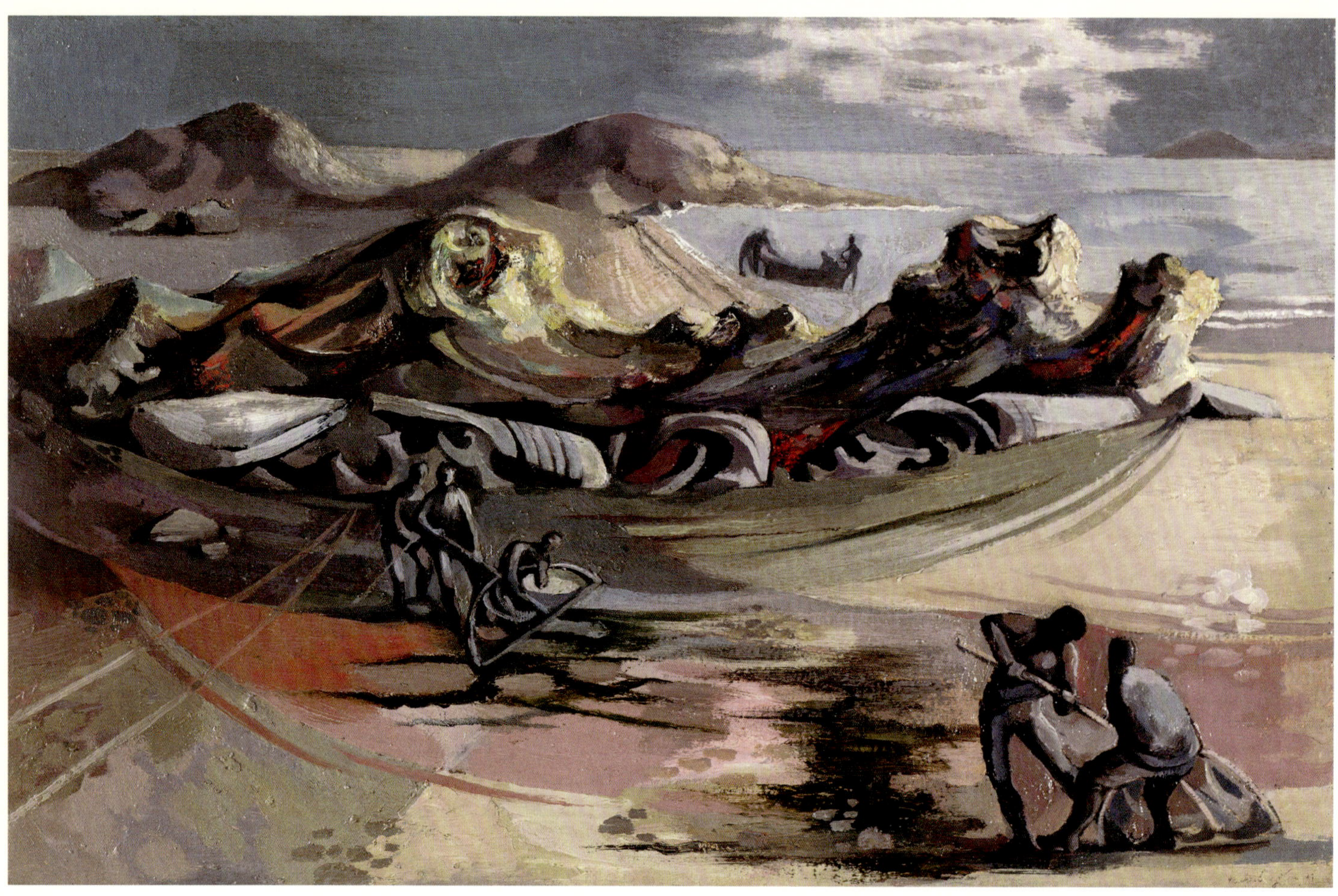

critic Roger Fry. Although the English Neo-Romantics were often linked to their Parisian counterparts by a common sensibility and attitude, their work nevertheless stood out on account of their particular thematic concerns, most notably the representation, or rather the *presence*, of landscape and natural forms. Their graphic style also drew inspiration from British pictorial traditions, including the works of outsiders from the turn of the eighteenth century who were rediscovered in the early twentieth century: Alexander Cozens (1717–1786), Samuel Palmer (1805–1881), and the visionary William Blake (1757–1827). Despite the tragic end of some of its adherents, such as Minton and Vaughan, English Neo-Romanticism flourished, albeit discreetly, within the closed world of British institutions, galleries and buyers, until the deaths in the late twentieth century of the last artists to be associated with the movement.

ABOVE: Michael Ayrton, *Ischian Fishermen*, oil on canvas, 36 × 57 cm (14⅛ × 22⅜ in.), 1947
OPPOSITE, CLOCKWISE FROM TOP: John Minton, *Figure in a Deserted Landscape*, gouache, oil, pen and ink on board, 50 × 73 cm (19⅝ × 28¾ in.), 1942; Samuel Palmer, *Early Morning*, pen, dark brown ink and sepia mixed with gum and varnished, 18.8 × 23.2 cm (7⅜ × 9⅛ in.), 1825; John Minton, *Surrey Landscape*, pen and ink on paper, 54.5 × 74.8 cm (21½ × 29½ in.), 1944

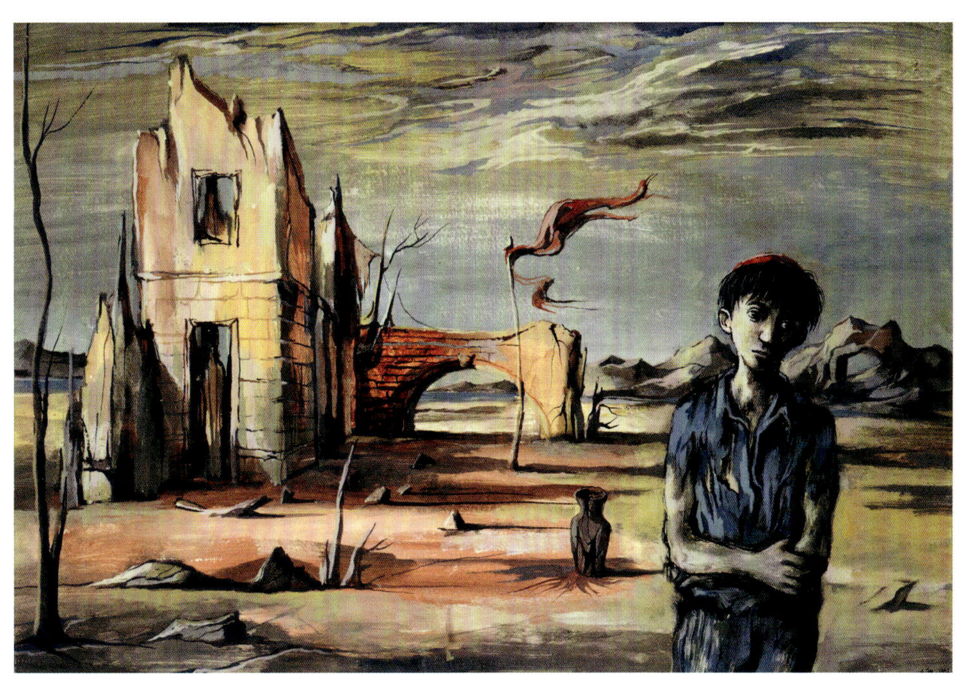

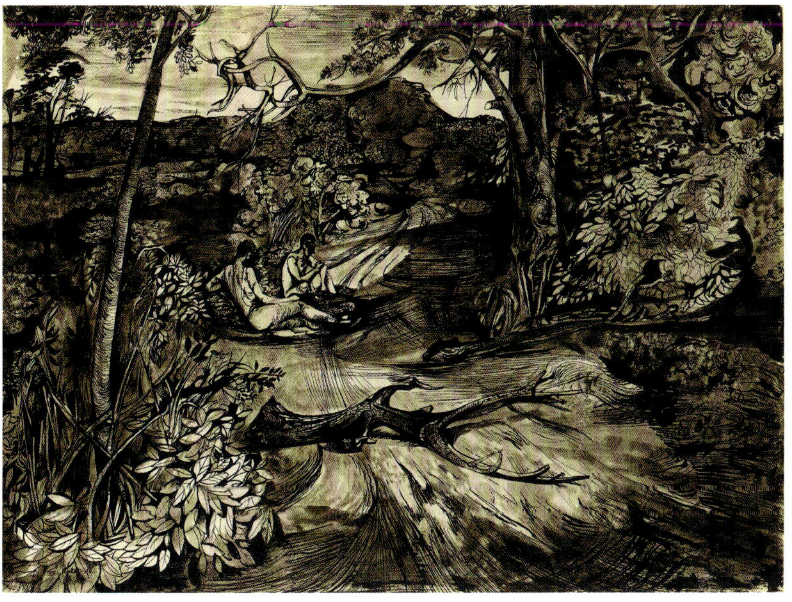

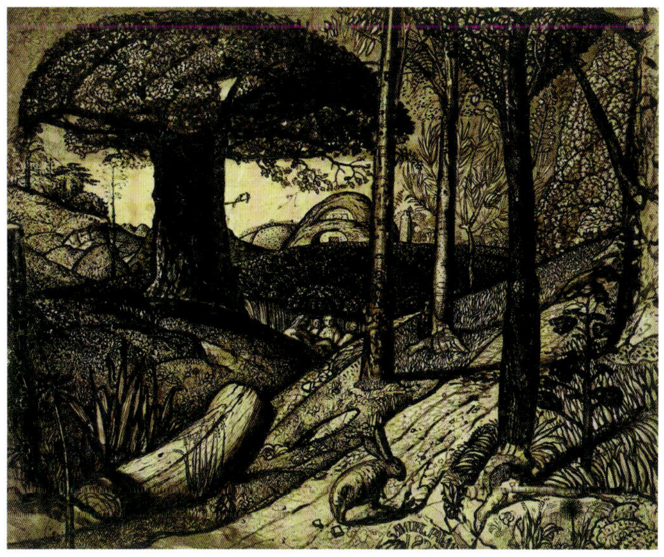

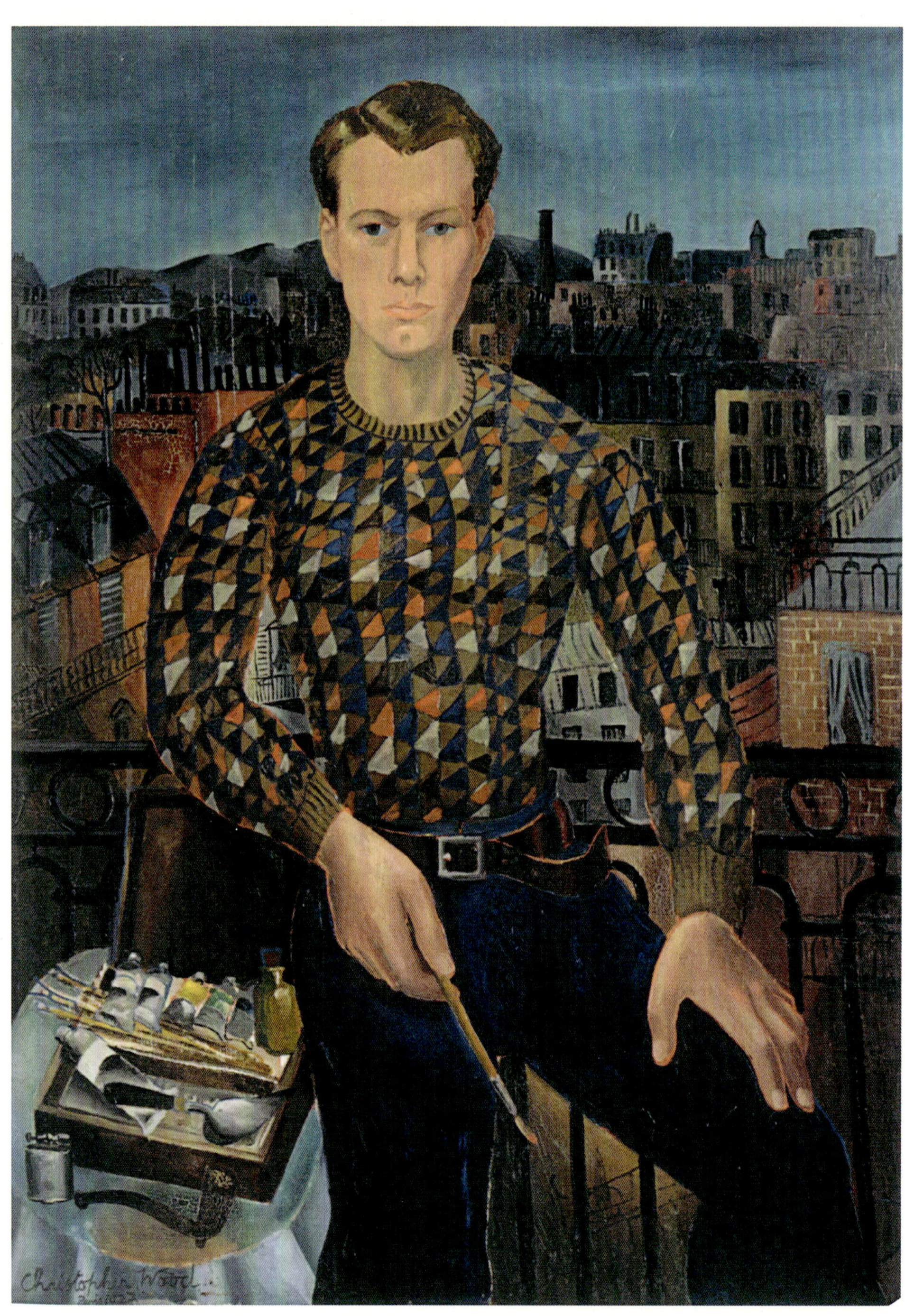

Christopher Wood, *Self-Portrait*, oil on canvas,
129.5 × 96 cm (51 × 37¾ in.), 1927

Kit Wood, the Outsider

We shall conclude this journey through the Neo-Romantic story, however, by lingering over another, even more marginal English artist: Christopher ('Kit') Wood (1901–1930). Despite the brevity of his life, Wood left behind a body of work of rare intensity. Furthermore, he was part of the original Neo-Romantic milieu in Paris, where he impressed not only Bérard but also Max Jacob and Cocteau, and he would eventually become a pivotal link between the English and French camps, and extend the movement's convergence lines, thereby opening up new territories. Shrouded as he now is in the aura of a tragic destiny, Wood stands as an enigma, open to all kinds of outlandish speculation. He was born near Liverpool, but when he turned nineteen he headed south to London, abandoning his architecture studies. He walked with a slight limp, as a result of a childhood bout of polio, but this seemed only to enhance his status as a model of romantic virility (a status he shared with Rupert Brooke, with whom he was often compared). As Francis Rose recalled, 'Kit was good, handsome [...] with a masculine build, a delicate nature, and the terrible fears of the poet.' And there is no doubt that his good looks and air of an eternal adolescent facilitated a succession of providential encounters that would determine the course of his short life.

The first of these, only a few months after his arrival in London, was with the great collector Alphonse Kann (1870–1948), a lifelong friend of Proust, who, astonishingly, has never been considered worthy of a biography of his own. Kann invited Wood to stay in his mansion on the Avenue du Bois in March 1921. A few weeks later, Wood moved to the city centre to study art at the Académie Julien and then at the Grande Chaumière. In this period, Wood also met the well-connected and versatile (and now unjustly forgotten) painter Adrien Étienne Drian (1885–1961), who helped him on his first steps into the world of fashion drawing.

Wood had another encounter in 1921 that would prove even more decisive: Kann introduced him to the Chilean diplomat Antonio ('Tony') de Gandarillas, who, like Kann, divided his time between Paris and London. Considered a kindred spirit by Cecil Beaton, Gandarillas was the nephew of Eugenia Errázuriz, an icon of austere elegance who was among the first to recognize Picasso's genius.

Gandarillas was unhappily married, with children, but, like the young Englishman, his sexuality was fluid. Moreover, he took advantage of his diplomatic status to free himself of certain social constraints. He started living with Wood, and their relationship would last six years, until the latter's untimely death. Under the mentorship of Gandarillas, who was some fifteen years his senior, Wood discovered Greece, Turkey, North Africa, Germany, Italy – and opium. Wood would eventually tire of this frivolous lifestyle, however, and found that even its many pleasures left him with a feeling of emptiness. He was ripe for new encounters…

The next ones would occur in late 1924, in a legendary intersection of literature, painting, loose living and drugs: the Welcome Hotel in Villefranche-sur-Mer (also deserving of a book of its own). Wood had come across the hotel's presiding spirit, the mercurial Jean Cocteau, in Paris, thanks to the latter's long-standing friendship with Gandarillas. The most enthralling account of life in the Welcome Hotel was written by Sir Francis Rose (a minor player in Neo-Romanticism whom we have already met) in his fascinating and idiosyncratic memoir (and fact-checker's nightmare). Gertrude Stein would later, rather puzzlingly, transfer on to Rose the hopes that had been dashed after her initial enthusiasm for Tchelitchew, Bérard and Berman, to the point of entrusting him with the illustration of her final books.

Rose went to the Welcome Hotel in 1925 to stay with his mother (who, among other unusual habits, would converse on a daily basis with the Archangel Uriel), and there he got to know the young Bérard, as well as Cocteau and his entourage, which included budding writers and artists such as Maurice Sachs ('Saks'), Jean Desbordes ('Desbordas') and Jean Bourgoint ('Bourgoin'). (Wood painted a superb portrait of Bourgoint, as well as another picture of him together with Gandarillas.)

In his memoir, Rose plays fast and loose with both dates and names, and he describes Wood first showing his work to Cocteau in Villefranche, whereas in fact the two had known each other for over a year and had even briefly shared a studio. Whatever its inaccuracies, however, his account is valuable for revealing Bérard's admiration for Wood (further confirmed by the despairing words that Bérard scribbled in a notebook on hearing of Wood's death): 'Bébé saw these paintings', wrote Rose, with reference to that time at the Welcome Hotel, 'and was enthusiastic about them and made himself enchanting to the lame and timid young man, with his strange handsome English schoolboy's face. When Bérard liked something he had a way of making it live. I can only describe this manner as eating what he saw, felt, or imagined.'

Wood was further encouraged by praise from Picasso at a meeting instigated by Eugenia Errázuriz in 1926, which surely contributed to the impressive burst of activity that marked the latter years of his life. This period was also convulsed by passionate love affairs, and further complicated by his continued intake of opium. After a stormy fling with Jean Bourgoint's sister, Jeanne (the inspirations for the siblings in Cocteau's *Enfants terribles*), in 1927 Wood launched into a turbulent relationship with Meraud Guinness (whom we have already met in relation to Waldemar-George during the war – a further example of the crisscrossing between the various players in this story). The portraits that Wood produced around this time – particularly those of Jeanne Bourgoint – display a remarkable precision and control of line, demonstrating skills that had blossomed in only a few short months.

After working on a project for Diaghilev that failed to come to fruition, Wood felt a need to return to England. He spent some time with Gandarillas in St Ives, Cornwall, before exhibiting in London. St Ives gave rise to further encounters that would mark Wood's final period, particularly with the artists Ben and Winifred Nicholson, whose support would help calm his nerves. Once back in Paris in 1928, Wood met a young Russian émigrée, Frosca Munster (1896–1963), who moved in the circles of the Ballets Russes and was a friend of Bérard, Kochno, Crevel and Cocteau. She finally provided Wood with a degree of emotional stability, to such an extent that he considered marrying her. (Munster would later be the long-term partner of Jean Hugo [1894–1984], a painter whose deceptively simple work is sometimes reminiscent of Wood's.)

A second spell in Cornwall in late 1928, and a meeting there with another outsider, the painter Alfred Wallis (1855–1942), further reinvigorated Wood: 'It is a great moment in my life. I feel things are becoming really vital and the studentship has passed. My work is becoming personal and sure and unlike anybody else's.' The works produced during this period of feverish activity, fired by the consumption of opium, furnished two exhibitions, only a few months apart, one in London and the other in Paris. These were well received critically but the sales did little to improve Wood's precarious finances.

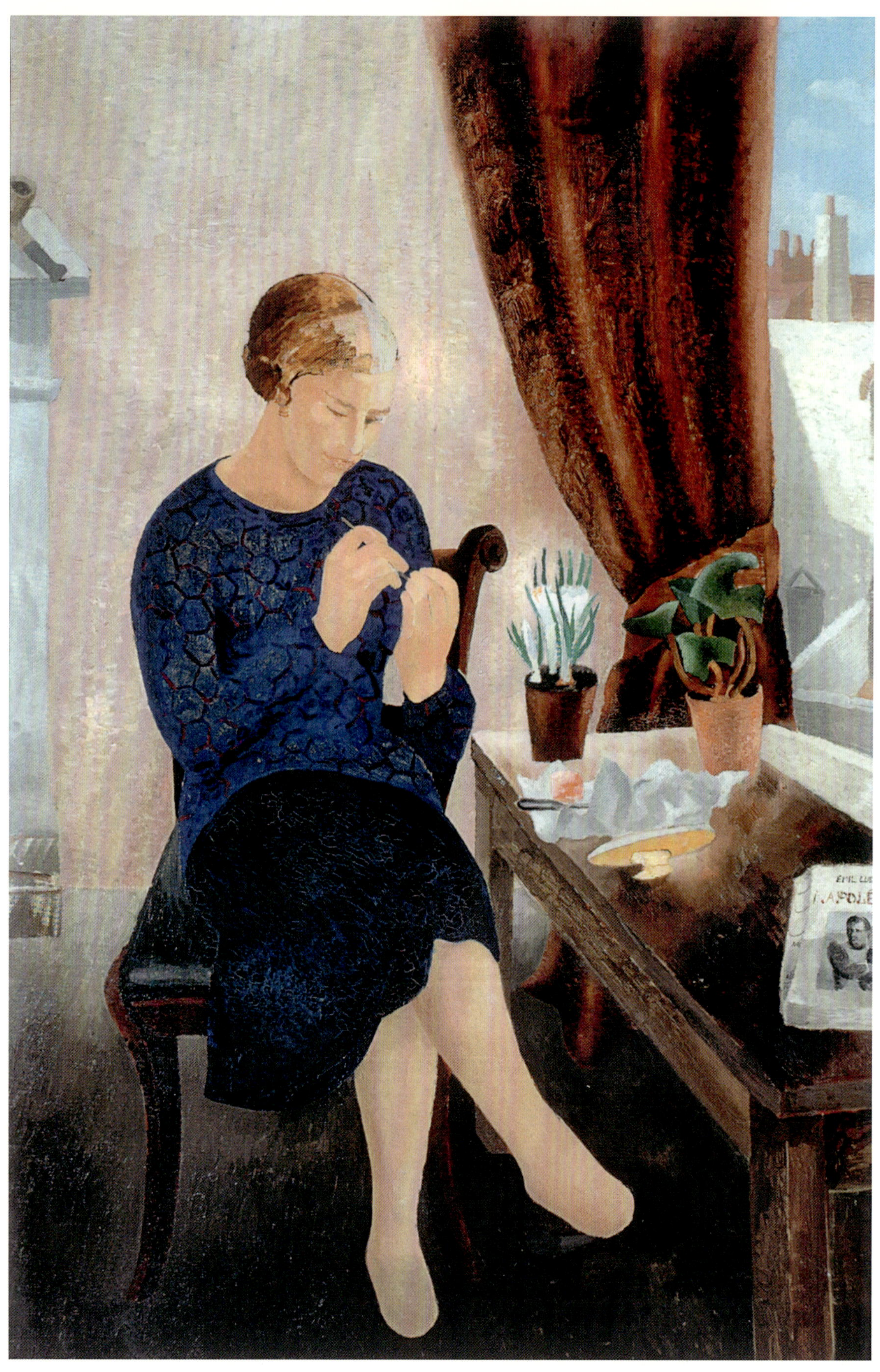

ABOVE: Christopher Wood, *The Manicure (Portrait of Frosca Munster)*, oil on canvas, 152.4 × 101.6 cm (60 × 40 in.), 1929
OPPOSITE: Christopher Wood, *Max Jacob*, oil on canvas, 81 × 64 cm (31⅞ × 25⅛ in.), 1929

Undeterred, he spent part of the summer of 1929 – and, later, some of 1930 – in Brittany, which turned out to match Cornwall as a source of inspiration. He spent several weeks close to the landscapes beloved of Thérèse Debains, in the small village of Tréboul (now absorbed by Douarnenez). Bérard joined him there, followed by Munster and one of the mentors of the Neo-Romantics, Max Jacob (1876–1944), who had been born in Brittany and, according to Virgil Thomson, was entranced by the young Englishman.

Wood maintained his frenetic creative output, as evident in a letter to his mother, who was always his principal confidante: 'I have several friends here. Christian Bérard the best of the young French painters and a very remarkable person is here, we spend most of the day together and work enormously. Max Jacob, one of the best poets and a great friend of Picasso is here too and several other minor lights.' Wood's biographer, Richard Ingleby, maintained that he and Max Jacob had already met, either in Villefranche or in Paris, and their friendship was strengthened by their shared Celtic roots. Although Wood did not reciprocate Jacob's feelings towards him, he nevertheless had great affection for him – as his portrait of the poet indicates. (Furthermore, given the direction of Wood's final period, he could not have remained unmoved by the mask of a tragic clown behind which Jacob, according to Jean Starobinski, would hide himself.)

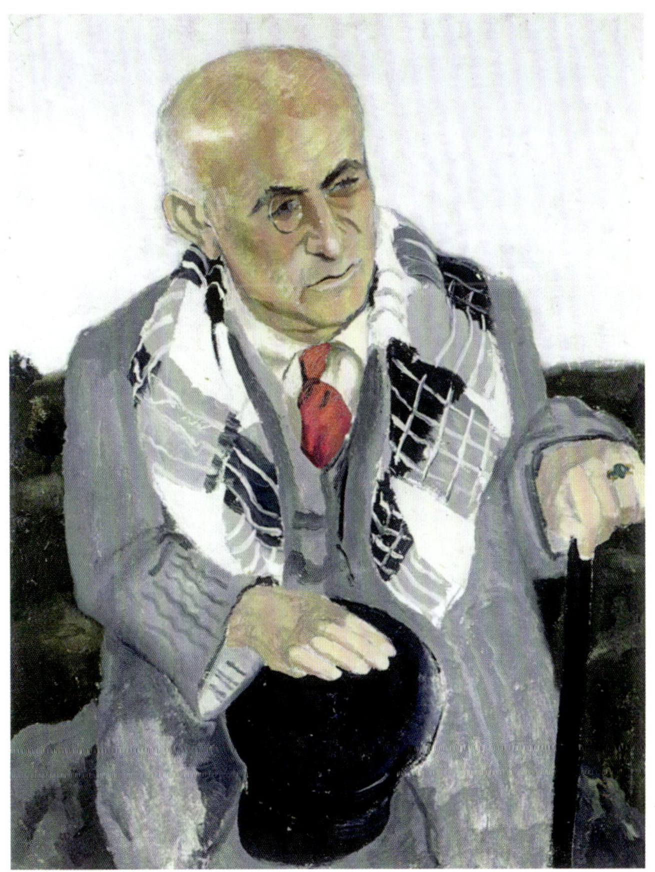

Among the 'minor lights' mentioned by Wood in his letter were Pierre Colle and Jacques Bonjean (who were interested in both his and Bérard's work), as well as the ever-restless Francis Rose, whose memoir vividly captures the few weeks that he spent in Brittany with Wood and Munster. Here, despite the opium fumes, conscientious application was the order of the day and tranquillity appeared to reign: 'At Douarnenez, the charming Frosca Munster, a friend of Kit Wood, met me. [...] Douarnenez, surrounded by a wild prairie of rocks and cliffs near Point du Bart [*sic*], fulfilled all my expectations. Kit, from a fishing boat, painted pictures of other fishing boats. He used Ripoleen house-paint, thinned with turpentine, and his colours were clear and pure. No real sail held as much of the brown and orange of a sun-lit sail as did those of his paintings.'

Wood's thick, textured surfaces, his use of frottage and generous application of varnish, as well as the ductility of the Ripolin paint, all recall the Neo-Romantics' predilection for bold gestures and technical experimentation with a wide range of materials. In contrast with the linear purity of his drawings, Wood's paintings relish materiality through an accumulation of scratches, smears and impasto. His portraits, landscapes, sea views and scenes from everyday life in Brittany and Cornwall, as well as his dreamlike compositions with distorted perspectives, are distinguished by inlaid, overlapping surfaces with no depth and brusque jumps in scale. These characteristics have led some critics to label Wood as a naïve painter (along with Wallis), but it is more appropriate to see him (along the same lines as Jean Hugo) as a knowing primitive. Two nudes of Francis Rose, painted during their stay in Brittany (now deservedly established among his best-known works), exemplify the qualities of Wood's final period: 'In a nude painting of me washing at a cheap basin,' recalled Rose, 'he scattered playing cards on a bed, and they really were the flowers of my painting. I do not mean these words to be "literary". Like the Douanier Rousseau, Kit knew the inside as well as the outside of flowers and playing cards and there was no impressionism about his statements; they were like the shop signs and painted advertisements on walls which have now disappeared.'

The last months of Wood's life were marked by an increasingly severe addiction to opium, which exacerbated the depression that would lead him to suicide. Wood thus entered the annals of the brief lives that have given sustenance to all romantic movements, while distracting from the reality of the work that they left behind. Virginia Button summed up his final hours thus: 'He was undoubtedly suffering the effects of withdrawal when he died in 1930. By all accounts in a state of extreme paranoia, induced by withdrawal from the drug, Wood jumped in front of an express train at Salisbury station on 21 August 1930.'

OPPOSITE: Christopher Wood, *Nude Boy in a Bedroom* (Sir Francis Rose), oil on hardboard laid on plywood, 53.8 × 65 cm (21⅛ × 25½ in.), 1930

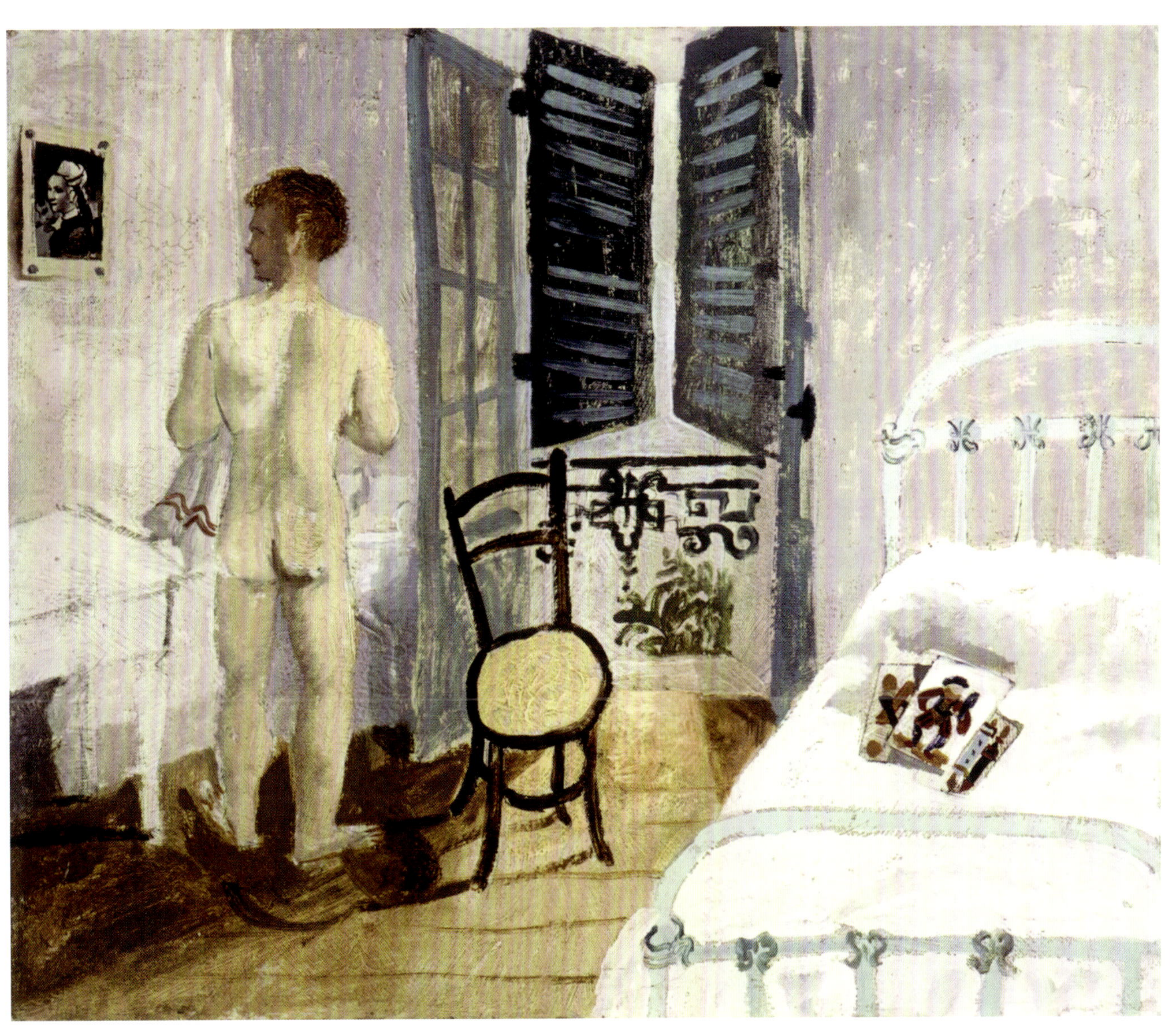

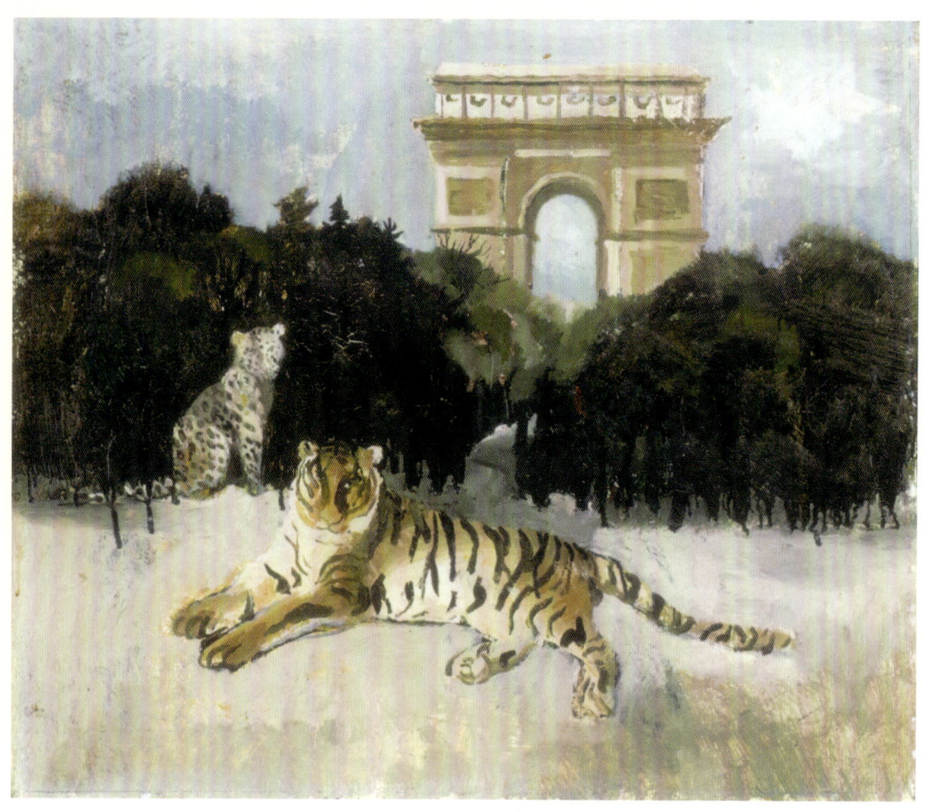

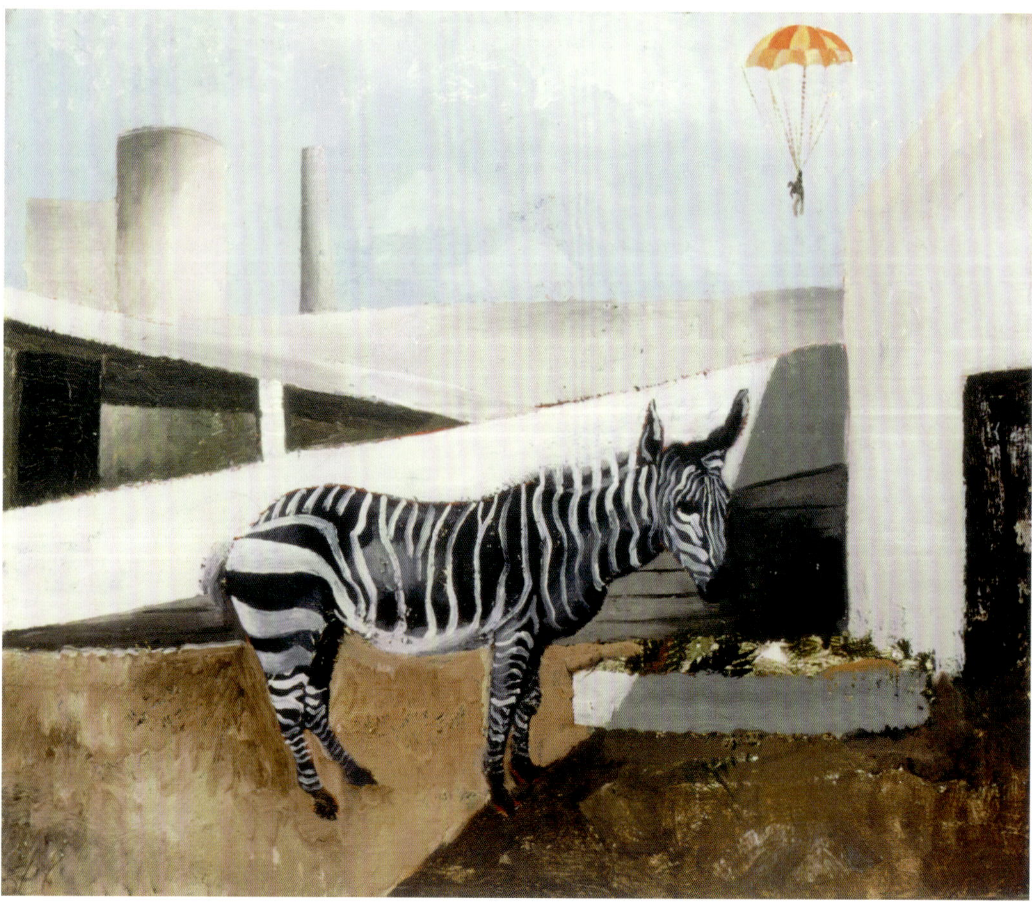

TOP: Christopher Wood, *Tigers and Arc de Triomphe*,
oil on canvas, 46.4 × 55.2 cm (18¼ × 21¾ in.), 1930
ABOVE: Christopher Wood, *Zebra and Parachute*,
oil on canvas, 45.7 × 55.9 cm (18 × 22 in.), 1930

The Art of Nuance

The effects of addiction can be seen in the sombre dreaminess and ominous atmosphere of Wood's final paintings, with their monsters, giants, harlequins, three-headed dwarves and unsettling acrobats, as well as their wild animals in incongruous architectural settings (*Tigers and Arc de Triomphe*, *Zebra and Parachute*, 1930).

These works represent one last variation on the theme of the circus and the *Commedia dell'arte*. This subject matter is endowed with a central importance in the inter-war cultural exchanges between France and England by Virginia Button (developing the thesis of Martin Green's groundbreaking study, *Children of the Sun*, published in 1976 amid some controversy). In England, it acquired a particular intensity in the literary and artistic milieus revolving around the Sitwells, which defied the trend toward realism and the 'vernacular' embodied by the likes of Hemingway and Somerset Maugham with a devotion to artifice and perpetual adolescence. 'Martin Green has convincingly argued', wrote Button, 'that the spirit of the Commedia dell'arte pervaded post-war culture, golden youth types such as the rogue and naif corresponding directly to the characters Harlequin and Pierrot. [...] According to Green, the assimilation of the Commedia into French high culture played a formative role in English perceptions of post-war French culture as innovative and liberating. The Commedia's three fateful protagonists, Pierrot, Columbine and Harlequin, enacted a self-perpetuating, comic-tragic triangular relationship, at odds with responsible, adult behaviour. Their imaginative world was governed by beauty and emotion, contrasting sharply with the ethos of such social institutions as work and marriage.'

Christopher Wood's tragic fate converted him – posthumously – into a model of the dandy aesthetic that was formulated visually by Beaton and verbally by Cyril Connolly in his freewheeling 1938 manifesto, *Enemies of Promise*. Here, Connolly exalted apparent failure and rejected conventional values in favour of non-achievement, in accordance with a 'Theory of Permanent Adolescence'. ('Whom the gods wish to destroy, they first call promising', he warned, in one of his most famous aphorisms.)

Although Connolly's 'Theory' was deeply rooted in the British class system and the privileges inherent in a public school and

Oxbridge education, it nevertheless chimes with certain aspects of a typically French dilettantism: a refusal to fit in or bow to authority, and a penchant for fantasy and formal experimentation.

'Permanent adolescent' would be an apt description of Bérard, in view of his attitude and lifestyle throughout his prematurely truncated time on earth. It would similarly fit Chick Austin, who combined his work as an enlightened curator with a career as a magician for high society, under the name of the 'Great Osram, Masked Master of Multiple Mysteries'. Austin built a Venetian villa not far from the Wadsworth Atheneum that was only one room deep, making it seem like a stage set even though it fulfilled a domestic function. ('The house is just like me', he said tartly, 'all façade.'). This militant immaturity, histrionic playfulness and embrace of paradox provides yet another reason to apply the epithet 'romantic' to the movement under discussion herein. The term designates an aesthetic stance – open to only a minority, by definition – that underlay its story and inevitably contributed to the opprobrium that would be heaped upon it.

*

This is not to say that Neo-Romanticism was completely brushed aside by the reconstitution of art (and its market) after World War II. As we have seen, the art world's centre of gravity moved from Europe to the United States, by which time Tchelitchew and the Berman brothers had already relocated there. And although Bérard could only view America from afar, he won recognition as a painter on the other side of the Atlantic, having been dismissed as a superficial virtuoso in Europe. As Waldemar-George explained in 1946 in the magazine *Quadrige*: 'The public knows Bérard for his fashion drawing and stage design but not for his painting. Very few French collectors are familiar with his pictures. (Most of them are to be found in England and the United States.) There are various reasons for this situation. Bérard has evolved on the fringes of the major currents in contemporary art. His position is a solitary one. Although his theatre sets, costumes and illustrations have helped shape taste, his painted work has remained misunderstood.'

The Neo-Romantic sensibility managed to maintain a low-key profile in the United States thanks to the continuous output of the three exiles based there and the support of a circle of cosmopolitan figures who had preserved ties with Europe: the unflaggingly supportive

Julien Levy; Charles Henri Ford, who spread the word via his magazine *View*; Monroe Wheeler, who exerted influence inside the Museum of Modern Art in New York; Virgil Thomson, now a music critic for the *New York Times*; Henry-Russell Hitchcock, an important voice in architectural circles; and, in various capacities, others such as Lincoln Kirstein, James Thrall Soby, Chick Austin and Glenway Wescott.

Neo-Romanticism's staying power was also enhanced by two American photographers who were working along similar lines to Cecil Beaton. The first was Horst P. Horst (1906–1999), who, under the auspices of his mentor George Hoyningen-Huene (1900–1968), had been close to the Neo-Romantics ever since their early days in Paris (as confirmed by Julien Green's *Journal*) and had posed back in 1933 for a superb portrait by Bérard. The second was George Platt Lynes (1907–1955), who was a friend of Lincoln Kirstein and his wife Fidelma, as well as her brother, the painter Paul Cadmus (1904–1999), and the Wadsworth Atheneum crowd. Both these men helped keep the spirit of Neo-Romanticism alive, not only by photographing its leading figures but also through the sophisticated and imaginative theatricality and lighting effects on display in their work for the leading fashion magazines.

The aquiline Diana Vreeland (1903–1989), the arbiter of New York taste in her roles as chief editor of, first, *Harper's Bazaar* and then, until the 1970s, *Vogue*, always kept works by Bérard and Eugene Berman in the legendary red room in which she loved to pose. She too had worked with them back in the 1930s, although in this case her support was a double-edged sword, as the connection with fashion served as an ideal weapon for the charges of 'superficiality' that were routinely hurled at the Neo-Romantics by the likes of Clement Greenberg.

*

By the time Eugene Berman and Tchelitchew returned to Europe after the war, their work – along with that of Bérard – had been shunted into the wings of the art world and was kept out of sight by museums, in storage. Their reputation for superficiality had stuck and they found themselves eclipsed by the luminaries of Surrealism. Nevertheless, they still enjoyed not only unwavering support from their dealers and galleries (particularly Alexandre Iolas, Lucie Weill

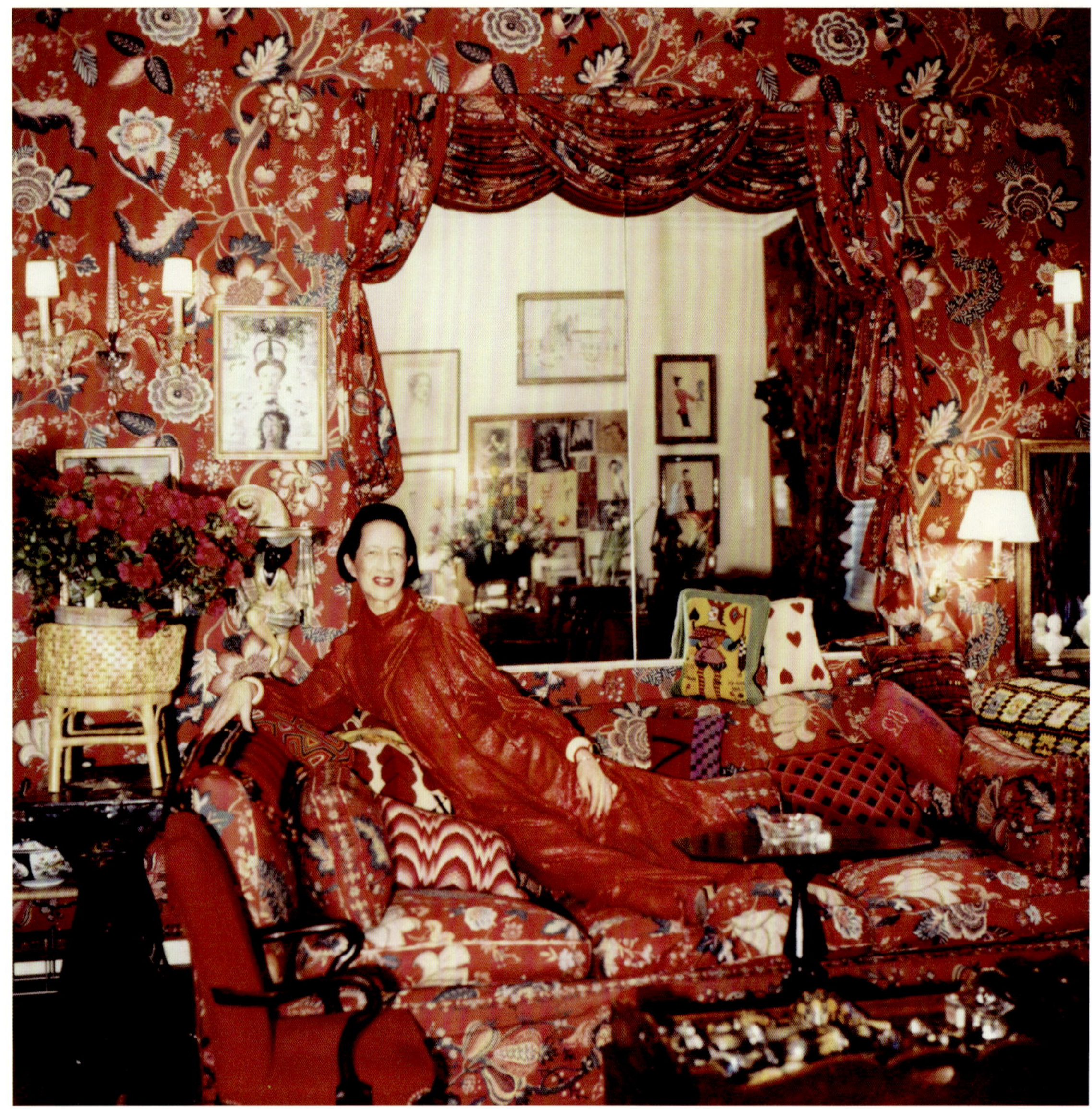

and the Obelisco) but also a particular aura, which lent them a degree of distinction (in every sense of the word). Unlike other painters or schools who depended for their patronage on collectors' aesthetic or speculative whims, interest in the Neo-Romantics designated membership of a private but dedicated club united by shared tastes. A select bunch of initiated collectors vied among themselves for these artists' works and used their names as shibboleths.

Having once featured in the collections of patrons such as Julien Green, Edward James and Peter Watson, James Thrall Soby and Lincoln Kirstein, Helena Rubinstein, Robert Piguet and Elsa

Diana Vreeland, photographed by Horst P. Horst, in her red Billy Baldwin-designed 'garden in hell' living room, 1979

Schiaparelli, the works of Bérard, Tchelitchew and the Berman brothers began to find new homes in the late 1960s as a new generation of illustrious admirers took up the torch. Appropriately, these buyers reflected an intersection of the worlds of art, literature, theatre and fashion, as they included the composer Gian Carlo Menotti, the fashion designers Yves Saint Laurent and Geoffrey Beene, the illustrator Pierre Le-Tan and the stage designer José Quiroga, who sought to transpose the Neo-Romantic spirit into his own work well into the 1970s.

Of all the artists who formed the initial Neo-Romantic circle in Paris, only Eugene Berman lived long enough to witness the effects of this continued enthusiasm and burgeoning re-evaluation – and, in February 1971, he was also able to take part in a homage to the 1926 exhibition, organized by the Lucie Weill Gallery in Paris.

While the Neo-Romantics never fell entirely into oblivion, they did lose favour with the art market. Conventional wisdom had it they represented the dialectical counterpart of 'modern' art, so they became victims of just the kind of schism that they had never sought, and in fact had deliberately rejected. As we have already seen on many occasions, the Neo-Romantics never saw their work as existing in opposition to that of their contemporaries. Furthermore, authoritative figures such as Julien Levy and the writers in *View* would speak of them in the same breath as undisputed champions of Modernism such as Gertrude Stein and Marcel Duchamp, Max Jacob and Jean Cocteau, Salvador Dalí and Joseph Cornell.

The Neo-Romantics were caught up in a dogmatic redefinition of aesthetic values and thus came to be sidelined from mainstream discourse, in universities as well as in art criticism and journalism, and left stranded by a vaguely teleological view of art and history that dismissed them as an encumbrance. Unlike the movements that would, in the coming decades, challenge the schematicism of such criteria and the primacy of abstraction over figuration (among other implicit dogmas) – the cheeky Pop Art of the 1960s and the Postmodernism of the 1980s, with its parodic elements – the Neo-Romantics never sought to affirm themselves through rebuttal or rejection. They were neither anti- nor post-modern, they simply reclaimed *another* modernity. Besides the professions of faith of Eugene Berman and Virgil Thomson, a final confirmation of this impulse can be found in the following description of Bérard (a few years before his death) by

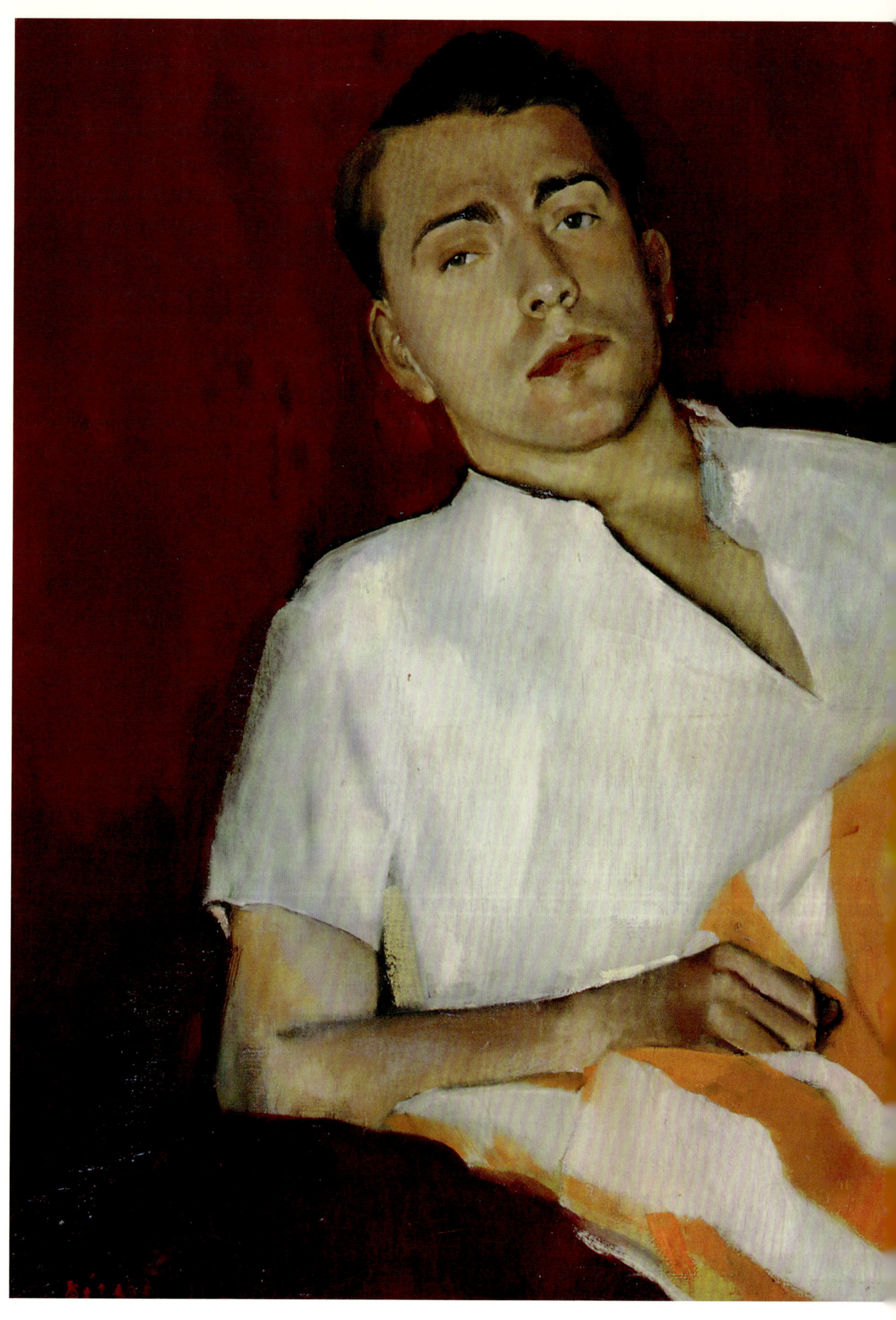

Christian Bérard, *Portrait of Horst P. Horst*, oil on canvas,
78.8 × 105.4 cm (31 × 41½ in.), 1933–34

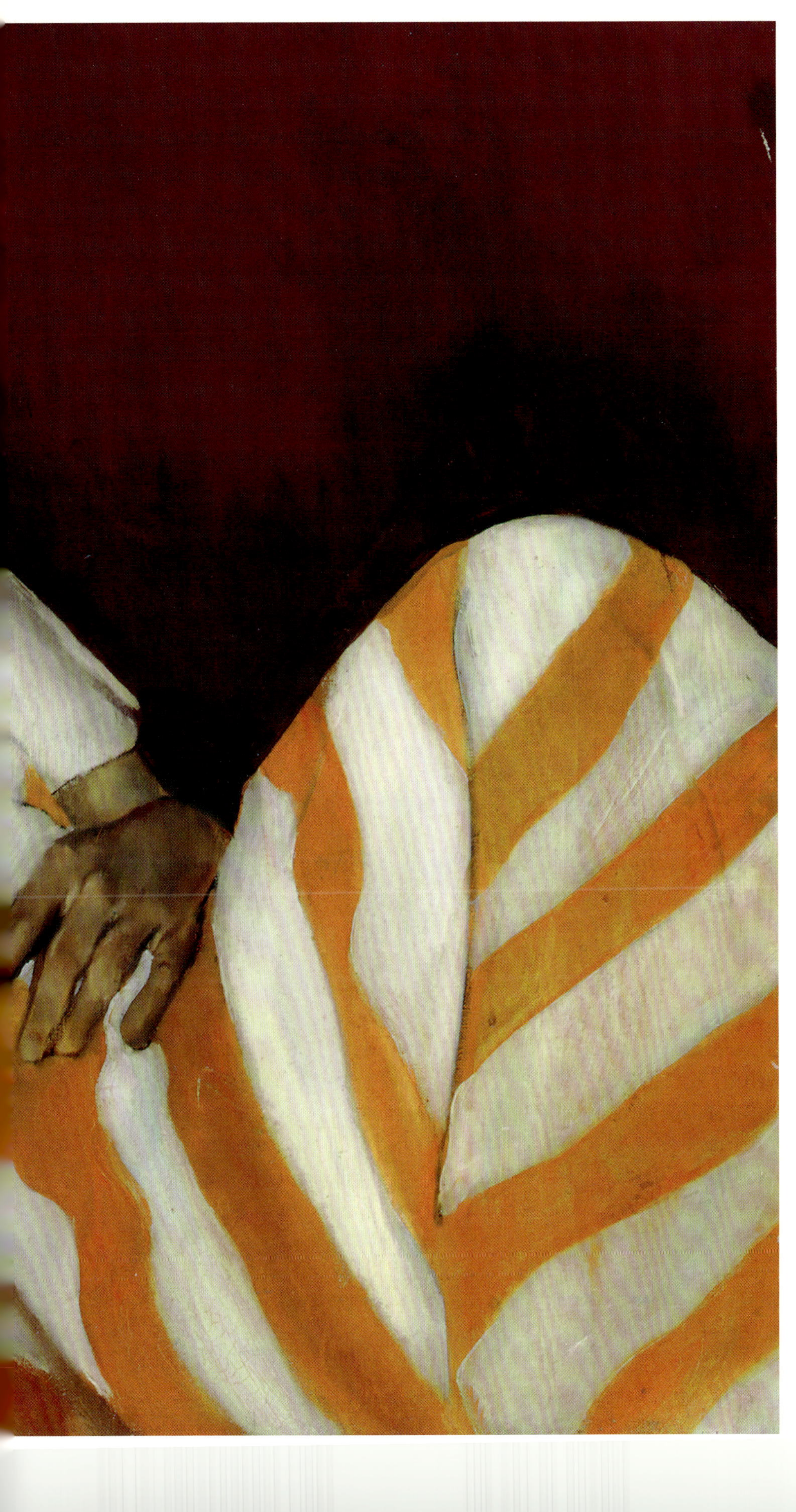

Waldemar-George: 'His reaction against those who have been called "the classics of the avant-garde spirit" has nothing willful or calculated. Christian Bérard has undoubtedly been brought up in the school of the Old Masters. At the age of seventeen, he was copying the paintings of Degas. He was inspired by Piero. He admired the divine Raphael. But, by reacting as he has reacted against the values of shock (I borrow this term from Valéry) and trying to rehabilitate the values of sensibility, Bérard is by no means behaving like a custodian who imitates the manner of the elders. He never evades his own generation. On the contrary, he retains its indelible imprint.'

The Neo-Romantic aesthetic of mix-and-match was entirely incompatible with the forces of simplification emanating from the media and the gallery circuit, which would increasingly intensify until they represented a veritable form of terror in the arts (to paraphrase the famous expression applied by Jean Paulhan to letters). One is reminded here of the despairing cry of Nietzsche that was taken up by Cocteau: '*Wehe mir! Ich bin eine Nuance*' (Woe is me! I am a nuance).

Every discourse is eventually bound to be exhausted, however, and thus the wilderness years around the turn of the twentieth century were marked by the 'deconstruction' of the received wisdom of the time with respect to artistic development. The reductive vectorization that had determined critical opinion for decades gave way to a more expansive model that opened up possibilities of fresh interpretations and the re-evaluation of unjustly overlooked artists. The Neo-Romantics are a shining example of such neglect, and it now seems possible to assess them on their own terms and not those of a skewed, all-embracing theory that relegated their singularity to a mere historical parenthesis. Now that 'modern' art has become, in its turn, an outmoded category or paradigm (superseded, in terms of the market, by 'contemporary' art) and the 'shock value' with which it had become synonymous has lost its strength (and its meaning, as a result of banal, knee-jerk acts of provocation), a new space has opened up for the allusive nostalgia and restless interrogation of Neo-Romanticism.

The prestigious dealers and collectors of Neo-Romanticism have gradually been replaced by new keepers of the flame, mainly born in the mid-twentieth century, after the group's glory days. These new enthusiasts were intrigued by the Neo-Romantic work that they came across in fashion and interior decoration magazines, or by the recycling of their stylistic traits undertaken by contemporary photographers in the early 1960s. The gaze is an effect of history and, like fashion, art is punctuated by cycles, complete with disappearances and resurgences, falls from grace and rehabilitations (let us remember how the Goncourts reawakened interest around 1850 in the art of the previous century, which had been totally discredited until that point).

As for the name 'Neo-Romanticism' itself, it is, as Soby declared back in 1936, a 'misnomer', and it should have faded away by now. However, it has resisted the passing of time (just like the torn posters so beloved of Berman). This persistence would be sufficient to demonstrate – if any demonstration were needed – that, despite the disparity of its members and their proximity to other movements (Surrealism, English Neo-Romanticism and American Magical Realism), the shared sensibility of Bérard, Tchelitchew and the Berman brothers was driven by a secret power, by criss-crossed resonances and a stubborn singularity. This fragile convergence of works, approaches and styles precipitated the spirit of a moment that was as fleeting as it was pregnant with meaning – and it is that spirit that these pages have sought to convey, a century after a handful of young artists improvised a makeshift exhibition on the walls of a gallery on the rue Royale.

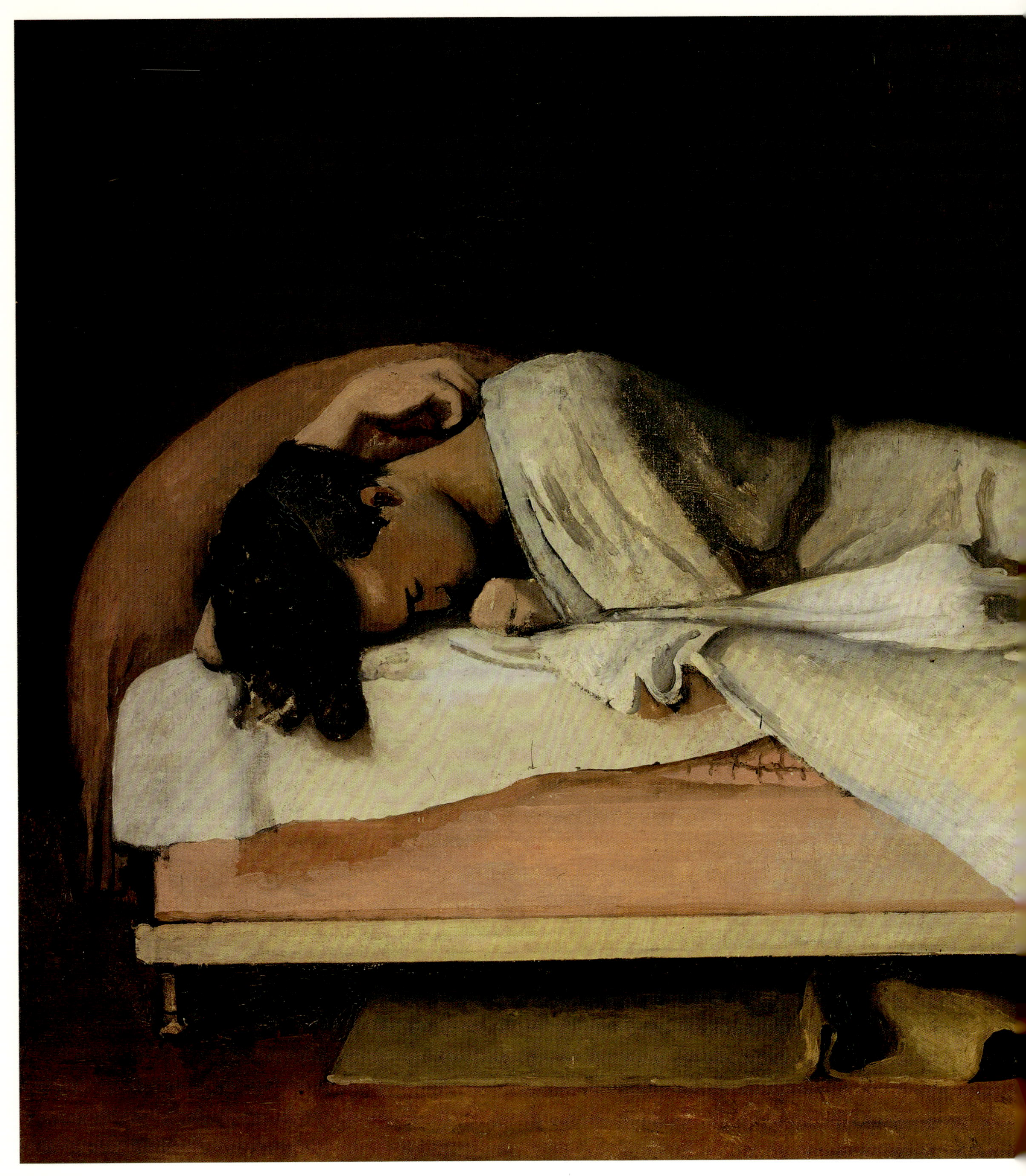

Eugene Berman, *Young Man Asleep* (Georges Hugnet), oil on canvas, 88.6 × 146.4 cm (34⅞ × 57⅝ in.), 1931

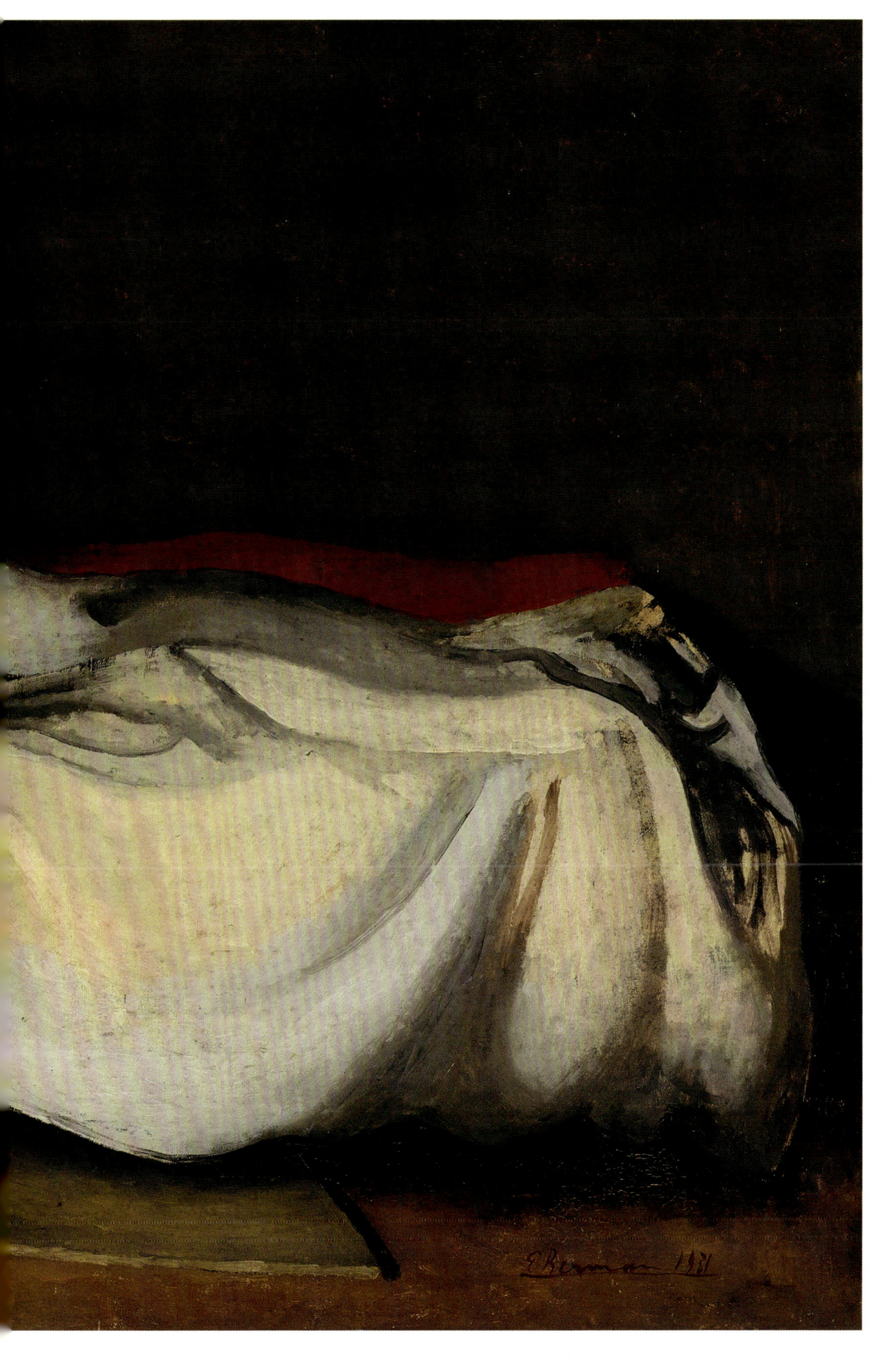

TOPOGRAPHY OF NEO-ROMANTICISM

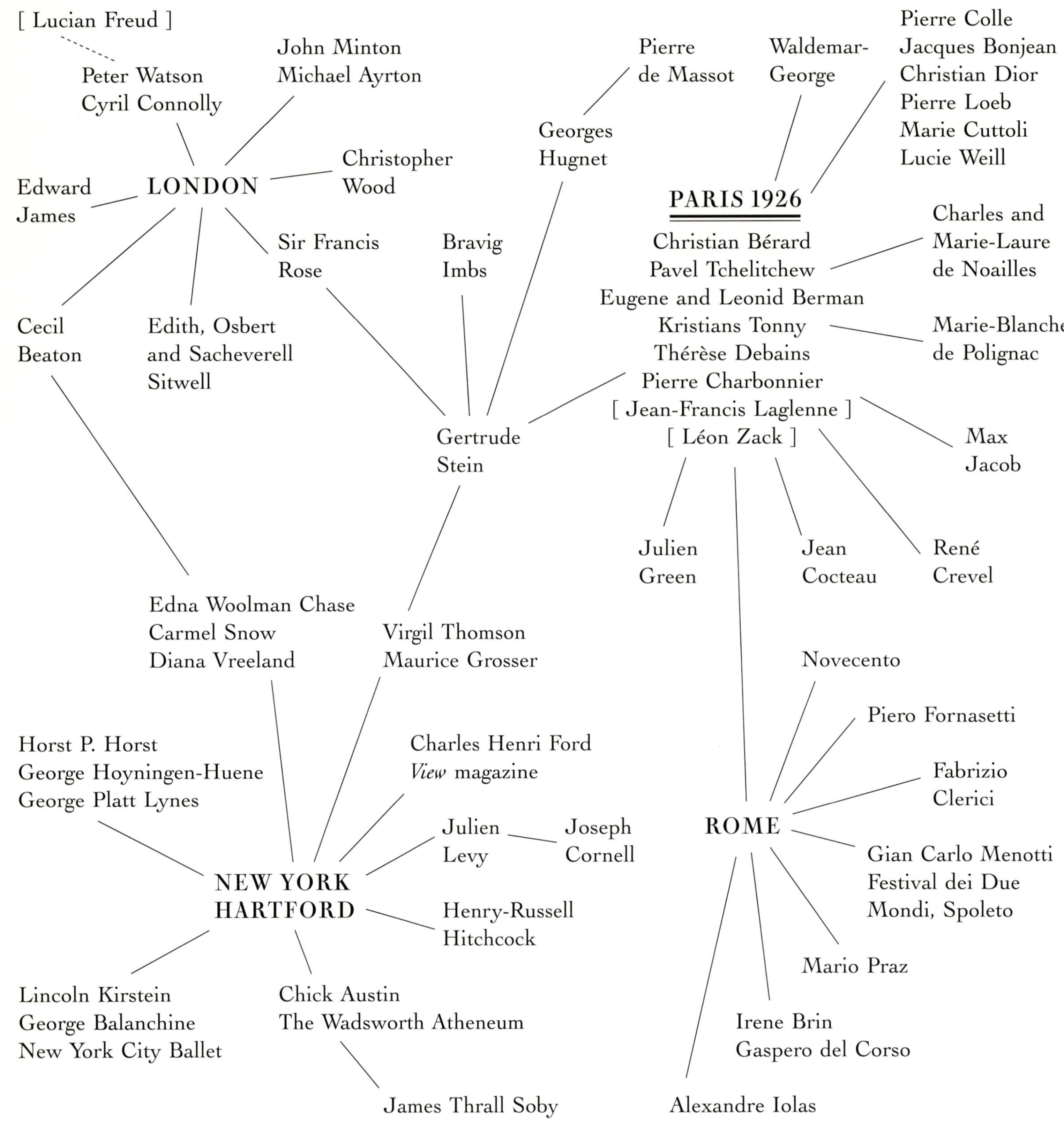

NOTES

p. 6 'thickly studded with direct quotations': Keith Thomas, *In Pursuit of Civility: Manners and Civilization in Early Modern England*, New Haven and London: Yale University Press, 2018, pp. 9–10.

EXILES

p. 24 'a season of *sturm und drang*': Leonid Berman, *The Three Worlds of Leonid* [hereafter: *The Three Worlds*], New York: Basic Books, 1978, pp. 141–2.
p. 24 'Two seventeen-year-old Parisians': ibid., p. 109.
p. 24 'pink baby with round cheeks': Boris Kochno, *Christian Bérard*, London: Thames & Hudson; New York: Panache Press, 1988, p. 8.
p. 24 'This summer': *The Three Worlds*, pp. 137–8.
p. 25 'a life of privilege': ibid., pp. 47–9.
p. 25 '[He] told us': Julien Green, *Journal intégral* [hereafter: Green, *Journal*], edition by Guillaume Fau, Alexandre de Vitry and Tristan de Lafond, Paris: Robert Laffont, 2019, pp. 837–8.
p. 26 'Anatole the visionary': *The Three Worlds*, p. 59.
p. 26 'because of the great number': ibid., pp. 108–9.
p. 26 'de Chirico's first solo show': It was a commercial failure (according to Leonid, not a single painting was sold).
p. 27 'Bérard came to see me': Green, *Journal*, p. 245. Another example of this animosity can be found in an exchange between Tchelitchew and Lincoln Kirstein during the latter's stay in Paris to see the Ballets 1933 at the Théâtre du Châtelet: 'Once again Tchelitchev was full of animated talk, generously sprinkled with inventive denunciation. Edward James was merely "an adorable child, delighted to be able to spend money." Kochno "had his uses as a stage man" but was otherwise negligible. There was "general hatred" for Bébé Bérard.' (Martin Duberman, *The Worlds of Lincoln Kirstein*, New York: Knopf, 2007, p. 168).
p. 27 'The other day': Green, *Journal*, p. 612.

LEONID'S TRAVELS

p. 29 'in greater detail': see also Matteo Fochessati and Gianni Franzone (eds.), *Anni venti in Italia*, Genoa: Sagep Editori, 2019.
p. 29 'We were most impressed': *The Three Worlds*, p. 124.
p. 30 'He [Eugene] preferred': ibid., p. 126.
p. 30 'More and more': ibid.
p. 30 'After his death': ibid., p. 145.

MISS STEIN'S PREVARICATIONS

p. 48 '[the group] was bound by': quoted by Tirza True Latimer, *Eccentric Modernisms: Making Differences in the History of American Art*, Berkeley: University of California Press, 2017, p. 16.
p. 48 '[They] deliberately renounced': James Thrall Soby, *After Picasso* [hereafter: *After Picasso*], New York: Dodd & Mead, 1935, p. 5.
p. 49 'more recently been interpreted': see Jane Stevenson, *Baroque between the Wars: Alternative Style in the Arts, 1918–1939*, Oxford: Oxford University Press, 2018, p. 17.
p. 50 'In *How To Write*': Gertrude Stein, *The Autobiography of Alice B. Toklas*, New York: Vintage Books, 1960, p. 225.
p. 50 'Jane Heap had been telling us': ibid.
p. 51 'Gertrude Stein was at first not interested': ibid., p. 226.
p. 51 'Virgil had in his room': ibid., p. 228.
p. 52 'As she used to explain to Virgil': ibid.
p. 52 '[W]e happened to go': ibid., pp. 228–9.
p. 52 'Berman is a bad painter': Green, *Journal* (28 January 1932), p. 371.

TEN PORTRAITS

p. 55 'to clarify her mind': Gertrude Stein, op. cit., p. 228.
p. 56 'I am once again': quoted by Tirza True Latimer, op. cit., pp. 32 and 129.
p. 56 'Bravig': the American critic and novelist Bravig Imbs (1904–1946), who formed part of Gertrude Stein's circle.
p. 56 'a personnel sufficiently tough': *Virgil Thomson by Virgil Thomson*, New York: Knopf, 1966, p. 165.
p. 56 'recent examinations': see Tirza True Latimer, op. cit., p. 40.
p. 57 'Tschelitcheff, Bérard, and Eugene Berman': *Virgil Thomson by Virgil Thomson*, op. cit., p. 92.
p. 57 'Their movement': ibid.
p. 58 'to Tchelitchew's impoverished bohemian circle': Boris Kochno, op. cit., p. 8.
p. 59 'Jean's room': Francis Rose, *Saying Life* [hereafter: *Saying Life*], London: Cassell, 1961, p. 57.
p. 62 'On the eve': Boris Kochno, op. cit., p. 28.
p. 63 'Curiously enough': *After Picasso*, pp. 17–18.

'THE BÉRARD ERA'

p. 69 'In partnership with a friend': Christian Dior, *Christian Dior and I*, trans. Antonia Fraser, New York: Dutton, 1957, p. 229.
p. 69 'a fair young fellow': ibid., p. 228.
p. 69 'Dior's gallery presented': *After Picasso*, p. 13.
p. 70 '1929': Christian Dior, op. cit., p. 231.
p. 70 'soon left poetry': ibid., p. 229.
p. 70 'acclaim that it aroused': This immediate success is also evident in a diary entry by René Gimpel, who was always on the lookout for new talent in his capacity as an art dealer: '30 April 1930. Christian Bérard. He is said to be the next great painter; we went to his place with Van Moppès, who knows him very well. He wrote to tell him that we were coming. He lives in a small hotel on [the street] Villa Spontini. Somebody from the family opened the door, and she said: "We ourselves do not know where he is. Letters like yours have been waiting for him for several days; he appears and disappears. It's impossible to know what he's doing."' René Gimpel, *Journal d'un collectionneur*, Paris: Calmann-Lévy, 1963, pp. 417–18.
p. 70 'the last show': Boris Kochno, op. cit., p. 79.
p. 71 'he had anticipated': ibid., p. 16.
p. 71 'The extreme instability': *After Picasso*, p. 16.
p. 71 'Bébé did what he could': *Virgil Thomson by Virgil Thomson*, op. cit., pp. 144–5.
p. 71 'self-indulgent': ibid., p. 144.
p. 73 'Solange knew him': Edna Woolman Chase and Ilka Chase, *Always in Vogue*, London: Victor Gollancz, 1954, p. 232.
p. 73 'Bébé usually appeared': ibid., p. 233.
p. 76 'Despite the fact': ibid., p. 235.
p. 76 'I was very much on the *qui vive*': Carmel Snow and Mary Louise Aswell, *The World of Carmel Snow*, New York: McGraw-Hill, 1962, p. 87.
p. 77 'Bébé's allegiance': ibid., pp. 127–8.
p. 77 'to do for his generation': *After Picasso*, p. 19.
p. 80 'To the extent that such failures': Tirza True Latimer, op. cit., p. 40.
p. 81 'Broadly speaking': quoted in Bruno Tessarech, *Villa Blanche*, Paris: Buchet/Chastel, 2005, p. 194.

TCHELITCHEW: WEIGHTINESS AND GRACE

p. 89 'He worked in both these fields': Donald Windham, 'The Stage and Ballet Designs of Pavel Tchelitchew', *Dance Index*, vol. 3, no. 1–2, 1944, p. 7.
p. 89 'His interest turned': ibid., p. 8.

p. 92 'he was painting': Gertrude Stein, op. cit., p. 225.
p. 92 'in most of his early pictures': *After Picasso*, op. cit., p. 24.
p. 92 'black, white': James Thrall Soby, *Tchelitchew: Paintings, Drawings* [hereafter: Soby, *Tchelitchew*], New York: Museum of Modern Art, 1942, p. 14.
p. 93 'Gradually the human face': ibid., p. 13.
p. 93 '[H]e piled up so heavy a texture': ibid., p. 17.
p. 96 'in the summer of 1926': see Patrick Mauriès, *Un Album de vacances*, Paris: Presses de Serendip, 2004.
p. 96 'The predominant color': Soby, *Tchelitchew*, p. 17.
p. 97 'At Alfred Flechtheim's': ibid., p. 13.
p. 98 'In contrast to the purely linear': *After Picasso*, p. 31.
p. 98 'Less sensual': ibid., p. 24.
p. 99 'grotesque tricks': ibid., p. 29.
p. 99 '*Ode*': show performed in the Théâtre Sarah Bernhardt, Paris, 6 June 1928.
p. 99 'Mannequins': Donald Windham, art. cit., p. 10.
p. 102 'London has been introduced': quoted in Soby, *Tchelitchew*, p. 18.
p. 102 'one of the leading figures': see Jane Stevenson, op. cit., passim.

TRANSPARENT BODIES

p. 107 'The circus continued to supply': Soby, *Tchelitchew*, p. 24.
p. 110 'Tchelitchew carried translucency': Donald Windham, art. cit., p. 13.
p. 111 'three distinct vanishing points': Parker Tyler, *The Divine Comedy of Pavel Tchelitchew*, New York: Fleet Publishing Corporation, 1967, p. 406.
p. 111 'The dry mother-of-pearl landscape': Soby, *Tchelitchew*, p. 26.
p. 115 'Tchelitchew's romanticism': ibid., p. 27.
p. 115 '[I]n terms of fairly direct analogy': ibid.

EUGENE BERMAN: DREAMING OF ARCHITECTURE

p. 123 'Eugene was born three years after Leonid': James S. Plaut and James Thrall Soby, *Eugene Berman: Catalogue of the Retrospective Exhibition of his Paintings, Drawings, Illustrations and Designs*, Boston: The Institute of Modern Art, 1941, p. 14.
p. 123 'It is art that tends towards architecture': Waldemar-George, *Formes*, no. 3, March 1930, p. 6.
p. 124 'when he met the architect and decorator': Julien Levy, *Eugene Berman: Paintings, Drawings and Decor*, New York: American Studio Books, 1947, p. V.
p. 124 'the avant-garde movement': Susan Day, *Jean-Charles Moreux*, Paris: Norma, 1999, pp. 31–2.
p. 125 'Eugene Berman's work': Waldemar-George, art. cit., p. 6.
p. 126 'pared down and free': ibid., p. 7.
p. 126 'I do know that on a subsequent visit': Julien Levy, *Eugene Berman*, op. cit., p. VII.
p. 127 'Breton's discomfort': Catrina Neiman, *View: Parade of the Avant-Garde*, New York: Thunder's Mouth Press, 1991, p. XV.
p. 127 'We did not have the feeling': Eugene Berman, *Appunti per un autorittrato*, Rome: L'Obelisco, 1959, n.p.
p. 128 'Joseph Cornell': see Patrick Mauriès, 'Cornell et les néo-romantiques', in *Joseph Cornell et les surréalistes à New York*, Lyon: Musée des Beaux-Arts, 2013.
p. 128 'Levy put on his first New York show': *Eugene Berman: Catalogue of the Retrospective Exhibition*, op. cit., p. 15.
p. 128 'visit to Berman': Green, *Journal*, p. 244.
p. 128 'the bridges of Paris': *Eugene Berman: Catalogue of the Retrospective Exhibition*, op. cit., p. 15.
p. 128 'The *clochards*': Julien Levy, *Eugene Berman*, op. cit., p. V.

A PAPER BALL

p. 131 'In America': ibid., p. IX.
p. 131 '[a]t the age of five or six': Alison Delarue, 'The Stage and Ballet Designs of Eugene Berman', *Dance Index*, vol. 5, no. 1, January 1946, p. 4.
p. 131 'impatient': Julien Levy, *Eugene Berman*, op. cit., p. 8.
p. 132 'No sooner had I landed': *A. Everett Austin, Jr.: A Director's Taste and Achievement*, Hartford, CT: The Wadsworth Atheneum, 1958, p. 48.
p. 133 'On that first visit': ibid., p. 49.
p. 133 'memoirs': This event was also mentioned in the *Journal* of the art dealer and collector René Gimpel, who met Chick Austin in Paris: '3 December 1928. Austin, the director of the museum in Hartford [Connecticut] comes to see me. He is around 24 years old and has only been in that museum for a year. The town was asleep, his youth and intelligence won everybody over and he got money pouring in. He has obtained around six hundred thousand dollars for this museum that had nothing. How did he work this miracle? By holding a ball in the museum. Everybody had fun and pledged themselves to him alone. Who knows what the destiny of this institution will be, thanks to this Don Juan, friend of the great masters.' (René Gimpel, op. cit., p. 373.)
p. 133 'Shall I add': ibid.
p. 135 'a series of magnificent mural decorations': Julien Levy, *Eugene Berman*, op. cit., p. IX.
p. 136 '"Of course," as Julien Levy has explained': Alison Delarue, art. cit., p. 7.
p. 137 'Berman used these decorative elements': ibid.
p. 137 '[h]e made innumerable sketches': ibid., p. 10.
p. 137 'the most completely theatrical': ibid., p. 9.
p. 137 'Theatre, it seems to Berman': ibid., p. 23.

MEDUSA

p. 145 'His busy imagination': Julien Levy, *Eugene Berman*, op. cit., p. X.
p. 145 'Strong impact': *Eugene Berman: Catalogue of the Retrospective Exhibition*, op. cit., p. 14.
p. 146 'Edgar Wind': see 'The subject of Botticelli's *Derelitta*', *Journal of the Warburg and Courtauld Institutes*, London, vol. 4, no. 1–2, pp. 114–17.
p. 146 'Just how much of despair': Julien Levy, *Eugene Berman*, op. cit., p. X.
p. 147 'in Igor Stravinsky's living room': see Michael Duncan, *High Drama: Eugene Berman and the Legacy of the Melancholic Sublime*, Manchester, VT: Hudson Hills Press, 2004, p. 134.
p. 152 'common to all': Julien Levy, *Eugene Berman*, op. cit., p. VIII.
p. 152 'Berman had already dreamed up': this trompe-l'œil is now in the Victoria and Albert Museum; see Ghislaine Wood (ed.), *Surreal Things: Surrealism and Design*, London: Victoria and Albert Museum, 2014.
p. 156 'Berman grasped the opportunities': see *Return from Egypt*, Knoedler, 1965.
p. 156 'He eventually settled in Rome': Eugene Berman, *Appunti per un autorittrato*, op. cit., p. 1.
p. 156 'passion for collecting': see Georges and Rosamond Bernier, *L'œil du décorateur*, vol. 2, Paris: Julliard, 1968, pp. 157–61; S. Carosi, M. Pozzi Battaglia and A. Russo, *Egizi-Etruschi, Da Eugene Berman allo scarabeo dorato*, Rome: Gangemi, 2017.

TWO MINOR ARCANA

p. 163 'We shall leave aside': see *The Three Worlds*, p. 141.
p. 165 'Two girls': ibid., p. 109.
p. 165 'I had been lucky to meet': ibid., p. 115.
p. 165 'Our little group from Rançon': ibid., p. 111.
p. 165 'what is certain': ibid., p. 118.
p. 169 'Actually, the needle': ibid., p. 122.
p. 170 'Before he was twenty': *After Picasso*, p. 45.
p. 170 'The newest excitement': Bravig Imbs, *Confessions of Another Young Man*, New York: Henkle-Yewdale House, 1936, p. 208.
p. 170 'In all essentials': *After Picasso*, p. 45.
p. 171 'A piece of paper': ibid., p. 47.
p. 171 'the time he painted everything': Bravig Imbs, op. cit., p. 213.
p. 174 'His portraits of Gertrude Stein': *After Picasso*, p. 49.
p. 174 'It was amazing': Bravig Imbs, op. cit., p. 300.
p. 175 'Tonny's biographers': see Frida de Jong and Laurens Vancrevel, *Kristians Tonny*, Amsterdam: Meulenhof, 1978, p. 26.

THE STRANGE CASE OF WALDEMAR-GEORGE

p. 179 'at the heart: ibid., p. 22.
p. 180 'the great imperatives': *Formes*, no. 11, 1931.

p. 180 'As [La Fresnaye's] strength': Waldemar-George, *L'Amour de l'art-Formes*, no. 4, April 1934.

p. 180 'Contemporary French art': Y. Chevrefils Desbiolles, op. cit., p. 100.

p. 181 'I declare that the Return to Rome': quoted in ibid., p. 58.

p. 182 'Romanity': ibid.

p. 182 'With the exception': Waldemar-George, *Formes*, no. 7, July 1930, quoted in ibid., p. 54.

p. 182 'some of [his] ideas': *La Revue mondiale*, no. 5, 1 May 1933, quoted in ibid., p. 55.

p. 183 'the South of France': see Claude Tollari-Martin et al., *Les chemins du silence: Jean Martin-Roch*, Arles: Actes Sud, 1994; Alladine Guevara, *Meraud Guinness Guevara, ma mère*, Monaco: Éditions du Rocher, 2007; Y. Chevrefils Desbiolles, op. cit., pp. 30–32.

p. 183 'his Fascism': Y. Chevrefils Desbiolles, op. cit., p. 34.

p. 184 'a representation': quoted in ibid., p. 73.

p. 184 'vehemence': quoted in ibid., p. 87.

p. 184 'the last chance': quoted in ibid., p. 93.

p. 184 'For George': Christopher Green, *Art in France, 1900–1940*, New Haven, CT: Yale University Press, 2000, p. 223.

THE INVENTION OF NEO-ROMANTICISM

p. 186 'Waldemar-George extracted': Y. Chevrefils Desbiolles, op. cit., p. 29.

p. 186 'When we speak': Jean Grenier, 'Le courant et le climat', *Preuves*, no. 3, 1960, pp. 73–4.

p. 187 'The twenties': *Virgil Thomson by Virgil Thomson*, op. cit., p. 151.

p. 187 'It was the choreographic stage': ibid., p. 153.

p. 187 'Characteristic of the whole new decade': ibid., p. 163.

p. 187 'Our new romanticism': ibid., p. 156.

p. 188 'Neo-Romanticism in painting': ibid., p. 158.

p. 188 '[J]ust as the surrealists': ibid., p. 164.

p. 189 'It is worthy of note': ibid., p. 165.

p. 189 'It was only at the end of the decade': ibid.

p. 189 'The grand return': ibid.

p. 190 'unashamed poignancy': *After Picasso*, p. 6.

p. 190 'as tiresome as': ibid., p. 2.

p. 191 'Few people thought': ibid., pp. 3–4.

p. 191 'the very elements': ibid., p. 11.

p. 191 'In reaction': ibid., p. 12.

p. 191 'cult for the incomprehensible': ibid., p. 7.

p. 191 'The painting of the Neo-Romantics': ibid., pp. 6–7.

NEO-HUMANISM IS A NEO-MANNERISM

p. 192 'In calling this book': *After Picasso*, p. XI.

p. 192 'Like Dalí': ibid., p. 5.

p. 192 'While Picasso's contempt': ibid.

p. 192 '[T]he reaction against': ibid., p. XII.

p. 194 'painters of reality': see Paul Jamot and Charles Sterling, *Les Peintres de la realité en France au XVIIe siècle*, Paris: Musée de l'Orangerie, 1934; Pierre Georgel, *Orangerie 1934: 'Les Peintres de la realité'*, Paris: Réunion des musées nationaux, 2006.

p. 194 'Some spirits': André Chastel, 'Résurrection du maniérisme', *Une semaine dans le Monde*, 2 November 1946.

p. 195 'Eugene Berman, Neo-Romantic': 'Review of Exhibitions of Charles Burchfield, Milton Avery and Eugene Berman', *The Nation*, 13 November 1943, in Clement Greenberg, *The Collected Essays and Criticism*, vol. 1, Chicago: University of Chicago Press, 1986, p. 163.

p. 196 'famously made a distinction': 'Avant-garde and Kitsch', *The Partisan Review*, Autumn 1939.

p. 196 'Towards the end of his career': see Chapter 6 of the present volume.

p. 196 'To a Canaletto': Eugene Berman, *Appunti per un autorittrato*, op. cit., n.p.

p. 197 'Berman thinks': Julien Levy, *Eugene Berman*, op. cit., p. XII.

LANDSCAPES OF FANTASY

p. 200 'It is not Berman's stays': Waldemar-George, 'Le néo-humanisme', *L'Amour de l'art-Formes*, no. 4, April 1934.

p. 200 'The journey to Rome': Jacqueline Munck (ed.), *Derain, Balthus, Giacometti, une amitié artistique*, Paris: Musée d'art moderne de la ville de Paris, 2017, p. 5.

p. 201 'post-catastrophe': Marcel Brion, *Art fantastique*, Paris: Albin Michel, 1961, p. 87.

p. 201 'Similarly': see Robert E. L. Masters and Jean Houston, *Psychedelic Art*, New York: Grove Press, 1968, pp. 111–12.

p. 201 'tragic paradox': Edmund Wilson, *Europe without Baedeker*, London: Chatto and Windus, 1986, p. 204.

p. 201 'This was especially true': see Vittoria Caterina Caratozzolo et al., *Irene Brin, Gaspero del Corso e la galleria L'Obelisco*, Rome: Drago editore, 2018, pp. 273–96.

THE LIGHTNESS OF LIFE

p. 202 'He would thus become': see Ilaria Schiaffini, 'La Galleria l'Obelisco e il mercato americano', ibid., p. 130.

p. 203 'In an illuminating text': Luciano, *Dialoghi e saggi, scelti da Alberto Savinio*, Milan: Bompiani, 1944; see also Alberto Savinio, *Scritti dispersi*, Paola Italia (ed.), Milan: Adelphi, 2004.

THE THEORY OF THE SALTIMBANQUE

p. 209 'the choice': Jean Starobinski, *Portrait de l'artiste en saltimbanque*, Paris: Skira, 1970, pp. 9 and 11.

p. 209 'In the language': ibid., p. 74.

p. 210 'everything occurs': ibid., p. 83.

p. 211 'That nomads' cart': letter to Schure, quoted in ibid., p. 106.

p. 212 'rather recklessly aristocratic disdain': *A. Everett Austin, Jr.: A Director's Taste and Achievement*, op. cit., p. 71.

p. 212 'the leap of the acrobat': J. Starobinski, op. cit., p. 126.

p. 212 'a world symbolically set': ibid., p. 131.

THE ENGLISH SCENE

p. 218 'Cecil had already started': *Saying Life*, p. 150.

p. 219 'portrayed by Tchelitchew': see Bonhams, *The Russian Sale*, 24 November 2008, no. 55.

p. 219 'Peter Watson': see Bonhams, *The Russian Sale*, 7 June 2010, no. 69.

p. 219 'the English Joan of Arc': quoted by Adrian Clark and Jeremy Dronfield, *Queer Saint: The Cultured Life of Peter Watson*, London: John Blake, 2015, p. 83.

p. 219 'a few months later': ibid., p. 82.

p. 219 '*beaucoup beaucoup*' (originally in French): ibid., p. 86.

p. 221 'impressive collection': ibid., p. 91.

p. 221 'For two young romantic English artists': Malcolm Yorke, *The Spirit of Place: Nine Neo-Romantic Artists and their Times*, London: Constable, 1988, p. 171.

p. 221 'packed in their mental luggage': ibid., p. 173.

KIT WOOD, THE OUTSIDER

p. 225 'Kit was good': *Saying Life*, p. 151.

p. 225 'Considered a kindred spirit': see Cecil Beaton, *The Glass of Fashion*, London: Weidenfeld and Nicolson, 1954, p. 174.

p. 226 'Bébé saw these paintings': *Saying Life*, p. 58; see also Richard Ingleby, *Christopher Wood: An English Painter*, London: Allison and Busby, 1995, p. 107.

p. 227 'It is a great moment': quoted in Virginia Button, *Christopher Wood*, London: Tate Publishing, 2003, p. 15.

p. 229 'I have several friends here': Richard Ingleby, op. cit., p. 217.

p. 229 'a tragic clown': see J. Starobinski, op. cit., p. 114. Francis Rose evoked a 'Max Jacob, who looked like Punch on the old covers of Punch, sometimes like the Punch of a Punch and Judy Show' (op. cit., p. 152).

p. 229 'At Douarnenez': *Saying Life*, p. 151.

p. 229 'Point du Bart': Rose was in fact referring to 'Pointe du Raz'.

p. 230 'In a nude painting': *Saying Life*, pp. 151–2.

p. 230 'He was undoubtedly suffering': Virginia Button, op. cit., p. 16.

THE ART OF NUANCE

p. 233 'Martin Green has convincingly argued': ibid., p. 35.

p. 234 'The house is just like me': Eugene R. Gaddis, *Magician of the Modern: Chick Austin and the Transformation of the Arts in America*, New York: Knopf, 2000, p. 124.

p. 234 'The public knows Bérard': Waldemar-George, 'Christian Bérard et l'homme, cet inconnu', *Quadrige*, no. 8, June 1946, p. 15.

p. 240 'His reaction': ibid., p. 16.

ACKNOWLEDGMENTS

The author and the publisher would like to thank the following for their assistance in the preparation of this book:

Elona Anidjar and Tajan Enchères, Paris
Stéphane Briolant and Auction Art, Rémy Le Fur & Associés, Paris
Laurence Disle-Couesnon and SGL Enchères, Saint-Germain-en-Laye
Jane England and England & Co, London
Lucie Faivre d'Arcier and Ader Maison de Ventes, Paris
Justine Hopkins (The Michael Ayrton Estate)
Josh Lynes (The George Platt Lynes Estate)
Simon Meynen, Paris
Dan Munn, The Michael Rosenfeld Gallery, New York
Emma Nichols (The Cecil Beaton Archive, Sotheby's, London)
Thierry Ollivier, Paris
Lisa Olrichs (National Portrait Gallery, London)
Richard Overstreet, Paris, and The Leonor Fini Archive (The Beinecke Library, Yale)
Irène Pliakas, Paris
Jacques Polge, Paris
Julie Rouart, Éditions Flammarion, Paris
Ilaria Schiaffini and Claudia Palma (Fondo Irene Brin, Rome)
Stacey Stachow (The Wadsworth Atheneum Museum of Art, Hartford, CT)
Andre Tchelistcheff, New York
Laurent Thareau, Nice
Jerry L. Thompson, New York

The author would also like to express particular gratitude to the following:

Thomas Neurath and Sophy Thompson at Thames & Hudson, Jules Estèves, Maria Ranauro, Jenny Wilson, Ramon Pez, Matthew Clarke, Adélia Sabatini and Lionel Leforestier. Without them, this book would not have found a home.

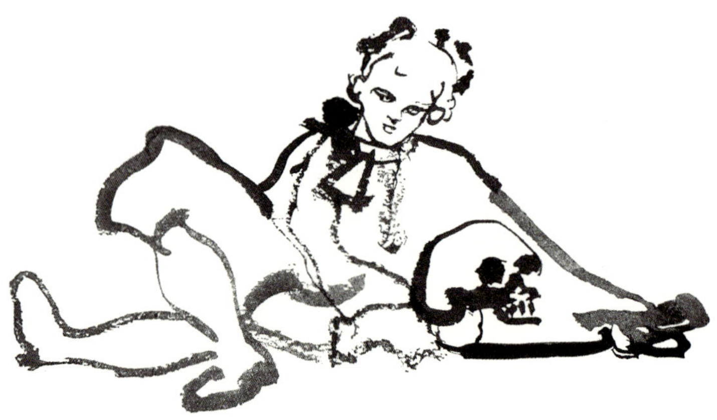

Christian Bérard, sketch published in *Art et Style*, no. 3, 1945

BIBLIOGRAPHY

Amberg, Georg, *The Theatre of Eugene Berman*, New York: Museum of Modern Art, 1947.

Antheil, Georges, *Bad Boy of Music*, New York: Doubleday, Doran & Company, 1945.

Balanchine, George, *Histoire de mes ballets*, Paris: Fayard, 1968.

Ballard, Bettina, *In My Fashion* (trans. A. Vincent, preface by F. Mitterrand, postface by P. Barillet), Paris: Séguier, 2016.

Battersby, Martin, *The Decorative Twenties*, London: Studio Vista, 1969 (repr., The Herbert Press, 1988).

— *The Decorative Thirties*, London: Studio Vista, 1971 (repr., The Herbert Press, 1988).

— *Trompe-L'oeil: The Eye Deceived*, London: Saint Martin's Academy ed., 1974.

Bauer, Gérard (ed.), *Théâtre des Champs-Élysées, cinquante années de créations artistiques, 1913–1963*, Paris: Olivier Perrin, 1963

Beaton, Cecil, *The Glass of Fashion*, London: Weidenfeld and Nicolson, 1954 (trans. into French by Denise Bourdet: *Cinquante ans d'élégance et d'art de vivre*, preface by Christian Dior, Paris: Amiot-Dumont, 1954).

Berman, Eugene, *Imaginary Promenades in Italy*, New York: Pantheon Books, 1956.

— *Appunti per un autoritratto*, Rome: Galleria de l'Obelisco, 1959.

— *Retour d'Égypte*, New York: Knoedler, 1965.

— *The Graphic Work of Eugene Berman* (preface and notes by E.B., introduction by Russell Lynes), New York: Clarkson N. Potter, 1971.

Berman, Leonid, *The Three Worlds of Leonid* (trans. Olivier Bernier), New York: Basic Books, 1978 (1st ed. 1962).

Bernier, Georges and Rosamond, *L'Œil du décorateur*, vol. 2, Paris: Julliard, 1968.

Bourgoint, Jean, *Le retour de l'enfant terrible* (ed. Jean Hugo and Jean Mouton), Paris: Desclée de Brouwer, 1975.

Bradford, Sarah, John Pearson, et al., *The Sitwells and the Arts of the 1920s and 1930s*, London: National Portrait Gallery, 1994.

Brion, Marcel, *Art fantastique*, Paris: Albin Michel, 1961.

Button, Virginia, *Christopher Wood*, London: Tate Publishing, 2003.

Carandente, Giovanni, *Eugene Berman*, Milan: Alexandre Iolas, 1968.

— *Eugene Berman*, Bologna: Galerie Forni, 1970.

— , and Robert Tobin, *Eugene Berman: A Retrospective Exhibit / retrospettiva neo-romantica*, Spoleto: Festival dei Due Mondi, 1973; Austin: University of Texas, 1974.

Caratozzolo, Vittoria Caterina, Ilaria Schiaffini and Claudio Zambianchi (eds.), *Irene Brin, Gaspero del Corso e la galleria L'Obelisco*, Rome: Drago Editore, 2018.

Carosi, Simona, and Massimiliana Pozzi-Battaglia, *Egizi-Etruschi, Da Eugene Berman allo scarabeo dorato*, Rome: Gangemi, 2017.

Chase, Edna Woolman, and Ilka Chase, *Always in Vogue*, London: Victor Gollancz, 1954.

Chevrefils Desbiolles, Yves, *Waldemar-George, critique d'art : cinq portraits pour un siècle paradoxal, essai et anthologie*, Rennes: Presses Universitaires de Rennes, 2016.

Clark, Adrian, and Jeremy Dronfield, *Queer Saint: The Cultured Life of Peter Watson*, London: John Blake Publishing, 2015.

Collectif, *Hommage à Marie-Blanche, comtesse Jean de Polignac*, Monaco: Jaspar, Polus et Cie, 1965.

— *Eugene Berman — Pavel Tchelitchew: Neo-Romantic Master Works from the 1930's & 1940's*, New York: Gallery of Surrealism, 2005.

— *Les réalismes*, Paris: Centre Pompidou; Berlin: Staatliche Kunsthalle, 1980–81

Connolly, Cyril, *Enemies of Promise*, London: Routledge, 1938.

Crespi Morbio, Vittoria, *Eugene Berman alla Scala*, Milan: Step, 2016.

De Jong, Frida, and Laurens Vancrevel, *Kristians Tonny*, Amsterdam: Meulenhoff, 1979.

Delarue, Alison, 'The Stage and Ballet Designs of Eugene Berman', *Dance Index*, vol. 5, no. 1, 1946.

Dior, Christian, *Je suis couturier*, Paris: Éditions du Conquistador, 1951.

— *Christian Dior and I* (trans. Antonia Fraser), New York: Dutton, 1957.

Duberman, Martin, *The Worlds of Lincoln Kirstein*, New York: Knopf, 2007.

Duncan, Michael, *High Drama: Eugene Berman and the Legacy of the Melancholic Sublime*, Manchester, VT: Hudson Hills Press, 2004.

Eaton, Robert (ed.), *Eugene Berman in Perspective*, Austin: University of Texas, 1975.

Faulks, Sebastian, *The Fatal Englishman: Three Short Lives*, London: Hutchinson, 1996.

Ford, Charles Henri, and Parker Tyler (eds.), *View*, New York, 1940–47.

Ford, Charles Henri, *View, Parade of the Avant-Garde*, New York: Thunder's Mouth Press, 1991.

— *Water from a Bucket: A Diary, 1948–1957*, New York: Turtle Point Press, 2001.

Foscari, Antonio, *Tumulto e Ordine, Malcontenta 1924–1939*, Milan: Mondadori-Electa, 2014.

Fox Weber, Nicholas, *Patron Saints: Five Rebels who Opened America to the New Art*, New York: Knopf, 1992.

Gélineau, Jean-Claude, 'Eugène Druet, un grand marchand d'art oublié', *La Gazette des amis de la maison Fournaise*, no. 12, 2016, pp. 14–17.

Green, Christopher, *Art in France, 1900–1940*, New Haven and London: Pelican History of Art, Yale University Press, 2000.

Green, Julien, *Dans la gueule du temps*, Paris: Plon, 1978.

— *Journal intégral* (ed. Guillaume Fau, Tristan de Lafond et Alexandre de Vitry), Paris: Robert Laffont, 2019.

Green, Martin, *Children of the Sun*, London: Constable, 1976.

Greenberg, Clement, *The Collected Essays and Criticism*, vol. 1, *Perceptions and Judgements, 1939–1944*, Chicago: University of Chicago Press, 1986.

Grosser, Maurice, *The Painter's Eye*, New York: Rinehart, 1951.

— *Critic's Eye*, New York: Bobbs-Merrill, 1962.

Harris, Alexandra, *Romantic Moderns*, London: Thames & Hudson, 2010.

Imbs, Bravig, *Confessions of Another Young Man*, New York: Henkle-Yewdale House, 1936.

Ingleby, Richard, *Christopher Wood: An English Painter*, London: Allison and Busby, 1995.

James, Edward, *Swans Reflecting Elephants: My Early Years*, London: Weidenfeld and Nicolson, 1982.

— *The Edward James Collection – West Dean Park*, vol. IV, *Pictures, Prints and Drawings* [sales catalogue], London, Christie's, 1986.

— *A Surreal Legacy: Selected Works of Art from the Edward James Foundation* [sales catalogue], London, Christie's, 2016.

Janus [pseud. of Roberto Gianoglio], *Berman*, Milan: Luciano Anselmino, 1978.
Joubert, Hélène, *Helena Rubinstein : La Collection de Madame*, Paris: Skira, 2019.

Kirstein, Lincoln, 'The Position of Pavel Tchelitchew', New York, *View*, no. 2, May 1942.
— *Pavel Tchelitchew Drawings*, New York: Bittner, 1947.
— *Pavel Tchelitchew, Pinturas y Dibujos*, Buenos Aires: Instituto de Arte Moderno, 1949.
— *Tchelitchew*, New York: Gallery of Modern Art, 1964.
— *Quarry: A Collection in Lieu of Memoirs*, Santa Fe: Twelvetrees Press, 1986.
— *Tchelitchew*, Santa Fe: Twelvetrees Press, 1994.
Kochno, Boris, *Christian Bérard*, London: Thames & Hudson; New York: Panache Press, 1988.
Kubler, George, *The Shape of Time: Remarks on the History of Things*, New Haven, CT: Yale University Press, 1962.
— 'Formes du temps réexaminé', *Artibus et Historiae*, vol. 2, no. 4, 1981, pp. 9–15.
Kuznetsov, Alexander, *Pavel Tchelitchew: Metamorphoses*, Stuttgart: Arnoldsche, 2012.

Lehalle, Évelyne, and Henri Wytenhove, *Christian Bérard*, Marseille: Musée Cantini, 1973.
Levy, Julien (ed.), *Eugene Berman, Paintings, Drawings and Decor*, London and New York: American Studio Books, 1947 (repr., Freeport, New York: Books for Libraries Press, 1971).
— *Memoir of an Art Gallery*, New York: GP Putnam's Sons, 1977.
— *Paintings, Drawings and Sculptures from the Julien Levy Collection* [sales catalogue], London and New York, Sotheby's, 1981.
— *Hommage à Julien Levy* [sales catalogue], Paris, Tajan, 2004.
— *Hommage à Julien Levy* [sales catalogue, part two], Paris, Tajan, 2006.

Masters, Robert, and Jean Houston, *Psychedelic Art*, New York: Grove Press, 1968.
Mauriès, Patrick, *Vies oubliées*, Paris: Rivages, 1988.
— *La boîte de Boris Kochno*, Paris: Maurice Imbert, 1992.
— *Un album de vacances*, Paris: Les Presses de Serendip, 2004.
— 'Eugene Berman, *Capriccio italiano*', *FMR*, new series, no. 3, November 2004, pp. 31–49.
— 'Leonid et la dynastie Berman', *FMR*, new series, no. 12, May 2006, pp. 45–58.
— 'Joseph Cornell et les néo-romantiques', in S. Ramond and M Affron (eds.), *Joseph Cornell et les surréalistes à New York*, Paris: Musée des Beaux-Arts de Lyon/Hazan, 2014.

Newton, Eric, *Christopher Wood, 1901–1930*, London: Redfern Gallery, 1938.

O'Higgins, Patrick, *Madame: An Intimate Biography of Helena Rubinstein*, London: Weidenfeld and Nicolson, 1971.

Pastori, Jean-Pierre, *Christian Bérard, clochard magnifique*, Paris: Séguier, 2018.
Plaut, James, and James Thrall Soby, *Eugene Berman: Catalogue of the Retrospective Exhibition of his Paintings, Drawings, Illustrations and Designs*, Boston: Institute of Modern Art, 1941.

Rava, Carlo Enrico, *Orientamenti della scenografia*, Milan: Görlich, 1960.
Rose, Francis, *Saying Life*, London: Cassell, 1961.

Sanchez, Pierre, *Les expositions de la galerie Eugène Druet*, Dijon: L'échelle de Jacob, 2000.
Sauguet, Henri, *La Musique, ma vie*, Paris: Séguier, 1990.
Sitwell, Edith, *Catalogue of the Collection of Works by Pavel Tchelitchew, the Property of Dame Edith Sitwell* [sales catalogue], London, Sotheby's, 1961.
Snow, Carmel, and Mary Louise Aswell, *The World of Carmel Snow*, New York: McGraw Hill, 1962.
Soby, James Thrall, *After Picasso*, New York: Dodd & Mead, 1935.
— *The Early Chirico*, New York: Dodd & Mead, 1941.
— *Tchelitchew, Paintings and Drawings*, New York: MoMA, 1942.
— (with Dorothy Miller), *Romantic Painting in America*, New York: MoMA, 1943.
— *Modern Art and the New Past*, Norman: University of Oklahoma Press, 1957.
— et al., *A. Everett Austin Jr., A Director's Taste and Achievement*, Hartford, CT: Wadsworth Atheneum, 1958.
Stein, Gertrude, *The Autobiography of Alice B. Toklas*, New York: Vintage Books, 1960.
— *Dix Portraits*, Paris: Éditions de la Montagne, 1930.
Stevenson, Jane, *Baroque between the Wars*, Oxford: Oxford University Press, 2018.

Tennant, Stephan, *The Contents of Wilsford Manor* [sales catalogue], London, Sotheby's, 1987.
Tessarech, Bruno, *Villa Blanche*, Paris: Buchet-Chastel, 2005.
Thomson, Virgil, *Virgil Thomson by Virgil Thomson*, New York: Knopf, 1966.
Tobin, Robert L., *Eugene Berman and the Theatre of Melancholia*, San Antonio, TX: Marion Koogler McNay Art Museum, 1984.
True Latimer, Tirza, *Eccentric Modernisms: Making Differences in the History of American Art*, Berkeley: University of California Press, 2017.
Tyler, Parker, *The Divine Comedy of Pavel Tchelitchew*, New York: Fleet Publishing Corporation, 1967.

Waldemar-George, 'Le néo-humanisme', *Formes*, no. 4, April 1934.
Watson, Steven, *Prepare for Saints: Gertrude Stein, Virgil Thomson and the Mainstreaming of American Modernism*, New York: Random House, 2012.
Wescott, Glenway, *Continual Lessons: The Journals of Glenway Wescott, 1937–1955* (ed. Robert Phelps and Jerry Rosko), New York: Farrar, Strauss and Giroux, 1991.
Wilson, Edmund, *Europe without Baedeker*, London: Chatto and Windus, 1986 (1st ed. 1947).
Windham, Donald, 'The Stage and Ballet Designs of Pavel Tchelitchew', *Dance Index*, vol. 3, no. 1–2, 1944.
Wood, Ghislaine (ed.), *Surreal Things*, London: Victoria and Albert Museum, 2014.

Yorke, Malcolm, *The Spirit of Place: Nine Neo-Romantic Artists and their Times*, London: Constable, 1988.

PICTURE CREDITS

Artwork dimensions have been supplied in captions where available.

a = above; b = below; c = centre; l = left; r = right

4–5 Courtesy Jane England/England & Co, London. © Estate of Sir Francis Rose, Photograph © England & Co, London; 8 Collection Denis Polge; 11 Collection Olivier Polge; 12 Metropolitan Museum of Art, New York. David Hunter McAlpin Fund, 1941 (41.65.20). Image 2021, Metropolitan Museum of Art/Art Resource/Scala, Florence. Used with permission of The George Platt Lynes Estate; 13 Private collection, Paris; 14 Philadelphia Museum of Art, Philadelphia. 125th Anniversary Acquisition. The Lynne and Harold Honickman Gift of the Julien Levy Collection, 2001 (2001-62-1111); 15 Museum of Modern Art, New York. Gift of James Thrall Soby (169.1941). 2021. Digital image, Museum of Modern Art, New York/Scala, Florence. © Man Ray 2015 Trust/DACS, London 2022; 16 Photo Hulton Archive/Getty Images; 17 Photo Archivio Cameraphoto Epoche/Getty Images; 18 Wadsworth Atheneum Museum of Art, Hartford, CT. Used with permission of The George Platt Lynes Estate; 19 Metropolitan Museum of Art, New York, Gift of Lincoln Kirstein, 1985 (1985.1087.16). Image, 2021, Metropolitan Museum of Art/Art Resource/Scala, Florence. Used with permission of The George Platt Lynes Estate; 20 Photo Cecil Beaton/Condé Nast via Getty Images; 21 Centre Pompidou – Musée national d'art moderne – Centre de création industrielle, Paris. Photo Centre Pompidou, MNAM-CCI, Dist. RMN-Grand Palais/image Centre Pompidou, MNAM-CCI. Dora Maar © ADAGP, Paris and DACS, London 2022; 22 Private collection, Paris; 24 Private collection, Nice; 25a World History Archive/Alamy Stock Photo; 25b Collection Albright-Knox Art Gallery, Buffalo, New York. Room of Contemporary Art Fund, 1940 (RCA1940:6); 26 Wadsworth Atheneum Museum of Art, Hartford, CT. Gift of the Austin House Committee, and Purchased through the gift of Henry and Walter Keney (1990.53). Photo Allen Phillips/Wadsworth Atheneum; 27 Private collection; 28a Private collection, Nice; 28bl, 28br Courtesy Tajan Enchères, Paris; 29 Church of San Francesco, Arezzo. Photo Scala, Florence; 32l, 32r Courtesy Tajan Enchères, Paris; 33 Courtesy Michael Rosenfeld Gallery LLC, New York, NY; 34, 35 (all), 36a Courtesy Tajan Enchères, Paris; 36b Wadsworth

The Ella Gallup Sumner and Mary Catlin Sumner Collection Fund (1934.8). Photo Allen Phillips/Wadsworth Atheneum; 37, 38 Private collection, Paris; 39al Private collection, Nice (formerly in the collection of Virgil Thomson); 39ar Courtesy Tajan Enchères, Paris; 39cr Private collection, Paris; 39b Private collection, Nice (formerly in the collection of Virgil Thomson); 40a Collection Denis Polge; 40b, 41a, 41c Courtesy Tajan Enchères, Paris; 41b Private collection, Paris; 42l Collection Denis Polge; 42r Private collection, Paris (formerly in the collection of Julien Levy); 43 Private collection, Nice; 44 Courtesy Tajan Enchères, Paris; 45 Courtesy Michael Rosenfeld Gallery LLC, New York, NY; 46 Wadsworth Atheneum Museum of Art, Hartford, CT. The Ella Gallup Sumner and Mary Catlin Sumner Collection Fund (1937.78). Photo Allen Phillips/Wadsworth Atheneum; 48 Museum of Modern Art Archives, New York (James Thrall Soby Papers, box 62. MA217). Photo Digital image, Museum of Modern Art, New York/Scala, Florence; 53 Gertrude Stein and Alice B. Toklas papers. Yale University, Beinecke Rare Book and Manuscript Library, New Haven, CT; 54 Private collection, Nice; 55 (all) Private collection; 58 Collection Olivier Polge. © Estate of Sir Francis Rose; 59 Collection Jacques Polge. © Estate of Sir Francis Rose; 60, 61 Private collection, Paris; 64–65 Museum of Modern Art, New York. Gift of James Thrall Soby (23.1960). 2021. Digital image, Museum of Modern Art, New York/Scala, Florence; 66–67 Collection Jacques Polge (formerly in the collection of Edward James); 68 Collection Denis Polge; 69 Courtesy Tajan Enchères, Paris; 71 Private collection, Nice; 72a Private collection, Paris; 72b Private collection, Paris. Alexandre Serebriakoff © ADAGP, Paris and DACS, London 2022; 74 Private collection. Photo Archives Charmet/Bridgeman Images; 75al, 75ar, 75bl Private collection, Paris; 75br Collection Olivier Polge; 76 Private collection, Nice (formerly in the collection of Georges Hugnet); 77l Private collection, Paris; 77r Courtesy Stéphane Briolant Photography, Auction Art, Rémy Le Fur & Associés, Paris, 78–79 (all) Private collection, Paris; 81l Photo Roger Schall. Courtesy Stéphane Briolant Photography, Auction Art, Rémy Le Fur & Associés, Paris; 81r Private collection, Paris; 82al Collection Denis Polge; 82ar Collection Olivier Polge; 82b Collection Denis Polge; 83 Collection Olivier Polge; 84 (all) Collection Jacques Polge; 85l, 85r Private collection, Paris;

88 Wadsworth Atheneum Museum of Art, Hartford, CT. Bequest of James Thrall Soby (1980.33.14). Photo Allen Phillips/Wadsworth Atheneum; 90 Private collection. Courtesy Michael Rosenfeld Gallery LLC, New York, NY; 91 Courtesy Michael Rosenfeld Gallery LLC, New York, NY; 92 Private collection. Courtesy Michael Rosenfeld Gallery LLC, New York, NY; 93l, 93c Collection Denis Polge; 93r Collection Olivier Polge; 94l Courtesy Michael Rosenfeld Gallery LLC, New York, NY; 94r Private collection, Paris; 95al Courtesy Michael Rosenfeld Gallery LLC, New York, NY; 95bl Private collection, Paris (formerly in the collection of Julien Levy); 95r Collection Olivier Polge (formerly in the collection of Edward James); 96, 97 Private collections; 98 State Tretyakov Gallery, Moscow; 100l Courtesy Tajan Enchères, Paris; 100r Courtesy Michael Rosenfeld Gallery LLC, New York, NY; 101a Detroit Institute of Arts, MI. Gift of an Anonymous Donor/Bridgeman Images; 101b Private collection. Courtesy Michael Rosenfeld Gallery LLC, New York, NY; 103l National Portrait Gallery, London (NPG 5875); 103r Gordon Roberton Photography Archive/Bridgeman Images; 104 Private collection, Paris; 105 Collection halley k. harrisburg and Michael Rosenfeld, New York. Courtesy Michael Rosenfeld Gallery LLC, New York, NY; 106 Museum of Modern Art, New York. James Thrall Soby Bequest (1253.1979). 2021. Digital image, Museum of Modern Art, New York/Scala, Florence; 108l Gordon Roberton Photography Archive/Bridgeman Images; 108r Private collection. Photo Art Resource/Scala, Florence; 109l New Orleans Museum of Art, New Orleans, LA. Courtesy Michael Rosenfeld Gallery LLC, New York, NY; 109r Columbus Museum, Columbus, GA. Courtesy Michael Rosenfeld Gallery LLC, New York, NY; 110a Christie's Images, London/Scala, Florence; 110b Private collection, Paris; 111l Wadsworth Atheneum Museum of Art, Hartford, CT. The Ella Gallup Sumner and Mary Catlin Sumner Collection Fund (1935.50). Photo Allen Phillips/Wadsworth Atheneum; 111r Wadsworth Atheneum Museum of Art, Hartford, CT. The Ella Gallup Sumner and Mary Catlin Sumner Collection Fund (1935.52). Photo Allen Phillips/Wadsworth Atheneum; 112 Christie's Images, London/Scala, Florence; 113 Private collection, Paris; 114 Collection of the School of American Ballet. Photo Jerry L. Thompson; 116a Private collection, Paris (formerly in the collection of Edward James); 116b Private collection, Paris (formerly in the collection of Julien Levy);

New York. Mrs. Simon Guggenheim Fund (344.1942). Digital image, 2021, The Museum of Modern Art, New York/Scala, Florence; 117bl Collection Jacques Polge; 117br Private collection. Courtesy Michael Rosenfeld Gallery LLC, New York, NY; 118 Collection halley k. harrisburg and Michael Rosenfeld, New York. Courtesy Michael Rosenfeld Gallery LLC, New York, NY; 119al Private collection. Courtesy Michael Rosenfeld Gallery LLC, New York, NY; 119ar Collection halley k. harrisburg and Michael Rosenfeld, New York. Courtesy Michael Rosenfeld Gallery LLC, New York, NY; 119b Wellcome Library, London; 120 Courtesy Michael Rosenfeld Gallery LLC, New York, NY; 121al, 121ar Private collection. Courtesy Michael Rosenfeld Gallery LLC, New York, NY; 121bl Courtesy Michael Rosenfeld Gallery LLC, New York, NY; 121br Private collection. Courtesy Michael Rosenfeld Gallery LLC, New York, NY; 122 Philadelphia Museum of Art. Gift of Briggs W. Buchanan, 1945 (1945-85-1)/Bridgeman Images; 124 Les Arts Décoratifs, Paris. Gift of Emilio Terry y Sanchez, 1965 (39997.A). Photo Les Arts Décoratifs, Paris/Jean Tholance/akg-images. Emilio Terry © ADAGP, Paris and DACS, London 2022; 126 Private collection. Giorgio de Chirico © DACS 2022; 129a, 129b Courtesy Tajan Enchères, Paris; 130 Wadsworth Atheneum Museum of Art, Hartford, CT. The Ella Gallup Sumner and Mary Catlin Sumner Collection Fund (1936.20). Photo Allen Phillips/Wadsworth Atheneum; 132 Wadsworth Atheneum Museum of Art, Hartford, CT. Gift of Mr. and Mrs. Russell Lynes (1989.67). Photo Allen Phillips/Wadsworth Atheneum; 133 Wadsworth Atheneum Museum of Art, Hartford, CT. Photo Ted Kosinski/Wadsworth Atheneum Archives; 134 Previously reproduced in Julien Levy, *Eugene Berman Paintings, Drawings and Decor*, American Studio, 1947; 135 Wadsworth Atheneum Museum of Art, Hartford, CT. Gift of James T. Soby in memory of his father, Charles Soby (1954.97). Photo Allen Phillips/Wadsworth Atheneum; 136l Courtesy Tajan Enchères, Paris; 136r Courtesy Tajan Enchères, Paris (formerly in the collection of Julien Levy); 138–39 (all), 140l Private collection, Paris; 140ar, 140br Courtesy Tajan Enchères, Paris; 141 Collection Denis Polge; 142 Private collection, Nice; 143al, 143ar Courtesy Tajan Enchères, Paris; 143b Courtesy Michael Rosenfeld Gallery LLC, New York, NY; 144 North Carolina Museum of Art, Raleigh, USA. Gift of the North Carolina State Art Society (Robert F. Phifer Bequest) in honor of Beth Cummings Paschal/Bridgeman Images; 146a Museum Boijmans Van Beuningen, Rotterdam. René Magritte © ADAGP, Paris and DACS, London 2022; 146b Palazzo Pallavicini Rospigliosi, Galleria Aurora, Rome; 147a Doria Pamphilj Gallery, Rome. Photo Peter Barritt/Alamy Stock Photo; 147b Musée du Louvre, Paris. Photo Josse/Scala, Florence; 148 Private collection, Paris; 149 Private collection, Paris (formerly in the collection of Bruno Caruso); 150 Courtesy Tajan Enchères, Paris; 151 Private collection. Courtesy Michael Rosenfeld Gallery LLC, New York, NY; 153l, 153r Private collection, Nice; 154 Philadelphia Museum of Art, Pennsylvania, PA. Gift of Mr and Mrs Henry Clifford/Bridgeman Images; 155 Private collection. Courtesy Michael Rosenfeld Gallery LLC, New York, NY; 158l, 158ar Collection Olivier Polge; 158br Collection Denis Polge; 159a Courtesy Tajan Enchères, Paris; 159bl Private collection, Nice; 159br Courtesy Tajan Enchères, Paris; 160l, 160r Private collection, Paris; 161al, 161ar Collection Jacques Polge; 161bl, 161br Private collection, Paris; 162 Collection Olivier Polge; 164 Private collection, Paris; 165 Courtesy SGL Enchères; 166al Collection Jacques Polge; 166ar Private collection, Paris; 166b Collection Denis Polge; 167al Collection Olivier Polge; 167ar, 167b Private collection, Nice; 168 Wadsworth Atheneum Museum of Art, Hartford, CT. Museum Purchase (1938.23a). Photo Allen Phillips/Wadsworth Atheneum; 172 Collection Olivier Polge; 173 Collection Denis Polge; 176–77 (all) Courtesy Tajan Enchères, Paris; 178 Private collection, Paris; 181 Casella Collection, Rome. Photo Scala, Florence. Carlo Carrà © DACS 2022; 182 Private collection, Nice. Reproduced courtesy the artist's estate; 184 Private collection, Nice (formerly in the collection of Lucien Rollin). Reproduced courtesy the artist's estate; 185a, 185b Private collection, Nice. Reproduced courtesy the artist's estate; 193a Musée du Louvre, Paris. Photo Scala, Florence; 193b Courtesy Tajan Enchères, Paris; 194, 195 Estate of Leonor Fini; 198a Collection Jacques Polge; 198bl Pinacoteca Nazionale, Bologna; 198br Vatican Museums, Vatican City; 201 Galleria nazionale d'arte moderna e contemporanea, Rome, Fondo Irene Brin, Gaspero del Corso e L'Obelisco, Part. 3, Serie 2, UD 5, Serie di provini di Leslie Gill. Su concessione del Ministero dei beni e delle attività culturali e del Turismo; 204–5 (all), 207 Private collection, Paris; 208a Metropolitan Museum of Art, New York. Bequest of Edwin De T. Bechtel, 1957 (57.650.366); 208b Courtesy Tajan Enchères, Paris; 210 Courtesy Michael Rosenfeld Gallery LLC, New York, NY; 211 Rijksmuseum Amsterdam; 212a, 212b, 213a Private collection, Nice; 213b Private collection, Nice (formerly in the collection of Leonardo Botta); 214 Pushkin Museum, Moscow. Photo Scala, Florence. © Succession Picasso/DACS, London 2022; 215a Private collection, Paris; 215b Courtesy Stéphane Briolant Photography, Auction Art, Rémy Le Fur & Associés, Paris; 216 National Portrait Gallery, London. Bequeathed by Sir Cecil Beaton, 1980 (NPG 5307); 220 © The Cecil Beaton Studio Archive; 222 Private collection. Photo Peter Nahum at The Leicester Galleries, London/Bridgeman Images. © Estate of Michael Ayrton; 223a Private collection. Photo Bonhams, London/Bridgeman Images. © Estate of John Minton/Bridgeman Images; 223bl Arts Council Collection, Southbank Centre, London/Royal College of Art/Bridgeman Images. © Estate of John Minton/Bridgeman Images; 223br Ashmolean Museum, University of Oxford/Bridgeman Images; 224 Kettle's Yard, Cambridge; 228 Bradford Museums and Galleries; 229 Musées des Beaux-Arts, Quimper, France; 231 Scottish National Gallery of Modern Art, Edinburgh; 232a The Phillips Collection, Washington, D.C.; 232b Tate, London; 236 Photo Horst P. Horst/Condé Nast via Getty Images; 238–39 Private collection. Photo Christie's Images/Bridgeman Images; 242–3 Museum of Fine Arts, Boston. Tompkins Collection, Arthur Gordon Tompkins Fund. (RES.32.4)/Bridgeman Images; 248 Private collection, Paris

INDEX

Figures in *italic* refer to illustrations

First published in the United Kingdom in 2022
by Thames & Hudson Ltd, 181A High Holborn,
London WC1V 7QX

First published in the United States of America
in 2022 by Thames & Hudson Inc., 500 Fifth
Avenue, New York, New York 10110

Theatres of Melancholy

Translated from the French by Matthew Clarke

For picture credits, please see pages 251–2

Designed by Jules Estèves

British Library Cataloguing-in-Publication Data
A catalogue record for this book is available from the British Library

Library of Congress Control Number 2021943190

ISBN 978-0-500-09407-5

Printed and bound in Italy
by Printer Trento SrL.

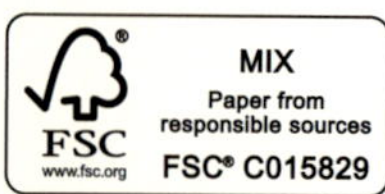

On the cover and endpapers:

TITLE TYPOGRAPHY: specially designed for this book by Jules Estèves from calligraphy by Boris Kochno on a drawing by Eugene Berman (see p. 140)

FRONT JACKET (FRONT): Eugene Berman, *Young Man Asleep* (Georges Hugnet), 1931 (detail). Museum of Fine Arts, Boston. Tompkins Collection, Arthur Gordon Tompkins Fund. (RES.32.4)/Bridgeman Images (see pp. 242–3)

FRONT JACKET (BACK): Christian Bérard, *On the Beach (Double Self-Portrait)*, 1933 (detail). Museum of Modern Art, New York. Gift of James Thrall Soby (23.1960). 2021. Digital image, Museum of Modern Art, New York/Scala, Florence (see pp. 64–65)

FRONT FLAP (FRONT): Christian Bérard, *Mozartiana*, sketch published in *Art et Style*, no. 3, 1945. Private collection, Paris (see also p. 248)

FRONT FLAP (BACK): Eugene Berman, *Trompe-l'œil*, 1939 (detail). Collection Denis Polge (see p. 141)

BACK JACKET (FRONT): Pavel Tchelitchew, *The Concert*, 1933 (detail). Christie's Images, London/Scala, Florence (see p. 110, above)

BACK JACKET (BACK): Eugene Berman, *View in Perspective of a Perfect Sunset*, 1941 (detail). Philadelphia Museum of Art, Pennsylvania, PA. Gift of Mr and Mrs Henry Clifford/Bridgeman Images (see p. 154)

BACK FLAP (BACK): Eugene Berman, cover design for *Town and Country*, 1939 (detail). Private collection, Nice (see p. 153, left)

FRONT ENDPAPER (1): Pavel Tchelitchew, programme cover for *Ode*, 13 June 1928 (detail). Private collection, Paris (see p. 113)

FRONT ENDPAPER (2): Eugene Berman, *The Masque of the Red Death*, 1945 (detail, reversed). Private collection, Paris (see p. 161, bottom right)

FRONT ENDPAPER (3): Christian Bérard, *Dancers*, n.d. (detail). Collection Olivier Polge (see p. 75, bottom right)

BACK ENDPAPER (1): Christian Bérard, lithography for programme cover for the Ballets des Champs-Élysées, April 1949 (detail). Private collection, Paris (see p. 79, right)

BACK ENDPAPER (2): Christian Bérard, studies for *Margot* by Édouard Bourdet, 1935 (detail). Private collection, Paris (see p. 75, above left)

BACK ENDPAPER (3): Eugene Berman, *Green Hunting Man*, 1941 (detail). Private collection, Paris (see p. 161, below left)

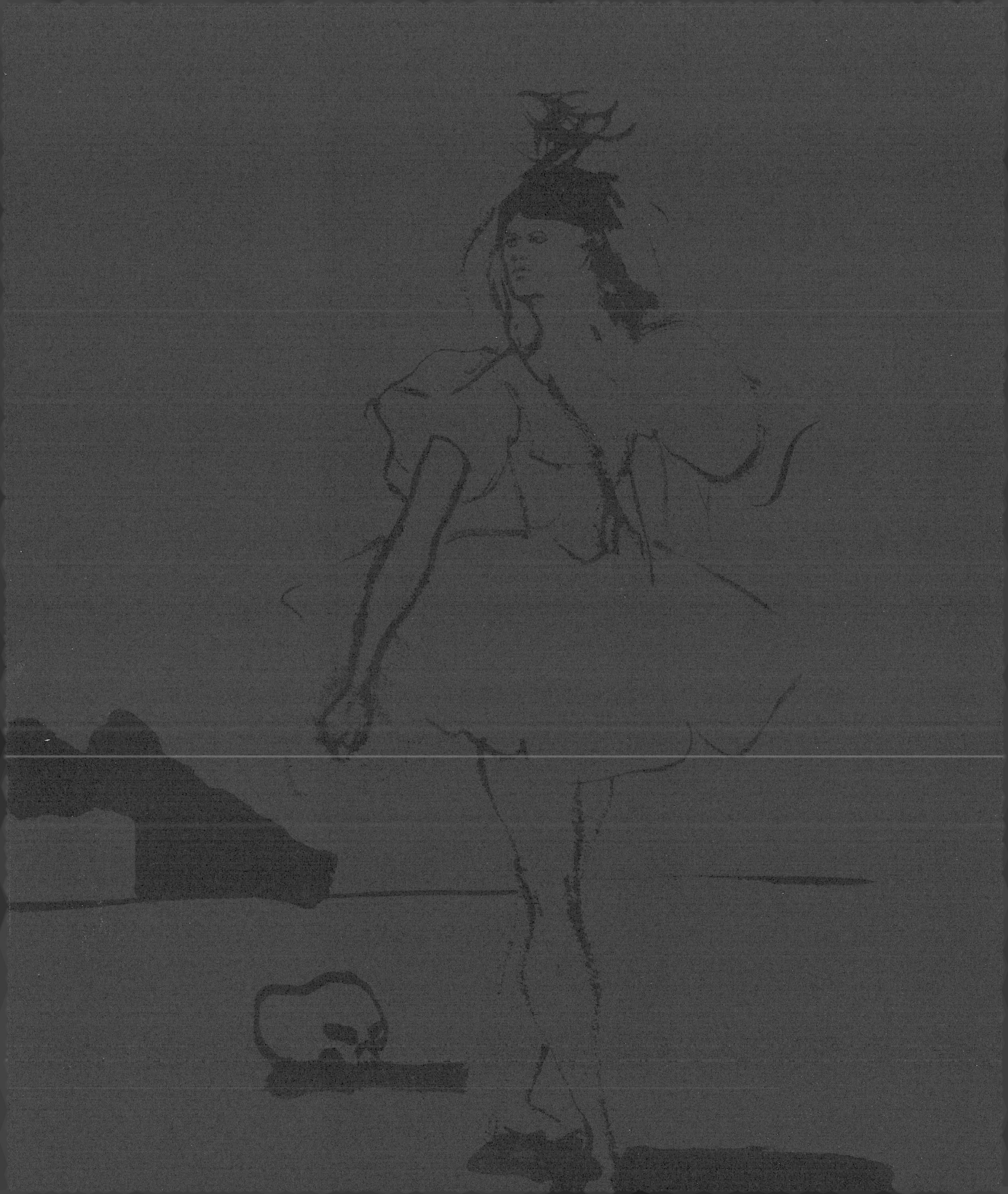

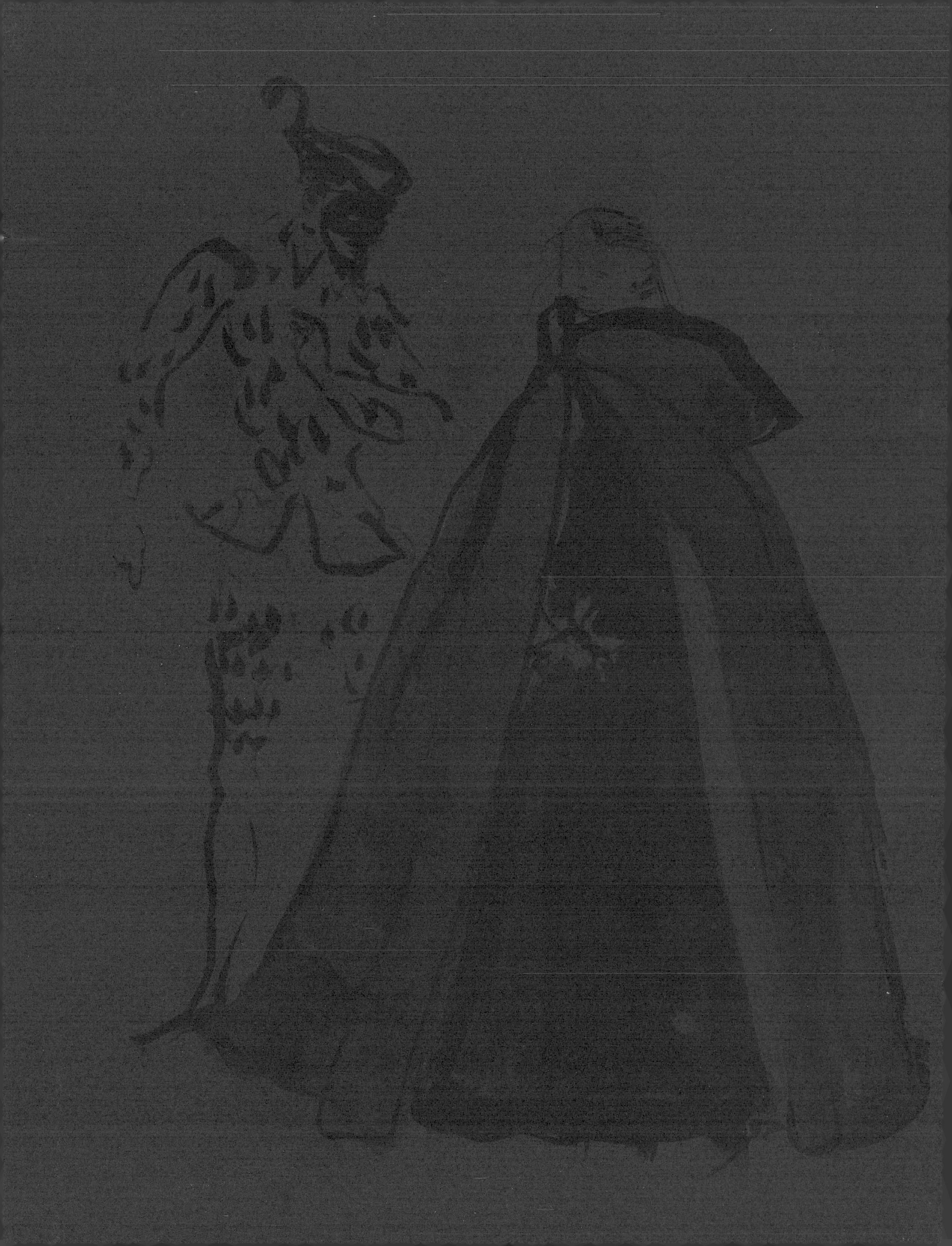